D0305354

THE ALPINE JOURNAL 2010 – 2011

Above the clouds on Impossible Wall: the first ascent, over 10 days in 2010, of this 850m wall above Greenland's Sortehul fjord earned climbers Oli and Nico Favresse, Sean Villaneuva and Ben Ditto and yacht skipper Bob Shepton a Piolet d'Or. Shepton tells their story in this Alpine Journal, page 121. (*Greenland Big Walls 2010 team collection*)

THE
ALPINE JOURNAL
2010 – 2011

The Journal of the Alpine Club

A record of mountain adventure
and scientific observation

Edited by Stephen Goodwin

Production Editor: Bernard Newman
Assistant Editor: Paul Knott

Volume 115

Number 359

Supported by the
MOUNT EVEREST FOUNDATION

Published by
THE ALPINE CLUB

THE ALPINE JOURNAL 2010 – 2011
Volume 115 No 359

www.alpinejournal.org.uk

Address all editorial communication to the Hon Editor:
Stephen Goodwin, 1 Ivy Cottages, Edenhall, Penrith, CA11 8SN
email: sg@stephengoodwin.demon.co.uk
Address all sales and distribution communications to:
Cordée, 11 Jacknell Rd, Dodwells Bridge Ind Est, Hinckley, LE10 3BS

Back numbers:
Apply to the Alpine Club, 55 Charlotte Rd, London, EC2A 3QF or, for 1969 to date, apply to Cordée, as above.

First published in 2011 by The Alpine Club
Typeset by Bernard Newman
Photo production by Tom Prentice
Printed and bound in India by Replika Press Pvt Ltd

A CIP catalogue record for this book is available from The British Library

ISBN 978 0 9569309 0 3

Foreword

Sat at my desk, about to begin this Foreword, I flicked to the BBC news website, an early morning reflex. Two suicide bombers had killed at least 80 people in Shabqadar, near Peshawar – the Pakistan Taliban beginning its deadly revenge for the killing of Osama bin Laden. Thrown by such tragedy it becomes difficult to find anything meaningful to say about a subject as seemingly frivolous as mountaineering.

Since the last *Alpine Journal*, the world has reverberated with the Gulf of Mexico oil spill, the Indus floods, the Japanese earthquake, dictators swept away in the 'Arab Spring', and war without end. For many of us, no doubt, part of the joy of being in the mountains is the relief it offers from this daily diet of woe. But this requires an increasingly thick pair of blinkers – even for those who cut the umbilical ties of internet and mobile phone. Greenland melts; guns, bombs and paranoid governments blight swathes of Asia. Ranges like the tantalising Cilo Dag in south-east Turkey have been virtually off-limits for decades.

Mountaineering and global politics become thus entwined. How should the *AJ* reflect this? It is occasionally said by those visiting mountains in countries ruled by oppressive regimes – Tibet for example – that their innocent guise as climbers is one way of seeing what is actually going on. But being a witness is pointless unless one actually *bears* witness.

Some, particularly in respect of China, might find themselves caught in the moral dilemma of speaking out or keeping the slate clean for future permits. Also such visits can keep doors open and be an assurance to friends and ordinary people in troubled areas that they are not forgotten. Nonetheless, for most of the world's mountains there is plenty of scope to give a broader picture of the places we climb, the circumstances of the local people and their environment, than is currently the case. I'm not looking for polemics: it would be lovely to turn up a climbing equivalent of the Polish master-journalist Ryszard Kapuscinski, however I'd be satisfied with an *AJ* that reflects mountaineers as not living in their own bubble.

New Zealander Pat Deavoll headed for unclimbed Karim Sar in Pakistan in March 2009. The mountain lies in the 'relatively' serene Hunza valley region. But en route Pat encountered columns of refugees fleeing the Swat valley where the Pakistani army and the Taliban were fighting house to house. 'Two million people displaced – that's half the population of New Zealand,' she observes in the opening feature of this *Alpine Journal*. A weary Pashtun is clinging to the running board of a truck and Pat ponders his fate. Then: 'For a split second we locked eyes and in that moment I realized we were irrevocably, eternally foreign to each other.'

The journal, to my mind, is doing its job with this 'big picture' approach to mountaineering. 'Scientific observation' has been embodied in our sub-title as part of the *AJ*'s remit since *volume I* in 1863, and in recent years this has increasingly focused on the effects of climate change. But as three Swiss scientists underline in this journal, the glacier melt and rockfall we see first hand as climbers should be heeded as a warning sign for all mankind. Their article is a summary of a major document, *Mountains and Climate Change: From Understanding to Action,* that went before the UN's Stockholm conference in December 2009. The summit was a profound disappointment, but the implications of the changes that Messrs Kohler, Maselli and Neu highlight here from the Andes and Rockies to the Hindu Kush and China cannot be wished away as a political inconvenience.

It is in fact one of the pleasures of the *AJ* that it has room to be discursive; so that in this volume as Andy Houseman describes his marvellous first ascent with Nick Bullock of the coveted north face of Chang Himal and Bob Shepton tells the skipper's tale behind the 2010 Greenland Big Wall expedition that scooped a *Piolet d'Or*, Peter Gillman can uncover early climbs on Ben Nevis by George Mallory and John Innerdale treat us to his artist's sketchbook on Bhutan. The new AC president, Mick Fowler, and ambitious Scot Bruce Normand take us exploratory climbing in the Chinese Tien Shan while Doug Scott ruminates on the seductions of Madame Fame. As the saying goes, 'all this and more'.

Discerning readers will have noticed that this is the first *Alpine Journal* since 1987 not to carry the logo of an outside publishing house on the spine. The decision to go it alone was part of a rethink sadly forced upon us by the death of AC member Peter Hodgkiss, whose Ernest Press had been joint publisher of the *AJ* since 1993. Exceptionally, there was little choice but to reschedule journal production and to label this volume '2010/11'. All being well, 'normal service' should resume with 2012.

Thankfully one thing that has not changed is the willingness (give or take a bit of arm-twisting) of mountaineers and others to share their stories with the *AJ*. Particular thanks are due here to assistant editor Paul Knott and his team of correspondents who supply the Area Notes on notable climbs worldwide, to production editor Bernard Newman who shapes the *AJ* image, and to proof reader Margot Blyth who spares our editorial blushes. I must also salute two loyal correspondents who bow out with this journal – Derek Fordham who has supplied the Area Notes on Greenland and Arctic exploration since 1969, and Chris Russell, whose '100 Years Ago' combings of the *AJ* archive have been a continuous feature since 1971. In accordance with the circularity of all things Chris ends, as he began, with Edward Whymper: the first '100 Years Ago' marking the centenary of *Scrambles Amongst the Alps* and this last recalling Whymper's death in 1911.

Despite the Jeremiahs telling us the book is dead, club journals are surely more relevant than ever in the information age: news of first ascents and so on is instantly relayed on sites like UKClimbing.com, magazines seem to focus increasingly on gear reviews and photo-led 'celeb' features (and ultimately end in the recycling bin) while the journals serve as a permanent record, not only of a year's outstanding alpinism, new routes and exploration, but of research and reflection on the mountain issues of the day. To all who have contributed to this 115th *Alpine Journal* – many thanks.

Stephen Goodwin

Contents

ARTS

SCIENCE

Illustrations

Obituaries

NOTES FOR CONTRIBUTORS

The *Alpine Journal* records all aspects of mountains and mountaineering, including expeditions, adventure, art, literature, geography, history, geology, medicine, ethics and the mountain environment.

Articles Contributions in English are invited. They should be sent to the Hon Editor, Stephen Goodwin, 1 Ivy Cottages, Edenhall, Penrith, Cumbria CA11 8SN (e-mail: sg@stephengoodwin.demon.co.uk). Articles should be sent on a disk with accompanying hard copy or as an e-mail attachment (in Microsoft Word) with hard copy sent separately by post. Length should not exceed 3000 words without prior approval of the editor **and may be edited or shortened at his discretion**. It is regretted that the *Alpine Journal* is unable to offer a fee for articles published, but authors who are not AC members receive a complimentary copy of the issue of the *Journal* in which their article appears. Preferably, articles and book reviews should not have been published in substantially the same form by any other publication.

Maps These should be well researched, accurate, and show the most important place-names mentioned in the text. It is the author's responsibility to get their maps redrawn if necessary. If submitted electronically, maps should be originated as CMYK in a vectorised drawing package (Adobe Illustrator, Freehand or similar), and submitted as pdfs. (Any embedded images should be at 300dpi resolution at A4 size.) Hard copy should be scanned as a Photoshop compatible 300dpi tiff at A4 finished size. This can be arranged through the production editor if required.

Photographs Colour transparencies should be originals (not copies) in 35mm format or larger. Prints (any size) should be numbered (in pencil) on the back and accompanied by a separate list of captions (see below). Pre-scanned images should be CMYK, 300dpi tiffs or Maximum Quality jpegs at A4 final size. Images from digital cameras should be CMYK, 300dpi jpegs or tiffs at the maximum file size (quality) the camera can produce. All images (slides, prints and digital) should have unique names/serial numbers that correspond to a list of captions supplied with your article or as a word processing document or via email.

Captions should include subject matter, photographer's name, title and author of the article to which they refer.

Copyright It is the author's responsibility to obtain copyright clearance for text, photographs, digital images and maps, to pay any fees involved and to ensure that acknowledgements are in the form required by the copyright owner.

Summaries A brief summary, helpful to researchers, may be included with 'expedition' articles.

Biographies Authors are asked to provide a short biography, in about 60 words, listing the most noteworthy items in their climbing career and anything else they wish to mention.

Deadline Copy and photographs should reach the editor by 1 January of the year of publication.

High Asia

1. John Innerdale, *Garula Kang, Bhutan*, chromacolour, 47 x 36cm, 1993.

PAT DEAVOLL

The Troubled Road to Karim Sar

In March 2009 I was in the midst of planning my third expedition to Pakistan in as many years when the Taliban invaded the Swat valley, causing a huge wave of refugees to stream south to camps in and around Peshawar, Rawalpindi and the capital Islamabad.

'What do you think?' said my expedition partners. 'Will we be able to get into the country? Out of the country? Are the media blowing things out of proportion?'

2. Police checkpoint on Karakoram Highway *(Pat Deavoll)*.

I consulted a couple of experts: Doug Chabot, who said he was cancelling his expedition, and Bruce Normand, who said he was glad to be leaving Pakistan via China. 'Islamabad airport could be under threat,' he said. 'If you do go, make other plans for leaving the country.'

At home in New Zealand, the computer screen reflected the team's puzzled faces as we trawled the internet for news of the conflict. We were bound for the south face of Kampire Dior, near the Taliban hinterland.

What if Islamabad is overrun by insurgents? What if the airport is captured while we are in the mountains? Will we be able to escape north to China? Should we get a Chinese visa just in case? What if the Taliban kidnap and behead us? What if we're caught up in a suicide bombing? What if...what if...what if?

3. Fleeing the fighting, refugees heading away from the Swat valley *(Pat Deavoll)*.

By May, two million civilians had fled Swat and the Taliban and the army were fighting house to house in the provincial capital of Mingora. The Taliban were posting assassinations of army personal on YouTube and rumours were spreading that the country's nuclear capacity might fall into their hands.

By the time we'd flown into Islamabad at the beginning of June, our team of four had dwindled to a team of two: Paul Hersey and myself. We'd switched to a new objective, Karim Sar, an unclimbed peak near the relative serenity of the Hunza valley. Ivo Ferrari, Yuri Parimbell and Fabio Valeschini attempted the mountain in 2007, but turned back because of bad weather.

I'd first seen Karim Sar a few years earlier from the top of a small peak by the Baltar glacier. Its ice-capped summit had shimmered in the rarefied distance, the midday light reflecting a grandeur surpassing its moderate size. Rock turrets reached to the sky; snow slopes curved down into the void. *Steep, elegant... and unclimbed.* At the time I was enchanted. But Paul and I would still have to travel north through a portion of Swat province to reach it.

4. Walking in to base camp (*Pat Deavoll*).

As we settled into our guesthouse in the capital, I recalled the previous year. A *whoomph* had sounded as my British climbing partner Malcolm Bass was sitting in his hotel room. The ground jumped and the windows rattled; a bomb had gone off just minutes down the road. When I arrived several hours later from

New Zealand to join him, he was still wide-eyed.

This year, soldiers and police with AK-47s lined the Islamabad streets. They wore black flak jackets and used mirrors with long sticks to search passing cars for bombs. They worked in pairs; one searching, face wooden with tension, while the other stood, rifle against chest, finger on trigger, gaze darting among the crowd. Barbed wire cordoned off the Marriott Hotel, once the cool retreat of air conditioning and post-expedition feasts of lobster and extravagant puddings. Five months earlier, a suicide bomber had driven his truck full of dynamite into the main entrance, killing 65. I wondered which of the smiling waiters I'd got to know by sight were now dead.

Baig, my friend and minder from previous journeys, hastened us through now empty streets. The Faisal Mosque, with room for 10,000 worshippers, was deserted – except for one small figure on the far side, sweeping the endless floor. Paul and I wandered gingerly barefoot over the scorching marble terraces before Baig hurried us on to the bazaar to do our pre-climb shopping. 'We must keep moving. There's no guarantee you will be safe. Don't go outside without me.'

5. Base camp – local shepherds come calling. *(Pat Deavoll)*

He sounded uncharacteristically serious, but kept further thoughts to himself. Paul fiddled with the beginnings of his moustache. 'Better do what Baig says.' He went off to his room to call his wife. I went up on the roof to smoke a cigarette. It was 45 degrees up there and the air hissed with heat. Distant blue hills wavered in and out of focus. The traffic sounded in the distance but the only person in sight was a road sweeper. He sat in the dust under a tree in his ragged clothes, flapping flies one-handed, his twig broom abandoned at his side.

Twenty-four hours later, Baig had hustled us out of the city. In an edgy voice, he'd said he wished we were flying north, but flights were cancelled. We drove north up the Karakoram Highway against a tide of refugees heading south from Swat. Families crammed into the backs of jeeps and onto the roofs of trucks and buses, while others struggled on foot, piggy-backing children and the elderly, and bundles of possessions. *Two million people displaced— that's half the population of New Zealand.*

A middle-aged man hung on the running-board of a truck. Beneath the brown Pashtun turban his sun-rugged features looked proud, but weary.

6. Karim Sar from the Baltar glacier: 'a grandeur surpassing its moderate size'. (*Pat Deavoll*).

7. The intricate south face of Karim Sar (6180m) (*Pat Deavoll*).

Where will he end up? In a refugee camp? What will happen to his home, his farm? How will he support his family? What if I had to leave my home and livelihood, not knowing when I'd return? For a split second we locked eyes and in that moment I realised we were irrevocably, eternally foreign to each other.

Guilt filled me, and I turned away. Near Chatta Plain, a kilometre-long traffic jam brought us to a halt. People clambered from their vehicles, greeting each other, laughing and gossiping in the heat and dust. Then news rippled down the line: *the Taliban have bombed the bridge.* A furore of shouting, blaring horns and diesel fumes erupted as the traffic tried to negotiate the rocky riverbed. I looked back. *Such a small bridge.* A large, jagged hole disfigured the far side. *I'm here to climb a mountain. This is their life. What would they think if they knew?* I didn't dare answer.

As we passed the eastern Swat town of Besham, bearded men stooped and stared through the windows, dark gazes of disapproval. I held my headscarf tight around my face and kept my eyes ahead. After several hundred kilometres and many security roadblocks, Baig sighed and finally let us stop for the night at a guesthouse. The next day, we reached Gilgit, the small northern city wedged between the Karakoram and the Hindu Kush, and Baig began to smile. We paused several times so he could hail friends. '*Assalam-o-Alekum.*'

The city was barricaded like a fortress, but on an impulse I rushed Paul to the bazaar to outfit him in the traditional *shalwa kameez* and the Hunza hat. He listened closely to the shopkeepers' words, and soon we had a small crowd of locals giving us advice. 'Sir you need a larger size! Oh you look very fine now. Sir, you must not pull the hat so low.' Paul looked good in an earthy smock that grazed his knees, a woollen hat jaunty across his forehead. Almost Pakistani.

Two days later, shepherds from the village of Budelas loaded our equipment onto tiny braying donkeys with large fluffy ears. Baig stood on a rock, laughing, conducting the donkey orchestra with a stick. The porters yelled affably as we meandered up the steep valley to our base camp beside the Shilinbar glacier, under the massive south face of Karim Sar. After a rowdy, impromptu game of cricket, they wished us much cheery good luck, '*Inshallah, Inshallah,* God willing…' and disappeared down the valley in a jovial, shambling, laughing mob. Our journey to the mountain was over. A different journey was about to begin.

The sun set behind the ridge and all was quiet except for the hum of the kerosene burner in the cook tent and the occasional phat-phat of rockfall. The air seemed to hang, waiting. At last, the south face reared 2600 metres above us; the intricate facets of rock, the labyrinth of snow gullies and traverses, the towering ice-cliffs lit by the last subtle rays of light. The twilight faded into night, into a timeless, unfathomable peace. There was no conflict here. The mountain was quiet, without emotions or judgment.

Finally, finally, we would go climbing.

As we acclimatised over the next week in snowy, unsettled weather, Paul struggled with the altitude. Summer was late to arrive and there was

8. Paul Hersey works his way up the steepening gully to high camp at 5100m. (*Pat Deavoll*).

vastly more snow than during the previous two years; we learned later that the Karakoram hadn't seen as much winter snow in 30 years. At base camp Paul came down with an undiagnosed illness, recovered, and then decided he didn't want to go onto the mountain. I felt a mix of despair, anger, and anxiety; the expedition was heavily sponsored and, for me, giving up without an attempt wasn't an option. I decided to try the mountain alone and succumbed to some angst-ridden, sleepless nights.

The morning of my departure for the summit, Paul announced he would come back up the glacier to advance base camp (4200m). I felt a flood of gratitude – even if Paul were thousands of feet below me it would be a huge relief to know he was there. Moving up through a dangerous section of the icefall, he climbed with new speed and confidence and next morning agreed to come a few hundred metres up the face to belay me through a rock band. But when we got beneath the short granite pitch, I realised that ice-cliffs, 1500m above, ringed the terrain. I decided to follow a gully system to the left that was overhung by a massive, but seemingly stable ice-cliff. It seemed the better of two evils.

To my surprise, Paul decided to continue, even though he had no overnight gear. At about 3pm I arrived on a small saddle at 5100m, dug a tent platform, and watched Paul slowly work his way up the steepening slope. The location was breathtaking: Rakaposhi and Diran to the south, Sangamarmar only a couple of kilometres east, and way in the distance the massive Hispar glacier.

We both spent a sleepless night; Paul because he was lying in a large plastic pack liner, and me because I was so damn nervous. At 4am I brewed up, handed my sleeping bag to Paul, and headed up a steep snow slope to the first obstacle, a small band of granite covered in loose snow. I bridged up a gully for a few metres, had an '*I can't do this*' moment, and climbed back down. Thwarted only half an hour from the tent! Taking a deep breath, I tried again and this time climbed the 20m to the top.

Another steep snow slope led to a 100m-high granite cliff. I headed right to circumvent it, then discovered I would have to traverse across a steep rock gully with a large drop beneath, and so scurried back left. Above me were two ice-cliffs and between them a steep, narrow gully of snow. I front-pointed 100m up the gully and found myself in a wide cwm rimmed by huge ice-cliffs 300m above. The cliffs seemed quiet, but it was early, and I decided to climb onto a broad ice rib on the right of the cwm to avoid any action. I tried to hurry, but with snow almost up to my knees progress was glacial. Conditions were better up on the rib and I sped up dramatically.

After climbing several hundred metres, passing some sizeable crevasses, I came to a large rock band that formed the base of the summit pyramid. From base camp it had looked as if this could be navigated on the left, but now I realised this would require a long traverse over steep ice with a 1500m drop to the Bar glacier below. Far too scary! I accepted glumly that I'd have to drop 100m, traverse right under the rock band, and try to summit from the east side. The exposure was frightening, and with every step loose, wet snow swished down alarmingly, gathering speed until it shot over the ice-cliffs. After what seemed like an eternity, the traverse ended and I was able to start climbing toward the ridgeline. By this time I was in the full sun and feeling tired.

At midday I hit the summit ridge above the east face. I could see the top and the only obstacle seemed to be a 60°-70° ice slope. 'I can rappel that,' I thought, and whizzed up the ice with renewed vigour. A five-minute wander along the final ridge put me on top. 'Yippee! Now I can go down,' was my reaction.

Two raps off V-threads got me nearly down the ice slope and another three off rock bollards saw me back to the start of the traverse. The snow had deteriorated further and by the time I reached the broad rib at the far end I was almost in tears. But progress down the rib was rapid and I soon cheered up. Back in the cwm, I sat behind a large block of ice, ate a bit and started to feel pleased with myself. I set off again with a big grin.

Reversing the steep, narrow gully between the ice-cliffs required concentration, followed by a nasty traverse back to the slope above camp. I spent 40 minutes cold-welding a stopper into a rotten crack for an anchor and 30m later repeated the procedure to rappel the final rock band. I could see the tent and soon Paul stuck his head out the door and waved.

I felt such an enormous sense of relief when Paul hugged me. He had water and food ready and vacated the tent so I could lie down. After 40 minutes he left to descend 1000m to advance base camp – another night in a plastic bag was beyond the call of duty. I fell sound asleep. At dusk I woke, made another brew, and then passed out till 7am. Descending the gully next day, my legs were like jelly. Paul was waiting at ABC and we packed up and made our way slowly back to base camp.

Back in Islamabad, I was happy to spend the time before my flight watching Wimbledon on cable in my hotel room. While we'd been in the mountains there had been further bombings in nearby Peshawar and Rawalpindi. Baig was ever adamant we keep a low profile. 'Only go out on the streets very early,' he said, 'and take me with you.' But when we did venture into the bazaar in the quiet of the morning, as vendors loaded their

9. Summit day: Pat Deavoll on the ice rib high on Karim Sar's south face (*Pat Deavoll*).

stalls and the first of the day's shoppers drifted by, we were approached by Pakistanis who thanked us for visiting their country. 'Thank you for coming in troubled times,' they said. 'It's not always like this. Really, we just want peace.'

Summary: An account of the first ascent of Karim Sar (6180m), Hunza region, northern Pakistan, in June 2009 by Pat Deavoll, accompanied to 5100m by Paul Hersey.

Acknowledgements: Many thanks once again to Nazir Sabir Expeditions for their superb logistical support and to Sport and Recreation New Zealand (SPARC Hilary Expedition Grant), The Mount Everest Foundation, WL Gore Ltd (Shipton/ Tilman Award), Mountain Hardwear, Southern Approach/Black Diamond, Berghaus, DHL and the New Zealand Alpine Club.

SANDY ALLAN

To Get Closer

Tenth July 2009. We're at 8125m, the summit of Nanga Parbat. I have semi-frozen hands, the weather is awful and Rick and I think we are a tad late to be in such a high place. It's 3pm and our top camp is long way down at around 7000m.

10. Nanga Parbat's Diamir Face, from base camp. *(Sandy Allan coll)*

Rick rushed his photos but I insisted on taking some better ones. While we had both already climbed several 8000m peaks, most of my photos are really poor. As it turned out my Nanga Parbat images are not much better, but there are at least some without thumbs or the inside of down mittens in the frame; one of Rick in fact is rather good and I know he likes it. That's how I partly froze my hands. The old ego trap was yawning again, a trap that for mountaineers can lead to poor decision-making with potentially grave consequences. I was putting my wellbeing at risk for the sake of a photo. Everyone, including me, seems to want a photo, a memento or

11. Rick Allen between camps 1 and 2 on the Diamir Face. *(Sandy Allan coll)*

perhaps nowadays a requirement to prove to others that we were there, like an attendance certificate from school days.

We had kept to our turn back time, but had stretched it to the maximum. Most of the Austrians and Italians had turned back ages ago, exhausted and disheartened by the continuing false bluffs and Cairngorm weather. Yet I felt an amazing calmness, an inner strength and surprisingly well. When the final Italian climber who had kept us company turned back at around 7900m I simply gave a hand sign in my big mittens to Rick not be influenced and to keep going. Rick read the sign and responded positively. We said our goodbyes to a sad Giuseppe and climbed on upwards. Less than an hour later we were forced to our knees, crawling the final metres in a strong cold wind. At the summit we could only sit or kneel; the wind would not let us stand.

Apart from the love of it, one of the reasons we had returned to Nanga Parbat was to peer down from the summit and see if there was a climbable way up from the Monzino Ridge side, which Rick and I had tried in 1995 on an Alpine-style expedition led by Doug Scott. However, due to the wind neither of us had the nerve to peer over what seemed like the very edge of our horizon.

After descending a short distance we sheltered behind a rocky protrusion while I massaged my hands back to semi-circulation, something the first aid manuals advise against but which invariably works if you catch the freeze early enough. We then scooted away downwards, meeting a large Korean team with some Pakistani and Sherpa high altitude porters who were making a concerted effort to get a 'Miss Go Mi-sun' to the summit. 'Wow! You're even later than us,' I said. 'It's wildly windy up there, we could not stand up on the summit. You should be careful.' I added a good luck and take care.

A few steps onwards and I recognised the face of Wolfgang who was part of a large, friendly Austrian team. He seemed calm and, when I asked, said, 'I am OK and with the Koreans.' I warned him that while 'you may think you are with the Koreans, the Koreans may not think you are with them'. I was incredibly concerned for him and knew he was far too late and was, in reality, by himself. 'Take care; you should come back with us,' I told him explicitly. But I knew his eyes were fixed on the summit and there was no way he was going to retreat. My thoughts were struggling with the knowledge that these people were actors entering their own 'perfect storm'. It was obvious that none were for retreating.

Rick and I continued down, moving fast and efficiently, the weather becoming even worse and it was starting to snow. The thought of having to cross a soft, deep, unstable snow-pack on the open slopes below was not something either of us relished. We were still feeling strong, and soon caught up with another famous Korean woman who had summited at least an hour before us and was being guided by Sherpas who were on oxygen. I recall one Sherpa in front of her and two behind, with tight ropes to their precious employer.

Miss Oh Eun-sun did not actually use bottled oxygen herself and was claiming that all her ascents were therefore 'oxygen free'. A literal interpretation if ever there was one; it seems that being hauled around by some of the highest paid Sherpas from Nepal, sucking oxygen from cylinders on their backs, does not really count as assistance. Nevertheless, as an enlightened Scottish Highlander I believe that our existence depends on our ability to build a harmonious, respectful global community and Miss Oh Eun-sun was a nice lady so I kept my thoughts to myself. I had spoken to her on a number of days before; we'd even shared a photo shoot and I was getting to know her quite well. On one occasion we chatted for ages while washing clothes by the stream at base camp. I was impressed that she did not send one of her minions to do her laundry. She explained that both she and Miss Go Mi-sun wanted to be the first woman to climb all 14 eight thousanders. While Miss Go was competitive with her, Miss Oh felt she was not competitive with Miss Go, she simply liked the idea of doing them all first. Misses Go and Oh were quite chatty and we often saw them on walks together around base camp. They had managers and a film team and their own teams of hyper-fit, quietly competent Sherpas. It was a bit of a circus. But the Korean teams fixed lots of rope and did a great deal of the work on the mountain from which we all benefited.

It was almost dark as we arrived back at our high camp at 7000m where my Vango tent was still standing. Two local porters were there, as originally I had been guiding the mountain until my client, Edward, went home after a couple of forays to Camp 1 at 4890m. Huge avalanches crashing down only metres from our camp, an incessant tummy bug and a pregnant wife back in London had won the day and Ed decided to go home. Immediately, with the help of Ali, our liaison officer, I told Mehrban and Quasim they could consider themselves on holiday with full pay. I had hired the two high altitude porters to assist me with fixing the mountain for Ed. However, I explained that Rick and I did not really need them; they could stay and climb the mountain for themselves or hang about and try and get work with the other teams, or simply go home. Mehrban was a wonderful guy who had already climbed K2 and was greatly respected by all the expeditions' porters and local staff. They operated independently and seemed to hang out with the porters of the much larger Austrian team, led by Gerfried Göschl.

I fully expected Mehrban and Qasim to have descended on our summit day but there they were on our return, offering us water to drink. It tasted of sweaty sock or something even worse so I vomited the first mouthful, then discreetly dislodged the large pot and began melting fresh snow. They were cool guys, good company and it was ace to have them around. However, in my opinion, while the Pakistan mountaineering agencies tell us their high altitude porters are good, they are still not equal to the Nepalese Sherpas.

That night at high camp I was awoken by a hullabaloo going on in the darkness. From the sound of it, people were trying to organise something. It transpired that the Koreans we met going up as we descended were now stuck up on the mountain between high camp and the summit. The news came as no surprise, but being reasonable men, rather than informing them it served them right we sent out a rescue party. Mehrban got up in what seemed like the middle of the night in freezing cold temperatures and went to help, joining forces with local staff from various expeditions who had been looking after the high camp. It was a sterling effort, moving by headtorch light, carrying freshly melted snow-water, spare food and clothing, and breaking trail for the Koreans back to Camp 4. They had extended the Koreans' lives. But being out overnight with limited food and water in terrible weather is not good for the human condition. Add to that the effects of extreme high altitude and the reader can work out that the tale does not end here.

The following morning Camp 4 was quiet. Rick and I got up early thinking that all was as good as could reasonably be expected and that all the climbers were back at high camp, in their tents warming up, re-hydrating and resting. We struck camp and headed down. We had spent enough time at altitude to know that it's best to hang out where there are good supplies of fresh water, thicker air and hearty meals. Rick also needed to get back to work and my daughter Hannah was graduating in Edinburgh so we both had good reasons to be back home.

The descent was made more complex by the lack of fixed ropes. While

2. Rick Allen on the summit of Nanga Parbat (8125m). *(Sandy Allan coll)*

Rick and I are not too fond of the fixed rope thing, they are actually really handy when descending. But as the weather window for the summit attempt had come faster than the commercial groups had planned for, they had had to pull the lower ropes to fix higher parts of the mountain for the aforementioned Koreans and their entourages. This resulted in some quite exposed down-climbing but being reasonably early the snow was in good condition. We struck my tent at Camp 3 (6500m) and went on to Camp 2 (6000m) where we again packed tents and tided up. Rick hung out at C2 for a while, but I wanted to get off the hill as soon as possible so declined the offer of tea from some high altitude porters, shouldered my huge sack and set off abseiling down the Kinshofer Wall and on to Camp 1. (I should mention that the Kinshofer Wall is an impressive bit of climbing, good Scottish grade IV at 5800m.) At Camp 1, I struck the old Salewa tent that Rick and I had bought second hand in Kathmandu for our new direct route on Pumori south face – that was back in 1986. It was sad seeing the faded flysheet in tatters although it made me realise that even with the occasional imperfection my own skin was holding out quite well under the circumstances. I tidied the camp up as best as I could, meanwhile melting snow and making a quick brew. Taking as much of the equipment and rubbish as I could by tying it to the outside of my Berghaus expedition sack, I left the rest for Rick.

I arrived back at base camp exhausted but happy. Rick and I were greeted like royals for, though we hadn't realised it, most people had turned back and did not make the summit. We had a few brews and some food, then went instantly comatose in our tents. Next morning we were updated on all the news. Miss Go Mi-sun had died; exhausted, she had fallen off on the descent somewhere above Camp 2 where a section of the fixed ropes had been removed for use higher up. Wolfgang Kölblinger, the Austrian we met intent on the summit, had also disappeared. There was a dreadful list of sad tales, all very human and unfortunately avoidable. Gerfried and some of his team turned up having climbed a new line to Camp 4 and then summited the next day, really looking for Wolfgang but all they found was a hat in the rocks. They presumed he had been blown off the summit.

The Korean budget was sufficient to charter two helicopters to search for Miss Go. This all added to the pandemonium. There were people milling about wearing the finest designer mountaineering clothing comprehensively adorned with sponsors' logos, taking photos and rushing to be the first with the bad, but potentially money-making news. It simultaneously amazed and disgusted me. They were really just ordinary people who wanted to climb a mountain yet who somehow were getting tangled up in the futile grabbing of associated fame, sacrificing empathy by being the first to get news out to some commercial website.

It made me sad and I was relieved to just hang out in my tent. The time alone allowed me to reflect on this 8000m peak bagging scene, so different from the Himalayan new routing I'm more familiar with. I saw many mountaineering people camped in the same remote but beautiful base camp as me, letting their sense of responsibility erode. Have these mountaineers, set on ticking eight thousanders by the normal route, fixing rope every step of the way, lost the habit of inwardness and open-hearted listening? So willing, or so it seemed to me, to sell their soul for a quick lucrative tit-bit.

Thinking back to our moment at 8125m, it was an amazing summit truly worked for, and we had it to ourselves. It was ace! And that was in line with much of our experience in Pakistan.

At the start of the expedition we had spent one night in Islamabad and then driven along the Karakoram Highway. We met amazingly friendly locals and travellers from distant lands; crossing into the Swat valley, we travelled in convoy with police and soldiers riding shotgun on our trucks; turning up in a village looking for beds in the middle of the night, the hospitality shown to us was humbling.

Walking out from base camp – Rick and me, Mehrban and Qasim – we met some holy men and invited them to share a hastily-made brew and our remaining biscuits. We sat together on boulders among green grass by the edge of a small stream. Once our biscuits were finished they shared their snack food with us. I talked about Pakistan, my ascent of Muztagh

3. Sandy Allan on the summit of Nanga Parbat: 'We could only sit or kneel; the wind would not let us stand.' *(Sandy Allan coll)*

Tower and journeys with friends on the endless Baltoro, climbing in these awesome mountains, jungles of inspiring ice-encrusted rock obelisks, cathedrals and spires, turbulent glacier-melt rivers, creaky bridges, ageing hand-painted jeeps with treadless, bulging tyres. Wonderful Pakistan; oily lentils, onion bhajis, goats and goat herders, stubborn mules, flies, apricot trees, irrigation channels and dusty chickens, well-intentioned people who do not necessarily believe that 'west is best' but understand that we are all simply different.

The conversation was amiable and engrossing. It became obvious that these spiritually rich men were also well-heeled and well-travelled. The leader of the holy men looked into my eyes and wonderingly asked why I wanted to go to the summit of Nanga Parbat? I replied, 'To get closer of course.' He nodded and smiled.

Summary: An account of how Sandy Allan unwittingly became the first Scotsman to climb Nanga Parbat. He and Rick Allen reached the 8125m summit on 10 July 2009 via the *Kinshofer Route* on the Diamir Face.

MALCOLM BASS

Ten Days on Vasuki Parbat

As the rock flew past me I knew it was going to hit Paul. I'd heard it come banging and whirring down the gully, bigger and noisier than the others. I'd screamed 'rock!' but Paul, tethered on the open icefield below, had nowhere to hide. It smashed into the ice a metre out from my stance beneath a roof, and then spun out, arcing towards its target. The impact was a muffled thud. Paul crumpled onto the anchors. It was 3pm on day 3 and the sun was beating full onto Vasuki Parbat's west face. Suddenly it was very quiet and I felt acutely alone.

But then Paul began to move. Moans drifted up as he righted himself, then stood back up to the stance.

'Paul, Paul … are you OK?'

'I think so.'

'Can you climb?'

'Give me a minute.'

I was desperate for Paul to start moving. I wanted to shout at him to get a move on (or words to that effect). We were at the bottom of a gully overhung by a 700m leaning wall of variable quality rock. For the last hour rockfall had been steadily increasing. The objective danger meter was swinging between 'Unjustifiable' and 'Suicidal'. But Paul knew all that: any delay on his part could more reasonably be ascribed to having just been hit by a 3kg boulder that had fallen several hundred metres than to a lack of appreciation of the urgency of the situation. So I shut up. Paul collected himself, took out the ice screws, and began to climb towards me, slowly and stiffly at first. It wasn't an easy pitch; tenuous hooks on small dusty edges; hard, black ice of the shattering type, loose sections, and the occasional death-dealing falling rock. I'd hated it, torn between the need to move carefully, to find some scant protection, and the need for speed. But Paul is an old hand at doing the business despite injuries sustained during our joint adventures; he'd rallied remarkably quickly after I'd inadvertently pulled him over a 20m sérac some years earlier, and so he did on this occasion. He soon began to move more freely, and before any more rocks could fall he'd joined me under the safety of a roof in the gully wall. We agreed on a pause for refreshments (a brew and some anti-inflammatories), to let the sun leave the face, and to gather our wits.

It had been a trying day. Our team of three had shrunk to a pair around noon when Pat, struggling with her recently broken back and acclimatisation problems, had wisely decided to descend. This had been a fraught few minutes for all of us. For Pat, the end of her dream of climbing the face after all her hard work. For Paul and I, the break up of the team. For me,

4. The west face of Vasuki Parbat, Garhwal Himalaya, showing the line of Bass and Figg's nine-day ascent. (*Satyabrata Dam*)

the loss of my friend and partner from so many recent climbs. With the sun just moving onto the face, a few minutes was all we had to think and talk it through, heads buzzing with racing thoughts and awash with emotions, then quickly sort the gear. Pat had taken the haul line, some screws, V thread kit, gas, food and a burner and set off down the snow slope to our previous night's bivouac site. I had taken the rest of the rack and headed up that hateful, bombarded pitch. Half an hour later the rock had hit Paul. A trying day indeed, and it was by no means over.

By rights we should have been nowhere near Vasuki Parbat. Our original plan had been to have another go at Janahut, a 6800m peak near the head of the Gangotri glacier, which the three of us, accompanied by New Zealander Marty Beare and Brit Andy Brown, had attempted in 2004. But whilst the Indian Mountaineering Foundation had happily given us a permit, the state of Uttarakhand, which now administers the Garhwal and Kumaon areas, had been less obliging, and by three months before we were due to travel it was clear that the vital state permit was not going to be forthcoming. A rapid email debate followed. 'What about that face in Sichuan we've always talked about?' 'If we go sub-7000m in Pakistan can we afford to ditch your ticket to India?' 'What about Himachal Pradesh?' It soon became clear that financial and permit considerations dictated an open list peak in India with equivalent kudos to Janahut. Vasuki Parbat was on Uttarakhand's open list. Mick Fowler and Paul Ramsden had got a permit for it in 2008. The IMF was supportive. And the west face had enough dramatic appeal to reassure grant-giving bodies that our new objective was worth funding. Administratively it was a winning plan. But as a climbing objective it made my blood run cold.

Firstly it was clearly very steep; try as I might I couldn't find a photograph which made the face appear to lay back even a little; it remained resolutely vertical. Secondly it didn't appear to be made of comforting Garhwal granite but of something much less pleasant. (Frankly I chose not to enquire too deeply into the geological question as Vasuki's proximity to the shale monstrosity of Satopanth didn't bode well). And thirdly it had seen off Fowler and Ramsden. Admittedly their 2008 trip had been dogged by ridiculous quantities of snow, but their *AJ* report (vol 114, 3-12) also spoke of challenging climbing, steepness, wild exposure, a rock fall (singular!), complex route finding and numbing cold. Such talk from alpinists of their calibre was somewhat daunting.

But we were committed and, bolstered by generous route finding tips from Mick in the form of photographs labelled 'Go this way to climb Vasuki', arrived in Delhi in lingering monsoon rain. After a two-day refresher course in the ways of Indian customs, a fine dinner at Mandip and Anita Soin's home, and an introduction to our prodigiously accomplished liaison officer Satyabrata (Satya) Dam (double Everester, both Poles on foot), we were on our way to the mountains. The roads were in terrible condition, a legacy of the horrendous summer of rain that had tormented the Subcontinent. The journey to Uttarkashi, normally a one-day drive,

15. Paul Figg and Malcolm Bass following the initial gully pitch on Day 1. (*Pat Deavoll*)

took two long days. We told ourselves that the frequent showers were the very last vestiges of the monsoon.

We had been travelling for no more than half an hour on the third day of the drive, from Uttarkashi to Gangotri, when, unbeknownst to us at the time, we encountered a Critical Moment. A mountain stream had washed away a section of the road ahead. A heavy truck had tried to negotiate the wash out, failed, and rolled onto its side, spilling its load of road repair gravel. The driver had escaped unharmed. We piled out of the bus and joined the crowd milling about in the heavy rain. After watching a few other vehicles attempt the wash out, our driver announced, with great foresight as it turned out, that he and his bus were going no further. What we didn't know then was that it was going to continue to rain heavily, and that the road up to Gangotri (the road-head) would close later that day and not reopen for over a week. Other climbing teams stuck in the traffic jam behind the rolled truck were to arrive in Gangotri a week later, or turn for home without ever reaching the mountains. But thanks to the quick thinking and local contacts of Khem Singh of Ibex Expeditions, we were soon on our way again, this time in two sturdy 4x4s. These were the last vehicles to make it to Gangotri before the road was closed.

Gangotri is normally a bustling place with a holiday atmosphere, crowded with pilgrims and tourists. But as the rain continued it grew to resemble an English seaside town in mid-January. Shops and cafés pulled their shutters down in the absence of business. At first we were relatively buoyant; we had plenty of time and a couple of days spent acclimatising would do no harm. But on the third day of continuous rain, as we watched the snow line dropping by the hour and heard that the track up to the mountains had been closed by the local authorities, our spirits began to sink. An attempt on an unclimbed mountain face at 6700m began to seem rather improbable if the weather wouldn't permit a walk along a paved track at 3500m.

But the next day dawned sparkling and clear. Those who knew the right people (and we did) would be able to set off up towards the hills the next day. We were on the move again.

Four days later we were ensconced in a fine little base camp more often used as ABC for teams on the normal route up Bhagirathi II. The team consisted of Satya; New Zealander Patricia Deavoll, who'd just recovered from breaking her back five months earlier; Paul Figg, a man who can keep going for ever as he proved on a 10-day 'up and over' ascent of our new route *The Prey* on Mount Hunter; Paul's partner Rachel Antill, our artist in residence; cook team Chandar Singh Negi and Shankar Thapa; and myself.

16. Malcolm studies one of Mick Fowler's photographs at the second bivvi. Fowler and Paul Ramsden attempted the face in 2008. (*Pat Deavoll*)

The mountains were deep in snow, but sunshine and a well-broken trail up gentle slopes on the eastern flanks of the Bhagirathis made by an Indian Army expedition allowed for acclimatisation. Pat wasn't acclimatising as well as she would have liked and was plagued by an incessant cough, but otherwise we were nearly back on schedule. The plan was for Paul, Pat and I to attempt Vasuki's west face, while Rachel painted and Satya photographed. We'd realised by now that it was going to be a very cold climb. We'd tried our lightweight sleeping bags on the acclimatisation foray, and even though I'd previously used mine on open bivouacs in winter in the French Alps, they'd proved far too cold for use here. So we packed big down sleeping bags and inflatable mats, and because with these loads we weren't going to be moving fast, we threw in seven days' food and nine days' gas.

In the pale dawn light of our first day on the face we reached the top of a snow cone and confronted the first pitch, a thin ribbon of water-ice snaking down a gully leading to the buttress we intended to follow. I made the first belay, a nut and a tri-cam; I can remember their placements even now. The deeply familiar routines of making belays, uncoiling ropes, and tying on contrasted, as they always do, with the strange and terrifying magnificence of embarking on something that will last for many days, of which you have dreamt for months, and which might well change you for ever.

Pat, as the strongest ice climber, led, and Paul and I followed with big sacs. The climbing was only moderate, but it felt hard with the sacs and altitude and I was glad when it was time to break out of the ice gully and make a rising traverse to a saddle on the buttress crest where we planned to spend our first night. But we were still low on the face and the ground was none too steep, so the snow was deep. We ploughed on through the afternoon, dreading our spells at the front trail breaking, to be rewarded by a flat, safe campsite.

Day 2 provided uneventful snow climbing. The barometer dropped more than expected so we camped a little early on another good site on a ledge to the right of the fall line. Next morning we set off well aware that we would be climbing into the crux section of the route – 300m of steep mixed ground. The cold was intense. We began by soloing in deep, cold snow, but gradually the ground steepened as we were funnelled into a gully dropping from the left edge of the steep buttress above. Snow gave way to ice; we roped up and began pitching. Pat brought us up to her stance:

'I could easily get down from here on my own.'

'Are you joking?'

'No, I mean it.'

Two hours later a somewhat battered Paul and a rather dazed Malcolm are sheltering beneath the roof drinking herbal tea and waiting for the gully to go quiet. Pat is back at the second night's bivouac ledge, safe for now, but worried about the rest of the descent, and plagued by contradictory thoughts about her decision.

Eventually the sun leaves the face after a brief golden finale, and in the gathering gloom and deepening cold I edge out into the silent gully. The ice is dark and hard, polished by rockfall. Covered by a veneer of grey grit, rock and ice are indistinguishable in my torch beam. The gully walls are worn smooth and our sole consolation is that the ice takes screws. We've planned to lead in blocks, and this one is mine. We're looking for a diagonal pitch that will take us onto what Mick had referred to as 'great squeaky white ice traverse pitches' leading rightwards to the buttress crest. At first we're convinced we'll see it soon, and then we're convinced we've missed it. For lack of better ideas we keep on up the gully. The climbing is brutal and ugly. We kick and hit hard. It's a nasty black gutter to be in on this dark, cold Himalayan night, but I'm gradually aware of feeling that all is well. It might not be pretty, it might not be clever, but I've done this before, I can do it again, and I can do it all night if that's what it takes. It's a strange place to find my flow.

17. Paul and Malcolm in the steepening snow gully on Day 3, shortly before Pat turned back. (*Pat Deavoll*)

Eventually the gully ends at an overhanging step. Randomly I swing out right onto steep rock, dry tool round a tricky corner, and find myself on a very nearly flat rock ledge. It's midnight. 'Paul, I've found our bivvi.' I pull a couple of slings over my head to make the belay. Unluckily one of the slings is actually my camera, which in my tired and over-excitable state I manage to drop. I watch it skitter away. I know Paul doesn't have a camera with him. I notice that just now I'm really not that bothered. We do the right thing and melt lots of snow for drinks, then spend the night sitting beside one another with our boots on constantly trying to keep our sleeping bags from sliding down. We don't really know where we are. We are worried about Pat. But basically things are under control.

With the first light of morning we're excited to see that we're perched only a little way above the Fowler/Ramsden ice traverse. We quite fancy some squeaky white ice, so Paul leads a descending diagonal pitch that takes us neatly onto the traverse. From here we see Pat pass the first night's bivouac site and disappear into the initial water-ice gully. Over breakfast coffee we'd planned on having an easy day traversing across to the bivouac site that Mick and Paul had found on the buttress crest. I did have an easy day: it was Paul's block. And Paul would have had an easy day too if every single one of our ice screws hadn't been blunted by the previous night's escapades.

The bivouac on the crest was everything we hoped it would be: aesthetic and comfortable. There's a good picture of it in the 2009 *AJ*. We set off next morning with high hopes of making big inroads into the meat of the route. But it was not to be. I led off, moving back left along the last section of the ice traverse to the bottom of a mixed groove cleaving the vertical walls above. Placing a piece of gear on a long sling, I began climbing the groove. The ice was superb, the rock helpful, and I was feeling good. After a few metres I paused to place another nut. Rather a low nut in retrospect, about level with the top of my right gaiter. On reaching down to clip it I fell off instead, an awful clattering fall that scared me whilst it was happening; out of the groove: straight over the ice traverse and on over a horribly steep wall. I ended hanging upside down, one nut stopping a long, long fall onto the belay, dilated pupils trying to take in the drop below me. Terrified for my life, I scrabbled frantically to get up the wall back onto the ice traverse. The wall was too steep, the moves too difficult, and I sagged back onto the rope, gasping for air from reaction, effort, and altitude. I hung there sucking and scared until fit to try again. More thought, less pedalling, and a very hard pull and lock-off got me a placement in the ice, and then I was up. I tottered back along the traverse to Paul on the pinnacle bivouac belay. And burst into tears.

My memories of the rest of that day are fragmentary. I remember spending a fair amount of time repeatedly telling Paul how much I wanted to get up the route, how sorry I was to have fallen, how we mustn't let it stop us (which nobody was suggesting) and crying. Then I fell asleep like some boring drunk who'd finally passed out. Paul diagnosed a, hopefully temporary, brain malfunction of some sort and prescribed a rest day. In putting the tent back up he dropped a tent pole. I wasn't strongly placed to berate him: I was probably insisting we go on to a club by way of the kebab shop. It turns out that First Light tents really only need one pole; take note you super-light fiends.

We set off next morning with the same high hopes, but with Paul in the lead. This proved a more successful strategy, and we gained height steadily by way of a couple of pitches of enjoyable mixed climbing just left of the buttress crest. The disembodied voice of our President warned us away from a tempting snowy traverse back left, and I took over the lead for an imposing, steep, dry, loose rock tower. Our timing was good, the sun was on the rock and I could climb barehanded. We kept our crampons on. Some very satisfying trundling (a 1000-metre drop, a personal best by far) removed the looser bits. I took my sac off for the rock pitches on the tower, so we slowed down dramatically as we hauled and cursed. It was getting dark as we reached the top of the tower to find a short sharp horizontal snow ridge leading to a little buttress. The next hour's climbing was intensely memorable.

Jan Babicz in his guidebook *Peaks and Passes of the Garhwal Himalaya* refers to 'the wild, vertical, West Face' (of Vasuki). This was the wild bit. Six days up a huge face; the dusk wind blowing strongly; vigorous *à cheval* progress with a kilometre drop either side; the world below, forgotten; the summit, forgotten; the only goal to move forwards to find a place to shelter and sleep.

As the cold intensified and the wind kept blowing, the need for shelter became urgent. We lashed ourselves to a rock outcrop and dug down into the sharp snow ridge. After an hour we had knocked enough off the top to make a narrow pitch, perfect for a one-pole tent. The nights in the little tent really worked well. Safe from objective dangers we were very mellow, Paul's calm presence a counterpoint to my greater exuberance. Warm in big bags we slept well and woke refreshed. We kept civilised hours, the early mornings being just too cold to get much useful done.

Day 7 began with a bit more horse work before the ridge ran into a short, steep barrier wall. Things looked grim as the initial section was smooth and overhanging, but a short traverse left found a steep groove that gave the technical crux of the route. Good nut cracks, sharp little edges on either side perfect for crampons, a long, locked-off reach to good ice, then a big heave and high kick and we were on the upper snow field. Bar a couple of short walls, we hoped the way to the summit ridge was open.

The altitude took its toll as we tried to move fast up the snowfield. Slacking, we stopped for an afternoon brew in a magical cave beneath a steep limestone wall. We stopped again an hour later because we'd found a perfect tent site under the overhanging limestone. It was like camping under Kilnsey.

Beginning our eighth day, a little rope tension allowed me to drop off the top end of the buttress/ramp into a gully. Perhaps we could have climbed this to the summit ridge, but it had hidden sections, so we crossed it and moved up and right. Even easy ground was hard work now, and our pace slowed noticeably. But we ground it out and late that afternoon reached the summit ridge.

It was a magnificent moment. As we crested the ridge our world suddenly expanded to include the Sundar valley on Vasuki's east side, the great pyramid of Satopanth and, to the north, over myriad mountains, the high brown plateau of Tibet. I was elated: the Himalaya hasn't granted me many summits, and to be on this untrodden ridge above such a compelling face felt glorious.

In Hindu mythology Lord Vasuki is the king of snakes, so it's no surprise that his mountain has a long, serpentine summit ridge. The summit lay

18. Paul and Malcolm (circled) on the upper section of the face on Day 9. (*Satyabrata Dam*)

north of where we'd topped out, so we moved off in that direction and camped in a little col between rocky towers, just short of the top. After a scanty meal (stretching our seven days' food to an eighth now) we discussed descent options. The east face is moderately angled snow and ice, but it was hard to read from above, covered with séracs and steepenings. Our blunt ice screws confirmed our instinctive Scottish winter climbers' wariness of wide expanses of snow and ice. The ascent route would have eaten our rack, so we opted for a long traverse of the summit ridge and descent by the north-west ridge, which we'd had a good look at from base camp. It's possible this ridge has been climbed to the summit. The Indo Tibetan Border Police claim to have climbed Vasuki in 1973, route unknown, and the scant details they provided have cast doubt on the claim. If they did make the summit it seems most likely it was by the north-west ridge as it's the most accessible route, and a natural for siege-style climbing (big ledges for camps). Since then there have been unsuccessful French and Welsh attempts on the ridge, and a successful Japanese climb of the east face, using fixed rope on its lower part.

The next morning began with a pitch of easy rock, a short section of snowy ridge, then the summit, an unspectacular hump in the ridge. As we climbed towards it I said, 'Paul, is it OK with you if we don't actually go to the summit? I've sort of promised Lord Vasuki that we wouldn't.'

'Funny you say that. So have I'

So we didn't.

The rest of the day moving north along the summit ridge was spectacular.

19. Descending deep snow on the north-west ridge, Day 10. (*Satyabrata Dam*)

The ridge was knife-edged, but not corniced. It had undulations and short, steep steps: the former wore out our legs, the latter wore out our psyches. We stayed roped and moved together, except for particularly nasty steps where we belayed. Often we had our tool shafts planted on the east face, our crampons on the west face. We were in deep snow most of the day and struggled to keep hands and feet warm even in our huge 'storm' mitts.

By late afternoon we had reached the junction of north-west and north-east ridges, and abseiled a couloir on the side of the north-west. As darkness fell we traversed a ledge onto the ridge proper and dug a poor tent site. Not much tea for us that night. For the first time, the cold prevented us from sleeping. We were going downhill in more ways than one.

The north-west ridge had looked easy except for the steep rock towers. In the event, abseiling the steep rock towers amongst rotting fixed rope was the easy bit. The level sections however were thigh deep in unconsolidated snow and we really struggled. Twice we climbed down steep gullies on the north flank. I dropped a stuff sac with my head torch, map and compass. We abandoned the ridge and committed to the lower part of the north face, needing steeper ground to maintain momentum. The snow got deeper. We plunged on down, rolling over little bluffs, glissading in our own powder avalanches. The angle was such, and the snow so deep, that we were virtually throwing ourselves down. As we reached the foot of the face the snow got deeper and progress slowed to a crawl. Hours later in darkness we reached Vasuki Taal, the lake whose shore is used for Satopanth base camp.

The stumble back over moraine ridges on steep, narrow paths with just one headtorch was purgatorial. We worked out that the best tactic was for Paul to walk on a few paces, stop, then turn around to light up the path as I walked up to him. I kept stumbling and falling, forcing me to use my hands to steady myself. I hated doing this, as we knew by now that we had some cold injuries.

At about ten o' clock on the night of the tenth day we saw the lights of base camp below us. Having only one torch showing we began shouting:

'There are two of us.'

'We've lost a torch.'

'We're both here.'

'Tea!'

Headtorches appeared from tents below. I was consumed with anxiety that everyone was OK.

We staggered down the moraine towards the lights. Rachel climbed up the moraine towards us, and we met with tears and hugs:

'Is everyone OK? Did Pat get down safely?'

'Everyone's fine.'

At that moment I finally relaxed. It was over. A few moments later we were down at camp, everyone hugging everyone else in the glow of a celebratory bonfire of rubbish. The smell of paraffin, the taste of tea, friendly faces, and everyone with their stories to tell; we sat in the mess tent talking long into the night. One by one people drifted off to bed. I was left alone. I tried to make some sense of the immensity of the experience. I couldn't. I smiled to myself, stood up stiffly and shakily, and tottered off to bed.

Postscript

When we unpacked Paul's sacs we found that one gas bottle had been crumpled by an enormous blow. This propane-butane air bag had saved him from significant injury or worse from the falling rock. We both had frost nip in 80% of our digits resulting in some blistering and a couple of months of numbness.

20. Malcolm Bass, exhausted, at base camp after the climb. (*Rachel Antill*)

21. Paul Figg and Malcolm Bass looking worn after 10 days on Vasuki Parbat. (*Rachel Antill*)

Summary: An account of the first ascent of the west face of Vasuki Parbat (6721m), Garhwal Himalaya, by Malcolm Bass and Paul Figg. Descent by north-west ridge; 4 to 13 October 2010, 1600m, rock-climbing of Hard Severe (loose), mixed climbing of Scottish VI. Expedition members: Patricia Deavoll, Malcolm Bass, Paul Figg (climbers), Rachel Antill (artist), Satyabrata Dam (liaison officer), Chandar Singh Negi (cook), and Shankar Thapa (assistant cook).

Acknowledgments: The team would like to thank the Mount Everest Foundation, the British Mountaineering Council, the Alpine Club, W L Gore (Shipton-Tilman Grant), Mountain Hardwear, DHL (freight), and Wayfarer meals for their support.
The ascent was one of six climbs shortlisted for a *Piolet d'Or* in 2011.

DEREK BUCKLE

In The Realm of The Bear and Snow Leopard

Most national parks positively teem with visitors but one of India's more recent additions, the Great Himalayan National Park (GHNP) does not fit into this category. Created in 1984, the park comprises a total of 1171 km^2 including its eco buffer zone. Prolific wildlife has attracted trekkers and bird watchers, but difficult access limits the aspirations of all but the very hardy to easier valleys such as that of the Sainj river to the south. While searching for a suitable venue for a joint expedition with the Himalayan Club in 2010, Harish Kapadia suggested that we should explore

22. Laura Millichamp arriving on the ridge of Snowcock Point. (*Derek Buckle*)

the remote Jiwa Nala region of the GHNP. In contrast to more peripheral areas, this valley has not previously attracted mountaineers and only the valley floor is well known. Prior to the establishment of the park, local villagers occasionally exploited the valley for grazing and for medicinal plants but neither is now permitted.

The Jiwa Nala is one of the three watersheds that comprise the GHNP - along with the Sainj and Tirthan further south. It is confined by steep mountain ranges to the north and south and by a glaciated, crenulated cirque to the east. A steep-sided, forested valley restricts entry from the west. Thus, the upper reaches of the Jiwa Nala can only be accessed via the southern Kandi Galu pass (3627m) or the northern Phangchi Galu pass

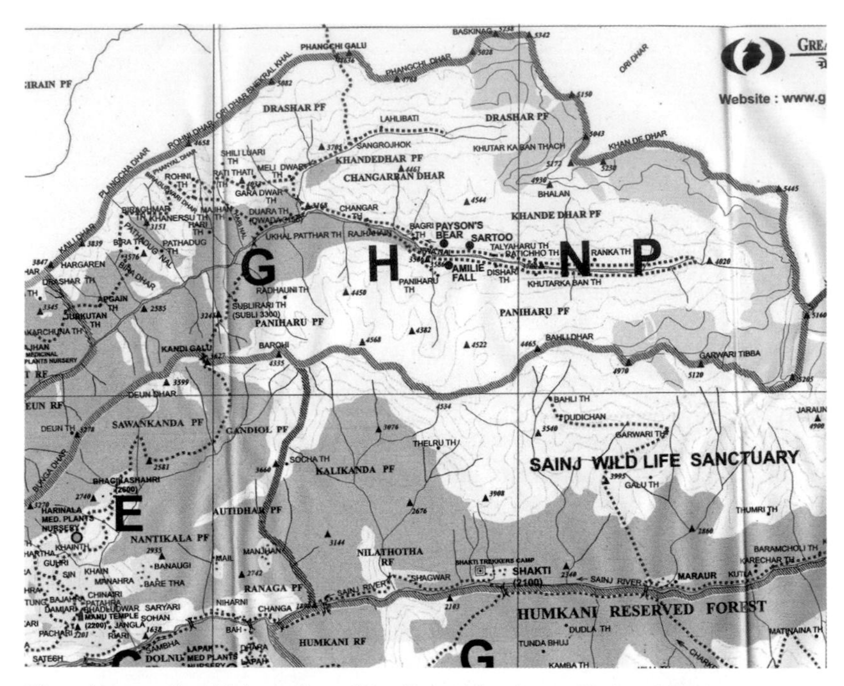

23. Above: Jiwa Nala region of the Great Himalayan National Park. *(Map courtesy GHNP).*

24. Google map of Jiwa Nala showing key locations.

25. Mike Cocker post-holing his way towards the summit of Tribulation Point, 5125m. (*Derek Buckle*)

(4636m). Both passes involve arduous four-day treks from their respective road-heads in Neuli or Pulga. Detailed maps are not officially available for this area, but the GHNP does offer a free electronic map on its web site that clearly shows the glaciated eastern head of the valley and indicates an array of peaks rising to a little under 5500m. Recently published Google Earth aerial photographs are even more informative and convinced us that considerable exploratory mountaineering opportunities existed.

Unfortunately, long before detailed planning got underway both Martin Scott, who had been intimately involved with the early discussions with Harish, and the Himalayan Club found that they were no longer able to participate and it became exclusively an AC expedition.

Following our arrival in Delhi in late September a four-hour train journey on the Shatabdi Express, during which we were continuously fed and watered, took us through the vegetated Indian plains to Chandigarh. From here an eight-hour drive through increasingly mountainous country led to the regional town of Kullu, close to the National Park headquarters. After a brief stay in Kullu we left early the next morning to take the comparatively short but winding road to Neuli on the Sainj river from where we started the four-day trek to our proposed base camp in the Jiwa Nala.

At Neuli we joined an enormous caravan of helpers: five Sherpas who would help establish camps and maintain BC, and a veritable army of 40 porters – comprising 29 Sherpas from Kullu and the remainder, including two guides, from Neuli. Needless to say, organising the group took some time and it was not until after 1pm that our entourage set off for Bhagi-

26. Derek Buckle all smiles having reached Tribulation Point. Snow Leopard Peak is in the background behind Derek. (*Mike Cocker*)

kashahri, the last village in the buffer zone. Following a well-defined wooded path it took around four hours to climb the 900m to Bhagikashahri. This area is famed for its medicinal plants and one in particular, cannabis, was freely growing in abundance. A colourful local puja, complete with litter-borne gods, drums and wind instruments, was underway as we arrived at which we were readily accepted spectators. However, the local children appeared more interested in us than the festivities, but perhaps they had seen something similar many times before.

This part of Himachal Pradesh is characterised by incredibly steep-sided valleys causing problems for both crop cultivation and habitation. With level land at such a premium we camped on the school playground but dismantled the tents during the day so that the space could be returned to its normal use. Leaving Bhagikashahri we walked through a mass of shoulder high cannabis before climbing steeply through deep forests of conifers, holly oaks, rhododendrons and deciduous trees to reach exposed open ground leading to the Kandi Galu pass. It was a magnificent effort on the part of our porters to ascend 1500m over such awkward terrain and a relief to get our first glimpses into the lower wooded reaches of the Jiwa Nala. A steep but relatively short descent from here led to our second camp near to the hut at Sublirari Thach (3350m). Machetes would have been useful to clear the 10 ft-high nettles and other plants for our tents although the Sherpas found that ski poles performed the task almost as well.

Descending steeply the next day the scant track gradually became less wooded as it neared the river, but it was evident that this was not a frequented route and we were grateful to have a local guide. Crossing to

7. Mike Cocker on Snow Leopard Peak, 5365m. (*Derek Buckle*)
8. Derek Buckle descending the rock chimney on Sentinel Peak. (*Mike Cocker*)

the Jiwa Nala's northern side, a considerably better path led to our third camp close to a bothy at Dwada Thach (3200m). It was here that the local porters returned to Neuli while the Kullu porters continued upstream past the Surtu glacial pond to the site of our base camp at Ratichho Thach (3725m: A on the satellite map). The valley bottom now assumed a glaciated U-shaped appearance rather than the steep-sided V-shape encountered below. Most visitors to the Jiwa Nala venture no further than the glacial pond, but judging by their abundant spoor Himalayan bears frequently do.

Base camp afforded good views of the icefall and glaciated cirque at the head of the valley, but these did not suggest which objectives to tackle or how to get to them. For this we made a foray up the slopes to the south, first fording the river before climbing a steep, grassy couloir to an undulating plateau. From a rounded knoll at 4315m a long lateral moraine (visible in satellite pictures) could be seen leading easily to the icefall from where we hoped to gain access to the upper glacier and its surrounding peaks. On 3 October we trekked easily up this lateral moraine to an extensive boulder field, stampeding a herd of 30-40 wild goats in the ablation valley to our left as we did so. With several potential sites for an advanced base camp available, and an encouraging route to the glacial plateau to the left of the icefall, we deposited a stash of technical gear before returning to BC.

With the help of three of our Sherpas (Lobsang, Tsering and Cheddar) we established ABC1 (4623m: B on the satellite map) two days later at the foot of the icefall and close to a prominent rock buttress. After a cold, clear night all bar John climbed the steep glacier on its left side (true right) close to the striated buttress under which we had camped to arrive at an extensive glacial plateau surrounded by a crenulated cirque of 5000m peaks. From here a southerly traverse led across the bergschrund to a steep snow slope to the right of a prominent col. With no easing of the gradient, Mike manfully led by post-holing the way to a compact airy top (5125m Alpine PD) that we have tentatively called Tribulation Point (C on the satellite map) on account of the effort required to get there. From here a route onto the upper glacier seemed possible by taking a steep snowy couloir immediately to the right (due north) of the upper striated rock buttress above ABC1. We returned to ABC1 intent on attempting this the following day.

After another cold night, on 6 October Drew, Mike and myself again ascended the lower plateau before turning north to climb the obvious 40° couloir we had noticed previously. This terminated in an undulating upper snow plateau surrounded by a continuation of the headwall cirque. Several climbing opportunities were evident, but we chose to turn southwest towards a pronounced rocky summit on our left which rose immediately above ABC1. An exposed upwards traverse led to a short (4m) rock chimney and the airy summit (5140m, PD+). Despite changing weather, which unfortunately obscured the panoramic view, we did notice several sets of snow leopard prints, and our next climbing objective. We tentatively called this Sentinel Peak (D on the satellite map) on account of its commanding position over the Jiwa Nala. After a short abseil in atrocious weather we returned to camp by the same route.

As Laura was still feeling the effects of altitude, and John continued to suffer from knee problems, Drew, Mike and myself left at 3am the next day in intensely cold conditions to attempt the dominant peak to the north (right) of the upper plateau that we had visited earlier. Following our previous tracks made the couloir easier, but Drew in particular suffered on the northerly snow traverse above by continuously breaking through the fragile crust. Encouraged by Mike and I on either end of the rope he was rewarded for his effort by leading up the left-slanting mixed ramp which terminated in a fine snow crest and eventually a tiny rocky summit (5365m, AD). The views, extending over a multitude of unclimbed peaks, were tremendous. Having seen many more snow leopard tracks we tentatively called this Snow Leopard Peak (E on the satellite map). We returned to ABC1 with all three of us post-holing across the upper plateau having decided that in the little time left we should explore other parts of the valley.

9. Laura Millichamp on the summit of Snowcock Point, 4890m. (*Derek Buckle*)

Dismantling the camp on 10 October we rejoined John and Laura at BC where the immediate plan was to investigate access to the peaks north of the valley. Setting off in two groups the next day, Laura and Mike climbed the broad couloir immediately above BC while Drew and I elected for another promising couloir a little further east. Both routes led to extensive, complex, waterless boulder fields with no obvious camping areas and no attractive mountaineering objectives within easy reach. We did, however, see several large raptors, an inquisitive pica and significant deposits of both goat and bear spoor. At 4600m Drew and I called it a day, but not before noticing that the lateral moraine to the west of the prominent triangular buttress a little further up the main valley led to another interesting, glaciated cirque to the south.

After relocating to ABC2 (F on the satellite map) at 4020m, all five of us followed the broad ridge of the second lateral moraine until reaching the glacier. The commanding spur leading south from the triangular buttress appears to offer some interesting climbing, but after leaving Drew and John to admire the view we carried on westwards over the glacier until it was possible to climb steeply to a small col overlooking the Sainj valley. From here a short easterly climb up a snowy arête led to a small rocky top where we could all sit *à cheval* to admire the view (4890m, PD). We tentatively called this Snowcock Point (F on the satellite map) on account of the flock of these birds that we disturbed near the summit. After returning to ABC2 we descended to BC the following day in order to prepare for the four-day trek out to Pulga in the north.

With the timely return of our porters on the 15 October we departed the next morning to descend first to Dwada Thach where we had camped on the way in. A steep ascent from here then led to our next camp at Lahlibati (3892m) before spending a very long day crossing the Phangchi Galu pass to camp in a meadow above Pulga at 2960m. The steep snow-covered descent from the pass caused some problems for the local porters but to carry heavy loads over such difficult ground for more than 10 hours was a Herculean effort on their part. After a relatively short drop down to Pulga we travelled by car back to Manali and Kullu before returning via Delhi to the UK.

It had been a real privilege to be the first mountaineers to visit such a pristine area as the Jiwa Nala. Once away from the valley floor we were always in uncharted territory and the mountaineering opportunities at all levels of difficulty are vast. The rock is a mainly a coarse mica-schist, which may be of dubious quality for climbing, but we saw few rockfalls, other than those in obvious detritus gullies, and even on steep ground the snow was stable during our stay. Climbing opportunities exist both to the north and south of the upper Jiwa Nala although sites for high camps are limited by the absence of water and the bouldery terrain.

Summary: In September-October 2010 five Alpine Club members, Derek Buckle (leader), Mike Cocker, Drew Cook, John Hudson and Laura Millichamp, visited the Jiwa Nala region of the Great Himalayan National Park. Various team members explored the glaciated upper reaches of the valley making first ascents of four major points on the crenellated eastern cirque. These were provisionally named: Tribulation Point (5125m), Sentinel Peak (5140m), Snow Leopard Peak (5365m) and Snowcock Point (4890m).

Maps: A detailed map can be purchased from the GHNP Office at Shamshi, Kullu, Himachal Pradesh, India or downloaded free from the National park's website: **www.greathimalayannationalpark.com**

Acknowledgements: The expedition is grateful for Alpine Club Climbing Fund support. We also thank Rimo Expeditions for in-country assistance, our Sherpas; Dan Kumar (cook), Tsering, Lobsang, Cheddar and Raj (cook's assistant) and Charan Johan (local guide).

DAVE WYNNE-JONES

Heat and Snow

Ski mountaineering in the Kullu Valley

30. Dave Wynne-Jones nearing the top of the Rohtang chute with the road over the Rohtang pass and the east face of Beas Rikhi (aka Dashaur peak) in the background. (*John Kentish*)

Arriving at Delhi in April with temperatures of 35 degrees and a ski bag on one's shoulder has to feel a bit odd, although the taxi driver seemed to accept it as yet another example of western eccentricity. Driving up to the Rohtang pass from Manali that oddness seemed less obvious until we noticed the age and condition of the skis and boots at the roadside stalls and that the 'fashionable' one-piece ski suits on offer were clearly local knock-offs. John H's eyes focussed on a particularly colourful display: 'That orange one I've got to have!' I refused to be drawn. We were soon to learn that even in Manali there is only a hazy grasp of the concept of skiing.

A year or two ago, I had been intrigued to learn of a guidebook to skiing in the Kullu valley of India. I eventually tracked it down on the author's website and acquired a copy. The book described a wealth of possibilities to get off the beaten track on ski and experience a real remoteness. In 2010 I organised a trip to the area for the Eagle Ski Club although the majority of the participants were also AC members. The long day's drive to Manali eventually put us at the heart of the skiing potential of the Kullu valley, described in CR Spooner's guidebook, but we began to realise that the heat experienced in Delhi was indicative of an early spring thaw and much of

31. Camp 2 in the Munsiary region with the East face of Rohtang Ri in the centre background. (*Dave Wynne-Jones*)

the potential would remain just that. A reconnaissance of the Solang valley suggested we would be doing a lot of walking, carrying our skis, to access what looked to be very thin snow cover. A foray above Gulaba brought us out onto rolling whaleback spurs where clouds of cabbage white butterflies, bright against the dark cedars below, looked for all the world as if they had been blown out of the very snow like living spindrift. There were impressive views but without any attractive mountaineering objectives. Also the ski runs down tongues of snow between trees looked unlikely to last more than a day or two, which would soon mean a steep mudslide back to the road. With continuous snow only likely above 3500m, we would have to go high and that meant the Rohtang pass.

Hiring a big jeep for the team and our kit looked like it had been a waste of time when we encountered a roadblock at Mahi around 3000m. However, despite the discouragement of a brusque NCO, the redoubtable JR Negi, who is i/c mountain rescue in the area, checked out our kit and authorised our access to the pass. Unfortunately our driver lost his nerve amongst deep ruts about 300m below the pass and left us to walk the rest of the way, assuring us that he would be at Beas Nala for the pick-up in four days' time. We trudged up the muddy road, shortcutting the hairpin bends on snowy tracks, until there was enough snow to skin on to the pass. Striking off from the barely cleared road, the team skirted a knoll and came upon an ideal campsite hard up against a rounded bluff with melt-water dripping off an overhang. We lost no time in setting up the tents and getting

32. Dave Wynne-Jones skiing the Rohtang chute. (*John Hayward*)

a brew on before turning in for an early night.

Our objective for the following day was Rohtang Ri, to the east of the pass. We skinned up snow slopes to the ridge bounding the northernmost little bowl that nestled under a cornice above the west face. There the steepness and condition of the snow suggested skis should be stashed before we booted up the increasingly rocky ridge to a cairned subsidiary summit. From there it was simple step kicking, and some post-holing, skirting the obvious massive cornice above the north face, to reach the main summit at 4697m. Afternoon cloud was beginning to bubble up so we quickly reversed the route to our ski depot and slid off the ridge onto the headwall of the bowl beyond. That led on down the north-west aspect of the west face until we cut back left via steep faces and over minor ridges to reach the campsite just before the first flakes of snow: a wonderful ski descent.

John K's health issues kept him in camp as the rest of us headed west for what was described as Dashaur peak by Spooner, although official maps gave it as Beas Rikhi. Steep skinning led to 4350m on the north face before we decided the angle was just too much and booted up. It was a glorious day but the penalty was that, even on this northerly aspect of the mountain, the softened snow would collapse, thigh-deep, at times. A large square cairn on the skyline had encouraged the idea that we were not far from the summit ridge but when we reached the cairn the summit ridge was still a good way beyond. We continued to kick steps, and sink, until we reached it. There a surprise awaited us: where the ridge narrowed and steepened to a series of exposed gendarmes a solitary but substantial mani stone had been placed, staking a Buddhist claim to this airy height. We climbed on to the highest of the gendarmes and took a break for lunch, enjoying the vista of snow peaks stretching into Lahaul.

33. John Hayward descending from the unnamed 4805m peak with Lee Johnson and John Kentish higher up the snow ramp in the background. (*Derek Buckle*)

John H and Lee had carried their skis as far as the mani stone and their reward was an exciting descent, carving bow-waves through soft snow to where Derek and I had left our skis. Then we launched ourselves down the north face, all the way to the point that the army had reached in their efforts to clear the road over the pass. While we were reattaching our skins a couple of officers turned up for a chat and told us that they were a month ahead of schedule in clearing the road: more evidence of global warming. We skinned back to camp to celebrate with John K.

Breaking camp next morning, we traversed easily east towards the Rohtang chute on increasingly steep ground until we found a break that allowed us to enter the chute at about one third height. We skied down to a rock island where all our camping kit was unloaded and stashed. The Rohtang chute is an extraordinary couloir that plummets directly between parallel rock walls from a break on the south ridge of Rohtang Ri. We were lucky to be able to skin to within about 50m or so of the top before having to carry our skis, but there were some tricky kick turns getting there and that top 50m was 50 degrees in places. The view over the knife-edge ridge revealed lots of scope for another camping trip although our thoughts were already focussed on the intimidating descent that we had just climbed. One by one we dived down the chute, regrouping in stages to ensure nothing untoward occurred in what turned out to be a brilliant descent, linking long sequences of swooping turns between the rock walls on snow that was a little heavier than perfect but still great fun.

Back at the rock island we reloaded our sacks and skied much heavier snow, following the river, down to gain the snowfields at Beas Nala. There we threaded our way through the day trippers, full of excitement at their first encounters with snow, to meet our car.

Two rainy days of temple visits in Manali and we were back at Beas Nala having braved the crazy hairpins and traffic jams as holiday crowds

34. Derek Buckle and Dave Wynne-Jones on the summit of unnamed peak 4375m with unnamed peak 4805m left and Khrei Ra Jot 4575 right in the background. (*John Hayward*)

fled the heat of the Punjab to play in the snow. At Beas Nala families wandered in ankle-length fake furs while the braver souls clicked into skis and were pushed off on gentle inclines by local 'entrepreneurs' who ran to catch them before they fell over. On the higher fringes a skier with more idea made cautious turns before climbing back up on foot for another go. We drew curious stares as we shouldered our packs and skinned steeply up the Sagu Nala past a waterfall waiting to unload the last of its fans and pillars of ice. Above, the snowed-up bed of the river that fed it led to a steep open chute that in turn led to a high bench below the peaks that we hoped to climb. We camped in a snow depression at 3960m in what Spooner describes as the Munsiary area.

It was impossible to ignore the sharp pointy peak in the distance, given 4805m on the map, although it entailed more than 3km of skinning across the high bench to reach its slopes. And what slopes! We gamely zigzagged up until the angle defeated our efforts to stay on ski, whereupon we strapped the skis to our packs and booted on to reach a snow ledge where the cornice curling from the ridge to our right met a sudden snow step at the base of the summit pyramid. There we left our skis and climbed up the step to gain a snow ramp left of a rocky spine falling from the summit. A short scramble led from that to the summit rock platform with a treacherous hollow cornice hanging over the precipitous north face. There was time to catch our breath and take in the view back towards the east face of Rohtang Ri and east towards 6000m peaks, Deo Tibba and Indrasan.

We scrambled back down to the skis. John H skied off the step and Lee skied off the cornice as an aperitif for an adrenaline rush that we all shared skiing down the face we had climbed. A sporting descent to camp quickly completed our day.

Another fine day saw us skinning up towards Khrei Ra Jot, a double-summit exceeding 4500m on the long ridge to the east. A steep couloir led to a small bowl below the col between the peaks where we left the skis. A rocky scramble up the broken ridge of the higher summit included a delicate slab that proved interesting in ski-touring boots before we gathered on the pleasantly sharp summit. Derek and I tackled the short snow slope and earthy rock ridge to the lower top although there did not seem a lot of point to it. The snow showed a tendency to slide so we spaced our runs carefully on the descent. Not carefully enough as it turned out because Lee began to catch Derek up and his attempt to take a less direct line led to the release of a small slide. It may have been small but still had enough mass to sweep Derek off his feet as he skied straight into its path. No harm done, but a few choice words were exchanged.

Our last day also dawned fine for a rapid skin up to a nearby 4000m peak we had scoped out on the previous day. The sun was taking its toll on the snow though and we preferred to trust ourselves to grassy rakes sodden with melt-water rather than the suspect snows of the couloir we had started to ascend. The slopes eased above, before a steep icy ramp led to the final summit at 4375m. A traverse further north on the descent led to another couloir with a less southerly aspect that proved a safer, if steeper option before a fast and fun run down the familiar return to camp.

It was much warmer and cloud was building so we packed up as quickly as possible and returned to Beas Nala along the line of our ascent of three days' earlier. The snow was turning to slush and proved challenging with packs still heavy with camping gear, but the only mishap was when Derek fluffed a turn in the steepest part of the chute and found himself hanging upside down from the buried heels of his skis. His attempts to recover resulted in his rucksack heading off down the slope for me to intercept while Lee skied over to give him a hand. Good teamwork! Back at Beas Nala, amongst the madding crowds, bedraggled white butterflies lay dead on the dirty snow as heavy drops of rain signalled an imminent downpour.

Rain stopped play for our remaining days in the valley so we drove out early enough to organise a visit to the Taj Mahal on our return to Delhi, rounding off our visit to India with the classic tourist experience that somehow remained an anticlimax.

Summary: An account of a three-week ski-mountaineering expedition to the Kullu valley in India in April 2010 with ascents of Rohtang Ri (4697m), Beas Rikhi (aka Dashaur peak, 4631m), Khrei Ra Jot (4575m), an unnamed peak of 4805m and another of 4375m. Party: AC members, Derek Buckle, John Kentish, Dave Wynne-Jones, and ESC members, John Hayward and Lee Johnson.

ANDY HOUSEMAN

More Than You Can Chew?

35. Nick Bullock approaching the first bivvi at 6000m, Day 1 (*Andy Houseman*)

Bent over my axes, I threw up in the snow – 'Not now!' I silently screamed. We'd both managed to keep well on the trip so far. What if I blew our only weather window? Standing in the dark silence, I shouted up to Nick, dreading his reply. It came without hesitation or the slightest note of anger: 'No worries youth, we can go down and give it a few days.'

36. Andy heading up the third pitch on Day 2, trying to find a way through the steep rock bands. *(Nick Bullock)*

There it was; a chance to run away. Was this what I'd been looking for? Was it all psychological? This was the biggest face I'd been on, and of course I felt nervous – anyone who says he doesn't is bullshitting. Nick's laid-back response almost made bailing too easy. It was our first day on the north face of Chang Himal. Out in front, Nick Bullock was zig-zagging up firm snow.

My climbing partnership with Nick had been forged over the previous few years, strengthened through friendship, mutual respect, and trust in each other in the mountains. Through the winter of 2006-7, we shared a flat in Chamonix, me the keen and inexperienced youth, Nick the wise old man. Conditions were favourable that winter and our route tally kept growing, the only problem being that neither of us had much enthusiasm for leaving a bivvi early.

Our choice of Chang Himal we owed to Lindsay Griffin and his contribution to the *Alpinist* article 'Unclimbed' (*Alpinist* 4). One of Lindsay's picks was the stunning 1800-metre north face of Chang Himal (6802m, also known as Ramtang Chang or Wedge Peak). Situated in the remote north-east corner of Nepal, it is one of many impressive mountains that form the Kangchenjunga Himal. We'd thought about going there in autumn 2008, but my attempt at a full-time job in the UK limited any time away. After a two-day jeep ride and 10-day trek to reach base camp, we would barely have had time to acclimatise, let alone attempt Chang Himal. Instead, we'd opted for the quickly accessed Hinku valley. And there, while resting at a teahouse down the valley, our base camp was robbed of everything apart from the garbage bag. We hadn't even tied into a rope.

One year later, luck seemed to be on our side. With no daily forecast

7. The 1800m north face of Chang Himal (6802m), north-east Nepal, showing the Bullock-Houseman route. *(Andy Houseman)*

being sent to us at base camp below Chang Himal, we had no way of knowing the good weather we experienced upon arrival would hold, but day after day it did. And we were lucky with conditions too. In 2007 a Slovenian attempt (the only proper shot at the face prior to ours) had failed at less than half height due to bad snow. We didn't have bomber, squeaky névé up the entire face, but we weren't complaining.

We had further good fortune in Buddy, our cook. Without a doubt, he made the trip. Day after day he produced pizza and chips, lasagne, fresh bread, apple pies, burgers – you name it, he'd cook it.

We arrived at base camp, situated at 5050 metres, above the Kangchenjunga glacier, in mid-October. The 10-day trek with three friends had been mellow and sociable; we could almost forget what we were there for. After our goodbyes at base camp, the trip suddenly took on a serious note; a kick up the backside, so to speak. The daunting north face of Chang Himal was just a couple of miles away over the jumbled chaos of the glacier. 'Umm… bitten off more than you can chew here,' I thought. From the time we woke to the end of each day acclimatising on the mounds of scree rising to 6000m behind base camp, Chang Himal was omnipresent – there was no escaping it.

For 10 days, we watched the face as our bodies slowly adapted to the altitude, Buddy producing tasty food day after day. With a route cairned across the glacier, the rack and food debate settled, and our kit stashed below the face, only an hour and half away, we were out of excuses. We spent a couple of days just eating, resting, and watching for any telltale signs of a change in the weather. None came and so, after a leisurely lunch, we took to our cairned path and settled down for the night in a small cave below the face.

Sleep came surprisingly easy. After an early alarm and a quick breakfast, at 2.30am we entered the rocky gully that leads on to low-angled snow slopes at the bottom of the face. Climbing onto the snow cone, we felt silent relief as we stood on a crust of firm snow instead of sinking to our waist in bottomless powder as we'd feared. We zigzagged up the slope, avoiding front-pointing till the last possible moment, saving our calves for what was to come. But instead of running up the firm snow, I moved as slowly as if I were wading through powder; I could barely keep pace with Nick as he kicked steps in front. I'd come out to Nepal not as fit as I'd have liked, but even so I'd felt better than this while acclimatizing.

38. Andy chopping the bivvi ledge on Day 2 at 6200m – 'and no, the ledge did not get any bigger!' *(Nick Bullock)*

In the anguished moments while throwing up, Nick's seemingly relaxed offer to go down was a temptation I had to resist. The drive was still there. 'I want to continue,' I shouted up. If Nick could kick the steps, I'd try to keep up.

We slowly soloed the steepening snow slope, moving as quickly as my weak body would allow through what we had dubbed 'The Narrows', the most threatened part of the route. By dawn we had started up the broad gully that eventually would lead us back left onto the central spur that was our key to the face. The odd steep step or a few moves on unconsolidated bottomless snow limited my daydreaming. The vomiting had stopped, but my body felt empty. Nick thought *giardia*. I wasn't sure, but the excitement of the unknown climbing above had taken over, keeping me going.

Nearly halfway up the face we stopped just to the right of the spur, chopping a small ledge for a rest and refuel. Feeling wasted but no longer ill, I asked Nick if he'd mind taking the first technical pitch of the route while I tried to down as much food and liquid as possible. I was feeling stronger with each bite. Above, Nick battled with steep snow and rotten ice, interspersed with time-consuming searches for gear in the shattered and blocky granite. This would be the norm for the rest of the route.

Feeling I should at least kick a few steps, I took the lead for the first time and ran out the ropes another 150m over steep snow to reach the crest of the spur, just over 1000m up the face. It was early, but we'd covered a lot of ground and were both tired. We set about chopping a ledge, knowing that

39. Nick coming up to a belay after a long section of simul-climbing on Day 3 before searching for an exit into the flutings that would eventually lead to the summit. *(Andy Houseman)*

a bivvi here would catch a welcome few minutes of warming sun at dawn.

'I'll head up this, I think. Looks straightforward.'

Nick smiled knowingly, but all he said was, 'Okay.'

Some minutes later, breathing hard, I looked a long way down at my last bit of decent gear as I searched for an axe placement at the top of the corner. Nick's sly grin filled my memory. After finding a good cam, I swung left and felt the reassuring 'thunk' of a pick in sound névé. Legs bridged wide to take the weight of the pack off my arms, I pulled a few moves over the bulge and the cam disappeared far below as I reached easier ground and started the hunt for a belay.

Pulling over the steep step, Nick glanced up with an I-told-you-so look and said, 'Umm, bet that was stimulating.' My payback was to hand Nick the rack for what turned out to be the crux pitch of the route – a long, steep corner with a capping overhanging of rotten ice. 'Watch me, youth!' That was daunting; I'd never heard Nick shout that in the mountains before. But the rope slowly ran through my belay plate, the jerk of a fall thankfully never coming. Dismantling the meagre belay, I started following as Nick moved up easier terrain, trying to find a belay. I pulled through the bulge on what usable thin ice remained, arms screaming and lungs bursting. An impressive lead.

The next four pitches were less steep but just as slow going as we tried to unearth protection and belays in the shattered rock. Leaving Nick's belay and a possible bivvi site, I started a long traverse to the right under a huge roof that had been obvious from base camp, a feature we hoped marked the end of the steepest section of the face. The ropes came tight, and while I waited a few minutes for Nick to start moving I got out my headlamp. Moving again, I passed the end of the roof but the beam from my head-torch showed no sign of a belay stance. I kept going towards a slight rib just discernible in the gloom, hoping to find snow deep enough to carve a bivvi ledge. But the rib proved useless and after placing two screws into bulletproof ice barely inches below the snow I slumped onto the anchor and brought Nick across.

Through the darkness we could just make out a snow arête above the roof we'd passed. Nick quickly led upward, hoping for a comfy ledge. But in the end we settled for a foot-wide stance just off to one side of the spur. A fitful night's sleep was ensured, though the hope that the hardest climbing was behind us made it slightly more bearable. We had climbed only 200 vertical metres that day.

Packing away one rope, we began the next morning moving together up a broad, right-trending snow ramp. Good névé and easy-to-find gear were a nice change. Soon we'd covered as much ground as we had the entire previous day. After traversing a couple of flutings, only one unconsolidated, rotten snow arête remained to negotiate before we'd reach a deep gully that we knew would lead to the easy-angled west ridge below the summit. Two attempts of levitating around the arête proved useless – clearly I needed a longer Peruvian apprenticeship!

Plan B was a short, rotten mixed step to reach one of the flutings directly above – more direct but, unlike the deep gully, with an unknown end. The rock step led into unconsolidated snow and a grovel over a few bulges before horrendous rope drag stopped me about 20m below the fluting's vertical headwall. Nick quickly took us up to the top of the fluting where we dug the biggest bivvi ledge of the route. (But still not big enough for the single-wall tent we carried and never used.) Brewing up that evening, just 300m below the summit, we feared we might have climbed ourselves into a dead end; the thought of rappelling and trying to find another way into the deep gully to our right wasn't too appealing.

We woke to a very cold morning, and Nick went for an exploratory

0. Andy Houseman coming up the final snow slope to the 6802m summit. *(Nick Bullock)*

'poke your head around the corner' look to the left. He returned to the bivvi ledge 10 minutes later with a grin that said it all. Another fluting appeared to lead straight to the west ridge. Stashing the bivvi gear, Nick left the ledge again, moving quickly with no pack. Following, I removed a screw from the last bit of ice we would find on the route and reached Nick, belayed to his axes and a not-so-inspiring bollard. As I took over the lead, I forgot the joy of being close to the summit and instead started contemplating down-climbing this Peruvian-style fluting on our descent, as it appeared that any chance of finding ice for rappel anchors would be fruitless.

Moving together, the rope between us pointless but for some reason still there, we pulled onto the ridge and into the full force of the wind that had been blowing long plumes off Kangchenjunga during the past two weeks. For the first time in four days we could see our summit, barely 150m away. I followed Nick's boot track up the 45-degree slope and quickly joined him on the knife-edge top.

What a feeling as we embraced and took in the full panorama: the gigantic north face of Kangchenjunga towering behind us, Jannu's impressive north face poking up in the distance, base camp a tiny dot below. After only 30 minutes on the summit, the cold and our anxiety about the descent forced us to leave. Easy down-climbing brought us to the point where we'd exited onto the ridge. Hoping to avoid the insecure snow flutings, we started digging as fast as the thin air allowed. However, after 20 minutes we'd found only rotten snow. Accepting defeat, I started down after Nick, plunging each tool as far as possible into the snow, holding my breath each

41. The much comfier bivvi at the end of Day 3 at approximately 6550m. *(Nick Bullock)*

time I weighted a foothold, expecting it to collapse. Finally we reached ice and quickly drilled a V-thread. A single 60m rap brought us back to the previous night's bivvi ledge. It was late in the afternoon, and since neither of us had the energy to chop another ledge lower down the face we spent a while on enlargement and settled in for one last night on the face.

After 14 hours of rappelling the next day, we crashed out in the cave at the base of the face, our rack gone but at last the true feelings of success sinking in. It was almost like standing on the summit again – but this time there were no niggling thoughts of unknowns still to overcome, just pure satisfaction.

42. Down safe! Bullock (left) and Houseman at the base of the face on Day 5 after 14 hours of abseiling and down-climbing. *(Andy Houseman)*

Summary: Alpine-style first ascent of the central spur (1800m, ED+ M6) on the north face of Chang Himal (6802m) (aka Wedge Peak or Ramtang Chang), Kangchenjunga Himal, Nepal, 29 October – 2 November 2009, by Nick Bullock and Andy Houseman. The pair bivouacked at the base of the wall before and after the climb, making a total of six nights away from base camp.

Acknowledgements: Bullock and Houseman would like to thank the following for their support: Mountain Equipment, Black Diamond, Scarpa, Mammut, DMM, Mount Everest Foundation, BMC, Nick Estcourt Award, W L Gore Shipton-Tilman Grant, Mark Clifford Grant, Lyon Equipment Award and SIS (Science in Sport). Also thanks to Loben Expeditions who provided a very professional and efficient service for the duration of the expedition.

MICK FOWLER

'Mind the Gap'

Steep and Deep in the Tien Shan

After 35 years of mountaineering, to find myself dangling deep inside a dark crevasse came as a new and unwelcome experience. Paul Ramsden and I had been descending an unnamed glacier in the Xuelian area of the Chinese Tien Shan. The range had been visited by mountaineers just twice before and the glacier just once. I find unexplored terrain and remoteness great attractions when I am pondering objectives in comfort back in the UK – but somehow such criteria felt less appealing now.

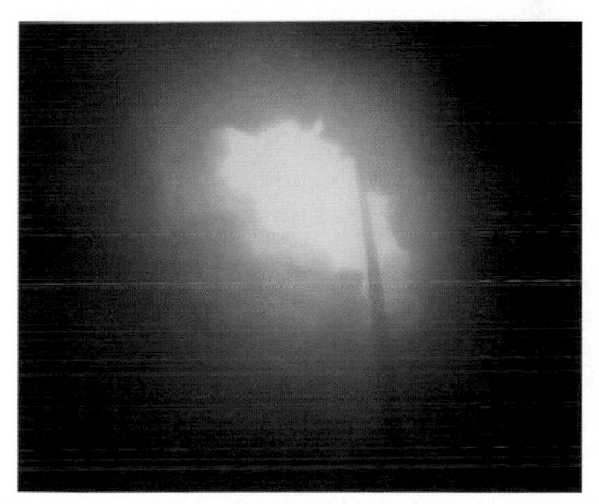

43. Daylight beckons or taunts. From within the crevasse. (*Mick Fowler*)

I had been probing cautiously when, suddenly, the snow around me collapsed and I felt as if I was being sucked into the dark bowels of the glacier. I came to a halt 10m down, rotating slowly among dripping icicles. As these broke off like organ pipes, it struck me that wearing snowshoes and with only ski poles in my hands, making a quick exit would be on the challenging side. I dangled forlornly, eyes slowly adjusting to the limited light filtering down through my small entry hole. Above me our single 7mm rope cut deeply into the overhanging eaves. I had learned about crevasse rescue techniques on an Austrian Alpine Club course back in 1969. Perhaps now was the time to see how much I had retained.

Below, a fragile-looking ice bridge hung between apparently bottomless voids whilst above, the walls converged in such a fashion that climbing up the side wall and bridging out looked a possibility. That, though, would require crampons and axes both of which were attached to the back of

44. A question of balance; Fowler tackles a challenging river crossing. (*Paul Ramsden*)

my sack. In the dim light, hanging frustratingly close to the ice bridge, I removed snowshoes and poles and clipped them into my harness. Swinging my rucksack in front of me, I then picked short-sightedly at the tight knot in the thin black cord that I had thoughtlessly used to tie my crampons to my sack. Getting kitted out without dropping anything was not a job to be rushed.

By the time I was ready with axes out and crampons on, my down jacket was soaked and I was getting concerned about what Paul must be thinking on the surface. Communication was impossible, the snow and ice seemed to absorb all sound of my shouts. To my relief though, the rope seeming to be taken in as I ice-climbed the side-wall, bridged up and finally thrashed inelegantly out of my entry hole. Gasping on the surface I felt distinctly like an exhausted seal emerging from a blowhole. Paul commented that I looked like one too. Falling in crevasses, I decided, is not to be recommended.

Paul and I were in the Tien Shan mountains in western China aiming for the first ascent of the north ridge of Xuelian East. And things were not going quite according to plan. The plan was that we would begin by spending a couple of nights acclimatising at around 5200m and then descend to base camp for a day of eating before tackling our main objective. Early that morning we had finished our acclimatisation nights and set out intending to get back to base camp that day. However, the best laid plans…

By lunchtime a foot of snow had fallen, Paul had dipped below the surface in a crevasse and an hour had been spent sitting in our tent on the glacier because we had no option but to wait for better visibility. My little crevasse incident then intervened and by nightfall we had only managed to descend to the main Muzart glacier – a distance that had taken a mere three hours on the way up. By the next morning the snow depth was up to a metre and by evening still more had fallen and we were still only halfway

5. Ramsden follows up on the mixed band, Sulamar north face, Day 1. (*Mick Fowler*)

back to base camp. By the time we arrived there on the third day we had been without food for two days – more stretching than we would normally expect on a straightforward acclimatisation exercise.

With a metre of wet snow on the lower glacier, and goodness knows how much higher up, the prospect of a 25km wade to the foot of Xuelian East's north ridge was unappealing. It was time to instigate plan B, the north face of Sulamar, a 5380m peak which had attracted our attention in a panoramic view of the range and had dominated our walk in to base camp. From what we had seen, the face sported an eye-catching steep buttress leading directly to a summit visited just once before, by the British/NZ team of Bruce Normand, Guy McKinnon and Paul Knott in 2008. For all the face was unclimbed, it adorned numerous posters and tourist literature in Xinjiang. In fact the more we contemplated, the more enthused we became at the prospect. The fact that none of the photographs we had seen, or the views we had obtained, showed the bottom section of the face was merely an added uncertainty to the usual raft of uncertainties that go with climbing in the greater ranges. There was though one greater uncertainty – which valley was the foot of the face actually in? Our rudimentary map had disintegrated when one of our horses fell into a lake on the walk in and the answer was by no means obvious.

It was, then, with a sense of exploratory excitement that Paul and I left base camp, retraced our steps along the walk in, confused local Kazakh

46. 'The rock was interesting or appalling depending on one's take on such things.' Ramsden gets to grips with the north face. (*Mick Fowler*)

herdsmen by wandering through their summer meadows wearing full mountaineering gear, and headed in the direction we hoped would lead to the north face of Sulamar.

Soon we were fording difficult watercourses, thrashing through lush, green vegetation and making crucial decisions about which way to go. Faced with such uncertainty, we were elated to exit from a long and delightful ablation valley late that afternoon in the knowledge that not only were we almost certainly the first mountaineers to pass this way but that we were in the right valley with no insuperable obstacles to reaching the foot of the face.

Pitching our little tent on snow at the foot of the face we ate noodles and crunchy fish heads (unable to understand the language, you never know what's in these Chinese food tins until you open them) and scanned the full face for the first time. There looked to be some stunningly steep ice sections on the first half and difficult looking mixed ground towards the top. The main thing that struck us though was how big the face was for a 5380m peak. The height interval of about 1600m was actually greater than the height interval on our original 6400m objective.

'4am alarm?' suggested Paul. 'Local time?'

The 'local time' bit is important in this part of the world as the Uyghur people use 'local time' whereas the majority Han Chinese population use Beijing time – which is two hours different. With both Chinese and Uyghur people involved in our trip the potential for confusion was high.

Local time or Chinese time aside, a clear night gave a good frost and we were pleased to be at the first difficulties, a steep band of snow-dusted rock, by daybreak. The difficulties and problems started immediately. The first pitch was mixed snow and ice and for reasons I still can't explain both my crampons started to come off at the same time. Paul watched with an air

47. 'Steep, uncompromising ground continued…' Ramsden on Day 2. (*Mick Fowler*)

of detached despair as the minutes ticked by while I perched stork-like on little steps cut in the ice, securing each crampon in turn. By the time I had completed the process I was beginning to feel a bit of an expert at attaching crampons in tricky spots like inside crevasses and part way up technical pitches. Concerned about a repeat performance, I tied safety cords to each crampon but all was secure thereafter and the cords served no purpose other than to regularly trip me up.

The rock was interesting or appalling depending on one's take on such things. It varied from coal-like black shale to shattered marble, both being equally unhelpful in terms of finding secure protection. With the benefit of hindsight it would have been easier to link together surprisingly crisp snow patches, but having committed ourselves to rock we persevered with time-consuming technical looseness, finally gaining what looked to be an icefield above rather later than we would have liked.

In fact the 'icefield' was initially rock slabs covered in powder snow, demanding care and not at all the fast ground that we had hoped for. Above, though, lay distressingly obvious ice in the form of two unusual and very steep cones. How these ice cones had formed prompted a fair bit of discussion. The left hand one was near vertical for about 100m whereas the right hand one was perhaps 75 degrees. We concluded that they were almost certainly the result of particularly severe spindrift (fresh snow sliding off the face) avalanches and we would do well to get above them before the regular afternoon electrical storms began. It was not long before

48. Ramsden pushes on in storm conditions, Day 2. (*Mick Fowler*)

we had failed in our race against the elements and our theory had been proved correct.

The deluge was huge. Some 900m of face emptied vast quantities of hailstones down the shallow gully above the ice cone. I was belayed just to one side of the flow but even so the noise was akin to standing next to a speeding express train and the air full of choking, wind-blasted snow. Paul had just pulled out of sight and I could only hang there well muffled on my belay and wonder how he was doing. Nothing happened for a long time. Eventually the rope started to be taken in and I could only assume that I was expected to climb. It transpired that Paul had managed to cross the main flow before it came down and was belayed on the far side – a situation that inevitably meant I had to climb directly through the maelstrom – another memorable experience I do not care to repeat.

A brief attempt at further upwards progress failed and instead we focused on digging out (literally) a sitting bivouac shelf from the impressively loose and fractured rock. Later the clouds parted momentarily and it was reassuring to see that we were now level with the unclimbed peaks on the opposite side of the valley.

A grey dawn prompted gentle grumbling. Paul's back was aching and

9. Paul Ramsden on Sulamar's summit ridge, Day 3. (*Mick Fowler*)

my ribs were distinctly uncomfortable after a less than graceful slip in the bath at our last hotel. Understandably Paul took every opportunity to remind me about this embarrassing incident.

On the bright side though the spindrift had stopped, upward progress was possible and challenging climbing is a great cure for aches and pains. The section that stopped us the previous day was quickly despatched and in improving weather we made good progress up a pleasant snow crest, across an insecure traverse and up a shallow couloir with great climbing up steep icy steps. Way above us we could see a prominent overhanging rock wall we knew to mark the top of the face.

Paul and I tend to adopt a relaxed 9-to-5 approach to mountaineering. We enjoy savouring our limited time in the mountains and have no desire to rush up and down as quickly as possible. Usually we start keeping an eye open for reasonable bivouac sites from mid-afternoon. Here though there seemed good reasons to make an exception to the rule. Above us it was pretty obvious that steep, uncompromising ground continued all the way to the top and comfortable bivvi sites were non-existent. Furthermore it seemed just possible to get to the summit ridge and a probable spot to pitch the tent before nightfall. The temptation was too much. We decided to climb into the night if necessary.

Having crossed this Rubicon, it was perhaps inevitable that the daily electrical storm should be earlier and more intense than usual. Clouds gathered, visibility shrank and the ground was regularly illuminated by wild flashes of blue followed instantaneously by ear-splitting cracks of thunder. The wind seemed to gust from all directions at the same time and around us the face was awash with spindrift. Regretting that we hadn't dug ourselves in earlier, we persevered. But it was hopeless. The combination of darkness, cloud and snow made the best route impossible to find. Cul de sacs abounded and there was nothing for it but to bivouac as best we could.

The chosen site from limited options was a small ice step under a slanting overhang. It was protected from the worst of the spindrift but inconvenient in every other possible way. After two hours we had fashioned an unattractively outward-sloping bucket seat and Paul had ripped his down jacket open on the jagged rocks of the overhang. The conditions remained wild and in an effort to keep crucial equipment dry and facilitate a quick exit if need be, we decided to don all our clothes, keep our boots on and not get into our sleeping bags. Having positioned ourselves within the tent fabric as best we could, we set about tying ourselves snugly into the belay loops that Paul's mother-in-law had expertly sewn through the corners.

50. Summit: Fowler (left) and Ramsden.

'She will be happy to know that her efforts are being put to good use,' commented Paul.

It was probably the last positive observation of the night. After less than an hour my fidgeting in particular was attracting adverse comment.

'What are you doing? Can't you sit still?'

I suppose Paul was justified in that a little fidgeting was indeed going on. At the time of his asking I was experimenting with a new position which involved a semi-inverted hang with my head down and knees and elbows against the slope. This went some way towards relieving pressure from my leg loops and restoring circulation in my legs but, as ever, it proved not to satisfactorily resolve the overall discomfort problem. Much to Paul's annoyance, I spent the rest of the night fidgeting badly in a never-ending quest for comfort.

Daybreak revealed that we had been hanging a mere 25m from an easy exit through the summit cornice. Even in the midst of the storm it wouldn't have taken more than 20 minutes to gain a spot where we could have escaped the face and fashioned a ledge for the tent.

1. Sulamar from above Xiate, Chinese Tien Shan. Sulamar and the north face centre stage. (*Jed Brown*)

But the difficulties were not over. Instead of a straightforward short ridge to the summit we were faced with a long and crenellated snow crest that was roasting hot on one side and frostily cold and windy on the other. Soon the snow on the sunny side was such that we convinced ourselves of the reasonableness of stopping earlier than our 3pm norm and enjoying an idyllic, relaxing afternoon brewing, reading and generally soaking up the view. In a pre-dawn start the next day it all seemed so much easier and an enjoyable ridge crest traverse in spectacular positions led to the summit.

Our descent of the previously unclimbed south ridge was very pleasant until we were seduced into descending an easy looking snow slope to the west. I shall refrain from detailed mention of memorable ice-cliff abseils and insecure soloing on shattered marble and simply conclude by noting that the sense of exploratory achievement and satisfaction of completing new climbs in rarely visited places is difficult to beat.

Back at base camp Abdul, our 'guide', had a celebratory beer to hand. We drank a toast with such enthusiasm that Paul cricked his neck and all further activity had to be put on hold for a day.

Summary: An account of the first ascent of the north face of Sulamar (5380m) in the Xuelian area of the Chinese Tien Shan, Xinjiang province, by Mick Fowler and Paul Ramsden, 30 August – 2 September 2010.

Acknowledgements: Fowler and Ramsden would like to thank all who helped to make the climb possible: the Mount Everest Foundation, the British Mountaineering Council, Berghaus, Black Diamond, Thermarest, MSR, Cascade and La Sportiva.

BRUCE NORMAND

The Great White Jade Heist

52. Bruce Normand acclimatising on the west ridge of Xuelian North-east, with the Muzart glacier far below. *(Jed Brown)*

There is a blank on the map of world mountaineering in the eastern Tien Shan. In contrast to the heavily visited ex-Soviet part of the range, the Chinese part has seen only a handful of expeditions in recorded history. At the centre of the blank is Xuelian Feng, in translation 'Snow Lotus Peak'. My 2008 expedition with New Zealanders Paul Knott and Guy McKinnon was the first ever to approach the mountain from the north. What we found was a paradise for exploratory alpine climbing: a vast and entirely unknown region of peaks and glaciers in which the complex Xuelian massif offers challenging route options on a wealth of ridges, buttresses and sub-summits, all for a single China Xinjiang Mountaineering Association (CXMA) peak fee. The horizontal and vertical distances are just right for tackling expedition-scale problems in alpine style. The administration is quite simple. The approach is amazingly straightforward, with motorways and paved roads for 1000km from Urumqi, an easy gravel road for

53. The north face of Xuelian West, Xinjiang Tien Shan, showing the line and camps of the Brown/Dempster/Normand route, *The Great White Jade Heist*. (*Bruce Normand*)

24km and a horse trek of only 22km in beautiful alpine scenery. The base camp at Hadamuzi occupies an idyllic, flower-strewn meadow with a jaw-dropping view directly into the biggest peaks. There's even a hot spring at the roadhead for soaking out the dirt, aches and odours at the end of a hard expedition.

On the down side, in summer at Hadamuzi it rains almost every evening, but then if it didn't there wouldn't be the flowers, streams flowing beside the cook tent or shower options where the water falls to the glacier. The local Kazakh horsemen tend to be stubborn, incompetent and usurious,

54. After the (first) storm: Dempster takes the air at breakfast on Day 3. (*Bruce Normand*)

demanding ridiculous fees, breaking agreed deals at any time and, when they do work, crushing loads and dropping them every kilometre. The spring and autumn seasons, which bring small numbers of trekkers to or through Hadamuzi, also seem to bring vast amounts of rubbish. In August 2008 we cleaned up everything we could find, but arriving in 2009 the place looked like a landfill. We removed more than 30kg of burnable garbage, 30 plastic drink bottles and 30 cans of cooking gas.

In 2008 the weather was not helpful, but a lot of glacier travel and snow-climbing took us to some 5400m viewpoints revealing much of the range. The Xuelian massif contains, in addition to the 6627m main peak, four distinct 6000m satellites and one major outlier (Yanamax, 6332m, which Guy and I climbed), as well as complete ranges of 5000m peaks to both north and south. While the north side of the massif has more than 20km of sérac-laden walls and ridges some 2000m in height, there is little doubt that its most compelling feature is the monstrous north face of Xuelian West, also known as Baiyu Feng ('White Jade peak'), which rises 2700m straight from the glacier opposite Hadamuzi.

In 2009 I was back to climb on Xuelian itself. Xuelian West would actually be the climax of a month of mountaineering, during which we'd acclimatise, reconnoitre and prepare by climbing the other satellites. I would climb mostly with Jed Brown, while our friends Kyle Dempster and Jared Vilhauer would work as a separate pair. After one acclimatisation trip to a 4800m peaklet, Jed and I tackled Xuelian North by its long west ridge, bivouacking at 5300m and working hard on precarious and rotten ridge snow. From its 6472m summit, we had what turned out to be the only view of the month beyond the Marble Wall to Pik Pobeda and Khan Tengri. One of our objectives was to reconnoitre the steep and exposed final rock step to Xuelian Main, a peak that has been awaiting a second ascent since the 1990 Japanese success from the opposite side. Another aim was to size up Xuelian West, of which we had a perfect bird's-eye view across and down the north face.

Turning to the east ridge of Xuelian East, we were surprised to meet a pair of climbers: Kyle and Jared, of whom we had seen no trace for a week because fresh snow kept blowing over all our tracks, had climbed a different line on the north side of the ridge. They joined us for the long trek up to the summit. Our arrival was marked by the biggest storm of the expedition, which forced us into a record-breaking bivouac featuring four men in a Rab Summit Extreme tent. Jed and I returned to Hadamuzi to rest before a bid on Xuelian North-east, where we found rotten snow and delicate rock on an infinite ridge, not difficult but desperately exposed, dangerous and so time-consuming that we were forced to give up at 5400m. Equally industrious, Kyle and Jared stayed on the upper glacier to climb an ice and mixed line on the untouched north face of Yanamax, which they pushed to the 6180m summit crest of its north buttress ('Yanamax 2').

Jared suffered frostnip to a toe on this last route and decided not to try any more big routes. Then, without warning, our liaison officer informed us that for bureaucratic reasons the expedition would end on 30 August – a loss of three days that put us under time pressure. There was weather pressure too, as after three weeks of generally unstable conditions it was now clear and dry all day, without even the high cloud banners we had watched all month. Thus it was that on 24 August, Jed, Kyle and I packed as little gear as we could justify, walked down from Hadamuzi, across the Muzart glacier and up the 5km side glacier leading straight to the base of the face. Perfect evening weather and light gave us a last chance to examine and photograph the route up the buttress towering above us.

The north face of Xuelian West is a little wider than it is high. It has a rocky half, swept clean by the west wind, and a snowy, sérac-ridden half, the obvious line of both weakness and safety being the shallow prow in its centre that divides the two. The bottom seemed to offer very long ice lines just to the left of the prow, while the top, above about 5400m, was split by what looked to be a snow couloir. For the middle section, mixed or rock climbing of unknown difficulty would be needed to get through the slab barriers separating the snow patches on the prow. The beautiful orange rock of the central Tien Shan (the best example is Khan Tengri) is of course not granite but a particularly compact type of marble, and protecting long slabs of it would be perhaps the biggest challenge of all.

Jed and I had camped under the face for days while doing the north buttress, but as I approached the tent site there was no tent... We found it reduced to a few strings of prayer flags, perhaps by a windstorm or an avalanche blast wave. The outer tent had been completely shredded, the

poles broken and splayed out around the wreckage. The inner tent was a sodden and sticky mess of burst instant-noodle sachets and half-dissolved sweets. I turned it inside-out: stove…still OK; rope…still OK; mountain tent…covered in sticky red chilli but apparently OK; poles…OK. This was inconvenient, but it wasn't a showstopper. Jed fired up the stove and started cleaning the sweet-and-sour tent with hot water. Kyle took charge of the hardware, choosing and cleaning what we'd need for the route. I worked on food, salvaging and re-bagging what we'd need for a five-day climb. We ate as we worked, so when Jed had the mountain tent serviceable again we piled in quickly and slept. We were still on track.

Jed and Kyle are both 26. Jed is from interior Alaska, so his ideas of cold weather and camping hardship match the

On *The Great White Jade Heist.*

55. Opposite top: Jed Brown on high-quality ice, Day 2. (*Bruce Normand*)

56. Opposite bottom: Kyle Dempster on rare positive rock, Day 1. (*Bruce Normand*)

57. Right: Dempster vanishing in spindrift on the M6 lead, Day 2. (*Bruce Normand*)

58. Below: Dempster tackles the crux pitches. (*Bruce Normand*)

Russian norm rather than mainstream European tolerances. He misspent his youth cross-country ski racing, so his aerobic capacity has no limit. Kyle is from Utah, where he misspent his youth frying brain cells on desert rock routes. His idea of hard climbing is around 5.13 or M10. Together with their shared experience of hard alpinism, it meant confi-

59. A constant presence: view of Xuelian Main (centre right) and the north buttress (left). (*Bruce Normand*)

dence to face the unknowns and technical difficulties of a remote wall was not in short supply. Three is a good number for alpine-style climbing: one rope team, two ropes and one rack, one stove and one small tent. Even with five days of food, only the two followers need big packs and the leader can climb truly fast and light.

Dawn found us at the foot of a snow cone leading into the lower right side of the prow; the rising traverse that won us the first 300m would be the last non-technical terrain for four days. Jed led the first block and we simul-climbed four pitches of moderate ice to arrive beneath a towering rock wall. The line we had chosen became narrow and steepened to vertical. Jed picked his way carefully over the thin ice, working hard to get sparse protection. Jed and Kyle switched leads and Kyle found thicker ice in the steepest part of the couloir, as well as good rock holds. Another four pitches of moderate snow and ice took us to the first moderately sized snowfield on the prow. It was 4pm and we'd done 10 pitches, but another 10 might be needed before we found a similar spot to bivouac. Two hours' chopping was required to fashion a platform in the ice decent enough for a good camp, enabling us to eat, drink and sleep in good style – the next chance for that might be three days away.

Next morning we'd done one and a half pitches before the sun came up. Jed was in the lead again, and his block took us through thin, breakable ice over slabs to gain several pitches of névé and finally two pitches of excellent alpine ice on thick flows over the slabs. We'd gained the major snowfield on the left of the prow which marks half-height on the wall, but it is topped by steep cliffs. It was time to move to the right side of the prow and tackle the slabs, so Kyle headed up the only ice line in sight. His second pitch steepened and required some wild bridging and leaning moves. Reasonable morning weather was giving way to thick clouds and light snowfall; spindrift avalanches began sweeping over the slabs. Our climbing options were also narrowing, with an aid wall above, endless snow over slabs to the right and a thin ramp running up to the left. We chose the last, and Kyle inched out along the narrowing ledge line, scratching to find tiny edges and periodically being deluged in spindrift. A virtuoso lead (we rated it M6) ended when he slapped an axe into some real ice on the crest of the prow. For Jed and me this was no longer a simple following exercise, as our bigger packs tried to pull us into a long, swinging fall.

Jed took the lead, but the ice streak was thin and brittle and the protection as shaky as ever. By the end of his pitch both the night and snow were falling fast. There was nothing in sight but 45-degree slabs with occasional snowfields. The risk of a night in the open in a storm was uncomfortably real, although as yet there was no wind. We were at the mental crux of the route. We voted to carry on, even if this meant climbing through the night. Headlamps on, Jed led us up the snowfield to the next rock spur. A smaller snow patch to the right was deep enough to make 60cm ledges. Then Kyle realised that the snow was so wind-pressed we could actually cut blocks of it. I dug two 60cm ledges, one above the other; Jed cut huge, solid blocks from the pressed snow and positioned them on the lower one; Kyle collected packs and hardware and rearranged our anchor. We piled side-by-side into the tent, harnesses on, backs against the wall and sleeping bags up to our chests, with the gear sitting on the blocks under our feet. The stove refused to work properly, perhaps due to oxygen deprivation, so we ate and drank only a little. Just as we were ready to sleep, the spindrift avalanches restarted, battering the tent against our faces and trying to push us off the ledge. We spent a miserable night pressing our backs to the wall and pushing snow off the canopy above our heads.

The morning was sunny but windy, and the avalanches were still pounding us. It was 11am when the wind died and the spindrift sloughs ceased some time later. Kyle and I stood outside on a beautiful morning while Jed used the opportunity to make the stove work perfectly, and plied us with food and hot fluid. We were still perched in the middle of an endless slab field, but the wall above was the last before the 'exit' snowfield at 5400m, beyond which the prow seemed to have a long snow gully; certainly the easy way off the face from here was to go over the top. It was Kyle's block again, and his lead meandered right and left, every move delicate but few truly difficult, and every pitch with only a few features in which to place gear. After six slow and careful pitches, we hit the snowfield, almost ran to its top, set two anchors in the rock and dug a full-width tent platform.

No sooner were we all installed in the tent than a series of flashes and rumbles began to pierce the night sky. The only lightning storm of the entire month had chosen this moment to pass right over our heads. From a distance, Jared shot video of the entire mountain lighting up like a flashing Christmas tree. From underneath, the risk of a lightning strike was irrelevant; another cataract of snow and hail cascading off the mountain tried hard to flatten the tent and take us down with it. I spent an hour outside in the torrent, heaving snow off the tent while Jed and Kyle gamely weighed it down from the inside, until the storm subsided.

The morning of day 4 was sunny but windy, and spindrift was still sluicing down the exit gully. After a quick, soloing start, we roped up again on encountering some of the slabbiest rock steps we'd seen on the whole route. Jed led another long, simul-climbing push with infrequent protection, until we emerged on the upper snowfields at 5900m in the early after-

60. On the summit of Xuelian West; from left, Jed Brown, Bruce Normand and Kyle Dempster. *(Kyle Dempster)*

noon. The hard part was over. This day was deteriorating too, and by the time I'd led a long, deep slog to the cornice guarding the west ridge, it was snowing again with visibility near zero. We decided to camp here (6300m), out of the wind, and try for the top and the unknown descent route in the morning.

Even as we set off at sunrise, a clear night was turning to clouds blowing over the ridge from the south-west. We hurried to the summit (6422m), but the white-out beat us to it. The wind was cold and the only view was of Jed and Kyle smiling and shaking hands. The risk of frostbite on the exposed ridge was real: we had to watch each other and warm up white patches on our faces. Soon we were below the clouds and wind again, following the south-west ridge and rappelling into the south-west face. A long, simul-climbing traverse took us back to the west ridge just above a point where we could descend a small, hanging glacier on its north side. Clouds and snow showers blew in. Three more rappels plus a deep slog down a steep, crevassed snow slope and we had threaded a route through the slots to the final col. The falling snow was turning to rain as we descended slush, mud and talus slopes to regain the flat glacier. We were back at our advanced base an hour after dark, soaked and exhausted from our five-day marathon,

61. Descending the south-west ridge of Xuelian West (*Bruce Normand*)

but warm and satisfied at a job well done.

In the morning our feet felt nearly as heavy as our packs as we staggered down the glacier with all our climbing and camping gear. This was the day the horses would come for the hike out, and indeed Jared and the staff had been packing for hours when we arrived. We changed our boots, added our packs to the loads and marched straight on. The journey out turned into something of a record: we were in Xiate Hot Springs by 9pm that evening, where the CXMA liaison officer had already rented a vehicle which took us to Zhaosu. The next day we were on the direct bus to Urumqi, where we arrived the following morning, just 70 hours after we'd topped out. With a getaway like that, it felt as though we'd just robbed a bank.

Summary: An account of the first ascent of Xuelian West, the west summit of Xuelian Feng, Xinjiang Tien Shan, China, by Scotsman Bruce Normand and Americans Jed Brown and Kyle Dempster. Their route *The Great White Jade Heist*, 2650m, WI5 M6 5.7 R, takes a direct line up the north face and was made on 26 to 30 August 2009. The ascent was one of two to be recognised by the 2010 *Piolet d'Or* awards.

Acknowledgements: The Xuelian Expedition members would like to thank the Mount Everest Foundation, the British Mountaineering Council, the Lyman-Spitzer Award of the American Alpine Club and W L Gore (Shipton-Tilman Grant) for their generous support.

Comment

62. John Innerdale, *Basingthang range*, Bhutan, chromacolour, 62 x 41cm, 2005.

DOUG SCOTT

Awards and Recognition in Climbing

The sweetest of all sounds is praise, commented Xenophon. And not only oneself but of one's children, if my parents are anything to go by. They entered me in a local baby show, August 1942, when I was 14 months old. It was reported in the *Nottingham Journal* that the actor,Tod Slaughter presented me with a rosette and the actress Patricia Hastings gave me a kiss for coming first in my category. Some are born famous, some seek fame, whilst others have fame thrust upon them, firstly in my case thanks to my doting parents.

Other awards have followed, and therefore in this exploration of the two issues of climbing as an Olympic sport and awards for alpinism, I am conscious my personal example comes under scrutiny.

My first certificate for climbing came from the Russians in 1974. Paul Braithwaite, Guy Lee, Clive Rowlands and I were presented with colourful certificates written in Cyrillic certifying we had climbed Peak Lenin in the Pamirs. The occasion was an international 'camp' set in the Achik Tash valley. Part of its purpose was to foster international relations amongst climbers and to gain foreign currency to enable Russian climbers to climb overseas. There was also a hidden agenda, and that was to persuade the IOC to admit high-altitude climbing as an event in the Olympic Games. When this proposal was voiced at any of the many meetings held in the 'camp' it was generally laughed out of court as for most visiting climbers the idea was anathema.

Pressure for climbing, in one form or another, to form part of the Olympics has never gone away – indeed, as I shall explain, mountaineering was within Coubertin's vision right from the start – however there is an important distinction to be drawn. The organisers of indoor climbing competitions and ice climbing competitions are working hard to gain entry into the Olympic arena. Most climbers, whatever their reservations, seem to think this is inevitable and not a problem so long as such competitions remain indoors or outdoors on purpose-built, artificial structures. What the mountaineering fraternity do question is the idea that there should be competition on natural rock and competitions in the high mountains.

Ed Douglas, in a balanced article entitled 'Faster, Higher, Stronger' in *Summit* (issue 54, 2009), raised the potential for an adverse impact on traditional recreational climbing should climbing become an Olympic sport and as a consequence the comprehensive work of the British Mountaineering

Council be compromised by too much focus on competition. The fear is that the organisers of competition climbing will have an influence on our sport out of all proportion to their numbers, as appears to have happened in the world of canoeing. Apparently access and conservation issues, for example, get sidelined as competition takes centre stage. Ed quoted one canoe stalwart as telling him that the British Canoe Union's relationship with competitions had become 'a case of the tail wagging the dog. It's the debate of the day in many clubs and is creating a lot of discontent.' The implication for climbing is clear; however as Ed concluded, 'competition climbing will only dominate the BMC if it's allowed to do so'. A weather eye needs to be kept on this developing situation.

There's quite a history to all this. Baron Pierre de Coubertin, the French idealist and father of the modern Olympic Games, suggested giving recognition for achievement in mountaineering since he considered such a noble pastime exemplified his Olympic ideals. In Paris, at the founding Olympic Congress of 1894, proposals were put forward to award an 'Alpinisme' medal for the most impressive climb made in the four years between the Olympics.

No awards were ever presented and little mention of it was made until in a postscript to the August 1911 *Alpine Journal* it was announced: 'Olympic Games of Stockholm 1912 Mountain Ascents. A gold Olympic Medal will be awarded for the finest performance between the years 1908-1911. The leading Alpine Clubs in the different countries have the right to propose candidates for this prize.' The Stockholm Olympics came and went without any award for Alpinism, since the Swede, Erik Ullen, who had been appointed a judge, counselled against giving any award because of the impossibility of comparing different types of climb and the performance of the 'athletes'. Ullen was the first of many, right up to the present time, to recognise that any judgement made on mountaineering achievements is bound to be subjective and open to debate. In effect, this established the fact that mountaineering was of a completely different character from mainstream, competitive sports.

The idea, however, lived on. Medals were struck and given to the 1922 Mount Everest expedition under the category of 'Alpine and Mixed Alpinism', mainly because the expedition achieved a new height record of 8320 metres. The Baron, now President of the Olympic Association, presented the prizes at the 'International Sports' Week' in Chamonix during the winter of 1924. This event later came to be recognised as the first Winter Olympic Games. Colonel Edward Strutt of the Alpine Club collected the silver–gilt medals on behalf of the team since the leader of the expedition, Brigadier General Charles Bruce, had already left for India as leader of the 1924 Everest expedition. Coubertin suggested that the British should take an Olympic medal to the summit of Everest – a suggestion that was accepted but never carried out.

The following were the members to whom these medals were awarded: Charles Granville Bruce, Geoffrey Bruce, George Finch, George Mallory,

Edward Norton, Howard Somervell, Tejbir Bura, Narbu Sherpa, Lhakpa Sherpa, Pasang Sherpa, Pemba Sherpa, Dorje Sherpa, Temba Sherpa and Sange Sherpa.

The Sherpa medals were awarded and given to their families posthumously since all seven had perished in the avalanche below the North Col that brought the 1922 expedition to an end. The whereabouts of the medals awarded to Charles Bruce, Mallory and Finch are known but not of those awarded to the seven gallant Sherpas from Darjeeling.

The brothers Franz and Toni Schmidt were awarded medals at the Los Angeles Olympics of 1932 in recognition of making the first ascent of the Matterhorn north face. The medals were collected on behalf of the Schmidt brothers by the President of the German Olympic Committee, Theodor Lewald, and were given to Franz and his father since Toni had been killed a few months earlier whilst climbing in the Alps.

Four years later at the 1936 Olympics, Günther and Hettie Dyhrenfurth were given Olympic gold medals for their mountaineering achievements in the Karakoram in 1934. On their International Expedition to the upper Baltoro glacier several first ascents were made including all four summits of Sia Kangri, the first of the great mountains of the Karakoram to be climbed.

There was general speculation that the ill-fated Austro-German team that attempted the Eiger north face in 1936 were hoping for an Olympic medal. The dramatic and very public death of the four-man team confirmed the suspicions of all conservative climbers, particularly in Switzerland and Britain, that attitudes to climbing prevalent in the eastern Alps were beyond reason. The censorious editor of the *Alpine Journal*, Colonel Strutt, had a field day, condemning not only the 'Munich Mechanisation' of climbing, but, through AC member Dr Oscar Hug of Zurich, he also aired condemnation of awarding of Olympic medals for 'Alpine Valour'. Hug wrote, 'An Olympic medal for mountaineering is to be deprecated at all costs. Mountaineering, as understood by Swiss and British climbers, is not an Olympic sport. Mountaineering contains some elements of sporting characteristics, but these are of a quite secondary nature in a form fostered by Eastern Alps' scrambling that smacks more of the Olympic Stadium where publicity is not unwillingly sought. Swiss and British mountaineers will have no dealing with Olympic medals.' The editor seemed to have forgotten that in 1924 he was in Chamonix collecting a whole clutch of Olympic medals.

In 1938, at the height of Nazi power in Germany and Austria, Hitler formally honoured Anderl Heckmair, Wiggerl Vörg, Heinrich Harrer and Fritz Kasparek for their first ascent of the Eiger north face. The fact that Hitler associated himself with awards in mountaineering may well have tainted the idea of awards in general, for none were given by the IOC for the next half century.

After the war, in September 1946, the IOC decided to abandon the idea of giving prizes for Alpinism as well as for Aeronautics. Alan Blackshaw and Roger Payne, on behalf of the UIAA, attempted to find out more about why precisely and who at IOC was behind this decision. So far no documentation has been found on the subject. It is hoped that alpine member nations of the UIAA may discover archival material on the subject.

Then in 1988, at the Calgary Winter Olympics, awards were given to Reinhold Messner and Jerzy Kukuczka for their ascents of all fourteen 8000m peaks. Each climber was given, unsuspectingly, a silver medal, which begs the question as to what a climber has to do to go for gold. In actual fact there does not appear to have been much interest from mountaineering clubs and organisations to encourage the IOC to again make awards for Alpinism.

However the idea of competitive mountaineering is far from alien in the former Soviet bloc where competitions were first promoted in 1948. Ronnie Richards, a participant in the 1975 Pamirs 'camp', summed up the situation in an *Alpine Journal* article of 1975 (vol. 80, p. 90): '... most Western climbers ...value just those aspects of mountaineering which set it apart from conventional sports. It was reassuring to find Eugene Gippenreiter and other Russian climbers sharing our views.

'Conditions peculiar to the Soviet Union explain the proposals: firstly the existing framework has developed attitudes and an administration structure whose officials would gain in power, status and prestige – their voice is presumably influential in a political climate where organised sport is encouraged at the expense of individually instigated efforts. Secondly, mountaineering is something of a poor relation compared to other sports – elevation to Olympic status would increase resources available for more and better equipment and clothing...'.

The Soviet attitude to mountaineering suffered a severe setback with the death of eight Russian women mountaineers set on making the first all-women traverse of Peak Lenin. They perished in a terrible storm at 7000m. They lacked the experience and suitable equipment, but also they were, it seems, blinded to the build-up of danger by their overwhelming ambition to succeed. They were locked into a pre-planned itinerary that made for inflexibility and determination to meet targets precluded changing direction as conditions dictated. The considerable back-up of guides out on patrol with radios and with helicopters in the area may also have induced a false sense of security. Here was laid bare, for all to see, the problem of external organisation and procedures subverting the small group from taking responsibility for their own lives through flexible self-reliance and prudent decision making.

This tragedy brought home to many the folly of promoting high-altitude mountaineering as another competitive, Olympic sporting event. If ever it was to become part of the Olympics, with the whole world looking on, one can only imagine the increasing number of similar disasters amongst teams of Olympic alpinists.

A year after the Pamirs camp came our successful ascent of the south-west face of Everest. No award was expected and none was received, at least not directly. Chris Bonington, our leader, had already been given a Gold Medal from the RGS in 1974; in fact I had stood with Don Whillans underneath the newly gold-embossed entry of Chris's name up on the panelling at the old entrance to the Society building. Don, who was not getting on with Chris at the time, since Chris had dropped him from his Everest plans, looked up and quipped, 'What exploring 'as he done? I've done all his exploring'. He then went on to quote Annapurna, oblivious to my suggestion that Chris had done a lot more than lead the successful climb of Annapurna's south face. These awards obviously don't go unnoticed and can cause consternation in others. However I heard no grumbling when eventually Chris was made a CBE: after all, he was with justification the main spokesman for British climbing, had climbed more than most and had probably sat on more committees than any other climber.

Rumour has it that Dougal Haston and myself as summiteers of Everest might have expected some recognition from Her Majesty if Dougal had not served three months in one of HM Prisons during his misspent youth. Still, we did get an invite to No 10 where we met Harold Wilson who asked us what part we had played in getting the summiteers to the summit! Many of the Everest expedition members were invited to the Man of the Year 1976 lunch and duly certificated as 'Men of the Year' after listening to the noble Lord Jack Ashley who, although stone deaf, spoke a lot of sense, much more so than the other speaker, the very tipsy Lord Boothby. It was surprising who you got to meet at such soirées.

In 1994 I received a letter from the Ceremonial Branch of the Cabinet Office, Westminster, asking if I would accept becoming a Commander of the British Empire. This came as a complete surprise as I had had no inkling from anyone that such a possibility was even being discussed. I have to say I accepted without a second thought and have never regretted doing so. My parents were overjoyed with my father saying, 'Thank God I have lived to see this day' – it being the culminating point in his lifelong ambition to see his son honoured for everything he did. In general being a CBE has only been of help in fundraising, helping friends abroad obtain UK visas and generally getting things done more quickly. It was rumoured that since Rebecca Stephens, a relative newcomer to climbing, had been awarded an MBE, the climbing establishment thought a token old timer should be awarded something too, hence my award.

It came long after I had done my most demanding climbs and was to honour a lifetime of climbing and unravelling the mysteries of Himalayan mountains rather than as a reward for one particular event. This was the case with fellow climbers, Chris Bonington CBE, George Band OBE, Pat Littlejohn OBE, and very recently Joe Brown CBE. None of us seems to have attracted any criticism so far for accepting these awards. Objections only seem to arise when such gongs are given directly after a spectacular event and especially if it is perceived that non-climbers are influencing events behind the scenes.

There have long been prizes given for exploratory mountaineering but the first awards made on a regular basis began in 1830 with the foundation of the Royal Geographical Society. Early recipients included Younghusband, Whymper and the Duke of the Abruzzi, and more recently, myself, 1999, Reinhold Messner, 2001, and Harish Kapadia, 2003. We all quite unexpectedly received the Patron's Gold Medal after the Queen had approved what in the UK is the highest honour, along with the Founder's Medal, for contributions to mountaineering and the knowledge of mountains.

In my acceptance speech I told of my consternation when sitting on the train, reading the *Daily Mail* on my way to the RGS, I had read that David Hempleman-Adams was our greatest living explorer, which must mean, I thought, that Wally Herbert (amongst others) was dead. I was able to announce the good news, after a few enquiries, that Wally Herbert was very much alive (sadly no longer).

Two friends with impeccable climbing credentials illustrate the pros and cons of accepting or rejecting awards. Voytek Kurtyka, one of the foremost mountaineers of the 20th century, turned down a request from the organisers of the *Piolets d'Or* to sit on the jury of what is arguably the best known international award in mountaineering. Voytek was approached by Christian Trommsdorff, President of the Groupe de Haute Montagne and the main organiser of the revamped *Piolets* of 2009, along with Manu Rivaud of *Montagnes* and Claude Gardien of *Vertical*. Christian himself has in recent years, with his great friend Yannick Graziani, made climbs worthy of a golden axe but being an organiser is ineligible for consideration.

Voytek said that he was sorry but he could not be part of the jury as he understood 'the world is suspended on a monstrous structure of wild competition and consequently of award and distinction ... this structure is an enemy of true art ... where award and distinction rules the true art ends.' For him climbing was a means to physical and mental wellbeing and towards wisdom, whereas award and distinction only led to vanity and egocentricity. 'Taking part in the game of award and distinction is dangerous for the climber ... I cannot accept your offer.'

Christian thanked Voytek for his 'sincere reply', adding, 'personally I totally agree with you about competition; this is not the spirit we want to promote at the GHM now but we choose to take an opportunity to be present in today's world and promote our values the best we can rather than to be absent and let others occupy the space ... people driven by competition ... maybe some of them could be inspired by people like you to change their attitude.'

Voytek did not take part but those who did, including myself as Jury President, saw to it that most of the revamped *Piolets* criteria were applied to the recipients. Paramount was that the awards should be given to those climbs exhibiting commitment, e.g. no drilling equipment carried, no fixed ropes and eschewing other aids that would diminish the uncertainty principle of the climb, such as walkie-talkies, satellite phones to weather forecasters, etc. Other key criteria were that the climb should be original, the 'leave no trace' principle should be observed, and local people treated with respect. The 2009 award in fact was given to three different climbs that more or less met the above criteria. Not having a single winner was seen as a step forward, lessening the competitive element of the *Piolets d'Or* and creating a system that endorses all those making inspiring climbs in an inspiring style; the 'winners' thus were not winners but ambassadors representing the best traditions of our sport.

With the revised charter and a new spirit established for the *Piolets*, Christian felt confident enough to approach Voytek again, this time to accept the 2010 Golden Ice-Axe Career Award to 'help promote our common values in Alpinism'. Voytek's reply was predictable: 'This is a devilish offer ... I always run to the mountains with great expectation that I can elevate myself above my human weaknesses and you try to put on me the most dangerous one ... the illusion that I am a person of distinction ... all my life is a sort of struggle with that illusion ... the greatest trap of our ego and a proof of vanity, I can't accept *Piolets d'Or*. The climber possesses an exceptional awareness of freedom. I hope you will understand my uneasiness in face of such a great honour.'

Christian, with understatement that would have impressed the British, commented to me and others: 'Maybe a little more work and he would accept?' We all have some sympathy for Voytek and with his statement that, 'seeking the distinction betokens vanity, rejecting the distinction betokens vanity'. It was a 'damned if you do, damned if you don't' dilemma for which he felt guilty. Voytek must know he is different from other climbers in that he has done what only a handful of other climbers could ever do. He is therefore distinct and cannot avoid the fact that everyone considers him so. Perhaps Voytek wanted to avoid a pitfall identified by Dr Johnson: 'Such seems to be the disposition of man that whatever makes a distinction produces a rivalry.'

The *Piolets d'Or* was the idea of Jean-Claude Marmier, President of the GHM, and Guy Chaumereuil, editor of *Montagnes* magazine. It came into being in 1991 with all the best of intentions and an idealism echoing that of Coubertin in launching the modern Olympics nearly 100 years before. It would salute the climbs that captured the imagination and essence of our sport. If the *Piolets d'Or* holds to this ideal it will remain the flagship award, a marker in the sand as to the best way forward to the good of climbing everywhere but especially to those former communist and far eastern countries where an outdated industrial ethos has clung on in mountaineering.

In recent years leading Russian climbers such as Alexander Klenov have questioned their country's system of high mountain competitions. He feels it has held back Russian climbing from breaking new ground in a committed style without bolts and fixed ropes. Anatoli Moshnikov is quoted on the web as saying, 'competitions today are not relevant and are displacing the essence of mountain climbing'. Ian Parnell in an excellent article in *Alpinist* entitled 'Victors of the Unwinnable' quotes the Russian Yuri Koshelenko as saying: 'The *Piolets d'Or* has helped me to understand better the ideals of European mountaineering.' So much so that Koshelenko made a valiant effort to climb Menlungtse's north face in alpine style.

The inaugural award went to Marko Prezelj and Andre Stremfelj who had climbed in impeccable alpine style the south-west ridge of Kangchenjunga South Peak – as original and committing a climb as the founders could have wished for. The problem was to keep the *Piolets* on course and that would depend upon the judgement of the jury members and the integrity of the sponsors. There needed to be eternal vigilance to ensure the award structure never lost the plot: was never diverted from the ideal for one reason or another.

If there is inappropriate motivation behind this award, or any award for that matter, because it has fallen into the hands of those who are ignorant of its *raisons d'etre* or with hidden agendas to gain power, wealth, fame, praise, increased status or to compete with other awards' organisers, then it will fail. If a recipient is chosen for political or financial reasons then the award will lose respect and create disharmony during the award ceremony and beyond. One thinks of Steve House lambasting the *Piolets* jury a few years ago for having chosen the Russian siege of Jannu over other more committing climbs including his own solo ascent of K7. This, and other controversial decisions have led to passionate debate. This is all to the good of the game for this constant scrutiny out in the public domain will help foster inspirational climbs well into the future. In 1998, Marmier resigned his patronage of the *Piolets d'Or* as he considered its original ideals had been compromised and devalued. Now that the award is back on course perhaps Jean-Claude would consider rejoining in some capacity?

Twenty years on from its inauguration, the *Piolets* organisers must ensure that they have full confidence in all those nominated for the award so it can be given with a full heart. It should also be presented without too much fanfare and razzamatazz from sponsors that would detract from highlighting the main reason that the award was set up in the first place – to celebrate the spirit of alpinism.

'Praise shames me, for I secretly beg for it,' wrote Rabindranath Tagore in his poem *Stray Birds*. Think about it.

Postscript: Shortly after filing this feature, Doug Scott received a further accolade in the form of 2011 *Piolet d'Or* 'Lifetime Contribution Award'. Previous recipients of this mountaineering Oscar are Walter Bonatti (2009) and Reinhold Messner (2010).

LINDSAY GRIFFIN

Playing The Game

What do we define as trad climbing in the UK? Until quite recently there was simply *climbing* and also sport climbing. The BMC, the representative body for climbing, mountaineering and hill walking in the UK, feels it is represented by a route with little or no in-situ protection or main belays. However, on certain trad routes extra protection (occasional pegs or bolts) will have been placed (and left in-situ) because of the perceived extreme difficulty of protecting the route with nuts and cams. This fixed protection will not significantly alter the character of a route. Even that can never be a clear statement, because it will be down to the first ascensionist to decide whether the natural pro on his or her creation is satisfactory, marginal or unsatisfactory.

Within the UK there are many areas, and indeed crags themselves, that have sport climbs and pure trad climbs – and even some crags that are a mixture of both styles. Two of the most well known venues featuring both are Malham in Yorkshire and the Llanberis slate quarries in North Wales. By and large, climbers in the UK are pretty comfortable with this and respect the different styles.

Before the 1960s climbers used to carry piles of little stones, which they placed in cracks and threaded, or used jammed knots like the Czechs on their sandstone towers. Then there were large machine nuts with the threads drilled out so they could be used on rope slings. John Brailsford, a blacksmith, made the first purpose-built nut in 1960, and a poor version of wired nuts followed a little later. Placing pitons on our crags has always caused ethical debate. But even when I was climbing in the early 1970s, many climbers would habitually carry a peg hammer and a few pegs for main belays. It wasn't 'the done thing' to place a peg for protection on a pitch, but establishing a good belay seemed acceptable.

In those days there was a lot more in-situ pro on the crags. Most of this rotted or rusted away and was never replaced, because equipment became more sophisticated in the form of small wires, RPs, cams etc. But as the gear was still generally poor compared to today, there was rather more jiggery-pokery; a bending of ethics that was rather glossed over at the time. However, the adventurous nature of the climb itself was not compromised.

Without sounding old-fashioned, because there are some fantastically bold young climbers around in the UK at present, the average climber in the early to mid 1970s was much happier on bolder climbs than the average climber of today; back then 'bold climbing' was simply the norm. You have to remember that this was the '70s when climbing was dangerous and sex was safe.

63. Aiguille des Pélèrins: A bolt placed here in 1980 by Michel Piola for protection on *Nostradamus* heralded a sea change in climbing in the Mont Blanc massif. (*Lindsay Griffin*)

In Britain, up until the mid '70s you rock climbed. If you progressed, you winter climbed in Scotland, and to continue further meant the Alps. That was it; with the exception of those with a surname such as Bonington, alpinists appeared unable to make the upward step to the Himalaya because (a) it was before the days of 'cheap' air travel and the entire cost of an expedition seemed prohibitively expensive, and (b) there was a huge psychological barrier, as few understood what was involved. That's a rash generalisation of course: there were certainly several people going to foreign venues, such as Yosemite, to rock climb. But it wasn't until the late '70s, when France was changing its philosophy from adventure to recreation, that a lot of top British rock climbers started to go to France and climb hard routes on fixed protection, mainly pegs but increasingly bolts. And they brought the idea back to the UK in order to push climbing standards.

So why did UK climbers preserve their trad climbing when the rest of Europe was overtaken by sport? It's a good question. It helps that we've always been a bit mad, but I think the main reasons reflect our very limited resource in the UK, and that virtually all mountain rock, certainly at the standard of the time, lends itself to natural gear. In addition, we seem to have, in general, a huge tradition and a great respect for the pioneers, both of which are perhaps not so strong in other countries. Certainly in the '80s and '90s the good sport climbers were, by and large, also good trad climbers, and realised that to improve the level of trad climbing, they had to work on bolts to better their ability and fitness.

At the close of the 1970s, with a growing acceptance in Europe of protection bolts and the incredible rise in free climbing standards, it was perhaps inevitable that someone would decide to take this new attitude into the mountains.

And where better than that crucible of alpine climbing, the Mont Blanc massif? In 1980 two young lads from Geneva climbed a new route on the north pillar of the Pélèrins. Previous rock climbs had more or less followed crack systems, where pegs, then latterly nuts, could be used for protection and aid. But in places the new Swiss climb involved very difficult (for the day – F6b+) steep open face climbing, with several sections of compact granite. On one of these they hand-drilled a protection bolt.

This was certainly not the first time bolts had been used in the Mont Blanc massif: in 1956 that great traditionalist Gaston Rébuffat placed one for a belay on his classic route up the south face of the Midi. A couple of months later a Swiss team used four bolts on a smooth wall near the top of their new route on the Petit Clocher du Portalet. But the drilled hole on the Pélèrins was more or less the first time a bolt had been placed solely for protection. The author, perhaps somewhat brashly, felt he was making a prophecy, and called the route *Nostradamus.*

And he was correct, because after Michel Piola placed that bolt in *Nostradamus*, climbing in the Mont Blanc massif would never be the same again.

Two years later the whole direction had changed. People were no longer looking at natural lines defined by crack systems but were purposely launching out onto compact slabs. Piola realized that an ideal venue for this was the knobbly rock of the Grand Capuçin. And so we got *Gulliver's Travellers* – still one of the great Mont Blanc classics – with a very minimal number of hand-drilled bolts.

This type of climbing needed an entirely different approach from traditional alpine work. These were hard technical climbs, levels unheard of before in the high mountains of the Western Alps, and the days of climbing in big leather boots and rucksacks were gone. These routes required a lightweight crag-climbing attitude. Again, this was not entirely original: Martin Boysen used rock shoes when he made the second ascent of the south face of the Fou in 1968, but at the time everyone said he was cheating. The lightweight approach would need leaving mountain boots and sacs at the base of the route. So how would you get off the summit?

The answer, of course, was sound, double-bolt belays.

This style proved to be very much the start of convenience climbing – people now wanted to enjoy the climbing without the awkward bits. I want to give you just one classic example, the west face of Petites Jorasses. I think when I climbed this face at the beginning of the 1970s, the classic *Contamine* was the only route. We took bivouac gear – because we were generally slow and incompetent – not so much for the ascent but more because the descent was complex and time-consuming. From the top

64. The Brouillard Face of Mont Blanc with the Right Hand Pillar centre stage (Bonington Harlin, Baillie, Robertson, 1965). But where should the route actually end? "Did we really climb it?" asked Baillie. (*Antonio Giani*)

you first had to rappel into a stone-swept snow couloir (which nowadays must be in dreadful condition throughout the summer), descend this while dodging rocks, make a difficult rappel over a large *rimaye*, cross a contorted glacier, and finally reach the remotely sited Gervasutti Bivouac in the dusk. Next day involved a long descent to the Val Ferret, a walk and hitchhike down to Courmayeur, and then back through the tunnel to Chamonix.

In the 1970s rappelling was always considered dangerous, something you did as a last resort when you were forced to retreat. A change in mindset was needed for the modern routes. But when Piola added *Anouk* – the first route in the Mont Blanc massif to use a hundred bolts – alongside the *Contamine*, it took away all the commitment. Now there was not only a rapid rappel on secure anchors from the summit but also the option of escape on route, at points where it was possible to reach *Anouk* by a traverse or diagonal rappel. I'm not saying this is worse; I can't say that it's better: it's just different.

This in turn led to a changing attitude as to what constituted a route. Traditionally a route had a 'logical conclusion', which was originally the summit, then the crest of a ridge, because the descent was different. Now the focus became the climb and the traditional values of a logical conclusion went out the window. For instance, many people climbed the Supercouloir on Mt Blanc du Tacul by what would become an accepted method: climbing to the end of the difficulties and then rappelling. But both before, and in the year or two after Gabarrou's first ascent in 1975, several parties climbed, more or less, to the end of the difficulties, which is not quite halfway up the face, before retreating in a storm. None of those felt they had climbed a route.

So, alpinists began to 'move the goalposts', in order to cut out the awkward bits. Most will feel this began in the '80s, but did it? No, actually you have to go back to at least 1965 and the first ascent of the Right Hand Pillar of Brouillard on the great south face of Mont Blanc.

In that year Rusty Baillie and Chris Bonington made two attempts on the pillar, which at that time was one of the 'last major unclimbed formations' in the range. On the latter they got to within a handshake of the top. They returned for third attempt with American John Harlin and Scot Brian Robertson. This time these four reached the 'end of the difficulties' and started up the mixed ground above to the crest of the Brouillard Ridge (unlike the Red, the Right Hand Pillar has no 'summit', it just merges into easier ground). A storm moved in, they descended, bivouacked, and next day rappelled their route. And they have always been credited with the first ascent. Nobody, even back in 1965, argued (part of this may have been to do with their status; at the time they were amongst the best alpinists in the business). And it was hard to imagine Baillie and Bonington having the motivation for a fourth attempt. However, as Baillie wrote, 'but did we really climb it? Does the Right Hand Pillar end at the summit of Mont Blanc, or on the Brouillard Ridge, or at the top of the Right Hand Pillar, or anywhere?'

The knock-on effect was interesting. When Roger Everett and I made the second recorded ascent in 1973, we got maybe 50m higher than the first ascensionists before bivouacking. I can't now remember how our discussion evolved, but when next day we started towards the Brouillard Ridge and saw an ominous bank of thick cloud moving in from the west, it was fairly easy to convince ourselves that we could go down from this point for tea and medals, happy with our 'ascent', because the precedent had been set. Bonington, innovative as always, had been ahead of the game in climbing 'to the end of the difficulties'.

Moving to the Greater Ranges, where traditionally it was assumed that people went for adventure and wilderness, what is the ethic concerning the use of bolts? Some while back the BMC came up with a statement that the UIAA subsequently adopted:

The UIAA believes that in the interests of protecting the future of World mountaineering, parties visiting remote mountain and wilderness areas should strive to minimise their use of drilled equipment and certainly refrain from using a power drill.

You can argue that a hole is a hole, but if you know it is going to take at least half-an-hour laboriously to hand drill and place a bolt in granite, then you think very strongly before doing so. The process is self-regulating.

Conrad Anker wrote the following concerning his 1998 first ascent of the west face of Latok II, at the time hailed as a landmark ascent – a pointer – in Himalayan climbing. I admit it's not the best example: firstly there are always two sides to a story and some of these details are disputed; secondly

65. The 2300m south face of Annapurna with the 7.5km east ridge forming the skyline: a forcing ground of exemplary high-altitude alpinism. (*Lindsay Griffin*)

it involves Alex Huber, who is undoubtedly one of the very best big wall free climbers around.

Anker envisaged leading up this wall with traditional gear, honouring the philosophy of Shipton or Mugs Stump. 'Alex said no. He'd failed in 1995 climbing in alpine style. Without the proceeds from a successful climb, he could lose his house. We'd take every guarantee we could find: fixed ropes, bolts, a power drill.'

And then later ... 'the fine orange granite seemed to welcome our gear, our portaledges, our camps. But when a hook blew, Alex got out the power drill, and "with a little hole, the move was outwitted". We lived on the wall for eight days and the hole count grew to 70. But in my mind we were killing the dragon.'

Contrast this with the ascent one year later of the *Norwegian Route* on the 1500m east face of Trango Pulpit at VII 5.11 and A4. Alright, it's nearly 1000m lower in altitude but the difficulties are far longer. The Norwegians spent 38 days in capsule style on the wall and placed only a minimal amount of bolts using a hand drill. Consequently the standard was very high, probably the hardest big wall route above 6000m at that time. Has it been surpassed? I don't know.

Recent years have seen a huge increase in 'goalpost moving' in the

Greater Ranges. Many climbers now simply seem to remove the awkward bits from the equation. We want to go into the wilderness, we want to have adventure, but essentially we don't want the commitment this entails; we want a compromise.

In the words of Rolando Garibotti, who is very much the guardian of ethics in Patagonia, these become 'valiant attempts' or perhaps 'superb efforts' that deserve widespread recognition. In the *American Alpine Journal*, that still champions traditional values, they are reported as incomplete ascents and, generally, any assigned route name goes unmentioned.

In some cases it might be logical to look at the question of intent. Did the climbers plan only to climb to the top of, for example, the pillar, or the middle of a long ridge, and then descend? Let's take a recent 'new route' in the Karakoram, claimed as such and given a name by its first ascensionists. The line lay on an unclimbed rock feature, but some distance below the top the leader fell and broke his ankle, so the party retreated. Their intent was most definitely not to descend from this point, so how does one define their attempt?

And what about the various styles of ascent? Intuitively, the purest is alpine style, an ethic now embraced by the new criteria of the *Piolets d'Or*. At really high altitudes this style is perhaps still best exemplified by the 1985 ascent of the west face of Gasherbrum IV. We don't really know in today's currency how hard it was technically; what we do know is that it was totally committing, precarious, had long sections with either little or no pro, and then a difficult descent on unknown ground. Almost as significant was the 1984 *Catalan Route* on the south face of Annapurna. Both are now one quarter of a century old, and although they may have been equalled, I'm not convinced they've ever been surpassed.

With other styles, when the going gets tough, things inevitably will get abandoned in the interests of safety – obviously. It's now no longer possible to make a true, committing, alpine style ascent of the *West Face Direct* on K2, or the north face of Jannu. Both are outstanding climbs and it would be very easy to argue that in the present state of our development there was perhaps no other way in which these could have been completed by climbers today. But it would be arrogant to assume that a two-man ascent in pure alpine style would not be possible in 10, 15 or 20 years' time. Let's hope there is still respect for those who have gone before; it would be the ultimate sacrilege in mountaineering if a team was to batter to death the north ridge of Latok I with a fixed rope ascent, a route that has been the goal of around 30 parties to date using a committing alpine or capsule style approach.

Our little game doesn't have rules, and of course the freedom to make our own choices is one of the reasons we all climb. But we have a sort of code of honour to protect the spirit of our activity, at least I think we do... I hope we do.

We live in an increasingly achievement-oriented world, and for a growing number of mountaineers, and climbers, winning the game seems

66. West face of Gasherbrum IV (7925m). In 1985, after making the first, highly committing, ascent of the 3000m face, Voytek Kurtyka and Robert Schauer descended the left skyline, exhausted and on totally unknown ground. (*Oriol Baro*)

to have become more important than how it is played.

Why we climb is completely personal, how we climb is communal. How we climb defines the future of mountaineering and also the mountain environment. Leave no trace, alpine style, doing more with less: many people can see intuitively that even if they can't climb this way themselves, it is progressive mountaineering – the way to go.

Part of this essay formed a presentation given at the 2010 International Trad Climbing Meet in Orco, northern Italy. It examines 'traditional values' in climbing; from Great Britain through the Alps to the Himalaya.

ROB COLLISTER

Cri de Coeur From The Alps

How many times can a man turn his head
And pretend that he just doesn't see? – Bob Dylan

The Aletsch Glacier, which flows out of the Bernese Oberland into the Rhone valley in western Switzerland, is the longest glacier in the Alps. It is fed by a number of ice streams emanating from peaks like the Äbeni Flue, Jungfrau, Mönch, Fiescherhorn and Grünhorn, most of them over 4000 metres. The point at which these tributaries merge to form the Aletsch is a plain of snow two kilometres wide known as Konkordiaplatz. At the geographical heart of the Bernese Oberland and of a UNESCO World Natural Heritage site, it has attracted mountaineers since the middle of the 19th century. The first hut was built here on a rock shelf a few feet above the ice in 1872 and it has been periodically enlarged and re-built ever since to cater for growing demand. Nowadays it accommodates up to a hundred people a night, especially during April and May when it is a popular base for ski mountaineers, and the term 'hut' is something of a misnomer. Materials for the original building would have been carried all the way up from the Rhone valley by porters or, conceivably, mules. Now, it is re-provisioned on a weekly basis by helicopter, and for the hut guardian and his family it is only a 30-minute ride on a skidoo uphill to the Jungfraujoch where the railway from Grindelwald terminates.

However, the biggest change has been to the glacier. There is nothing new about glacial recession: it has been going on for 150 years, but the process has accelerated recently. In the case of the Aletsch, the glacier has not actually retreated very much, but its surface has dropped dramatically as its volume shrinks. Konkordia in the summer becomes by midday a swamp of rotten snow cut by rushing melt-water streams. Where once climbers could walk onto the ice, there is now a metal staircase zigzagging almost 100 metres up a vertical rock face. At the end of a long day, it comes as a sting in the tail, especially at 2800 metres above sea-level. Every few years, as the glacier level falls, the Swiss Alpine Club is obliged to fit a new section of staircase. In the 30 years since I first visited the hut, the ice has dropped as much as it did in the previous 100. This is not my imagination. At bends in the staircase small signs indicate the year in which this was the surface of the ice. About 10 years ago I counted the number of steps out of curiosity. There were 360. Two years ago I counted again. This time, there were 433, 450 including a ladder lashed to the bottom. It is a graphic illustration of the effect of global warming on the landscape, but it is far from unique. The same story is being repeated all over the Alps, indeed all over the world. Many small glaciers have disappeared completely; others have become no more than snow patches. Elsewhere, what used to be a smooth surface of snow has become a ridge and furrow of ice covered with rock debris. Access to and from larger glaciers becomes increasingly problematic, with treacherously loose moraine walls or ice-polished slabs to negotiate.

For most people in the West, climate change is not urgently present in their lives. It is still something to be read about in the papers, something that will affect other people, at some time in the future. But for mountaineers, one would have thought, the reality of global warming cannot be denied. The evidence is before our eyes every time we set foot on a glacier. Yet many, if not most, do appear to be in denial. The adventure travel industry is booming; the number of climbers and hikers jetting off to Greenland, Antarctica, South America and the Himalaya on a regular basis shows no sign of diminishing. easyJet and Ryanair continue to post handsome profits; the heli-ski industry, though banned in France and Austria, flourishes in Italy and Switzerland; weekend jaunts to the Alps for both skiing and climbing are very much in vogue. Climate change? What climate change?

Satish Kumar, a former monk and editor of *Resurgence* magazine, who once walked 8000 miles from India to Washington via Moscow, Paris and London on a pilgrimage for peace, with no money and nothing but the clothes he stood up in, believes that, in relation to planet Earth, we are all either tourists or pilgrims. We regard the Earth either as a resource available for our gratification or as a miracle of beauty and complexity to be marvelled at, valued and protected. One would expect mountaineers to be pilgrims. Mountains have been, and still are sacred in many cultures. Traditionally, even in the West, they have been sources of inspiration, symbols of aspiration and metaphors for personal quest. The early alpine climbers were, for the most part, pilgrims, entranced by what they saw and found, revelling in the discomfort and effort required. They were mountain travellers, excited by crossing a col into a different valley as much as by reaching a summit. Significant numbers were clergymen and academics seeking validation of a faith undermined by Darwin. Today, the notion of mountains as natural cathedrals, proposed by Ruskin, is deeply unfashionable. Respect, reverence even, has been replaced by a view of mountains as commodities to be marketed for the benefit of local communities and as trophies to be collected by visitors. It is an attitude to be found at all ends of the mountain spectrum from Everest to Snowdon. In the Alps it has resulted in rack-railways, cable-cars and chair-lifts to make life easier for skiers in winter and climbers and walkers in summer, in fixed ropes to make climbs of the Matterhorn, the Eiger and countless other peaks more accessible and, most recently, in the metal clutter of *via ferrata* that have sprouted on the cliffs behind every alpine village, it seems, to provide thrills without the need for skills.

There is a paradox at the root of mountaineering that was expressed succinctly many years ago by a French alpinist, Jacques Lagarde and quoted by Lindsay Griffin in his Introduction to an AC guidebook:

Ever since man has been drawn to the mountains by a love of wild nature, rigour, solitude and the unknown, all of which he found in that final refuge, he has done everything to eliminate precisely what he sought.

Today, comfort and convenience, those twin pillars of consumerism, have prevailed in the mountains as they have everywhere else. Duvets, hot showers, beer on tap and freshly-baked bread are becoming the norm in huts, diminishing the delicious contrast and sense of appreciation that return to the valley used to bring. Bolts, GPS, radios and mobile phones have removed much of the uncertainty, and with it the adventure, of alpine climbing and ski mountaineering. Digital cameras, BlackBerries, iPhones, heart-rate monitors, and altimeter wrist-watches to record every conceivable aspect of progress, all ensure that the modern mountaineer, festooned with electronic equipment, is only fleetingly, if ever, truly in the present. And if all this displacement activity should prove insufficient, we can always plug in to an iPod to avoid hearing whatever the mountains have to say. There is little time or space for that 'sense of joy, awe and wonder' of which Satish Kumar speaks and which has been described so feelingly over the years by mountaineers as diverse as John Muir, Eric Shipton, Bill Murray, Arne Naess and Jim Perrin.

However, it is easy enough to venture off the tourist's beaten track. We have but to leave the gizmos behind to emerge from a cocoon and be at once more acutely aware of our surroundings, more in tune with the mountain world and, as a result, probably safer also. To visit the Alps out of season when the huts are closed apart from a 'winter room' (more than half the year in fact) is to quickly re-discover 'wild nature, rigour, solitude and the unknown'. I would not wish to deny that there is value and enjoyment in the exercising of skill, judgement and experience to overcome difficulties and achieve a goal, be it a summit or a journey, or that there are plenty of occasions in the Alps when weather or snow conditions dictate that speed is of the essence. But to travel sometimes in a spirit of quietude rather than bent on accomplishment, as explorers rather than conquistadors, is to allow mountaineering to become less a matter of success or failure, and more an opportunity to notice, to observe and to be absorbed into a marvellous world. We might then come to feel more readily a part of the mountains ourselves and to feel wounded by what has been done to them and what is happening to them. We might even find it in our hearts to comprehend the plight not just of glaciers but of the whole planet and of those millions, if not billions, less fortunate than ourselves.

These sentiments may resonate with some members of the Alpine Club. Others will ridicule them as the ranting of a hair-shirt killjoy. Yet ultimately we are talking not about how we choose to spend our holidays but about social justice as well as conservation in its widest sense. Over the last few years, through a mixture of concern, self-interest and coercion most of us have made changes to the way we live our everyday lives. We recycle our paper, glass, tin and plastic; we are learning to turn off lights, TVs and computers when not in use; we see the sense of insulating our lofts and excluding draughts from windows and doors; we share transport when we can. Nobody is perfect but most of us are trying. Mountaineering, however, seems to be a compartment of our lives exempt from wider concerns. The mountaineering community needs to accept that its activities do impinge seriously on others and that changes in behaviour and life-style do make a difference, even if only by adding momentum to a very slowly rolling ball. We need to ask questions about how we travel and how frequently, about how and where our clothing and equipment are made, and from what materials, and how often does it really need to be replaced. We need to make choices based on human and environmental cost rather than on pounds or dollars. Perhaps a start would be some form of carbon-rationing, which would have to be self-imposed as government has shied away from the idea since the recession. (Is there a role here for the AC?) An approach of 'less is more' to all aspects of our travelling and climbing could actually be enriching, enabling us to rediscover a simplicity and authenticity that used to be at the core of mountaineering. We could even find ourselves again on the pilgrim path which, returning to Satish Kumar, 'is to be on a path of adventure, to move out of our comfort zones, to let go of our prejudices and pre-conditioning, to make strides towards the unknown'.

Ends of The Earth

67. John Innerdale, *Towers of Paine*, Chile, chromacolour, 50 x 60cm, 2002.

DAVID HAMILTON

Ski Mountaineering on The Frozen Continent

8. Mt Vinson summit, looking north to Mt Shinn, Mt Epperly, Mt Tyree and Mt Garner. *(David Hamilton)*

Long after all the other mountains in the world have been documented and climbed there will still be unexplored ranges in Antarctica. The logistic challenges, extreme climate and high costs of Antarctic exploration mean that only a few lucky climbers visit the interior of the icy continent each year. I have been fortunate to work as a guide in Antarctica for six seasons, mostly leading groups on two popular programmes: 'Last Degree' ski trips from 89° South to the South Pole (four times), and ascents of 4892m Mount Vinson (12 times).

Antarctica's highest peaks all lie in the Sentinel Range (part of the Ellsworth mountain chain) at S 78° 30' W 86° 00'. Basic 1:200,000 USGS maps have been available for this area since the 1960s. The recently produced 1:50,000 Omega Foundation map has more detail and greater accuracy. Studying this new map gave me the idea of making an exploratory ski mountaineering journey among Antarctica's highest mountains.

The key to travelling self-sufficiently for two weeks lay in using lightweight plastic sleds to transport our equipment. I had used a variety of sleds in other environments and knew that we needed an effective way of controlling the sleds during ski descents. A little research led me to Ed's Wilderness Systems in Minnesota, USA, where I purchased rigid fibreglass towing bars plus aluminium stability fins for the sleds.

I convinced my employer Antarctic Logistics and Expeditions (ALE) to allow me to range freely for two weeks at the end of the 2009/10 season

69. Starting out from Vinson Base Camp at 2,100m on the Branscomb glacier. *(David Hamilton coll.)*

and I persuaded Patrick Bird, a suitably fit and capable climbing friend, to join me for the trip. I led a 'Last Degree' ski trip from 20 December to 1 January followed by a few days as manager at Vinson Base Camp (VBC). On 7 January Patrick arrived and we were ready to start our trip.

In the afternoon we made a short trip from VBC at 2100m to Ski Hill 500m above to get a feel for the landscape and snow conditions. We followed an easy ridge line and were surprised to trigger a large surface layer avalanche in the bowl to our right as we climbed. Conventional wisdom holds that avalanches are very rare in Antarctica but in recent years ALE guides have observed several slides of recently deposited, wind-transported snow. The descent was fairly typical for high altitude Antarctic snow: variable breakable crust in places and a hard windblown surface in others. I hope that I am never asked to write advertising copy extolling the virtues of Antarctica's highest peaks for skiing. The truth is that while the base can be over 3000m deep, the surface layers rarely offer great skiing. Smooth, hard and windblown is usually as much as can be hoped for. Just occasionally a few centimetres of new snow on top of this can give a good surface. More frequent are patches of polished blue ice and iron-hard sastrugi. A ski trip to Antarctica's Ellsworth Mountains will always be about the unique location and magnificent scenery. Rarely will the quality of the skiing justify the formidable economic and logistic challenges of getting there.

It is possible to overplay the extreme nature of the Antarctic environment to make any expedition sound like an epic feat of endurance. Certainly those involved in very long unsupported crossings of the continent may experience conditions that can overwhelm even the best clothing equipment. A short trip at the height of the Austral summer need not be a traumatic experience. Temperatures at VBC vary from -10°C to -20°C during the climbing season and Vinson summit is normally around -30°C to -40°C. Used correctly, modern 8000m clothing can cope quite comfortably with these temperatures. Strong winds need to be treated with considerable respect as they are the main enemy of both comfort and safety.

My clothing system has been tested on the summits of Everest and Vinson many times. I was confident that it worked well and ensured that Patrick was similarly equipped. My one concern was for my feet. Leaving my trusted 8000m boots behind, I had to find a way of making my ski boots work at -40°C. For anyone with feet smaller than a size 12 the solution is simple: a shell one size larger than normal with extra insulation added via customised inner boots and extra socks. When one is already using the largest ski boot shells available the options are more limited. The answer was a combination of lightweight inner socks, vapour barrier liners, lightweight wool ski socks, custom-made intuition ski boot inners and a neoprene overboot. It took a bit of work to perfect this system. It was only when I removed the ski boot tongues and attacked the inner boots with a craft knife that the correct mix of comfort and performance was achieved.

Patrick and I left VBC on 8 January following the standard climbers' route on Vinson along the Branscomb Glacier as far as Low Camp. We each took about 40kg of supplies split into 10kg in a rucksack and 30kg on a sled. Under a cloudless sky and a merciless sun we were very hot on the long, gentle climb. Later that evening as the sun disappeared behind the bulk of Vinson the temperature in the tent dropped below -20°C.

Most of our planned route lay on the high-altitude plateau, above 3700m, that makes up much of the central Sentinel Range. The first challenge we faced was to get our supplies and equipment up to this height. We did this by making two carries on consecutive days to High Camp on Vinson's standard route. After the first carry we descended to Low Camp by ski. It is debatable if there was any advantage in using skis here given that we had to carry the extra weight uphill for the slim reward of a difficult descent on a steep slope with crusty snow. After two big load carries we were ready for a rest day but the weather forecast persuaded us to try and snatch the summit of 4660m Mount Shinn (Antarctica's third highest peak) before a predicted period of poor weather. Mount Shinn is one of my favourite Antarctic peaks and this was my third ascent. The route is varied and interesting without ever being difficult. The summit ridge is spectacular with several false summits and very large 'stable' cornices. From the summit

70. Patrick Bird skiing down the route of the fixed ropes between Camp 2 and Camp 1 on Mt Vinson's 'normal route'. *(David Hamilton)*

there are great views northwards towards 4852m Mount Tyree and 4575m Mount Gardner, the second and fourth highest peaks in Antarctica. We struggled a bit with the altitude but the weather conditions were ideal: clear skies, bright sunshine and little wind. We reached the summit in 7 ½ hours and made a ski assisted return to camp in three hours.

We appreciated our delayed rest day the following day, and then had a second rest day imposed upon us by low clouds and strong winds. It was still quite windy on the morning of the 14th. By early afternoon conditions had calmed and we were able to pack up camp and load the sleds. We followed the standard route towards the summit of Vinson. This climb is not steep and gains 1200m over 6km, but it was a real struggle to pull the heavily laden sleds up the icy sections of the route. After a day of sun and clear skies we were enveloped in swirling winds and mist just before reaching our intended campsite at 4700m on the col between the main summit of Vinson and a satellite peak called Sublime. In poor visibility we set up the tent in a cold shaded wind-scoop fearing that we would be hidden from the sun the following day.

At 10.30 the sun appeared from behind a rocky ridge. The tent soon warmed up and we were able to enjoy breakfast in some comfort. By 12.30 we set off to follow the straightforward ridge to the summit of Vinson, reaching it 90 minutes later. The air was still and clear. We could see the entire length of the Ellsworth Mountains stretching to the north and south. To the east and west the flat expanse of the Antarctic ice sheet extended as far as the eye could see. The view was not unlike looking out over a sea of clouds below; only in this case what we were seeing was not a cloud inversion seen from above but an uninterrupted sea of ice that stretched for thousands of kilometres in all directions.

We descended to camp for lunch before packing the tent and loading the sleds ready to continue our journey south-east. We crossed the high-altitude plateau of the Vinson Massif with its dozen subsidiary summits before the ground fell away into a gentle slope leading to Hammer Col. The sleds behaved reasonably well on the descent with only a few flips. Soon

1. On the summit ridge of Mt Shinn, looking towards the peaks at the northern end of the Sentinel Range. *(David Hamilton)*
2. Mt Tyree (Antarctica's 2nd highest peak) seen from the summit slopes of Mt Shinn. *(David Hamilton)*

73. Leaving the Corbert/Clinch Col at 4700m on the Vinson Massif. *(David Hamilton)*

we were adept at keeping them upright even as we executed some fairly aggressive ski turns. Camping at 3850m on the Hammer Col was unbelievably warm. There were no surrounding peaks to cast their shadows over the camp and it was exposed to 24-hour direct sunlight. The temperature in the tent never fell below 20°C. It was so hot and bright throughout the night that we found it difficult to sleep.

The next day was clear and sunny on the high peaks although we could see some distant clouds at lower elevations. Leaving the tent and sleds behind we set off on the gentle 8km climb towards the Craddock Massif, which culminates in Antarctica's ninth highest peak. We knew that the highest point, 4477m Mt Rutford, had received only one previous ascent via the steep west ridge. Although our ski approach from the north was a considerably easier climb it was a new route on the peak and the first ski ascent. The summit was just out of view for almost all the climb. The wind would threaten to increase and then die down. The clouds would threaten to obscure the route and then clear. There was just enough uncertainty about the climb that we were never quite sure if we would succeed until we removed skis 70m below the top and set foot on the final steep tower of rock and ice.

The summit block was the strangest piece of mountain architecture that I have ever seen. A huge crack split the overhanging summit rock block. A snow cone piled on top of the block had been eroded by wind channelled up through the crack. This had created a symmetrical concave feature in the snow resembling a modern sculpture. We photographed this for several minutes and looked along the lengthy summit ridge linking the other three principal summits of the Craddock Massif before descending to collect our skis.

The climb had taken 5½ hours. The ski descent took only 1½ hours and this included several stops to take photographs and admire the views. After another warm night in Hammer Col camp we started our homeward journey retracing our route back to the Vinson Plateau 6km distant and 1000m higher. The winds grew steadily from the west as we climbed and the heavy sleds slowed our progress. By the time we reached our intended campsite on the col between Corbet Peak and Clinch Peak the wind was gusting at 30-40 knots, funnelled through the gap in the mountains.

We searched in vain for a sheltered spot to pitch the tent and settled for a small shelf partially protected by a low ridge of rocks. The wind and spindrift howled around us as we struggled for more than two hours to cut a platform for the tent and pitch it. We dragged the heavy sleds into the flapping fabric to hold it in place while we fought with the poles and stakes. Finally, with three ice axes, two snow stakes, and a heap of rocks we secured the tent in place and crawled inside. We had been looking forward to completing a 'hardship free' expedition but the Antarctic weather was not going to let us leave without a taste of what a serious low temperature storm feels like. We were happy to be safely inside the tent with no cold injuries as the wind continued to shake the tent throughout the night.

By the morning the wind had dropped to 20-30 knots. We loaded the sleds inside the tent, dropped the tent quickly and 'rafted' the sleds together for the start of the journey. A few hundred metres lower we escaped the worst of the wind. We separated the sleds, reconfigured our loads and started to ski. We expected a quick simple downhill run to regain High Camp on the regular Vinson route. Few things in Antarctica work out exactly as planned. It took several hours of frustrating work to drop 900m over 7km to reach our goal. Along the way we encountered hard blue ice and giant sastrugi. Inaccurate altimeter readings caused us to drop too low before a crucial traverse. Wearily we resorted to skins to facilitate the climb back to the correct line of travel.

By 6pm we skied into High Camp and met almost 20 other climbers. We had grown used to having the entire mountain range to ourselves and it seemed strange to be back in the company of others. The forecast for the following day was good. Although we had accomplished all of our goals we had not done as much 'proper' skiing as we had hoped. Neither pulling sleds up or down really meet the requirement for 'enjoyable' skiing. So I suggested that we make a repeat ascent of Vinson the next day, unencumbered by sleds, before descending to VBC. Patrick was initially surprised by this idea, but realising that we were well acclimatised quickly agreed.

We made a fast ascent to the summit carrying light loads in five hours. To make a change from our earlier ascent we followed the 'Right Hand Variation' that deviates from the standard route 250m below the summit. This enabled us to see a different side of the peak and make a traverse of the summit. It was -35°C on the top with moderately strong winds so we did not stop for long before heading down the standard route to a point where we could put on skis at 4750m. From here we made a swift return to camp in less than an hour.

We were looking forward to a quick descent to VBC but our difficulties were not over. We had not appreciated how hard it would be to lower the sleds down the fixed ropes from High Camp to Low Camp. Abseiling with the conjoined sleds was a tough challenge and it took three hours to get from 3500m to 2800m. Low Camp was enjoying the evening sun but the route to VBC was shrouded in low-lying mist. We had been anticipating a smooth ski down gentle slopes to VBC. Instead we endured a tense descent

74. Patrick Bird (left) and David Hamilton on the summit of Mt Shinn. *(David Hamilton)*

through fog with visibility of no more than a few metres. Only the faint marks left by the ski poles of a previous party and an occasional marker wand indicated the correct path. After a 13½ hour day we staggered into VBC to be welcomed by the ALE camp staff with a bottle of champagne and a hot dinner.

The trip had lasted 14 days. We had covered 90km, much of it above 4000m, and summited three of the highest peaks in Antarctica. Patrick added up the figures and concluded that we had climbed a total of 8125m and descended 6625m on skis. I reminded him of our conversation six months earlier. When I had invited Patrick to ski with me in the Vinson Massif he had said that it sounded like a lot of money to climb one mountain. I had replied 'you get yourself down there and I will make sure you get a chance to climb more than one mountain'. I had kept my side of the bargain and we both agreed that it had been a great trip.

Summary: An account of a ski mountaineering expedition in the Sentinel Range of Antarctica's Ellsworth Mountains by David Hamilton and Patrick Bird in January 2010, including ski ascents of Mt Vinson (4892m), Mt Shinn (4660m) and Mt Rutford (4477m).

DEREK BUCKLE

Chile Relish

The 2010 Alpine Club expedition to Chile

It was hot when we arrived in Santiago at the end of January, in marked contrast to the cold prevailing in the UK at the time. It was here that we met up with Carlos Bascou, our Chilean member who had worked hard on planning our itinerary. He and Mike Soldner had conceived this expedition some years previously and had eventually decided on exploration of the mountains surrounding Tupungato from a base in the upper reaches of the Rio Colorado. Both had visited this area once earlier as part of their preparation for the first Chilean expedition to Nanga Parbat in 2007. At

75. Alpenglow on Tupungato (6570m), one of the highest peaks of the Chilean Andes. (*Derek Buckle*)

6570m, Tupungato is one of the highest of the Andean peaks, yet it does not attract the hoards regularly seen on Aconcagua, its close neighbour and the highest mountain in South America, despite being only 70 km from Santiago. The relative remoteness of Tupungato compared with many other Chilean mountains undoubtedly accounts for some of its reduced popularity, but the need for access permits to the upper Colorado valley is a second factor. Permits are required from both the Chilean border control agency and the Alfalfel power plant harnessing the waters of the Rio Colorado. As Carlos had arranged these prior to our arrival in Chile our access to the valley was a remarkably smooth affair.

Suitably equipped with detailed maps and a vast quantity of food, we left

Santiago for the mountains on 2 February. A short drive of only two hours took us east from the city to the vast opencast mine at the road-head hamlet of Chacayal where we met with the *arrieros* and mules that were to take our loads over two days to a base camp at 3160m. Neither day was particularly arduous but a flood-damaged bridge over the Rio Azufre, a significant

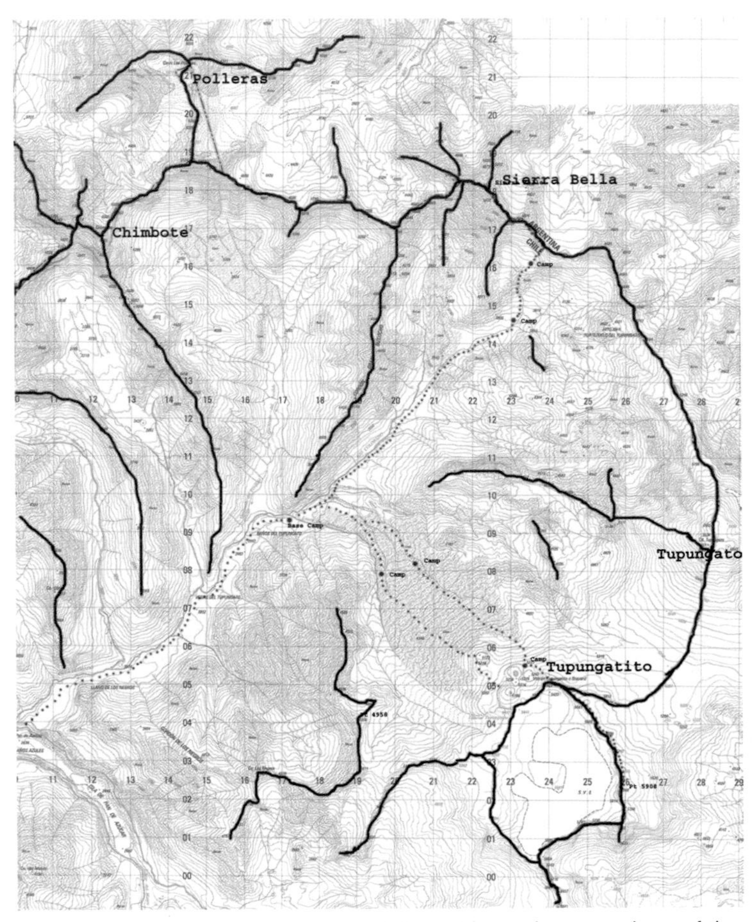

76. Tupungato region with routes followed by various members of the Alpine Club expedition indicated.

tributary of the Colorado, necessitated an early horse-assisted river crossing that limited the distance travelled on the first day. By necessity therefore we made our first camp on a grassy plateau watered by a mineral spring. The scenery became typically volcanic and would become progressively more so as we gained height. Crossing the Azufre before noon the following day was an exciting affair, particularly for those unused to horse riding. My own very limited experience had already demonstrated that I had little control of horse behaviour and it was fortunate that the horses were roped

7. Kai Green negotiating densely packed *penitentes* on the descent from Sierra Bella. (*Derek Buckle*)

for the crossing, especially when even they stumbled in the fast-flowing muddy waters.

Safely transported across the Azufre, we generally followed the Colorado for a further six hours until a rightwards branch led to Baños del Tupungato where we sited base camp. Despite the dust, this camp afforded stupendous views of Rabicano (5334m), Chimbote (5493m) and Polleras (6024m) to the north-west in addition to Sierra Bella (5275m) and Tupungato (6570m) to the north-east and east respectively. Chimbote, the only major unclimbed peak in this panorama, was one that we had hoped to attempt until we learned that a number of competent Chilean parties had been defeated within 100m of the summit by steep, unconsolidated rock. We were later to experience some of this loose rock and it more than vindicated our decision to leave Chimbote well alone. Previously climbed Polleras on the other hand looked an attractive mountain, but earlier ascents had been made from the west and it was unclear how we could access this side of the mountain from where we were, bounded to the south as it was by a seemingly impregnable wall. Rabicano was too far away to

78. Derek Buckle and Kai Green approaching the south summit of Sierra Bella (5223m, Alpine D) (*Carlos Bascou*)

79. Sierra Bella (5275m), an early objective of the AC expedition. (*Derek Buckle*)

even be considered. Faced with this scenario we focused on Sierra Bella and one of the satellites of Tupungato called Tupungatito.

Having decided to attempt Sierra Bella first, Carlos, Kai, Dave and I continued up the main valley on 4 February following the well defined northerly *voie normale* to Tupungato until a side valley led leftwards at ~3700m. Here we left a stash before returning to BC. Unfortunately Dave was by now unwell so the following day only three of us returned to establish a camp on a level gravel patch immediately across the river from the stash. From here Kai and Carlos still had the energy to prospect a route up the steep, boulder-strewn northerly couloir as far as the glacier snout before turning in. The next day full loads were carried up the couloir from where we traversed rightwards over progressively larger *penitentes* until five hours later we reached a rounded boss a little below a major rock band at 4461m. The effort required to traverse closely-packed, 0.5 to 1.5m high *penitentes* while hampered by heavy packs necessitated that we camp here. Some two hours later, after collapsing the upper *penitentes* onto those lower down, we had a level platform on which to pitch the tent surrounded by a magnificent panorama comprising literally billions of *penitentes*. It seemed that the whole face on the Chilean side of the range comprised these intriguing ice pinnacles that are formed at higher altitudes in the Andes as a result of differential ablation.

We left camp at 4.15 the next morning, clambering over frozen *penitentes* in the dark until we crossed the bergshrund. From here the slope steepened to approximately 40 degrees for some 300m before we joined the frontier ridge. Fortunately this slope was free from significant *penitentes*, but they reasserted themselves with a vengeance on the ridge. After cresting a prominent snow dome, however, it was possible to cross a shallow col to a scree-lined outcrop that led in about 1km to the rocky south summit of Sierra Bella (5223m, Alpine D) that we reached after more than seven and a half hours. The final 10m involved delicate climbing on highly unstable, poorly protected ground, a phenomenon which appeared to be typical of most of the exposed rock in this area. The main summit, around 50m higher and a further 1km on, lay to our right over a narrow rocky arête that we estimated might take a further two hours to reach. Needless to say we did not attempt it.

On account of the *penitentes*, the return to top camp took almost as long as the ascent, exacerbated somewhat by our tired state. Scrambling down over unstable ice pinnacles more than a metre tall was a salutary experience that none of us was anxious to repeat. It was with some relief that we eventually stumbled back into camp too tired even to prepare a cooked meal. Sleep was not long in coming that night.

We returned all the way to BC the following day, pausing only to collect surplus gear from the lower camp. On arrival we learned that most parties had opted to climb Tupungatito, although by a variety of routes. Tim and Cherrie had climbed to the first caldera in a heroic two-day stint taking a route just left of the prominent north-west flowing glacier while others had

80. Chimbote (5493m), at the time of writing the only major unclimbed peak above the expedition's base camp at Baños del Tupungato. Steep, unconsolidated rock near the summit has proved a barrier. (*Derek Buckle*)

opted for a more northerly route that gave access to the col between Tupungatito and its more elevated parent. They were still in the process of establishing their high camp when we arrived back. Rather disappointed by the poor quality rock, John T made the decision to descend with Carlos that same evening and Tim and Cherrie left for the same reason the following day. Unfortunately, after making an ascent of the 4958m peak just south of the Tupungatito glacier, a slip resulted in Les losing his passport which meant that he and Paul also had to descend in order to arrange a replacement. Somewhat like the 'ten green bottles sitting on a wall,' the remaining group was now reduced to 10.

On 10 February Kai moved up to join Henry, Gemma, John R and Mike at the left hand camp on Tupungatito while Annabelle, Margaret, Pru, Dave and I made tracks for that nearer the glacier where Tim and Cherrie had stayed earlier. A prominent dead cow constituted an obvious way mark where the two tracks diverged. After consolidating these upper camps located at around 4200m, various parties climbed the miscellany of summits on Tupungatito. The complex topography of these active caldera made it difficult to ascertain the dominant summit of the volcano and it appeared that all parties reached different points. Because of their more northerly location, Gemma, Henry, Mike, Kai and John R followed the northern crater rim past a prominent crater lake from where Kai and John R established a further camp on the ridge itself. Unhampered by *penitentes*, they then traversed the frontier ridge in a southerly direction to make the first ascent of a prominent 5908m peak (Alpine AD) that is as yet unnamed. The higher 5933m peak nearby unfortunately eluded them. We subsequently learned from a scientific team from the University of Maine that joined us later at BC that the uncharted region marked on the Chilean maps was in fact an icecap filling yet another crater from which the glacier emanated.

Dave and I meanwhile traversed the right-hand rim of the first sulphurous crater to a high point of 5388m (GPS reading) beside an even greater caldera. This crater gushed steam with the loudness of a jet engine while at the same time supporting numerous *penitentes*. Due to a later start, Annabelle, Margaret and Pru just failed to reach the crater rim, stopping a little short of 5000m, but it was a fine effort nonetheless.

Both camps returned to BC on Saturday the 13 February where the final drama was enacted by Pru. After a fall on large, unstable boulders she unfortunately tore a lateral knee ligament that reduced her progress to a painful plod. Thankfully, *arrieros* attached to the scientific team came to our assistance by transporting her back to BC on horseback. After one more day at BC, during which our own *arrieros* returned with mules, we returned to the road-head where Carlos was ready to ferry us back to Santiago, naturally stopping en route for beer and a meal at a traditional Chilean restaurant.

Thanks are due to Carlos Bascou and Mike Soldner for organising this unique expedition to a part of Chile rarely visited despite its closeness to the capital, Santiago.

Participants:
AC members: Carlos Bascou, Annabelle Barker, Derek Buckle, Margaret Clennett, Henry Day, Kai Green, Gemma Hagen, Paul Hudson, John Rushby, John Temple, Tim Whiteley, Dave Wynne-Jones.
Guests: Pru Cartwright, Mike Hale, Leslie Holbert, Cherrie Whiteley.

Maps
Chilean 1:50,000 maps; IGM 5-84-05-0061-00 Tupungato and IGM 5-04-05-0060-00 Rio Olivares.

Summary
In February 2010 sixteen AC members and their guests visited the Tupungato area of the Chilean Andes where various team members climbed Tupungatito and the south summit of Sierra Bella. In addition, probable first ascents were made of two peaks on the frontier ridge with Argentina, one of 4958m and the other of 5908m, both unnamed.

Acknowledgements
The expedition is grateful to the Alpine Club Climbing Fund for support.

PAUL KNOTT

Fairweather Friends

Blue skies exploring in Alaska

The Fairweather range is one that climbers often pass on their way to more frequented mountains. I did just that on my first visit to southeast Alaska in 1993, but from the summit of Mt Augusta the distant view of Mt Fairweather somehow left a lasting impression. Despite this, for more than 15 years this compact range remained a remote prospect as I struggled to persuade first myself, then a suitable climbing partner, to brave its notorious maritime storms. The potential for prolonged storms makes climbing here a high-commitment activity, as the mountains can only be reached by ski plane or by undertaking sea-to-summit adventures.

81. Paul Swanstrom (left) and Paul Knott arrive at base camp on the west shoulder of M Abbe. *(Paul Knott collection)*

When I looked for suitable unclimbed objectives in the range, it didn't take long to find the striking north ridge of Mt Crillon (3879m). This summit stands proud in the west arm of Glacier Bay, well south of the main Fairweather massif. It was the venue for two of Brad Washburn's early exploits in 1933 and 1934, which culminated in its first ascent. Amazingly, the 1934 route has yet to be repeated, and the only additional route on Mt Crillon is

Above: Mt Bertha from the descent to the Johns Hopkins glacier. The north-west ridge faces the camera, dividing light and shade.
Below: Pre-summit plateau of Mt Bertha at sunrise on summit day, looking towards Mt Fairweather. *(Paul Knott)*

the west ridge. A number of parties had attempted the north ridge, but had either been unable to get near it or had retreated low down. What potentially gave us a good chance was an offer by Haines-based ski plane pilot Paul Swanstrom to land us inside the Johns Hopkins glacier basin, which looked from maps and photos to provide more promising access. I became rather excited about this possibility when it became apparent that despite being one of the major glaciers of the west arm of Glacier Bay, the Johns Hopkins was essentially unexplored from a climbing perspective.

Guy McKinnon and I arrived in Haines in mid-April 2009. This is early in the season, and snow lay around the town and even on the beach in places. Amazingly, the weather maps promised prolonged stable conditions, and after a couple of days a crisp and calm morning created a great sense of anticipation. The next couple of hours would be crucial to where we could land and what we could climb.

As Mt Crillon emerged from the haze, my fears about the descent ridge were realised as a series of large séracs loomed up. At least one of these looked as though it would have to be tackled directly, and made a fearsome sight when we flew past at close range. Equally concerning was the lower access to both the route and descent ridges, which featured an icefall with at best only a tortuous way through. The ridge, too, looked sporting, with a rocky crux high up and avalanche-prone lower slopes linked by a sustained corniced section. A back-up plan was needed, and fortunately the long and unclimbed northwest ridge of Mt Bertha presented itself as a more accessible option. But only if we could land in the Hopkins basin. The options for this are limited as the upper névés are very broken and the lower glacier undulates and is prone to melting out. Instead, Paul (our pilot) had scoped out the possibility of landing on the west shoulder of Mt Abbe. As well as being a rather inconvenient 650m above the glacier, this felt like a small target as Paul scoped out the landing. It was cause for celebration for all of us as we set down on this elusive prize.

Our elevated campsite formed a superb vantage point. The main Fairweather massif was surprisingly close, with Mts Quincy Adams, Fairweather, Salisbury and Lituya set out before us. Below to the north was the Johns Hopkins Inlet, a popular destination for tour boats. Despite its proximity, several parties, including the teams of Wickwire/Givler/Jagersky/Marts in 1977 and Haberl/Haberl/Mair/Blackwell in 1983, had found that it does not provide access to the main glacier, which is very broken below about 300m. Only on the far side of Mt Abbe has a team climbed from the Inlet, namely Walter Gove and Bill Pilling on their 1991 ascent of Mt Abbe via the Gillman glacier. Opposite us lay the cirque formed by the north sides of Mts Bertha and Crillon, and this too had previously eluded attempts at access, not only from the Inlet but also via cols between Mts Abbe and Bertha. For us, these difficulties were now all but circumvented.

Keen to take advantage of the stable weather forecast, we prepared ourselves to tackle the north-west ridge of Mt Bertha (3110m). Our first challenge was to find our way onto the main glacier. From the air, we had

Summit and rock spires of Mt Abbe from 6300ft on the north-west ridge of Mt Bertha. *(Paul Knott)*

spotted a crucial snow ramp through a lower set of bluffs, but the convex slopes hid it from view. Once we found it, the ramp was straightforward, but below us on the glacier loomed a crevassed area we had to cross. This took on added significance due to the low elevation of 650m and our reliance on snow bridges. Reaching the benign-looking glacier beyond represented something of a milestone.

A short distance up the glacier, we crossed a distinct set of bear prints. Apparently the bears have found an access route, even if people cannot.

As we continued towards Mt Bertha, views unfolded of a series of steep, monolithic rock pillars on the south and west sides of the Mt Abbe chain. This light-coloured, featured granite was completely unlike the dark, poor rock we saw elsewhere. The 1977 Wickwire party climbed this side of Mt Abbe and the striking rocky peaks to the south-east, having approached from the Brady glacier via two linked cols. As with many other potential climbs in this area, access may be a problem as the hanging glacier below these peaks looks quite broken. The 1977 route to the north summit of Mt Abbe looked as if it might no longer be viable.

At the base of Mt Bertha, we navigated around a crevassed area and camped. Above us was an undulating four miles of ridge rising 2165m to the summit. This was soon to become a trial of stamina as we found ourselves first wallowing in unconsolidated winter powder, and then breaking through melt-freeze crust. The 900m of height we gained that day was a struggle, and our camp seemed low on the mountain with much unseen ground above. We were travelling light on food, and the next day would be crucial to the attempt. It was a beautiful morning with an inversion, and we quickly crossed a 'schrund, regained the ridge, and topped a fore-summit. At last it felt as though we had left behind the lower slopes and were tackling the upper mountain. Still, the long ridge ahead of us was an intimidating sight as it sharpened and I feared narrow cornices and awkward drop-offs would slow our progress. As we continued, these typical south-east Alaskan features added interest, but not technicality, and sustained trail-breaking from Guy late in the day took us through compressible wind deposits to a camp high on the upper snow dome. With only the final cone to negotiate, we reached the summit on our fourth climbing day, 26 April. The view over to the south was exquisite, as the sun glinted on the expansive Brady icecap and the ocean beyond. The contrast was striking with the narrow valleys and mixed alpine faces of the Mt Fairweather group to the north. We were the fifth party to stand on this summit, the first being Bradford Washburn's party in 1940. All the previous ascents had been from the Brady glacier to the east. Having virtually exhausted our supplies, we descended rapidly, retracing our steps. Towards the base of the ridge, we found that the winter powder on the shady side had turned into deep slush.

After two days refuelling our bodies at base camp, we were spurred into action by a forecast promising several more days of stable weather. This gave us time to tackle the unclimbed 2621m peak north of Mt Crillon and east of Mt Orville, which was a particularly striking sight from our camp. We had seen an expedient route on this from Mt Bertha, taking the shallow east rib to the south face of the summit triangle. In warm conditions, we waded up the isothermic snow on the rib, and by 8am on our second day had reached 2304m in the bowl below the upper south face. We put the tent up and spent the day watching avalanches let loose on the face. Early on 2 May, we crossed the bergschrund above the bowl and continued up the south face via a frozen couloir and snowed-up rock rib to reach the summit in pre-dawn light. I had already thought of a name – somewhat

6. North and east faces of Peak 8599ft ('Fifty Years of Alaskan Statehood'). *(Paul Knott)*

tongue-in-cheek – based on commemorations we had seen on our travels: 'Fifty Years of Alaskan Statehood'. Mindful of the weather, we packed our high camp and continued our descent. The day warmed so rapidly that when we descended the lower east rib in mid-morning, we left a one metre trench through soaking wet snow that threatened to slide. The prospect of crossing major snow bridges at 650m in these conditions did not appeal, so we stopped on the glacier in the hope of an overnight freeze.

Early next day, warm air flowed ominously down the glacier. Our south-west facing re-ascent to base camp started up a collapsing snow tongue over an increasingly exposed and meltwater-covered rock band. A sense of impending reversion to stormy southerly conditions continued that afternoon with cloud caps over the summits followed by flattening light and snow flurries. The barometric pressure had fallen 22mb. Amazingly, the storm held off, and we decided to fly out while we still could. Within an hour of landing we were aboard the ferry down the Lynn Canal. As I stood in the rear deck watching the sunset over the retreating hills, I already knew I wanted to return. I like the sustained adventurous immersion these mountains provide, which is nowadays easily missed in the pursuit of short, sharp experiences and a quick return to the city – and today's technology makes fly-in, glacier-based expeditions more civilised than ever before. Back in Juneau, the next day dawned cold, wet and windy, while the *Juneau Empire* reported the passing of record high temperatures.

86. Guy McKinnon on the summit of Peak 8599ft at sunrise, with Mt Bertha behind (north-west ridge facing camera). *(Paul Knott)*

Summary: An account of two climbs in the Fairweather range, south-east Alaska by Paul Knott and Guy McKinnon – the north-west ridge of Mt Bertha (3110m), a new route, 23-27 April 2009; and the first ascent of Pk 8599ft (2621m) via east rib and south face, 30 April - 3 May.

Acknowledgements: Knott and McKinnon thank the Mount Everest Foundation for financial support for this expedition.

BOB SHEPTON

Greenland With The Wild Bunch

The Skipper's Tale

87. Straight off the deck of *Dodo's Delight* and onto *Seagulls' Garden* (E5 6a). (*All photos from the Team Collection*)

The email read, 'Bob, do you know where there are any big walls to climb in Greenland? We did some on Mt Asgard in Baffin last summer and would like to do some in Greenland in 2011.'

'Well yes' I do know where there are some big walls on the west coast of Greenland but I am not going to tell you where they are as I want them for

88. Sean Villaneuva and Olivier Favresse approaching the first hanging dihedral on *Red Chilli Crackers* (E6 6b).

myself and my teams. But … it so happens I left my boat in Greenland for the winter, what about this year?'

'Ah, we'll have to think about that, and get back to you.'

To misquote Caesar: they cogitated, they came, they saw, they conquered.

As one of my 2009 crew said: 'I can't believe you have world-class

Above: the west pillar of Angagoq Tower, Quvnerit Island, Cape Farewell area, showing the lines of *Chinese Gybe*, scene of Nico Favresse's fall, and *Chloé*. Figures give scale!

Above right:Impossible Wall, Sortehul, near Upernavik, showing the line of *Devil's Brew* (E7 6c, 5.12d, 850m).

Right: Red Wall, Agparssuit, southern end of Sortehul, showing the lines of *Red Chilli Crackers* (left) and *Seagulls' Garden*.
(See Summary for technical details).

92. Ben Ditto on *Seagulls' Garden*. The dihedral of *Red Chilli Crackers* is below to the left.

93. Below: exiting the third portaledge camp on Impossible Wall; Olivier Favresse jumaring, Sean Villaneuva waiting.

climbers on your boat this summer.' Ignoring the implied insult – why shouldn't I have world-class climbers on my boat? – the team then were the Favresse brothers, Nico and Oli, from Belgium, Sean Villaneuva O'Driscoll, parts Irish, Spanish and Belgian, and Ben Ditto, American. World class? We would see; I just dubbed them 'the Wild Bunch' after all those high fives and yells at the top of climbs on their website – and to keep them in their place of course. They enjoyed that. So 'Greenland 2010 – Tilman International' was born.

The boys duly arrived in Aasiaat on the plane and immediately that afternoon took over the Greenland National Day celebrations at the party at the boatyard, entertaining the staff with their musical instruments and song. Next day we went out for an afternoon's sail in my boat, *Dodo's Delight*, a 10 metre Westerly Discus, literally to learn the ropes as two of them had never sailed before, and then next day finally put out for the passage to Upernavik.

It proved a rather arduous passage for us all and especially the two novices. We motored across Disko Bay. There was a breeze at last so we turned the engine off and sailed. But thereafter the engine would not start and we had to sail whether there was wind, however strong, or none at all, and there was the occasional iceberg looming suddenly out of mist. It was particularly frustrating in the dead calms, of which there are many in Greenland. Sean was heard to comment 'This must be the low point of the expedition.' I hoped he was right and there would be nothing worse. It took us five days to sail the normal two day passage, and we had the final indignity of sailing very slowly through a lot of icebergs in full view of the settlement of Upernavik, and then had to negotiate coming alongside the wharf on sail alone. 'Well, you wanted to learn how to sail, lads, didn't you?'

Upernavik

Solving the problem of starting the engine proved embarrassingly easy; sorting the alternator did not. But obviously the team wanted to get quickly to the climbing so I bought a portable generator which was far too big and heavy for a small boat but was the only one available, and we set off for the big walls. We started on Red Wall, the headland of Agparssuit, at the southern end of the Sortehul. Apparently the Greenlanders call it 'the cliff where the guillemots stand in line', and so they did, like black sentinels on parade. I got the impression that the Wild Bunch were not too used to sea cliff climbing as they seemed put off by the seagulls wheeling and squawking around. But they stepped off the boat up against the sheer cliff, and into the dinghy moored at the bow, and so onto the rock to start the climbs. They had chosen two well defined dihedral and crack lines straight up the cliff, and completed them in one big 30-hour push. Thus *Seagulls' Garden* (400m) at E5 6a sustained or 5.11 and *Red Chilli Cracker* (350m) at E6 6b sustained or 5.12a became the first routes ever to be done on this wall with all its potential. The only problem was that to save weight they had not taken a radio with them and when finished had to walk all the

94. The steep first pitch after the first portaledge camp on Impossible Wall.

way round the fjord behind the headland to where I had anchored the boat. The first I knew of their arrival was when Sean swam, in the nude in arctic waters, across to the boat in the early hours next morning.

'Oh, I'm sorry, I was asleep.'

'Not at all, I wanted to swim.'

After a brief visit back to Upernavik I dropped them off for another climb on a dramatic face halfway between Upernavik and the Sortehul, this time by a short dinghy ride. I returned to Upernavik to deal with the alternator problems whilst they set up camp and then put up another superb route on this face, *Brown Balls* at 5.12a (sustained 5.11, with two pitches of 5.12a) , 450 metres. It became a team effort, as Nico had come up to a huge pillar which looked just too close to giving way for comfort; he and Sean went down to the high point of the other two, who then abseiled off and left them to finish the route. So the final route takes the continuous line just to the right of the obvious central pillar. They described it as 'a superb line with Yosemite-type cracks', and all the harder on this first ascent owing to having to clean sand and earth from the cracks. It was then a combined on sight free ascent, though Nico confessed to one pull on gear on a 10-metre wet section of wall.

But the team's *tour de force* in this area was the first ascent of Impossible Wall. I had had my eye on that wall for many years now but, as I told them, I had never had a team good enough to climb it before, hence the name. Their route – *Impossible Wall and the Devil's Brew* (there are stories behind all the names) at E7 6c or 5.12d was simply the steepest and hardest climb on the wall, and probably in this whole area, comprising 850 metres and 19 pitches

95. Ben Ditto leading on *Chinese Gybe*, Quvnerit Island, Cape Farewell.

96. Olivier Favresse heading for the team's biggest cam on *Chloé*, Quvnerit Island.

97. The vast sweep of *Impossible* Wall, showing Ben Ditto and Sean Villaneuva on the first pitch of *Devil's Brew*.

with each pitch sustained. They started by simply stepping off the boat, moored alongside on a couple of cams into cracks; this was the first time a 'Garden of Eden' had been planted on my boat, with all the grass and earth thrown down as the boys climbed and cleaned the route above. There was no let-up in standard and it took 10 days to complete the climb with three portaledge encampments on the way. True, three of those days were spent stuck on their portaledges owing to bad weather but this was initially no problem as they had included their musical instruments in the haul bags and fell to 'jamming' and composing new songs. But gradually the infa-

3. Between rock and ice: The Skipper returns with *Dodo's Delight* to see how the team is doing on Impossible Wall.

mous black hole above (coincidentally Sortehul also means Black Hole) began to drip more and more water on them. Three days later Sean, our loose rock, wet rock, grass, lichen expert – it doesn't matter as long as he can just keep on climbing – managed to lead the black greasy hanging chimney crack. Nico also had his moments. The Greenlandic name for this wall is Seagull Cliff or Bad Seagull Cliff, and they were. He *had* to get onto this ledge but the fulmar simply wasn't having it and kept ejecting that foul smelling slime all over him. It took repeated swings with a number 4 cam before the fulmar finally relented.

The hard penultimate pitch also proved interesting, especially as Nico had to keep emptying the contents of *his* stomach, in ways I would rather not describe (but very awkward in the midst of a hard climb), owing to the seagulls having polluted the water supply. They topped out to a well deserved dance together on the summit and a toast in champagne when I picked them up round the back of the mountain in the boat. Funnily enough it had only been eight days for them, as their days were 30 hours long!

Nico was heard to remark later: 'I think that must be the greatest adventure of my life so far,' and a knowledgeable authority has subsequently commented that it was 'probably the hardest climb done in Greenland to date.' It *was* a landmark climb, and hopefully these groundbreaking ascents will open up the tremendous potential of this area for climbing, at almost any standard, for the future.

Whilst they had been on the wall I took myself off to explore eastwards towards the icecap, and to survey some other possible big walls we had been told about. As usual in Greenland the distances were further than

99. The Skipper enjoying himself high above the water on *Never Again!* (E2).

100. Opposite page: Above the clouds on Impossible Wall.

expected, and there turned out to be only one possibly interesting big wall anyway. I did however find some other useable anchorages, one of which was a beautiful remote keyhole anchorage, well worth the effort. These have now been reported to the Royal Cruising Club Pilotage Foundation, which is in any case in the process of conducting a comprehensive survey of sailing in arctic waters. I also discovered another aspect of exploration in Greenland: on two occasions I nearly hit isolated rocks in deep fjords, the water going from 100+ metres to four, three, two metres in a matter of seconds. Either they were in the wrong place on the charts, or my boat was in the wrong place on the chart plotter.

The team were keen to look at other areas and had heard especially of the potential around Cape Farewell in the far south. We went south first to Aasiaat to sort out gear we had left and then made the rather arduous 500 miles plus passage to the Cape Farewell area. The wind refused to blow or was 'in our faces', and we had to make the whole passage on engine, with a difficult evening weaving in heavy swell through ice – growlers, bergy bits and icebergs – streaming out of the Sermilik glacier and fjord south of Paamuit. We called in at a couple of 'towns' and inspected the occasional big wall possibility on the way, but to no avail. One advantage of having a boat is that exploring and investigating is possible, but this time the team had to get their kicks by skinny dipping in arctic waters amongst the ice floes! We re-stocked at Nanortalik, read past expedition reports from the Tourist Office, and made our way round to the Cape Farewell region.

Cape Farewell

We immediately noticed the difference. At Upernavik it had been big sea cliffs; here the terrain was Alpine in character. We did five new routes. The first two were on a wall beneath an unnamed peak north-west of Tikaguta on the Saga map, which the boys only found because they got lost in the morning mist. It had involved a 5km walk-in, carrying all that gear, from the boat anchored in the Torssukatak, and gave 'two classic, clean, direct lines on excellent rock' at E4 or 5.11, both of 450m. They were kind enough to name the main summit Shepton Spire, and then completed the traverse of the ridge at D-TD to a subsidiary summit.

Two further routes were made on the wall at the northern end of Quvnerit Island. Both were clear-cut off width cracks – *Chinese Gybe* and *Chloé*, both 550m E5 6b or 5.11+. The names? On the first, Nico, eight metres above a stance with no protection, pulled on a huge block of some 200lbs which came away in his hands. He struggled to hold onto it and find purchase somewhere somehow, but in the end had to push it away and take a 16m plus fall, ending upside down with 400m of void below him. The rock hit the wall and burst but mostly missed Ben on the stance, who only took a badly grazed ankle but later found the blade of his pocket knife snapped in half in his sack, presumably by the shrapnel. Both were considerably shaken. Chloé was a close friend of the group, the Belgian boulder champion, who was killed in a fall in the Alps on the very day of this ascent.

The final ascent was a mistake, at least by the skipper who foolishly allowed himself to be persuaded to go out with Nico and Sean. The route on Angnikitsoq at E2 and 500 metres was too long and too hard for an old man, however expertly guided, who survived, exhausted, but named the route *Never Again!* Seventy five seemed a good age to retire, again. However he was able to join the Wild Bunch victory dance at the top and become a full member!

Atlantic

We stopped at Saft Wall on the way out but the weather turned gnarly and only bouldering was done. We made our way down Prins Christian Sund, enjoyed the hospitality and Danish pastries at the Weather Station and headed out for the Atlantic crossing, 'for the experience' as the lads put it. They were not disappointed; it was quite a tough crossing with a lot of headwinds before we could work south and pick up favourable westerlies to bowl us along to Scotland. We hove-to, to sit out Post Tropical Storm Danielle and another vigorous double depression later. And again to repair the steering at sea which had worked rather loose. We finally came up to Mingulay and Pabbay and inspected the cliffs with a view to climbing, before anchoring off a remote beach with a huge colony of seals lining the water's edge. But the next day the skipper overruled the climbing for fear of weather and we eventually arrived at Oban in a full gale. Welcome home!

Summary of climbs

Upernavik Area: (Saga map 14 Upernavik) Sortehul Fjord. Agparssuit: Red Wall (our name), Greenlandic – 'where the guillemots stand together in a row'.

Seagulls' Garden, E5 6a sustained or 5.11, 400m, 12 pitches, Nicolas Favresse and Ben Ditto.

Red Chilli Cracker, E6 6b sustained or 5.12a, 350m, 11 pitches, Sean Villaneuva, Olivier Favresse. Start: GPS 72^0 39.4N 55^0 52.8W. Two clear-cut straight up and down dihedral and crack lines.

On sight free ascents – one pitch on *Red Chilli Cracker* redpointed after a fall when grass gave way. One bolt placed on *Seagulls' Garden* for protection on a slab.

Umiasugssuk: Intermediate Wall (our name) on the north face of Spot Height 620 south of the narrow channel of Torssût, GPS 72^0 46.3N 55^0 56.2W.

Brown Balls, E5/6, 6b or 5.12a (sustained 5.11, 2 pitches of 5.12a), 450m. A superb line with Yosemite-type cracks (harder on first ascent owing to having to clean sand and earth from the cracks). Route takes the line just to the right of obvious central pillar. On sight, combined free ascent (though one pull on gear on a 10-metre wet section of wall); first part O Favresse and Ditto, second part N Favresse and Villaneuva.

Tingmiakulugssuit: Impossible Wall (our name), Greenlandic – 'Seagull Cliff' or 'Bad Seagull Cliff'.

Impossible Wall and the 'Devil's Brew', E7 6c or 5.12d, 850m – 19 pitches, all sustained, (O and N Favresse, Ditto and Villaneuva). GPS 72^0 39.6N 55^0

45.9W. Takes the steepest and hardest line up Impossible Wall; 3 portaledge encampments, 10 days.

101. The Skipper, Bob Shepton, brandishes a bottle of Devil's Brew, a Vietnamese concoction, complete with cobra and scorpion, presented to him by the four climbers, and which gave the name to their stunning route on Impossible Wall.

Cape Farewell (Kap Farvel) Area: (Saga map 1 Qaqortoq/Uummannarsuaq). Unnamed Peak (60⁰ 03.1N 44⁰ 31.5W) north-west of Tikaguta.
Corned Beef, E4/5.11, 450m, (Villaneuva and Ditto).
Condensed Milk, E4/5.11, 450m, (N and O Favresse).
The ridge was then followed at D-TD to the eastern summit. Main summit kindly named Shepton Spire. (The names of the climbs describe the skipper's favourite foods aboard a boat.) Two classic clean direct lines on excellent rock. Approach: 5km walk in from the boat anchored in the Torssukatak (60⁰ 02.9N 44⁰ 31.3W), or up the valley north from Frederiksdal (longer still).
Quvnerit: (northern end of island, on face of Spot Height 1180, Angegoq Tower).
Chinese Gybe, E5 6b or 5.11+ (off-width), 550m, 15 pitches, (N Favresse and Ditto). One bolt found – previous Swiss team had abseiled off. FFA on sight.
Chloé, E5 6b or 5.11+ (off-width), 550m, 14 pitches, (Villaneuva and O Favresse). On sight, free ascent. Obvious clear-cut off-width cracks below right hand summit. The summit ridge to main and subsidiary summits was completed after an overnight bivvi at TD, but not claimed as a first ascent.
Angnikitsoq: (SE corner – Angnikitsoq qoqa by Spot Height 670).
Never Again! E2 5c, 500m, 12 pitches, N Favresse, Villaneuva, Bob Shepton. Start 60⁰ 02.48N 49⁰ 01.58W. Scramble up to rock face, follow cracks through huge rounded slabs between two main crack or chimney systems. This leads to an almost direct crack system steepening steadily all the way up and including a small roof (crux).
www.xpedition.be gives another account from the protagonists with some fine pictures.

Note: the expedition was one of two recipients of a *Piolet d'Or* for 2011. The other went to Yasushi Okada and Katsutaka Yokoyama of Japan for their 2500m route on the south-east face of Mt Logan (5959m), Canada.

Surveys

102. John Innerdale, *High Atlas, Morocco*, chromacolour, 40 x 32cm.

PAT LITTLEJOHN

Trad (For Now) on Gran Canaria

103. Crags above Ayacata – 'a bit of a Mecca' for trad climbers. (*Pat Littlejohn*)

Where can you go in the depths of winter to rock climb in warm weather? Spain can be great of course, but recently it has suffered several freezing-cold periods, as has the eastern Med'. Places like Joshua Tree, Mexico and South Africa are safe bets but they take a lot more time and cash.

So it can be worth heading south of the regular Spanish crags to the Canary Islands, and that's where Steve Sustad and I took a quick trip in winter 2009/10. There are many attractions: cheap flights with easyJet or Ryanair, a balmy climate with temperatures hovering around 20-25 degrees, loads of cheap accommodation and hire cars at £12/day. So why aren't the Canaries more popular with British climbers? Well, the sport climbing, though good and plentiful, doesn't quite match southern Spain for quality and is a little more scattered. However having sampled it on Tenerife and Gran Canaria, I can confirm that the latter is far better, with many more cliffs and climbs. And Gran Canaria has something else which might surprise you – very impressive and adventurous traditional climbing.

Though blighted with the usual tourist developments on its southern shore, most of the land area of Gran Canaria is a beautiful and mountainous national park, rising to nearly 2000m in the centre where the volcanic cores of several mountains give rock scenery that is a cross between the Dolomites and the canyons of Arizona. This area has seen

104. Roque Nublo – the basalt monolith offers quality bolt routes. (*Pat Littlejohn*)

traditional mountaineering since the 1930s but never a guidebook as far as I know, with information being kept with the local climbing club (*Federación Gran Canaria de Montañismo*, **www.fgcm.org/**) and more recently stored on the internet at: **topatras.eresmas.com/Escalada.htm** It's in Spanish so use Google Translate to get the gist of it – and have a really good laugh at the robotic English.)Sport climbing exists all over the island, but for trad the central group of rocky peaks around the village of Ayacata is a bit of a Mecca and has a rather interesting history. In the early days routes were established by traditional alpinists using pitons for protection and aid. We couldn't find any information about these but stumbled across them whilst doing our own explorations. We'd be climbing a line thinking it might be a first ascent, then right near the top after several challenging pitches we'd be humbled by discovering a rusted piton (more often than not an old Charlet Moser offset, one of the worst-designed pitons of all time). These climbers were obviously pretty bold and skilled at climbing on all forms of basalt.

In the early '80s, when bolts were going in by the thousand in the crags of southern France and the Costa Blanca, climbers in Gran Canaria were making hard trad ascents which can only be compared with adventurous climbs at South Stack or the sea cliffs of the South-west. Topos for these can be found in the central café/bar in Ayacata and they make impressive reading. The routes are big, up to eight or nine pitches, and have hard, naturally protected free pitches (up to Fr 7a) as well as occasional aid sections up to A3+ (probably desperate). On many of the topo-diagrams the first ascensionists make a point of stressing that their routes were climbed without bolts and without hammers, so among some teams there was a strong 'clean climbing' ethic. This ethic may or may not be still alive and well on the island (we did hear that some older routes had now been equipped with bolts) but it was refreshing to find an area that had not yet succumbed to all-out bolting. It's my guess that many of these routes await second ascents and that they would give fantastic sport to people who would enjoy an enhanced 'Gogarth experience' in the middle of winter in a warm climate. I know I'll be back for more trad climbing there. It seems that equipping routes for sport climbing began on the Roque Nublo, a superb

5. The massive cliff of Los Quemados on the south side of Montaña de Ojeda where Littlejohn and Sustad essayed their 13-pitch route *El Cardonal*. (*Pat Littlejohn*)

monolith of hard, weathered basalt perched at almost 2000m on the highest plateau of the island. There about a dozen bolted climbs here now, all good quality, as well many others on rock formations in the vicinity.

As it was, on this trip the main objective for Steve and I was a big mountain escarpment he'd spotted just before my arrival. This was the south side of a peak called Montaña de Ojeda, where it forms a massive tiered cliff called Los Quemados. We had no idea whether anything had been climbed here, so we just went up with all the gear and took a look. From a distance it seemed that there would be several possible lines, but up close we weren't so sure

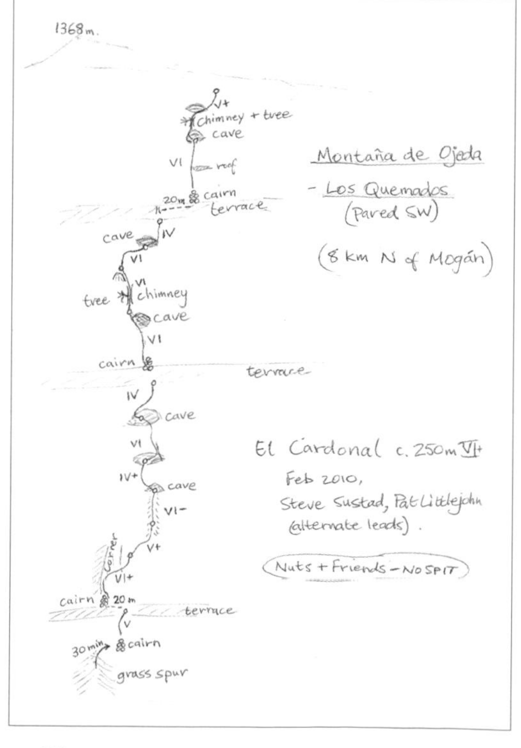

106. Steve Sustad on Pitch 5 of *El Cardinal*. (*Pat Littlejohn*)

107. Opposite: Pat Littlejohn bridging on the crux Pitch 2 (VI+). (*Steve Sustad*)

– many nice features petered out into blank, protectionless rock. With bolting gear many things would have been possible, and that may be the ultimate destiny of the cliff, but for us the challenge was finding a way that would go in our preferred style, i.e. no bolts, pegs or hammers, just a good old British trad rack of nuts and Friends. We found a cairn at the base of the cliff below a likely-looking line so we wondered if climbers had beaten us to it, but after five metres of climbing it was obvious that no-one had touched this line before and that the cairn was probably marking a path.

Steve kicked off up the first VS pitch, a little snaking groove which gained the base of the very big and impressive main tier. We wandered up and down this for a while before deciding on the line to attempt. For me it was straight in at the deep end – I was in recovery from a knee operation and hadn't done any rock climbing for four months, so I wasn't prepared for the 20m of sustained technical bridging that started the next pitch. This turned out to be the crux of the route at about E2/3 5c, or UIAA grade VI+. We had to break right to reach some more grooves, which gave really good climbing on perfect rock for two further pitches, but after this we realised we were in no shape to continue – we had made too late a start on a baking hot day, and we had not brought enough water. Too close to sunstroke for comfort we retreated, pleased to have found a very promising line.

Next day an 'alpine wake-up' saw us approaching the crag at dawn, with six litres of water between us. Above our high point the line linked a series of scoops and caves before landing us below another steep and imposing tier. By now the sun was beating down again and the crag felt truly African. We had hit some unusually hot days. As I led another technical groove with some memorable finger-tip layback moves, Steve roasted on the belay and warned that he was overheating again. Luckily his pitch took him into a chimney and he was able to stuff his head into some shade for several minutes, after which he felt better. My next pitch was a thin crack which

108. Steve Sustad starting Pitch 7 of *El Cardonal* (XS). (*Pat Littlejohn*)

looked nice from below but turned out to be nasty and crumbling – the rock had taken a sudden turn for the worse, as basalt can. After struggling for a while I realised I could swing right to reach a big wind-eroded scoop which had been invisible from below – now the way was clear to the top of the tier, above which loomed the final 50m wall.

We were now three quarters of the way up the face so the desire to finish it properly up the final tier was strong, even though the terrace below it promised an escape of sorts. There was a possible line straight ahead but after 15m it was blocked by a rotten overhang, and to press on into XS territory at this point would have ruined a potentially fine route. Luckily, a groove 20m to the right turned out to have better rock and better gear than had been apparent from below. It led past an overhang to an amazing 'bell' of rock formed where wind erosion had hollowed out material behind the hard outer layer of basalt. By striking it with a karabiner you could play different notes in different places. I took cover in a cave stance while Steve dealt with the final pitch and soon we were on the great shelf where the cliff terminates, enjoying a breeze and views of the peak and the island's interior. The result of our efforts was *El Cardonal*, a 13-pitch route that was sustained but nowhere too hard, definitely a worthy objective for people wanting to experience a long, adventurous trad climb on Gran Canaria.

At the present time (and provided the well-meaning but misguided bolting zealots don't destroy all the traditional climbing) Gran Canaria offers a fascinating mix of different types of climbing and is a good venue to enjoy both styles in the depths of winter. I know it's tempting just to throw a bunch of quick draws in a bag and jump on a plane, but taking trad gear gives you the 'freedom of the hills' and a more varied trip, and I think we all know which routes will be the most memorable.

MARTIN GILLIE

Alpine Climbing in The Mountains of Cogne

109. The ENE ridge of La Grivola from near the Balzola hut. (*Jonathan Halliday*)

The mountains of Cogne appear to have been forgotten by British alpinists. Apart from the Gran Paradiso, the highest peak, which is well known for being amongst the easiest of the 4000m peaks to climb, few British climbers could name any mountains in the area. However, there are more than 20 peaks between 3500m and 4000m that offer fine alpine

110. L-R: Torre del Gran San Pietro, Roccia Viva and Becca di Gay. The two couloirs leading to the summit of Becca di Gay are clearly visible. (*Tom Burslem*)

routes mostly at the classic Facile-Difficile grades. The most recent guide in English to these peaks was published in the 1960s and even the Italian definitive guide is 30 years old. Although there are some recent selected guides in Italian, up-to-date information on the alpine routes in English has not been readily available for some time. This article aims to bring the area to the attention of British alpinists again by describing the history and geography of the area, and by giving current descriptions of routes to the main peaks.

The Cogne peaks lie to the south-east of Mont Blanc in the Aosta valley region of Italy. On the main alpine ridge they form the most substantial group of peaks between the Little St Bernard Pass and the Mediterranean. Most of the main summits lie on two ridges that run roughly north-south and drain into several of the tributaries of the Dora, the main river in the Aosta valley. For their height the peaks are heavily glaciated, for example, the Glacier de la Tribulation on the north-east flank of the Gran Paradiso covers more than $4km^2$. Consequently, although some smaller glaciers (and the snow-cover on some faces) are retreating rapidly, most climbs still require glacier crossings and have a full 'alpine feel' to them. There are a variety of rock types in the area with gneiss being found most widely on the main peaks. This varies in quality and perhaps as a result most rock routes follow ridges rather than faces or buttresses, with obvious exceptions being the rock climbs on the Becca di Moncorve.

In contrast to the recent lack of interest, British climbers were very active in the exploration of the mountains with only two of the main peaks (Roccia Viva and Becca di Gay) being first ascended by local climbers. Surprisingly, given its seriousness and the amenable nature of some other peaks, La Grivola was the first of the main peaks to be climbed in 1859 by Ormsby and party, after a near miss by Tuckett a month earlier. The Gran Paradiso

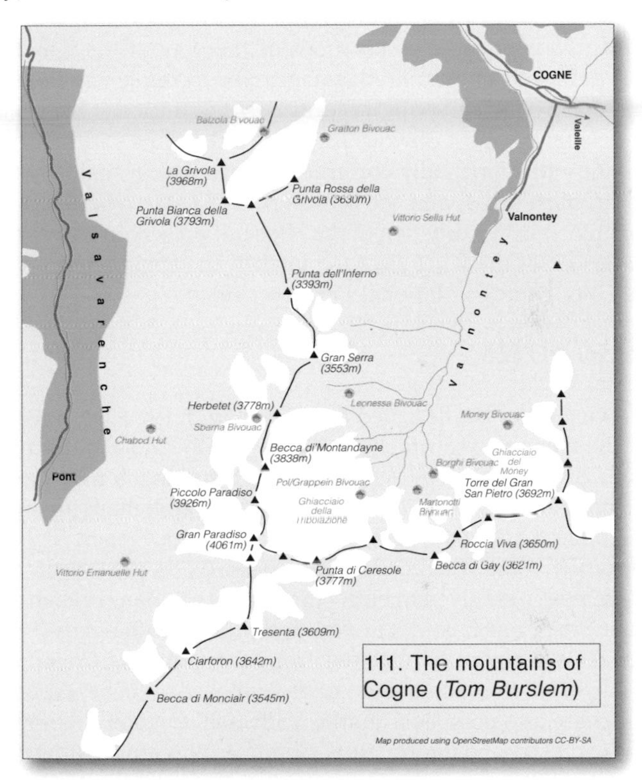

111. The mountains of Cogne (*Tom Burslem*)

followed in 1860 after which there was relatively little activity until Yeld and the ubiquitous Coolidge arrived in the 1870s. Between them this pair climbed dozens of routes in the period 1878-1900 and also published a climbers' guide to the area. Mummery too was active during this period during which the Cogne mountains seem to have been regarded almost as highly as the Zermatt and Chamonix peaks. Mallory climbed around Cogne in 1911 but since then the mountains have been largely forgotten by British mountaineers.

The Aosta valley has a very distinctive culture, having over centuries been pulled between Italian and French influences – as recently as the 1940s there was a significant chance of it being annexed by France. Its inhabitants are therefore generally bilingual in French and Italian and have a strong sense of regional identity. From the mountaineer's perspective this can occasionally lead to confusion because all the peaks have at least two names that are not always similar. But this is completely offset by the hugely welcoming and relaxed attitude to visitors, and also by the excellent and distinctive food and wine that is widely available, including in all the manned huts.

The area has long been noted for its scenery and wildlife. The kings of Savoy (later Italy) were the first to appreciate these aspects and acquired the entire area as a private hunting ground. Although early climbers were required as a consequence to keep out of the way of the King's hunting trips, this did result in certain advantages; for example Coolidge noted in 1898 that the 'The telegraph is no longer reserved for the King's use'! For modern visitors the most obvious benefits of the King's former ownership are the mule paths, originally constructed for hunting, that lead to around hut level in most areas; and the prevalence of *stambeccos* (ibex) that were once threatened with extinction in the Alps but preserved within the King's land. In the 1920s the King gave the land to the Italian nation and it has been the Gran Paradiso National Park ever since.

CLIMBING NOTES

The following notes are designed to be used with the *Excusionista* 1:25000 maps of the area that are widely available locally and also from specialist retailers in Britain. However it is hoped that the sketch map on p145 will provide enough detail for planning. The *Excursionista* maps are much superior to all other maps of the area but show names in French. This contrasts with the locally, more widely used, Italian names. In these notes the names of the main peaks are given in both languages as Italian/French. For other features just the French names are used, in line with the maps.

The peaks are normally accessed from the valley of Cogne (in which there is a town of the same name) or from Valsavarenche. Approaches to some peaks are also possible from the Valle dell' Orco in Piemonte but the author has no first-hand information. Cogne itself is a substantial town with shops, banks, hotels etc. The Cogne valley has several tributary valleys, most notably Valnontey containing a small village of the same name with two campsites and a shop, and the uninhabited but scenic Valeille. Valsavarenche has several villages and campsites along its length. The small village of Pont at its head has a shop and campsite. All the villages in the area are well served by reliable and cheap public transport, with Aosta being the hub for most services.

Accommodation for climbers is provided by three wardened huts and numerous bivouac huts. All the manned huts are very comfortable. However, two primarily serve the normal route to Gran Paradiso while the third (Vittorio Sella) serves just a few alpine routes. Consequently most climbs are started from bivouac huts. These vary in size from 4 to 12 bunks and all have mattresses and blankets. Generally parties will have bivouac huts to themselves or will share with just a few others. They thus offer a happy medium between overcrowded, manned huts and the effort of lugging bivouac equipment on the approaches to climbs.

2. The North ridge and NE face of Gran Paradiso taken from the Piccolo Paradiso. (*Tom Burslem*)

Huts

Vittorio Emanuele II 'VE' Hut (2734m, 150+ bunks, 2hrs) The largest manned hut in the area and the usual base for Gran Paradiso, La Tresenta and Ciarforon. Well run and with a choice of 4 bed 'cabins' or dormitory accommodation. Easily reached up the well signposted mule track from Pont in the Valsavarenche.

Chabod Hut (2710m, 85 bunks, 2½hrs) An alternative, probably more comfortable, base for the Gran Paradiso and also well-placed for Herbetet. Approached via a well maintained mule track that leaves Valsavarenche at point 1829.

Vittorio Sella 'VS' Hut (2579m, 143 bunks, 2½hrs) More of a hamlet than a hut. It consists of several buildings formerly used as a hunting lodge by Italian kings. It has a separate bar and a resident cat. Well-known for its excellent food, particularly at lunch. Approach from Valnontey by the well marked track that leaves the village from behind the alpine gardens.

Leonessa Hut (2910m, 12 bunks, 4hrs) A large bivouac hut well placed for Herbetet. From Valnontey follow the main valley path to a bridge near point 1845. Cross this and continue on the old mule track which doubles back on itself at point 2060 before ascending to the national park Herbetet lodge at point 2441 in a series of easy zigzags. Above, a rougher path leads up Vallon de l'Herbetet. At about 2850m this crosses the stream and paint flashes lead over rough ground to the hut. Water is available about 10min behind (south) the hut.

Pol/Grappein bivouacs (3183m, 12 bunks total, PD-, 4½-5hrs from Valnontey) Two huts, old and new, splendidly placed on a rocky prow overlooking Valnontey. Where the approach to the Leonessa hut doubles back, continue directly up the valley. After 300m fork right (sign) and follow a faint, steep path up the moraines at the head of the valley. At about 2300m the path traverses several small streams horizontally (bridges in place) before continuing very steeply up a moraine crest to a rock buttress. Gain this by use of staples and chains and continue on traces of path to a cave. Above the cave turn sharp right and climb the edge of a boulder-filled gully to exit rightwards at the top (chains). Scree and rubble lead to a rocky shelf ascending right to left across the rock buttress above. Take this shelf to the extreme left edge of the buttress. A traverse line then leads almost horizontally back right across the buttress (occasional paint marks then chains). The huts are now visible and can be reached either by climbing easily straight up the buttress to the glacier which is crossed (crevasses) or by crossing a wide gully and ascending the rock buttress directly beneath the Pol hut, steep but easy.

Money Hut (2872m, 8 bunks, 3½hrs) Situated on a rocky eyrie with superb views of much of the range. From Valnontey follow the main valley path to about 1km south of the hamlet of Vermiana where there is a sign-posted path to the left. Take this which climbs steeply to the picturesque Money pastures. At point 2340m take the left fork and follow a faint path (paint flashes, cairns) that leads up the moraine to below the rock spur on which the hut stands. At about 2700m the path traverses left to a rock step (chains) and the hut. Water is available from the stream behind the hut.

Gratton Hut (3198m, 9 places, 5hrs) Located on Col Pousset this is a possible starting point for La Grivola and also the trekking peak of Pointe Rousse. Start from either Cogne or Cretaz and reach Pousset Dessus by any of many possible routes through the forest on well-marked paths. The route then continues directly to the hut with a steeper rocky section near the col. If there is little snow it may be necessary to descend some distance from the hut for water.

Balzola Hut (3475m, 4 places maximum, 6½hrs from Cogne) A very small, remote and old hut in a wild location on Col de Clochettes. It serves the ENE ridge of La Grivola. From the Gratton hut, traverse horizontally from the col at 3198m on the west flank of the ridge for about 150m. Cairns and paint flashes lead down to chains and the glacier. The last few metres of descent are awkward, even with the chains, and a rope is recommended. Cross the glacier and reach the rubble slope below the Col de Clochettes. This is very loose but easy. It is probably best to reach the ridge slightly left of the col and then follow the crest to the hut, which is located slightly right of the col and not easily visible from below. Water may not be readily available in dry conditions.

Other bivouac huts in the area include the Borghi and Martonotti huts that serve Roccia Viva and Becca di Gay, the Antoldi hut in the Valeille and the Sberna hut on the Valsavarenche side of Herbetet. There is also a new hut on the Valsavarenche side of La Grivola but no first-hand details are available.

3. Herbetet from near the Leonessa hut. The S ridge is the left-hand skyline of the sunlit peak, the East ridge faces the camera and the NNE ridge is the right-hand skyline. (*Stuart Campbell*)

ROUTES

Gran Paradiso/ Mont-Grand Paradis (4061m)

The most famous peak in the area with a variety of worthwhile routes.

Normal route from Valsavarenche (F+, short steps of II on summit rocks). This very straightforward route from the Vittorio Emanuele II hut up the Glacier de Laveciau is clear from the map and details are readily available elsewhere. There is normally a trench all the way up the glacier that is followed by dozens daily. It is also possible to approach from the Chabod hut up the other branch of the glacier.

Normal route from Valnontey (PD+, steps of II/III). This is a much superior alternative to the Valsavaranche normal route. From the Pol huts traverse the Glacier de la Tribulation south then west to the foot of a snow ramp (near point 3625). Ascend the ramp south to reach Col de l'Abeille (2½hrs) From the col older descriptions recommend climbing to Fenêtre du Mont Roc direct but this has never looked in any way appealing (steep, loose and threatened by cornices) to the author, who has always climbed the couloir between the twin peaks of Mont Roc, directly above Col de l'Abeille. The couloir can be taken direct or a steeper section avoided by steeping out right and climbing the left bank for a few metres. From the top of the couloir, the Glacier de Laveciau is easily reached and the Valsavarenche normal route followed for a few minutes. (2hrs, 4½hrs)

North-west Face (D –.) A classic and objectively safe face route. Best approached from the Chabod hut from where the route is clearly visible. About 55° and 400m from the bergshrund.

Cresta Gastaldi/Crête Gastaldi (AD-, III-) An alternative approach to Col d'Alpe. Start as the Valnontey normal route but keep following the glacier south to reach the col at point 3688 (1½-2hrs). Follow the ridge west from the col over various towers and pinnacles to Col de l'Abeille (2hrs), where the Valnontey normal route is rejoined. The initial steep section from point 3688 is best taken right, then back left to the crest. (III-, 2hrs). It is possible to lengthen this route at the same grade by including other peaks on the southern edge of Glacier de la Tribulation, with the full circuit from Tête-de-Valnontey giving the most satisfying traverse.

114. The view from the Pol hut. (*Tom Burslem*)

East Face (AD) The line of the first ascent from the Cogne side, a very bold undertaking for the time (1869). In earlier descriptions the face is described as threatened by séracs but these are no longer apparent. Instead a 45-50° snow/ice slope leads almost to the summit from a narrow section low on the face. The approach is that for the Valnontey normal route until point 3625.

Gran-Piccolo Traverse (AD+) A superb, long and varied ridge route. From the summit follow the N ridge to Col du Mont Petit Paradis. This is mostly a fine narrow snow arête but with a couple of rock steps – a short abseil may be useful. From the col ascend the rock ridge (step of III+) to gain the snow slope leading to Mont-Petit-Paradis (2hrs). From its summit a series of rock towers (some named) form a section of almost horizontal ridge before a snow descent leads to Col di Montandayne. Climb or turn the towers according to taste (mostly II, 3hrs) At the col the traverse can be abandoned by descending the north-west flank (this may be icy). Better is to continue to the Becca di Montandayne. From the col this is gained by following the ridge for a short distance before being forced out on to a ledge line on the right flank. Follow this briefly before a fine crack (sustained, steep III) allows the crest to be regained near the summit. A short descent from the summit leads to the top of a snowy couloir leading to the Glacier de Tsasset which can be followed to reach the Leonessa bivouac hut (3hrs). This itinerary in reverse is clearly possible, as is a further extension to include Pointe de l'Herbetet by its south ridge – this would result in a truly huge day, first completed by Captain Percy Farrar's party in 1898.

Herbetet/Pointe de l'Herbetet (3778m)
A classic horn peak with several worthwhile ridges.

North-North-East Ridge (PD+, II+) The normal and easiest route. From the Leonessa hut follow the north edge of the Glacier de l'Herbetet to the foot of a couloir descending from the southernmost of the two Cols de l'Herbetet. Gain the col by some horribly loose mud/scree slopes, thankfully quite short – abseil possible in descent. Once the ridge is gained it is followed on or near the crest on mostly good rock (II+) until it merges with a snow/ice field on the N face. Climb this until the rocks forming the flank of the north-west ridge are reached and then briefly followed (II) to the summit. In descent it is important not to follow the north-west ridge for long but to start descending its flank shortly after leaving the summit in order to gain the snowfield. This is obvious in good visibility but not in mist (4-5hrs).

East Ridge (AD, III) Highly recommended, particularly in combination with the NNE ridge. From the Leonessa hut take the Glacier de l'Herbetet to reach the ridge at a shallow col just west of point 3272 – the final slope to the col may be icy. Perhaps due to glacier change, gaining the ridge from here now requires a steep rock step to be climbed. This is best done by stepping left (looking up the ridge) about 15m on to the Glacier de Tsasset glacier and then climbing a groove line on the south flank of the ridge (20m, sustained III). Once on the ridge follow it mostly easily turning any obstacles on the right. Near the top some harder sections (II/III) are best taken near the crest (4½-5½hrs).

South Ridge (AD+) An apparently fine rocky ridge from Col Bonney but no first-hand information. The Col can be reached from either the Leonessa or Sberna huts.

La Gran Serra/Grand-Serre/Gran Sertz (3553m)
An easy training peak and excellent viewpoint with the comfortable Vittorio Sella hut at the base of the normal route.

South Flank (F+/PD-) From the VS hut cross the stream via the bridge behind the hut and almost immediately leave the main traverse path to the Leonessa hut to start climbing steeply towards the Glacier du Lauson (faint path in places). Cross the glacier towards a steep snow/rock transition that leads to the higher Glacier Grande Vallon. Ascending the transition further left is less steep but may be bare loose rock in dry conditions in which case steeper snow to the right is preferred. Cross the Glacier Grande Vallon to directly below the summit rocks that are ascended to the summit (II-).

La Grivola/Mont Grivola (3968m)
A serious but superb and isolated peak. A 'nearly 4000er'. It is often

approached via the Gratton hut and Glacier du Trazo although starting from the Vittorio Sella hut is also possible.

South-East Face (PD+) The normal route but not particularly appealing because of loose rock. Probably the most reliable descent route. Looked at from Glacier du Trazo the face has a series of ribs running upwards. The route uses two of these to climb the face, crossing between them at about one-third height and exiting on to the easier upper section of the *ENE Ridge.* From the Glacier du Trazo reach the foot of the rib running to just left of the summit. Climb this from 150m before a vague rising traverse crosses the couloir on the right and allows the next rib to be gained. Climb this to the upper section of the *ENE ridge.* In descent paint flashes indicate the point at which the *ENE ridge* should be left.

ENE Ridge (AD, III or IV) An excellent ridge route on mostly sound rock, approached from either the Gratton or Balzola huts. From the Balzola hut follow the ridge more or less on the crest to the summit. There are numerous towers and pinnacles to negotiate on the way (steps of III). A large green tower that overhangs slightly is the first major obstacle. A traverse line leads right under the foot of this to a left-slanting snowy couloir that allows the crest to be regained. Somewhat higher there is a steep red tower. Either climb this via its front face to an exit leftward (IV, piton), or turn it to the left (III) on poorer rock. It will be helpful to abseil into at least two of the notches on the ridge (4-6hrs).

Other routes appear to be seldom used today. The classic north ridge (AD+) looks very fine viewed from the Balzola hut but approaches are awkward. The options are a long ascent from the Gran Nomenon Chalets or a committing descent from the Balzola hut to the Glacier du Mont Grivola. These approaches would also allow the north-west face (D) to be gained. From the south and Valsavarenche the mountain can be climbed from Col du Mont Grivola by a complicated route (AD), mostly on the south-east face in order to avoid the steep and loose steps on the south ridge.

Torre del Gran San Pietro/Tour du Grand Saint Pierre (3691m)

The highest point on the ridge forming the east flank of Valnontey. It is an excellent viewpoint. Approaches from Valnontey are described below but it is also possible to approach from Valeille and the Antoldi bivouac hut. Note, however, that the traverse between these two valleys over Coupe de Money is probably best avoided because of the loose ground on the Valeille side of the col – the Col de Money is a better option.

SW Ridge (AD-) From the Money bivouac descend the short step on the access path before making a rising traverse (loose rubble) towards point 3053 and the Glacier Coupe de Money. Traverse this at around 3200m close under the end of Cote Paganini to reach Glacier du Money before heading south to reach Col de Money (2hrs). From the col follow the ridge with interest over a variety of snow and rock peaks, generally on the crest, until the final gap below the summit pyramid. Traverse right (south-west)

5. The North face of the Ciarforon from the Vittorio Emanuele hut. (*Louis Wallace*)

almost horizontally from the gap for about 70m before ascending directly (crux) to the summit (III, 2hrs, 4-4½hrs).

N Ridge (PD+) Follow the *SW Ridge* route until beyond the end of Cote Paganini. Then cross the glacier south-east and ascend the couloir leading to the col at 3558m. This requires good snow. From the col ascend the ridge on the crest (III) to the summit. A line slightly left (south-east) of the crest is easier but very loose in places (3½hrs).

Full Traverse of the Apostoli Peaks (AD) A full traverse, either from the Col de Money to Tour de Saint Ours (3610m), or the reverse, is the most fulfilling route on the mountain. Tour de Saint Ours is climbed or descended via its steep NW flank, which can be icy. Saint Ours is a local saint.

Ciarforon (3642m)

The characteristic dome-shaped peak clearly visible from the Vittorio Emanuele hut. It has two summits, one rock, one snow, with a frozen lake between them.

NE Ridge (PD+) From the VE hut cross the stream and follow moraine path east-south-east to reach the Moncorve glacier. Cross this south-east to point 3347 on the ridge, slightly above the col between Ciarforon and La Tresenta. Follow the ridge mostly on the crest and then slightly on the left to a steepening; traverse horizontally right to reach the right side of the crest and then snow slopes which are followed to the summits (3-3½hrs).

N Face (AD/D-) A good alternative to, the NE face of the Gran Paradiso. Reduced snow and ice cover has changed this face considerably with the ice bulge visible in older photographs now replaced by a continuous band of rock at about two-thirds height. This band is loose and may become problematic if the snow cover continues to reduce. The line is very obvious from the VE hut. Difficulties are likely to vary with snow conditions.

The *NW ridge* is reputedly a fine climb (III+) in its upper sections but the lower section above point 2935 is dangerously loose. It is perhaps best approached in good snow cover from the lower portion of the N face.

Other Peaks

La Tresenta is a good training peak easily accessed from the VE hut. A traverse is possible. The Becca di Gay and Roccia Viva are difficult to access from the Valnontey side but offer two couloirs (L-hand, R-hand), a N face and ridge routes accessed from objectively threatened approaches. The Becca di Monciar is well seen and easily approached from the VE hut. The W ridge is PD and the N face AD+.

ACKNOWLEDGMENTS

The author wishes to thank Luca Signorelli who read a draft of this article and was able to provide many missing details and to correct errors. Thanks are also due to Tom Burslem who produced the accompanying map and made suggestions for improvements to the text. Darcey Gillie is to be thanked for helping the author explore the area and for commenting on a draft of the article.

BIBLIOGRAPHY

Andreis E, Chabod R, Santi M C (1980) *Gran Paradiso*, Club Alpino Italiano/Touring Club Italiano. The most recent definitive guide to the area. Masses of detail with good diagrams but becoming dated. Difficult to obtain and in Italian.

Collomb R G (1969) *Graians East*, West Col Productions. The most recent guide to the area in English. May be available in reprint form but now very dated.

Stefano A (2008) *I Rifugi Della Val D'Aosta: 125 Rifugi E Bivacchi*, A catalogue of all the huts and bivouacs in the Aosta valley with notes on approaches, and climbing and skiing possibilities. In Italian.

Yeld G, Coolidge W A B (1893) *The Mountains of Cogne*, Conway and Coolidge's Climbers' Guides, London. The first climbers' guide to the area. Detailed and still of use if it can be obtained.

Yeld G (1900) *Scrambles in the Eastern Graians in the Years 1878-1897*, Fisher Unwin. A narrative account of exploration and first ascents in the Cogne Mountains. Quite widely available second-hand.

Reflections

6. John Innerdale, *Jungfrau from the Hardergrat*, watercolour, 40cm x 30cm, 2009

PETER GILLMAN

'The past is a foreign country . . .'

It certainly feels like a foreign country when I think back to it, if not another planet. I remember traversing a frozen landscape where cold and wind reigned. Tom and John were ahead of me on the path that led to the glistening western flank of Quinag. It was March 1969 and Tom had his eye on yet another new route. This one followed a gully that rose from the crest of a tongue of scree and culminated in an overhang festooned with candelabras of ice. I edged up the steps Tom had carved with his axe, balancing on my crampons and reassuring myself that I was in good hands. Then Tom launched himself on to the candelabra pitch, slivers of ice dislodged by his axe showering down. I saw his crampons slithering and heard him call down: 'I think we'll have to give the mountain best.' But he pressed on and disappeared beyond the overhang.

Typically for a Patey foray, it was already late in the day; barely an hour remained before nightfall, giving me the opportunity, in the hallowed journalistic phrase, to make my excuses and leave. John stayed to follow Tom up his new route, while I tip-toed back down the gully and across the glen, head braced against the wind, to the point where Tom had parked his battered Skoda. Tom and John arrived just as the last of the light disappeared, their faces burnished by the cold and wind, telling of the hurricane that assaulted them on the top, threatening to lift them off their feet as they searched for the line of descent. They called the route *The Windpipe*, to evoke the weather encountered on the top. We headed back to Ullapool, though my guess is we stopped for a dram of Glen Morangie on the way; that detail eludes me 40 years on.

So what was I, a neophyte journalist of modest climbing abilities, doing in such extreme circumstances? Much of the responsibility lies, as so often, with John Cleare. I was working regularly for *The Sunday Times* magazine, then a power in the land of journalism for the quality of its writing and photography, and in partnership with John had proposed an article about Scottish winter climbing, hoping to convey its delights to a lay readership. It was John who devised our itinerary, insisting that we spend time with Tom and report on his drive to snatch as many new routes in the uncharted far north-west as he could in the time left over from attending to his duties as an Ullapool GP.

I recall a tousled figure with unkempt climbing equipment and a voracious determination not to waste a moment. Since Tom had no climbing partners in or near Ullapool, he justified his readiness to climb solo by

117. Top: John Cleare and Tom Patey – Tarbet, Sound of Handa, Sutherland, November 1966. (*John Cleare*)

118. Below: First ascent of *The Windpipe* (VS, II), west face of Quinag, northern Highlands, led by Tom Patey. John Cleare brings up third man Peter Gillman, March 1959. (*John Cleare*)

claiming that it was no more dangerous than climbing with a rope, since the rope was likely to break in any leader fall. I felt the argument was specious but accepted it as a pragmatic attempt to justify a course of action for which he had no viable alternative. He told me that he felt the finest mountaineering route anywhere was the Heckmair route on the north face of the Eiger; he admired the way it probed for the line of least resistance even on such an outlandish mountaineering challenge. More of the infamous *Nordwand* later.

I was in awe of figures such as Tom – not the ideal mode for a journalist, I admit, particularly as I often felt tongue-tied in his presence. But I managed to ask enough questions to elicit the necessary quotes. Otherwise I was content to tag along to wherever Tom and John had decided we should spend the day. Thus I was present on the day Tom made the girdle traverse of Creag Meagaidh, at that time ranked as one of the 'Last Great Problems' of the Scottish winter (*The Crab Crawl*, 2400m IV, 4). After another delayed start, Tom and John embarked on the route at midday, together with Jim McArtney, Mary Ann Hudson and Allen Fyffe.

John believed that the attempt was being made for his benefit, to enable him to take photographs for our article, but Tom had other ideas.

119. Creag Meaghaidh, Central Highlands: Jim McArtney and Mary Ann Hudson (leading) working on the first crux pitch of *Crab Crawl* (IV,4). Tom Patey had already gone ahead solo to complete his classic girdle of the entire cliff. (*John Cleare*)

Having posed briefly for John's cameras shortly after the start, he told the others he would push on a little to see what lay around the next corner. He never looked back, completing the route solo, although he had enough of a conscience to acknowledge Jim's dismay when he realised he was going to be left behind. I meanwhile was watching the proceedings from below the crag, only too aware that – just as on Quinag – this excursion was way beyond my abilities. My absence enabled Tom to create a joke for his subsequent article, Creag Meagaidh Crab Crawl:

Peter Gillman, John's Press Colleague, announced that he had all the necessary material for his article, and that he ought to be getting along. Since this was the first time he had been within conversation range and had not yet started to climb, we were impressed by his talent for improvisation.

None of this was true, but I did not mind; as journalists also like to say, never let the facts get in the way of a good story. Hamish MacInnes once confided that his own role in Tom's mythmaking was often precisely reversed. Tom recorded that Hamish would telephone and leave a message instructing him, for example, to be at the Skye ferry in three hours time in order to launch a winter assault on the Cuillin ridge. In truth, Hamish told me, it was Tom who would call him with impossible demands. It was easy to forgive Tom, because he was such a superbly witty and sardonic writer.

I should add that I was not always a passive spectator. In that same week I went foraging with Tom and John for new routes on Sgorr Ruadh. When we reached the crag he generously pointed out an unclimbed gully and offered it to John and myself, while he searched out something more testing. This time it was John's turn to feel torn, for he agreed to lead me up it although he would rather have been climbing with Tom. Thus it was

120. Eiger North Face 1966. Left: Dougal Haston and John Harlin II. Right: Neophyte photo-journalist Chris Bonington snaps Mick Burke. (*Peter Gillman*)

that my one new winter route – *Easy Gully*, 180m II - was inscribed in the guidebooks.

I entered this world of climbing celebrities by being – to cite yet another journalistic aphorism – in the right place at the right time. I was in the second year of my career as a journalist when John Harlin II persuaded the *Daily Telegraph's* weekly colour magazine to help fund his attempt to climb the *Eiger Direct* in the winter of 1965/66. I was a junior staffer on the magazine having been made redundant from my previous job on a glossy London magazine a year after leaving Oxford. Harlin's deal with the *Telegraph* followed an unsuccessful attempt by John Cleare, the Svengali of media spectaculars such as the Old Man of Hoy, to win coverage from the BBC. Accordingly John and I set off for Leysin to meet Harlin and prepare an article for the *Telegraph* magazine on the build-up to the climb. Sadly for John, he was later jettisoned from the venture, to be replaced as 'official' photographer by Chris Bonington.

In February 1966 I found myself in Kleine Scheidegg with Harlin, Bonington, Layton Kor, Dougal Haston, Don Whillans and Mick Burke. I had never before reported any news story and I had been climbing for just two years, making the customary weekend forays to Snowdonia in a Renault Dauphine or Austin A35, with HVS the limit of my abilities if not yet my ambitions.

I knew of Bonington and Whillans, of course, from their exploits on the

21. Eigerwanderers (l to r): Peter Gillman, Dougal Haston, Roland Votteler, Rolf Rozenzopf, Sigi Hupfauer, Günter Schnaid, Jörg Lehne, Peter Haag, Layton Kor, Chris Bonington.

self-same Eiger; and from Whillans' already legendary partnership with Joe Brown. Chris I recall as being unfailingly friendly and helpful towards this 24-year-old journalist who was abruptly part of the Eiger team, despite the contempt with which the mountaineering world views most journalists.

It was a critical time for Chris as he attempted to devise a way of earning a living from mountaineering in the wake of his abortive careers as army officer and margarine salesman. He had turned down Harlin's invitation to join the climbing team but had somehow parlayed that into the commission to take photographs for the *Telegraph*. Even so the boundaries between roles were rapidly blurred. Chris became so determined to live up to Robert Capa's key dictum – if your pictures aren't good enough, you're not close enough – that he made one of the crucial leads of the ascent, the ice gully beside the newly-named Central Pillar that opened up the route.

Don Whillans was supposedly Chris's photographic assistant but managed to spend most of his time – and a large slice of the *Telegraph's* money – at ease in the restaurant at the Kleine Scheidegg hotel, where my principal memory is of him imbibing pitchers of beer as he sat with his feet up next to the bar. The scene did not strike me as incongruous at the time, although later I reinterpreted it as a metaphor for the growing ambiguities of the Don's climbing career. Before long Chris replaced Don with Mick Burke, who was working at Harlin's climbing school at Leysin. It was Mick who accompanied Chris to the summit via the West Flank in time to greet

122. Dougal Haston on the First Band icefield on the Eiger north face *Direct* route during the filming of the BBC documentary *Last Blue Mountain*, March 1968. (*John Cleare*)

the victorious team, helping Chris to capture stunning images of their ice-crusted faces as they subsided in the snow. I remember Mick as friendly, open, no-nonsense, never inhibited about speaking his mind.

Dougal Haston was the enigma. I was drawn to him at first, this taciturn figure who seemed immensely confident and self-possessed. We had both studied philosophy and had earnest conversations about our university courses. He gave glimpses of his inner steel and his certainty about his goals in life, namely to climb the hardest routes by the purest means. His resolve was revealed to me most dramatically during the agonised radio conversations that took place after Harlin fell to his death while jumaring up the fixed ropes below the Spider.

The assumption among the group below the face, who included Bonington, Burke and Kor, was that the attempt should be abandoned. Since I had witnessed Harlin's death, I shared that feeling, although it was not my decision to make. It was Haston, then at the Spider, who argued pivotally that to renounce the climb would be to waste the monumental effort expended thus far – buttressing this argument to the effect that this is what Harlin himself would have wanted, and that the climb could become his memorial. There was an element of *realpolitik* in Haston's reasoning, since he figured that a significant coterie of the rival German team was equally determined to continue. In the event, the conjoining of the two national groups and their arrival on the summit provided the perfect redemptive narrative, which I can appreciate now, even if I was less attuned to such constructs at the time.

I came to know Haston more closely the following winter, when I accompanied him, Burke, Martin Boysen and Pete Crew to Patagonia for an attempt on Cerro Torre. By now I had been sacked from my job at the *Telegraph* following a spectacular row with its notoriously psychopathic editor, John Anstey. (I readily concede that while losing one's first job may be regarded as unfortunate, losing the second undoubtedly ranks as carelessness). I was then, perforce, a freelance, writing for the *Sunday Times* magazine and newspaper, and Mick and Dougal asked me to enquire whether the paper would back their attempt. Dougal and I were taken to lunch at the Savoy – this was still the glorious era of boundless Fleet Street expenses – where Dougal produced a blurred photograph of Cerro Torre. The news editor wrote the headline in an instant: 'The Worst Mountain In the World'. The *Sunday Times* agreed to pay £1500 into the expedition coffers, a sufficient sum in those days to make all the difference, and I was paid a magnificent £60 a week.

The British Cerro Torre Expedition of 1967/68 lasted 10 weeks and most of that time, both for myself and the climbers, was spent at base camp below Cerro Torre's glacier while the Patagonian weather surpassed itself in the ferocity of the storms lashing the FitzRoy massif. One of my abiding memories is of the wind roaring through the trees like an express train; another is of the ground reverberating as séracs toppled into the lake above the camp. Not only did this inactivity present a writing challenge, I also had a challenging time conveying my admittedly spare dispatches to London. In that pre-technology era, I had to walk for six hours to the road-head and then embark on a three day round trip in a borrowed pick-up to the nearest postal office, where my dispatches were telegraphed to London at hideous expense. These excursions became more important towards the end of the trip, as the expedition ran out of both money and food, and I was dispatched to ask the *Sunday Times* – via another horrifyingly expensive telephone call – to wire more of the former in order to acquire supplies of the latter.

It was thus at these intimate quarters that I had further insights into the personality of Dougal Haston. His determined selfishness was revealed in such matters as the nightly bridge school, where he resolved to exclude me from the proceedings. None of the others were prepared to stand up for me and I did not make a fuss as I already felt in an awkward position: as a supposedly objective journalist, was I of this expedition or not? I tried to steer clear of the group dynamics, particularly when they fractured as the expedition petered out in the unrelenting Patagonia weather. I was nonetheless the principal accused in a kangaroo court that investigated the disappearance of a tin of peaches after the empty can was found buried near my sleeping bag. It was evident to me that the culprit was the Argentine climber who had been assigned to our group, Jose Luis Fonrouge; but

I had a sticky time persuading my four colleagues of my innocence.

Of the others, I remember Mick being frank and jovial as usual. Pete Crew, so his team-mates intimated, was apparently out of his depth, having failed to adapt his sublime rock-climbing skills to the vagaries of mixed climbing in so hostile an environment. Martin Boysen listened to BBC World Service, singing along to the classical melodies that rose and fell on the ether. He suffered his customary wretched luck when he sprained an ankle in a juvenile game of jumping over the base camp stream, compelling him to languish in base camp with me while the remaining climbers, following a further bout of storms, made their final attempt. His frustration almost boiled over at times but was eased when his colleagues stomped back into camp one nightfall. They reported that the expedition's fixed ropes, so painstakingly put in place a month earlier, had been shredded by the wind and the attempt was officially at an end.

By this time I'd had enough of the BCTE. My excuse was that I had to get back to Buenos Aires to file my report on the end of the expedition. But once the homing urge took hold I hardly stopped moving until I reached London a few days later.

Of the four, I stayed in touch with Dougal for a time; I think I was intrigued at seeing his inner character so starkly revealed and was inclined to forgive it as the ruthlessness leading climbers required to achieve their aims. Our relationship effectively ended when he sent me a letter steeped in anger over an article I had written lamenting the death of Dave Condict, the school friend who had introduced me to climbing just as I left Oxford. Dougal told me it was sentimental and self-indulgent, and this time I felt I had seen enough of the recesses of his soul.

By contrast I established a friendship with Mick Burke that went beyond mountaineering, particularly as I observed his determination to establish a career as photographer and cameraman. It was these ambitions that, sadly, lured him into extreme danger on the summit ridge of Everest in 1975, when he went on alone – after Martin Boysen turned back because of problems with his oxygen apparatus – to fulfil his ambition of recording the first movie film at the summit of Everest. Even more poignantly, he almost certainly achieved his goal before, most likely, walking through a cornice on the descent.

I saw nothing of Peter Crew after Cerro Torre, either as a climber or in his new guise as an archaeologist. I thought my relationship with Martin Boysen had ended in the same way until he wrote a generous letter complimenting *The Wildest Dream*, the biography of George Mallory I wrote with my wife – in which he also revealed that for him to write a letter to anyone was a rare event.

Forty years on, I still look and wonder if the youthful, ingenuous figure in John Cleare's marvellous photographs can really be me. But my continuing love affair with Scottish mountaineering has remained a tangible legacy. I am now well into the bus-pass generation, but Scotland's call remains strong as ever and I'm planning for Glencoe as I write. After long abstinence, I have decided to try to add the 'new' Munros to my tally, having completed the original list shortly before it was revised. It was John who pointed me to the top of my first Munro, Cairn Gorm, when we were preparing an article about a winter survival course based at Glenmore Lodge shortly before the Eiger Direct affair in 1965/66. We were back in Scotland the following year, when I met Tom Patey for the first time and had the privilege of him escorting me up my first winter climb, *Aladdin's Couloir* on Coire an t-Sneachda. He took his responsibilities seriously too. I slipped and was about to make an ice-axe brake when he held me on the rope.

I believe that was also the day when I was introduced to the delights of Rowanlea, the hotel in Carrbridge where, after a day on the hill, Tom would produce the accordion he carried in the Skoda and entertain us with his singing. His ballads, with their gallows humour and their irreverence towards the celebs of the climbing world, had a wit and invention to rival Burns. Closing time had no meaning at Rowanlea; when the hour came and went, landlord Jimmy Ross would simply dim the lights and lock the door. Drinking and singing would continue into the wee small hours. Finally it would occur to Tom that he had to be in Ullapool for morning surgery. He'd gulp a handful of amphetamines and hit the road, leaving himself just enough time to change his shirt and don a tie and so present the face of respectability to his patients.

123. Peter Gillman (*Seth Gillman*)

I was delighted to hear the recordings of Tom at a ceilidh at the Clachaig, retrieved by Dennis Gray from Bill Brooker and re-mastered by Paul Cherry (reviewed on page 398). The timbre of Tom's voice had been distorted in my memory, assuming a rasp that it did not have in reality; I had also forgotten how Tom had difficulty articulating his Rs when he sang. But the lyrics shone out, taking me back to Carrbridge and from there out on to the snow-covered hills that provided such thrilling encounters for a young man in his 20s. Each time I return to Scotland those sensations flood back, providing a window to some of my most precious memories.

DICK ISHERWOOD

A Year Off Work

I hope and believe that one day it [Everest] will be climbed. Then when no higher 'altitude record' is possible, mountaineers can turn to the true enjoyment of the Himalaya, most likely to be found at about 20,000 feet or less.

Tom Longstaff, *This My Voyage*

124. Dorje Lakpa, Jugal Himal, from the south, showing our two camps on the west ridge (*Dick Isherwood*)

In mid 1979, after 10 years of varied work in several countries of the Far East, I found myself at age 35, still single, unburdened by employment or other responsibilities, with a bit of money in the bank, and a desire to climb a few more Himalayan peaks before I got too old. Geoff Cohen had a sabbatical year coming up at Edinburgh University. Sabbaticals are meant for mind-enlarging study at other academic institutions but Geoff had just discovered that there was in fact no rule to that effect, and reckoned he could expand his mind in the mountains as well as anywhere.

When we met in Manchester I had a brand new copy of John Cleare's *Collins Guide to Mountains*, autographed by the man himself, with whom I had just led a Baltoro glacier trek. The cover had a photo which had got my attention. Dorje Lakpa is in the Jugal Himal, almost directly north of Kathmandu, and is one of the most striking mountains you see from the plane window as you fly in. It was reportedly unclimbed, apparently not too hard, and at 6966m about the right height for a small light party. Tilman had been almost all the way around it in 1950, but he was there in the monsoon and never even saw it. The approach from the south went via Panch Pokhari, a pilgrimage site and occasional trekking destination, so we had a cover story in case anyone wanted to see our permit. With good luck we could cross the col Tilman had used and come home down the Langtang valley. It seemed the perfect objective for a discreet trip. Dave Broadhead and Ann McIntyre were taking a year off from teaching in Scotland so we had a team.

We met in the Kathmandu Guest House in early October, bought our food locally, including an enormous round cheese, arranged 15 porters through Mike Cheney, and caught the bus to Chautara, east of the Kathmandu valley and at the end of the road. The monsoon ended obligingly a day after we set out. The porters took us, over several days, to a group of summer grazing shelters at around 4500m, close to the moraines of the glacier descending from Dorje Lakpa, and right below where John had taken his cover photo. Ann guarded the camp while Dave, Geoff and I looked for a way up the mountain.

We first explored up the main glacier but it was a mess of moraines and melting ice. The ablation valley on the left was much better, but we had to leave it where a side glacier came in, and descend some steep moraine. On the other side we re-ascended to a hollow with a pair of tridents by a pool – the holy men even got up here. We now had access to the branch glacier leading to the west ridge of Dorje Lakpa.

We found a way through an area of crevasses and made a camp right below the ridge at around 6000m. After a bit of acclimatisation time we started up the ridge that was initially easy snow. We found an ancient fixed rope on terrain we were wandering up solo. It steepened and narrowed, and we made a dump on a high point, beyond which things got a bit more serious. A couple of days later we came back with all the gear and camped in a spectacular spot. There was barely enough room for the tent, and only then because we had piled rocks under one corner. We were sleeping three in a two-man tent – it was a bit cramped, but very cosy if you got the middle berth.

The ridge now became corniced and rather steep on its flanks. We roped up for a while, then went back to soloing on the southern side, on excellent névé. There was an area of bare green ice which came rather close to the cornice at one point, but the corridor between was wide enough, and we found ourselves on a flat snow platform, below a large bergschrund, at just the right time to stop for the night. It was a perfect campsite as it got all the evening sun. Next morning we were off in the dark, leaving the tent, and Geoff led a steepish ice pitch above the 'schrund. I led us into some rather rickety snow – three dimensional lattices of icicles, very close to the cornice at times – and we reached a basin of deep soft snow, up which we ploughed slowly to the summit.

A layer of cloud had come in during the day, and we were at the very top of it. The sun was on us and we could look over the cloud layer, but it didn't clear enough for a view. As it was after 4pm we couldn't wait longer. We got back to the tent in the very last light. An extremely slow descent over the next two days took us back to the base camp.

Geoff and I climbed Bauddha (6151m) with some exciting soloing near the top. We got separated on a fluted snow face and chose separate flutes. As mine steepened I wished I had a rope, but too late. Each little flute was hard ice on one side and loose powder on the other, and the layer of hard stuff was disturbingly thin. We reunited for one steep pitch to the summit and came down more conventionally.

We had done what we'd come for and the food was running out – even the cheese. We packed everything up and set out, with loads of 30kg or so, for the obvious col west of Bauddha. Just below the col we had to cross a gully in the snow down which some stones were falling. The plan was to choose a quiet moment, drop into the bed of the gully, and run across and up the other side. It wasn't very far but at 5800m with big packs it was easier to plan than to execute. Three of us made it safely but Ann got a blow on her upper arm from a brick-sized rock. We thought she might have broken a bone, but it was just badly bruised. The rest of us took her load and we continued over the col and down into the upper Langtang above Langsisa. We waded the Langtang Khola and finished our last scraps of food before descending to Kyangjin Gompa the next morning. The route we had taken has become widely known as Tilman's Col, but if you look at the original edition of *Nepal Himalaya* it's clear that Tilman crossed a different col, further east and right at the foot of the west ridge of Dorje Lakpa. He even has a photo of the tridents by the pool. The way we went was probably easier.

It was mid November and the weather was fine. Geoff and I thought we just had time to get another trip in before the winter snow came. We bought three weeks' food and set out with three of Mike Cheney's finest to carry it all, bound for the Rolwaling valley. We had some wonderful views of Gaurishankar from the approach, and some exciting moments on the trail – in those days the main footpath to Beding used three bendy tree branches to negotiate a rock wall above the river. The boys got us up to a base camp above Nar and overlooking the Rolwaling lake, took their pay and scampered off. There were a few thin high clouds around.

We'd decided to try a peak called Tsoboje (6689m) which is right above the north side of the lake, by now very frozen. We had no idea whether it had been climbed but it had an attractive ridge dropping down from its eastern end toward the lake. We were camped in a tiny hollow right below this ridge and thought we were well set. Unfortunately it then snowed.

It snowed for two days and we dug the tent out more than once. Then it cleared, the sun came out, and – guess what next – it all started to thaw. I emerged in the morning sun, looked up and saw a huge icicle, dripping water, right over the tent. Time to move, fast. We dragged everything

25. Dave Broadhead at the first ridge camp on Dorje Lakpa. (*Dick Isherwood*)

down the slope and found a safer place.

Off up the hill, through various rock bands, to another campsite on an area of scree before the real ridge. This was very steep on our side but we found a neat way out to the sharp ridge crest and round on the other side things looked a bit better. Geoff led one of the more impressive pitches in my memory, up a steep rock groove with very little protection, in double boots and with a 15kg sack. We ended the day in a reasonably good position, in a little saddle on the ridge with maybe 500m to go to the top.

We'd brought the inner tent as a bivvi bag, and work was needed to make a ledge big enough for it. Unfortunately the snow we stood on rapidly gave way to ice as we dug. The ice was mixed with rock and I broke the pick of my axe. We dug on, but by the time we had a platform big enough to use there was light in the eastern sky. We got in anyway, and slept, after a fashion, still roped up.

It may have been the short night, but in the morning I was not feeling at all brave. There were lenticular clouds coming from the north-west, which is where the snow comes from in Nepal in the winter. Geoff wanted to finish the job but I am ashamed to say that I chickened out. He was very good about it but we missed a great opportunity, as we were almost certainly above all the difficulties and the weather in fact did nothing much for days.

We descended and camped above the lake. It was a calm night but suddenly the tent was rocked by a series of wind gusts. Then it all calmed down again and we slept well. When we got out in the morning we saw that a huge icefall had come down, within a hundred metres of the tent, and made a mighty hole in the ice on the lake, which was a couple of feet thick. There but for fortune… We attempted to cross the Tesi Lapcha, with rather large loads, but it snowed some more. Winter had come. We gave up and went to India, where we bought traditional single speed bicycles and toured Rajasthan – but that is another story.

Eventually, after a short trip to the Valley of Flowers, it was time to do some real climbing in the Karakoram. In early July we travelled by train from Delhi to Lahore, enduring a wait of four hours at the Wagha border while the Indian customs checked the baggage of travellers *leaving* India. In Rawalpindi we met Des Rubens who had just flown from the UK.

As usual the flights to Skardu, on little propeller planes which had to fly around Nanga Parbat, were chaotic. We kept showing up at the airport very early and got on a plane on only our third day. We had managed to hit the start of Ramadan, but it proved to be a bonus – double breakfasts for us on the plane as the Moslems weren't eating. Having no permits of any sort, we kept a low profile and got out of town as fast as possible in a rented jeep to Khapalu, and the roadhead below Hushe.

We had various loose ideas for climbing. One was an attempt on Masherbrum by the original southern route, but when we saw it from the Hushe valley we thought it was a bit big for us.

It seemed a better idea to go up the Charakusa Glacier, to the east. With five porters we headed up the valley, past flowering roses and small cypress trees – this bit of the Karakoram is quite well vegetated. The trail led to summer grazing settlements to which people were just beginning to bring their cattle. Beyond, big lateral moraines flanked the glacier and granite walls appeared out of the mist – the weather was not great. We paid off the porters, with the usual difficulties, and were glad to be alone in great scenery. The whole valley was one of the most beautiful I have ever seen. We camped among yellow poppies and looked at the enormous and very steep north face of K6. This was obviously too much for us, though it was fun sketching theoretical lines up it. More realistic was a peak on the north side, 21,700 feet on our map, and apparently close to K7, which we had difficulty identifying.

A side glacier led up to a face on Pt 21,700 which didn't look too steep, at least from well below, so we decided to give it a try. We put a camp in a snow basin at around 5000m and plotted a route up a series of snowfields and rock bands. It didn't look hard at all, but we got a series of shocks. The granite here is very monolithic, with few cracks, and the rock steps were deceptively steep and uncompromising. We found ourselves repeatedly climbing runnels of ice between big bald chunks of rock. Geoff did some impressive leads on the first day that took us to a tiny snow ledge, just big enough for the Vango tent.

We had gained about 700m and decided to leave the tent here, as there was unlikely to be a place for it any higher up. Des was feeling the altitude, having just come out from the UK, and this may be why he left his sleeping bag in the tent the next morning. Not a great idea.

On the second day we took ages to climb the next (fourth) rock band, first up a very steep chimney full of ice, then a traverse across some steep

26. K7 West, showing the high point reached. (*Dick Isherwood*)

ice with bits of rock sticking out of it – almost a hand traverse. We got out onto a steep snowfield which led to a notch in the west ridge of the mountain, but by now Des was very slow – falling asleep on the stances – and the weather was not looking good at all. Geoff found a ledge on the rocky ridge crest just big enough for three to sit on. The view down to the Kaberi glacier on the other side was enough to give me nightmares. We organised ourselves in the twilight and were lucky to drop no more than Des's mug. We put him in the middle, since he had no sleeping bag, and huddled together. The boots got passed to me at one end and I hung them all by their laces from a big chock placed in a crack – at least I thought I did. We had a surprisingly warm night, though it was all a bit cramped. In the morning I carefully passed the boots back and discovered that I'd failed to clip in one of Des's – it had spent the night merely wedged between two others. I didn't dare confess to this and sat in silence as Geoff said speculatively:

'I wonder what would happen if you dropped your boots from here?'

Des replied:

'I doubt if you'd get down.'

I spent the rest of the climb wondering just what we would have done.

Above here it was steep – like overhanging – for the next 20m or so. Geoff tried manfully to climb it directly, then we decided to traverse around the steep bit. We went down and across for a couple of rope lengths, then back up left in some icy cracks and onto a rock ramp. Seven hours of effort saw

127. Des Rubens on Drifika, Karakoram. (*Dick Isherwood*)

us 30m directly above our bivouac. It might have been quicker just to peg up the overhang, even at this height.

At this point Des very nobly decided to opt out. He was still going very slowly, so he abseiled down directly back to the bivvi ledge. We let him take one of the two sleeping bags and the stove and pot. Geoff and I continued, initially up straightforward snow, but then onto rather hard green ice with a cover of loose powder. By the time it eased off again, below a sérac wall, it was sunset – the clearest evening we'd had so far – and I had trouble dividing my attention between the climbing and the tremendous views – north to K2 and the other Baltoro peaks, east to the Golden and Silver Thrones, and west to the huge mass of Masherbrum.

We found a snow hollow under the séracs and shared the one sleeping bag and one Karrimat. Supper without a stove didn't take long. Above us was a huge hanging disc of ice which might have wiped us out if it had decided to fall, but we were too tired to care. Amazingly I slept fairly well.

We knew we were close to the top, but in the morning it was snowing and we could see very little. I led a pitch up the ridge above and was surprised when the mountain hit me in the face – the visibility was so poor I couldn't see that it had suddenly steepened. Time to reconsider. It was extremely frustrating, as through gaps in the cloud I glimpsed the edge of a big snowfield, crevassed but basically easy, that seemed to lead to the summit. However with no stove or food, and only one sleeping bag we couldn't wait it out, so we went down.

We picked up Des and descended very slowly to the tent, doing some impressive abseils over the rock bands. Our uneaten shrimp curry from three days ago tasted great, even with bits of ice in it. The descent the next day should have been efficient but somehow wasn't. The rope got stuck after one big steep abseil and Geoff did some desperate rock climbing back up a very steep groove to free it. On the next abseil it happened again and Geoff was again the hero – both Des and I were far too shattered for this. Somehow I had lost both front points off one of my crampons by now. We shambled down across the bergschrund and into the lower gully, which we got out of just ahead of a large avalanche.

We had been five days on this climb and we were all very tired. I had slightly numb and tingling fingers and toes, and lay in the grass feeling as if I was in a shell. My body didn't want to do anything but my mind was very active, thinking of all the things I could do in the future provided I continued to survive experiences like this.

We went down to our dump for more food, taking two days over what should have been a four hour round trip, then considered our options. We really had to get to the top of something. The only peak of respectable height in this valley system which looked any easier than the one we had just failed on was marked on our map as 21,150 feet. It was a sharp pyramid, looking a bit like the Obergabelhorn, and was up the southern branch of the glacier, to the south-west of K6. After a couple more days' rest we set out, working through a messy icefall, and taking two days to a camp at around 5700m below the north-west ridge of the peak. We found we were following a trail of Japanese debris – someone had been here before. They had left the label from a quart of Suntory whisky, but no sign of the contents. From this camp we could look back at Pt 21,700 and realise just how close we had been to the top.

Next morning was fine and clear, and we soon reached a col on the west ridge, from which we had a magnificent view of a large part of the Karakoram. Good snow continued to within 300m of the top, then it got steep. We climbed a rock chimney, initially trying to ignore bits of Japanese fixed rope but eventually using them. Des led a very scary pitch across steep rock slabs with a thin and fragile ice cover, and we reached a narrow and very corniced summit ridge. It was almost horizontal but of course

128. Geoff Cohen on K7 West. (*Dick Isherwood*)

the real summit was at the far end. Sections of fixed rope peeked out of the snow and we clipped our rope into them, having no idea what they were attached to.

Somehow it was 5pm when we got to the top. We had probably the best long distance mountain view I have ever had – most of the Pakistan Karakoram, dominated by K2, Chogolisa and Masherbrum, a huge extent of the Indian Karakoram, and some very steep granite pillars closer to hand, south of K6. We could see Nanga Parbat to the west and distant peaks in Sinkiang beyond K2. We took a few photos and wondered what to do as we were clearly not going to get down to our camp. I must have been very tired as I wanted to dig a deep snow hole right there on the summit ridge, but I was rightly overruled. We began abseiling down, rather diagonally. I was last off the ridge and I eyeballed the piece of line looped around a granite spike sticking out of the snow, willing both of them not to fail. Crossing the rock slabs was very skittery, especially with front points on only one crampon.

Then it got dark. We had very limited headtorch batteries and Geoff proposed that only the first man down should use his – the other two could just follow the rope down in the dark. This worked for a bit, then all the torches failed when we were still on steep ground. We cut three modest thrones in the ice, belayed to bits of rock and an ice peg, and made the best of it. We had very little bivouac gear and it was too exposed to take off your boots or anything, so we all had a miserable night. We had only one more serious diagonal abseil to do in the morning, for which Geoff again pulled out amazing reserves of energy. By 11am we were asleep in the tent.

This peak now goes by the name of Drifika (6447m). We probably did the second ascent and by now it has had several more. Pt 21,700, now known as K7 West (6858m), had its first ascent by Steve House and party, taking a different route, only in 2007.

It was a very memorable year. I can hardly believe it was 30 years ago. We may have gone a bit over 20,000 feet, but I think we were doing very much what Tom Longstaff had in mind.

). Geoff Cohen on the south-east ridge of Tsoboje, Rolwaling, Nepal. (*Dick Isherwood*)

History

130. John Innerdale, *Matterhorn from Ried*, watercolour, 40 x 30cm, 2007.

HENRY DAY

Annapurna Anniversaries

– and that picture

The twentieth of May 2010 was the 40th anniversary of the ascent of Annapurna I by the British Army Mountaineering Association Expedition; it was also 60 years since the French made the first ascent of the mountain. Or was it? Two books have caused me to look again at our experiences of 1970 and compare them carefully with the details of the first ascent.

131. North face of Annapurna 1. *(Henry Day)*

David Roberts in his book *True Summit* (2000, Constable, p216) wrote:

> *Ever since 1950 there has been a small cadre of skeptics within the mountaineering community who doubted that Herzog and Lachenal reached the summit on June 3. The doubt springs in part from the celebrated summit photo.*

Which caused Reinhold Messner to spring to the defence of Herzog in his

132. Gerry Owens's heels and the summit ridge stretching east. Manaslu is 50km away. *(Henry Day)*

own book *Annapurna: 50 years of Expeditions in the Death Zone* (Mountaineers Books), also published in 2000. Messner says he wrote it because:

> *In 1996 a literary feud directed against Maurice Herzog began in France, which I found unfair. Naturally there were still unanswered questions about the report on the Annapurna ascent published in 1950, but Herzog's summit success remains an indisputable fact… In 1996, when Herzog was almost 80, that nobody was prepared to come to his defence is sad – and it is only because of this that this book was written.*

However, Messner does not address the issue of whether they reached the summit; he just accepts that they did. My photographs have never been published alongside those by Lachenal and they will be compared later in the conclusion to the article to see if they illuminate the matter. Co-incidentally, it was one of my photographs that illustrated the dust cover of the Roberts book and it was John Cleare, who had arranged it, who alerted me to the controversy that had totally passed me by.

But first let us recall our Army expedition of 40 years ago.

Our team arrived at Pokhara on the King's Flight. The aircraft was a WW2 vintage DC3 Dakota, one of only two planes belonging to the King of Nepal, and we had chartered it. A hooter sounded when the plane was heard to alert a small boy whose job it was to shoo away cattle grazing on the grass airstrip. We had been told there was no motorable road to Pokhara so everything had to be transported by porters or mules or by aircraft. We arrived to find we were sharing a Gurkha compound with Chris Bonington's Annapurna South Face expedition.

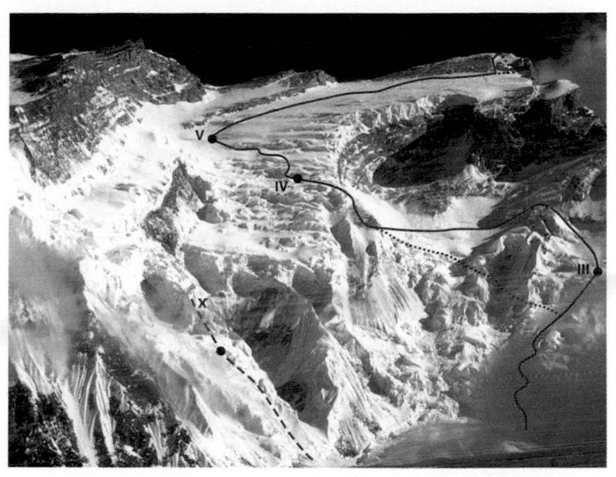

133. North Face of Annapurna:
——— AMA Route with camps.

-------- AMA attempted new route, X – high point.

••••••• French Route where it cuts the corner below The Sickle. Last section to the summit was to right of AMA line. Dutch Rib is low down, taking the prominent fin to the right of the AMA attempt. *(Henry Day)*

Nick Estcourt and I had overlapped in the Cambridge University Mountaineering Club for two years and I had even tied onto his rope for a few routes, including *Kipling Groove* in a snowstorm on one memorable December climbing meet. At the time, we both lived in Cheshire as did Chris, to whom I had been introduced. Meeting up again in Pokhara, they took us over to meet some of the other glitterati who made up their team, including Don Whillans, Dougal Haston and Martin Boysen.

The South Face team's sea freight and not arrived and we helped extricate them from a morale-sapping delay by lending them enough hill food to get started on the route. After the climb they were able to pay us back in kind, leaving a cache of food where our paths rejoined. We found their rations a welcome change but frugal; I remember eating a complete pack as a snack as we walked along the trail. Don's memorable remark to me later about rye bread in the ration was: 'Pumpernickel, f...ing pumpernickel, just like donkeys' crap.'

A few weeks later a mail runner sped into our base camp at the head of the Miristi Khola on the north side of the mountain with a big smile on his broad Gurkha face. Major Bruce Niven, a Gurkha officer and our expedition commander, had brought with him a few of his soldiers to support us, as well as a delightful manner that smoothed the way through many challenges with the line of supply. What Purna-bahadur handed me I treasure to this day: a letter from Maurice Herzog himself. I had written to let him know we were planning to try another ascent from the north (though not necessarily by the French line) and had studied his account with great care. What he wrote underlined one of a number of lessons we had drawn from his book: *'Buvez de l'eau. Encore et toujours plus.'*

Not drinking enough water had been only one of the mishaps that befell the French summiters, one following on from another in terrible succession. On a small card in my pocket I had listed that they became dehydrated, anoxic, lost, frostbitten and drugged. Our small team had talked through all of this and planned as best we could how to avoid suffering the same.

134. Modiste blanking out Annapurna South. *(Henry Day)*

Whether to take supplementary oxygen was one issue. In the same letter Herzog had written:

> *I congratulate you that you succeeded without oxygen on [the ascent of] Tirich Mir, which is at a very similar altitude as Annapurna, but any way it is better to have the apparatus [oxygen bottles] available on the spot either in order to be able to go through a particularly hard area or in order to recuperate in case of exceptional fatigue.*

Only nine months before, three of us had gasped our way to the top of Tirich Mir, at 7784m 'only' a thousand feet lower than Annapurna. Gerry Owens and Richard Summerton had been going more strongly than me that day for the first time on the expedition. Clearly I had to do something to keep up with them this time. Also judgement had suffered. On the way down a nice, even snow slope, at the sort of angle you'd ski down without a thought every winter, I decided on a sitting glissade. Bad decision! The only thing that stopped me accelerating down 3000m to the South Barum glacier was a small ledge we had cut into the slope where we had spent the night at more than 7000m with no tent or bivvi bag. No wonder I had frost bitten toes – another judgement thing. On that ledge, trying to breathe again after being winded by the thudding stop, I resolved to try supplementary oxygen if ever near 8000m again. Gerry, however, did not approve, a purist ahead of his time.

The end of my toe, complete with nail, had lifted off neatly a month or so later when we were waiting somewhere in the Gulf for the RAF to fly us home. Our doctor was most put out that I had not kept it for him to exhibit. Double boots had just become available commercially and mine had inners of leather, which had proved inadequate. Graham Tiso gave me a replacement inner made of felt and this was much warmer. We all had similar boots for Annapurna and no further cold injuries were suffered.

The dehydration problem was directly linked to stoves. The only small gas stoves then available that we knew of used Camping Gaz cartridges

5. Dhaulagiri 30km away. View to the west past the Fang. *(Henry Day)*

containing butane which would have been frozen solid most of the time. Propane-butane mix only became available some years later. So we were using kerosene stoves with all the palaver of pricking and priming. We became obsessed with keeping the stoves going. As I fell asleep the night before going for the summit on Annapurna, I rehearsed in my mind the exact procedure for the dawn start. Matches in top breast pocket, solid methylated spirits 1 (1½ sticks) in priming bowl, pricker to the right of it... I can remember it all so perfectly. So we were well up to speed on drinking plenty. Oh yes, and a pee bottle (each) by the knees, halfway down the tent wall.

Our build-up of camps on the north side of the mountain went quite well. We rapidly reached the foot of the Sickle, a huge band of séracs topping a curved rock cliff that covered most of the north face of Annapurna I. Richard and Gerry had an early taste of what it threatened when they were engulfed in the tail-end of a sérac fall one morning as they were brewing up breakfast. The blast was strong enough to blow away a tent full of stores that were never found again. Richard and Gerry were peppered with ice shrapnel and well shaken.

Partly because of this, but also because we wanted to pick a new route for ourselves, we set about probing the left side of the huge face where a series of ribs promised an elegant line that outflanked the worst of the ice avalanche danger below the Sickle. We took turns in pairs to prepare the route – we only had five climbers by then, having lost one to pneumonia on the way in. First Dougie Keelan and I, and then Gerry and Richard fixed ropes up the blue polished ice, but after 10 days of this we gave the route on the north-east buttress best and returned to the French line under the Sickle. It was good to see that one of the ribs was completed a few years later by a Dutch team. However our bodies had continued to acclimatise and the Sickle had not avalanched for those 10 days.

Our Sherpas had now caught up as they were no longer needed to supervise porters over the difficult route from Choya, each section of which had had to be traversed five times by the 32 men we had been able to

136. Manaslu top right, looking east along the Central and East summits of Annapurna I. *(Henry Day)*

recruit. They had also heard of the loss of some friends on Everest and viewed climbing the Sickle with misgiving. However, with great diplomacy, Bruce Niven, who was now running things from base camp, together with Sonam Girmi, our sirdar, were able to persuade them to carry on, to our great relief. The Sherpas took part in the key carry up to Camp IV on 18 May. Sonam and Pertemba, together with Dougie Keelan and Andy Anderson, Gerry and I, spent that night there at 7100m. Pemba Norbu and Ila Tashi who had also carried a load up immediately descended as planned. Pertemba was to reach the summit of Everest with Pete Boardman in 1975 by the south-west face and Sonam was to be our sirdar on the South Col route the following spring. Next day six of us laboured up another 400m and sited the tent at 7500m, leaving Gerry and me dug into the open slope with everything we needed.

We were not sure how things were progressing on the south face at this stage. Through our Gurkha signallers, part of Bruce's team, we were able to relay messages to and from their base in Modi Khola and by that means were able to offer the possibility of a traverse of the mountain for their summiters should they wish to give a try. I had sent a message to them, in military terms:

> *18 May 70. Camp 4 at 7100m. For Bonington from Day. We hope to establish Camp 5 at 7700m tomorrow and send pairs of climbers to the summit on 20, 21 and 22 May. The route will be marked with yellow flags and Camps 4 and 5 will be left in place. Camps consist of (sufficient for 2 men for one night). Nil oxygen. Let me know asp if you are still interested because we will pull out quickly if successful.*

137. The iconic photo of Maurice Herzog taken by Louis Lachenal on 3 June, 1950.

Breathing supplementary oxygen led to a great night's sleep, at least for me. Next day, Gerry demonstrated his distain for the apparatus by ignoring the controls. The clumsy masks obscured our vision and until I hauled Gerry to a stop and found he was on four times greater flow rate than me I struggled to keep up with him.

Low winds and perfect weather transpired as forecast, added to which snow conditions mostly made for good, but ankle-breaking cramponning. It took us around an hour and a half to cover a kilometre of ascending traverse to the foot of a broad rock band, split by a snow-filled gully. We kicked steps up progressively steeper snow and ice, eventually escaping left through the top of the rocky band onto a final steeper ice slope, and then up to two mushrooms of a cornice on the ridge that proved to be the summit.

I took a complete round of photographs as well as a few of Gerry, perched as high as he dared on the cornice, which he cut part way through on our side. Peering over the south face, we could see Modiste staring back at us as well as Machapuchare floating below on a sea of puffy white cumulus cloud that obscured any possible view of the other expedition. Dhaulagiri had been visible on our right for the last few days but now we could see Manaslu as well in the opposite direction. Gerry slipped a small Nepalese flag onto his ice axe shaft and pushed it in the snow for a picture. I slipped a Union Jack onto mine and passed it up so he could hold it up like the French had done. It was much later that we spotted it was upside down, a distress signal. This was not intentional, but perhaps appropriate as the tribulations of the French while getting down were much in mind and I was certainly anxious. I took a few more photos of Gerry as we carefully descended, one at a time, the steeper summit ice slope – not without both of us having small falls on the way. Gerry collected a few stones from the sides of the gully to take home as presents. It did not take long to get back to Camp 5 which we reached after about five hours' round trip. It had taken us only three hours to reach the top, compared to Herzog and Lachenal's eight, which gave some indication of the benefits to us of supplementary oxygen. Meanwhile Dougie and Andy had laboriously returned to Camp V where they insisted on looking after us with brew after brew although they were probably in worse shape than we were, not having the advantage we had had of breathing 'English air' for a night and a day.

In due course we met up again with the South Face team in Pokhara and Gerry and I were soon buttonholed by Dougal and Don who took us off to the other side of the airstrip for a beer. We exchanged experiences, with us telling them all about what we had seen and found. They had topped out on their route in a whiteout and in due course published a grainy still photograph, enlarged from 8mm movie film to show where they had reached. A photo in Messner's book shows the same view of Erhard Loretan on the summit from the ridge. (The full video clip of it is significantly clearer and shows much better what foul weather conditions they had). Don's account appeared in *Mountain* magazine and Dougal's in Chris Bonington's *Annapurna South Face* (1971). It was interesting to read that some of our tracks were visible a week later in spite of the heavy snow we experienced in the intervening week. They had not spotted the yellow RiRi flag we left on top. Strong winds could easily account for both these things.

138. Gerry Owens on the summit of Annapurna I at 11am on 20 May 1970. *(Henry Day)*

At the Alpine Club dinner at the Café Royal in London in December 1970 the guest of honour was Maurice Herzog. Gerry and I presented both him and the AC with a small piece of limestone mounted on a wooden base with a silver label saying where it came from. In return he wrote in my copy of his celebrated book:

> *For Captain H. Day, who gave me the great pleasure to bring me a stone of the Annapurna that I was unable to take myself. With my gratitude. Maurice Herzog.*

Returning to the matter of the summit photographs, Lachenal's diary for 3 June says:

> *A little below [the top] of the north face a rock bench received us, so that we could take the several official photographs we had to take …*

Looking at my photo of Gerry descending the summit slope), the skyline is not dissimilar to that in Lachenal's photo of Herzog minus the mushrooms. Lachenal's rock bench camera position could be where the couloir gave onto the summit ice slope within a few rope-lengths of the crest. Given the way the appearance of terrain can change from day to day as the wind affects snow and ice cover, let alone in the 20 years that had elapsed between the two photographs being taken, the rock exposed at the time of the two ascents as shown in general views of the north face are remarkably

139. Summit icefield in descent. Note flag left on the top. *(Henry Day)*

similar. The configuration of the skyline is too similar for the French photo to have been posed anywhere else except nearly at the summit.

As to whether they actually trod the summit, or at least crested the corniced ridge as we did, I subscribe to the traditional view that if they said they reached the summit, then they did. I salute the French expedition and Louis Lachenal and Maurice Herzog in particular for their great achievement and rejoice that all four of us got down to tell the tale.

Postscript: Statistics compiled by Elizabeth Hawley and given in Messner's book make for sober reading. Annapurna I has been the least ascended of the fourteen 8000m peaks. Fatalities exceeded the number of successful expeditions for many years (38 ascents up to 2000 and 57 deaths) and this grim ratio was the worst of all the eight-thousanders. Five Britons have reached the top so far, of whom Gerry Owens and Dougal Haston were killed in the mountains and Don Whillans died of a heart attack. Alan Hinkes and I are still alive.

STEPHEN GOODWIN

Everest Revealed?

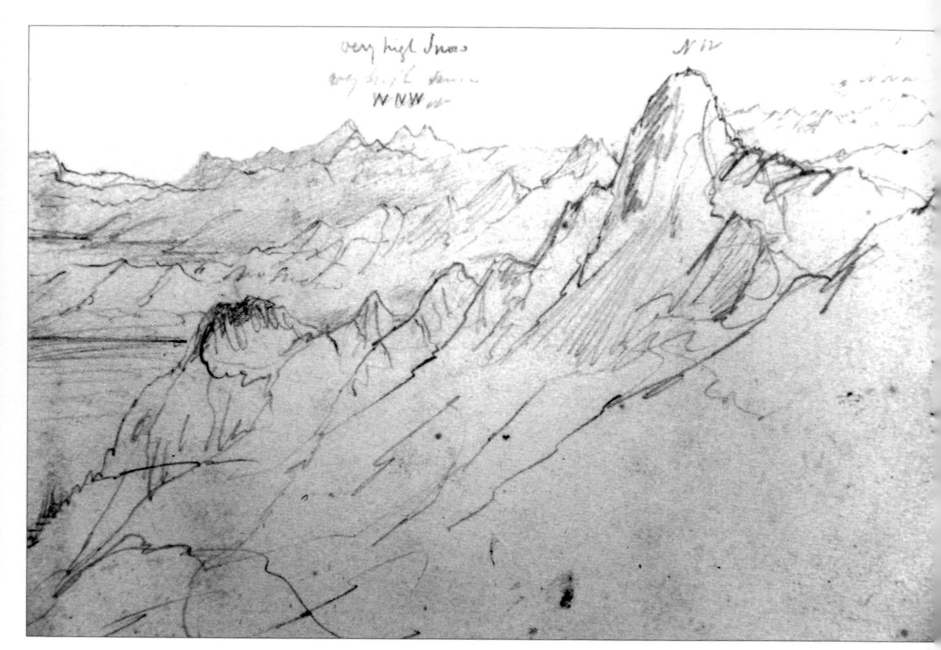

140. Sketch by Joseph Dalton Hooker from 'Choonjerma pass', Nepal, 1848. (*Courtesy o Royal Botanic Gardens, Kew*)

Is this 1848 sketch by Joseph Dalton Hooker the first recorded view of Mount Everest by a European? Drawn in situ on the 'Choonjerma pass' – now generally referred to as the Mirgin la – in eastern Nepal, it has, for many years, lain unidentified in the archives at the Royal Botanic Gardens, Kew. Its 'discovery' adds one more facet to the remarkable accomplishments of Hooker during his three years of exploration and research in the eastern Himalaya.

The Mirgin la is an old trade route linking the valley of the Simbuwa Khola, flowing from the Yalung glacier on the south side of Kangchenjunga, to the valley of the Ghunsa Khola, draining the mountain's west and northern flanks. Reaching some 4500m, today the pass is used by trekkers linking the routes to Kangchenjunga's north and south base camps.

Hooker and his party crossed southwards from the Ghunsa valley on 5 December 1848, the botanist rhapsodising about the view in his *Himalayan Journals* and comparing the sunset to the effects achieved by J M W Turner.

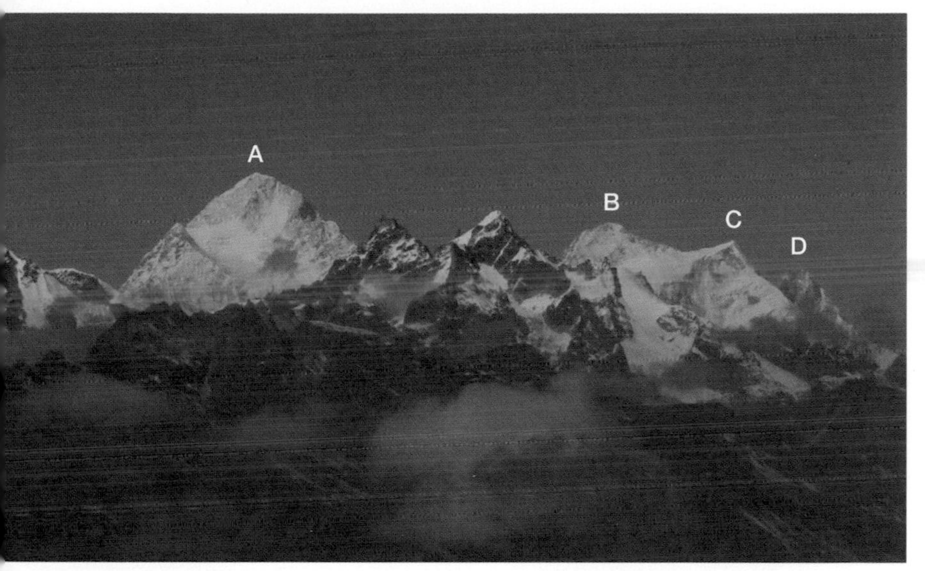

11. 'Gigantic forms': the upper east face of Makalu (A) dominates this view westward from the region of the Mirgin la. Everest is marked B with the South Summit just visible, C is Chomo Lonzo Main and D and is reckoned to be Chomo Lonzo Middle. Lhotse is hidden by the foreground rock peak. (*Courtesy of Royal Botanic Gardens, Kew*)

As it [the sun] sank, the Nepal peaks to the right assumed more definite, darker, and gigantic forms, and floods of light shot across the misty ocean, bathing the landscape around me in the most wonderful and indescribable changing tints. As the luminary was vanishing, the whole horizon glowed like copper run from a smelting furnace, and when it had quite disappeared, the little inequalities of the ragged edges of the mist were lighted up and shone like a row of volcanos in the far distance. I have never before or since seen anything, which for sublimity, beauty, and marvellous effects, could compare with what I gazed on that evening from Choonjerma pass.

Hooker had earlier noticed what he called 'the most lofty group of mountains in Nepal' lying 'a little to the north of west'. They were subtended at so small an angle that he could not measure them with a sextant, however he added, 'judging from the quantity of snow, [they] must be prodigious'.

Though the crossing is today generally referred to as the Mirgin la, there are actually three passes and a good deal of uncertainty over their respective names and heights. For what it's worth, the Nepa 1:100,000 map I used for a crossing in 2001 gives the northernmost pass as the Sinion la (4440m), the central pass as the Mirgin la (4480m) and the southernmost, and highest, as the Sinelapche la (4640m). However our Sherpas called this last one the Sinion la. According to Chandra Das, the name Choonjerma refers to none of these passes but to the terrace between the Mirgin la and the southernmost pass, and means 'collection of cascades'. For the trav-

142. Watercolour by Walter Hood Fitch, c1850, based on Hooker's observations from Choonjerma pass. (*Courtesy of Royal Botanic Gardens, Kew*)

eller, it is the sense of traversing a rough moorland balcony, crags to the east and wooded valleys and distant peaks to the west, which is strongest.

Hooker's impressions of the scene were captured in a watercolour (above) by Walter Hood Fitch, the botanical artist who illustrated Hooker's writings. Believed to have been painted in 1850, it captions the view as from the Choonjerma pass and the height as '16,000 ft', which seems a bit high, but gives no information on the distant peaks.

The watercolour appears to include Makalu and the Everest group, though it would be another two years (1852) before Radhanath Sikhdar, the Bengali chief computer, rushed into the office of the surveyor general of India and declared he had 'discovered the highest mountain in the world', and 15 years before the name 'Everest' was adopted by the Royal Geographical Society.

Hooker was director of Kew between 1865 and 1885, and it was there, at the end of 2010, that a documentary filmmaker, Peter Donaldson, unearthed Hooker's Choonjerma sketch and its significance was realised. Written above Makalu and the Everest group are the words 'very high snows WNW'. These are presumably the same peaks he writes of in his journal as being 'a little to the north of west'.

Whilst it is possible earlier illustrations or sketches may exist, attempts by Kew's illustration team to locate anything have been fruitless. Professor Stephen Hopper, Director of the Royal Botanic Gardens, said: 'We have a vast collection of illustrations here at Kew and curation is an ongoing job. It is always wonderful when we turn up a hidden gem of such historical importance. To our knowledge there are no other earlier representations of Everest by a European, in which case, this discovery could be one of the most important findings in Kew's archive.'

GEORGE RODWAY & JEREMY WINDSOR

Ama Dablam – 50 Years On

March 2011 saw the 50th anniversary of the first ascent of Ama Dablam. The ascent via the south-west ridge by Bishop, Gill, Romanes and Ward arguably marked the beginnings of technical alpinism in the Himalaya. However, in the years since, hundreds of mountaineers have reached the summit and the route is now regularly climbed by commercial expeditions using fixed ropes and the support of Sherpas. Ama Dablam's reputation today as a trade peak stands in stark contrast to the perception of those who first tried to climb it.

143. The 'Silver Hut' (at 5800 m) with Ama Dablam in the background. The south-west ridge route is roughly up the left-hand skyline. (*Courtesy of Jim Milledge*)

Until Michael Kennedy's excellent article on Ama Dablam in *Alpinist* no. 10,[1] it would have been all too easy to overlook the unique early history of this striking peak. Set in the heart of the Solu Khumbu region of Nepal, Ama Dablam first came to the attention of western mountaineers in the early 1950s as they essayed a route to the south flank of Everest. In his book *Summit: 150 Years of the Alpine Club*,[2] George Band recalls New Zealander George Lowe commenting during the 1953 Everest expedition, 'that peak [Ama Dablam] will never be climbed' (p.168). This was a reasonable prediction given what was to follow a few years later. The

144. Long telephoto from near Tengboche showing two ropes of two (Gill, Romanes, Ward and Bishop) on summit fluting of Ama Dablam, 13 March 1961. (*Courtesy of Mike Gil*

peak's first attempt in the October of 1958 was by a British-Italian team led by Alfred Gregory. The climbers found the difficulties of the SW ridge and the growing cold of autumn a severe challenge:

> *After extremely difficult climbing the attempt was abandoned at about 20,000 ft. [~6100 m] due to great technical difficulties of steep rock and ice. Following this a journey was made around the mountain and all ridges and possible routes examined. We found no feasible way of climbing the mountain; with the weather becoming increasingly cold, all idea of climbing this very difficult peak was given up.*[3]

Despite Gregory's verdict, just a few months later, in May 1959, another British-led attempt chose the mountain's north-east spur and north ridge as their objective. Close scrutiny of photographs showed that this possible route levelled out in the last part of the climb, and the last 300m or so of ascent appeared to be at a relatively easy angle.[4] The team made astonishing progress on a route significantly more difficult than the south-west ridge and very nearly succeeded in making the first ascent. However, tragedy struck when Michael Harris and George Fraser disappeared high above their 6400m camp as they neared the easier summit slopes. The north ridge would not be climbed in its entirety until 1979.

The first ascent of Ama Dablam in 1961 had unusual beginnings. Rather than travelling to Nepal with a mountain already in their sights, the first ascensionists arrived as members of the highly ambitious 1960/61 Himalayan Scientific and Mountaineering Expedition. Led by Sir Edmund Hillary, the expedition had several objectives. During the autumn months of 1960 Hillary accompanied a party in search of the yeti before eventually returning the following spring to make an attempt, *sans* supplemental oxygen, on Makalu (8463m). In the intervening months, leadership of the expedition passed to Griffith Pugh, a physiologist based at the Medical Research Council's laboratories in London. Pugh, with a small party of scientists, oversaw a set of human physiology experiments that would become the 'gold standard' for high altitude field studies.

The site of the laboratory could not have been more extraordinary. At 5800m on the Rakpa glacier, close to the head of the Mingbo valley and the south-west ridge of Ama Dablam, a small cylindrical prefabricated 'Silver Hut' just 6.7m long and 3m wide was erected. This structure had been designed and built in the UK from marine plywood containing 8cm of plastic foam insulation, and each section could be conveniently carried as a porter load.[5] Mike Gill, one of the participants and the only surviving member of the first ascent party, wrote to one of the authors recently:

We were in the unusual position of living and working ... in the Silver Hut at the head of the Mingbo which meant that we just took days off work when we could be spared – not the usual assault mode where climbers are either at base camp or above. You could say that the Silver Hut was our base camp!

Over the course of the long winter months, Pugh and his colleagues, with the aid of some of the most sophisticated research tools then available, painstakingly recorded the subtle changes that occurred to the body's organs at high altitude. Whilst the impact of altitude on the heart and lungs occupied the vast majority of their time and energies, it was the studies performed on a single research subject that provided Pugh with what some would argue were his most astonishing results.[6]

On a cold January evening, a 35-year-old Nepali called Man Bahadur arrived at the foot of the glacier and asked if he could stay to complete a religious pilgrimage to the mountains. He was dressed only in thin cotton clothes and a large turban. The group urged him to descend to the warmth and safety of the valley far below. Ignoring their advice, Man slept close to the Silver Hut for four nights, enduring temperatures as low as –15°C without the benefit of shoes, gloves or shelter of any kind. The expedition members were so impressed by this that they allowed him to stay and sensing that this was someone special, Pugh persuaded him to take part in a series of studies. For the first experiment, Man was crisscrossed with 11 temperature probes and sat on a canvas chair whilst his bare feet were rested on a sheepskin rug. At temperatures hovering around zero C the pilgrim sat patiently for three hours whilst Pugh looked on shivering in his thick down suit. The results were startling – the subject's core temperature remained unchanged and his average skin temperature fell by only

3°C. Jim Milledge, a scientist who stayed in the Silver Hut throughout the winter of 1960-61 recalled many years later:

It was amazing. It [the cold] didn't shut down his periphery, as it would for you or I. He kept his skin temperature just above freezing and he didn't have violent shivering. He just had a very slight shiver, like a dog shivers, and that seemed to be enough to keep his metabolic rate up and keep him warm.[7]

In the second experiment Pugh made a series of measurements with a sophisticated gas analyzer in order to measure the pilgrim's metabolic rate. The findings were most notable. Sitting almost motionless, Man was able to almost triple his metabolic rate and generate enormous amounts of heat in the process. Normally, such a feat would only be possible with a painful degree of shivering. Man had instead found a different way to keep warm, and to this day it is still not totally clear to scientists how this extraordinary physiological act was accomplished. Whilst Pugh and his team resumed their planned experiments, the mountaineers amongst them became increasingly distracted. After several months studying the mountain, a possible route was finally identified:

At first we had hoped there might be an unseen easy way around the back but in this we were disappointed. Then one day it dawned on us that the obvious route was directly up the front of the mountain, up the Mingbo (SW) Ridge and the fluted snow-face that we had been gazing at ever since we arrived in the Khumbu [virtually adjacent to the Silver Hut – see photo].[8]

Slowly, plans for a serious reconnaissance of the south-west ridge were hatched. On 18 February, a break in the research finally arrived and a close inspection was begun. The climbing team was composed of New Zealanders Mike Gill and Wally Romanes, American Barry Bishop, and Englishman Mike Ward. Jim Milledge, who had made the first ascent of nearby Puma Dablam (6340 m) a few weeks before, related later:

We all felt that the chances of success were small. However, over the next three weeks they worked their way slowly along the knife-edge ridge, over rock towers, to the snow and ice section. We were able to follow their progress by watching them through the telescope and by radio contacts. On March 13, all four reached the summit.[5]

Milledge's early pessimism was well founded. No sooner had Ward and his team established Camp 1 than a series of difficult obstacles were encountered. A 'gully with an overhang' and, 'a series of ragged and jagged turrets', needed to be overcome before the foot of the steep and intimidating Yellow Tower was eventually reached.[9] Here, faded nylon ropes marked the high point that John Cunningham had reached two and a half years before with Gregory's team. However, using a combination of aid and free tactics, the tower was quickly climbed and a series of ropes and wire ladders were fixed amongst the overhanging rock. Ward was impressed with the route, writing later:

Ama Dablam seemed to be a mountain of Alpine calibre; the route…providing climbing of every variety. By and large the difficulties had to be overcome rather than avoided, and there were sections of artificial rock and artificial ice climbing.[9]

Beyond the Second Step the route quickly changed. The rotten sections of steep rock that had characterised the lower part of the ridge were now replaced by a series of towers smothered in loose snow and a series of smooth icy walls. Nonetheless, after almost three weeks on the mountain, the four climbers finally gathered at the foot of the snowfield that masked the mountain's south face. Stretching for almost 500m, this was to prove the final obstacle. From the vantage point of their snow cave the team was able to trace out a series of flutings that offered a safe way to the summit. Fortunately, snow conditions were perfect and they took little more than six hours to reach the summit. The mountain had finally relented. In recognition of Mike Ward's leadership of this demanding climb – in many ways the vanguard for technical alpinism in the Himalaya (and a route not repeated until 1979) – Mike Gill wrote to the authors in August of 2010:

It really was Mike's climb. He saw the route, was the first to start climbing on it, and it was Mike who put the route up the first rock buttress which is the most technical part of the climb.

However, news of their success on the mountain was greeted with political outrage in Kathmandu. Nepal had recently instituted a peak permit/fee system and this ascent was made without 'official' government permission. Hillary had not been in Nepal during mid-winter, but when he returned late in the season to prepare for a spring attempt on Makalu, he was faced with an angry Nepalese government that was preparing to throw him and all of his expedition companions out of the country as an example to others. Hillary subsequently spent the next 10 days meeting with countless officials and government ministers in an attempt to limit the fallout. In the end his powers of diplomacy reigned supreme, and he escaped with a number of stern lectures and a fine equivalent to about US $60.[10]

Lest we forget the primary reason why these mountaineers/scientists spent numerous winter months in the Khumbu, Jim Milledge provides a summing-up some of the most valuable scientific observations from the work in and around the Silver Hut:

I suppose the overall statements that we could make about the limits of long-term [altitude] residence [were very important]… 5800m [the Silver Hut altitude] is certainly too high to acclimatise in the long term…now we say if you want to have super acclimatisation the thing is to go and live somewhere around

145. Mike Gill, Wally Romanes, Mike Ward, and Barry Bishop (L–R) on summit of Ama Dablam, March 13, 1961 (*Courtesy of Mike Gill*)

> *4000-4500m with frequent trips to higher altitude to boost acclimatisation – but spending most of the time below 5000m.*[7]

Milledge also suggested that the work done on the distinctive breathing differences between Sherpas and the scientists shed important light on human physiological variation in those native to low altitude vs. those native to high altitude.[7] The finding that the Sherpas have a much lower ventilatory (breathing) response to hypoxia led Milledge and a colleague to conduct an in-depth study of this (and other) phenomena in the Khumbu just a few years later.[11] These important physiological findings would be integral to shaping acclimatisation strategy and climbing tactics for high altitude mountaineering in the following decades.

The 1960-61 Himalayan Scientific and Mountaineering Expedition was unique. Not only did Griffith Pugh and his scientific colleagues complete some of the most important research ever undertaken at high altitude, but a few of the mountaineers in the group successfully climbed a difficult virgin peak in a bold and imaginative style. For scientists and mountaineers alike, this expedition most certainly set a high standard for all others to follow.

References

1. Kennedy M, Mountain profile: Ama Dablam, *Alpinist* magazine, 2005(10):22-41.
2. Band G, *Summit: 150 years of the Alpine Club*, Collins, 2006.
3. Gregory A, Ama Dablam, *American Alpine Journal*, 1959, 11:326.
4. Jones JHE, Ama Dablam, 1959, *Himalayan Journal*, 1959-60, 22:13-21.
5. Milledge JS, The Silver Hut Expedition, 1960-1961, *High Alt Med Biol*, 2010,11:93-101.
6. Pugh LGCE, Tolerance to extreme cold at altitude in a Nepalese pilgrim, *J Appl Physiol*, 1963,18:1234-8.
7. Rabbitts R, *Extreme medicine: A history of high altitude scientific research*, University of Birmingham 2008.
8. Gill M, *Mountain midsummer: Climbing in four continents*, Hodder and Stoughton, 1969.
9. Ward M. The uses of adversity, *The Mountain World* 1962/63, Rand McNally; 1964. p. 70-91.
10. Hillary EP, *View From The Summit*, Pocket Books, 2000.
11. Lahiri S and Milledge JS, Sherpa physiology, *Nature*, 1965, 207:610-2.

PETER GILLMAN

Mallory on The Ben

At Easter 1906, during his first year at Magdalene College, Cambridge, George Mallory went climbing on Ben Nevis. He had two companions: Graham Irving, the schoolmaster who introduced him to climbing at Winchester; and Guy Leach, another former Winchester pupil who was at New College, Oxford. The three men spent 10 days in Fort William, where they lodged at St Andrew's Choir School. They went on to the Ben five times, during which, apart from a distant sighting of a couple in Allt a' Mhuillin glen, they had the mountain to themselves. The Ben was in full winter condition and they climbed five routes, culminating in the second winter ascent of North-east Buttress, first climbed by Naismith and others 10 years before.

The Ben Nevis excursion is significant in the Mallory story, since it was his first full climbing trip in the British Isles. (He was aged 19 at the time; Leach was 20, Irving 29.) Yet it has, until now, escaped the notice of Mallory biographers, including this one. In *The Wildest Dream*, written with my wife Leni, we asserted that Mallory's first British climbing was undertaken in Snowdonia in September 1907, in the company of Geoffrey Keynes and Hugh Wilson. Mallory's five days on the Ben, which predate the Snowdonia trip by 17 months, have come to light thanks to the resurfacing of the Book of Minutes of the Winchester Ice Club. The club was formed by Irving at Winchester in 1904 and the minutes were used to record its visits to the Alps. The 1904 and 1905 accounts include written contributions by Mallory himself. Irving wrote the entire account of the 1906 Ben Nevis expedition, filling 57 pages of Volume Two (there are six volumes in all).

For a long time the whereabouts of the minutes was a mystery. They had been purchased from a dealer in 1967 by a US collector, Wilbur Smith, who had them rebound and planned to publish them. But the project foundered and Smith died in 1988. In 2009, a firm of solicitors found the bound volumes in their archives, and passed them to the Alpine Club Library.

Irving's record of the Ben Nevis trip thus fills a gap in the roster of Mallory's climbs. His account is revealing in other ways. Mallory's energy and enthusiasm shine through, speaking of the character that was to be demonstrated on Everest two decades on. There is also an ingenuous quality about Irving's description of their visit to 'the greatest of our British mountains' that is both appealing and surprising, for he appears unaware of the activities of Scottish Mountaineering Club members in the preceding decade.

The SMC was founded in 1889 and started publishing its journal in

146. Orion Face and Tower Ridge, Ben Nevis, showing routes where George Mallory, Graham Irving and Guy Leach were active in 1906. (*Andy Nisbet*)

1890. The 1902 edition comprised a Ben Nevis Guide, edited by William Inglis Clark. The decade from 1896 brought intense activity on the Ben, with climbers of the stature of Clark, Harold Raeburn, Willie Naismith and the Rev A E Robertson advancing snow-and-ice standards to new levels. Yet Irving appeared ignorant of any of this, or of the existing names of the Ben's features and routes. He overcame this lacuna by coining his own terms for both the features and climbs. Identifying their modern names required assiduous detective work, in which I was valuably assisted by Ken Crocket, SMC member and co-author of the definitive history *Ben Nevis: Britain's Highest Mountain* (Crocket & Richardson, SMT, 2009), who also provided details about the *Scottish Mountaineering Club Journal*; Robin Campbell of the SMC; the Fort William guide and guidebook writer Alan Kimber; and AC stalwart John Cleare. At the end of this process we were confident that we had cracked Irving's code.

As Irving records, he and Leach arrived at Fort William railway station on the morning of Tuesday 3 April, 'well sated by an ample breakfast of ham and eggs' served on the train. They were met by their host, Mr Thompson, schoolmaster and organist at the Choir School in Fassifern Road. Mallory – 'in his eccentricity' – journeyed by sea from his family home in Birkenhead to Clydeside, arriving by train that evening. 'The expectations of those who met him were doomed to disappointment, as he had enjoyed the smoothest of passages and his health was in no way impaired,' Irving wrote. Once at the Choir School they met Mrs Thompson who 'amply performed all the duties of landlady and attendant, with the assistance of several daughters and a small Aberdeen terrier. The cooking was quite adequate and the rooms most comfortable.'

During their 10 days at Fort William, the three climbers were blessed with good weather. The sky was mostly sunny, fresh snow fell just once, and the approach to the Ben was 'comparatively dry'. In his preamble to the climbing accounts, Irving describes the northern aspect of the Ben. 'Here is a long precipitous face, extending perhaps for a mile and a half and averaging about 1500 feet in height: from it vast buttresses of rock stand out and afford unbounded scope to the climber for satisfying his ravenous appetite.'

Irving identifies two features by their current names: the North-east Ridge, 'the most huge of all the projecting buttresses'; and Tower Ridge, rising in the centre of the face. Both were named on the six-inch OS edition published in 1902 which has to be the map Irving refers to in his account. However Irving was clearly not equipped with the 1902 *SMCJ* Ben Nevis guide, which included the OS map marked with an additional 25 features and routes. He thus coined names for two features, the 'Zmutt Ridge' and the 'Intermediate Ridge', whose identities were the subject of some of our detective work. Irving noted that the snowline began around 2,000 feet and that the snow was up to 30 feet deep around the summit. 'Every gully or corner was filled with snow and the rocks of the Tower and N E Ridges were thickly plastered over with a coating of ice.'

The three went on to the Ben for the first time on 4 April. They set out at 9.45am to attempt Tower Ridge, first climbed in winter conditions by Norman Collie and two companions in 1894 and graded until recently at III. At 12.45 they reached the foot of a 'vast snowfield' at 2800 feet, as measured on their aneroid barometer. After stopping 35 minutes for lunch they resumed climbing, roping up at 'the foot of a snow couloir which run upwards in a S E direction'. They cut steps to a notch at 3400 feet above the first prominent peak in the ridge. They followed the crest of the ridge until they reached 'the foot of a steep mass of rock which appeared to be the Tower: as this was completely wrapt in a thick coating of ice, further advance that way was soon seen to be hopeless.'

This was almost certainly the pillar known as the Little Tower. They attempted a detour but finished on a secondary ridge that led them back to the Tower. 'All attempts to discover a route by which this ice-covered mass could be turned were fruitless: not an inch of rock was visible.' At 5pm they headed down, Mallory clearing out the steps they had cut as he led the descent, secured by Irving on an ice-axe belay. It took them two hours to reach the notch and a further hour to descend to the glen. They returned to the choir school at 10.30 to be greeted by an 'anxious landlady at the gate – no search party however had yet been organised.'

The three had an 'off day' on 5 April which they spent rowing across Loch Linnhe 'through tremendous waves' to Loch Eil, returning to Fort William in time for tea. They were back on the Ben on 6 April, this time following a line to the left of the Tower. 'The snow was good and not too steep for good nails: so progress was fairly rapid. When some fresh snow

147. George Mallory (1886-1924): a youthful outing on Ben Nevis helped shape Mallory's taste for adventure.
(*Alpine Club Photo Library*)

was reached, often with very hard stuff below it, G.H.L.M took up the running and with his usual energy kicked some ample steps.'

Although they did not know its name, it is most likely that they were in Observatory Gully, and after an hour they reached the juncture where it divides between Tower Gully and Gardyloo Gully. Both were marked on the 1902 *SMCJ* map and both had their first winter ascents in 1897 – achieved, what's more, by three Alpine Club members, led by none other than Walter Haskett Smith. Once again, Irving was clearly unaware of any of this. He considered the left-hand gully (Gardyloo Gully, Grade II) 'very steep and almost impossible' and so they followed the right-hand gully (Tower Gully, Grade I).

After they roped up, Irving took the lead, cutting steps across 'a very steep slope which lay above a small rock face' that reminded him of the Ice Wall on the Grand Combin. He eventually reached the heavily-corniced crest of the ridge, making a steep traverse until he could haul himself on to the summit plateau. He brought up Mallory and Leach and they reached the summit at 3.20. 'In such perfect weather the view was wonderful and, as this was the first ascent, the party was deeply impressed.' They descended via the path to the north-west, undertaking several long glissades, and reached their lodging at 5.50.

On 7 April, preferring 'a gentle day's climbing elsewhere', they climbed the neighbouring peak of Stob Bàn (3274ft). They followed the corniced main arête to the summit which they reached at 1.30pm. They had intended to return via Mullach nan Coirean (3077ft) but lost their way in cloud. Abandoning their plan, they glissaded back to Glen Nevis, marvelling at 'that wonderful dark purple hue in which the hills at the top of the Glen were dressed in the late afternoon'.

On Sunday 8 April, after attending 'divine service', they took a rowing boat on to Loch Linnhe and into the Caledonian Canal. They returned to the Ben on 9 April, where – 'with a long day in view' – they hired a wagonette to cover the first two and a half miles along the road. They first climbed Carn Mor Dearg (4002ft) then glissaded back to the glen where they decided to attempt 'one of the ridges W of the Tower' which they dubbed the 'Intermediate' Ridge. This was almost certainly North Trident Buttress, first climbed by Harold Raeburn and three others in 1904 and now rated Grade III.

What is curious about Irving's description is that he did not report the same level of difficulty the party met on the two other Grade III routes they climbed – perhaps because snow conditions had ironed out some of the problems. The party roped up at 2pm with Irving taking the lead. The toughest pitch proved to be 'an uncomfortably steep and narrow rock-chimney choked by a jammed stone at the top.'

Halfway up the pitch Irving removed his rucksack and dropped it, assuming that Mallory would catch it. Mallory assumed in turn that it was attached to Irving's rope and it fell past him. The rucksack, which contained a large plate camera, sweater, cake and honey, 'sped down the snow and bounding nimbly from rock to rock vanished into the distant unknown.' Irving eventually levered himself past the chockstone, and the party reached the plateau at 6.25. After a brew of cocoa they pressed on to the summit in time to witness a transcendental sunset.

On 10 April they opted for an easy day, selecting a feature they called the East Zmutt Ridge, one of a pair of ridges that they named after the Zmutt Ridge on the Matterhorn. They most likely climbed *Ledge Route* on Number Five Gully Buttress, first ascended in 1895 and rated Grade II. From Irving's account it was the easiest route they climbed. They also retrieved Irving's rucksack, discovering to their amazement that the camera was almost undamaged – although there was 'general sorrow' at the loss of the honey and cake.

They took another rest day on 11 April, again venturing on to Loch Linnhe. This time they headed with the tide towards the sea, enjoying a copious lunch, and then returning with the tide in the afternoon, 'with a brief halt for tea on the W shore'.

12 April brought their final climb and their toughest objective. This was North-east Buttress, first climbed in winter conditions by William Naismith and four others at Easter 1896. It was recorded in the *SMCJ* that year, and is now rated Grade IV. In 1906, that remained its only winter ascent. Irving wrote that the North-east Arête of Ben Nevis, 'which had hitherto defied all [our] ideas of climbing by its forbidding aspect, was at last put to the test. The task thus imposed upon the Club was of the severest possible nature.'

They left their lodgings at 8.30 and started up the route at midday, leaving their stove at its foot and taking 'one piece of cake and one sandwich per head'. They roped up with Irving in the lead and reached the crest of the arête at 3.30pm. From there they made arduous progress, rendered more testing when Irving dropped his ice-axe while clearing a rocky projection of ice.

As Ben Nevis habitués will know, the two crucial pitches – the vertical

148. The six volumes of the Book of Minutes of The [Winchester] Ice Club, now held in th Alpine Club Library, which include a hitherto forgotten account of what is believed tc be George Mallory's first full climbing trip in the British Isles. (*Peter Gillman*)

wall known as the Mantrap, and a 40-foot corner – occur near the near the top of the route. Irving was most likely describing the Mantrap when he wrote how 'what seemed an impassable wall loomed in front and threatened to bar progress completely.' Irving overcame it via a steep couloir that led to a 'still steeper broad ice-chimney which became quite vertical at the top' – probably, the 40-foot corner. Irving wrote: 'Again and again it seemed that the leader must be baffled despite his vigorous efforts' but after a 75-minute struggle he reached the top.

Progress from that point was less demanding and they were at the summit at 8.25 as the last light faded. Their ascent of the route had taken eight hours, compared to the seven required by Naismith and his party. They were back at Fort William at 10.30, where Mrs Thompson served 'a hearty supper', consumed 'with that intense feeling of satisfaction which is the constant companion of success'.

On 13 April the weather broke, bringing rain in Fort William and snow on the tops. Even so, Mallory returned to the Ben to search for the stove and the lost ice-axe. He found the former but not the latter, returning from his round trip in just under four hours.

'The whole party,' Irving concludes, 'left Fort William by the afternoon train, hoping to arrive at their respective destinations early on the following morning, but owing to the vagaries of the Good Friday train service, and the stupidity of the Glasgow porters, they were compelled to spend the night in Edinburgh; and it is perhaps not unworthy of record that the Castle Temperance Hotel, Prince's Street, displayed an admirable combination of cheapness and comfort. Thus ended the first visit of the Ice Club to Ben Nevis.'

So also ended George Mallory's first British climbing expedition. Although Irving mostly took the lead, it was an episode in which Mallory's determination and taste for adventure were being shaped. There was a pioneering element to the enterprise which Mallory must have savoured, together with a collective tenacity and reluctance to be thwarted. As for Mallory's character, there was a further revealing moment on the first day, when the three men missed the bridge across the River Nevis. While Irving and Leach retraced their steps for half a mile, Mallory, 'with his usual agility effected a crossing by large boulders'. Irving's minutes also evoke nostalgia for an innovative period of mountaineering. Those who inspect them in the AC library are likely to savour the spirit of the age they describe, together with the glimpses of Mallory provided by his mentor, Graham Irving.

With the party's routes identified, one puzzle remains: why was Irving unaware of the previous activity on the Ben? He was a member of the Alpine Club and so, I had presumed, would have had access to the SMC journals at the AC library. However, scrutiny of the *Alpine Journals* of the time reveals that this was apparently not so. The *AJ* lists those clubs that donated copies of their journals and while they included the Alpine clubs of France and Italy, and even of Russia and Holland, the SMC was not among them. Nor, with one brief exception in 1895, did the *AJ* record any climbing by its members on Ben Nevis. Nonetheless, it still appears remiss of Irving to have done no further research – unless he preferred to remain ignorant and thus have the thrill of climbing as if on virgin ground.

Mallory continued to climb with Irving, notably in 1911, when they spent two weeks in the Alps, together with Harry Tyndale, another Ice Club alumnus who was married to Irving's sister Oriane. After Mallory's death in 1924, Irving wrote of him as 'an ever-young and singularly lovable personality'. Irving continued at Winchester until his retirement in 1937. A prominent AC member and a prolific writer, he died in 1969.

As for Guy Leach, the least experienced climber of the three on the Ben, he became a schoolmaster – as did Mallory – after leaving Oxford. And like Mallory, he served in the First World War, in Egypt and France, rising to the rank of Captain and winning the Military Cross. He died in Hampshire in 1957, aged 72.

* *For the full story of how the Ice Club minutes were retrieved, I am indebted to AC archivist Glyn Hughes. The minutes appeared in the catalogue of H M Fletcher, a book dealer in Cecil Court, in 1967. Wilbur Smith, the American collector who bought them, was a banker and mountaineer then working in Beirut. He had the minutes rebound and, some 20 years later, proposed publishing them in a facsimile edition. He signed a contract with a London publisher; Irving's son Robert, music director of the New York City Ballet, provided an appreciation of his father; and Roger Chorley, AC president, wrote a foreword. The plan was to print 500 copies and to start printing once there were 300 orders. They went as far as producing a flyer, intending to distribute several thousand copies in the UK and USA.*

At that point the plan disintegrated. Smith had a row with the publishers, complaining that they had failed to distribute the flyers. As the proposed publication date approached, only 24 firm orders had been placed, and the project was abandoned. Smith died a year or so later, in 1988. The minutes finally reached the Alpine Club after a firm of London solicitors found them while clearing out their archives. The solicitors called the ACL in July 2009 and their offer of the minutes was accepted with gratitude.

C A RUSSELL

One Hundred Years Ago

(with extracts from *The Alpine Journal*)

> Unkind things have been said about this winter, but the ski-runners will long remember it with affection; for the first time for several years they have not had to bewail an insufficiency of snow.

With favourable snow conditions skiers were out in force at the principal Alpine resorts during the early months of 1910. Experienced ski mountaineers and winter climbers were active in the high mountains where many notable expeditions were completed including, on 21 January, the first ski ascent[1] of the Gross Wannenhorn by Karl Steiner and P Trümpler. On 25 March Alfred von Martin and Hermann Rumpelt made the first winter ascent of the Weissmies and four days later, accompanied by the guide Oscar Supersaxo, the first winter and ski ascent of the Alphubel. Other high peaks were climbed for the first time in winter: the Aiguille d'Argentière on 9 January by M Cottier with Maurice Crettex; the Aiguille des Grands Charmoz by C Sauvage with Joseph Ravanel[2] on 11 January; and the Dent d'Hérens on 16 January by Mario Piacenza with Jean Baptiste Pélissier and G Carrel.

The cold and wet conditions experienced in many Alpine regions during April and May continued without respite throughout the summer months.

> The climbing season of 1910 will long be remembered as one of the worst and most unsatisfactory ever known, both for persistent unsettled weather and for the troublesome condition of rocks and snow.

Although many parties were confined to the lower peaks several expeditions of note were completed during brief spells of fine weather. In the Mont Blanc range on 29 July Marcel Kurz and Steiner made the first ascent of the steep north face of the Aiguille de l'A Neuve, above the Saleina glacier. On 19 August H O Jones with Henri Brocherel and a porter made the first complete traverse of the Rocher du Mont Blanc, the long rock ridge between the Mont Blanc and Dôme glaciers and above the Quintino Sella hut.

In the Pennine Alps on 18 August Geoffrey Winthrop Young and Marcus Heywood with Josef Knubel made the first complete ascent of the west-north-west face of the Dent d'Hérens. On the next day an interesting variation of a famous route on the Matterhorn was followed by Maud Meyer with Christian Jossi junior and Dévouassoud Gaspard who left the hut on the south-west, Italian ridge to continue the ascent to the summit. Finding

9. Hoher Göll, west face. (*S M Russell*)

that the upper section of the ridge was out of condition they traversed the west face some distance below the *Galerie Carrel* to complete the ascent by the north-west, Zmutt Ridge which was reached at a point 'more than an hour from the top.'

In the Bernese Alps on 8 July a traverse across the upper slopes of the Fiescher glacier to the Bergli hut by a large party led by the great guide Alexander Burgener ended in tragedy. Starting from the Eismeer station of the Jungfraujoch railway[3] with the intention of ascending the Jungfrau on the following day, they had reached the rocks below the hut when a massive avalanche swept Burgener and five other members of the party to their deaths. Christian Bohren senior, the guardian of the Konkordia hut, who happened to be at the Bergli and had descended to meet the party also lost his life.

In the Bregaglia district on 8 August Harold Raeburn and W N Ling established a new route on Monte Disgrazia, climbing the rib now known as the *Spigolo Inglese* at the west edge of the north face to reach the north-west ridge.

In the Eastern Alps several outstanding new routes were completed. In the Dolomites on 18 July the summit of Cima Una – the Einserkofel – was reached by Guido and Max Mayer with Angelo Dibona and Luigi Rizzi who forced a direct line up the north face. On 29 July Josef Klammer, Richard Kroher and Max Zeller made the first ascent of the imposing west face of the Hoher Göll above Berchtesgaden.In the Julian Alps on 22

August H Tuma with Jože Komac opened the *Slovene Route*, an early climb on the north wall of Triglav.

During the year many parties were active in other mountain ranges. In Norway on 30 July Carl Rubenson, Ferdinand Schjelderup and Alf Bryn made the first ascent of Stedtind (1381m), the famous rock pyramid in the Tysfjord district. In the Caucasus Walter Fischer, Viktor von Friedrichs, Gustav Kuhfahl and Oscar Schuster travelled to the Kasbek region where they engaged a local hunter named Inaltico Kalagoff and completed a number of climbs including, on 28 July, the first ascent of Suatisi Khokh (4470m). On 8 August Fischer and Schuster scaled Kaltber (4408m) by way of the Kaltber glacier and the east ridge. Other visitors to the range included Oscar Hug and Casimir de Rham who on 2 September climbed Nakra Tau (4277m) and traversed the three summits of Dongusorun (4452m).

In the Punjab Himalaya in September Dr Arthur Neve, the Rev Marcus Wigram and a local man named Ahmdhu reached the summit[4] of Peak D41 (5945m), one of the peaks on the west ridge of Nun (7135m). In Garhwal C F Meade accompanied by the guides Pierre Blanc and Alexis Brocherel explored the western approaches to Kamet (7756m), reaching the saddle at the head of the Khaiam glacier before being forced to retreat.

In the Southern Alps of New Zealand on 7 January the Australian climber Freda Du Faur and L M Earle with Peter Graham made the first complete ascent of the long west ridge of Mount Malte Brun (3176m). A few days earlier Earle and Bernard Head with Jack Clarke and Alex Graham had continued their successful expeditions[5] by making the second ascent[6] of Mount Sefton (3159m), reaching the summit by way of the Copland Valley and the west ridge.

In the Canadian Rockies Tom Longstaff and his sister Katharine attended the annual camp of the Alpine Club of Canada, held on this occasion in Consolation Valley near Moraine Lake to the south of the Canadian Pacific Railway. On 4 July with the guide Rudolf Aemmer, Longstaff completed a notable new route by making the first ascent of the north-west face of Mount Assiniboine (3618m). Another visitor to this region was J E C Eaton who on 28 July with Bruce Otto and the guide Heinrich Burgener made the first ascent of Mount Pilkington (3285m) in the Freshfield group, one of the high peaks near the Continental Divide.

Further north on 3 April William Taylor and Pete Andersen, members of a party[7] from Fairbanks, reached the north, lower summit (5935m) of Mount McKinley or Denali (6194m) where they hoisted a flag on a large flagpole[8] – a remarkable exploit for the period.

At home leading climbers of the day were active in all the principal regions. In Wales J M Archer Thomson established two new routes of note: *Chasm Route* on Glyder Fach with H O Jones and L Noon at Easter; and, in September, with Jones and K J P Orton *The Gambit Climb* on Clogwyn y Ddisgl, one of the cliffs above the Llanberis Pass. In Scotland on 18 September Harold Raeburn, accompanied on this occasion by S M Cumming, F Greig and D H Menzies, returned to Buachaille Etive Mor to make the first ascent of *Crowberry Gully* under summer conditions.[9]

A welcome event was the publication of *Climbing in the Ogwen District* by Archer Thomson, the second of a series of guides issued by the Climbers' Club. The guide was an immediate success and received a favourable review in the *Alpine Journal.*

> Each climb is described in sufficient detail to enable any one visiting the mountain for the first time to find it, gauge its difficulties, and see how they are to be overcome, and identification is further assisted by photographs and diagrams.

Other books published during the year included *Twenty Years in the Himalaya* by C G Bruce and *The Call of the Snowy Hispar* by Dr William Hunter Workman and his wife Fanny Bullock Workman.

At the end of the year a notable expedition was undertaken by Marcel Kurz and Rudolf Staub who completed the first recorded ski circuit of Piz Bernina. Starting from the Bernina Hospice on 29 December they crossed the Palü, Fellaria, Scerscen, Sella and Roseg glaciers and descended Val Roseg in darkness to reach Pontresina the same evening.

* * *

In the following weeks further expeditions of note were undertaken with the aid of ski. On 14 January 1911 Kurz and Professor F F Roget accompanied by Maurice and Jules Crettex, Louis Theytaz and Léonce Murisier completed a section of the high-level route – the Haute Route – reaching Zermatt from Bourg St Pierre. Staying at the Valsorey, Chanrion and Bertol huts the party crossed a number of passes including the Col du Sonadon and on 13 January made the first winter ascent of the Dent Blanche.[10] On 8 January Staub, Karl Steiner and Guido Miescher completed the first ski ascent of the Gran Zebru - the Königspitze - in the course of a circuit of the Ortler group. Other peaks climbed for the first time in winter included the Tour Noir, ascended by Jean de Rufz with Joseph and Camille Ravanel on 24 January and Mont Dolent, scaled on 12 March by G Couchepin, O Dehms, J Sautier and R Schanze with Maurice Crettex. On 31 January C F Meade accompanied by Josef Pollinger and Josef Lochmatter reached the summit of the Matterhorn, encountering a violent southerly gale and intense cold during the descent.

The rain and low temperatures experienced during the spring and early summer were followed by an 'extraordinary spell of unbroken fine weather' which continued for much of the climbing season. Many parties were able to take advantage of the favourable conditions and successful expeditions were undertaken in all the principal regions. In the Mont Blanc range H O Jones and Geoffrey Winthrop Young with Josef Knubel completed an outstanding series of climbs. On 9 August they joined forces with Karl Blodig[11] to open a classic route on Mont Blanc by ascending Picco Luigi Amedeo and the south-west, Brouillard ridge from the Col Emile Rey.[12]

150. Lötschberg Tunnel, 31 March 1911. Chief engineers Rothpletz (*wearing cap*) and Moreau meet after the breakthrough. (*Gesellschaft für Ingenieurbaukunst, Zürich*)

Two days later Jones and Young with Knubel and Laurent Croux made the first descent of the north-east, Hirondelles Ridge of the Grandes Jorasses – a ridge which at that time was still unclimbed. On 14 August, after a brief rest in Courmayeur, Jones, Young and Knubel reclimbed the peak from the Col des Grandes Jorasses to make the first complete ascent of the west ridge.

A few days later, on 19 August, the same party with the addition of Ralph Todhunter and the guide Henri Brocherel made the first ascent of another classic route – the east, Mer de Glace face of the Aiguille du Grépon. Young wrote later[13] that for him this day formed 'the close of the most perfect season of our alpine lives'.

Other notable new climbs in the Mont Blanc range included the first ascent of the long north-west, Tricot ridge of the Aiguille de Bionnassay by the mixed party of Eleonore Hasenclever, Helene Wirthl, Max Helff, Günter von Saar and Richard Weitzenböck on 27 July and, in August, the first complete ascent of the south-south-west, Cosmiques ridge of the Aiguille du Midi by the brothers George and Max Finch.

As the magnificent weather continued classic routes were established in other Alpine regions. In the Pennine Alps on 7 July Dietrich von Bethmann-Hollweg with Oscar and Othmar Supersaxo made the first ascent of the steep north-north-east face of the Lenzspitze, following a line up the east side of the face. Later in the season, on 9 September, Mario Piacenza with Jean Joseph Carrel and Joseph Gaspard completed the first ascent of the south-east, Furggen ridge of the Matterhorn, forcing an indirect route round the difficult upper step. In the Bernese Alps on 30 July Albert Weber with Hans Schlunegger senior reached the summit of the Jungfrau from the Jungfraujoch after making the first ascent of the north-east ridge.

In the Eastern Alps on 11 August Richard Gerin and Otto Pitschmann opened a new route on the Grossglockner by climbing the north-east ridge, between the Pallavicini couloir and the north face. In the Dolomites notable new routes included the east face of the Campanile Basso – the Guglia di Brenta – by Paul Preuss, solo, on 28 July and the exposed south-west edge of the Torre Delago, one of the Vajolet Towers, on 9 August by Irma Glaser with Tita Piaz and F Jori.

Elsewhere in the Alps further progress in connection with a major engineering project was reported on 31 March.

> The Lötschberg Tunnel was pierced early this morning. The two boring parties met at 3.50am ...
>
> On January 14 the two parties of workmen, one boring from Kandersteg on the north, the other from Goppenstein on the south, first heard the detonations of explosives through the thousand odd yards of mountain dividing them, but progress was slow owing to the hardness of the rock. Blasting was continued on both sides to the last, communication between the two galleries being kept up by telephone overland.

In July Walter Fischer and Oscar Schuster returned to the Kasbek region in the Caucasus, accompanied on this occasion by the artist Ernst Platz. Assisted by a local man named Michael Gabulow they undertook a number of expeditions including the first ascent of Tsmiakom Khokh (4177m), climbed by Fischer and Schuster on 3 August.

Early in June Dr and Mrs Workman left Srinagar to commence the seventh of their mountain journeys. Accompanied by Count Cesare Calciati as topographer, an assistant named Dante Ferrari, the guide Cyprien Savoye and three porters[14] from Courmayeur, the Workmans spent several weeks exploring the Kondus and other glaciers to the south and east of the Masherbrum and Chogolisa groups. In the middle of August the party crossed to the Siachen glacier where they carried out further exploration and ascended a peak of some 6400m from which 'a very extended view over the Siachen and its tributaries was obtained.'

To the east Dr Alexander Kellas accompanied by local men spent three months in Sikkim where he continued his extensive exploration and made the first ascent of several high peaks including Sentinel Peak (6470m) on 21 May, Pauhunri (7125m) on 16 June and Chomiomo (6835m) on 12 July. He also reached a point less than 50m below the Nepal Gap (6300m) on the north ridge of Kangchenjunga (8586m) before being forced to retreat. Kellas then travelled to Garhwal where he examined the approaches to Kamet (7756m), climbing a peak of some 6150m near the Khaiam saddle on 22 August before leaving for home.

151. Author-Explorer-Mountaineer
Edward Whymper's grave at Chamonix. (*J M Russell*)

During the summer Dr Ernest Neve continued his exploration of the Kolahoi group in Kashmir. On 21 June he made the first ascent of the south peak (5110m) accompanied by Kenneth Mason, an army officer seconded to the Survey of India, and two Gurkhas.

Later in the year Theodor Herzog, a German botanist, and the Swiss climber Carl Seelig spent several weeks exploring the Cordillera Quimsa Cruz in Bolivia. During their travels they undertook a number of climbs, making the first recorded ascent of Inmaculado (5312m) and reaching a point some 15m below the summit of Jachacunocollo (5820m), the highest peak in the range.

In Britain, where the coronation of King George V took place on 22 June, climbing continued apace and many new routes were recorded. In Wales during August Guy Barlow and E W Steeple accompanied by H E Bowron, A H Doughty and A G Woodhead completed *Grooved Arête*, a popular route on the east face of Tryfan. On the Isle of Skye a classic expedition was established on 10 June when A C McLaren and Leslie Shadbolt made the first traverse of the main Cuillin Ridge from Glen Brittle to Sligachan.

On 16 September at Chamonix the death occurred of Edward Whymper whose name will always be associated with the early climbing history and first ascent of the Matterhorn. Although in later life Whymper presented a formidable and austere figure he is also remembered for many acts of kindness and, as Sir Arnold Lunn observed,[15] 'it is impossible to deny him the unmistakable imprint of greatness.'

This account, the last in the present series, is concluded with the extract from Whymper's famous book *Scrambles Amongst the Alps* which was quoted in the first account in the series. Now, as then, for the mountaineer the following lines from *Scrambles* require no alteration.

> If I could blot out every reminiscence, or erase every memory, still I should say that my scrambles amongst the Alps have repaid me, for they have given me two of the best things a man can possess - health and friends.
>
> The recollections of past pleasures cannot be effaced. Even now as I write they crowd up before me. First comes an endless series of pictures, magnificent in form, effect, and colour. I see the great peaks, with clouded tops, seeming to mount up for ever and ever; I hear the music of the distant herds, the peasant's *jodel*, and the solemn church-bells; and I scent the fragrant breath of the pines: and after these have passed away, another train of thoughts succeeds – of those who have been upright, brave, and true; of kind hearts and bold deeds; and of courtesies received at stranger hands, trifles in themselves, but expressive of that good will towards men which is the essence of charity.

References

1. A ski ascent is defined by Sir Arnold Lunn as 'an expedition on which ski were used until the foot of the final rock or ice ridges'.
2. The famous guide Ravanel, *le Rouge*.
3. At that time the upper section of the railway to the Jungfraujoch was still under construction.
4. The small cairn on the summit found by Neve and his companions had been built by members of Dr and Mrs Workman's party to mark the first ascent of the peak on 14 August 1906.
5. Earle had established a new route on Mount Cook (3764m) - see *AJ 114*, 240, 2009 - and Head, accompanied by Clarke and Alex Graham, had made the first ascent of Mount Aspiring (3036m) in the Haast range on 23 November 1909.
6. The first ascent had been completed by E A FitzGerald with Mattias Zurbriggen on 14 February 1895.
7. The other members were Thomas Lloyd and Charles McGonagell.
8. The flagpole was a seasoned spruce sapling 'full 14ft long'.
9. Raeburn had completed the route under winter conditions on two previous occasions; see *AJ 114*, 241-242, 2009.
10. The peak had been climbed by O G Jones with Antoine Bovier, Pierre Gaspoz and a porter on 25 April 1893; see *AJ 98*, 223, 1993.
11. On reaching the summit of Picco Luigi Amedeo Blodig realised his ambition to become the first climber to ascend all the summits in the Alps of 4000m or over recognised at that time, narrowly beating the engineer Hans Pfann, who achieved the feat on the same peak two days later, and Dr Ernst Pühn who climbed the peak on 18 August.
12. The brothers G B and G F Gugliermina and Joseph Brocherel, who on 20 July 1901 completed the first ascent of the Brouillard ridge, had reached the summit of Picco Luigi Amedeo from the Mont Blanc glacier by way of the north-west face.
13. Geoffrey Winthrop Young, *On High Hills*. London, Methuen & Co Ltd, 1927.
14. The porters were Siméon Quaizier, Cesar Chenoz and Emile Gléry.
15. Arnold Lunn, *A Century of Mountaineering*. London, George Allen & Unwin Ltd, 1957.

Arts

2. John Innerdale, *Chomolhari and ruined Dzong from base camp*, watercolour, taken from John's Bhutan journal, 1997

JOHN INNERDALE

The Hidden Kingdom

A Painter's Story

We leave Kathmandu at midday and fly due east to Bhutan. At once we are amid spectacular snowy peaks and the moustachioed pilot of our Druk Air plane of the King's flight keeps us informed and entertained. Paro, he says, is the toughest airstrip to negotiate in the world and as he speaks I am kneeling at the feet of two Bhutanese monks in an attempt to take photographs through their window; what must they be thinking?

Diana and I are sitting close to George and Susan Band. It is the 1991 Alpine Club expedition to Bhutan comprising nine mountaineers and nine trekkers (among whom 10 are AC members) hoping to attempt a group of unclimbed peaks in the remote Basingthang region of the eastern Himalaya.

As we fly past Mount Everest, George begins an unforgettable commentary. Using binoculars he points out historical routes, identifies and remembers details of the 1953 expedition. We can see the South Col clearly and could that be the Hillary Step? Probably not. As we pass I notice the wispy afternoon clouds beginning to glow around the summit.

Later we pass close to Kangchenjunga. I sit captivated as George points out the route he took, tells the story of the final crack close to the summit with Joe Brown, reminds us of the momentous day when he and Joe looked across to Makalu, Lhotse and Everest, resisting the temptation to venture on to the summit of the 'Untrodden Peak'.

We begin the descent in a series of steeply banked turns, between ever-closer mountainsides, finally gliding gently into the Parucho valley, winding sinuously and shimmering in the afternoon light. The airport is tiny, hand-painted in bright primary colours, with a picket fence. A single room barely copes with our party, but everyone is calm, peaceful, smiling.

I manage a quick sketch; as unofficial expedition artist it is the first of numerous attempts to capture the place, the people and the landscape of the Kingdom of the Thunder Dragon.

Weight limitations restrict my palette to eight watercolours and six water-based chromacolours. Capturing the essential characteristic of mountains has long posed me problems. Usually seen from some distance in a constantly changing light they have to be illustrated on a small canvas or watercolour pad. The translucency of the pigment, speed of drying and the way the paper captures the ambient light of the landscape makes watercolour the most satisfactory medium.

The aim of the expedition is to combine nine trekkers and nine mountaineers together in a walk-in with an extended trek for the non-mountaineers during the climbing phase of the expedition, together with some cultural sight-seeing at the beginning and end. The trekkers split off at Lingshi and continue along the strenuous but spectacular Laya-Gaza to Punakha and Thimpu, arriving the same day as the mountaineers.

The trek begins in the Paro valley - an enchanting place. It's bucolic nature enhanced by the transparency of the air and the silence. The houses here are considered to be the most beautiful in the country, mostly three stories high, gaily decorated in rich vibrant colours, shingled roofs covered with chillies drying in the sun.

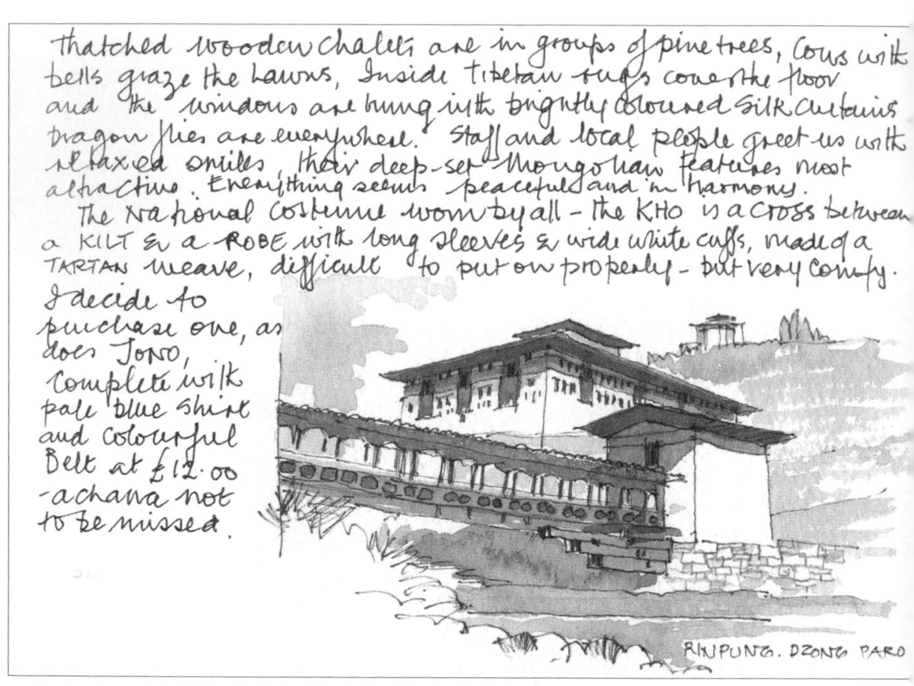

153. From John Innerdale's Bhutan journal (1991), showing Rin Pung Dzong with cantilever bridge in foreground.

Along the way children are emerging from school, wearing uniform in the style of the national dress, which by law everyone must wear. Men wear a *gho* and women a *kira*, which look like a cross between a kilt and a dressing gown. It becomes clear that the rich deep colours woven into national dress are used in the general decoration of buildings. These are pure, warm, peaceful colours, easy to paint.

We cross a giant cantilever bridge, emerging into a valley with walled-in paddy fields. Here and there vast farmhouses stand handsomely on the hillside. They are elaborately carved and painted, fret-work panels enclose ventilated roof spaces supported by finely dressed, tight stonework. We pass fields of millet, alpine flowers, English garden flowers and abundant marijuana. Swallow Tailed and Bhutanese Blue butterflies surround us as we walk.

I am aware we have come to a very special place. The thin atmosphere enhances the landscape, intensifying the colours, emphasising the effect that 'purple, violet and ultramarine blue has on everything we see'. *Ruskin*

We stop at the Rin Pung Dzong, a fortress built in 1646, the outer walls of which are trapezoidal masonry, six storeys high. This is Himalayan architecture of a cyclopedian style and scale. We speak in hushed tones as monks in crimson robes surround us praising Buddha with their chanting. A gong is sounded, an old monk emerges with a whip and boy monks

4. John Innerdale, *Rin Pung Dzong, Bhutan*, watercolour 31 x 23 cm, 2007.

scamper quickly away. I make a sketch of the courtyard with deep purple shadows, blood red decorations set against cobalt violet sky. Monks form a chattering, happy queue as they enter a chapel.

We continue along the valley rising through resin-fragrant woodland, passing numerous white-washed chortens. These represent Buddha's mind and are consecrated. At last we cross a meadow and climb through a forest of oak and rhododendron to a plateau festooned with white fluttering prayer flags.

We look across a deep valley to the black cliff face upon which the Taktsang Lhakhang clings, overhanging the valley 800 metres below. This breathtakingly beautiful view is an unmissable chance to paint. It is the

155. John Innerdale, *Taktsang temple, Bhutan*, chromacolour, 26 x 32cm, 1991.

most venerated pilgrim site of the Himalayan world. Known as the 'Tiger's Nest' it is an intensely spiritual place where in the eighth century, Guru Rinpoche miraculously flew on the back of a tigress from Tibet to convert the Bhutanese to Buddhism. I am reluctant to leave this place and before doing so spin the prayer wheel in the nearby chorten, the bell ringing with each turn of the drum, sending blessings out ceaselessly.

The following day we assemble at the Drugyel Dzong, a burnt-out castle where Bhutanese armies locked horns with Tibetan invaders.

We load up 35 ponies and for several days follow the river through forest and meadow acclimatising until reaching the Chomolhari base camp. This is where the adventure begins.

Chomolhari's south-east face towers over the camp, blindingly white. As I attempt to paint this majestic view, there is an inner tension; is the attraction more as a climber than an artist? The links are strong but which is the dominant?

I am confronted with a vast white vertical surface which I'm attempting to record on a small white vertical surface; so where to begin? As usual, with the sky, which dominates so much of my work.

Leaving the camp we climb to the summit of the Nyile La (4890m) eventually leading to the unclimbed summit of the Nyile Le (5090m) and from here together with Band, Lovatt and Langmuir I can see the entire northern range bordering Tibet including Jitchu Drake (6989m), Tserim Gang (6526m), Takaphu (6523m) and Garula Kang (6574m).

The final day, before the climbers and the trekkers part company, is spent visiting the Lingshi Dzong. It is a gem; built in 1668 it has been under siege several times by Tibetans and its masonry walls are peppered with holes for defence. Beneath are prison cells to house temple robbers. I enjoy a leisurely afternoon sketching and painting in the shadow of a comfy wall accompanied by a lonely monk who hums and whispers to me as I work.

The following morning five of the nine climbers set off over the Yale La (4940m) to the Basingthang valley, traversing high above the river Chu to an idyllic base camp site. Our team of Singye (sirdar) and six assistants set up the village of mess, cook, toilet and five sleeping tents. This is a most happy energetic team who for two weeks looked after our every need. Here too is a perfect location for landscape painting. As we acclimatise the weather is set fair and we work out a strategy to set up two tented camps for each group of mountains. This will enable as many of us as possible to attempt significant routes.

With the arrival of four more climbers we are now ready to go. The first party of Band, Blacker, Langmuir, Mould and Nixon make the first ascent of Ngum Tang Gang III (5640m). Over the next 10 days first ascents are made of Wohney Gang (5589m) by Mould, Lovatt and Langmuir and Ganae Gang I (5487m) and Ganae Gang II (5460m) by Nixon, Band and the Innerdales.

On our rest day at base camp, George Band and I climb the Riburi Ridge where George finds a perfect set of blue sheep horns. I manage a half day painting the Wohney Gang headwall and the Ganae Gang group. As I work George explains the geological history of the range we have climbed, revealing what lies beneath the snow and ice that I am struggling to portray.

The face of Ganae Gang is wondrous, with the sun setting and a golden light emphasising the shadows from the ridge. I sit entranced painting in haste as a deepening blue Bhutanese sky emphasises and compresses the shadows. As the light fades we reach base camp to find Eric, Jerry and

156. John Innerdale, *Lingshi Dzong, Bhutan,* watercolour 17 x 14cm, 1991.

Peter back from their abortive attempt on Peak 5567, which was part of the exploration around the Pubukang glacier from Camp III. Here we came across footprints of blue sheep, bear, pugs of snow leopard and large prints of a biped that Singye says are 'Mountain gorilla or Yeti'. I photograph these, placing my ice axe beside them to give true scale. They are massive.

After a relaxing walk out we are reunited with the trekkers for a week of relaxation, some celebration, visits to important monasteries and spectacular *dzongs*. Eventually we journey across the kingdom to Bumthang to enjoy the annual 'Black Hat' Buddhist Festival of Dancing, yet another chance to paint and absorb the beauty, peace and harmony of the Kingdom of the Thunder Dragon.

Later, on our return to Paro, we visit the Minister for Home Affairs and put before him a list of the mountains the expedition has climbed together with proposals for the names of each peak, hitherto shown as altitude points on the simple map we had of the region. These are translated into Bhutanese, are accepted and now form part of the updated survey of the country.

Note: An account of the climbs accomplished as part of this expedition appeared in *AJ* Vol 97, 'Exploring in the Hidden Kingdom', by Peter Mould.

TERRY GIFFORD

Noyce's Cambridge Mountaineering Poets

FR Leavis dominated my formative years at Cambridge and his stringent approach to criticism effectively delayed my publishing, if not actually writing poetry, for decades. When so few writers, and even fewer poets, could be admitted to the Leavis canon, how could any contemporary young scribbler hope to write 'literature'? Of course, for such intimidating delays the literary world should be, not only grateful, but more relieved than it could imagine. My early poetry was an extended recovery of the long-stifled expressions of adolescence. But, having broken through several glass cornices, assailed the mountains of the mind and glimpsed the real cliffs of fall, no-man-fathomed, and wanting to deal with that steep as far as is personally possible (i.e. up to HVS), I'm an advocate of mountaineering poetry. Either seeking control of language at the edge, or being playful with the dangerous sublime of forms, mountaineering poetry claims a space for man's 'mounting spirit in his bone-house', to continue the Gerard Manley Hopkins metaphors. It is to poetry that we turn to understand the pull of mountains, sometimes in the guise of prose. And it is the editors of the glossy magazines and journals who are scared stiff by the stuff, bold mountaineering gatekeepers that they are. But no such fear in that most astute of literary mountaineers, the Kingsman, Wilfrid Noyce, whose anthology, *The Climber's Fireside Book* (Heinemann) published posthumously in 1964, I'd like to revisit to consider the eight Cambridge mountaineering poets he included there.

If you're still with me, I'd better come clean. None of my books of mountaineering poetry has been short-listed by the Boardman Tasker judges. I was not a student of Leavis's at Downing in the 1950s, but I was taught in the early 1960s by recent students of Leavis who'd got jobs at the Cambridge Grammar School for Boys (notably by Frank Glover Smith, later of Sussex University, who let us Sixth Formers doing English listen in the lunch-hour to the first records by one Bob Dylan – not altogether irrelevant here). Then I went to Sheffield to train to be a teacher because, first, it was a real place like those where most of the working people of England lived and, second, it was close to crags.

The Boy Scout leaders who ran a troop up Newmarket Road in Cambridge had taken us to the Lakes and hired Des Oliver to take us climbing on Glaciated Slab in Combe Ghyll. To these two inspirational forces - Leavis disciples and Scout leaders - at work outside the university for the children of college servants like me, I am only now learning to be truly grateful. By such wonderfully strange and generously given routes does a grandchild of the Fens (my father was the first generation to move from the orchards of Cottenham to the big city) and son of the spade (my dad was Head Gardener at King's, 1961-86) come to be drawn to comment on the sensibility witnessed by a part of the mountain poetry included within a forgotten anthology. You need to know where the sensibility of the commentator is located.

At first glance Noyce's anthology appears to be a wholly romantic one. This is no surprise, since he had little else from which to choose in the early 1960s and the literature of the sport is, as we know, rooted in Romanticism. Noyce includes a sonnet by Keats that takes mountain mist as a metaphor for the 'vague' state of human self-knowledge. The potentialities of 'Thought and mental might' remain 'challenged', as we now might say, by 'mist and Crag'. Indeed, such vagueness, to use Keats's term, in the poetic expression of a sense of connection between human sensibility and the mountain environment is what has commonly come to characterise the Romantic movement of which Keats was a part. But after this sonnet Noyce can't resist adding three unlinked couplets by Keats that are the opposite of vague. Noyce says, 'Rare as they are, some of Keats's "mountain" lines are among his most evocative':

> Crag jutting forth to crag, and rocks that seemed
> Ever as if just rising from a sleep ... (*Fireside Book*: p 40)

Clearly Noyce is really seeking a sharply accurate representation in which language works hard to jolt the imagination of the reader into a new perception of the reality and meaning of mountains that transcends the vagueness associated with the Romantics. In 1964 what was not available to Noyce was the Rock and Ice backlash against the whole university-educated, middle-class, romantic establishment of mountaineering that had its literary expression in the anti-establishment, under-stated humour of Tom Patey. But what Noyce did have available to him was a poetic movement towards enlightened realism that made possible a disciplined imaginative enquiry into the work of the eight mountaineering poets from Cambridge included in his anthology. The work of Michael Roberts (Trinity), Christopher Isherwood (Corpus Christi) and Noyce himself (King's), is linked by the best of the post-Romantic poetry of Geoffrey Winthrop Young (Trinity) back through some observant lines of Tennyson (Trinity) to the parodist Romantic Byron (Trinity) and the founding father of rock-climbing poetry, William Wordsworth (St John's). To be fair, the journey out of Romantic mountain poetry that Noyce was seeking had its contributions from the Oxford-educated poets W H Auden and William Bell. Ironically, the final poem in the anthology by Geoffrey Sutton (Peterhouse, CUMC President 1953-4) from the 1960 *Climbers' Club Journal* is a throwback to romanticism. In 'Exequy' Sutton claims that the deaths of Bob Downes (Clare) on Masherbrum and George Fraser (King's) on Ama Dablam in 1957 are transcended by the sparks of their lives from their knights' lances against death's windmill. Romantic heroism as the poetic fallback position in grief is hard to kill. But the line out of that kind of easy palliative which Noyce sought in the poetry in his anthology has come to provide a more reliable and lasting guide to the writing of mountaineering poetry than anything that followed it had to offer - the emotional evasion and linguistic repression of what I call 'the literary Rock and Ice era'. Patey's songs were never intended to be anything other than lightweight. Unless I've missed something, we had to wait until the climbing poetry of David Craig (Downing) in *Native Stones* (1987) to find a mountaineering poetry that continues where Noyce's search left off.

So that's my thesis and here's how the evidence unfolds in my reading of it. In 1783 the young Bill Wordsworth was with a gang of local farmers' lads, including one called Birkett, who were climbing to a raven's nest on Yewdale Crags, Coniston when the leader got cragfast and had to be rescued (Thompson, *Wordsworth's Hawkshead*, Oxford University Press, 1970: p 211 et seq). The churchwarden paid four pence for an egg or a dead chick, so rock-climbing for the kids of Wordsworth's time had modest economic and farming conservation rewards as well as aesthetic ones when informing the rock-climbing section of the Prelude Book I. As 'a plunderer then/ In the high places' of what we now construct as 'the Lake District' Wordsworth's bird-nesting gave him the sharp experience of detail that only rock-climbers can fully appreciate:

> Oh, when I have hung
> Above the raven's nest, by knots of grass
> And half-inch fissures in the slippery rock
> But ill sustain'd, and almost, as it seem'd,
> Suspended by the blast which blew amain,
> Shouldering the naked crag ... (1805 edition, line 341ff)

It doesn't require one who knows the secrets of finger-locks in half-inch fissures to feel the exhilaration of that iambic rhythm and alliteration that sustains an emphasis on the 'ill-sustain'd' danger and delight of such a situation. Bob Dylan's exhilarating wordplay can't match it for conveying a real experience.

But Noyce chooses the ecstatic, visionary Snowdon passage from the *Prelude*, followed by the apparently contrasting gloomy evocation of the Simplon Pass. He chooses a building rhythm of thought and experience: 'Among all Wordsworth's mountain poetry, his vision on Snowdon in the *Prelude* seems to me supreme; the more striking after the pedestrian start' (p 23). Stalking a summit sunrise, it's actually moon-power upon the mountain that Wordsworth finds. Its contrasts of 'silent light' and 'dark abyss' give him a sense of 'Nature's mind', the dynamics of which are evoked in such struggling, inadequate phrases as 'interchangeable supremacy' and 'mutual domination'. This is the unity in difference that makes the paradox of danger and delight possible in the notion of the sublime. Wordsworth

157. Wilfrid Noyce (1917-62): 'disciplined, imaginative enquiry' into the work of his fellow Cambridge mountaineering poets. (*Alpine Club Photo Library*)

is aware that this is dangerous physical and mental territory and struggles with the imaginative discipline of poetic language and form to reach into it. Seen from the 'gloomy Pass' of the Simplon, the same 'interchangeable' creative-destructive dynamic ('Of woods decaying, never to be decayed') emerges as a poetry of more explicit unity that anticipates James Lovelock's Gaia theory. Postmodernist literary criticism fails to express contradictions as powerful as this. But the historically post-modern mountaineering poet knows the paradox that Wordsworth knows: 'that all/ The terrors, all the early miseries [...] should ever have made up/ The calm existence that is mine when I/ Am worthy of myself' (1805 edition, line 355ff).

I'm going to gallop along here because I want to get to the now neglected Michael Roberts. But one ought to recognise in passing that the voice of Patey is gleefully, to use Byron's own word, anticipated in the passage from Byron that Noyce has wittily given the title 'The Romantic' (p 26). Having it both ways, as usual, Byron parodies and celebrates the 'altar [of] high places', knowing that so-called civilisation below is 'circumscribe[d]' in its forms of worship, but probably preferring them. This is an energised and necessary stage in the journey towards a post-romantic mountaineering poetry that Noyce is charting here. Tennyson's typical contribution is to be simply smitten by the Alps, at a safe distance, in what Noyce titles 'The Dawn from Milan', but in a vividly descriptive, tightly rhymed, two stanzas (p 49 et seq).

In many ways the poetry of Geoffrey Winthrop Young, which I think of as romantic in sensibility, is actually Victorian: plainer in speech than the Romantics, using short lyric rhyming forms and full of loss and nostalgia, as though wanting to recapture the Romantic vision and failing. His best-known climbing poem is probably 'The Cragsman':

> In this short span
> between my finger-tips on the smooth edge
> and these tense feet cramped to the crystal ledge
> I hold the life of man.

(*Collected Poems*, London: Methuen, 1936: p 129)

But Noyce's line of thought, if I'm right, leads him to choose two poems that are dependent upon the reader knowing that most of Winthrop Young's mountaineering life was achieved without the leg he lost in the First World War. (He famously re-climbed the Matterhorn with an artificial leg.) So the choice of 'After the Battle on Monte San Gabriele, 1917' that appears to be more about the general use of limbs 'lent by life' than mountaineering itself, has its poignancy in the idea that 'life may halve the loan' (p 110). 'Be then content/ to live new music by their altered measure' has a resonance for readers of *The Climber's Fireside Book*, for whom Winthrop Young would be a figure famous for his fabled Pen y Pass Easter climbing parties and as the founder of the BMC. In Noyce's time he says that the most quoted poem of Young's is the second one he includes, which also alludes to the two halves of Young's mountain days. 'I have not lost the magic of long days', says the poet, because 'I dream my feet upon the starry ways;/ my heart rests in the hill' (p 111). In our own time perhaps the most quoted poem of Young's is 'High Hills', which Noyce also includes. There is a reaching back for Wordsworth's sense of a 'larger rhythm and line,/ moving between the eternal mode and mine' (p 123), but the images are abstract and there is a more forceful presence of 'the circles of our discontent'.

Noyce dates this poem as published in 1938. What was not widely known until the publication of Alan Hankinson's biography (*Geoffrey Winthrop Young: Poet, Educator, Mountaineer*, London: Hodder and Stoughton, 1995) was the fact that Young worked secretly with liberals in Germany during this period to try to counter the momentum of Hitler's politics. So some of the 'brief ills' of which this poet was aware in 1938 turned out not to be so brief. Indeed, Noyce's comment on the co-written work of his next Cambridge poet indicates Noyce's willingness to include political satire in *The Climber's Fireside Book*. *'The Ascent of F6'* was a strangely prophetic play', wrote Noyce (p 157). In 1936 Auden and Isherwood characterised, not the Germans, but 'the finest flower of English Mountaineering' as those who would sacrifice their lives to make the first ascent of F6 for the glory of the nation. Auden and Isherwood highlighted the class function within Britain of national expeditions, against which the Rock and Ice era would later offer an alternative. The characters Mr and Mrs A in the play are clearly the parents of the future Rock and Ice generation. Mr A is given the following quatrain:

> Cut out the photos and pin them to the wall,
> Cut out the map and follow the details of it all,
> Follow the progress of this mountain mission,
> Day by day let it inspire our lowly condition. (p 159)

It is clear from the last line that Auden and Isherwood make no attempt to create an individual voice for Mr A, such is their confidence in their middle-class literary audience. Their intervention in the class war is thus less than convincing and was, indeed, only a modish passing phase. Much more integrity, to use a phrase familiar to such readers of Dr Leavis as might still live, could be claimed for the poetry of Michael Roberts on several fronts.

Michael Roberts read Mathematics at Trinity and became a science teacher at the Royal Grammar School in Newcastle-upon-Tyne, but is best known as the editor of the first *Faber Book of Modern Verse* (1936), a definitive retrospective on Modernism from the 1930s. He published three collections of poetry which has been called 'austere', but which Leavis might have called 'serious'. His alpine exploits are reflected in the mountaineering classic of his wife: Janet Adam Smith's *Mountain Holidays* (1946). Noyce includes four poems by Roberts, one of which, 'Everest 1948', marks the closure of Tibet, the later closure of Nepal and the tension in the Himalayan regions following Partition. In engaging with the politics of the mountain environment in this poem Roberts achieves more than the Punch and Judy knockabout comedy of F6. Precise images carry allegorical weight as the poem balances the 20 years that led to the first ascent of Everest with the 'new clouds/ that cover India and Pakistan'. A tone combining simplicity and symbolism echoes that of Roberts' mentor, T S Eliot. Above and within all these tensions, which connect the highs and lows of human endeavour in all cultures, stands the 'Mother of all snows, Chomolungma, Everest'. Quite simply, 'The time is not propitious'.

The complexity of the mountaineering experience and its contexts expressed in the apparent simplicity of the poetry could hardly be carried further than in the poetry of Michael Roberts. For other readers his poem 'La Meije 1937' might be his major achievement, his honesty and humility undercutting the breathtaking challenges for both mountaineer and poet:

> A man should use every nerve and muscle,
> A man should puzzle out the hardest questions,
> A man should find words for the thoughts that no one knows.
> (p 167)

What this poem 'finds words for' are a complex mixture of contradictory thoughts – beauty and death, stillness and clattering noise, pride and self-doubt, arrogance and humility. Mountaineers tend to despise the tourists, but this poem ends by admitting that in the hamlets above La Grave the English mountaineers were 'the intruders' upon a life of quiet dignity and grace. For others the celebratory lyric 'St Gervais' might be all encompassing - the trams and slums of Newcastle are not excluded from the memory of 'Coming out of the mountains/ singing'. For others again, the sweep of vivid images in 'The Secret Springs' might evoke the complexity of contrary forces of which 'mossy walls', 'water on brant and slape', 'the green glacier-ice', 'history' and 'the huge/ Slow movement of a nation's mind' are all apart and a part. There is much more here than the cold mind and portentous images of Modernist poetry, with which Roberts is associated through his *Faber Book of Modern Verse*.

It seems to me that the poetic journey charted by this group of poems in Noyce's anthology, that happen to be by Cambridge poets, bring him to a desire for humility and integrity within the larger tensions engaged by the mountaineering experience. His preference is for a plain language and an inspirational image that would outflank the vagueness and self-indulgence associated with the weaknesses of Romantic poetry. The poem of his own that he chooses to include is 'A Prayer for Everest, 1953 (Written before the mountain)'. It is in his characteristic short lines and whilst including storm, cold and fatigue, the poem is a prayer that friendship will overcome his weaknesses, even to the point that 'no envy bleed,/ when – for I know my heart -/ others succeed' (p 221), as indeed, they did.

By 1960 Noyce could look backwards and forwards to quite different eras of mountaineering literature and culture. He himself was part of a kind of boldness in climbing unthinkable to earlier generations. In fact, he was thought by his contemporaries to be accident-prone (Perrin, *Menlove*, London: Gollancz, 1985: p 148) and he died in his fourth serious accident (on the Anglo-Russian expedition to the Pamirs in 1962). He was taught to climb by his cousins Guy and Colin Kirkus, then by Menlove Edwards, whom he met in the Climbers' Club hut Helyg. Next day (and their first out together) they came across Winthrop Young, 'driving forth the legions of the Easter party to the rocks', as he remembered in *Mountains and Men* (London: Bles, 1947 p 21). In that same book he wrote a sentence that anticipates the very kind of climbing poetry that was to come later: 'The thing, then, that we cannot watch, of everyday, is our body fitting itself to this world surrounding' (*Mountains and Men*, London: Bles, 1947: p 148). This exactly describes the achievement of Cambridge mountaineering poet David Craig's poem 'Into Rock' in *Native Stones* (Secker & Warburg, 1987: p 6). To my mind this poem is one of the best to be written thus far about the rock-climbing experience.

In *Scholar Mountaineers* Noyce speculated that one day mountain writing 'will no longer be a sideline of men normally engaged in other spheres, but an occupation itself fully satisfying' (London: Dobson, 1950: p 20). And what kind of mountaineering poetry, one wonders, would such a new era produce?

Science

158. John Innerdale, *Horns of Paine*, Chile, chromacolour, 64 x 48cm, 2002.

THOMAS KOHLER, DANIEL MASELLI & URS NEU

Mountains and Climate Change: A Global Concern

Mountains are among the regions most affected by climate change. Alpinists are front line itnesses to some of the most obvious signs of a warmer world: glacier retreat, increased rockfall ıd the formation of glacial lakes. But the implications of climate change will reach far beyond ountain areas, with profound consequences. The article that follows is based on the first and ıal chapters of an 80-page brochure entitled 'Mountains and Climate Change: From Underınding to Action', prepared at the Centre for Development and Environment, University of rn, Switzerland, for the Swiss Agency for Development and Cooperation and presented at a le event at the United Nations Climate Change Conference in Copenhagen on 12 December 09. The Alpine Journal is grateful to the editors, Thomas Kohler and Daniel Maselli, for rmission to publish this summary on an issue that should concern us all.

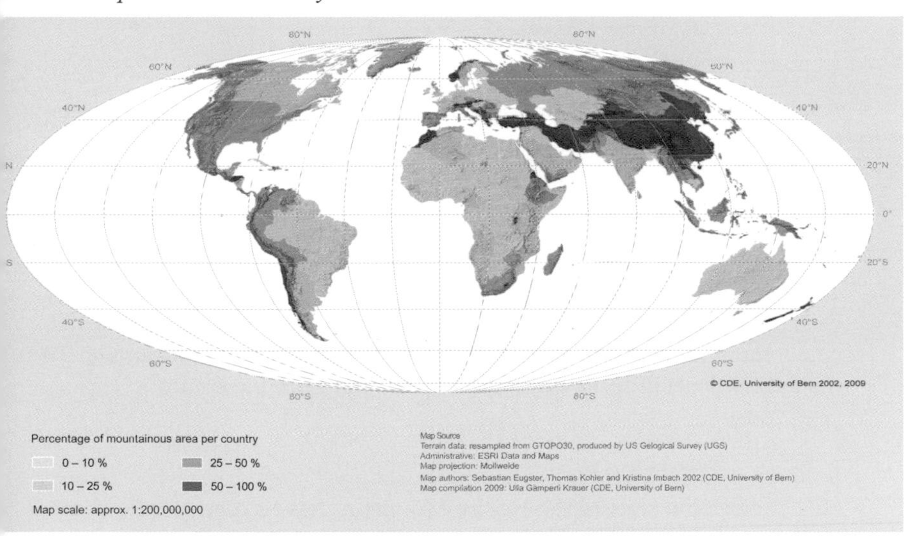

9. The map shows the countries of the world classified according to the percentage their mountain area. Countries with a high percentage of mountains are found on all ntinents, and range from large countries such as China and Iran to small ones such Lesotho, New Zealand, Switzerland, Norway and Slovenia. Other countries such the United States or Russia, or India, Canada and Algeria with important mountain eas have a lower percentage due to their large plains and lowlands. The underlying hill ading shows that even countries with low percentages of mountains – Australia, Brazil, Thailand – do have mountains, which play a much more important role than their land rcentage would indicate, for example for the provision of fresh water. The map therefore dicates that mountains play a key role in global development, feature prominently in the ading economies, and that climate change in mountains is a key concern for humankind at needs to be addressed in all regions of the world.

Man-made greenhouse gas emissions are expected to lead to average global warming in the period 1990-2100 of between 1.1 and 6.4°C, depending on the global release of greenhouse gas emissions. This warming will not be uniform but will vary considerably between different regions. In general, it will be greater over land and in high northern latitudes. The most robust precipitation projections are for increases in the monsoon regions and in middle and high latitudes, and a decrease in the subtropics. The area of snow cover will decrease in general, while snowfall may increase in regions with very cold temperatures such as high mountains. Most glaciers and ice caps will lose mass or disappear in the long term.

Climate change is a reality today, and some of the best evidence such as melting glaciers comes from mountain areas. Many scientists believe that the changes occurring in mountain ecosystems may provide an early glimpse of what could come to pass in lowland environments, and that mountains thus act as early warning systems.

Regional Climate Projections For Mountain Regions

ANDES

Annual precipitation is likely to decrease in the southern Andes, with relative changes being the greatest from June to August. For the rest of the Andes, future precipitation changes will depend heavily on changes in El Niño patterns, which are poorly understood at present.

A recent regional climate model study for the tropical Andes shows more warming at higher elevations and an increase in inter-annual temperature variability for scenarios with greater global warming. Glaciers in many parts of the tropical Andes may disappear over the next few decades, which could entail severe problems in water supply – in Peru, for example, 10 million residents of Lima depend on freshwater from the Andes.

ROCKY MOUNTAINS

Higher elevation sites in the Rocky Mountains have experienced a three-fold increase in warming compared to the global average during the last few decades.

Climate models show above-average warming with the greatest warming at high latitudes from December to February, and from June to August in the mid-latitudes. Annual mean precipitation will increase, except in the South, but precipitation is influenced by El Niño and the North Atlantic Oscillation, for which predictions are unreliable. There will be earlier snowmelt in spring and a shift from snowfall to rainfall, particularly at middle and lower altitudes. Moreover, the incidence of forest wildfires has increased significantly in recent decades; this is closely associated with increased spring and summer temperatures and with earlier spring snowmelt.

HINDU KUSH HIMALAYA

As the largest high-elevation land mass in the world, the Himalaya-Tibet massif plays an important role in global climate and climate change. Warming is predicted to be well above the global average, which can be seen even in global climate projections. Many climate models project that monsoonal flows will weaken, which would lead to a precipitation decrease. However, it seems probable that this effect is more than offset by enhanced water transport due to greater moisture in warmer air. Model projections show an increase of precipitation in December, January and February. These projections are uncertain, as they depend on poorly understood changes in the monsoon regime and El Niño patterns.

EUROPEAN ALPS

In general, Europe has shown a greater warming trend since 1979 compared to the global mean, and the trends in mountainous regions are still higher (Böhm et al. 2001). Regional climate projections indicate warming of about 1.5 times the global average, with greater warming in summer. Precipitation is projected to decrease in summer and on an annual average, and to increase in winter. General warming is expected to lead to an upward shift of the glacier equilibrium line by between 60 to 140 m per °C temperature increase, along with a substantial glacier retreat during the 21st century. The duration of snow cover is expected to decrease by several weeks for each degree C of warming at middle elevations in the Alps region.

Mountains: a Key Concern on The Global Climate Change Agenda

Mountains provide freshwater to half of the world's population. Climate change will affect the availability of water. In many cases, this will mean less water when it is most needed. Regions with the most mountain land are also the regions where mountain water for surrounding lowlands is most important – including the countries across the Eurasian continent from the Middle East to China, the Andean countries, the Nile Basin, and western North America. Also, many countries with less mountain land critically depend on mountain waters for specific regions or uses. Climate change in mountains will thus have important implications for irrigation, urbanisation and industrialisation, and hydropower generation. This will mean using water more efficiently, increasing storage capacities, and establishing, or re-visiting, institutional arrangements for sharing water equitably within and between nations.

Mountain areas are typically exposed to multiple hazards. Climate change is likely to increase this exposure, as extreme events such as storms, landslides, avalanches, and rockfalls are likely to become more common and more intense in mountain areas, threatening both livelihoods and infrastructure. Hazards cannot be prevented, but mountain regions can be supported

160. The climate of the European Alps is warming at 1.5 times the global average. Glaciers here, as in many other mountain areas, have been reduced close to their minimum extent during the climate optimums of the past 10,000 years. This pair of photographs of the Eiger glacier, Switzerland, with the Eiger and Mönch in the background, illustrate the marked retreat of the ice over one century. Top photograph taken around 1900. *(Photochrom picture from private collection of Samuel U Nussbaumer)* Lower photo taken 12 July 2009. (*Samuel U Nussbaumer*)

in managing the risks emanating from these hazards. This support begins with preparedness and ends with recovery; key ideas include effective early warning systems, land use zoning, and strategies for intervention.

Half of the global biodiversity hotspots are in mountain regions. They are an important global heritage that is being threatened by climate change and human action. Impressive achievements have been made in safeguarding this heritage; protected areas have been the fastest growing land use category in recent decades, especially in mountains. While mountain biodiversity is thus increasingly seen as a global common good by many, local communities who directly depend on its services must be included in stewardship of this valuable resource. Mountain communities should see more tangible benefits from conservation efforts than has been the case in the past. Payment for Environmental Services is a way to achieve this aim.

Mountains are home to about 10% of the global population. The large majority of mountain people live in developing countries. One third of them are food-insecure, a high proportion in global comparison. Mountains are often limited-choice environments due to harsh living conditions and a marginal position in terms of economic integration and political decision-making. External support is needed in order to reduce poverty levels. As temperatures rise, however, climate change might hold prospects for mountain agriculture – for crops previously not grown or limited to lower altitudes – provided that water, land, labour and capital through credit schemes or remittances from migrants are available to exploit such opportunities, and that access to markets is assured.

The Importance of Moving Beyond Climate Change

Much recent and current debate on adaptive capacity and vulnerability has been driven by the climate change agenda, but understanding the multidimensional nature of drivers of change, responses and feedback mechanisms is essential. This also applies to mountain regions, which are exposed to a wide range of mainly external drivers of change, including political, economic, and socio-cultural forces. Climate change action must therefore be embedded into a more general framework as provided, for example, by the concept of sustainable development. Any such framework will have to take note of the great diversity of mountain development contexts relating to environment, people, economies and cultures. Specific and tailored strategies will therefore be needed when it comes to climate change action. Human factors such as governance need to be considered in order to avoid simplistic projections about the impacts of climate change.

Many mountain countries, especially those with a high percentage of mountain territory, are developing countries with lower levels of industrialisation, and many are smaller nations. For these countries, adaptation is the main answer; they are far less the cause of the problem than they are the victims when it comes to climate change. For them, this change is a huge externality that will mean substantial additional costs in future. As adaptive measures are designed and implemented, the involvement of mountain populations is a must, as they have important knowledge and will be among those most directly affected by climate change and remedial action. As case studies show, the involvement of local people is increasingly becoming a reality.

Adaptation will have to be supported by mitigating measures that address the root causes of climate change: the emission of greenhouse gases and other substances that cause global warming. The involvement of economic and population centres outside mountain regions in industrialised, emerging and developing economies will be critical for achieving a tangible reduction of these emissions, as a major share of the greenhouse gases are released in these areas. Some of the largest emissions of greenhouse gases come from countries with a significant proportion of mountain areas, such as China, the US, and Russia (*see map*).

The Way Forward

At the global level

Chapter 13 of Agenda 21, with its focus on mountain areas, as well as the UN Framework Convention on Climate Change and its Clean Development Mechanism (CDM), provide frameworks for concrete action to tackle the drivers of climate change and to mitigate its impact. As many mountain countries are smaller developing nations, they have not benefited much from the CDM programme and the carbon market, due to institutional constraints and the complexity of accessing funds. This requires urgent re-examination. Mountains and money do not easily come together. Technological, financial, and institutional support for development in mountain countries thus need be strengthened. Mechanisms for coordinating and extending such support include the *Global Environment Facility* (GEF), the *National Adaptation Programmes for Action* (NAPA), and the *Global Climate Change Alliance* of the EU, to mention but a few mechanisms already in place.

At national and regional levels

Many countries have established national focal points and regional bodies for managing climate change and have carried out impact assessments to determine how climate change is likely to affect them. However, progress on mainstreaming climate change adaptation has been limited, especially in relation to key development concepts such as poverty reduction policies, land use planning and zoning, and national development strategies. There is a growing number of Payment for Environmental Services (PES) programmes with proven track records in industrialised and developing countries. PES relating to watershed management, water regulation for hydropower and irrigation, biodiversity conservation, and hazard prevention are a means for ensuring that mountain communities can benefit from the implementation of measures to maintain environmental services that are important for lowland areas and their large population centres. Many of the efforts made to date in climate change adaptation are generic. Proven practices that could be upscaled are as yet lacking. Documentation and lessons learnt will thus be crucial for establishing a body of sound experience tailored to the specific needs of mountain regions.

The importance of research

The research community has a responsibility to sensitize policy-makers and the public about climate change in mountains and its implications in wider highland-lowland interactive development contexts. Research should also focus on designing integrated mitigation and adaptation measures. Given the paucity of reliable and long-term data on mountain climates and resources, especially in countries of the South and East, there is a need to establish long-term observatories and monitoring mechanisms that will allow more accurate projections of climate change, more precise assessment of impacts, and documentation of existing adaptation strategies in and beyond mountain regions. For the research and education communities, capacity development and trans-disciplinary approaches will be important components of all these activities.

Now is the time for action in addressing climate change issues in mountains. This could help transform currently perceived problems into opportunities for a better future in mountain regions and in the many lowland areas that depend on their services.

The editors of 'Mountains and Climate Change: From Understanding to Action' were Daniel Maselli (Swiss Agency for Development and Cooperation) and Thomas Kohler (Centre for Development and Environment [CDE], University of Bern). The first chapter, 'Climate Change in the Mountains', which forms the first part of this article, was written by Urs Neu of the Forum for Climate and Global Change, Swiss Academy of Science, Bern. The second part was written by Thomas Kohler with members of the Mountain Focus Group of CDE, Bern. The full brochure can be downloaded at www.cde.unibe.ch/Research/MA_Re.asp

Area Notes

161. John Innerdale, *Machu Picchu, Peru*, chromacolour, 78 x 60cm, 2005.

Area Notes

COMPILED AND EDITED BY PAUL KNOTT

LINDSAY GRIFFIN

The Alps 2009

These notes would not have been possible without the help of many of the climbers mentioned in the text, and the wisdom of Luca Signorelli.

1. Climbing through the upper rock buttress on *Le Reveil de L'Ours* (de Leo/Sanguineti, 2009). The snow and ice arêtes of the Brenva Spur are visible at the top of the picture. (*Marcello Sanguineti*)

Mont Blanc massif

Italians Sergio de Leo and Marcello Sanguineti climbed a new route along the right flank of the popular *Brenva Spur* of **Mont Blanc**. Another Italian team repeated it two days later. Both were ascending a line that had been followed before, but in the opposite direction.

In June Sebastien dc Sainte Marie (Switzerland) and Pierre Tardivel (France) skied from the summit of Mont Blanc to the top of the *Brenva*

163. Day 2 on the first ascent of Punta Baretti's *South-west Ridge*. Duncan Tunstall on the grooved arête (Pitch 24) above the Gray Tower. (*Simon Richardson*)

Spur, weaved a difficult course through the séracs below, and then continued down the north flank of the spur, finishing via the *Güssfeldt Variant*. Tardivel named his line *Les Brenvitudes* and reported sustained slopes of 45-50°.

De Leo and Sanguineti later followed *Les Brenvitudes* in reverse but with a significant difference. In the upper section de Sainte Marie and Tardivel had skied quickly below threatening séracs and a rock buttress. The Italians found the safest route at this point was to climb through the rock buttress, sandwiched between the spur (on the left) and séracs to the right. This gave three pitches, with a crux section of F6b. Above, they made a long rightward traverse below the final séracs. Other than the rocky crux, the new route, named *Le Reveil de L'Ours*, is similar in difficulty to the Brenva Spur (AD+/D-).

Four Frenchmen made the third free ascent of *Divine Providence* on the **Grand Pilier d'Angle**, but like Slovenians Andrej Grmovsek and Marko Lukic, who made the second free ascent, they agreed that the original free grade felt somewhat overrated; more like F7b than F7c.

Although technically not the most difficult of the 4000m peaks in the Alps, **Punta Baretti** is certainly the most remote and inaccessible. On May Day 2006 Tardivel, Jeremy Janody and de Sainte Marie made the first ascent, and then ski descent, of the *South-west Couloir*. With a height of 1100m, this is one of the longest couloirs in the massif and Tardivel aptly named it *Couloir au bout du Monde*. It is largely straightforward 40° snow to a steeper and narrower upper section, where a short 70° rock step must be bypassed (Tardivel made a 10m rappel here during the ski descent). In 2009 Italians Mara Babolin, Francesco Rota Nodari and Roberto Rovelli made the second ascent. The main danger of this route is stonefall, but as the couloir lies in shade until after midday, climbing early on a cold day can minimise this. From the summit the three traversed north along the rotten rock ridge and over Mont Brouillard to Col Emile Rey, from where they then descended west to the upper Mont Blanc glacier and an unguarded Quintino Sella hut.

AC member Simon Richardson had noted the unclimbed SW ridge to the left of the couloir in 1992 but was put off, as no doubt were other alpinists, by the access; a long approach followed by a tortuous climb up the lower, highly chaotic, Mont Blanc glacier. However, on examining photos published by the Italians he could see that global warming had turned the lower icefall into a smooth and benign ice slope. So, later in the season he climbed the South-west Ridge with Duncan Tunstall. The pair climbed 40 roped pitches to the summit, starting with three pitches up the South-west Couloir and then cutting left onto the crest via a steep gully. Several towers were negotiated and there was sustained V and V+, with a couple of sections of VI. The route was graded ED1, and felt comparable with, though rather more sustained than, the North-east Rib of the Finsteraarhorn in the Bernese Oberland. They also descended to Col Emile Rey but then continued east across the upper Brouillard glacier to the Eccles Bivouac, from where they eventually regained the Val Veni.

Spanish Basques Josune Bereziartu and husband Rikar Otegui made the first free ascent of the 1994 Motto-Piola route *La Leggenda* (320m: F7a+ and A0) on the SE face of the **Aiguille Croux,** near the Monzino hut. The route takes the full height of the face and probably features its best granite but Motto and Piola were only able to climb one pitch with aid/rest points. This pitch was on-sighted by Otegui and then flashed by Bereziartu. Due to the boulder-problem nature of the crux, the climbers are unsure of the grade – either F7c or F8a. Remaining pitches were confirmed as having maximum difficulties of F7a+, and the route as a whole relies on a mix of trad and bolt protection. Bereziartu was the first women to redpoint F9a and has also climbed V15 boulder problems.

Making what has become an almost annual pilgrimage to the 'quiet corners' on the Italian side of the range, AC member Tony Penning put up three new rock routes with partner Ali Taylor. He first inspected the lower NE face of **Mont Noir de Peuterey**, at the end of the long East Ridge of the Aiguille Noire, and came away with the unfinished *Zig Zag* (TD). This entire section of wall below the Brenva glacier had no previously recorded rock climbs but the reasons quickly became apparent when Penning discovered the loosest rock he has encountered on all his new lines this side of the range. Although there were several good pitches, the route is disappointingly forced along large vegetated ramps. In the 560m of climbing, there was bold British 5b and a section of E3 5c, pulling hard on a giant detached flake with a cam in the side the only protection. The route was terminated approximately halfway up the face. Better was *Sorgente Pepper*, a 200m ED1 further to the left, climbing the right wall of a giant Y-shaped chimney with several pitches of E3 and E4. *Sorgente*, a pun on Sergeant, is the Italian word for a spring or source.

The pair also added *The Aging Gunslinger* (560m of climbing: TD: E3 5b) on the SE face of the **Evêque** above La Vachey in the Val Ferret. This proved a complex, three-day affair in wild terrain, the long approach up loose rock and precipitous grass slopes not recommended even to chamois, according to Penning. In 2004, with Nic Mullin and Robin Wilmhurst-Smith, he had explored this approach to a small snowfield below the face, and then climbed an 11-pitch E2 5b on the right side of the headwall. The meat of his new route involves climbing diagonally across the upper wall, right of the 2004 ascent, the psychological crux being a very poorly-protected, big undercling into a groove at a grade of around E3 5b. This rarely ascended face has an interesting history. In 1940 three soldiers and active mountaineers, part of a group of Italian military deployed in the valley during the Second World War, took time off to pioneer the desperate approach to the face, and then scrambled up immediately below it to reach the crest of the East Ridge on the right, which they followed to the summit of the Eveque. Their total time from valley to summit was just seven hours: no one since has been able to understand how they did it.

Talented Slovenian alpinists Andrej Grmovsek and Marko Lukic made the second free ascent of *No Siesta* on the N face of Pointe Croz, **Grandes Jorasses**. The pair took three days, from 17 to 19 March. They'd hoped to climb it faster but conditions were not perfect and they were surprised by the difficulties and time-consuming nature of the 'easier' (M5/M6, 70°) pitches. They found the hard pitches to be more technical than physical, rating the 1100m ascent M8, AI 5 and UIAA VI+. Grmovsek feels it may well be the hardest, long mixed route in the Alps when climbed all free.

Above the approach to the Triolet (Dalmazzi) hut, Philippe Batoux and Patrick Gabarrou completed an old project on the **Paroi de Titans,** a fine rock wall best known for the 1996 10-pitch Motto-Piola classic *Venus, ou bien Venice*. The pair first climbed a few pitches of their new line in November 1996 but then more or less forgot about it. Eventually, in October 2009, they completed all eight pitches to the top of the wall at F6c, 6b obl. The route has bolts but also needs natural gear, and the pair have named it *13 Ans de Réflexion*.

In late July Swiss Xavier Schacher and Nicolas Villet tried to repeat the *South-west Pillar* of the **Aiguille Sans Nom,** a route put up in 1998 by Doré Green and Simon Richardson (450m: ED1, F6c and A1). However, they went too far up the couloir leading to the Brêche Sans Nom and on discovering their mistake, decided not to descend but follow a slim hidden couloir rising up the left flank of the *South-west Pillar*. They climbed this at M6 to join the upper section of the *British Route*, where they were able to free climb the A1 corner, which was wet on the first ascent, at F6c/6c+. The route was named *Initiation 4000* and the climbers continued up the Sans Nom Arête to the summit of the Aiguille Verte.

Ecrins

In mid-June Hélias Millerioux and Robin Revest completed an interesting climb when they made only the second summer ascent of the *1964 Route* on the N face of Pointe Puiseux, the main summit of the **Pelvoux**. The line

4. Marko Lukic dry-tooling a difficult rock section on *No Siesta*. (*Andrej Grmovsek*)

was originally graded ED, VI and 65° but the two French, climbing in cold, snowy conditions, report 80° snow, ice and mixed, and sections of poorly protected F6a on equally poor rock. The face is more than 1000m in height and the two found only one in-situ piece of gear – an old peg. This wall has an awesome reputation for loose rock, as do many other big north faces in the Ecrins, and prior to 2009 had only received two more known ascents, both in winter.

After climbing seven pitches in 2001 and adding another six in 2003, stopping at the Glacier Carré, Christophe Moulin finally completed his long-standing project on the S face of the **Meije**, left of the classic *Allain Route*. In 2009, with Laurent Laboudigue, he added three pitches on the summit pillar at F6b/c, 7a and 7a, and then returned later with Paul Michas and Simon Rémy to add three more pitches (F7a maximum), to join the *Allain Route* on the final ridge. The 800m route, named *Mitchta* (F7a, 6b+ obl.), is steep throughout its length, and is considered one of the most serious rock routes to date in the massif. The lower section will be exposed to any rock or ice falling from the vicinity of the Glacier Carré (or from parties on this section of the *Normal Route*). The climb mostly uses trad protection.

Bernese Oberland

The main event on the North Face of the **Eiger** was Robert Jasper and Roger Schäli's first free ascent of the *Japanese Direttissima*, 40 years after it was first climbed. With technical difficulties of F8a and M5, some poorly protected pitches, ice and mixed climbing, plus the ever-present threat of stonefall, it is now arguably the most demanding route on the North Face. The technical crux is the Rote Fluh but above the Second Icefield it climbs an 800m headwall, which involves two successive pillars of steep, friable rock, the second – Sphinx Pillar – right of The Fly.

Earlier in the season Stefan Siegrist, no newcomer to hard climbing on the North Face, made the first redpoint ascent of *Magic Mushroom*. He climbed the 21-pitch route with Thomas Theurillat and Ralph Weber over two days, with a night in a portaledge. In 2007 first ascentionists Christoph Hainz and Roger Schäli made obligatory moves of F7b on the upper section of the overhanging wall leading to the 'mushroom', a characteristic rock formation on the West Ridge that Eiger BASE jumpers use as a launch site, but they were unable to complete the redpoint. Siegrist was more successful, completing this section at F7c+, and then using a parachute, that he had brought up the climb, to finish the day with a classic BASE jump.

On the nearby **Scheidegg Wetterhorn** Swiss climbers Denis Burdet and Nicolas Zambetti added another hard rock route, when they created *Into The Wild* up a compact 450m buttress on the N flank of the lower NE pillar. The 10-pitch route was completed in two and a half days and then later redpointed at F7b+, 7a. While the route is bolted, a selection of Friends is essential. Burdet and the Zambetti brothers are also responsible for *Baston Labaffe*, a 34-pitch route on the true North Face, eventually redpointed in 2005 at F7c, F7a obl. This is one of the most difficult big Alpine climbs on Swiss limestone and the ambience is serious: stone fall and verglas are not uncommon.

Valais Alps

In mid June French alpinists Martial Dumas and Jean-Yves Fredriksen, and the well-known Swiss guide Jean Troillet, climbed a new line on the North Face of the **Matterhorn**, though did not reach the summit. This completed an attempt in 2006 by Troillet and Sébastien Gay, which was defeated by stonefall. The two had planned to return when conditions improved but sadly, just a few weeks later, Gay was killed above Verbier while skiflying. The lower part of the route takes the vertical or sometimes overhanging terrain between the initial sections of the classic 1931 *Schmid Route* and the 1965 *Bonatti Direct*, joining the *Schmid* after c500m. At 600m, at the approximate level of the Shoulder and after three days on the wall with bivouacs in 'old school' hammocks, a storm forced a traverse to the Hörnli Ridge. Although new ground is less than half the face, the line has been given a name, *Voie Sébastien Gay*, and has difficulties reported as ED2/3, F5, A2 and 85°. The climbers appear to have been unaware of the

1972 *Czechoslovak Route*, which is the most direct line on the North Face, climbing the lower wall between the *Schmid* and *Bonatti*, then keeping almost equidistant between the two before joining the *Schmid* for the last 250m. The 2009 route takes a parallel line to the right, before crossing the *Czechoslovak Route* to join the *Schmid*. Curiously, the *Czechoslovak Route* has been omitted from definitive Swiss Alpine Club guides to the mountain and although their topo shows difficulties of V and 70°, the climbing is likely to have been predominantly mixed, and specific mixed grading wasn't around in those days. It remains unrepeated and most likely a climb somewhat ahead of its time.

Further east on the **Dent Blanche,** Simon Deniel and Patrick Gabarrou added another line to the NNE face, though failed to complete their original objective due to strong winds and extreme cold. *Merci* follows a parallel line right of the *Vaucher Direct* to the upper rock barrier, where they were forced to traverse left to join the *Vaucher*, and then finish via the *Winter Direct*. Gabarrou has given the route a conservative grade of TD+, commenting that there was great mixed climbing and some committing rock at F5 that was particularly trying as they had to keep gloves on the whole time.

In 2005 Gabarrou and Nicolas Zambetti climbed *Sulla Piaggia* on the East Spur of the SE face of the **Breithorn Central Summit.** The route is partially equipped. In 2009 Gabarrou returned with Michel Coranotte to add the seven-pitch *Le Sourire de Romain* up the wall and vague pillar left of the Spur. Three pitches of relatively easy ground lead to a superb section of F6a and F6b. Though the route is bolted, a few cams will prove useful.

The South-east Face, which receives plenty of sun, is a series of fine rocky pillars and broken mixed ground some 320m high. Apart from the original 1964 Italian route in the middle of the wall (AD, III on solid rock), there are several good routes of around AD+ (IV and IV+) put up in the early 1980s by local guide Marco Barmasse. All are easily accessible from the Kleine Matterhorn Téléphérique.

Bernina

Unclimbed faces are at a premium in the Alps, especially on well-known mountains, but on the first official day of spring Luca Maspes, Emanuel Panizza and Christian Turk made the first ascent of the ESE face of **Piz Morteratsch**, just to the north of Piz Bernina. The new route climbs the left flank of the upper NE ridge, or *Crest of Hope*, an established classic that has become rather less popular in recent years. As the 600m face has predominantly dreadful rock, it would be too dangerous to contemplate in anything less than cold, snowy conditions. On the day of the ascent the summit temperature was close to -25°C and while the route was certainly free from objective danger, the climbers struggled to keep hands and feet from becoming totally numb. They took 13 hours for the round trip from the Boval hut and named the route *Il Grande Freddo* (The Great Cold).

On the Main (South) Summit of the **Piz d'Arlas** Maspes and Panizza climbed a short new line on the W face between the 1981 *West Couloir* and the 1993 *West Face*. The 300m route was completed in early April and while certainly not extreme, involved delicate climbing on snow-covered slabs. This face is easily accessible from the Diavolezza téléphérique station.

On the Italian side of the range, above the Scerscen glacier, guidebook author and local guru Giuseppe Miotti, with Moris Milivinti, opened a new eight-pitch variant start to the classic *Corti Route* on the SW pillar of **Pizzo Sella**. Fine climbing on sound rock follows the initial section of pillar that the original 1928 route avoids. The new direct start is VI but the route above no more than IV/IV+ and has a total height of 500m. The 1928 route is considered to be one of the finest rock climbs in the Bernina, and comparable in difficulty and quality to the *North Ridge* of Piz Badile.

Dolomites

Confirming that the Dolomites are still far from worked out, Manuel Stuflesser and Norbert Weiss put up a fine new route on one of the region's most popular formations, the **Second Sella Tower**. Surprised to discover that apart from the ultra classic 1935 *Demetz-Gluck* start to the NW ridge, there were no recorded routes between this ridge and the standard 1930 *West Face Route*, the pair spent four days working their line on the left side of the W face, weaving through the prominent roofs at mid height. The result, the 10-pitch *Batajan* (the nickname of Franz Stuflesser, killed on the Third Sella Tower) has fine climbing on excellent rock. It is generally sustained at VI- to VI+ with one pitch of VII and one of VII+. Within three days of the ascent the route had received two repeats, both parties commenting on the excellent quality.

Prolific Dolomite activists Florian and Martin Riegler made the second ascent and first on sight of *Karies*. At the time of the first ascent in 2003 by Karl Unterkircher and Adam Holzknecht, the eight-pitch *Karies* (F7c) on the **Zahnkofel** of the **Sassolungo** was considered possibly the hardest route in the massif.

The most notable ascents on the south face of the Marmolada were the second and third free ascents of the magnificent *Via della Cattedrale* on **Marmolada di Roccia.** Originally climbed in two stages during 1983 and '85 at A4 and VI+ (no bolts), the route had a free ascent in 2004 from Pietro dal Pra, who rated the crux F8a+ and two other pitches F7c. In 2009 Florian Riegler climbed the route in 21 pitches with Rebecca Finch, Reigler echoing dal Pra's sentiments that it was the finest route he'd ever climbed in the Dolomites. Shortly after it was the turn of Hansjorg Auer and Much Mayr, who completed the route in just 10½ hours. Both climbers led the crux and pronounced it more like 8a, but agreed that the climb was 'superb, with reasonably good protection and perfect Marmolada limestone'.

On the **Pilastro del Serauta**, which lays towards the right side of the Marmolada's S face, Tizziano Buccella and Geremia Vergoni redpointed their 2008 route, *Opus Pocus* (200m), at F8a, 7b+ obl. Most of the route is climbed with natural protection, but the third pitch, where there is no

5. The North Face of the Civetta (3220m) in winter: (A) Col Coldai. (B) Torre di Coldai (2600m). (C) Torre d'Alleghe (2649m). (D) Torre di Valgrande (2715m). (E) Pan di Zucchero (2780m). (F) Punta Civetta (2920m). (G) Punta Tissi (2992m). (H) Monte Civetta (3220m). (I) Piccola Civetta (3207m). (1) *Chimera Verticale* (Beber/Bau/Geremia/Matteraglia, 2007-08: FFA Bau, 2009: 600m: IX). (2) *Captain Skyhook* (Crippa/Spreafico, 1987: c600m: VII+ and A2). The major crack systems on either side of *Chimera Verticale* are the *Andrich-Fae* (to the left) and *Aste-Sussatti*. (*Claudio Cima*)

possibility for natural gear, is completely bolted.

On the E face of **Sass Maor** in the Pale Group, Rolando Larcher and Fabio Leoni made the first winter ascent of *Masada*, a 1250m route put up in 2001 by Marco Canteri, Davide Depaoli and Samuele Scarlet at F6c+ and A0/A1. The legendary Dolomite climber, Scarlet, who passed away in 2010, was 60 at the time. *Masada* cuts through the classic *Solleder Route* and features an exposed but completely bolted 35-45° overhang some 800m above the ground. During the summer Riccardo Scarian eventually managed to free this pitch, and hence the entire route, at F8b.

Over on the great **Monte Agner,** Renzo Corona and Ivo Ferrari climbed a new direttissima on the NW face, up the wall and black dièdre left of *Pilastro Bee*. Although no grade has been voiced for the 750m *Tango per Marinella*, the pair felt it was perhaps the most beautiful route on the Agner, and destined to become an absolute classic.

On the **Civetta** one of the most significant players currently playing the game of opening big, bold, new routes in the Dolomites, Alessandro Bau, finally completed a redpoint ascent of *Chimera Verticale* on the NW face of **Punta Civetta,** on the wall between the classic *Aste-Sussatti* and *Andrich-Fae* routes. Bau had worked on this route with various partners over the previous two years but free-climbed the 15 independent pitches above the *Andrich/Aste* common start with his two brothers at IX, VIII obl. There is little in-situ protection.

A few days later Bau made only the third ascent, but first solo, of *Captain Skyhook*, a hard route up the steep compact wall between the *Aste* and 1931 *Comici* routes. First ascentionists Paulo Crippa and Dario Spreafico climbed the route in 1987 at VII+ and A2. On the second ascent in 1992, Roland Mittersteiner redpointed it at IX- (F7b+). After one failed attempt Bau completed the route at the original grade with just one bivouac (and liked it so much that he was back in March 2010 with Nicola Tondini to make the first winter ascent – in a 28-hour round trip from the hut).

On the **Torre Trieste** Andrej Grmovsek and Lukic Kranj made the third free ascent of the 750m *Donna Fugata* on the SW face. The Slovenian pair climbed this route, which takes a direct line though the friable yellow overhanging rock on the lower central section of the wall between the 1959 *Piussi/Redaelli Direttissima* and the classic 1934 *Carlesso/Sandri*, in one day on their first attempt. It has a hard crux pitch of F8a.

In the less frequented Feltrine Group, Jenny Lavarda and Marco Ronchi spent two months working on Maurizio 'Manolo' Zanolla's highly exposed 2006 route *Solo per Vecchi Guerrieri*, a four-pitch line above a very steep approach on the N face of **El Colaz**. The crux is the final pitch, a thin crimpy wall at F8c/8c+, a grade confirmed by the second and third ascentionists, Mario Prinoth and Riccardo Scarian. The route has obligatory climbing of F7c/7c+.

Finally, on the famous **Cima Scotini** in the Fanes Group, Florian and Martin Riegler made only the second redpoint ascent of *Zauberlehrling*, a 23-pitch route on the SW face put up as long ago as 1990 by Christoph Hainz and Oswald Celva at F7c. The brothers spent all day on this 550m route, finding some pitches psychologically demanding due to friable rock.

DEREK FORDHAM

Greenland 2009

In 2009 weather and snow conditions on the Inland Ice were particularly bad. Twenty-eight applications were made for permission to attempt the crossing between east and west coasts and of the 11 who started from the east eight had to return or be airlifted out, indicating either the severity of the conditions or a general lack of preparedness.

One of the first parties to cross from **east to west** was Ian Hall and Alistair Shawcross (UK) who started up the Hahn glacier on 7 April and reached point 660m (the normal point of arrival and departure for parties heading to or from Kangerlussuak on the west coast) on the 1 May after 25 days on the ice. The weather was a problem and poor visibility and large sastrugi slowed progress for much of the journey. The pair spent two days tent bound due to high winds and 'white-out' and both suffered from minor frostbite. The exit off the Russell glacier at Pt.660 was found to be relatively easy and gave good access to the waiting 4x4 taxi from Kangerlussuak Tourism! On 23 April a Swiss team of Moritz Hermann and Sonja Meier left Nagtivit heading for Ilulissat. They encountered strong easterly winds and experienced delays due to unusually warm temperatures which gave rise to poor snow and visibility. They altered their destination to Kangerlussuak but after discovering their Norwegian telemark boots were not warm enough they decided to abandon their trip and return to Tasiilaq. In early May a Tangent Expedition group crossed from east to west in 27 days but no further details are available and later in the season Norbert Pokorski and Rafal Krol (Poland) crossed from Nagtivit to Pt.660 in 27 days, starting on 17 August and finishing 12 September having experienced no delays or problems.

One of the first expeditions to start from the **west coast** was a six-person Finnish team led by Timo Stenros who left Pt.660 on 28 March. After four days one member had to be evacuated by helicopter and the remaining five continued in windy weather with temperatures down to -44°C. After leaving DYE2, the abandoned early warning station on the Inland Ice, on 14 April it was necessary to evacuate another member of the team and only four continued, enduring two days tent bound before breaking a ski some 100km from the east coast and repairing it with the aluminium frying pan – 'no pancakes any more' as their diary records. The weather and travelling conditions were much warmer as they neared the east coast towards the end of April. The west coast was not without its failures. Christophe Periard with a companion started from Kangerlussuak on 21 April but after one week his companion was taken ill and both men were airlifted out. Hvitserk, the Norwegian expedition group made a crossing between 8 May and 4

June encountering more snow than usual on the first few days. Two clients were evacuated due to hypothermia on 24 May. Australians Chris Weyers and Phil Hannam, as the Ice Wings 2 Expedition, left Kangerlussuak on 29 May with the aim of achieving a double crossing of the Inland Ice with the aid of power kites. After the failure of their satellite phone shortly before the halfway point they headed south-west to DYE2 where they were able to advise their base that they were in good shape. They then kited back to Kangerlussuak having been out for about a month and covered 500km. Described as, 'a cold trip and very full on!'

An expedition which never reached Greenland is worthy of mention for its aims if not its achievement. The Carbon Neutral Expedition under Raoul Surcouf set sail from Portsmouth on 19 April with the intention of sailing to Umivik and from there making a double crossing of the Inland Ice and sailing home again. Unfortunately they were struck by a force 11 storm in the Atlantic and capsized three times before being picked up by an oil tanker. It makes the Inland Ice seem quite tame! Danes Fleming Lund and Sverri Warm using tractor kites and ski sails left Narssaq in south Greenland on 28 June and reached Qaanaaq on 31 July after spending 29 days skiing the length of the Inland Ice. They covered 200km per day at speeds of up to 75 mph, encountered no problems and after their month on the Inland Ice felt 'ready to re-join the rat race'.

In the **Staunings Alps** a strong five-man team from the French Federation of Alpine Clubs (GUMS) led by Anthoine Melchior made a fine north – south ski traverse which commenced with gaining access to the Skjoldungebrae from Alpefjord and continued to Nordvestfjord, finding an alternative to the difficulties of the Col Major. The total traverse was 335km and took 34 days including crossing 16 passes of which two were totally new and five were crossed on ski for the first time. A few summits were climbed but access was generally limited by adverse weather and poor snow conditions. The expedition started from Alpefjord on 11 April and during the first week enjoyed fine weather and temperatures between -20°C and -30°C. The weather then worsened with much cloud and 2 metres of snowfall slowing progress and increasing the avalanche hazard. They reached Nordvestfjord on 7 May and the airfield at Constable Pynt on 15 May.

To the west in Nordvestfjord in August a four-man team from Imperial College London led by Dominic Southgate planned to climb peaks in **NW Renland**. The expedition's start was delayed by the non-arrival of some of their equipment but once underway they reached by boat a point on the north coast of Renland from where they set up a base 1.5 km inland. Both the main glaciers of the area were explored as well as access to the ice cap and having solved problems of crossing glaciers and rivers the party climbed four peaks between 1636m and 1950m. An attempt at an additional route on one of the peaks was turned back by deteriorating snow conditions.

Also on Renland but at Skillebugt in the south-east was a four-man Dutch party from 8 August to 30 August. Niek de Jonge and Jelle Staleman hoped to make the ascent of a 900m pillar known as **The Cenotaph** and Martin

Fickweiler and Gerke Hoekstra aimed to make a big wall style ascent of a direct line on a peak called **Shark's Tooth**, which subsequently proved to be inaccessible due to impassable rivers. De Jonge and Staleman were turned back on The Cenotaph after 600m (UIAA VII) where to continue would have required extensive bolting. They then joined the others and made a free ascent of a line of least resistance on The Cenotaph. Two further peaks of 2000m and 1000m were climbed from the Apusinikajik glacier. Both were of mixed terrain and the higher gave a grade of TD/TD+.

On the west coast, Bob Shepton and four companions continued his Tilman-type boat based explorations. In August they sailed from Scotland across the Atlantic, first to the **Akuliarusinguaq peninsula** at Lat 71' 50"N in west Greenland. Here they located a prominent cirque not previously explored on the south-west of the peninsula and made the ascent of 10 unclimbed peaks before pursuing the main thrust of the expedition which was the exploration of **Northumberland Island** at Lat 77' 23"N. They made ascents of nine peaks, six of them via a technically difficult ski mountaineering traverse by Tom Howard and Andy Prosser along almost the full length of the island. They survived two big storms and finally the boat was left in Aasiaat after winter had arrived early.

Also travelling by boat, but on the east coast was the *Jonathan IV*, an ex BT Challenge yacht with 10 people on board. On 24 August they left Longyearbyen in Svalbard to explore the Fjord region of north-east Greenland. With various trips ashore they sailed through Kejser Franz Josephs Fjord and Geologfjord, slowly working south to Ella Island and Kong Oscar Fjord. They reached Scoresbysund on 8 September and left for Iceland on 13 September.

Responsibility for Greenland expeditions has from the beginning of 2010 passed from the Danish Polar Centre to the Greenland Home Rule Authorities in Nuuk and this seems like a good time for me to pass on the baton of these notes. In preparing the notes I have noticed an increasingly casual attitude to expedition organisation, particularly some of those planning to cross the Inland Ice. It has been more and more common to find groups setting off too early, relatively poorly prepared and relying heavily on other people and technology to get them out of the inevitable problems. This contrasts with the level of preparation and self-reliance normal some years ago, as exemplified perhaps by my journey across the Inland Ice in 1971, and other expeditions of that period, when we had a small radio for time signals only, navigated by sextant and 7-figure log tables, and were for three months totally out of contact and independent. My consuming enthusiasm for Greenland and the Arctic, where I have taken part in many happy expeditions of my own remains undiminished and I trust the *AJ* will be well served by my successor. I send my grateful thanks to all who, over the years, have generously responded to my requests for information. I have thoroughly enjoyed being party to your achievements!

[Editor's note: Derek has been reporting on Greenland and Arctic exploration and adventure in the Alpine Journal since 1969 – a most impressive feat]

SIMON RICHARDSON

Scotland Winter 2009-10

According to the weather forecasters, 2010 was the coldest winter in Scotland for nearly 50 years. The snow arrived in earnest at the end of November, the mountains turned increasingly wintry and by late December the landscape was coated in a uniform blanket of white, to the delight of climbers and skiers alike. The sustained cold weather lasted into the middle of March and as a result more than 40 new Grade VII and VIIIs were climbed, nearly double any previous year, and there were dozens of significant repeats. Highlights included the development of Coire Scamadal on Skye, the astonishing first winter ascent of *Anubis* (XII) on Ben Nevis by Dave MacLeod and big additions on the Minus Face and Creag an Dubh Loch.

The Finest Ice Climbing Venue in Scotland

The vertical basalt crags of Coire Scamadal on the north side of The Storr are dripping wet most of the year but have the potential to be a natural ice trap. Facing north-east, and easily visible from the main road north of Portree, they have attracted the attention of ice climbers over the years, but most have been thwarted by their relatively low altitude and proximity to the sea. They were finally breached by Mike Lates who climbed an icy gully cutting through their left side in two instalments in the late 1990s. *Scamtastic* (V,5) saw a second ascent by Mick Fowler and Dave Turnbull last season.

Well aware of the potential of the corrie, Lates was determined to return as soon as conditions became good. The cliff started to ice through December, and finally after New Year the ice was thick enough to climb. On 4 January, Lates enlisted Andy Huntington for the first ascent of *Top Scam* (V,6), the central ice line topped by an ice umbrella. Lates returned four days later with Martin Welch to add *Scamadaladingdong* (IV,6), the prominent icy recess to the right of *Scamtastic*.

Other teams had been alerted to the potential, and on Saturday 9 January, Robin Clothier and Doug Hawthorn picked *The Fine Line* (VI,6), the plum route on the crag, up the vertical ice sheet on the imposing right side of the cliff. The following day, Alasdair Fulton, James Sutton and Ben Weir joined the fray and added another major line – *The War Path* (VI,6), whilst Clothier and Hawthorn climbed *The Shard* (VI,6), the huge hanging cigar to the right of *Scamadaladingdong*. After a brief thaw, Martin Welch and Stewart Anderson climbed *Vertigo Gully* (VI,7), the prominent incised corner on the right of the cliff whilst Hawthorn and Weir added the equally impressive *Slilverpine* (VI,7) up the hanging chimney to the right of *The Fine Line*. This concluded a remarkable 10 days of development and the establishment of one of Scotland's steepest ice climbing areas. No doubt

56. Dave MacLeod approaching his highpoint on his second attempt on *Anubis* (XII) in January 2010. MacLeod succeeded on his next visit a few weeks later. (*Andy Turner*)

these superb routes will attract considerable attention next time there is a major freeze.

Anubis – A Pointer to The Future

Late in February, Dave MacLeod stunned the winter climbing world with the first winter ascent of *Anubis* (XII), a summer E8 6c, high up in Coire na Ciste on Ben Nevis. MacLeod made the first summer ascent of the route, which follows an intermittent crack-line running up to a huge roofed prow on the front face of *The Comb*, in July 2005. He had dreamed of climbing it in winter ever since, and after completing his long-term project to free the nearby aided winter route *Don't Die of Ignorance* (XI,11) in March 2008, he turned his attention to *Anubis*. Unlike *Don't Die of Ignorance*, which took six attempts, Dave succeeded on *Anubis* on his third visit. After climbing the long crux section, which overhangs 12m over its 35m length, he tied his 70 metre ropes together and continued up icy grooves, with the rope just clipped to the belay as a runner, until he was on Grade IV ground. He then untied and soloed to the top.

Anubis opens a door to a new future for the world of winter climbing. MacLeod has taken M-climbing tools and techniques and combined them with Scottish ethics to produce a climb that is quite unique across the world. *Anubis* is equivalent in difficulty to the hardest pre-protected M-climbs and represents a quantum leap in the development of the sport. M-climbing will never be the same again and MacLeod can justifiably claim to have climbed the most difficult traditional mixed route in the world.

Cairngorms – Super Route for Dubh Loch

Creag an Dubh Loch's 200m-high Central Gully Wall is one of the great Scottish cliffs. This maze of steep slabs and overlaps rarely builds up with snow and catches the morning sun, so not surprisingly it is rarely in winter condition. Until this season it had only been climbed in winter on three occasions. The first was in January 1980 when the strong Edinburgh team of Hamilton, Taylor and Spence made a winter ascent of the VS *Mousetrap* at VII,8. Their ascent benefited from unusually icy conditions, but even so it was an astonishing feat for the era.

The route was repeated in January 1986 by Dougie Dinwoodie and Jeff Hall in similarly icy conditions, but the ascent of the day was the first ascent of *The Rattrap* by Andy Nisbet and Sandy Allan. This pair started up the 5c cracks of *Dubh Loch Monster* before veering right to gain a line of ice near the upper section of *Gulliver*. Their 19-hour ascent, climbing the upper pitches by moonlight has entered Scottish winter climbing legend as one of the greatest winter climbs of the 1980s, and was one of the first Scottish Grade VIIIs to be recorded.

In recent years, *The Rattrap* saw a couple of repeat attempts by Pete Benson, but they failed due to poor conditions at mid-height on the face. After accompanying Benson on one of these attempts, Guy Robertson resolved to climb a direct line up the face based on the line of *King Rat*. This summer E1 classic follows VS cracks for the main part, except for a wide 5c roof at the start of the second pitch. Above the roof, Robertson had noted that it was possible to climb a more direct line up the crack system, avoiding some of the devious wandering left and right taken by the summer line.

Robertson made two attempts on the line earlier in the season with Pete MacPherson. They reached a high-point five pitches up, below an overlap level with the second crux section on *King Rat*. After a brief thaw and re-freeze Robertson and MacPherson were back on 18 February. This time the grooves were lined with helpful snow-ice and after a 6am start the pair were on top of the crag before dark. 'The route was stunning,' Robertson enthused. 'Not the slow powdery verglas grind of last time but really elegant, thin and icy climbing, interspersed with very strenuous bulges (and, of course, the roof). For me it was one of the best, if not the best, of all the long hard routes I've done. You can imagine the two of us sitting watching the sunset, after all that effort, to be rewarded with conditions and such an immaculate day. We were tickled pink.'

The eight-pitch long *Super Rat* (IX,9) is one of the finest Scottish winter additions in recent years taking a strong natural line and needing a precise combination of snow, freeze and thaw to make it possible. Ross Hewitt was also rewarded that day with an ascent of *Mousetrap* with Tania Noakes. Three days later, Iain Small and Simon Richardson added *Danger Mouse*, which starts up *Mousetrap*, then follows *Kraken* and *Waterkelpie Wall* to join the upper pitches of *Super Rat*. At VII,7 it is the easiest line on the wall but as with the other three routes on the face it will only be possible when the 'easier' upper pitches have consolidated snow or ice. The front face of

67. Left: Iain Small climbing the *Subtraction* groove on the first ascent of *Integration* (VIII,8), Minus One Buttress, Ben Nevis. (*Simon Richardson*) Right: Pete MacPherson climbing steep cracks on Pitch 4 during the FA of *Super Rat* (IX,9), Creag an Dubh Loch. The route continues up the cracks and bulges to the right of the ice smear high up and left. (*Guy Robertson*)

Central Gully Wall has now been climbed six times (on four separate days) in the last 30 years and remains one of the most elusive winter objectives in Scotland.

Minus One Buttress Comes of Age

In early March, the Minus Face came into its best condition for over 20 years, and the much-prized Minus gullies saw many ascents together with two new winter routes on the legendary Minus One Buttress. The original line on this superb feature (*Minus One Buttress* – VII,7), was first climbed by Arthur Paul and Norrie Muir in April 1977 and has only been repeated a couple of times. According to climbing folklore the pair were climbing on the Ben on a horrible sleety day, but that night it froze, so they headed back up next morning to find the mountain coated in a climb-anywhere coating of polystyrene ice. Their route was repeated a day or two later by Jerry Smith and Graham Little, and then in 1988 by George Armstrong and Alan Shand but, since then, all other attempts on the route have failed.

Iain Small and Simon Richardson followed the first three pitches of *Minus One Direct* and then continued up the summer line of *North-eastern Grooves* to below the huge overhanging corner slicing through the upper part of the buttress taken by the summer E1 *Subtraction*. Small made an outstanding lead of this long and demanding crux pitch, and they eventually arrived at the top of *Integration* (VIII, 8) on the crest of North-east Buttress at 8pm with eight sustained pitches and 13 hours of climbing behind them.

Three days later, Guy Robertson, Nick Bullock and Pete Benson followed their footsteps up the lower part of *Minus One Buttress* before breaking out right to follow a continuous crack-line leading up the buttress. This stunning line (VIII, 8) approximates to the summer *Minus One Direct* with the *Serendipity Variation* (E1). 'The route was never particularly hard,' Robertson said afterwards, 'but this is possibly the finest winter climb I've ever done. The climbing and the line were simply superb.' Unfortunately these routes were only in condition for a few days before a slow thaw set in and the ice peeled off and crashed into the lower reaches of Observatory Gully.

Second Ascent Fever

Significant second ascents included *Against All Odds* (VII,7) in Glen Coe (Robertson-Fyffe), *Hung, Drawn and Quartered* (VIII,8) on Am Basteir on Skye (MacPherson-Parnell) and *The Godfather* (VIII,8) on Beinn Bhan (Small-Stone). In the far north, Pete MacPherson and Iain Small made the second winter ascent of *Marathon Corner* (VIII,8) on Ben Loyal. This vegetated E1 climb was first climbed in winter by Guy Robertson and Pete Benson in 2004 and has the distinction of being the most northerly winter climb in the country

The most important repeats however, were two ascents of *The Tempest* in Stob Coire nan Lochan in Glen Coe by Andy Turner and Dave MacLeod. *The Tempest*, which takes the diamond-shaped wall on Summit Buttress to the left of Broad Gully, was first climbed by Neil Gresham in January 2001 after top rope practice and pre-placing gear. The route caused a furore at the time, but it was a genuine attempt to raise Scottish winter standards in line with the rest of the world. The route was graded M9, and together with *Logical Progression* in the Southern Highlands, which was climbed in similar style, it set a new technical level for Scottish winter climbing.

The Tempest was repeated shortly after Gresham's ascent by Innes Deans, but since then it has not been climbed. Scottish technical standards have risen considerably in the intervening nine years, often by climbers who have applied skills learned on M-climbing venues elsewhere in the world. As a result, the Scottish ground up ethic has emerged even stronger than ever, and it was time for a re-appraisal of *The Tempest*.

Enter Andy Turner who realised that to make a ground-up ascent, placing protection as he climbed, he would have to remove the original in-place nuts and pegs that were now in poor condition. Turner spent a couple of days climbing *Scabbard Chimney* and *Spectre*, so he could abseil down the route to remove the gear. He then succeeded on leading the route on his second visit. His first attempt failed at a bold section at three-quarters height, but on his return he managed to find a couple of wire placements to protect the committing icy top section. Turner felt that in its traditional state the route was worth hard IX,9, possibly even X,9 for the difficult-to-find gear and run out climbing.

A few days later, Dave MacLeod set off up the route, eager to make an on-sight ascent. He also stalled at a point six metres below the top, having run out of the correct sized protection. 'I didn't fancy a major peel from the final moves without gear but was desperate not to lose the on-sight either,' he explained on his blog. 'Solution? Down-climb the whole thing taking

168. Iain Small on the FA of *Danger Mouse* (VII,7), Creag an Dubh Loch, which takes the easiest way up the great front face of Central Gully Wall. (*Simon Richardson*)

the gear back out and come back after a rest.' A day later MacLeod was back on a typically foul Scottish day, and he battled up the route fighting through spindrift avalanches to record the first on-sight ascent. Both ascents were highly significant. Turner demonstrated that it was possible to climb the wall without working the moves and MacLeod climbed the route in perfect style. These two ascents alone are a clear demonstration of how far Scottish winter standards have progressed over the past decade – who can guess what the next 10 years will bring?

PAUL KNOTT

Kyrgyzstan 2008-10

This report covers developments taking place in Kyrgyzstan during 2008-10, excluding all peaks of the Pamir Alai. The report has been compiled with the assistance of the Alpinist newswire, American Alpine Journal, BMC International News, Climbing.com news, mountain.ru, and russianclimb.com.

From 20-29 2009 August, Russian climbers Vitaly Gorelik and Gleb Sokolov made the first ascent of a steep 2400m buttress on the N face of Pik Pobeda (7439m). On the route they encountered very hard ice and a shattered band of yellow rock with thin ice, both of which made for slow progress. They reached the top of the buttress on 27 August and continued over Pobeda West (6918m). During the climb, they experienced high winds and temperatures around -17°C.

In August 2010, Alexander Kirikov and Gleb Sokolov made the second ascent of the little-known 1982 *Ukrainian Route* on Khan Tengri (6995m). This follows a logical line up the SW face between the standard *Pogrebetskogo 1931 Route* (F5a) up the west ridge and the 1964 *Romanov Route* up the SSW or *Marble Rib* (F6a). Also in the Central Tien Shan, on 28 August 2008 Denis Urubko, Gennady Durov and Boris Dedeshko completed an F6a, 33-pitch new route alpine style on Eight Women-climbers Peak (6110m). The mountain appears to have been untouched since its first ascent in 1974, which was by the S ridge.

In July 2010, a UK/US party climbed in the almost-unexplored Djangart region, south of Karakol and close to the border with Xinjiang. Virtually the first recorded climbing visit to this range was by the UK team of Ingrid Crossland and Graham Sutton in 2004 (*see AJ 110*). In 2008, a Moscow team climbed Pik 5291m. The 2010 team approached via the border post at Uch-Koshkon and the Kaichi valley, and two days with horses from the usable road-end took them to the Djangart river near the outflow of the Akoguz glacier. From the Djangartynbashi glacier, Dan Clark, Matt Traver, and Mike Royer climbed Pik 4766m (41°37' N, 78°51' E) via a 700m icy couloir on the NW face which they named *Horseman's Horror* (D+, 80°) after discovering their horse team had cut 20m from one of their ropes. They propose naming the summit Pik Howard-Bury, after the British explorer who visited the Tien Shan in the early 20th century. From the same glacier on 27 July, Traver and Royer climbed Pik 5048m (41°35' N, 78°52' E) via the N ridge and NE face at AD+, 650m, proposing the name Peak of Illumination for the summit. From the N2 glacier, they climbed the E face of Pt 5080m (41°39' N, 78°59' E), which they christened Pik Sutherland, via the southernmost couloirs at TD-, 700m, retreating from just below the

59. Pik Howard-Bury (4766m), Djangart region, showing the line of the first ascent via *Horseman's Horror* on the NW face. *(Michael Royer)*

summit due to high winds.

In 2009, Pat Littlejohn, Adrian Nelhams, Vladimir Komissarov and party made a return trip to the Kuilu range, which they first explored in 2000. From a base camp on the N side of the Kuilu river, they made the first ascent of Ak Sakal (5020m) via a snow shoulder at 4500m, of the more technical Bakshi (4434m), and of Pk Koopsyz (4755m).

A number of parties have continued exploration of the central part of the Western Kokshaal-Too. In July 2008, a team of Slovenian mountaineers climbed from the Fersmana glacier, having approached the area via Naryn. At the head of the glacier, Arne Jeglic and Anze Cokl made the first ascent of Pik Zastava (5070m), via *FAT Couloir Direct* (VI/4, 600m) on the N face. They descended to the west with eight abseils on Abalakov anchors. On the unclimbed Pik Byiely (Grand Poohbah, 5697m), Arne Jeglic and Jaka Ortar attempted the S ridge and couloir with difficulties up to V/3-, ending above all notable obstacles but 300m below the summit. Jaka Ortar, Jani Skrinjar and Janez Rutar climbed the face of Pik 5230m, reaching 5017m via a route they called *Missed* (50-60°, 350m). Bor Sumrada and Janez Rutar made the first ascent of Pik 4905m, which they named Pik Plaza, via the west couloir and north ridge (80°/40°-60°, 350m). Two separate groups reached the summit of previously unclimbed Pik Anin (4805m) via the N face. Jeglic and Cokl with Tadej Orazem climbed *Bloody aurikelj* (V/5, 350m), while Ortar and Sumrada, Skrinjar and Rutar climbed *Waterfull*

(IV/4, 300m). The party also made a number of ski descents, including of the lower summit (5130m) of Pik Neizvestniy (5230m), and made the first ascent of Pik 4627m as acclimatisation.

In August 2009, the Polish climbing party of Rafal 'Waldorf' Zajac and Michal Kasprowicz made the first ascent of Pik Granitsa (5370m), taking a line towards the R side of the N face that they named *Nordic Walking* (AI5/5+, M4/5, 800m+). They descended the centre of the face on Abalakov anchors. Earlier, the same party climbed a new ice route *Z-K* (600m, 60-80°) on the NW face of Pik Plaza (4905m). Also in August 2009, from the adjacent Sarychat glacier, the UK party of Martin Jones, Edward Lemon, Gareth Mottram and Jacob Wrathall made five first ascents after a long moraine approach: Pik Lyell (4864m GPS), Pik Thornes (5014m GPS; 4989m on maps), Pik Katherine (4840m GPS), Pik Sylvia (4910m) and Pik Hilarie (4928m). The last two of these link via a snow ridge to still-unclimbed Fers III (5210m), which the team did not have time to attempt. A little further west, in 2008 Pat Littlejohn, Adrian Nelhams, Vladimir Komissarov and team made several first ascents from the Kotur glacier basin. Different groups climbed two variants on the previously unclimbed S ridge of Pik Judith-Brian (4986m) at PD+ and AD+, and made an ascent of adjacent Pik Pyramida (5140m).

The Kyzyl Asker glacier was the venue for a strong Minsk-based party in August-September 2009. The troika Sergei Nilov, Mitya Golovchekno and Sergei Mikhailov attempted a new route on the SE face of Kyzyl Asker (5842m), climbing from 22-29 August and reaching 5560m before retreating in the face of prolonged severe storms. The team of Stas Shabunya, Nikolai Golovchenko, Alexander Lukyanov and Ludmilla Gaidukovka made the first ascent of the summit Babocha (Butterfly, 5300m). Nikolai Bandalet, Sasha Malakhovskiy and Tanya Frolova climbed a new route on Panfilov Division (5280m), finding the summit note left by the Yu. Popenko's first ascent party in 1980. Earlier, on 17 August Bandalet, Nilov, Malakhovski, Golovchenko and Mikhailov reached the summit they named Verniy (Faithful, 5250m by GPS; also known as the Tien Shan Petit Dru or Sabor, meaning Cathedral) via its remote central NW wall at 6B, 700m, 80-90°. The team spent four nights on the wall. Also in the area in August 2009, Dave Gladwin and Tom Stewart made the first ascent of the N ridge of the N summit (c 5500m) of Kyzyl Asker at ED2/3, VI WI3/4 M6+/7, 2000m, from 24-26 August. They descended the unseen W face, and subsequently named the summit Sculptura Chokursu. On the NNE face of the c4800m summit between Piks Zuckerman and Carnovsky, Gladwin and Stewart climbed a new route *Sarah's Daddy* (ED2 WI5, 500m), with some ground in common with *Beefcake* and *Fire and Ice*. Tom Bide and Carl Reilly climbed Pik 5046m via the W face and S ridge at TD/TD+. Bide and Urpu Hapuoja climbed the N ridge of Pik 4863m at AD.

Finally, in August 2010 a party of Polish mountaineers including Tomasz Owerko explored the neighbouring Dzhirnagaktu glacier basin at the far western end of the range. They climbed a number of peaks, including Night

'0. North face of Pik Granitsa (5370m), showing the line of first ascent via *Nordic Walking* (solid line) and the abseil descent line (dotted). *(Michael Kasprowicz)*

Butterfly (5056m) from the S, Raven Peak (5370m) via the N face, and Rock Horse (5186m) by the W ridge. The latter summit, and other smaller peaks on the eastern side of the glacier, may have been climbed from the Kyzyl Asker glacier by Kazbek Valiev's 1985 team.

Further west again in the Torugart-Too range, in July-August 2010 John Proctor and Robert Taylor made the first ascent of a peak they named Mur Samir (5008m on Russian map; 5035m by GPS), via the NE ridge at AD. Taylor with Adam Russell then climbed Pk 4820m immediately north of Mustyr (5108m) via the N ridge at PD+, naming it Karyshkyr. Proctor and Russell also attempted Pik 4850m from the Teke-Lutor glacier, finding an AD snow/ice route to a subsidiary summit. Meanwhile, Mark Weeding, Misha Sukhorukov and Glenn Wilks made first ascents of Pik 4470m (40°37'58" N, 74° 31'45" E), Piks 4510m and 4616m (40°39'10" N, 74°28'54" E) along the same ridge, Pik 4318m and Pik 4378m, all accessed from the Karakol river. In the same range in August-September 2010, James Monypenny, Sam Leach and Tom Nichols made a further three first ascents: Toroloc (4870m) via the N face at D, 600m; Free Tibet (4700m), PD; and Peak Abu (4495m), F. They also climbed a new route *Diligent Epiphany* (TD, 900m) taking a couloir on the N face of Mur Samir.

Also in the Naryn region, in 2010 Pat Littlejohn's ISM teams made a number of new ascents from the S side of the At Bashi range. In August a group climbed from the Mustabbes river, climbing peaks Stefan (4480m, PD), Bashnya (4690m, AD), Darshana (4570m, AD), and Beersh Berkut (4600m). Another group in September from the Kensu valley climbed 11 new peaks/routes including the S ridge of Sumashedshaya (4510m) at D+, the E ridge of Pik Ara (4595m) at AD, the N ridge of Ekilik (4496m) at AD-, and a new route on the highest peak Kensu (4757m) via the S ridge. Active in the same range in August 2009 were Sally Brown, Eddy Barnes, Sari Nevala and Vanessa Wills, climbing from the Kaeyndi valley. The party made probable first ascents of Dove Peak (4311m), Crow's Nest (4155m), Chook Mountain (4063m) and Icarus (4537m), all at PD- / AD+. They also climbed the new ice route *Wills-Brown Couloir* (D, 70-80°) to the ridge between Shark Peak (4249m) and Crocodile Peak (4352m).

An interesting recent development in this part of Kyrgyzstan is alpine rock climbing in several accessible venues, all explored by Pat Littlejohn and Adrian Nelhams with various teams. Prominent amongst these is the Son Kul canyon, which has limestone routes potentially up to 900m, with around 20 routes climbed to date – up to 8 pitches and British E2. Routes reported in 2009 include the N ridge of the main 3450m summit, with steep HVS sections, and *Manaschi Rib* on a smaller subsidiary peak, also at HVS with 14 pitches plus 150m of scrambling. The 600m ridge to the right of this yielded *Friendly Buttress* at V-. Shifting to the unexplored east side of the canyon, over the river, Pat found *Eastern Spine* with some 5a pitches. The hardest route was in another canyon further west – *Striker* (E2 5c), climbed by Pat with John Vlasto. Geoff Hornby and David Barlow also visited the Son Kul area in 2009 and report climbing a 650m HVS, a 100m E2 and a 200m VS.

Littlejohn's parties have also explored two further alpine rock venues. The Nomad Domes area near Arashan has seen a number of 3-pitch routes developed. The Tash Rabat valley north of the At Bashi range also appears to have good potential; the 2010 ISM party climbed five limestone routes up to 500m and HVS standard.

Elsewhere in Kyrgyzstan, in August 2008 Mikhail Kleslo's Czech team made the first ascent of Korumdy East (6384m) in the eastern Zaalay Pamir.

DICK ISHERWOOD

Pakistan 2008-10

Thanks are due to Lindsay Griffin, and to several of the climbers mentioned below, for assistance with these notes.

2008

One of the most notable ascents in Pakistan during 2008 was an alpine-style new route on the Rakhiot (NW) Face of **Nanga Parbat**. Italians Simon Kehrer, Walter Nones and Karl Unterkircher first acclimatised by climbing two subsidiary peaks on the NE ridge of **Chongra South** (6448m) and **Chongra Main** (6824m), the latter via a new route to make only the second ascent of the mountain. They then embarked on the Rakhiot Face by a line up its centre below the Silver Plateau. After some steep ice climbing they reached a snow shelf at 6300m where Unterkircher, searching for a tent site, fell 15m into a crevasse carrying the party's only rope and satellite phone in his sac.(How many of us have come close to doing this?) His companions found him dead, and managed to retrieve the rope and phone, though not his body. As they were feeling relatively good themselves, they decided, after a conversation with Unterkircher's agent in Italy, to continue. They reached the Silver Plateau at 7500m and descended the 1953 Buhl route, with some variations, partly on short skis, which they had carried up the climb. They were eventually rescued by helicopter from 5400m. Their 3000m route was graded IV-V, M4+, with ice up to 70-80°, and was named for Unterkircher, a very experienced Himalayan and Karakoram climber.

On **K2**, the weather in July was unusually bad so expeditions were backed up and things became crowded on the Abruzzi Spur route above the Shoulder, with no less than 10 groups hoping to reach the summit at the same time. There seems to have been some confusion over the fixing of ropes up to and through the Bottleneck, largely done by Sherpas and high-altitude Pakistani porters, but in the end 18 climbers from six parties reached the summit on 1 August. An avalanche then removed most of the fixed rope. Several people died in falls and another sérac fall claimed four more. In all 11 climbers were killed, the worst year for fatalities on K2 since 1986, when 13 died.

The Russians Valerie Babanov and Viktor Afanasiev climbed new routes on both **Broad Peak** and **Hidden Peak**. Their route on Broad Peak followed a steep buttress well to the left of the original route, through a steep sérac barrier at around 7000m, and traversed to join the original route in its upper part. Their climb on the SW face of Hidden Peak took a new

171. The summit snow ridge of Batura II (7762m). In the background is a rare photo of the summit of Batura I (7785m). (*University of Seoul expedition 2008*)

line, largely on ice, and left of the 1983 *Polish route*, to join the 1977 *Yugoslav route* at 7200m on the SW ridge. They also planned another new route on Gasherbrum II but decided they were a bit too tired.

Two Polish climbers made an alpine style traverse of Hidden Peak, from south to north, starting up the Spanish 1983 route on the SW face and joining the original American 1958 route high up, after four nights in one camp waiting out bad weather. They reached the summit after 10 days and descended to the north, presumably on or close to the *Messner/Habeler route*. They had planned to continue their traverse over Gasherbrums II and III but had to descend due to lack of food and fuel.

Batura II, at 7762m one of the highest unclimbed summits left in the world, was finally climbed, after many attempts, by a Korean party from the University of Seoul, led by Kim Chang-Ho, in part to mark the university's 90th anniversary. The climb took the S face above the Muchuhar and Batokshi glaciers, and involved a steep 700m rock headwall. They used 2400m of fixed rope.

The American Kyle Dempster climbed the impressive 1300m W face of **Tahu Rutum** (6651m) in the Hispar Mustagh solo – really solo, as he had no support at all for seven weeks. He started up 640m of steep ice then climbed on rock, using a continuous loop technique with 280m of rope, sleeping on a portaledge, and hauling his gear. After 21 days on the face he reached 6500m on the final ridge in darkness and high wind, decided not to continue to the summit, and descended in more bad weather, taking two days to abseil down the face and three more on the snow-covered glacier, all with no food, to reach his unmanned base camp. This seems to have been one of the more extreme solo adventures of recent years.

Two Slovenian climbers, Dejan Miskovic and Pavle Kosjek, climbed a new line on the NE face of the **Mustagh Tower** (7284m), from the Younghusband Glacier, up steep ice, snow and mixed ground at a standard of WI5 M5. They reached the top of the face at 6900m in one long day and bivouacked in a snow hole, then gave up on the summit in poor weather and decided to descend the 1956 French route on the SE ridge. While soloing down, Kosjek fell through a cornice to his death, carrying their only rope. Miskovic did still have the satellite phone, however, and called Slovenia for help before the batteries died, then descended to 5400m where he was eventually picked up by a helicopter. This is the nearest yet to an alpine style ascent of the Mustagh Tower.

172. The Korean route on the north-west face of Spantik (7027m), 2009. (*Kim Hyung-Il Collection*)

A Norwegian party of four repeated the famous Norwegian 1984 ascent of the **Great Trango Tower** over 30 days. The climbing, in often poor conditions, was very difficult, but unlike the first ascensionists they did manage to descend alive.

Three other Slovenians made the second ascent of **K7 West** (6858m) following the first ascent by Steve House and companions a year earlier. Three other climbers in the same group attempted a steep route on the rock pillars of the S face, reaching 5700m.

2009

Fewer parties climbed in Pakistan in 2009, due to security concerns. It was also a very heavy snow year in the Karakoram. No one reached the summit of K2 but there was, at least, only one fatality. There were several ascents of Nanga Parbat, Hidden Peak and Gasherbrum II, but only one success on Broad Peak.

Five climbers from a large Austrian/Canadian group climbed a new route on the Diamir Face of **Nanga Parbat**, covering 2300m of new ground and joining the 1962 *Kinshofer route* at 7250m. They continued to the summit, looking for a comrade who had ascended the *Kinshofer route* with a Korean party and become separated from them. It transpired that he had fallen toward the Mummery Rib to his death.

Spanish climbers Alvaro Novellon and Oscar Perez made the first complete ascent of the NW ridge of Latok II (7108m), which had many previous attempts going back to 1987. They reached the summit after four

173. Aymeric Clouet traversing the south-east face of the Ogre at around 6300m in 2009. (*Julien Dusserre*)

bivouacs and descended the same route. Perez fell on an unstable snow slope and pulled Novellon off too, but their rope snagged on a snow crest. Perez was severely injured and Novellon, after trying unsuccessfully to lower him, descended alone, using a cut rope for many short abseils. He called his climbing club in Spain, which mounted a rescue effort but bad weather prevented them reaching Perez, over a week after his fall. Their ascent was graded VI 6a M6.

Two Czech climbers, Jiri Pliska and Ondrej Mandula, made a new route on the SW face of **Latok IV** (6456m) above the Baintha Lukpar glacier in a single day in July. They took a steep line left of the Japanese 1980 route, which was the first ascent of the peak. The Czechs descended by the same route, in deteriorating weather from just below the summit and above all the difficulties.

A French team (Aymeric Clouet, Julien Dusserre and Jerome Para) attempted the **Ogre** (**Baintha Brakk**, 7285m) by its SE face from the Choktoi glacier. After two days of steep mixed climbing they reached the base of the final steep rock wall on the east ridge at around 6250m, then made a long traverse left to the SE ridge. They then had to retreat from the foot of the final tower at 6800m in bad weather, descending this ridge, which was first climbed to the same point by Canadians Jeff Relph and Jon Walsh in 2006 but has not so far been completed to the summit.

Three Korean climbers made a new route on the NW face of **Spantik** (7027m) to the right of the 1987 *British route* (the *Golden Pillar*). They climbed in alpine style and took seven days, grading it VI WI4 M8. As on the British route, some of the climbing was very insecure and good belays were hard to find. They descended by the SW ridge further right, the descent used by the British and by others since, and first climbed upwards by a Japanese party in 2004.

Pat Deavoll from New Zealand made a solo first ascent of Karim Sar (6180m) in the Batura Mustagh after her companion became ill. The route, on the south-east side of the mountain, above the Shilinbar glacier, involved steep rock and ice, and some bad snow conditions. She climbed it in a long day, up and down, from a camp at 5100m.

A Canadian party attempted the so far unclimbed East Summit (c 6900m) of **Pumarikish** in the Hispar Mustagh, but were deterred by avalanches and instead made the first ascent of **Khani Basar Sar** (6441m) by its SW rib, taking 24 hours from a bivouac at 4800m.

On the rock towers of the Baltoro, Tomas and Alexander Huber, with two companions, made a completely free ascent of the famous *Eternal Flame* on the 6251m **Trango Tower**, a route first climbed in 1989 by Kurt Albert and Wolfgang Güllich. The first ascent was largely free but did use a bolt ladder on one pitch near the top. The Huber route bypasses this at a standard of 5.12d, and an altitude of around 6000m. As the climb was already named they gave names to their individual new free pitches, which is perhaps a novel practice in the big mountains.

In the Charakusa valley above Hushe a Swiss party made the first ascent of **Farol Far East** (6200m), a rock peak which had seen several previous attempts. They fixed some rope on its east ridge and found more difficult rock (6c+ M6+) near the summit, which they reached on the Swiss national day, 1 August.

Also in this valley, an Italian team attempted a new route on the impressive SW pillar of **K7 West**, climbing at up to 7b A2, but descending from 5700m, fully 1000m below the summit. There are now three partial routes on this pillar but none has reached the 6200m sub-peak of K7 West, let alone the main summit.

2010

Relatively few parties managed to climb in Pakistan in 2010, due to the security situation and also to the catastrophic floods, which affected not only the lowlands of the country, but also the Indus valley as far up as Ladakh.

On **K2** there were no successful ascents this year. The Swedish climber and extreme skier Fredrik Ericsson was climbing with Austrian mountaineer Gerlinde Kaltenbrunner on the Abruzzi Spur when he slipped somewhere above the Bottleneck and fell over 3000 feet to his death. His plan, believe it or not, was to ski down from the summit. Kaltenbrunner, who is trying to become the first woman to climb the fourteen 8000m peaks without oxygen, turned around and safely climbed down to camp four on the shoulder and then continued down to base camp.

The Austrian climber Christian Stangrl claimed the only ascent of K2, in what appeared to be a remarkable solo push, but was doubted by several people and eventually admitted that he had not been very near the summit at all. He seems to have turned back below the Abruzzi Shoulder. His account included a sighting of a snow leopard somewhere well above the base camp, which in itself is highly improbable. The Austrian media have nominated him for the 'climbing lie of the decade' – though this decade has a way to go.

In August two Russian climbers, Vjacheslav Ivanov and Oleg Koltunov, finally succeeded on the steep granite west face of **K7 West**, though it is not clear at the time of writing whether they continued up the difficult mixed ridge to the summit 600m higher. An Italian pair attempted the same face but retreated after 10 days when their portaledge was destroyed in a rockfall. They then climbed a steep 900m new line on the W face of **Farol West** (6370m).

The Pakistan authorities are putting up their peak fees for 2011, though not by very much. The 50% discount that has been applied to most of the high Karakoram peaks since 2002 has been cut to 40%, which means, for instance, that a K2 permit for up to seven climbers will now cost $7200 instead of $6000. Peaks in Gilgit, Ghizar and Chitral (except Spantik) are offered at 90% off for anyone brave enough to go there. Peaks below 6500m still require only a $50 per person trekking permit, which is very liberal compared to China, India or Nepal.

For those interested in the **Hindu Kush** a new and detailed sketch map of the Tirich Mir massif at a scale of 1:70,000 is now available from a Spanish source, including a panoramic sketch of the mountains based on a photograph taken by Kurt Diemberger.

For more information, visit **www.sgim.drac.com**

HARISH KAPADIA

India 2009

4. Zanskar peaks, L to R: Pk 5780, Rungofarka (6495m) (on Rungofarka glacier) and Lingsarmo (6955m) (on Lingsarmo glacier). Taken from a chorten near Gelmothungos. *(Harish Kapadia)*

The best news of 2009 was that the Indian government opened 100 new peaks for climbing. Though the notification came in early 2010, the process was undertaken throughout 2009. It is almost 17 years since a number of new peaks have been opened to climbers. All the peaks are in the Zanskar and Ladakh area. Many of them are along the road which runs from Kargil-Sankoo to Padam. This passes Panikhar, Parkachik, Ringdom, and the Pensi la to reach Padam. South of this road lie several smaller valleys which are on the watershed between Zanskar and Kishtwar. The peaks that lie in these valleys like **Gelmothungos**, **Chilung**, **Durung Drung**, **Hagshu** and **Nun** and **Kun** (both above 7000m) were open but now many other approaches to these peaks are possible. **Lingsarmo (6955m)**, a high peak in the Nun-Kun massif is now open. In the Shafat glacier, peaks opened include **Rungofarka I (6495m)**, **II (6395m)**; Chilung nala, **Chiling Pk I (6253m)** and **II (6349m)**; Hagshu valley **Peak 6515m**; and in the Durung Drung valley **Peak 6485m**. Moreover, due to the road passing by the mouths of these valleys one only has to step down from one's trans-

175. Zanskar peaks in the Lalung valley (third valley from Ringdom to Pensi la): Pk 6152 (left) and Pk 5844m. *(Harish Kapadia)*

port and cross the Suru river or Doda river to set up a base camp. Peaks are not more than two days away, thus allowing climbing in very light style, economically and with the ability almost to change base camps by road. Some photographs were published in the *Himalayan Journal,* Vol 65, and a complete list of 104 newly opened peaks with co-ordinates and map references is available.

In 2009 there were 64 Indian and 37 foreign expeditions to the Indian Himalaya, a total of 101, one of the largest numbers in recent years. However, many Indian expeditions were to peaks that have been climbed often (Satopanth, Chhamser Kangri) and many foreign groups were commercially organised trip to well-known peaks, including Nun and Kun. Stok Kangri retained its record as the most climbed 6000m peak in the world with the added tag of one of the dirtiest base camp seen (or smelt) anywhere.

In Garhwal, one of the best climbs was that of **Mukut Parvat (7242m)**, by a French team. It is significant that a team of foreigners was allowed to climb a peak that stands on the border with Tibet. Martin Moran solved the challenge of **Changuch (6322m)** rising above the Pindari glacier. Many teams in the past, and even in 2009 failed, sometimes with fatalities. An Indian team climbed **Deoban (6852m)** and the leading Slovenian alpinist Marko Prezelj, with two young climbers, climbed **Bhagirathi II (6512m)** and **III (6454m)** above the Gangotri glacier. They climbed the south and south-west faces respectively in alpine style.

Sikkim was also opened to allow a British team to attempt **Kellas Peak (6680m)**. Though they did not ascend the main peak, the party reached Kellas Col (6380m), a snow saddle on the border ridge south of Kellas Peak, and climbed an unnamed peak of 6252m. On nearby **Tingchen Khang (6010m)** tragedy struck a Mumbai team soon after the ascent of the peak. A freak fall killed two young climbers, while two badly injured Sherpas with them were rescued.

In the eastern Karakoram, two high virgin peaks were attempted in adjoining valleys. An American-British-Indian team attempted **Saser Kangri II (7518m) Eastern Peak**, while an American-Indian team attempted **Plateau Peak (7287m)**. Both attempts reached half way up their respective mountains.

Both leading mountaineering organisations in India had new Presidents. Ramkrishna Rao, former Director General of ITBP, was elected President of the Indian Mountaineering Foundation, while leading Indian mountaineer Col Ashok Abbey took over the reins of the Himalayan Club. The Himalayan artist Serbjeet Singh passed away during the year, leaving a legacy of many fine paintings. He was painting at the Zozila pass in Kashmir as a war artist when Indian guns were firing on Pakistani troops. He produced several sketches of the Himalaya, based on maps, which were remarkably true to reality.

And finally, the Indian Himalaya was severely affected by changes in the weather, such that one can use the cliché that the only certainty about the weather was its uncertainty. The dry spells had effects on villagers' psyche too. The villagers of Langja in Spiti have always been suspicious about the weather being affected by the mountain above their village and have given it the romantic name Chau Chau Kang Nilda – 'Blue Moon in the Sky'. This year the villagers stopped some expeditions from proceeding to the mountain as they believed the presence of climbers was affecting the crops. A curious effect of global warming!

SIKKIM

Kellas Peak (6680m)

Team: British; leader, Jeremy Windsor. For the first time in more than 75 years, a party of climbers obtained permission to retrace the footsteps of historic British explorers such as Douglas Freshfield, Alexander Kellas and Frank Smythe, visiting the mountains of north-west Sikkim. Graham Hoyland, Mark Lambert, Anindya Mukherjee, George Rodway, Dukpa Tsering Sherpa, Phurba Sherpa, Thendup Sherpa and Jeremy Windsor headed north from Gangtok by 4WD to the district capital of Lachen, then on to the roadhead just beyond Thangu. With the help of the Indo-Tibet Border Police and a number of bemused yak herders, the party moved west across the Lugnak la to the Lhonak valley, then made a series of camps up-valley in an attempt to make the first ascent of Kellas Peak (6680m) on the Tibetan Border north of Jongsang (7462m).

176. Kellas Peak (6680m, left) and Lhonak Peak (6710m, right) from the Lhonak valley. Kellas col (6380m) is the snowy col on the far left. *(Jeremy Windsor)*

During the 1930 Kangchenjunga expedition, Günther Dyhrenfurth, Frank Smythe and other members named this shapely mountain after the prolific Scottish explorer Dr Alexander Kellas, who visited the mountains of Sikkim from 1907 to 1921. Kellas made a prodigious number of climbs in the region and in 1910 completed no less than 10 first ascents over 6000m, including Pauhunri (7125m), at that time the highest summit reached by man. Through his professional interest in chemistry, Kellas became an authority on the effects of high altitude on the human system, and questioned whether Everest could be climbed without the use of supplementary oxygen. In 1921 he explored approaches to Kabru (7338m) to the south of Kangchenjunga and returned to Darjeeling just a few days before joining the first British Everest expedition. Sadly, during the approach through Tibet, he suffered a heart attack and died. One of the great British mountain explorers of the time, Kellas was a retiring character who most often climbed with local Sherpas and, unfortunately, wrote almost nothing about his mountaineering experiences.

The 2009 party reached Kellas Col (6380m), a snow saddle on the border ridge south of Kellas Peak first gained by Kellas during one of his unsuccessful attempts to climb Jongsang. Members of the party also made the first ascent of Pt 6252m, but frequent avalanches and difficult hidden crevasses put them off making a serious attempt on Kellas Peak. The expedition was able to identify a large number of attractive unclimbed peaks in the Lugnak, Muguthang and Lhonak valleys, which should attract mountaineers for many years to come providing access to this area remains possible. *(report by Lindsay Griffin)*

Tingchen Khang (6010m)
Team: Indian; organisers, Chakram Hikers, Mumbai; leader, Mangesh Deshpande. A team of five mountaineers attempted this peak in the Sikkim Himalaya. At 1.30pm on 19 October, Mangesh and Sekar along with two Sherpas reached the summit. After descending around 100m on the slopes they slipped and fell about 50m. Both the members were fatally injured and died. Sherpa Mingma and Sherpa Ang Dorjee were also severely injured. Rescue operations were launched with the help of local government and military authorities and high-altitude Sherpas. The remoteness of the area and weather conditions made rescue operations difficult. Both Sherpas were evacuated to hospital by Indian Air Force helicopter and survived.

UTTARAKHAND – KUMAUN HIMALAYA
Nanda Devi East (7434m)
Team: Polish; leader, Jan Lenczowaski. Since the first ascent of this peak in 1939 by a Polish team the climbers from Poland have had a special affinity with this high peak. The 10-member team established base camp at 4300m in the Lawan valley. They followed the south ridge and put up Camp 2 at 6400m on 22 May. They reached 6900m, however constant bad weather, insufficient time and the sickness of one member forced them to call off the attempt.
Changuch (6322m)
Team: British; leader, Martin Moran. Many attempts have been made on this unclimbed peak and some have ended in disaster. Finally the mountain selected its climbers and the six-member British team was successful in reaching the coveted summit in the pre-monsoon season. After establishing base camp at 4275m in the Lawan Gad, ABC at 5150m and the summit camp at 5800m, they followed the NW ridge of the mountain. On 9 June, Martin Moran with Rob Jarvis, Paul Guest, Leon Winchester with LO Ludar Singh reached the summit. They estimated the climb to be Alpine D-. They also attempted Nanda Devi East but too much snow, lack of campsites and illness of two members halted them at 6050m.

Team: Indian; organisers, Mountaineers' Association of Krishnanagar; leader, Basanta Singha Roy. Unlike the British, the seven-member team from West Bengal was not successful in climbing the peak. They crossed Trail's pass en route and entered Lawan Gad from the Pindar valley. High camp was established at 5640m on 29 August on the north-west ridge connecting Changuch with Nandakhat. Technical difficulties stopped the attempt at that point.

Team: Indian; organisers, Altitude High Adventure; leader, Anit Sah. This 14-member Indian team also failed in the post-monsoon season due to bad weather and snowfall. They reached 300m above their Camp 2 established at 5180m.
Kalanka (6931m)
Team: Netherlands; leader, Michael Robert van Berkel. From Jumma, the three-man Dutch team established base camp at Bagini Kharak (4400m) on

19 August. They reached ABC at 5000m but could not proceed due to lots of snow. As a consolation, they climbed an unnamed peak (6505m) near their base camp on 21 September.

GARHWAL HIMALAYA – GANGOTRI AREA

Bhagirathi II (6512m) and III (6454m)

Team: Slovenian; leader, Marko Prezelj. The renowned Slovenian alpinist visited the Garhwal with two young climbers, Rok Blagus and Luka Lindic, in the post monsoon season and climbed both the peaks in alpine style. Bhagirathi III was climbed by its south-west face, all three reaching the summit on 22 September. Bhagirathi II was tackled from its south face followed by south ridge and all three climbers stood on top on 1 October.

Kedarnath (6968m)

Team: Italian; leader, Giordani Maurizio. On 12 August, all 11 members of this Italian expedition reached the summit of this peak above the Gangotri glacier. They followed the traditional route from their base camp at Tapovan.

Meru Shark's Fin (6450m)

Team: Slovenian; leader, Silvo Karo. Another well-known name from Slovenia, Karo attempted the Shark's Fin of Meru with two friends, Andrej Grmovsek and Marko Lukic in August–September 2009. They established ABC at 5160m but reached only 5800m on the east face before heavy snowfall forced their retreat.

Unnamed (6172m) and Swachand (6721m)

Team: Italian; leader, Giambattista Villa. This unnamed peak is located on the left bank of Swachand glacier. In August 2009, this Italian team followed the traditional path from Gangotri – Bhojbasa – Tapovan to Sunderban following the Gangotri glacier and established base camp at 4600m. Bad weather stopped any further progress.

CENTRAL GARHWAL

Chaukhamba I (7138m)

Team: Indian; organisers, Summiters, Kolkata; leader, Satyajit Kar. This large team from Kolkata approached this high mountain from Mana. After reaching the Bhagirath Kharak glacier, they established base camp at Ghoracha (4200m). Three further camps were established with Camp 3 at 6100m above the icefall. They attempted north face and reached just 40m below the summit on 25 June. Bad weather stopped them reaching the top.

Deoban (6852m)

Team: Indian; organisers, Ordinance Factories Mountaineers & Trekkers; leader, Samrat Basu. The nine-member team approached Deoban, in the Amrit Ganga valley, in the post monsoon season. They established base camp at Eri Udiyar on the right bank of Amrit Ganga. Camp 3 was established on Upper Bidhan glacier and summit camp at 6320m. Ascending via the north-west ridge and finally via the west ridge, the leader along with Ashim Ghosh, Tapas Dey, Prosenjit Bagchi and four high-altitude supporters reached the summit on 28 August.

Mukut Parvat (7242m)

Team: French; leader, Lionel Albrieux. The eight-member team approached this high mountain from Ghastoli. After entering Khati nala they reached the Pachhimi (West) Kamet glacier, established base camp at 4800m, ABC at 5300m and the summit camp at 6500m on the south ridge. Climbing alpine style, Albrieux with Damien Cabane, Sebastien Giacobi, Didier Jourdain, Emmanuel Pellissier, Marion Poitevin and Sebastien Bohin reached the summit on 2 October at 11am. Mukut Parvat was first climbed by a New Zealand expedition in 1951, but from the Dakhhini Chamrao glacier and NW ridge. They had tried the west Kamet glacier approach but found it too challenging. Edmund Hillary was a member of the team and the climb was one of the reasons he was selected for the 1953 Everest expedition.

Ronti (6063m) Team: Indian; organisers, The Natures' Foundation; leader: Debabrata Dutta. This seven-member team approached from Wan following the route through Ranak Dhar – Gairuli Patal – Ali Bugial – Baidani Bugial – Pathar Nachuni – Kailubinayak – Baguabasa – Huniathar – Rupkund – Giunargali col to base camp at Silasamudra. They established Camp 1 at Dodang and then crossed Bara Homkund. On 29 August they reached the Ronti Saddle and finally the summit at 1.30pm.

HIMACHAL PRADESH

Fluted Peak (6159m), Losar valley, Spiti

Team: Indian; organisers, Jadavpur University Mountaineering and Hiking Club; leader, Atanu Krishna Pathak. The team of eight members approached from the Losar nala and established two high camps. On 27 June they reached to beneath a cornice at 5800m and could not proceed.

Indrasan (6221m)

Team: Indian; organisers, Tarit Memorial Mountaineering & Trekking Association; leader, Partha Majumder. A seven-member team attempted this attractive mountain near Manali in June. After establishing Camp 1 atop Duhangan col (5100m) the team had to return as bad weather and excessive snowfall stopped the attempt at 5300m on 12 June.

Menthosa (6443m)

Team: Indian; organisers, BEAS Sodepur; leader, Amiya Sarkar. The seven-member team followed the Urgus nala and established two high camps. From their top camp (5850m), on 30 July they attempted on the summit but a big crevasse at around 6005m could not be crossed and they retreated.

Papsura (6451m)

Team: Indian; organisers, Bhadrakali Padatik; leader, Prosenjit Mukherjee. This eight-member team from West Bengal established base camp at 4500m on the Tos glacier. They put in four high camps with a summit camp at 5850m. From here they reached 6100m on the NW face. Bad weather and lots of snow prevented them from continuing. An attempt on nearby

Devachen also failed for the same reason. On 8 June, Arun Sen, Dipankar Ghosh, Rajib Bhattacharya, Soma Paul, Jyotilal Soren, Santosh Singh and Subrata Das reached the top of an unnamed peak (approx. 6000m) via the north ridge. This peak was located west of their Papsura summit camp.

Rubal Kang (6187m)

Team: Indian; organisers, Kolkata Trekkers Youth; leader, Ashim Kumar Ghosh Chowdhury.

This peak is located in the West Dibibokri glacier, and was attempted by an eight-member team from West Bengal. They established two high camps on the mountain. From the top camp at 5836m, Kakali Majumdar and Mohar Singh Thakur reached the summit on 27 August.

Shiva (6142m)

Team: Indian; organisers, Climbers' Circle; leader, Tapan Kumar Mukhopadhyay. Shiva is located in the Pangi valley of Chamba district. From Cherry village the team of nine members followed the right bank of the Garotu nala and reached base camp on 27 July. They established Camp 1 (4800m) on the SW ridge on an icy patch, Camp 2 (5400m) on the broken west ridge and summit camp (5800m) again on the NW ridge. On 7 August, after crossing an icy hump, the leader with Sushanta Mandal, Laxman Singh Rana and Kendru Singh Rana reached the true summit.

Unnamed Peak (6184m) near Gangstang

Team: British; leader, Jonathan Preston. The 11-member British team began walking from Darcha and after passing through Palamo and Doll established base camp at 4284m. ABC was at 5008m and Camp 1 at 5606m. Two members suffered AMS and were brought down by the liaison officer and high-altitude supporters. Other members continued the attempt. From summit camp, they climbed the S face and on 5 October the leader with Robin Thomas, David Bingham and Benjamin Fry reached the summit. This was the first ascent of this peak located at 32^0 49'25" N, 76^0 58' 91" E. They have proposed to name the peak 'Sarasvati'. Their GPS showed the summit to be at 6165m.

Unnamed Peak (6060m) near Karcha Parvat

Team: Japanese; organisers, Tokai Section of Japanese Alpine Club; leader, Tsuneo Suzuki. This three-member Japanese team followed the Karcha nala and set up base camp at 4420m. Camp 1 (4700m) and Camp 2 (5200m) were established and on 18 July at 2.50pm, Ritsuyu Matsubara with three high-altitude supporters reached the summit via the NW face. They proposed he peak name 'Lower Karcha Parvat'.

EASTERN KARAKORAM AND LADAKH

Saser Kangri II (7518m)

Team: Indian American; leaders, Motup Goba and Mark Richey. This joint Indo-American-British expedition included Indians Chewang Motup (co-leader), Ang Tashi, Konchok Tinles, Dahn Singh and Tsering Sherpa; Americans Mark Richey (co-leader), Steve Swenson, and Mark Wilford; and British climber Jim Lowther. The goal was to climb the east summit of

177. South face of the unclimbed Saser Kangri II Main (7518m) showing the 2009 route from its base at 6000m to the high point at 6800m, with the three bivvi sites marked. The intended continuation, which the team consider safe and feasible, follows the upward rightward sloping break in the face to linked icefields at the top. The Main summit is the left hand of the two prominent points on the summit ridge. *(Jim Lowther)*

Saser Kangri II. The west summit was climbed by an Indo Japanese expedition in 1984. According to the team's maps and information, the east summit is higher and therefore should be referred to as Saser Kangri Main, which would make it the second highest unclimbed peak in the world. Mark Richey reports:

'The expedition left the Nubra valley (3050m) near the village of Tigur on 7 August. Two days were spent hiking up the Chameshan Lungpa valley to the snout of the Sakang Lungpa glacier. Base camp was established in a side valley on 11 August above and SE of the Sakang Lungpa glacier at 5180m. To reach our intended objective of the East (Main) Summit of Sasser Kangri II, we needed to cross over onto the South Shukpa Kungchang glacier which was the next valley east of our base camp. We made acclimatisation and reconnaissance trips up the unnamed glacier behind base camp on 12-13 August and established a camp on an unnamed pass above the South Shukpa Kungchang glacier at approximately 6000m. We dropped onto the South Shukpa Kungchang glacier on 14 August to explore the route to the base of the south face of Saser Kangri II. We returned to base camp on 16 August in deteriorating weather and waited there until 24 August when the weather improved enough to go back onto the South Shukpa Kunchang glacier. We spent two nights camped high on the glacier at 6500m to acclimatise and then returned to base camp.

After a period of rest in bad weather, on 6 September we climbed back to the pass in cold and windy conditions. We decided to use the short weather window to go up on the route for a day and reconnoitre the route and assess snow conditions. On 7 September we made an advanced base camp below the face and on 8 September we climbed up the south face to approximately 6700m before rappelling back down. The bottom of the south face is at about 6000m and the map shows the east summit at 7513m. The face is all hard water ice and no snow so the lower slopes were all technical ice climbing. The rock on SKII is high quality orange granite. It is a safe route with nothing above you to fall on you, provided you stay along the far right side of the couloir as we did.

Bad weather kept us from attempting the peak again until 19 September when we started up the face with the intent of going for the summit. We reached a good bivouac site early in the day at 6700m and spent the night there since there did not appear to be any good bivouac sites until a ledge system at 7000m. On 20 September we climbed up steep ice slopes in the main gully system to where we veered to the right into some mixed climbing that would take us onto the major ledge system halfway up the face. We had a poor bivouac that night on small ledges chopped out of the ice and we were not able to erect the tents. On 21 September we made progress onto the large ledge system and established a better bivouac by spending nearly 4 hours chopping a ledge out of the ice. That night it snowed and due to the poor, cold and windy weather we decided to descend on 22 September. Climbing this high in late September was very cold. We had nighttime temperatures of -13 to -17 C and highs during the day if we had sun of -5 to -9 C. We left base camp on 25 September and arrived at the road in the Nubra valley that same day.'

Plateau Peak (7287m)

Team: Indian – American – British; organisers, The Himalayan Club; leaders, Divyesh Muni and Marlin Geist. This five member Indian-American team approached this unclimbed mountain from the Sakang valley. No expedition was reported to have entered this valley since a 1985 Indian-Japanese team to Saser Kangri II. The team faced many difficulties in route finding and ferrying loads to base camp near the snout of Sakang glacier at 4800m. ABC was at 5400m on the moraines of the glacier and Camp 1 at 5760m at the base of the wall leading to the col between Plateau Peak and Saser Kangri III. The team started fixing ropes on the wall in turns and reached around 6600m on 15 August. On the same day both leaders with Rajesh Gadgil and Sudeep Barve reached the Sakang col (6100m) overlooking North Shukpa Kungchang glacier. The weather turned bad, with heavy snow and the team decided to retreat due to threat of avalanches.

On 26 August, Divyesh Muni with Rajesh Gadgil, Samgyal Sherpa and Mingma Sherpa completed a first ascent of **Tsumzong Kangri (6010m)** in

8. The first (and only) decent bivvi site at around 6700m on the 2009 attempt on the south face of Saser Kangri II Main (7518m). *(Mark Richey)*

alpine style. The peak is located near the junction of the Sakang glacier with its subsidiary glacier near its snout. One high camp was established and from there the climbers followed first the north ridge and then the west ridge to the summit.

DICK ISHERWOOD

Nepal 2009-10

I would like to thank Elizabeth Hawley, Lindsay Griffin and Tsunemichi Ikeda, in addition to a number of the climbers mentioned, for their help with these notes.

2009

The spring season in Nepal and on its northern border was again influenced by restrictions and uncertainty on the Tibetan side of the Himalaya. March 10th was the 50th anniversary of the 1959 Tibetan uprising, followed by the flight of the Dalai Lama, and the Chinese government severely restricted access for both climbers and tourists, but subsequently, in April, restrictions were eased and a number of expeditions were able to get permits just in time for the season.

Perhaps the most significant climb of the season was by Denis Urubko and Boris Dedesko from Kazakhstan, who made the second ever ascent of the avalanche prone 2400m SE face of **Cho Oyu**, by a new route, over five days. Their climb took a very direct line well to the left of the 1978 Austrian route on the same face, and included some very steep rock at over 6000m, which was partially climbed with aid but also with free sections at up to American 5.10. They graded the route F6b A2/3 M6. They took an additional four days to descend by the same route. Both climbers lost around 10kg of body weight. Denis Urubko became the eighth person to climb all fourteen 8000m peaks without oxygen, and he has done several of them by non-standard and often difficult routes.

The Americans Joe Puryear and David Gottlieb made the first ascent of **Jobo Rinjang** (6778m) south of the Nangpa La by its S face, largely on ice up to 75 degrees, with one bivouac on the ascent. They tried to traverse west to the highest peak in this group (6895m, provisionally named Lunag I, and also unclimbed) but ran into very bad snow conditions on the ridge crest and eventually bivvied again on the summit of Jobo Rinjang before descending the way they had come up with a long series of abseils from threads in the ice.

Earlier in the year, in early January, Inez Papert and Cory Richards climbed a new line on the N face of **Kwangde Shar** (6091m) in Solu Khumbu over four days. This is no less than the seventh line on the continuous N face of Kwangde Lho and Kwangde Shar, overlooking Namche Bazaar, which was first climbed by David Breashears and Jeff Lowe in 1982. It shares some ground with a 1996 French route. It was graded a mere TD (!) but also WI5 M8.

In far NE Nepal the Spanish climber Salvador Garcia-Atance led a

9. The route on the south-east face of Cho Oyu taken by Denis Urubko and Boris Dedesko, with bivouacs marked. *(Denis Urubko)*

party on what may have been the first ascent of **Dome Kang** (7264m and a subsidiary summit of **Jongsang Peak**, 7483m).They climbed the SE face of the Jongsang massif to the extensive summit plateau with 1500m of fixed rope, in what appears to have been largely a repeat of a Slovenian route climbed alpine style in 2001.

Joseph 'Dodo' Kopold from Slovakia made an impressive solo ascent of the east face of **Annapurna South** (7219m) by its central pillar, which had been attempted at least twice before. His climb involved very steep water ice, difficult rock and insecure snow and he graded it V+, WI6, M5. He reached the north summit of the peak, traversed to the main summit, and descended by a route to the south and east, close to the original Japanese ascent route of 1964, largely in the dark, during which he fell 5 metres into a crevasse. His round trip took only 40 hours from the Annapurna Lodge in the Sanctuary.

Kopold, with Martin Minarik and Elizabeth Revol, had originally intended an alpine style ascent of the 1970 British route on the S face of Annapurna I, but they were defeated by bad weather. Minarik and Revol then climbed the E ridge of **Annapurna** from the Sanctuary to the 8026m East Summit. Their ascent route involved dangerous snow conditions, so they decided to descend the north side of the range toward Manang, from the 7100m col between Roc Noir and Tarke Kang. However they became separated. Revol reached Manang village safely but Minarik, who was going very slowly and apparently suffering from oedema, disappeared. He

180. Dodo Kopold's route line on Annapurna South, seen from the Sanctuary. (*Dodo Kopold*)

had previously climbed seven 8000m summits, which shows yet again that no one is immune to the effects of very high altitude.

On **Everest** a Korean team led by Park Sung-Yeok climbed the SW face by a new line, to the left of that taken by a Russian party in 1982, and joining the W ridge high up. Four climbers reached the summit using large amounts of both fixed rope and oxygen. The upper part of the new line reportedly included rock climbing of 5.9 standard at 8100m. The same team had tried the route unsuccessfully in 2007.

Total numbers on Everest were down a bit from recent years, with a mere 457 successful ascents, mostly via the South Col. Conditions were unusually dry and some commercial expeditions used a few bolts for security on the Yellow Band – apparently a first for the Nepalese side, though at least one Russian expedition used lots on the north side in 2004. As usual several fatalities occurred, some of them clearly due to the physical inadequacy of certain paying customers. One death was attributed to 'chronic heart disease'.

Dhaulagiri had more ascents than usual, with 30 people reaching the summit in eight expeditions, all on the original NE ridge route. 22 people succeeded on the original route on **Kangchenjunga** and there were also successful ascents of Annapurna, Makalu and Lhotse beside large numbers on both Cho Oyu and Manaslu.

Tragically, in the post monsoon season, the outstanding Slovenian climber Tomas Humar died while attempting a solo ascent of the S face

181. The line on Pasang Lhamu Chuli (Jasamba) taken by the Anthamatten brothers and Michael Lergen-Dangen in autumn 2009, with bivouacs marked. (*Simon Anthamatten*)

of **Langtang Lirung** (7234m). He apparently fell at around 6300m on the south side of the SW ridge, possibly broke some bones, was unable to descend and froze to death. His body was recovered by helicopter. Humar had an impressive record of ascents on Himalayan faces, several of them solo, most notably the S face of Dhaulagiri in 1999.

In the Kangchenjunga range, also in the post monsoon season, Nick Bullock and Andy Houseman climbed the N face of **Chang Himal / Wedge Peak** (6802m, and now officially named **Ramtang Chang**). They took three bivouacs on the ascent of the steep mixed face, and a fourth while descending by the same route. They graded it ED+, M6. (*See p45*)

In Solu Khumbu Simon and Samuel Anthamatten and Michael Lergen-Dangen made an alpine style ascent of the SSE face of **Pasang Lhamu Chuli** (7351m, also known as **Jasamba**) near the Nangpa La, another difficult mixed route. They reached the summit on 29 October after three bivouacs. This is the third route on this side of this peak, and is a considerably more direct way to the summit than the others. They rated it VI, M5 with 90° sections.

The Japanese climbers Fumitaka Ichimura and Genki Narumi made an impressive traverse of **Taboche** (6501m), ascending by a new route on the north face, to the right of the pillar climbed by Mick Fowler and Pat Littlejohn in 1995, then descending by the south and east faces to Pheriche. They climbed in late November and encountered much steep ice on the face, and poor snow conditions at the top; the latter prevented them reaching the actual summit. One abseil on the descent was from a distinctly improvised deadman – 'a buried stuff bag filled with snow, which moved slightly as I descended'.

Polish climbers Wojtek Kozub, Marcel Michalek and Krzystof Starek climbed the 1400m N face of **Melanphulan** (6573m), in the Nare valley, which is just south of Ama Dablam and the Mingbo La, over five days in October. This was a very steep ice face, up to 85°, and took them four days, but they were forced to descend from the corniced ridge just below the summit. As they had placed Abalakov threads at the belays on the way up their descent was fast and efficient.

Joe Simpson climbed a new route on the S ridge of **Mera Peak** (6470m, and a very popular trekking peak by its ordinary route) solo in October. He estimated its standard to be similar to the Route Major, and named it 'In Memoriam' after two of his former climbing mates.

Three Italian climbers, Enrico Bonino, Nicolas Meli and Francesco Cantu, made difficult new routes on **Kyajo Ri** (6186m) and two lower peaks in the area south of Gokyo late in the post monsoon season. They graded their 800-meter route on Kyajo Ri M6+ WI4+ 6b [5.10d] A2, 85°, which may set a new record for grading complexity.

In Manang two parties attempted the beautiful pyramid of **Nemjung** (7139m) which had only had one previous ascent, by its E ridge in 1983. A Japanese group led by Osamu Tanabe climbed the WNW face on steep snow and ice in two days, descending by the same route. (Tanabe, sadly, was killed in an avalanche on Dhaulagiri I in 2010).

The French climbers Christian Trommsdorff and Yannick Graziani attempted a new route on the S face. They spent six days on 'a route of around 2400m, 45 pitches, mostly ice/mixed, a few pitches of just rock, many very delicate snow ridges, walls, flutes to climb or traverse, fantastic gullies, many vertical sections, a very committing route'. Unfortunately they had to retreat from around 7000m after Trommsdorff was hit on the helmet by a large chunk of ice.

2010

In June 2010 the China Tibet Mountaineering Association (CTMA) issued a new regulation limiting the age of Everest climbers to 18 to 60. This follows ascents by the 13-year-old American, Jordan Romero, with his father and others in May 2010, and by a 16-year-old Nepali who suffered significant frostbite. Nepal currently has a minimum age of 16 and no maximum. The upper age record is currently 76 but an 80-year-old former Nepali foreign minister is said to be planning a challenge. Further crazy projects will doubtless follow.

A British swimmer, wearing only a standard Speedo, swam one kilometre in 2°C water across Pumori Lake, at 5300m and close to the Everest Base Camp, in order to highlight the dangers of global warming. One hopes there was a good fire waiting for him in his trekking lodge.

Apa Sherpa has now reached the summit of Everest 20 times.

182. The 2009 Japanese line on the WNW face of Nemjung (7139m). (*Nobosuke Ohki*)

A South Korean woman, Oh Eun-sun, reached the summit of Annapurna in April and claims to be the first woman to ascend all fourteen 8000m peaks. She is only 5'1" in height, which possibly sets yet another record. However there is some doubt about her ascent of Kangchenjunga in 2009, as her climbing speed was remarkably fast and her photos were inconclusive. (Have we heard this story before?) Of the three Sherpas accompanying her (!) one said they made it, one said they didn't, and the third has not given an interview.

The Spanish Basque Edurne Pasaban completed her 14 peaks barely a month later, apparently without controversy.

In the spring Denis Urubko climbed Lhotse from the South Col solo, by a new variant, climbing largely on rock and joining the standard Lhotse Couloir route at 8300m just below its top. He took only five hours from the South Col to the summit.

On **Makalu** a Ukrainian expedition made a route starting on the 1975 Slovenian route on the SW face then ascending new ground, largely on steep slabby rock, to join the 1971 *French Route* on the West Pillar at 7500m, which they then followed to the summit. They used 3000m of fixed rope but no oxygen or climbing Sherpas. Three of the ten climbers reached the summit.

Three Russian climbers made a new and very steep mixed route on the 1400m N face of **Cholatse** (6440m) in Solu Khumbu in March 2010. Their route is largely independent of the 1995 French route on this face, but joins it near the top and continues to the W ridge.

Early in the spring of 2010 David Gottlieb and Joe Puryear made the first ascent of **Takargo** (6771m and also known as **Dragkar-Go**) in the Rolwaling valley by its E face, reaching the summit on 12 March after three bivouacs. This was apparently the first ascent of this conspicuous and attractive peak just west of the Tesi Lapcha. Sadly Joe Puryear was killed in October 2010 on Labuche Kang in southern Tibet.

Also in the Rolwaling area, four French climbers made a difficult mixed route on the SE face of **Lunag I** at a standard of IV/V F5. After two bivouacs they reached the summit ridge at about 6830m. They did not continue to the 6985m summit, which is thus still unclimbed, but bivouacked a third time and descended the next day with 22 abseils.

A Japanese party climbed the remote peak of **Kojichula Chuli** (6489m) in the Mugu Karnali area of far west Nepal. They climbed the upper part of its east face that appears to be just in Tibet. Three previous parties had failed on this mountain.

In the 2010 post-monsoon season the Italian climber Walter Nones was killed in a fall while attempting a new line on the SW face of Cho Oyu with two companions. He was, as they say, a very experienced mountaineer.

Also in the autumn season Americans Joel Kauffman and Jarad Vilhauer climbed a very difficult new line on the SW face of **Lobuje East** (6119m) in the Khumbu Himal. They reached the summit after 27 hours on the face and descended by the standard SE ridge route on this trekking peak. They graded it 'VI WI 5+ AI 4 M7 85°', which again demands a more advanced degree in mountaineering studies than your scribe possesses.

The Everest scene continues unabated. One development is the increasing use of helicopters to ferry well-heeled clients directly from Kathmandu to various points in Solu Khumbu so they don't have to do too much walking, or suffer delays at the Lukla airport. Russell Brice, who knows more about the commercial Everest business than most, now puts his clients in the Kathmandu Hyatt, which is out on the edge of town, away from all the temples, etc, as it is the only hotel with its own helipad.

Another development is the appearance of increasing numbers of mainland Chinese climbers in Nepal, perhaps a sign of the rapidly growing middle class there. One Chinese team put eight climbers plus eight Sherpas on the summit of Dhaulagiri I in May, but lost three members on the descent, while several others suffered frostbite.

* * *

Andy Parkin endured ferocious winter weather, frostnip and three sleepless nights in January 2011 to accomplish what has been recorded as the first ascent, solo, of the north face of **Dingjung Ri** (6249m). Recounting what would also be the first calendar winter ascent of the mountain, Parkin said it was one of the hardest trips he could remember. 'The climb vindicates all I have been trying to do with my trips and shows what will be the future trend – winter climbing on unclimbed peaks or faces; hard climbing in wild places at a time of year when there are no people around.'

Technically in the Rolwaling Himal, Dingjung Ri is situated west of a point midway up the Nangpa valley (Bhote Kosi), which runs south from the Nangpa La to Thame. It was first climbed, from the west, by Peter Boultbee and Dennis Davis during Alf Gregory's productive 1955 Merseyside Himalayan expedition. This three-man team was ostensibly reconnoitring Gaurishankar but climbed five or six other summits, including Parcharmo, Ramdung and Pimu.

Parkin set up base camp on pastures above the Nangpa valley. After one acclimatisation outing, he returned to his tent to find clothing had been stolen. That night he was attacked: rocks, some of them as large as half a kilogramme, were thrown through his tent. He scared off the assailant and later moved down to the house of a yak herder, Phu Tensing, where he had no further problems.

It was Phu Tensing who pointed out to Parkin the mountain he knew as Dingjung Ri, a peak indicated on the Schneider map as point 6263m. Later an older Sherpa said the peak was called Rima Mayo, which Parkin says translates as 'left-hand mountain'. It was this peak he climbed. (Heights and names are notoriously inconsistent and confusing on maps of Nepal's mountains.)

A heavy fall of snow at the end of December made moving around difficult, but once Parkin accessed the north face, conditions improved. 'The climb was steeper than the Grandes Jorasses north wall – 85° in places – with this line of ice, névé and snow threading up and left to curve back to the summit,' Parkin said. After two extremely cold and windy bivouacs, he was able to travel light to the summit – an amazing dollop of névé on pure ice – that he reached on 17 January.

He abseiled through the night with frostnipped fingers to his lower bivouac site, where he had left a gas cylinder. Next day he reached the base of the mountain after a total of three and a half chilly days on the face. 'Zips froze and broke on my boots, all systems were collapsing and I was so tired that staggering back to ABC I would rest the weight of the sac on a boulder and promptly doze off, saved from freezing by my down suit.

'The day after I carried on down, carrying all the gear – 25/30 kilos – bent double against the gusting wind, to make BC in time for the porters who were due. My yak herder friends sheltered me and fed me *dhal bhat*; all the people from the village of Thame Tenge (upper Thame I suppose) were really good to me.' *SG*

Correction: *The photo on p 284 of the 2009 Alpine Journal was unfortunately miscaptioned. It should read 'High risk climbing under séracs high on the Japanese Route on the north-east face of Teng Kangpoche (Yasushi Okada)'*

JOHN TOWN

China and Tibet 2009-10

The past two years have continued to be difficult ones in Tibet, though one or two teams have managed to find a way through police and permit problems. The main activity has been in Sichuan and Xinjiang where climbers continue to break new ground on routes that are often at the cutting edge. Other ventures seem less in tune with current trends, with a 6500m peak in the Kangri Karpo succumbing to a party of 17 supported by 10 porters, and a team on Siguniang making extensive use of skyhooks and a drill when free climbing became impossible. A more welcome development is the appearance of Chinese climbers climbing independently for the fun of it. Many gained their skills on state controlled and initiated mega-expeditions, but this no longer seems to be a constraint on individual initiative. One only has to stroll through the endless array of outdoor shops in Chinese cities to see what is coming.

QONGLAI SHAN

Attention centred on the formidable S face of **Siguniang (6250m).** In December 2008 Li Hongxue, Yan Dongdong, Liu Yunfeng, Wang Ting and Zhou Peng and a second team consisting of Gu Jie, Luo Biao and Sun Bin both made attempts on different lines in the area of the central couloir. Cai Yu, Ji Xing, Peng Xiaolong, Zhang Yusheng, Zhao Jianshan and Zheng Chaohui made an unsuccessful attempt on the SE ridge. Yan Dongdong and Zhou Peng returned for a further go at the central couloir line in February before finally succeeding on this impressive route in November 2009. Alexey Gorbatenkov and Svetlana Gutsalo had tried a month earlier but retreated in the face of a storm.

In October 2009 the Russians Vladimir Molodozhen, Andrey Muryshev, Valery Shamalo and Denis Sushko climbed a new route on the NW buttress of **Siguniang.** The 1150m line took 18 days and when the weather made free climbing impossible they continued, making extensive use of skyhooks and the drill on a section of 100m at around half-height. Evgeny Bashkirtsev and Denis Veretenin retreated from a different line in the face of the storms.

Another Russian group, consisting of Anfisa Krasheninina, Sergey Lyagin, Andrey Mikhailienko and Igor Sherstnov were avalanched at about 5100m on **Luotuo (aka Camel) Peak (5484m)** at the end of October. Krasheninina and Sherstnov did not survive. A Chinese guide was killed on **Celestial Peak (5413m)** when an abseil piton failed, but his client managed to make his own way to safety.

Yan Dongdong was in action again in February 2010, this time with the female climber Li Lan in the Changping valley, where they made the

183. 5800m peak in the headwaters of the Dongchu Tsangpo, Kangri Karpo range. *(Tamotsu Nakamura)*

first ascent of the multicoloured **Wuse Shan (5430m)** via the south face and an unsuccessful attempt the previous month on the west side of **Chibu (5430m).** In September, two US teams climbed new routes in the area. Chad Kellogg and Dylan Johnson made the first ascent of **Seerdengpu (5592m)** at the third attempt via the NE ridge and made an attempt on a 5086m spire. **Toby Grohne** and **Jesse Huey** climbed the impressive NE (Forlorn Ridge) of **Celestial Peak.**

DAXUE SHAN

There were two fatal accidents in this region in 2009. In May, Johnny Copp, Micah Dash and filmmaker Wade Johnson were avalanched in a deep gorge below the SE face of **Mount Edgar (E Gongga, 6618m)**. Hungarians Peter Csizmadia, Veronika Mikolovits, Balazs Pechtol and Katalin Tolnay left their base camp in the Gangou valley, to the east of **Ren Zhong Feng (6079m)** on 17 October 2009. No trace of them was found but rescuers found evidence of recent avalanches in an area extremely exposed to sérac fall.

The Danish team of Carsten Cooper-Jensen, Martin Ploug and Kristoffer Szilas followed the unfortunate Hungarian team on the eastern approach to **Ren Zhong Feng.** Ploug and Szilas reached the summit on 25 November 2009 via the E face and N ridge; Ploug took a 30m fall down one side of the ridge but was stopped by Szilas, who jumped over the other side. The height of the peak as measured by GPS and altimeter was c5800m, rather less than the official 6079m.

Russian climbers Mikhail Mikhailov and Alexander Ruchkin made the first ascent over 12 days in May 2009 of **Pt 6134m,** which lies north-west of Mt Edgar, close to Mt Grosvenor, via the 1100m SW buttress.

In October 2010, Kyle Dempster (US) and Bruce Normand (UK) made the first ascent of the west face of **Mt Grosvenor** (aka **Riwuqie Feng, 6376m**) in a single day. They followed this up by a successful attempt on the east face and south ridge of **Mount Edgar (E Gongga, 6618m)** in an eight-day round trip. Their companions Jean Annequin and Christian Trommsdorff reached 5700m on a line further right before retreating in high winds.

Penny Goddard, Lydia Bradey (NZ), Kenny Gasch and Mark Jenkins (US), made an attempt in April 2009 on the unclimbed **Nyambo Konka (6114m).** A liaison officer, Chen Zheng Lin, forced upon them by the Ganzi Tibetan Autonomous Prefecture Mountaineering Association, did his best to foil their efforts and they were finally halted by poor weather and conditions. They did however manage the first ascent of a 5020m peak in the neighbouring Qionglai, navigating by BlackBerry.

A further sign of the growth in independent climbing was the first ascent by Chinese mountain guides Xiaolong Peng, Jie Gu and Yang Liu of **Peak 5662m,** 17km south-west of Kangding, on 24 July 2010.

SHALULI SHAN

Yangmolong (6066m) still remains unclimbed, despite two further attempts in the autumn of 2009. Dave Wynne-Jones with Derek Buckle, Dick Isherwood and Peter Rowat suffered hostility and multiple thefts from local people before having their ambitions thwarted by bad weather and technical difficulties. John Otto, Tim Boelter (US) and Su Rongqin (China) had similar problems with the locals in the Sanglongxi valley and moved to the Zhongba valley. The south face of the mountain proved too dangerous but they were successful in making the third ascent of **Dangchezhengla (5830m)** via the south glacier, south-east face and north-east ridge.

A Joint Expedition from the Kobe University Alpine Club and the China Geosciences University Mountaineering Association, comprising 17 members and 10 porters, made the first ascent of **Lopchin (Kangri Karpo II 6703m)** on 5 November 2009. Tibetan students Deqing Ouzho and Ciren Danda were the first to reach the summit, followed two days later by Koichiro Kondo and Masanori Yazaki.

NYENCHEN TANGLA EAST

In November 2009 Tamotsu Nakamura, with Tsuyoshi Nagai and Tadao Shintani, explored three new areas of the Nyenchen Tangla East: the Aigagong glacier above the Nye Chu, Lake Jambo Tso and the Maraipo glacier in Jingling District, and the North Yuri glacier in the Botoi Tsangpo. They also visited the Dongchu Tsangpo, south-west of Songzong in the Kangi Karpo. The expedition returned with a stunning array of photographs of new and unclimbed peaks, as well as documenting a rare tree burial site. John Town and Jerry Lovatt succeeded in entering the Yigrong Tsangpo gorge from the east by the new road but were turned back by police at the village of Talu. Bruce Normand and a companion attempted to cross the Shargung La to the Jingling area but were turned back at Bemba (Pelbar).

TANGULA SHAN

The Tangula Shan lie to the north-east of Central Tibet, forming the barrier over which the main road and railway must pass to reach the rest of China. In September 2007 a five-man Japanese expedition made the first ascent of **Peak 6543m**, 5.4km south-west of the main peak of the Geladaindong massif. Three of the team set off from the top camp, but due to strong winds only Osamu Kato reached the summit.

QILIAN SHAN

This glaciated range lies to the north of Qinghai on its border with Gansu Province. A three-man Chinese expedition consisting of Li Yong, Yuan Wei, Huang Zonghua attempted the first ascent of the **West Face** and **South Ridge** of highest peak **Kangze'gyai (c5800m)** in 2009. Li and Huang reached the summit on 7 October.

TIBETAN PLATEAU

Reports have been received from Sweden of a variety of remote ascents in 2007 and 2008, approaches being made on foot and by mountain bike in the company of a variety of other climbers.

In 2007, on the Chang Tang, a Canadian-Swedish party made the ascent of **Kangzhagri (6,305m)** (N 35°33'25", E 89°34'40") on 26 June via the WSW face, after a 27-day unsupported approach. In September two ascents were made in American company from the Aksia Chin road connecting Xinjiang with the far west of Tibet.

Sirenshou (N 35°49'33", E 79°13'42") was climbed on the 2 September by the north ridge, after a three-day approach on foot, and **Jiao Feng** (aka **Qierlizuoke South**, N 35°58'09", E 79°26'33") on the 9 September by the north-west ridge after a two-day approach on foot.

Between 4 and 8 October a number of ascents were made in German company in the Toze Kangri range, after a one-week approach. These included **Toze Kangri South-West (6356m)** (N 34°44'20", E 82°19'51"), **Toze Kangri North-East (6356m)** (N 34°46'32", E 82°21'52") and **Toze Pyramid (6329m)** (N 34°41'44", E 82°12'56") – the latter two being solo Swedish ascents.

In 2008 two further ascents in the Chang Tang were made after an epic approach by foot and bike.

Kukushili (6360m) (aka **Songzhi Ling** N 35°39'48", E 85°37'03"), was climbed on 28 June via the south face by a Canadian-Danish-Swedish party, after a 36-day unsupported approach. **Purog Kangri (6436m)** (aka **Purog/ Zangser** massif: N 34°25'00", E 85°38'03") followed on the 9 July from the south after a further nine days of travel.

In October 2009 Grzegorz Chowla from Poland made the first ascent of **Mayer Kangri I East (6035m)** by the east ridge, accompanied as far as 5865m by Janusz Majer. The pair had first tried to reach the village of Nyima via Shigatse and the Kiku La (5120m) but were stopped on this pass by Chinese police. They then tried a different route, first via the Lhasa-

Golmud highway to Nakchu and then driving west past Baingoin and Serling Tso (lake) and over a 4900m pass to the village of Rongma. They then crossed a second pass to place their base camp at 5057m on the south-east flanks of the range.

KUN LUN

Russians Diana Borisova, Pavel Demeshchik, Vasiliy Ivanov, Ivan Muyzhnek, Anna Pereverzeva, Sergey Zayko and Otto Chkhetiani made the first ascent of **Qong Muztagh East (c6970m)** on 6 October 2009. During previous explorations in 2006 they had discovered this second major peak of this massif, which is about the same altitude as Qong Muztagh itself. Although the group started from the northern Taklaman side of the range, it had to cross over to the south, before circling round to approach the massif from the south-east, making a round trip of over 500km. While they were on the mountain, Chinese authorities confiscated nearly all of their cameras, photos, GPS and maps.

CENTRAL TIBET

The unnamed Swede (see Tibetan Plateau above) began his 2008 efforts with solo ascents in March and April of **Jietanzhouma (6008m)**, (N28 51' 40" E 90 08' 10") which lies just south of the Gyantse Road and Noijin Kangsang massif, and of the south-east ridge of **Pulha Ri (Maphu Kangri 6404m)**, which is situated just east of the road between Tingri and Lhaze, not far from Lhagoi Kangri.

HIMALAYA

The well-known American climber Joe Puryear was killed when a cornice collapsed on **Labuche Kang (7367m)** in October 2010. Together with climbing partner David Gottlieb he was attempting to make the second ascent of the peak.

Kazuya Hirade and Kei Taniguchi deserve special credit for reaching **Gaurishankar (7135m)** from the north in October 2009, talking their way past several police and army groups. After four days on the north-east face of the south summit, they were defeated at 6850m by the rock band just below the summit ridge.

TIEN SHAN

The Xuelian massif of the Central Tien Shan has continued to draw attention. Following his successful visit in 2008, in 2009 Bruce Normand (UK), with Jed Brown (US), made the first ascent of **Xuelian North (6472m)** by the west ridge, and **Xuelian East (c6400m)** by the east ridge. At the same time, Kyle Dempster and Jared Vilhauer (US) climbed **Xuelian East** by the north flank, having previously made the first ascent of **Yanamax II (6180m)**. Normand then teamed up with Brown and Dempster to climb the impressive 2650m north face of **Xuelian West (6422m)**. (*see account p 62*)

In September 2010, Mick Fowler and Paul Ramsden made the first ascent

184. Western summit of Mount Hua Shan (2160m), Shaanxi Province. *(Ondřej Žváček)*

of the N face of **Sulamar (5380m)** in the Xuelian massif. The 1000m route took six days and they followed this by exploring the nearby Chulebos range. (*see account p 53*)

SHAANXI PROVINCE

Leo Houlding, Carlos Suarez and Wang Zhi Ming received special permission for their 600m tree and rock route on the revered **Mount Hua Shan (2160m).** They were able to bathe their wounds in the temple/hotel complex that adjoins the summit.

Sources: *American Alpine Journal, American Alpine Club, Climbing, Mountain Info, BMC, Tamotsu Nakamura.*

KESTER BROWN

New Zealand 2009-10

This report covers developments in the New Zealand mountains from July 2009 to December 2010.

The Darran Mountains, in Fiordland National Park, have continued to attract much attention from those interested in exploring new climbing terrain.

During the winter of 2009, Allan Uren, Ron Dempster and Max Gough climbed a three-pitch ice and mixed line in the **Macpherson Cirque** which they named *The Celtic Connection* and invested with a technical grade of 7, a first for the Darrans. The winter of 2010 also saw some climbing activity, with one new route being established, this time by Matthias Kerkmann and Alejandro Mora Munos. The route, dubbed *Reunion Invernal,* was established over two days and takes a striking line on the upper wall of Crosscut in **Cirque Creek.**

In between the two previously mentioned events, the Darran Mountains were graced with a summer that included numerous high pressure weather systems, during which the alpine rock climbers came out to play. In the **Lake Terror** region, Nick Flyvberg and Tony Burnell climbed a 255m, grade 23 route on the wall that rises directly from the lake; they used an inflatable raft to access *Terrabilita.* Next, the pair added a third route to the north wall of Mt Terror. They named their second new climb *Terra Firma,* and graded it 21.

Over in the **Central Darrans,** Richard Turner, Richard Thomson and Bruce Dowrick occupied themselves with two new rock routes: *Parallel Lines* (22, 6 pitches) is on the north-west flank of **Karetai** and *Nature Identical Dave* (22, 4 pitches) is on the south face of **Te Wera.**

On **Moirs Mate,** Nick Cradock, Murray Ball and Dave Shotwell opened *Lucky Strike,* a seven-pitch grade 20 climb that is quickly becoming the most popular route in the Darrans, probably due to the amenable nature of the bolting, the quality of the stone and the ease of access.

For the more traditionally inclined, a major new route was completed on the north face of **Mt Grave.** Rob Frost, Andrei van Dusschoten and Guy McKinnon climbed the North Rib over two days, encountering loose rock, big commitment, a forced bivvi and some real adventure.

Heading east now, over the main divide to the **Wakatipu Region,** and back to the winter of 2009, five new alpine mixed lines were established on the west face of the **Telecom Tower,** in the **Remarkables Range.** Tony Burnell, Aaron Ford and Sally Ford climbed *Saturday Morning Special* (M3/4) and *Equinox* (M5+), and Sally and Tony climbed *Number One*

185. Tony Burnell abseiling into the upper section of *Terrabilita* (23), Lake Terror, Darran Mountains. *(Nick Flyvberg)*

Gulley (M3). Dave Bolger and Greg Larkin added *Growling Dog* (M5) and Rupert Gardiner and Niall Mueller contributed *State of the Nation* (M5). During the same period, Mike Rowe and Andrew Finnigan completed a new route that tackles the full west face of the **Remarkables**, it's called *Shooting the Breeze,* is 1700m long and is graded at MC4.

The following winter saw Ben Dare frequenting new terrain on the shady side of **Single Cone.** Ben soloed the first ascent of *Fire in the Sky* (M6) on the west face before teaming up with Steve Leake to open *Stairway to Methven* (M5), on the south face. But those routes may have just been a warm-up for

186. Sally Ford on the first ascent of *Equinox*, Telecom Tower, Wakatipu Region. *(Tony Burnell)*

Ben, as he subsequently soloed a major new line on the south face of **Mt Earnslaw**: *Right Next Door to Hell* is 1750m long and graded at WI4+ M4.

Over in the north branch of the **Routeburn Valley,** Andrew Finnigan and Julian Webster found a real gem on the west buttress of **Mt Somnus.** Their climb, *Mid-Winter Christmas,* is 9 pitches of mostly moderate water-ice, with brief crux sections of grade WI3+ and M5 terrain. Ben Dare had spent some time solo on Earnslaw the summer prior to his winter climb; he established a new route on the west face that he graded III/3.

The biggest hills in New Zealand saw an increase in new route activity in the period covered by this report. In **Tai Poutini Westland National Park,** the winter of '09 saw an ice line added to the south-west face of the West Peak of **Mt Haast**: *Swimming with Sharks* (III/4) came courtesy of Jono Clarke and Matt Quirke. The climb must have been a good one, as Jono went back the next winter with Jamie Vinton-Boot to add *Talula Does the Hula from Hawaii* (III/5+), further to the right on the same face. Nearby, and just a couple of weeks later, Allan Uren, Penny Goddard and Dave Williams added an alternative left-hand finish *to The Vision* on **Conway Peak.** Continuing with his variation theme, Allan Uren teamed up with Ben Dare and veered left on *Lust for Life,* on the south face of **Barnicoat,** to create an alternative to that route.

The 09/10 summer at **Aoraki Mount Cook National Park** saw a new route completed on **Aoraki Mt Cook** itself by Lachie Currie and Stuart Holloway. *Resolution* (MC6) consists of great rock and is in a fantastic position on the left side of the Bowie Buttress.

And finally, in July 2010, Kieran Parsons and David Manning made the first ascent of the S. Face of **Mt Travers** in **Nelson Lakes National Park.**

ANTONIO GÓMEZ BOHÓRQUEZ

Peru 2008-9

Translated by Paul Knott

This report documents new routes and significant repeats in the Cordilleras Blanca and Huayhuash, Peru, between June 2008 and September 2009, plus climbs in the Cordilleras Vilcanota and Jatún Chacua in the dry season of 2009.

To write it, I have analysed, challenged and synthesised data from the *American Alpine Journal,* Andes Info archives and personal communications with Anthony Barton, Hugo Sifuentes, Koky Castañeda, Richard Hidalgo, Silvia Vidal and Vicente Bárcena.

CORDILLERA BLANCA 2008

Cerro Huaytapallana II or Central, East Summit (c5025m)

On 19 July, Britons Anthony Barton, Jim Sykes and Oliver Metherell reached the head of the Huaytapallana gorge, also called Quebrada Rajururi. That day, they climbed seven long pitches on the west side of this peak on excellent rock and crossed to the north-west ridge for another long pitch until they reached an impasse in the form of a long rocky gendarme. They then made three rappels to the bottom of the face and, although they had finished at the ridge, named the route *Copout* (560m, 10 pitches, TD+ E1 5a or 5.9 R/X).

Five days later, Barton and Metherell climbed to the col that separates peaks Huaytapallana I and II, where they found an 'enormous wedged block to the right of a large tower'. They reached the top of the block by a narrow chimney to gain the eastern ridge. Having passed the crux they followed the ridge, which they found 'delightful, exposed, and airy but not too difficult'. On the East Summit (somewhat lower than the main) they found no evidence of previous ascents. They named this route *Last Exit*, 375m, 7 pitches, TD E1 5a or 5.9R. After down-climbing to a large terrace, they made four rappels to reach the bottom of the face just left of the descent from their previous climb.

Huascarán Norte (6654m) to Triángulo Este (c6150m)

From 23-30 July, Catalan (Spanish) Silvia Vidal and Swiss Youri Cappis carried food and equipment up the Quebrada (ravine) Anqosh to an advanced base camp (c5500m) and fixed 200m of rope. They then climbed capsule style. As Cappis was inexperienced in big-wall climbing, Vidal led all the pitches. They set up C1 at end of the 5th pitch (c5500m), C2 at the 10th (c5750m) and C3 at the 14th. On 9 August, after 18 days on the

187. 'Triángulo del Huascarán Norte'. Silvia Vidal's line on Corominas/Baró's photo. *(Andes Info collection)*

wall, they reached the apex of the eastern rock triangle (c6150m). They had intended to reach the summit of Nevado Huascarán Norte (6654m), but gave up. Adverse weather conditions forced them to rappel from that apex down the ascent route, which they named *Entre Boires* (*Between Mists*): starts at about 5350m; 800m vertical; 970m long; A3/F6a+, 80°.

Chopicalqui (6354m) to SE ridge (c6000m)

On 26 June, Matic Obid, Pavel Ferjancic, Jernej Arcon, Vladimir Makarovic and Mitja Glescic ascended by the Quebrada Ulta to the east face of Chopicalqui and camped at about 5000m. On 28th, they left at 2am and reached the base of the face three hours later. They climbed about 100m of 50° – left of the route of *Johnson-Pohmajevich* (1988) – followed by another 100m of rock on the left side of a small couloir. Afterwards they climbed 350m (50°-70°), trending left, and 50m of mixed to reach the SE ridge. The Slovenians were planning to follow this ridge – climbed by Clarbrough and Wayatt in 1969 – to reach the summit, but stopped at this point (c6000m) due to deep snow, and descended. They named this climb *Burros Eslovenos*: 600m with general difficulty M5 50° -70°

Nevado Ulta (5875m) to eastern ridge (c5800m)

On 16 July, Basque (Spanish) Aritza Monasterio and Slovenian Viktor Mlinar departed from a small bridge (c3885m) between Ulta Passage and the village of Pompey, and went up the Quebrada Cancaracá Grande to a moraine camp (c4625m) at the foot of the glacier south of Nevado Ulta. The next day they crossed the crevassed glacier and camped at 5110m next to a rock pillar. On 18th at 5am they started on the south face. They passed two bergschrunds, a 60° slope, a pitch of 80°, and icefalls of 90°-95° to reach the eastern ridge at about 5800m. The climb ended here, because the rest of the ridge to the summit looked very dangerous. They made eight rappels with 60m x7mm ropes. They named the route *Andinista-Rifnik*: 650m, MD+/ED VI/4+.

Hatun Ulloc (Ulloc Grande, c4420m)

In late July, Americans Dave Anderson and Brady Robinson camped in the Quebrada Ishinca. They spent several days going up and down the 'gully' right of Hatun Ulloc to reach the top of the third prow (c4420m). From here, they abseiled and removed vegetation to prepare the cracks for subsequent free climbing, and placed a protection bolt in what could become pitch 13. They returned to the camp with the idea of repeating the ascent of Crill and Gallagher, to complete it with the five pitches that were missing up to the third prow. (This ascent in 2004 ended at the first of the three prows of the peak [see *AJ* 2005, p342 and *AJ* 2006 pp320-321]; in 2005 Wood and Wellman continued to the second and estimated that they were about 60m below the third.) Anderson and Robinson fixed three rope lengths and then, when the weather allowed, continued a further 14 pitches to the top (c4420m) with free climbing, although they pre-protected the key roof pitch of Crill-Gallagher. They named the full route *Astroman of Peru*, maximum difficulty 5.11c in pitch 13. *Correction: in AJ 2006 p320, where it says c4800, read c4420m.*

CORDILLERA HUAYHUASH 2008

Puscanturpa Chiquita (5066m)

From 10-13 July, Slovaks Vlado Linek and Patrik Barjak climbed on the north side of **Puscanturpa Sur** (see *AJ* 2006 p324) on a small tower called 'Puscanturpa Chiquita'. Their route, *Burro Loco* (Crazy Donkey), has seven pitches (UIAA 6+, 8-, 8-, 4, 5, 8, 2) and 300m. They placed 11 belay bolts and seven in the pitches, and used fixed ropes. Future climbers will require large Camalots on the third pitch and will have to rappel the route, unless they decide to rappel to the col behind the needle and open a way to the nearest snow-capped summit.

CORDILLERA VILCANOTA 2008

Nevado Tinqui or Tinki (5450m)

The claimed 4 October ascent of 'Nevado Pucapunta (5490m)' by the Peruvian aspirant guides Raúl Laveriano, Willy Alvarado, Beto Pinto, Claudio Lliuya and Steven Fuentes was, without doubt, the Nevado Tinqui (5450m) as seen in route line photographs published by different specialised media. The future guides reached the base of the S face, climbed trending right for 120m on packed névé and another 240m of hard ice to

188. From left to right, Nevado Tinki (5450m), Caracol (5619m), Concha del Caracol (5630m) and Pachanta (5727m) *(Antonio Gómez Bohórquez)*

reach the gully right of the upper rock band and hence the snowy SE arête, which led (by its right side) to the summit. They graded the climb at TD, 65° and called it *Magno Camones*. They descended the SE ridge to reach the col of Nevado Caracol and descended diagonally to the south glacier.

This mountain became known outside of Peru thanks to a photo by Piero Ghiglione published in *Mountain World* in 1953, plates 50-51, with the caption: 'Unnamed 19,600ft between Ausangate and Cayangate ...'. The same picture by the Italian explorer is between pages 30-33 of his book, *Nelle Andes of South Peru,* 1953. Günter Hauser's book, *Ihr Herren Berge* (1959), between pages 80-81 and 95-97, shows the as yet unnamed summit (5450m on the attached map) to the left (E) of Nevado Caracol (5619m). This last picture is expanded in *Mountain World* (English) and *Berge der Welt* (Germany), 1958/59, Photo 24. Also, the sketch map of Cronk and Wortis in *Alpine Journal* 1959, p.40, includes the peak in question, but without a height or name. *Le Ande,* by Mario Fantin, p.4, records the name and altitude of each of the three neighbouring peaks east of this summit: Caracol (5619m), Concha de Caracol (5630m), and Pachanta (5727m). The latter is named 'Nevado Puca Punta' (no elevation given) on ING Peru sheet 28-t Ocongate, which points to the NNE of the Paso del Campa and the SSW end of 'Nevado Collque Cruz'!

The same occurs in the sketch (trekking topo) Cordillera Vilcanota, Tinqui-Auzangate, drawn by Healey and printed by South American Explorer Club in 1985. The toponymy of the sheet 28-t – like the sketch based on it – is consistent with common usage and leads to confusion because **a)** it appears that the three peaks receive the same name as one (Puca Punta)

189. Nevado Tinki of the Cordillera Vilcanota with the Peruvian line. Photo taken from the summit of Nevado Campa I on 20 July 2008. *(Antonio Gómez Bohórquez)*

located SSW of these glaciers and several summits to the south, **b)** calls Nevado Cayangate 'Nevado Collpa Ananta' (6110m), and **c)** names 'Nevado Collque Cruz' a series of peaks located between Nevado Puca Punta and Nevado Collpa Ananta, when in fact the real Collque Cruz is 8km NE of Nevado Cayangate. This can be seen by comparing, for example, sheet 28-t Ocongate with the topo of Wilkinson and Rubens published in *Alpine Journal* 2005, p48. Note that the bottom left of this sketch indicates (with no height or name), E of the three summits, the peak in question. This peak was named 'Tinki' (5450m) by the German expedition that climbed it in 1966, perhaps in honour of the Tinqui hacienda on the approach to base camp. This first ascent by several members of the Akademische Alpenverein München was noted in *AAJ* 1967, p396: 'On June 16 we made the first ascent of Tinki (17,881 feet), which lies just east of Caracol'. The ascent of the S face in 1980 is also recorded in *AAJ* 1981 p230: 'On July 21 [Rainer] Bassler and I [Herbert Weinzierle, Deutscher Alpenverein] made a new route on the Nevado Tinki (5450m, 17,881 feet), the direct south face, which averaged 60° and was 70° near the top'. Therefore, when we know the exact line of the latter route, or other later routes not recorded in the literature, we will know whether the ascent by the Peruvian mountaineers is the first, a variation or a repeat.

Nevado Campa II (5611m)

The 4 October ascent of 'Nevado Qampa (5500m)' by aspirant guides Johan Zárate and Alberto Hung probably corresponds to Campa II (5611m) on the Hauser map cited above. The Campa peaks, also called Kampa, Q'ampa and Jampa in various publications, are named 'Nevado María Huamantilla' on ING Peru sheet 28-t Ocongate. The two Peruvian climbers left from a base camp (c4600m) next to 'Alcacocha' (lagoon) at 2.45am. They reported ascending via the north-west side between peaks 5300m and 5390m and by the north-west ridge to reach the summit of Campa at 9.05am. Recall the routes mentioned by Bernard Amy – in *AAJ* 1971, pp411-412, and in *La Montagne et Alpinisme,* No84, October 1971, pp131-138 – whose group climbed in July 1970 by the NW slope to the summits of Campa I (5485m), Campacito (5390m) and Campa II (5611m). But if the Peruvian pair 'climbed the south-west face and the long ridge to the summit' – as published *AAJ* 2009, p182– then their route runs between the peaks 5260m and 5450m reported by Hauser and follows the NE ridge to the summit of 5611m. In any case, the pair estimated that they climbed 150m of III 65° between those peaks to reach the ridge, and named the route *YAS Gael.*

Mariposa (5818m)

Named 'Nevado María Huamantilla o Chilenita' (5808m) on ING Peru sheet 28-t, this summit was climbed on 4 October by three pairs of Peruvian aspirant guides by different lines up the north slope. Melesio Escolástico and Marco Lliuya (who died later on Huascarán) graded their climb TD III 80°; Darío Alva and Flavio Mandura graded theirs TD V 80°; Miguel Gamarra and Willy Huamán graded theirs TD V 60°. The lines of these three climbs are drawn in *AAJ* 2009, p182, in a picture for which the caption notes 'no other routes are thought to exist on this face'. In relation to this comment, and to which of these Peruvian climbs may be new, recall that Herbert Oberhofer, of the Akademische Alpenverein München, reported in *AAJ* 1967 p396: '[..] the same day [June 26th] making [with K. Winkler] the second ascent of Mariposa (19,089 feet) by a new route, the north ridge'.

With such a brief explanation, it is hard to know which ridge the German alpinist referred to because the summit Mariposa does not have a north ridge as such according to the Hauser map. From the summit one ridge goes down to the north-west and another to the north-east to join a pronounced col to Peak 5630m south-east of Ausangate Chico (5700m). The latter summit was climbed in 1970 by Christian Choquet and Bernard Amy, who recorded this ascent in *La Montagne et Alpinisme,* No. 84, October 1971, and in *AAJ* 1971, p412: 'Chico (5700m or 18,701 feet) traversed from west to east with a bivouac, followed by the ascent of Mariposa (5818m or 19,089 feet) on July 14 and 15'. *AAJ* 1975, p171 recorded the next ascent, by German climbers in 1974: 'Mariposa (19,056 feet) via north face by Vogl, Volkl, Konnerth, Forster on August 28'. Also *AAJ* 1979, p246 reported another ascent of the face: '[... Carl] Heller, [Terry] Moore and I [Robert Rockwell] climbed Mariposa (19,090 feet), a sustained climb up the north face culminating in 1200 feet of 45' to 60' snow and ice.'

CORDILLERA BLANCA 2009

Urus Central (5495m)

On 16 October, Beto Pinto and Eric Albino Lliuya, students on a Peruvian (AGMP) mountain guides course, left a moraine field (c4600m) in the Quebrada Ishinca at about 6am, and climbed the S face by a possible new 360m route they called *El vuelo del Inca* (*Flight of the Inca*), MD+, 6a, II, M5, 70°-90°. They reached the summit about 12.30 and descended by three rappels and by down-climbing the E ridge.

Ranrapalca (6162m)

On 27 August, Eloy Máximo Salazar Obregón (guide), Octavio Salazar Obregon (aspirant) and Eric Albino Lliuya departed at 11pm from a moraine field (c4800m) in the middle of the Quebrada (gorge) Cojup (Qojup) and ascended the glacier to the S. Shortly after midnight on 28th they crossed two bergschrunds and climbed the S face in lightweight style. They found soft snow (50°-60°), mixed terrain, hard snow, ice, an overhanging area (90°-95°), and finally a couloir (80°) to the SW ridge. They followed this ridge and reached the summit at 6.30pm. They descended first by the NE ridge, then on the E face with two (maybe three) rappels and down-climbing to the col Ranrapalca-Ishinca. From here they reached the moraine camp around 4pm. They estimated that this route is 850m, difficulty ED, 50°-90°/95° and named it *La paliza del Ranrapalca* (*The beating of Ranrapalca*). It remains to be determined whether it is new route, a variant to the SW ridge, or coincides with the line taken by Nicholas Jaeger (TD 750m) in seven hours (bergschrund-summit) on 13 June 1977.

Pucaraju (5346m)

On 26 July, in the Yanamarey massif, Americans Nate Farr and Marcus Donaldson climbed 300m on the S face to the N ridge only. The climb *Game of Kings* (TD+, WI4, M6, 5.8) is to the right of the 1995 *Meynet-Cordier* line. They descended the ridge to the next gully, where they rappelled to the base of the S face.

CORDILLERA HUAYHUASH 2009

Puscanturpa Norte (5652m)

From 27-29 June, from the head of the Quebrada Huanacpatay (Huanacupatay), Basque climbers Mikel Bonilla and Aitor Avendaño opened a 10-pitch variation on the SW face to reach the French route *Macanacota* (Arrisani-Faure-Paurrage, 2000), after which it took five long pitches to reach the top. In the photo with the route line reported by Bonilla and Avendaño it appears that two of these pitches (the last two) are from the other French route opened between May and June 2000 by Daudet, Lombard and Baudry (see *AAJ* 2001 p284). The Basque climbers named this route *Barne Sua* (French 7c+ and 6c obl), which is about 750m up this rocky summit, and descended by rapelling the line of *Macanacota*.

Cordillera Jatún Chacua

From 21 July to 1 August, Basques Koldo Zubimendi, Koldo Rodríguez, Gaizka Barrutia, José María Garcés, Gorka Olabarrieta, Iker Iriondo and Vicente Bárcena departed the town of Oyón for Pucayacu. From here, after a two-day approach, they camped in a plain called Hualmay by the locals and Pistag on sheet 22-j Oyón of ING Peru. This base camp (c4400m) is one km E of the Jatunpata lagoon. They ascended seven peaks of the Cordillera Jatún Chacua, located south of the Cordillera Raura, north of the Cordillera de la Viuda and between the E and S chain of summits called

190. Nevados Cuchpanga NW (5195m) left and NE (5203m) right. Iriondo-Olabarrieta-Zubimendi, red line. Rodríguez-Barrutia and Bárcena-Garcés, blue line. *(Bárcena coll.)*

'Cordillera Rumi Cruz' on this map sheet. All ascents were one-day returns to base camp. The climbs are summarised below in chronological order using names that the explorers gave the peaks and summits and the GPS altitudes they recorded.

Cuchpanga NW 5195m and NE 5203m

Cerro Cuchpanga (5154m) on sheet 22-j of the Peruvian ING lies NE of the Pistag lagoon, S of Huisi Huaganan (5158m) and N of Tuganga Machay (5030m). On 21 July, after 5pm, seven climbers circled the N side of the Pistag lagoon and entered the adjacent valley to the E. They reached the glacier at about 8.30 and, divided into three ropes, crossed to stand under the S face of Cuchpanga NE.

The rope of Iriondo-Olabarrieta-Zubimendi then ascended the snow slope directly and the couloir above (65°) to reach the NW top and traverse to the NE. Due to the unstable snow set off by this trio, roped pairs Rodríguez-Barrutia and Bárcena-Garcés crossed to the right (E) and ascended the adjacent couloir. They reached the two peaks, and all descended toward the NW ridge. Two séracs let loose, and they turned to the W, finding traces of their ascent down on the moraine.

Chacua Grande 5094m

Named 'Cerro Chacua Grande' (without height data), this lies NE of the Pistag lagoon on sheet 22-j of the ING Peru. The seven Basques left base camp on 23 July at 7am, arrived at 9am at the base of the S ridge and climbed it in three hours. The ridge had little difficulty (only two steps

191. Nevado Chacua Grande from the east. *(Bárcena coll.)*

of UIAA IV+ or V-), but plenty of loose rock. From the top they down-climbed the ridge as far as a gully descending SE and, where this ended, found a way down to the E. They then found a suitable abseil anchor which allowed them to lose 40m, then a traverse S led to the scree by which they descended to the base of the S ridge.

Pistag Machay 4951m

Without name or number, this summit is NNW of the Pistag lagoon on ING Peru sheet 22-j. On 24 July, Zubimendi, Barrutia, Iriondo and Bárcena climbed easily up rock, always seeking the ridge that rises from S to N and near the top came to an area exposed to the E. They reached an altitude measured by GPS at 4951m with a 4m margin of error.

Huisi Huaganán 5158m

The summit named 'Cerro Huaganán' (no altitude given) is NNE of the Pistag lagoon and E of Totoracocha on ING Peru sheet 22-j. On 25 July at 8am, Zubimendi and Bárcena went ahead of the rest of the group for approximately two hours along a route they spotted the previous day from Pistag Machay. They tried to gain the N ridge from the SW, but a vertiginous section forced them to retreat. The rest of the group joined them and all climbed more to the north-east, to try to gain the ridge higher up. They then came to a gully which ascended almost parallel to the ridge. Iriondo and Barrutia continued the ascent to the N, gained the ridge, and were the first to reach the 5158m summit. Meanwhile Olabarrieta, Zubimendi and Vicente progressed up the gully. This turned into a rock wall on the E face, which they climbed by a succession of dihedral, terraces and cracks to 100m below the summit, completing the most exposed pitch of the route. After this, a series of terraces led to the summit. Here they joined their companions in descent of the N ridge.

Conchamarca Machay 4960m

This is P 4922m situated S of Pistag lagoon and SW of the Huatay (Huatay-cocha) lagoons on ING Peru sheet 22-j. On 27 July, Garcés, Zubimendi, Olabarrieta, Barrutia and Bárcena set off to the S looking for high valleys to the north of 'Cordillera Callejón' on the Peruvian map. They reached a col SE of the Conchamarca (possibly Cochamarca) lagoon and E of Cerro Yanamachay. They continued south and ascended the N ridge of the twin rocky peaks (north 4947m and south 4960m) 4922m and unnamed on the above map. For this reason, they proposed to ING Peru the name Conchamarca Machay taken from the largest lake at the foot of these peaks. They descended to the north-west to skirt the W and N edges of the lake and hence to base camp.

Ashcac Oriental 5204m

This is P 5165m on ING Peru sheet 22-j. On 28 July, the seven approached it by Hualmay along the E and N of Pistag Machay. From the col north of Pistag they descended to the Cuchpanga lagoon and continued N, entering the gully that divides and forms the spurs of Ashcac Occidental (Western) and Oriental (Eastern). They climbed a gully with rock, talus and snow, which climbs in its final part to smooth, rounded boulders and to the SW of the glacier snout. They divided into three ropes to cross the glacier, climbed the S slope, and at the steepest point of the climb, overcame a crack. They reached the summit at 11.15 am and descended by the same route.

Tuganga Machay 5030m

This lies NNE of the Pistag lagoon and S of Cuchpanga on ING Peru sheet 22-j. On 1 August at 7.15am, Barrutia, Olabarrieta, Iriondo, Zubimendi and Bárcena left by the road they had taken as far as Cuchpanga. They then turned SE at the northern end of the Pistag lagoon and, at another point SE of this, turned NE to reach the foot of the S ridge. They climbed with little difficulty (UIAA III+) without using the rope and reached the W summit, recorded by GPS at 5030m with a 4m margin of error. They did not continue to the E summit of similar altitude, because this would have meant an abseil to the ridge connecting the summits with overhanging climbing on one side and snow to the S. They down-climbed their ascent ridge, descended to the S shore of the Pistag lake and returned to base camp.

MARCELO SCANU

Argentine Andes 2009-10

NORTHERN ARGENTINE ANDES

The 6029m volcano **Volcán Salín**, Salta, was first ascended by pre-Columbian Indians. Hans-Martin Schmitt from Germany and Adrian Germishuizen from South Africa climbed it on 20 May 2009, opening a new route on its NE face. This is the 5th overall modern ascent, the first being by Argentineans Sergio Bossini and Carlos Mas in 1960.

The west glacier of **Pissis** is the largest in the region, with an area of 40km^2, and before 2009 had not been ascended in its entirety. It can only be reached after a difficult 200km off-road ride. The only previous attempt was in 1994 by Mexicans who reached a point NW of the highest point. In March 2009, a team directed by Guillermo Almaraz erected base camp at 5000m (27° 43' 04.5" S, 68° 54' 00.8" W) in the valley that gives access to the glacier. The team was completed with Eduardo Namur, Daniel Pontín and Nicolás Pantaleón. The ascent continued by a penitentes-covered valley to a camp at 5600m beside the glacier (27° 44' 03.1" S, 68° 51' 40.8" W). Next day they traversed the 7km glacier, camping at 5950m near the ridge used by the Polish on the 1937 first ascent (27° 44' 48.3" S, 68° 48' 45.5" W). The final summit bid was made by Almaraz, Pantaleón and Namur ascending the snowed face to reach the ridge that is the last part of the Polish route. They continued via the W face of minor summit Gendarmería Nacional (6675m) to reach the main summit just past midday on 14 March. The group used the latest unofficial height measurement, 6795m; the official figure is 6882m.

Cerro La Coipa (5050m) is an elegant triangular summit on the access to Pissis. It has been known by this name (a kind of mineral) from long ago and appears on ancient maps. The Instituto Geográfico Militar Argentino marks as La Coipa a nearby summit some 100m higher that isn't well seen from the slopes. The locals point to the 5050m summit as the real La Coipa. On 23 November 2009, Jose Luis Querlico and Marcelo Scanu erected a base camp at 4150m its eastern slopes. On 27 November Scanu left alone from base camp at 7.45am taking the south-east ridge, and summited in windy weather at 2.45pm, completing the first ascent of this summit. There were no traces of other ascents. At 4.15pm he was back at camp and by 5.30pm the team was back in Fiambalá at 1500m.

Argentines Andrés Martínez Infante, Fernando Arranz, Guillermo Bianchi and Glauco Muratti made the first ascent of the virgin summit **Gram Bicentenario** (5785m), which may be an old volcano, west of Volcán Pissis near the Argentine-Chilean border. They travelled to base camp (4500m) by all-terrain vehicle. On 17 November 2010 they departed very early and climbed via the long N ridge, which has many terraces and a plateau that seems an ancient crater. They arrived at the top at 3pm and obtained a GPS reading very similar to the official map height.

CENTRAL ARGENTINE ANDES

A group has been very active in the area of **Cordón de la Jaula**, W of the Cordón del Plata, Mendoza, near to Aconcagua but much more isolated. On 17 October 2009, Pablo González, Gabriel Barral and Alcides Massa left from a 4000m camp on a moraine. They ascended the W face of a virgin 5147m peak that is christened as **Pico El Fede** in honour of Fedrico Campanini, who died on Aconcagua. They then traversed west and ascended two other peaks, making the second overall ascent of **Pico San Esteban** (5168m) and **Pico Rosa** (5165m). On San Esteban they found the first testimony, 45 years old. On all three peaks they had 40° snow slopes. To reach the area, they ascended the El Plata-Vallecitos col and Quebrada del Peine, taking after the Quebrada de la Jaula. Pablo González has made many other interesting first and second ascents in this area. With his brother Federico, he climbed **Cerro Aguila Blanca** (5250m), the highest summit in the north sector of La Jaula. They summited on 23 March 2008 and found the testimony of the first team directed by Peterek in 1956. Some days before Pico El Fede was climbed, a group formed by Gabriel Moretta, Matías Cruz and Pablo Ruiz made the first ascent of a peak that they called **Pico Campanini**, also in honour of Federico Campanini. The groups didn't know the existence of one another so the naming of the peaks was coincidental. Pico Campanini has a height of 5245m and neighbours El Fede. The group climbed a 700m, 40-70° ice couloir with a crux 20m sérac with 90° passages to a ridge that finishes on the summit.

In January 2009 Mercedes Garrido, Antonio Pontoriero and Marcelo Scanu tried to find access to a fine virgin 5774m summit in the **Cordillera de Olivares**, Agua Negra zone in the Argentine Province of San Juan, very near to the border with Chile. In February 2010, Pablo González and I reached the summit. On 7 February an old pickup of the road crew left us at 4200m in the Quebrada San Lorenzo. Next day we followed a destroyed mine trail to camp at 4625m. On 9 February, González climbed a new route on the S face and ridge of **Cerro Bifurcación** (5223m), first ascended by Scanu and team in 1991 (see *AAJ* 1992, p161). On 10 February we erected the last camp at 4850m, near the Portezuelo (Col) de Olivares. In 1817, a military group supporting San Martin passed by here, helping gain control of Chile. On the 11th we set off early in good weather, climbing the west face, which was reminiscent of Aconcagua. We reached the 5774m summit, naming it **Cerro Presidente Perón** because the three-time Argentine president was a climber and supported many expeditions in Argentina and abroad. This ascent was part of the programme '200 años de Patria, más de 500 de montañismo' (200 years of the country, more than 500 years of climbing) marking the Argentine Bicentennial and over 500 years since the first Inca climbers on the highest South American peaks.

Argentine climber Gabriel Fava and Frenchman Henry Bizot climbed a new and interesting route on the Central Summit of **La Mesa** (The Table), in the Cordillera de la Ramada whose highest mountain is Mercedario (6770m). In December 2009, they reached the 6150m summit by its NE ridge, calling their route *Verónica y sus 6 hijos* (1100m, 35/55°, AD+/D).

The mountain now named **Cerro Comandante Cabot** (5865m) is located in San Juan Province near Cerro Presidente Perón (5774m), also ascended for first time this year. Comandante Cabot was a military officer who passed from here to Chile supporting San Martin´s actions to free that country from the Spaniards. Late on 18 December 2010, Argentine Pablo González and his wife reached Pircas Negras in the Agua Negra Pass and ascended to camp at 4043m in the Quebrada de San Javier o de la Pirca. On 19th, González soloed the mountain via the east face, avoiding ice (this was a dry year with little snowfall), and reached the pyramid-like summit at 3.45pm.

Between Bonete and Pissis volcanoes in Provincia de La Rioja, there is a ridge called **Cordón de los Pioneros** with many unexplored volcanoes raising more than 6000m. A team consisting of Argentines Guillermo Almaraz, Eduardo Namur, Juan Labra, Lelio de Crocci, Claudio Valva and Daniel Pontín ascended one of these mountains during the expeditions marking the Argentine Bicentennial. Beginning on 31 October 2010, the expedition acclimatised by Laguna Brava, a salty lake with Inca ruins, old geysers and an old crashed airplane. First they made the second ascent of **Chepical** (4646m, see *AAJ* 2005 p276) and Cerro Pilar (5032m) with an Inca altar in its summit. Afterwards they travelled to base camp, crossing the Pampa (plateau) de Veladero and through the Quebrada del Medio to camp at 5100m. Next day they ascended a creek up to a plateau, camping at 5570m. Early on 7 November they began the ascent of the virgin N peak of the Cordón de los Pioneros, taking the SW ridge to the south col and continuing the S ridge in high winds. The summit was defended with great rock blocks. Finally they reached the 6092m summit, calling it **Pico Bicentenario** (Bicentennial Peak), 27° 55' 16.2" S, 68° 45' 12.2" W.

The impressive peak of **Pico Polaco** (c6000m) lies in the Cordillera de la Ramada, Provincia de San Juan, near the Mercedario massif, and is the nicest peak in the ridge and one of the best in all the Central Andes. It was named 'Peak N' by a Polish expedition in 1934, but was climbed for the first time in 1958 by Beorchia and Yacante from San Juan. They christened it Pico Polaco (Polish Peak) in honour of the 1934 expedition. The old height of 6050m has been lowered; some give the mountain 6020m, others 6001 or 6000m, or even less than 6000m. Two young climbers, Gabriel Fava from San Juan and Iván Rocamora from Mendoza climbed a new route on the NE wall. The expedition began on 5 October 2010, reaching base camp the next day in Pirca de los Polacos (3600m). On the 7th, the pair departed to the base of the wall with only one sleeping bag, using a precarious stone wall as a bivouac at 4750m. On the 8th they began the climb at 6.15am, taking easy rock to reach an ice line through rock towers to a very steep 30m icefall with hard ice at 5400m, which they avoided on the left via 55m of poorly protected 4th class rock. They continued up a series of ice and snow couloirs steepening to 55/60°, with up to 4+ rock in between, to eventually reach the summit ridge. They finally ascended

192. The north summit of Pico Polaco (c6000m), showing the line of *Cheto Alpino* (1000m, D+, 75°, 4+). *(Gabriel Fava)*

some rotten but easy rocky steps to reach the N summit (Cumbre Norte) at 6pm. They named the route *Cheto Alpino* (1000m, D+, 75°, 4+). For the descent they took a couloir that falls directly east, with some steps of 60°, beside the 1958 route, to a bivouac at 4800m on the moraine. Unfortunately, Rocamora died on Mercedarios South Wall some days after. With Fava, he was trying to enchain the 6000ers of the range.

TIERRA DEL FUEGO

Activity near Ushuaia: **Torres del Río Chico** are rocky towers at the end of el Valle del Río Chico at 54° 43' 1.81" S, 68° 19' 5.02" W. Nacho González, Martin Steinhaus and Federico Ruffini made a new route, the third route and the third overall ascent to the Torre Inferior del Río Chico on 11 March 2009. They named it *Prefiero ser flogger*, 6b, 380m. It was snowing a little with a temperature of -7°C. On the Domo Blanco (White Dome, 1200m), Mariano Rodriguez and Ibai opened a new route that they called *Piedra, papel o tijera*, 250m on 90° ice. We don't have the exact date of the climb.

PHIL WICKENS

Antarctica 2009-10

93. The Three Pigs (Antarctic Peninsula) - the new line '*42 Balais et Toujours pas Calmé*' is the snow/ice gully on the left (*Phil Wickens*)

Despite an increase in the number of yachts visiting the Antarctic Peninsula, very few climbing parties have attempted new routes or unclimbed peaks. The major achievements of the 2009-10 season were by two French parties, led by Ludovic Challeat, aboard the yacht *Podorange*, and Patrick Wagnon, aboard Isabelle Autissier's *Ada II*. After unsuccessfully trying to reach Mt Francais (2822m) from the north via the Iliad Glacier, Challeat's team moved to Brabant Island, where they made the third ascent, on skis and over two days, of **Mt Parry** (2522m) from the south and east on 13 January. They then moved to the Antarctic Peninsula proper, where they climbed Scheimpflug Nunatak (1150m), and attempted Pulfrich Peak, from Andvord Bay. They then moved to the Penola Strait where, in addition to ascents of the frequently climbed Mt Demaria, Mt Scott, and Mt Shackleton, they ascended the Wiggins Glacier to make the fourth ascent of **Mt Peary**, which at 2080m was more than 200m higher

194. Wandel Peak (980m) on Booth Island showing the line of *La Mystique des Corniche.* (*Phil Wickens*)

than the official height.

Meanwhile, Wagnon, together with Lionel Daudet and Mathieu Cortial, aboard *Ada II*, successfully climbed the dramatic 1600m west ridge of **Mt Foster** (2105m) on Smith Island in 15 hours, a route they named *Vol du Serac* (ED+). Notorious for its bad weather, the main summit had been reached, after various attempts, via the south-east face in 1996 by Greg Landreth's New Zealand team. The French headed for the unclimbed and slightly lower north summit. The upper section of the 1600m route proved to be the crux, where Cortial took a roped fall, a sérac collapse left Daudet hanging on his rope, and the summit mushrooms provided some entertaining tunnelling to surmount. After a 15-hour descent, the group then headed to Brabant Island where they started up the equally impressive and unclimbed north-west ridge of **Mt Parry** (2522m). After sitting out a storm partway up the route, they were successful in making the fourth ascent of Mt Parry, with the upper section and summit mushrooms again providing a precarious crux. After a 19-hour descent of the same line a large wave hit their landing site and washed away most of the food and gear, prompting them to name the 2500m route *Nouvelle Vague* (New Wave: ED).

Behind Port Lockroy towers the west face of **Savoia Peak** (1415m), the highest mountain on Wiencke Island that was first climbed in 1905 by Charcot's expedition. Although the summit has been reached numerous times since, no attempt had been made of the west face. The French headed for an obvious and striking gully on the left side of the face, which gave 800m

95. Savoia Peak (1415m) on Wiencke Island showing the line climbed by Wagnon/Daudet (ascent on left, descent on right). (*Phil Wickens*)

of water ice, finishing through cornices and rime-mushrooms to reach the final 300m ridge, from where they descended the easier south side of the mountain. They named their route *Bon Anniversaire Tristan,* ED+.

Further to the south, at the entrance to the Lemaire Channel, lies False Cape Renard and the towers commonly known as **The Three Pigs**, up which the Pou brothers created their route *Azken Paradizua* in 2007. A strikingly straight snow and ice gully splits the western side of the western-most tower and this was climbed by Cortial, Daudet, and Wagnon to give *42 Balais et Toujours pas Calmé* (ED-). Wagnon's team then turned their sights to the peaks on Booth Island that line the western shore of the Lemaire Channel, climbing the attractive gully, which they named *La Mystique des Corniches.....ons* (TD+), that drops almost directly from the summit of **Wandel Peak** (980m).

Ada II continued southwards, beyond the Antarctic Circle and into Marguerite Bay, where they finished their very productive expedition by making the probable first ascent, via a gully on the west-north-west face, of **Statham Peak** (1120m), which lies on the western side of Pourquoi Pas Island. Heavy sea-ice and poor weather prevented them from reaching Alexander Island, far to the south, and so they sailed south-west to the rarely visited Peter 1 Island. After landing, they were unable to reach the summit of the highest point, **Lars Christensen Peak** (1640m), due to bad weather and large crevasses. They returned to *Ada II* and two weeks later, after 75 days away, were back in Argentina.

196. Mount Ashley (1145m) from the northeast, looking across the Lucas Glacier. The rightmost summit is the highest. The 2009 route reached the col left of the summit from behind, and continued along the skyline ridge. (*Crag Jones*)

SOUTH GEORGIA

In late October 2009, Skip Novak and Crag Jones sailed on *Pelagic Australis* to Salisbury Plain on the north-west coast of South Georgia. Although most of South Georgia's significant summits have been climbed, **Mount Ashley** (1145m), which lies between Salisbury Plain and King Haakon Bay, remained unclimbed since it is outside of the main Allardyce and Salvesen ranges. On 30 October, from the Grace Glacier to the north-west they ascended on skis to the headwall, which they climbed to reach the main south-east ridge, reaching the summit after 9 hours.

Mount Everest Foundation Expedition Reports

SUMMARISED BY BILL RUTHVEN

The Mount Everest Foundation (**www.mef.org.uk**) was set up as a registered charity following the first successful ascent of Everest in 1953 and was initially financed from the surplus funds and subsequent royalties of that expedition. It is a continuing initiative between the Alpine Club and the Royal Geographical Society (*with the Institute of British Geographers*).

The main object of the Foundation is the support of expeditions planning the exploration of mountain regions of the earth.

The MEF has now distributed more than £950,000 to some 1600 British and New Zealand expeditions planning such exploration. Most of the grants have been awarded to ambitious young climbers who help to maintain Britain's reputation as one of the world's leading exploratory nations, but some have also been awarded to teams planning scientific research in a mountain environment.

All that is asked in return is a comprehensive report. These reports are eventually lodged in the Alpine Club Library, the Royal Geographical Society, the British Mountaineering Council and the Climbing and Mountaineering collection in Sheffield Central Library established in memory of Alan Rouse.

Each year the Foundation holds a fund-raising lecture at the Royal Geographical Society, but donations to assist in its work are always welcome, particularly from those who have benefited from MEF grants in the past, so why not include a bequest to the Foundation in your will?

The following notes summarise reports from the expeditions supported during 2009 and 2010, and are divided into geographical areas.

REPORTS FROM EXPEDITIONS IN 2009

AMERICA – NORTH & CENTRAL

British Ruth Gorge Gavin Pike with James Clapham; April-June 2009
Although the spectacular glacial rift known as Ruth Gorge is well explored, there are still plenty of opportunities for new routes in the surrounding area. This was proved by this duo who, after warming up on the classic *Shaken, not Stirred* (V A15) on the south face of Moose's Tooth, headed for the unclimbed east face of Peak 11,300 (3444m). Climbing mostly by night to minimise the risk from an overhanging sérac, they put up *Night of the*

*Raging Goose (*1500m, V WI5) on its central couloir, eventually returning to camp via the south ridge after 25 hours on the go.

A week sitting out storms gave them time to recover before heading for the north face of Mt Church (2509m), climbed for the first time by a Japanese team in 2008. Pike and Clapham elected for the central line up the face, resulting in some hairy moments (plus serious bruises when a 'bus-sized' cornice collapsed), but eventually achieved a new route, which they named *Amazing Grace* (V AI4). MEF Ref 09/02

British/New Zealand Alaska Extravaganza Vivian Scott with Tony Stone plus Steve Fortune (NZ); May-June 2009

The main objective of this team was *Z Buttress* on Mount Hunter (4441m), but on arrival in the area, they learned that a Swiss team had beaten them to it and made the first ascent one week earlier. However, they decided to warm up by climbing *Moonflower Buttress*, which they achieved in good style, descending by the west ridge, the round trip taking three days. The Swiss team had reported dangerous cornices and ice mushrooms on the north face of Mt Hunter and the weather forecast was not good, so with the aim of maintaining some acclimatisation, they skied up to spend a night at the 11,000ft (c3350m) camp on the W buttress of Denali. Back at base with the weather still good, Scott and Fortune made an enjoyable traverse up the SW ridge and down the E ridge of Mt Francis (1531m). As the bad weather arrived they assisted in the evacuation of a sick climber on Denali, but after several days of snow, left the mountains altogether, and went rock climbing on the granite tors of the Chena valley. Fortune then went home, but with a few days left and an improvement in the weather, the others returned to the Ruth amphitheatre where they climbed *Cobra Pillar* on Mt Barille (2331m). MEF Ref 09/07

British Kluane Icefields – Staircase Glacier Glenn Wilks with Jenny Foister, Peter McCombie and Mark Weeding; May-June 2009

Virtually nothing was known of the mountains around the Stairway Glacier (part of the St Elias range) in the Kluane Ice Fields NP suggesting that this team might have been the first climbers to visit: prior to departure, they identified 15 possible objectives. Access was by ski-plane flying from Silver City which dropped them on the glacier; from three separate camps they made first ascents (up to Scottish grades II/III) of nine of the peaks with heights ranging from 3160m to 3490m MEF Ref 09/16

Glacier Bay Climbing Paul Knott (UK) with Guy McKinnon (NZ); April-May 2009

Glacier Bay National Park lies in SE Alaska, and the Johns Hopkins – although possibly never previously visited by climbers – is one of its major glaciers, surrounded by the major summits of the Fairweather Range. This team hoped to make the first ascent of the N ridge of Mt Crillon (3879m) and then complete a traverse of the mountain, but aerial reconnaissance

from their ski-plane approach revealed serious icefalls and séracs; they therefore decided to attempt the unclimbed 6km NW Ridge of Mt Bertha (3110m) instead. From their drop point at 1200m on the broad snowy west shoulder of Mt Abbe, their trip started with a difficult descent to the south arm of the glacier; after two days to recover, it took them four days of unusually good weather to reach the summit of Mt Bertha – probably only the fifth team to do so.
With time to spare, they then made the first ascent of the striking Peak 8599ft (2621m), which lies N of Mt Crillon and E of Mt Orville, proposing the (strictly unofficial) name of '*Fifty Years of Alaskan Statehood*' in line with Russian tradition. (*see article p114*) MEF Ref 09/11

British Ruth Gorge Jon Bracey with Matt Helliker; May 2009
Although this duo hoped to climb a new route on the South Face of Mount Bradley (1017m) in Ruth Gorge, when they arrived in Alaska they found that unusually warm temperatures made anything but north faces too dangerous, so they turned their attention elsewhere. They were successful in climbing two new routes: on the 1300m N face of Mt Grosvenor (2572m) they climbed *Meltdown* (VI, grade 6+ ice/mixed, ED3) and on the 1150m N face of Mt Church (2509m) – only two weeks after the visit by Pike and Clapham (see above) – *For Whom The Bell Tolls* (V, Grade 6 ice/mixed, ED2). They also repeated the Japanese Couloir on Mt Barrill (2332m) while searching for two missing climbers, who later turned up safe and sound after spending a grim night out near the summit. MEF Ref 09/24

British St Elias Range Simon Yates with Paul Schweitzer; April-May 2009
This team was originally hoping to make the first ascent of the west ridge of Mount Hubbard (4577m) in the remote Wrangell St Elias Range on the Yukon border with Alaska. However, when they heard that this had already been climbed, at the suggestion of local activist Jack Tackle they turned their attention to Mt Vancouver – in particular the 2400m SW spur of its S summit, Good Neighbor Peak (4850m), which forms the border between Alaska and Canada. (Although previously climbed by a large Japanese team in 1968, this had been from the Canadian side in very snowy conditions, and used fixed ropes for most of its length. Three team members were killed in avalanche.) After negotiating problems concerning bush pilots crossing the border, they were eventually dropped by ski-plane in a small glacial basin at the base of the ridge, where they set up their base camp. From here, climbing in strictly alpine-style over a period of five days, they followed the west side of the ridge up 3000m of ice and mixed climbing to the summit. This was very serious and committing (overall Alpine ED with up to Scottish V ice and 6 mixed), with retreat virtually impossible in the second half. Moving east along the frontier ridge, they reached the top of the original line on Good Neighbor, the 1967 Centennial Route on the SE Spur, which they descended over two days in storm conditions. (*see article AJ 2009 p26*) MEF Ref 09/29

AMERICA – SOUTH & ANTARCTICA

British San Lorenzo Mick Fowler with Steve Burns, Ian Cartwright and Es Tresidder; Sept-Oct 2009
Cerro San Lorenzo (3706m) is the second highest peak in the Patagonian Andes and was first climbed by an Italian team in 1941. It has received a number of subsequent ascents, but this team hoped to make the first ascent of its south face. However, on arrival in the area, it was immediately obvious that this year séracs would make any attempt on the face too dangerous.
Alternative objectives attempted include a big gully between Pilar Sar and Cumbre Sar, which was abandoned below the bergschrund because of deep snow etc, and the east side of Cerro Penitentes (2967m), abandoned for the same reason. Although an attempt on Cerro Hermosa (2450m) was contemplated, strong winds and heavy snow made any further climbing unsafe. MEF Ref 09/20

British Apolobamba Kris Hill with Adrian Dye, Matt Griffin and Simon Wyatt; July-August 2009
After acclimatising in the Condori range this team moved to the Cordillera Apolobamba on the northern tip of the Bolivian Andes, where they hoped to make first ascents of peaks over 5000m. In particular, they hoped to climb a peak they had named 'Rock Peak' but were unsuccessful due to the conditions – in particular the lack of snow which they had anticipated would enable them to climb a section of rubble. In fact, they decided that 'Rubble Peak' would be a more appropriate name. They did manage other climbs, including a 5255m rocky peak named 'Cherro' and a rocky ridge 'Wompa Ridge' (PD+) to a point just below the summit of Cherro. They also attempted routes on the north face of Canisaya and on the SW face of Charquini, but failed on both. MEF Ref 09/30

HIMALAYA – INDIA

Indo-American/British Saser Kangri II Jim Lowther (UK) with Mark Richey, Steve Swenson and Mark Wilford (USA) and Chewang Motup, Ang Tashi, Konchok Tinles Dahn Singh and Tsering Sherpa (India); August-Sept 2009
With access to the Indian Karakoram largely forbidden to foreign expeditions, many of the stunning mountains in the area remain unclimbed, including the east (ie Main) summit of Saser Kangri II (7518m) – reputed to be the world's second highest unclimbed peak. This team planned to recce the area and hopefully make its first ascent.
After finding a route to the peak's south face, they spent four days climbing steep ice (55°-60°) and mixed ground until they were stopped at 6700m by the combined effects of slow progress, technical ice climbing, a lack of bivouac sites and extremely cold, deteriorating weather. MEF Ref 09/18

HIMALAYA – NEPAL

British Chang Himal North Face Andy Houseman with Nick Bullock; Oct 2009

Although Chang Himal (aka Wedge Peak, 6802m) in the Kangchenjunga Himal is reputed to have been climbed from the south, this team planned to make the first ascent of the 1800m central spur on its north face which Lindsay Griffin had described as an 'unclimbed gem' in a magazine article. (A Slovenian team had attempted the line in 2007, but had been forced to retreat at less than half-height due to poor snow conditions.)

This team established a base camp at 5050m on a very windy grassy plateau above the Kangchenjunga glacier, directly opposite (and NE of) their objective. After acclimatising on Pk 6215, and a rest, they started on the route, reaching the summit on the fourth day.

Descent was by abseiling and down-climbing the ascent route, which they graded ED+ M6. This expedition received the Nick Estcourt Grant for 2009. (*see article p45*) MEF Ref 09/04

CHINA AND TIBET

Xuelian Feng Bruce Normand with Jed Brown (USA); July-August 2009

For Normand this was a return visit to the Chinese Tien Shan. He planned to climb new routes on the satellite peaks of Xuelian Feng (6627m), the highest group in the area away from the border peaks of Pobeda etc.

The central peak, Xuelin Main, had been climbed from the SE by a Japanese team in 1990, but none of its subsidiaries had been touched.

After acclimatising on a 4850m peak, Normand and Brown climbed Xuelin North (6472m) by its west ridge, then Xuelin East (c6400m) by its east ridge (summiting with two other US climbers completing a different route) and finally Xuelin West (6422m) by its north face, the last with the addition of Kyle Dempster from the US team. MEF Ref 09/10

New Zealand Nyambo Konka Penny Goddard and Lydia Bradey (both NZ) plus Kenny Gasch and Mark Jenkins (both USA); April-May 2009

This team planned to explore the Daxue Shan Range of West Sichuan, and hopefully make the first ascent of Nyambo Konka (6114m). They attempted the peak's east face from the Bawangou valley, and moderately technical mixed rock snow and ice brought them to the summit ridge at 5800m.

Unfortunately, this presented them with hard, steep blue ice with many crevasses, which they deemed impassable. No other route on the peak looked more feasible, so following a period of bad weather they turned their attention to a c5020m peak in the Qionglai mountains to the east where, using an (illegal) BlackBerry as their main navigation tool, they made what was probably its first ascent via a route involving mainly steep rock scrambling. MEF Ref 09/19

British Yangmolong Dave Wynne-Jones with Dr Derek Buckle, Dick Isherwood and Peter Rowat; Sept-Oct 2009
Yangmolong (6066m) is one of the few remaining unclimbed 6000m peaks in Sichuan, and has become something of a target for this leader. In 2007 (MEF Ref 07/22A) he attempted an ascent via its north face but was stopped at 5400m by steep and difficult terrain with sérac barriers. However, during the trek out, the team spotted what appeared to be an approach from the east, so this return trip was to investigate further. They noted three possible lines on the east ridge, although soon discounted two of them. Despite poor weather (rain up to 4000m and heavy snow at 4900m) which held them up for a full week, they established a high camp at 5400m, but were prevented from tackling the technical summit. Unfortunately, early in the trip, they discovered a dramatic attitude change in the local people, who not only stole from their tents, but also extorted money with menaces; the local police seemed powerless, and none of the team is keen to return to the area. MEF Ref 09/23

PAKISTAN

New Zealand Charakusa Big Wall Bruce Dowrick with Jonathan Seddon from NZ and Adrian Laing and Scott Standen from Australia; July-August 2009
These experienced big wall climbers visited the Charakusa valley intending to attempt to free-climb a new route on the 1300m west wall of Nafee's Cap, a sub-peak of K7. Although they did not actually reach the summit due to heavy icing and snow, they were successful in their aim, creating *Naughty Daddies*, a 19-pitch route up to grade 25 (F7b), which they believe to be the hardest free technical rock route climbed at altitude by New Zealanders or Australians. A new 10-pitch line (F6a) was also climbed on Nayser Brakk (5200m), a beautiful spire above their base camp. With its excellent rock and little precipitation, the team feel that the Charakusa area still has a lot to offer. MEF Ref 09/17

New Zealand Batura Glacier Pat Deavoll with Paul Hersey; (June-July 2009) Although the initial submission was for a three-person team planning to explore and hopefully make the first ascents of the south faces of Kampire Dior (7142m) and Kuk Sar (6934m), the political situation put these out of bounds, and by the time it took place, it was two people, Deavoll and Hersey, hoping to make the first ascent of Karim Sar (6180m), on the southern side of the Batura massif. This had been the subject of a failed attempt by an Italian team in 2007, but all attempts to contact them prior to departure were unsuccessful. After a two-day walk-in up the Shilinbar glacier from the road-head at Budelas, they established a base camp at 3535m, directly under the peak's south face. The area had experienced more snow in the previous winter than for many years, and when Hersey suffered an undiagnosed illness, the prospects of success looked poor. Nevertheless, he agreed to set off with Deavoll, and actually reached c6000m before leaving her to continue alone. This she did with great trepidation, climbing a mixture of deep snow and 60°-70° ice until she reached the summit. (*see article p3*) MEF Ref 09/28A

CENTRAL ASIA AND THE FAR EAST

Western Kokshaal-Too Carl Reilly with Tom Bide, Dave Gladwin, Graeme Schofield and Tom Stewart plus Urpu Hapouja from Finland; August-Sept 2009
The main aim of this team visiting Kyrgyzstan was to make the first ascent of the north ridge of Kyzyl Asker (5842m). After meeting in Bishkek they spent a few days acclimatising in the Ala-Archa National Park, which offers an impressive range of high quality climbing. The journey to the Kokshaal-Too area was in a massive 16 tonne vehicle, which despite having 6WD managed to get trapped up to its axles in a bog at one stage, taking almost 24 hours to dig free. Once in the area, the team operated as separate climbing pairs. Gladwin and Stewart tackled Kyzyl Asker, and after three 18-hour days on the 2km-long, 1400m-high north ridge reached the summit, taking another day to descend to BC. They graded the route WI3/4, Alpine V/VI, M6+/7. Meanwhile, Bide and Hapuoja climbed the north ridge on Peak 4863m (AD) and Reilly and Schofield climbed the north ridge on a peak not shown on the map (D). Finally Bide and Reilly climbed the W face/S ridge on Peak 5046m (TD/TD+). The above heights are as marked on the American Alpine Club 1:50,000 Climbers' Map which they found very clear and easy to read, although their own altimeters recorded up to 400m difference from some spot heights. They noted that the weather in August tended to be colder but more stable than in July when most previous expeditions had visited. MEF Ref 09/08

Anglo-New Zealand Zartosh Simon Woods with Graham Rowbotham and Adam Thomas plus Jock Jeffrey from NZ; July-Sept 2009
Although there were rumours that Zartosh (6128m) in the Muzkol Range of Tajikistan has already been climbed by a team from the Eastern Bloc, these were unconfirmed, so this party hoped to make the first definite ascent. The 700m north face had already repulsed three attempts by Kenyan climbers but nevertheless was the first route that the new team attempted reaching c5650m before unconsolidated snowpack, thin ice and powder snow on top of rock forced them to retreat. They subsequently reached the summit via the west col on a route consisting of mixed technical ground, but found no trace of any previous ascent. MEF Ref 09/09

Kara Gakar Exploratory Mountaineering Sally Brown and Eddy Barnes from UK plus Sari Nevala from Finland and Vanessa Wills from Australia; August 2009
This team had intended to explore and climb in the remote Dzhalgal-Mau

valley of the Borkoldoi range in Kyrgyzstan, but as they arrived in the area hunters on horseback informed them that this was their territory and prevented entrance. Faced with a swift decision on an alternative location, the team stood at the highest point on the plateau to try and select an area to which access looked feasible. They moved first to the Western Kokshaal Too, and later to the Acha Kaeyndi valley in the At Bashi range, for neither of which had they maps or done any planning, thus ensuring that this was a true exploratory trip. Nevertheless, they reached the summits of 16 peaks up to 5250m, but it will take some time to ascertain how many of them were first ascents. MEF Ref 09/14

Zhungar Alatau Stuart Worsfold with Jamie Goodhart, Liam Hughes, Paul Padman and John Temple plus two Kazakh nationals; August 2009
The area south of the Koksu river in the Zhungar Alatau region of Kazakhstan has had few visitors, so offered a good destination for this exploratory expedition. River crossings prevented them from establishing their base camp in the planned location, so they had to make do with a lower site, which naturally increased the length of walk-ins, although it also added flexibility. They spent four days climbing in the valley of the Kyoabl-Kapacau river and then five more in the valley of the Tblwkah river. With relatively good weather during their 17 days in the area, the team climbed a total of 16 peaks up to 4162m, nine of which may have been first ascents. However they feel that the area still has plenty of scope for further exploration. MEF Ref 09/21

09/22 - 21st Century Altai Tim Moss with Marc Bullock, Matthew Freear, Nancy Pickup, Spike Reid and David Tell; May-June 2009
Although a number of teams, primarily Soviet, have previously visited most parts of the Russian Altai, little is known about their achievements, so this team of non-technical climbers felt it would offer scope for considerable exploration leading to a simple guide to the area. After establishing a base camp in the South Kurai range they climbed five peaks (c3100m) graded F to PD, four of which were possibly first ascents. Some team members also spent a few days in the Northern Chuysky range at the end of the trip, where they traversed the Teacher Horseshoe. MEF Ref 09/22

Kings College Alumni MC Western Kokshaal-Too Edward Lemon with Martin Jones, Dr Gareth Mottram and Jacob Wrathall; July-August 2009
This team originally planned to base their expedition on the Malitskovo glacier, but then discovered that many of the peaks in the area were climbed in 2007, so decided to use the Sarychat glacier instead. Access was delayed by a driver who did not know the area, eventually dropping them 30km short of their intended base camp. Once established they were further disappointed to find that, instead of being good quality limestone, the local rock was shale. Nevertheless, they climbed three mixed routes ranging from Scottish II to V. They reached five previously unclimbed summits,

the highest being Peak 4989m, although their GPS recorded it as 5014m. MEF Ref 09/27

MISCELLANEOUS

Glaciological investigations in the Kebnekaise Alessio Gusmeroli and Prof Tavi Murray from Swansea University with Tatiana Enzinger, Marco Fransci, Daniel Hjelk and Riccardo Scotti from Stockholm University and supported by Peter Jansson and Henrik Tornberg; March-April 2009
Although the MEF does not normally support expeditions to mainland Europe, it was felt that this work on one of the biggest glaciers in Sweden deserved encouragement, as it was utilising the latest developments in ground-penetrating radar. Based at the Stockholm University Research Station at Tarfala (one hour's skiing from the glacier) the team was very fortunate in having good weather throughout most of their stay in the area, enabling them to take continuous records. The new data will be compared with that obtained during previous surveys to determine how polythermal glaciers are responding to recent climatic warming. MEF Ref 09/01

REPORTS FROM EXPEDITIONS IN 2010

AMERICA – NORTH & CENTRAL

Baffin Big Walls, Canada Mark Thomas with Stuart McAleese and Mike (Twid) Turner; May 2010
Sail Peaks form a series of mostly unclimbed gigantic rock faces rising very steeply on the southern side of the Stewart Valley on Baffin Island. Access was a nine-hour trip by skidoo from Clyde River, and after setting up base camp, the team fixed 400m of rope to the base of the wall. They then had 20 days of very difficult (mainly serious aid) climbing, covering 1400m of rock in cold, snowy conditions to reach the summit. They called the route *Arctic Monkeys*, and graded it VI, A4, V+. An early thaw prevented skidoos reaching base camp at the end of the trip, so they were forced to wade through frozen slush for 25km to make their escape. MEF Ref: 10/03

Kichatna, USA Adrian Nelhams with Dean Mounsey; May 2010
Hoping that his third visit to Alaska's Kichatna range would be lucky, Nelhams planned to climb new routes on the W Face of Mt Jeffers (c2440m) from the Tatina glacier and/or a similar route on the NW Face of Middle Triple Peak (2693m) from the Monolith glacier. But he had reckoned without the unseasonably warm temperatures and lack of an overnight freeze that resulted in an unstable snowpack. Although several attempts were made on Mt Jeffers, each was abandoned due to frequent avalanches. They were more fortunate on the other side of the valley, which had a different aspect, and two 1000m mixed routes were climbed. The first

was a beautiful 800m line to a summit c2300m: they called the route *Beat Surrender* and graded it ED2. The other route was a curving 1000m ED1 line *Metronome* to a summit c2360m. MEF Ref: 10/05

Barkley Ridge, Wrangell St Elias, USA Stuart Howard and Dave Swinburne; July-August 2010 Although May and June are normally chosen for climbing in the Wrangell St Elias range, as teachers they were forced to go later, finding the snow softer, but not unmanageable. They had originally hoped to make the first ascent of Peak 9270 (2825m), the highest point of the Barkley Ridge, but with unsettled weather in the area, they followed the recommendation of their bush pilot and transferred their attention to the rarely visited upper reaches of Granite Creek. Once dropped off, they lost no time in tackling as many peaks as possible. They reached the summits of three, Peak 8329 (2539m) at AD-, Peak 7679 (2341m) at AD, and Peak 7178 (2188m) which gave an easy ascent on ski: all were assumed to be first ascents. An attempt at Peak 7890 (2405m) was thwarted by a large wall some 150 metres below the summit. They felt that there is still plenty of opportunity in this area of Alaska for exploration and first ascents of moderate difficulty. MEF Ref: 10/09

Sim-Griffith Ruth Gorge, USA Will Sim with Jon Griffith; April-June 2010 On their first visit to the Greater Ranges, this team had hoped to climb new routes on Mount Dickey (2909m) and/or the East Face of Mount Dan Beard (3127m). However it snowed almost constantly whilst they were in the area. On one of the few days of good weather they managed to climb 400m on Peak 11300 (3444m) before Griffith fell 20m, injuring his back and forcing a retreat. In search of better weather, they flew over to Denali base camp on the Kahiltna glacier from which, to acclimatise, they first climbed the 800m East Ridge of Mount Francis (3185m) and the 1000m SW Face/Couloir of Kahiltna Queen (3773m). They then attempted a single push ascent of the Moonflower Buttress on Mount Hunter (4442m), reaching 'The Vision' in 16 hours before making the agonising decision to descend without completing the route. This expedition also received an Alpine Club Climbing Fund Grant for 2010. MEF Ref: 10/14

AMERICA – SOUTH & ANTARCTICA

NZ Antarctic Peninsula Lydia Bradey with Penny Goddard and Dean Staples; Jan-Feb 2010
A few days before leaving New Zealand this team learned that a French team had just made the first ascent of the West Ridge of Mount Parry (2520m) on Brabant Island, their intended objective. Undeterred they continued, and after sailing from Ushuaia to the Antarctic Peninsula they looked around for an alternative, and selected a classic line on the West Face of the First Sister of Fief (986m) on Wiencke Island. Ice cliffs prevented a landing near to the peak, but access only took half a day on

skis. Although at 12 pitches it was shorter than the route on Parry it was far more technical, as it followed a central line of steep ice and snow rather than a ridge: they graded it NZ Alpine Grade 5. Descent was by seven abseils down a gully between the First Sister and Mt Luigi to complete a 14-hour day. Penny Goddard holds dual NZ and UK nationality, and was awarded the Alison Chadwick Memorial Grant for 2010. MEF Ref: 10/02

HIMALAYA – INDIA

Janahut Malcolm Bass with Paul Figg from UK and Pat Deavoll from NZ; Sept-Oct 2010. Although the original intention had been another attempt to make the first ascent of Janahut (aka Jankuth 6805m) at the head of the Gangotri glacier, this year they were refused a permit, but fortunately managed to obtain one for Vasuki Parbat (6792m). After acclimatising on the nearby slopes of Bhagirathi II they started up the West Face of Vasuki Parbat, following a line attempted by Mick Fowler and Paul Ramsden in 2008. At approximately half-height on the third day, Deavoll chose to descend, but the other two continued, despite Figg being hit on the shoulder by a large rock and Bass sustaining concussion in a 10m fall. On day eight they reached the long summit ridge, and on day nine followed it north, over the main summit to descend the North-west Ridge, passing a metre below the highest point in homage to Lord Vasuki – King of the Serpents. This was probably the third ascent of the peak, although the IMF does not recognise the first ascent claimed by the Indo-Tibet Border Police in 1973. (*see article p18*) MEF Ref: 10/06

Jopuno Geoff Cohen with Bob Hamilton, Dick Isherwood, Steve Kennedy and Dave Ritchie plus Paul Swienton USA); April-May 2010
Although Jopuno (5936m), has had three previous ascents, they had all been via its ridges; this team hoped that the recent designation of certain peaks in western Sikkim as 'Alpine Peaks' would allow them to explore Jopuno's unknown east side. However, they found the approach unfeasible due to extremely difficult vegetation, so turned to nearby Lama Lamani. Cohen and Swienton climbed the SW spur to a notch, then traversed left on snow to gain the North summit (5655m), while Hamilton and Kennedy continued up the harder mixed crest to reach the summit ridge which they followed to the top at PD or AD-. All four descended via the NW Face. They also climbed a peak of c5500m near the col between Jopuno and Lama Lamani, and investigated the West Ridge of Jopuno, but were climbing too slowly to reach the summit. MEF Ref: 10/12

Imperial College Obra Valley Jonathan Phillips with Boris Korzh, Phil Leadbeater, Kunal Masania and Andy McLellan; Sept-Oct 2010
The Obra Valley is situated in the far Western Garhwal, and being little visited offers plenty of scope for exploration and first ascents. Although heavy rain and landslides delayed access, once established the team expe-

rienced 16 days of settled weather. From a high camp at 4900m they made the first ascent of Pt 5480m via its SW Ridge (500m, AD-). Moving camp 200m higher, they then climbed the valley's highest peak, Pt 5877m, thought to be known locally as Dauru, via the NW Ridge (700m, AD). After moving camp again, they crossed a col on the SW Ridge of the shapely Ranglana (5554m) and descended a short distance towards the Maninda valley, before traversing to Ranglana's South Ridge and following it to the summit (900m, D-). MEF Ref: 10/13

Singekang Valley Jeremy Windsor with George Carlton, Sandra Kennedy, Alan Tees and Andrew Tees from UK plus Martin Boner from Ireland; Oct-Nov 2010. Although adjacent to the Spiti River Highway, the Singekang Valley appeared to be unvisited by western travellers until this team arrived. Their exploration identified a number of accessible peaks and a potential crossing towards the east at the head of the valley. They had hoped to make the first ascent of Singekang (6031m) via its West Ridge, but were stopped 400m below the top by unconsolidated snow, low temperatures and steep ice towers. However, they did make the first ascent of Snaght Kang (5500m) whose summit lies at the end of the north ridge of Peak 6091m on the southern rim of the valley. MEF Ref: 10/19

HIMALAYA – NEPAL

Parkin-Saunders Khumbu Winter 2009-10 Unclimbed Peaks Andy Parkin with Victor Saunders; Jan-Feb 2010
Although most climbers visit the Himalaya in summer, the winter months sometimes offer more settled – albeit colder – conditions. This pair hoped to take advantage of this to make the first ascent of Peak 5943m (via its SE Face) from the Chola valley before moving south to Pangboche and establishing a camp up the Minma Khola from which to climb Peak 6424m (a shoulder of Kantega North West) at the head of the Omoga glacier. However, with the winter being so dry, neither of these routes looked feasible, so the pair decided to try the unclimbed North Face of Lobuje West (6119m). Unfortunately, while carrying a heavy rucksack to the bottom of the face, Parkin fell on the moraine and hurt his back. Although he decided to continue, the pair had to give up at 5600m when the injury proved too painful. MEF Ref: 10/01

Chamlang North Face Graham Zimmerman (NZ/US) with Hayden Kennedy and Cory Richards (both US); Nov-Dec 2010
The original objective of this team was to visit the remote area between the Khumbu and Barun valleys, to attempt the North Face of Chamlang (7319m). However, in view of heavy snowfall and reports of failures and accidents on other northern aspects, they decided to attempt a new route on the South Face of Nuptse (7861m) to the right of the infamous *Cobweb Wall,* which appeared to be in good condition. After acclimatising on nearby

peaks, they carried gear to the foot of the route, and took detailed photographs of the face. Examination of these revealed that large sections of the route were devoid of ice, exposing loose, slabby rock. With higher than normal temperatures, more and more ice was melting, creating dangerous conditions on all peaks, so it was reluctantly decided to abandon the expedition. MEF Ref: 10/11

Annapurna III Nick Bullock with Pete Benson and Matt Helliker; April-May and Oct-Nov 2010
Annapurna III (7555m) has always proved a challenge and this team's first attempt did not even reach Base Camp. Undeterred, they returned in the autumn, when additional sponsorship enabled them to fly in by helicopter. They soon discovered that the SE Ridge, their original objective, consisted of very loose rock, with its approach threatened by avalanche and sérac fall. Hoping the East Ridge would provide a safer option, they climbed to a shoulder at 5900m and stashed gear for a later attempt. Bad weather and extreme cold kept them in BC for the next week, and although they managed to reach the cache again, they realised they had insufficient time to safely attempt the climb and return to base camp, so reluctantly abandoned the expedition. MEF Ref: 10/20

CHINA AND TIBET

Chinese Tien Shan Mick Fowler with Mike Morrison, Paul Ramsden and Rob Smith; August-Sept 2010. The Xuelian range lies in Xinjiang Province close to the borders of Kazakhstan and Kyrgyzstan, and although it forms a major part of the Chinese Tien Shan, it is little visited. The prime objective was to make the first ascent of the NW Ridge of Xuelian East (c6400m) but bad weather with heavy snow prevented the team getting to within 25km of the glacier, so they concentrated on their back-up, Sulamar (5380m). Despite regular thunderstorms and more snow, in a 6-day round trip Fowler and Ramsden were successful in making a traverse with the first ascent of the North Face and descent via the unclimbed South Ridge at a grade of TD sup. (This was the second ascent of the peak, which was originally climbed in 2008 by Bruce Normand's team: they had named the peak Khanalak 2, but the locals know it as Sulamar.) Fowler and Ramsden went on to investigate the potential of the Chulebos peaks, while Morrison and Smith explored the previously unvisited side glaciers feeding the Muzart glacier. (*see article p53*) MEF Ref: 10/07

International Sichuan Bruce Normand (UK) with Kyle Dempster (USA), Jean Annequin and Christian Trommsdorff (France) and Gu Qizhi and Yan Dongdong (China); Oct-Nov 2010
When his planned expedition to Tibet was refused permission by the local authorities, Normand managed to organise an alternative trip to the Minya Konka area of Sichuan. He had three objectives in mind: the West Face

of Mt Grosvenor (aka Riwuqie Feng, 6376m), the East Face of Mt Edgar (6618m) and any route on the unclimbed San Lian Feng (6684m). In a 24-hour push, Dempster and Normand made the second ascent of Grosvenor, climbing the Central Couloir on its West Face, while the French pair reached 5700m on a route further to the right before high winds forced them to retreat. In an eight-day marathon of highly technical climbing on Mt Edgar, Dempster and Normand climbed the left side of the E Face to the S Ridge (M6 and ice to WI5) to what in a white-out appeared to be its highest point: again this was a second ascent. Meanwhile the Chinese pair attempted a route on the N Face, but were forced to cancel due to cold weather and inadequate equipment. Although the mountains of Sichuan are no longer 'unexplored', the team reported that the Minya Konka range still contains about a dozen 6000m peaks that are either unclimbed or have only had one ascent. MEF Ref: 10/22A

PAKISTAN

Tahu Rutum, Pakistan Luke Hunt with Hamish Dunn and Tom Ripley (plus Holly Mumford to Base Camp); July-August 2010. For their first venture into the Greater Ranges this young team chose an area north of the Hispar glacier intent on first ascents of routes in the Khurdopin group, in particular the beautiful NW Ridge of Tahu Rutum (6651m). Unfortunately, in 2010 the monsoon travelled further north than usual, causing extensive flooding in parts of Pakistan and confining the team to their tents for much of their time at base camp, so that they never progressed beyond the foot of the mountain. This expedition received the Nick Estcourt, Mark Clifford and Jeremy Wilson grants for 2010. MEF Ref: 10/08

CENTRAL ASIA AND THE FAR EAST

N Wales Western Kokshaal-Too, Kyrgyzstan Matt Stygall and Dave Rudkin; August-Sept 2010

This team visited the Fersmana glacier in the Western Kokshaal-Too region of the Tien Shan with the intention of exploring and hopefully climbing Pic Byeliy (aka Grand Poohbah, 5697m) and possibly Pic Granitsa (aka Border Peak, 5370m). Although the weather was good when they arrived, it soon turned against them, with storms and heavy snowfall. To acclimatise, they attempted the West Ridge of an unnamed peak of 5200m, but retreated from 5000m due to poor rock. An attempt on the North Face of Pic Granitsa was abandoned at the bergschrund due to poor weather/snow conditions and the risk of avalanche. In view of this they felt that conditions on Pic Byeliy would be too dangerous, so they moved to the Ak Sai National Park, where they climbed the classic 700m Route Schwaba on the West Face of Bachichiki (4516m) at HVS (5.8-5.10). This expedition also received a Mark Clifford Award. MEF Ref: 10/10

Scottish Wakhan, Afghanistan Alan Halewood and Neal Gwynne; July-August 2010
Much of Afghanistan is ravaged by war, but the eastern end of the Wakhan Corridor ('Little Pamir') is relatively safe. Following consultation with Mountain Unity International which has set up facilities for trekkers and climbers visiting the area, they concentrated on the Pamir-i-Wakhan Range to the west of the Waghjir valley. They were affected by the heavy monsoon rains that struck the Pakistan area so badly, but nevertheless climbed several easy walking peaks up to 5000m, and also Koh I Iskander (5562m), a more serious peak with a pitch of Scottish III. They left the area via the 4895m Garumdee pass (aka Uween e Sar), with a detour to climb a peak of 5327m, which they named Koh I Khar (Peak of the Donkey). Both peaks are thought to have been previously unclimbed. MEF Ref: 10/15

Untouched: First ascents in the Djangart, Kyrgyzstan Matt Traver with Dan Clark and Jamie Maddison plus Chris Parenteau and Mike Royer from USA; July-August 2010. The Djangart region of Kyrgyzstan's Kokshaal-Too range has seen little activity from western mountaineers, so seemed an ideal venue for an exploratory expedition. Prior to departure, the team identified three peaks of particular interest, and although they experienced rain almost every day, they did indeed climb three peaks – but not those originally contemplated. First success was on Pt 4766 on which Clark, Royer and Traver climbed the 700m *Horseman's Horror*, D+ on its NW Face. During the approach to the second peak, Pt 5080, Clark became unwell and (accompanied by Maddison) returned to Bishkek for medical treatment. Meanwhile Royer and Traver climbed the 700m *Will your anchor hold?* TD- on its E face, and finally on the N Ridge of Pt 5048, the 650m *Postcard for the Chief*. Names for each of the peaks have been proposed to the Kyrgyz Alpine Club, viz 'Peak Howard Bury', 'Peak Sutherland' and 'Peak of Illumination'. MEF Ref: 10/16

Torugart-Too, Kyrgyzstan Sam Leach with James Monypenny and Tom Nichols; August-Sept 2010. The Torugart-Too range in SE Kyrgyzstan had attracted few expeditions, so gave this team plenty of scope for exploration and first ascents. In this they were successful, making the first ascent of Pt 4870 (Torolok) by its N Face at Grade D, and climbing new routes on the N Face/NW Ridge of Pt 5008 *(Diligent Epiphany*, TD-), *Free Tibet* on the N Ridge of Pt 4700, and on the S Ridge of Pt 4495. They were also pleased to report how smoothly they progressed through the various checkpoints involved. MEF Ref: 10/21

Reviews

197. John Innerdale, *Rébuffat Route, Aiguille du Midi,* watercolour, 40 x 30cm, 2008.

Reviews

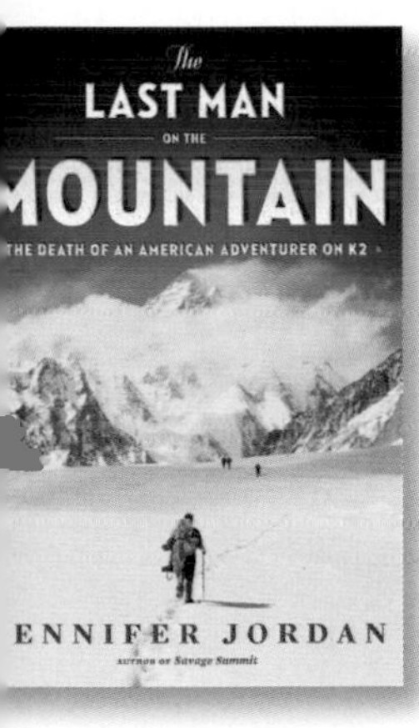

The Last Man on the Mountain: The Death of An American Adventurer on K2

Jennifer Jordan

WW Norton and Company, 2010, pp320, £18.99

To misquote Oscar Wilde, to review one K2 book may be regarded as a misfortune, to review two looks like carelessness, and to review five together almost certifiable. But here goes.

Of the five, three deal more or less with the 2008 tragedy and two with events long gone. Let me take the earliest first. *The Last Man on The Mountain* by Jennifer Jordan is essentially a biography of Dudley Wolfe, who died on the infamous Fritz Wiessner expedition in 1939. Ms Jordan has written about K2 before in *The Women of K2*. I fear that, for all their good points, both books suffer from the same flaws. Some are quite inexplicable, given that the author has twice travelled the long, hard road to K2 Base Camp. She should know that, for instance, K2 is *not* composed of 'volcanic rubble', nor did Bill House lead his eponymous chimney 'without a rope or any fixed protection'. Wiessner and Pasang did not 'rappel each other down': from their high point they *rappelled*, and whenever they had to down-climb they would presumably have *belayed* each other. Wiessner, in his attempt to rock climb the mixed ground to the left of the Bottleneck Couloir, most certainly did not solve 'the last riddle of this confounding mountain that had eluded men for generations'. There had only been one serious attempt (Houston and Bates) the year before, and when the mountain *was* climbed in 1954, it was via the Bottleneck. Wiessner's exact route has, as far as we know, never been completed.

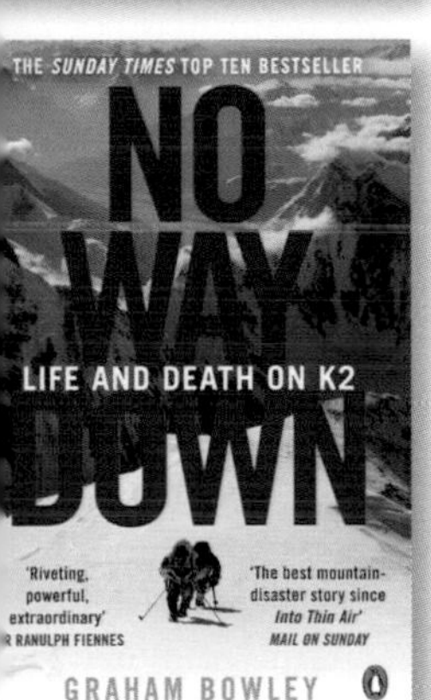

o Way Down:
fe and Death on K2
raham Bowley
king/Penguin, 2010,
280, £18.99

All this (and much more) does raise questions about the rest of the book, which is a shame. It is a detailed, and as far as I could tell, well researched account of Dudley Wolfe's 'Great Gatsby' lifestyle. Jennifer Jordan seems to be much more at home with the New York *glitterati* of the 1920s and '30s than she is with the harsh world of the Karakoram. If she had got a veteran of K2 to read the relevant chapters she would have corrected what at times

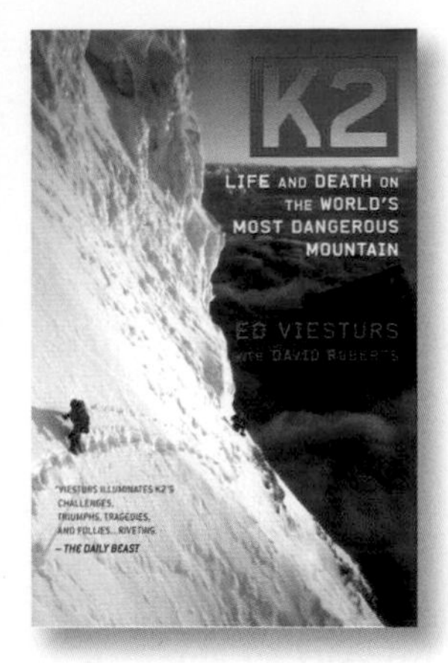

K2: Life and Death on the World's Most Dangerous Mountain
Ed Viesturs with David Roberts
Broadway Books, 2009, pp352, hardcover US$26, paperback US$14.99

can only be described as schoolboy howlers. Her analysis of the blame, if any, attached to Wiessner is probably the best section of a disjointed book.

The other history book has the off-putting title *K2: Lies and Treachery*, by Robert Marshall, an Australian surgeon obsessed with the treatment of Walter Bonatti during and after the summit climb by Compagnoni and Lacedelli in 1954. Marshall, a non-climber, learnt Italian to understand all the ramifications of statements, libel actions and court cases that have periodically erupted since the first ascent. This book claims to be the truth about the expedition. Unfortunately the very first sentence contains an error, referring to the 13 deaths on K2 in 1986 happening in the same week, not the whole summer. This, like Jordan's book, sets the antennae quivering for any other factual mistakes.

Marshall is a self-confessed devotee of Bonatti, who, in his eyes, can do no wrong. What I found worrying about the book is that he never refers to other expeditions, comparing events on the summit day, and I can't help wondering if he has ever read about them. It seems to me that Bonatti has long since been exonerated from the controversies centred on his attempt to carry oxygen cylinders to Lacedelli and Compagnoni, and the exact circumstances of his forced bivouac with the porter Mahdi.

Marshall spends page after page discussing how, when and where the summiteers' oxygen ran out, and postulates that it might have been on the descent. Even today oxygen regulation is not an exact science and it is quite likely that every bottle would have varying amounts of gas available. Exactly when it ran out can only be a matter of conjecture. The summiteers' accounts may or may not be accurate, but are almost certainly clouded by exhaustion, oxygen deprivation and the passage of time. To endlessly analyse their accounts half a century later seems to be self-defeating.

Bonatti was certainly treated unfairly by Compagnoni and the autocratic leader Ardito Desio, but the whole unpleasant affair had (I thought) been resolved. What Marshall calls 'lies and treachery' I would describe as yet another high-altitude cock-up, combined with extreme emotions of disappointment, jealousy and elation, all added to by the insidious effects of altitude. There *were* lies and treachery, but most of them came after the expedition.

That grand old veteran of K2, Charlie Houston, once told me that 50 years after his epic attempt on K2, he was amazed that on re-reading his own classic book *K2: The Savage Mountain,* how much he had forgotten, or worse, had got it wrong. I hate to say this, but without first-hand experience, in the strange, distorted world of high altitude, it is almost impossible to have any real understanding of what goes on. Like a policeman interviewing two drunk drivers after a car crash, evidence has to be treated with a huge pinch of salt.

I say 'almost' but Graham Bowley, an English journalist working for the *New York Times*, is an exception. What started as an article for his paper turned into a fully fledged book – *No Way Down: Life and Death on K2,* in which Bowley tells, as far as possible, the whole story of the 2008 disaster, when 11 climbers died in 48 hours.

Graham Bowley treats the hugely complex series of events with great clarity and objectivity. Only occasionally does his self-confessed non-climber status show. (Apparently those unfortunate climbers killed in crevasse falls were 'mystified' and the Shoulder of K2 is not flat nor is it a mile long.)

Inevitably the book will be compared with Jon Krakauer's *Into Thin Air.* I think it is better: Bowley's 'outsider' status works in his favour. Having no (ice) axe to grind, he makes few judgements and sets down sometimes conflicting stories side by side. If his accounts are not 100 percent accurate, it is not for lack of trying: Bowley flew from the States to Ireland, Norway, Holland, France and Italy to interview survivors of the tragedy, and then completed a personal pilgrimage by trekking to K2 Base Camp to see for himself the magnetism and beauty of the mountain. His book was short-listed for the 2010 Boardman Tasker Award.

Another book dedicated to the events of K2 in 2008 is a personal account by Wilco van Rooijen. In *Surviving K2,* the Dutchman (who lost almost all his toes to frostbite) describes his previous attempts on K2 in 1995 and 2006 before describing in detail his own 2008 epic: a bivouac not far below the summit and above the sérac barrier that avalanched twice. Then, facing snow blindness, and losing the route, he descended well to the left of the Cesen route before being rescued after a second night out. Maybe it was because I read the book after Bowley's that, despite the ordeal that van Rooijen suffered, I was less impressed with the way he told his story, horrible though it undoubtedly was.

Inevitably there were controversies about how and where people died. The first Irishman to climb K2, Gerard McDonnell, shared the bivouac with van Rooijen then, on the descent, apparently tried to rescue two Koreans and a Sherpa, entangled in ropes and almost beyond help. The exact circumstances of McDonnell's death are not known; Bowley and the Italian Marco Confortola have different opinions but, like the endless arguments surrounding tragedies on K2 in 1986, it doesn't alter the facts. But, one chilling remark by van Rooijen to Bowley concerns the account of Confortola, about the death of McDonnell: 'Shame about Marco, though, that he gets it all wrong. He was exhausted. His mind had obviously gone. He may have ...exaggerated.' Yet this is coming from a man who spent two nights bivouacked, the first of these above 8000 metres. It reminded me of almost the same words spoken by Kurt Diemberger about Willi Bauer. Both men were seemingly oblivious to the fact that they themselves were

K2: Lies and Treachery
Robert Marshall
Carreg Publishers, 2009, pp232, £20

Surviving K2
Wilco van Rooijen
G & J Publishing CV, 2010, pp165, US$35 (signed, from author's website)

exhausted and their judgement and memory equally, if not more, impaired.

I am leaving the best until last. Ed Viesturs's *K2: Life and Death on the World's Most Dangerous Mountain,* written with David Roberts is by a country mile, the most accomplished book and, with Roberts at the helm, so it should be. Viesturs has one huge advantage over the rest of the field in that he has climbed all the 8000 metre peaks, and his opinions carry a lot more weight. He is not afraid to criticise from a position of strength, and the book does contain a lot of informed opinions. Before I go any further, I have to admit that the author frequently refers to my own two K2 books, which is very flattering. I have tried to ignore this and make the point that Viesturs is in a better position to comment on the K2 controversies than I ever was.

The book starts with the 2008 disaster, then gives an incisive potted history of the mountain, dealing only with major events and ignoring many of the expeditions that add little or nothing to K2's history. Viesturs is rightly scathing about some of the self-justifying actions of K2's would-be suitors, and has no hesitation in calling to task those climbers who don't know how to turn back. He admits that on his ascent in 1993 he made a mistake in pushing on for the top beyond his 2pm deadline. Climbers who don't summit until 6 or 7pm, or even later, are significantly stacking the odds against their survival, as well as putting others at risk.

Of the 2008 disaster, Viesturs retells the story with his own cryptic comments about the decision-making – or lack of it – on the fatal day. He bemoans the lack of humanitarian values in the last few years. Strangers thrown together by circumstance seem unable to act in any sort of caring way when things go wrong. He also makes the important point that, as so often happens in Himalayan history, the Sherpas are the real heroes, even laying down their lives for their employers.

Viesturs does occasionally reveal a strange attitude to European climbers. Of Aleister Crowley's absurd comment that '...the south face, perhaps possible theoretically, meant a complicated climb with no halfway house', Viesturs thinks that Crowley actually imagines that there should be an alpine hut halfway up! More important, but equally curious, is his assertion that, for European climbers, carrying marker wands is not 'chic'. He quotes Kurt Diemberger as saying 'they're no protection against avalanches', but omits to say that on the very next page of *The Endless Knot* Diemberger writes that both Al Rouse and Julie Tullis pick up a bundle of wands, which sadly were still not enough to help the pair extricate themselves from the Shoulder in the prolonged storm and whiteout of 1986. But these are minor criticisms.

Viesturs is at his best when he sums up the reasons behind the tragedies, making the point that climbing must always be deregulated and (rather pessimistically) there is no way that the events of 1986 or 2008 can be stopped. He makes the point that after the storm on Everest in 1996, about which Jon Krakauer wrote so vividly, instead of the deaths acting as a deterrent, the numbers of would-be clients willing to pay up to 75,000 dollars each actually increased. I fear it is inevitable that the same thing will happen on K2. It is worth saying that in 2008 all the climbers involved in the catastrophe were experienced. But, and it is a big 'but', none of them could be described as an outstanding mountaineer of the day.

If there is one image that sums up the tragedy of 2008 for me, it is a small photo in Rowley's book. It shows a long line of tiny figures on the traverse above the Bottleneck. With a magnifying glass I could count at least 18 people spread out under the sérac that was the cause of such carnage later that day. To see such congestion on a bank holiday on Striding Edge, or on a July day on the Hörnli Ridge of the Matterhorn would be fair enough I suppose, though I wouldn't want to be part of it. But at 8000 metres on K2? Have the lunatics taken over the asylum?

Old fossils like me were brought up to understand that before attempting Everest or K2 you had to have proved yourself in the world's great ranges first. Now it is not uncommon to claim to be the youngest (or indeed the oldest) successful summiteers, Everest has been ascended as a first (and possibly last) climb by people who have no experience whatsoever. Yet the more likely you are to die, the more alluring K2 and Everest become.

But I am straying away from these books. Reading them has been an absorbing, and occasionally a painful task, bringing back terrible memories of 1986. All five are well worth reading, but probably not all at once. If you can only read one, it has to be Ed Viesturs. If want to go to K2, think very carefully, then read them all – twice.

Jim Curran

Journal of the Italian Expedition to K2 - 1954
Pino Gallotti (Spedizione italiana al K2 - 1954 - Diario Alpinistico)
Family-produced edition, 2009

On 31 May 1954 at his base camp Ardito Desio, leader of the Italian expedition to K2, announced the names of the climbers chosen for the two teams who would attempt the summit. Members of the expedition voted unanimously not to communicate the names of the men who would reach the top before the release of the official report. They wished to avoid all the interest of the public being focused on two people rather than on the whole expedition. In the same spirit, when joining the expedition all had signed their agreement not to release any declaration, nor to publish any report or journal concerning the expedition.

So it was that when Desio's book of the expedition appeared later in 1954, it reported the version of the two men who made the summit, Achille Compagnoni and Lino Lacedelli, and disregarded completely Walter Bonatti's account of what was to become a hot controversy in the following years. Desio had not even cared to listen to Bonatti's version.

The story has become well known. On 30 July, Bonatti and Erik Abram with Hunza Amir Mahdi had been charged with carrying spare oxygen bottles to Compagnoni and Lacedelli who had gone ahead the day before to set up Camp 9. After a few hours Abram gave up; Bonatti and Mahdi went ahead, but when they reached the point where their comrades and the camp where they planned to spend the night ought to have been, there was no tent and no living soul. Compagnoni and Lacedelli had unexpectedly chosen a higher place for the camp. There seemed no logical reason; however it later seemed likely that it was to prevent Bonatti from reaching them, in fear he would join their bid for the top.

Bonatti called loudly; Lacedelli shouted back: 'It is too dangerous, leave the bottles and go back.' But it was already dark and Bonatti and Mahdi were compelled to bivouac above 8000m with no tent and no bivouac equipment. They survived, but Mahdi had his fingers and toes frostbitten and later amputated.

Of course the episode would be disturbing in the official book of the glorious expedition, so no wonder Desio left it out. But what was worse, in the following years Compagnoni, breaking the agreement signed when joining the expedition, declared that he and Lacedelli had run out of oxygen before reaching the top because Bonatti had sucked it from the bottles. This was impossible because Bonatti had neither mask nor regulator. However it took 53 years before justice was officially rendered to Bonatti in a definitive report by the Club Alpino Italiano.

Pino Gallotti was one of the members of the expedition. He died in 2008 and the following year his K2 journal was published by his family. It is a private journal and I set to read this newly disclosed account with much emotion and high expectations. Not one of the members of the expedition had backed Bonatti in his desperate want of rehabilitation. Perhaps all of them were intimidated by Desio's overwhelming personality and powerful position in society? Or they were inhibited by the agreement they had signed? But I thought it likely that in their journals they would have written what they had seen and heard, and what they had thought. I went through the journal excitedly, looking for clarifications from a first-hand witness... But nothing. It is a lovely, detailed day-by-day account of the expedition from its departure to its return, but there are no descriptions of what happened other than what Gallotti himself did. Bonatti and Mahdi's enforced bivouac is reported in a few lines and the ascent to the summit by Compagnoni and Lacedelli receives just a few paragraphs, with no comment. I did not find anything of what I was looking for.

But then I realised that I had started off reading the book on the wrong foot

– or better, with the wrong eye. Basically when somebody keeps a diary he has no intention of publishing, he writes for himself, noting what he thinks he would like to remember in the future. From that perspective Gallotti's journal is the perfect record of all the emotions and the enthusiasm of a man called to take part in a great event, the greatest adventure of his life. Lacking the attention of a publisher and of an editor taking care of the text, the journal is not a masterpiece of literature, but it is enjoyable for its genuineness and total lack of rhetoric. Some episodes, such as the interment of Mario Puchoz who died of pneumonia at Camp 2, are particularly touching. And there are lots of charming small details. 'Here, on a ledge covered by debris, I find a book of English poems. It is all crumpled but still legible. I remember that at the second American camp, I found Chekov's *Cherry Orchard*...'

Mirella Tenderini

One Mountain Thousand Summits: The Untold Story of Tragedy and True Heroism on K2
Freddie Wilkinson
New American Library, 2010, pp352, $24.95

Four voices spoke in the night.
With this simple, yet evocative sentence, Wilkinson draws the reader into his white-knuckled climbing narrative with ease.

One Mountain Thousand Summits chronicles the 2008 climbing disaster on K2. When eleven men perished on its slopes in August of that year, it was one of the deadliest single events in Himalayan climbing. The story made headlines around the world. But media coverage of the event was contradictory and confusing, for it seemed that none of the surviving climbers could explain what had happened, their memories sheathed in a spider's web of exhaustion, hypoxia and grief.

Wilkinson, a New England-based climber, mountain guide and outdoor writer, had recently written a report of the accident for *Rock & Ice* magazine. He was headed to Nepal for a climbing expedition when he decided to stop in Kathmandu and personally meet Sherpas Chhiring Dorje and Pemba Gyalje, two of the climbers he had interviewed by email and phone. Based on the meeting, he realised that they were more reliable witnesses than most western climbers whose stories dominated the headlines. *One Mountain Thousand Summits* is his almost defiant response to those poorly researched media reports and suspect conclusions.

When Wilkinson decided to expand his research for the book, he didn't limit his research to the western climbers. Quite the opposite. He concentrates a large part of his book on the stories of the four Sherpa climbers who were largely ignored by the mainstream media in the aftermath of the tragedy. Two of them lost their lives during the incident, and their heroic efforts saved the lives of at least four climbers. He makes a strong case that the Sherpas (both those who were guiding and those who were climbing as members of the expeditions) were not given adequate credit for their actions on the mountain.

The early part of the book gives a blow-by-blow description of the events on the mountain. One by one, the climbers straggle out of Camp 4, bound for the summit of K2. And one by one, they perish on the mountain. Some slip off its icy slopes and fall to their deaths; others are swept away by avalanches or falling séracs. While recounting the unfolding tragedy on the mountain, Wilkinson explores the mental stamina required, as well as the technical skills and physical endurance needed for a mountain like K2. Perhaps even more interesting is his close and unflinching look at the racial dynamics and communication landmines inherent in guided and professional climbing at 8000 metres and higher.

He doesn't limit himself to the events on the mountain. Wilkinson gives a detailed account of the experiences of teammates and loved ones at home, glued to their computers, desperately scouring the internet for news. This, more than anything, connects the almost otherworldly events on the mountain to real people back home whose lives are shattered by the unfolding tragedy.

The second part of the book examines the role of Sherpas and high-altitude porters in the climbing world. It is here that the voices of Sherpas Chhiring Dorje and Pemba Gyalje are clearest and most convincing. It is a welcome change to see equal attention paid to the Sherpa climbers, not only to their actions, but also to their thoughts and feelings and analysis of what happened.

Later in the book, Wilkinson concentrates on one of the most compelling characters to emerge – Gerard McDonnell. McDonnell, who was well known in both the climbing and Irish music worlds, became the first Irishman to summit K2 on 1 August 2008. After an overnight bivouac on his descent, he and Italian climber Marco Confortola discovered three climbers trapped upside down in a tangle of ropes above the Bottleneck, the steep ice couloir above Camp 4. Confortola and McDonnell tried for several hours to free the men before Confortola decided that it was futile. He began to descend, and was confused to see McDonnell heading up instead of down.

McDonnell's partner, Annie Starkey, was devastated by early reports of the incident that suggested McDonnell had abandoned the stranded climbers who were near death. Based on hers and some of the survivors' interviews, combined with Wilkinson's painstaking minute-by-minute reconstruction of what *could* have happened, it appears that McDonnell probably stayed behind to assist the others – not abandon them. Confortola later recalled that it was while McDonnell was above them that the three stranded climbers managed to untangle themselves and begin their descent. He concluded that McDonnell had likely climbed up in order to release the tension on the ropes of the entangled climbers. After spending several hours working alone on the ropes, he managed to loosen them, finally allowing them to free themselves. Tragically, shortly after they began their descent, they were killed by the release of an avalanche. McDonnell was killed as well, by a falling sérac.

Wilkinson tries to do a lot in this book. In addition to recounting the events on K2, he gives a history of climbing on K2 and tackles the topics of climbing ethics and expedition politics. He educates on high-altitude physiology and Sherpa climbing traditions. He delves into the characters of both the climbers and those closest to them. And he tries to solve the mysteries of what really happened in the last hours of Gerard McDonnell's life as well as the courageous actions of Dorje and Gyalje. It's all extremely interesting, but the transitions from one theme to the other are sometimes confusing.

Although Wilkinson was not on K2 when tragedy struck, and has never even been to K2, his story is painstakingly researched. Wilkinson is a seasoned journalist and an experienced climber, but this is his first book. His meticulous research, passion for the subject matter and unique approach shine through. I say, bravo!

Bernadette McDonald

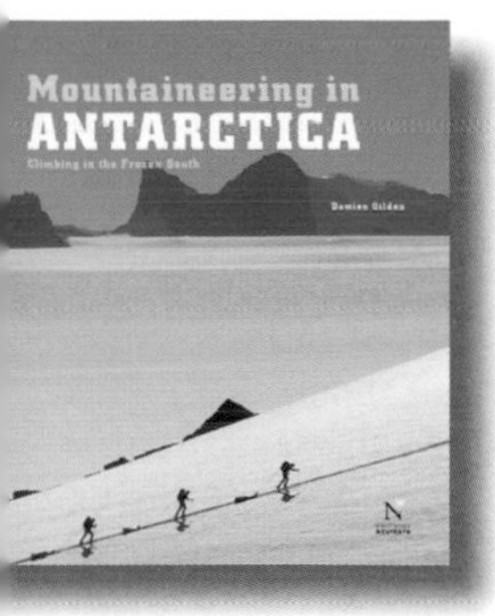

Mountaineering in Antarctica: Climbing in the Frozen South
Damien Gildea
Editions Nevicata, 2010, pp 192, £30

Many people, climbers included, envision Antarctica as a large, flat continent, covered by enormous ice sheets and glaciers. Whilst this is true for vast regions of Antarctica, it is also home to some of the remotest mountain ranges on earth, and they include a massive number of beautiful and unclimbed mountains.

Since publishing the *Antarctic Mountaineering Chronology* in 1998, which is regarded as the authoritative listing of ascents since the first explorers set foot on Antarctica, Damien Gildea has kept track of virtually all climbs that have been undertaken in Antarctica. As an active climber with 10 seasons of Antarctic mountaineering under his belt, Damien has been in a unique position to not just monitor climbing activity, but to meet and interview many of the climbers themselves. Readers of the *American Alpine Journal*, *Alpinist* and *Climb* magazine will be familiar with his reports, but this coffee-table book goes much further. Illustrated with stunning photographs and informative maps, it brings together a vast wealth of information, and accounts and stories of expeditions that have ventured south.

Mountaineering in Antarctica reads like a journey through these mountain ranges, detailing not only the climbs that have been attempted and completed, but also the exploration and geography of the different ranges. It comprehensively summarises activity in each area, and in doing so exposes those areas that have not been explored by climbers, to the extent of giving tantalising hints of suitable objectives. Damien's enthusiasm for climbing in Antarctica is apparent throughout the book; in fact, it is so great that he can't even keep the unclimbed areas and mountains to himself.

The extent of mountain exploration and climbing revealed in this book is breathtaking, from that undertaken by those working for government research bodies, such as the British Antarctic Survey, to small private groups travelling to Antarctica by yacht or aircraft. In addition to ascents on the Antarctic continent, Damien also covers the sub-Antarctic islands, such as South Georgia and Peter I Island, making this a very comprehensive publication indeed.

This is a unique, well-researched and much-needed compendium on Antarctic mountains and the climbing that has been undertaken on them. It will be of interest to climbers, history lovers and armchair explorers alike, and is an invaluable resource to those hoping to climb on the great white continent.

Phil Wickens

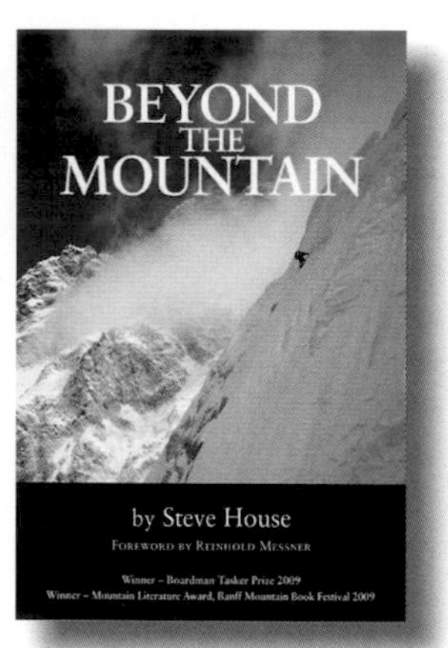

Beyond the Mountain
Steve House
Patagonia Books, 2009 (USA), pp285,
republished in UK, 2010, by Vertebrate Publishing,
£12.99

In his prologue to *Beyond the Mountain* Steve House writes, 'When I stood on the greatest summit I've ever achieved, success vaporized.' There is, contained in those simple words, a truth and a melancholy that summarises this book, one of the best works in mountain literature to come along in a while. It's not by accident that it was the winner of both the 2009 Boardman Tasker Award and the 2009 Banff Mountain Book Award for Mountain Literature. It is a thoughtful book of remarkable insight.

Beyond the Mountain successfully captures the truth, ambition, dedication, loneliness and also sadness present in the high-stakes and very deep play that is pure alpinism. The prologue – a single page that is complete, poetic and without drama or hyperbole – sets the stage and the tone for the whole book.

House uses his landmark alpine-style ascent of the Rupal Face of Nanga Parbat in 2005 as the vehicle and backdrop to describing his growth and development as a world-class alpinist and doesn't shy away from the selfishness that journey entails. In a first-person narrative style, House assembles nearly 20 years of climbing like a well-edited film, revealing first his current reality and then the paths and interruptions that led there. The writing is cathartic, and the reader wonders if House isn't dissecting himself, his life, with the same surgical precision he would apply to his rucksack and gear rack before the hardest routes. While at times some of the content can appear elitist – indeed the core group of climbers who operate at this level has always been tightly knit, occupying a somewhat private sidewalk only a few tread – more often it is humble, reflective and passionate.

Alpinism is a demanding art painted on a demanding and often unforgiving canvas, one that is often full of dilemmas. That is where the biggest messages in *Beyond the Mountain* come through. Passion and drive lead to success, but we pay high hidden prices for our dreams, beyond the obvious threat to physical wellbeing. Success momentarily slakes ambition, then at once is a new empty hall echoing with the sounds of once was and is now gone. It is clear that the ascent of the Rupal Face, the highest wall, by a pure line, in the purest of style, was emblematic of a man whose life dream and inner compass is defined by such moments. Reinhold Messner wrote 'Each goal achieved is equally a dream destroyed.' Success is 'vaporized' as House puts it. Ultimately the tension that carries the reader through *Beyond the Mountain* comes not so much from the descriptions of gripping adventures, but from the descriptions of the voids that are left inside following such intense experiences.

Jon Popowich

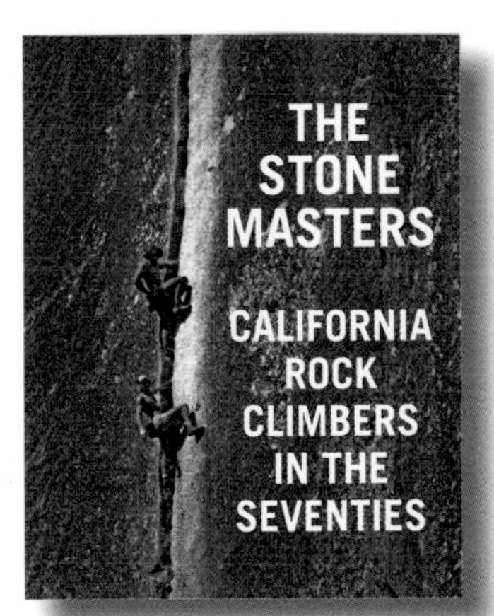

The Stone Masters: California Rock Climbers in the Seventies
John Long (text) and
Dean Fidelman (photographs)
Stonemaster Press, 2009, pp196, US$60

The Stone Masters is an unashamedly romantic book. It describes a world with no boundaries, and a world where rules are dictated only by experiences. That fact that this world is limited to the rock walls of Yosemite and mountain walls wherever they exist helps to shape a clear and remarkable consistency of purpose for this generation of climbers. The characters who write stories for this compilation are the larger than life heroes of 1970s American rock climbing, men and women who conceived a world that transformed the great walls of Yosemite into canvases and pages on which to write the history of extreme rock climbing, and to discover who they were in the process.

At its best the writing is intense, revealing, inspiring and makes you want to be 20 again. That 'being 20 again' wish is important for this reason: What inspires people to climb? Before the advent of climbing walls, when seasoned climbers were asked, 'Whatever made you want to climb a mountain?' most would shrug their shoulders and say something like, 'Well I read a book and got inspired'. Future generations may very well say, 'I read a book called *Stone Masters*'.

The Stone Masters is masterful both in the way it is put together and in recalling a bygone (but not long ago) age. An 'art' book in presentation, it has some terrific, vibrant writing, and wonderful images that capture the chaotic, out of focus nature of years characterised by the Vietnam war, Watergate, pipes full of weed and a climbing revolution that extended well beyond southern Cal', especially for anyone who shared even a small part of those years. It is the perfect 'heritage' book to carry forward the spirit of adventure and discovery of the Camp 4 heyday rock scene into the future.

The first 20 pages of pictures and captions set the scene for what follows, a montage of impressions in a book dedicated: *to all those with a restless spirit and a dream, who step into the unknown and find some thing miraculous, fun, and for keeps.*

The publishers quote Emerson's 'There is no history, only biography', and shape the book through the characters who shared 'common experiences but radically different histories'. The essays that provide the biographies and autobiographies are a mix of both the re-found and reworked. Interspaced is new material that reflects upon the historical pieces and helps weave them together into a whole and reflective work, both historical and current.

For this reviewer, the best and most consistent writing comes from John Long. Apart from the publisher's efforts, Long's inspired writing is in many ways the main driver of this book. I suspect the way this book came together was rather like a climbing project – if you are going to do it, work hard and do it with style. Long's writing is stunningly original and unashamedly romantic – hence my opening comment. When he had the inspiration for this book project he decided that rather than include old essays re-worked for magazines, he would search out the earliest possible drafts to get close to the true and raw essence of the age.

There are also excellent pieces from John Bachar, Lynn Hill, Mike Graham, Tobin Sorensen and other legends of that period. There is a well-worked short history by Roger Breedlove and a number of individual short biographies, such as Randy Vogel's portrait of Rick Accomazzo. Each writer seems to be able to capture the individual while simultaneously stirring them back into the great and complex stew-pot of emotions and experiences that were their common history.

The book is also beautifully conceived as a montage, a mix of images and words. Individual captions have a way of expanding a photo and of saying it all. The Valley walls in winter are captioned as, 'marvels to look at, miracles to climb'. That's why we do it. And the wonderfully captured photos of individuals in action – John Bachar, John Yablonski, Lynn Hill, et al – carry words that give a person, a climb, or an experience new perspective, and breathe life into individuals who are no longer here and places that have changed forever.

Jeff Jackson's introduction just about reviews the book as well as sets the scene:

I'd known Long's work since 1977, when I was 13 years old, hunkered like a mage over a book of spells, completely entranced by the beauty and strangeness of climbing. There were no mountains or hills in Parker, Texas, and 'sports' consisted of slamming men and animals onto the ground and dominating them – in other words hunting, football and rodeo. The stories in the climbing magazines, on the other hand, were full of people climbing in the most beautiful places on earth – massive and sublime slabs of granite and sandstone and snow, and the object of the game was not to dominate but to meld with your adversary. The articles – and especially Long's essays – suggested climbing wasn't about victory. It was about style.

The fact that style, like adventure, is an essential part of romanticism is one of the tricks that keeps Long's writing stimulating and enlivening without it becoming sentimental or self-centred. The romantic spirit that runs through this book is refreshing because it is always looking outward, always trying to see the essential value of action without trying to justify it or measure it. The book is almost completely without a grade. It is about the activity of climbing, what can be learned, how you work and help friends, have fun, survive difficulty and death, and use that unquantifiable mix as a creed by which to live. You become a rock athlete, a stone master, to find adventure, to survive and to meld and be human. And it also warns that to become obsessed is to lose the lessons.

The book carries a health warning: 'climbing is inherently dangerous – always climb with a rope.' Yet the absence of ropes is a feature of the book, as it was for many southern Cal' climbers of the 1970s. Unless you are prepared to allow your kids the freedom of adventure, the proximity of reality to death, and all the mind-bending experiences that are part of life's journey, don't let them read this. Death is 'part of the deal' as John Long's life-long, dying mentor Paul Gleason so poignantly reminds his pupil in one of the final essays in this book.

This book is the real deal if you believe that adventure should not be defined and that to risk all is not fatalism. *The Stone Masters* won the Grand Prize at the Banff Mountain Literature Festival in 2010 and also won the award for Best Historical Mountain Book. That is a good indication of its scope and quality. The book is beautifully conceived and portrayed by Dean Fidelman. He is one of the lesser-known spirits of that age, both as a climber and photographer of human beauty and frailty in a harsh world. Mike Graham apparently published the book, although there are no credits given. Some of us will remember Mike from our crossover days at Al Harris's during our shared period of inspired, nihilistic engagement with everything above the horizontal.

John Porter

Snow and Mixed Climbs:
Vol 1 Ecrins East, Cerces, Queyras
Sébastien Constant
Editions Constant, 2010, pp352, €35

Seb Constant is without doubt one of the Ecrins region's most prolific winter alpinists and ski mountaineers. A fully accredited IFMGA guide, he knows the area in winter as well as anyone and so it is not surprising that he has included here not only all of the classic lines but also plenty of the best of the new routes put up over the last 15 years. And several of these masterpieces are of Seb's own creation.

Gauging opinions on the guide, I found out that most if not all of the local 'alpine gods', including guides Francois Lombard, Stef Troussier, Seb Foissac and Tony Lamiche, agree that *Snow and Mixed Climbs* is a major step forward over existing publications such as the definitive GHM/Francois Labande *Guide du Haut-Dauphine*, and John Brailsford's *Ecrins Massif* Alpine Club guide (up till now the only English guide book to the area).

On the back cover of Constant's guide it says: 'The aim of this guide is to unveil the possibilities offered by this vast corner of the Alps and present all the normal (worthwhile) routes… (for) every keen mountaineer and ski mountaineer.' To put these words into perspective you have to understand first that this guide covers just three areas – the eastern side of the Ecrins Massif, the Massif Des Cerces, and the Queyras Massif. And just one of these three areas – the Ecrins Massif – is 30 times bigger than the entire Chamonix Valley. So with only 344 routes covered this guide is by no means definitive. It is the author's personal perspective and hence personal choice of routes.

So what is the book like to use? The first thing to say is that working out where the actual routes and ski descents are has been made incredibly easy thanks to the author's generous use of amazing full colour photos. And importantly it is all in English, so no problem for the linguistically challenged.

Seb is a professional mountain photographer and he has clearly used this expertise to great effect. The book is rich in glorious full colour shots that clearly and simply explain the layout of the various massifs, the approaches and descents and the routes themselves. As a 'local', having lived in the area since 2003, I find this an absolute godsend. The photos have been taken by a variety of approaches – on skis, on the routes, and whilst climbing on adjacent peaks. The result is very easy to use topos that get you quickly and efficiently to the right climb or ski on the right peak.

Moreover all the photos were taken within the last few years. Because of glacial retreat and the general effect of global warming, the southern Alps, like all other alpine areas, have changed drastically over the last 15 years.

This has rendered the old guides pictorially out of date. And so again Seb's collection of mountain photos are all the more useful.

In terms of route descriptions the guide also scores highly. I compared the route descriptions for a number of lines in the Labande topos to Seb's work and found *Snow and Mixed Climbs* to be generally more accurate and detailed. The same was true in comparison to the Brailsford guide.

The guide aims to cater for the occasional alpinist, the dedicated ski mountaineer and the extreme climber in search of classic adventure and/or new gems. For alpinists, it's all that you will need. Though it is not definitive, with 344 listed routes there is more than enough for 99 percent of climbers' appetites. It is intended for summer use too, especially on normal routes and classics.

Ski mountaineers, however, may want to consider definitive ski guides such as Toponeige's *Ecrins Est* and *Ecrins Sud*, especially as many of the ski descents Seb includes are serious affairs requiring a higher level of skill than that generally possessed by the visiting Brit on a two-week winter foray. Even so, because the photo diagrams are so clear and easy to understand, ski mountaineers, like alpinists, will greatly benefit from this guide.

A big point that I feel Seb makes well is that mountaineering is about personal choice and judgement. As he says in his introduction, 'the days of pigeonholing routes and the style in which they should be done have passed'. Seb leaves it up to the climber and skier as to what can be climbed or skied or indeed how the itineraries are accomplished. He simply includes details of the approach, the climb and the descent. If a line has been skied he gives all the relevant info including a ski descent grade and then leaves it to individuals to make their own decision. Seb also subtly attempts to widen the motivated skier's horizons by making many references to the amazing exploits of his partner Hervé Dégonon; one of the Ecrins' great extreme skiers. Hervé is continually pushing the boundaries by descending on skis whenever he can. In this respect the guide is very encouraging for ski tourers and the sport is given a lot of space within the book, right from the front cover showing a couple making a rising traverse on an alpine route carrying skis.

Seb employs the same 'open' philosophy on 'when' to climb etc, following the modern view that there are no set seasons and the classic approach tools of snowshoe, ski, snowboard or boot are employed as conditions and the route that day dictate. This is especially relevant here in the southern Alps where ice and mixed gullies can be in condition as early as October or as late as May; 'winter' is a very relative and changeable season in the Ecrins.

The guide's modern and refreshing feel is further enhanced by some interesting additions. For instance, there's a hefty 15-page intro covering everything from the logistics of getting to this alpine paradise to grading charts, mountain risks unique to the region, survival techniques, a typical Ecrins gear rack, and how to modify gear such as ice-axe picks and shafts. Again all clearly explained using photo diagrams.

I also really love the 'Free Expression' essays dotted throughout. These are full-page anecdotal musings by well-known local mountaineers and skiers regularly operating in this area, including Patrick Gabarrou and Christophe Moulin. I particularly like Patrick's personal account of the classic 'Gabarrou/Marsigny' on the south face of Pic Lory. These are really inspiring pieces that in combination with some great thumbnails excite and motivate the reader – well they worked for me anyway.

The view from my bedroom widow looks straight out onto the Pic de Bonvoisin – a major 3000m peak in the Vallouise sector – and one that visiting Brit Mick Fowler commented on as looking 'particularly appealing and favourably challenging'. Now armed with this new guide I know exactly where all the recent lines have been added and more importantly what is still left to be tried. I for one can't wait to get stuck in and start using this guide in earnest.

Snow and Mixed Climbs is an essential tool for anyone contemplating winter alpinism and/or ski mountaineering in the southern French Alps. Grab a copy and book your flight today.

Jerry Gore

The guide is available from outdoor shops in the Ecrins and direct from the author's website: **www.sebastien-constant.com**

Evening Light
Roger Hubank
The Ernest Press, 2009, pp286, £12

George Hazard summarily abandoned his wife and child in order to continue to pursue his mountaineering ambitions. The marriage he had 'somehow blundered into' suffered the same demise as all his other personal relationships; he seemed unable to comprehend what was expected of him, off the rock. For him, nothing had ever compared with the exhilarating simplicity of devoting all his attention to a knife-edge traverse or the almost mystical experience of becoming aware of his absolute insignificance in the face of the power of Nature at her most furious and destructive – or at her most beautiful.

Then, whilst returning to England in old age in order to write the autobiography his publishers had commissioned, a truck accident puts him into a coma. When he finally awakes, it is his daughter, Calon, who he first sees. During the years of her father's absence she found emotional salvation both by creating her own large family and by becoming a member of her husband's – the populous Redfern 'tribe'. Hazard's initially reluctant involvement with these strangers draws him into the catastrophes which invade their lives and thus gives him an insight into the quiet power generated by the emotional support the 'flatlanders' provide, which he has so long scorned. This leads him to the gradual realisation that the love – of Nature, of wild places, of self-forgetting – which he drove himself to embrace in the mountains did not wholly afford him the truth he had sought, but that it also lay elsewhere, in sharing others' losses, triumphs and preoccupations.

Indeed, the Redfern family seem to endure more than their fair share of loss, and it is when considering this weight that the narrative feels somewhat overburdened. Nevertheless, there are careful and often illuminating parallels between Hazard's life and those of the stricken family members. Hugh Redfern, the handsome, genial patriarch is lost when a volcano he is exploring erupts, another consequence of risk, another casualty of obsession. Shortly after his death his widow, Philippa, discovers that his preoccupations were not confined to his vulcanology as she uncovers evidence of repeated infidelity while sorting through his private papers. Philippa's conviction that her innocence had facilitated Redfern's dalliances, later transmuting into feelings of failure and inadequacy, enables both Hazard and the reader to understand the depth of his betrayal in fleeing from his wife and baby daughter in order to pursue his self-centred ambitions.

The literary device of Hazard's memory loss ensures that he must research and evaluate the events of his climbing career in order to illuminate those that remain clouded. He slowly comes to feel some disdain, even disgust, for the man he was, the man who left two climbers to die on Mont Blanc in order to reach his own place of safety, the man who 'hardened himself... grew steely' and withdrew from others in order to find inner freedom for himself. His ruthlessness in pursuing his mountaineering ambitions and his subsequent emotional severance from the world others perceive as reality made him quite unable to comprehend that 'a man was forever what he had been at any time for others'. Hazard's life-long assertion had been that the mountains stripped one of self-delusion, allowed one to acquire self-knowledge, to live truthfully. Now, in frail old age, with accusations about his ambitions in the mountains blinding him to the safety of other climbers, this certainty is no longer clear-cut and he begins to question the emotional code which has governed his life.

This realisation is embedded in the book's title: *Evening Light* was a new gritstone route Hazard wanted to put up to reassure himself that his prowess on rock was still intact. Faced with an intractable problem on the route he chipped a hold in order to surmount it. When his malpractice was exposed and the route subsequently climbed clean, he determined to prove himself by means of the ultimate challenge of climbing all the 8000-metre peaks. By disappearing into this endeavour he escaped both his critics and his own dishonesty. His life's premise, then, was built on a profound deception, the worm in the apple of his success, a denial of a basic truth.

Now, with his first real forays into family life, he realises that it is the things which limit us which make us what we are – most immediately, 'the solidarity with others'. Yet he does not attempt to annihilate the conviction his mountaineering career strengthened in him but, instead, to adjust his perspective, to find the worth in that 'different order of reality' of which he had been such a prominent part. It, too, has its truths; the revelation for Hazard is that they are not the only signposts to a man's completeness. Love of his 'other world' did not exclude those other more socially integrated attachments of family and friends but added another dimension to the narrow road he had travelled.

Evening Light firmly grasps the mountaineering nettle: emotional detachment enables climbers to survive in high and hostile territory but can stifle the richness and complexity of attachments in the flatlands. The lines demarcating success and failure are far less starkly drawn in the shifting sands of marriage and family life and those who depend on clarity and view existence as a series of personal challenges which confirm identity and purpose may have no frame of reference in this emotionally cluttered life. What Hazard comes to realise is that the mountains did not contain the definitive code for existence; the mystery he saw embodied in them which he spent a lifetime's travail pursuing is part of a greater whole and it is the openness to that belief which ultimately sets a man free.

Val Randall

Medicine for Mountaineering
& Other Wilderness Activities, 6th Edition
Edited by James Wilkerson, Contributors Ken Zafren and Ernest Moore
The Mountaineers Books, Seattle, 2010, pp 384, US$29.95

The *AJ* Editor lives down the road from my surgery so I suppose it was inevitable that one day a medical tome would arrive with the simple instruction to write a review for the journal.

Opening the used envelope revealed perhaps the most famous wilderness medicine book of them all – *Medicine for Mountaineering* – now in its 6th edition. The first edition in 1967 was revolutionary, pushing first aid beyond a couple of bandages into new fields such as diagnosis, prevention, planning and much more. Since then it has become established practice that the scope of mountain medicine, even for the non-health care professional, encompasses drugs, reductions of fractures, and treatment for shock and hypothermia. The reason was clear in the 1960s and to an extent remains so today: mountaineering is an activity with inherent risk that takes place away from roads. Participants therefore need to be self-reliant, resourceful and confident to manage injuries and illnesses for hours or even days. Here, though, we encounter the dilemma of what is safe and effective in the mountains when the operator has been instructed on paper and perhaps on a specialised first aid course but has never encountered the problem *in the flesh*.

This book, along with the myriad of competitors, has to draw a consistent line for its target audience over many topics, between educating the reader to think like a doctor or provide a protocol-driven, problem-based system of management. An example may help. I am climbing in northern Italy on one of those long remote icefalls. My partner momentarily has a lapse in concentration, slips on the ice, falls over and his ice-axe impacts onto his chest. It hurts but in a couple of minutes he can talk in short sentences and says he feels OK. An educated reader will consider the options – simple broken rib; traumatic pneumothorax, that may be simple or 'tension'; haemopneumothorax; left lower chest – spleen injury, right lower chest – liver injury, front of chest – cardiac injury etc, etc. Now experience will tell us what is common, what injuries go together, and what signs are reliable at ruling a diagnosis in or out. And so by the hypothetico-deductive method a working diagnosis is made and treatment given.

The critics of this approach will argue that our diagnosis is nevertheless inaccurate as the signs on which it is based are not as good as we think and neither are our treatments specific. Why not ask: Is the patient 'big sick or little sick'? 'Big sick' patients are deadly pale, cold and sweaty, anxious, restless and often the quiet one at the back; 'little sick' patients though in pain are none of the above. You manage 'big sick' in one way – usually by rapid evacuation, oxygen and supportive measures – and 'little sick' another way – reassurance, pain relief and a timely evacuation.

So returning to our casualty with his painful ribs, he is 'little sick' so benefits from a few painkillers and not having to carry his rucksack down. I don't have to worry about missing a tension pneumothorax; as long as his condition does not deteriorate he remains 'little sick' whether or not he has a pneumothorax.

Medicine for Mountaineering uses a doctor's approach, an approach that requires serious study and many pages of text if it is to be successful. These attributes are not ingrained in modern man, who prefers, to paraphrase Mark Twight[1], to go 'light, fast and high' by using pre-event training, minimal but the best equipment, and efficient techniques. *Medicine for Mountaineering*, as its odd title implies, is removed from the modern way, though the associated e-book will go some way to overcoming the 400 pages and 750 grams of the printed book.

Readers might reflect that this is the first book review of mountain medicine (despite many new publications) in the *Alpine Journal* since my book *Casualty Care in Mountain Rescue* featured in 2002. What chance then that lay readers will engage in the medical journey when the 'big sick, little sick' approach along with a satellite phone is an option? My colleague, Dr David Hillebrandt, describes instructing a urinary catheterisation remotely in such a way.

Does *Medicine for Mountaineering* fulfil its objectives? In general it does, and I enjoyed the chapters to which I, as a member of an organised rescue system, was drawn. These included the psychological responses to wilderness accidents, and rescue and evacuation. The section on eye disorders

1 Mark F. Twight. *Extreme Alpinism*. 1999 The Mountaineers, Seattle.

was particularly good and has important advice for persons having corrective surgery for short-sightedness. Detailed clear instruction is given for important life-saving techniques, such as cricothyroidectomy. It is easy to pick holes in the detail but this reflects my knowledge rather than errors. Most of the information is inevitably anecdotal rather than based on firm evidence and there is a lack of discussion when there are variances to accepted practice. For example, in a dramatic case report of an accident on the Western Breech of Kilimanjaro the authors 'speculate that wrapping the climber's pelvis and awaiting transport on a firm stretcher could have been life saving'. Perhaps, but the absence of the caveat that wrapping of the pelvis is a developing technique for which no evidence of survival benefit has been published as yet (October 2010) is regrettable in such a book. In other areas, clear advice is hard to find; for example, water disinfection techniques are well described but there is no drawing together of the information even if it is to say that no single method is superior and comparison studies are lacking.

North American tones come through in many places reflecting that only two of 24 contributors are from outside that continent. For example, in the introduction we are advised that: 'All participants in wilderness activities should undergo regular examinations by a physician knowledgeable about and sympathetic to their interests.' A European text would stress more targeted advice and the use of the internet for knowledge of local illnesses, health services and emergency numbers.

So in conclusion, interesting for the well-read expedition medic and as a summary for the doctor, though Auerbach's reference book *Wilderness Medicine*,[2] at 2316 pages and 5kg (DVD enclosed) will keep the doctor happy for longer. But for a small trip of mates, an expedition leader who prefers Mark Twight's approach may want to check out *First Aid and Wilderness Medicine* by Jim Duff and Peter Gormly.[3] Here we have a *British* book in a concise bullet-point style; at 248 pages and 250g, it punches above its weight.

John Ellerton

John Ellerton is a GP in Penrith, Cumbria, medical officer with Patterdale Mountain Rescue Team and Mountain Rescue England and Wales, and a member of the International Commission for Alpine Emergency Medicine (ICAR MEDCOM).

2 Paul S. Auerbach. *Wilderness Medicine* 5th ed. 2007 Mosby Elsevier, Philadelphia
3 Jim Duff and Peter Gormly. *Pocket First Aid and Wilderness Medicine* 10th ed. 2007 Cicerone Press, Cumbria.

Monte Rosa: Königin der Alpen
Daniel Anker and Marco Volken
AS Verlag, Zurich, 2009, pp336, €39.80

The young Winston Churchill, visiting Zermatt in 1894, insisted on an ascent of Monte Rosa rather than the Matterhorn, not only because of its superior height but also because the guides' fee for Monte Rosa was substantially less than that for *Das Höre*. Then, as now, I presume it would also have been less crowded.

My own first taste of Monte Rosa remains indelible. It had been a very long day and the final climb along the summit ridge to the Dufourspitze, at 4634m the highest of Monte Rosa's tops, had been tricky in strong winds and with a lot of ice-glazed rock to negotiate. We'd wished we'd had more than one ice screw. Back on skis, legs soon became tired. The middle section of the descent is a long schuss down the Gorner glacier. For much of its length it was rutted sheet ice. My abiding memory is of struggling to keep control on wobbly legs while directly ahead the setting sun painted the sky with dark fire behind the silhouette of the Matterhorn. Pain, panic almost, and a deep pleasure all wrapped together.

This splendid monograph from the AC's Swiss friend Daniel Anker revives the pleasure without the pain. It also brings the realisation that despite my having approached Monte Rosa each time from the Zermatt or Saas valleys, it is much more than a *Swiss* mountain. In fact, whisper this since the Swiss revere it as their highest summit, Monte Rosa is best appreciated from Italy – '*la Regina delle Alpi*' might be a more appropriate sub-title.

There is a superb double page photograph at the front of this book, taken across the Lago di Varese on a crystal winter's day with the whole massif rising into a clear blue sky. Another remarkable photo taken in almost the reverse direction, at night from the Albergo Gugliermina, looks out over snowy ridges to the electric light sea of greater Milan. It really drives home the fact of the Alps as an island in the heart of urbanised Europe.

Monte Rosa is a feast of illustration, providing more than sufficient reason, I would say, to buy the book even if you don't read German. Archive photos, landscapes, modern climbing action and extreme skiing, sketches and paintings bring to life the story of the mountain told in chapters based on its four villages – Gressoney, Zermatt, Macugnaga and Alagna – and on the huts and bivouacs above them plus of course the multiple summits of the massif.

Members of the Alpine Club figure prominently in the Monte Rosa story and are well represented here. Edward Whymper's well-known engraving *The Club Room at Zermatt* is juxtaposed with a group photograph taken during the club's 150th anniversary gathering in the resort. The Monte Rosa hotel looks much the same in the background. Only one of the dozens of people in the 2007 photo is named – our then president, Stephen Venables, seated cross-legged at the front, even though looming above him is the unmistakeable form of Kurt Diemberger. Lots of you are there – a magnifying glass helps.

Stephen Goodwin

New Monte Rosa Hut, SAC
Self-sufficient building in the high Alps
ETH Zurich, 2010, pp224, CHF65/€45

This fine monograph provides a detailed and fascinating account of the design and construction of the new Monte Rosa hut opened in September 2009.

This remarkable, futuristic eco-hut sits in a spectacular location 2883 metres high above the Gorner glacier, slightly above the site of the old hut, in the shadow of the Matterhorn, enjoying, some would say, an even better view. From a distance, the building has the appearance of a space station: the extraordinary shape, almost crystalline in form is based upon the cross section of an orange. Trapezoidal shaped segments create the plan form.

The project was launched in 2003 as a project of the Swiss Alpine Club (SAC) to mark the 150th anniversary of Zurich's Federal Institute of Technology. The SAC was founded in 1863 following a resolution which stated 'the Association, will erect huts at suitable locations in the High Alps so as to accommodate the growing ranks of pleasure seekers bound for the high mountains and glaciers'.

Today SAC membership exceeds 125,000 and remains faithful to this undertaking, currently maintaining 153 huts in the Swiss Alps.

The first hut in this location known as the Bétemps was completed in 1895 and comprised 25 beds plus warden's accommodation. The last hut, in which many AC members must have stayed, had a capacity of 160 beds and this was demolished in 2010.

So what has inspired the architects to create such a striking shape? Clearly there were major challenges, extreme climatic and topographical conditions combined with the search for a shape that would reflect this spectacular local landscape. Could they design a structure that acts as a point of reference in an environment in limitless scale, a building that shows approaching mountaineers the way over the glacier. The answer is clearly in the eye of the beholder for there is no doubt that the solution is controversial, admired by many, undeniably avant-garde in style.

The five storey prefabricated building is built on stainless steel foundations with a timber framed superstructure clad externally in shimmering silver aluminium. On the southern facade sits an integrated photovoltaic system; this generates more than 90% of the energy requirements making it the greenest hut in Europe.

But by far the biggest challenge the architects faced was the timing and method of construction. With construction only possible from mid May to September, the building had to be a prefabricated frame capable of transport by train and helicopter and being completed in five months. The solution was a computer-aided design (CAD) masterpiece, comprising a complex spatial puzzle of 420 elements delivered by train to Zermatt followed by 3000 helicopter trips to the site where 35 technicians lived throughout the summer.

The SAC has a limited history of commissioning visionary buildings that define the spirit of the age, but in tackling this unique project in such an innovative way has laid down a marker for mountain huts of the future.

Critics will say a low carbon technological integration of the photovoltaic system imposes an architectural vocabulary alien to the mountain landscape; I would disagree. The overall integrity of the design shines through, it sits comfortably in hostile surroundings, a beacon of futuristic architecture for the enjoyment of future generations of mountaineers.

John Innerdale

The Hut Builder
Laurence Fearnley
Penguin (NZ), 2010, pp246, NZ$40

Fiction which is based on mountaineering experience either uses it as foreground or background. This novel, which was short-listed for the Boardman Tasker Award 2010, is in the latter camp in that it is more about camping than mountaineering. Note that I have resisted suggesting that this is camp fiction, which it is definitely not, partly because it is a little limp-wristed about sex, and generally understated emotionally. But I also resist going so far as to say that it is frosty, although its crux is a long period spent in a snow cave when the central character Boden Black's taciturn male companion, Walter, Opens Up.

Walter had let slip the fact that he was in prison, which has disturbed the very conventional Boden Black, who can barely admit to himself that he has inclinations towards being A Poet. It turns out Walter was imprisoned for being a Conscientious Objector. But the real horror is that he was interned with Rex Hillary, the younger brother of the National Hero. Something of the Boden Black mentality is indicated by what the author presents as Black Thoughts:

> *This man, Edmund Hillary – a man who represented everything that was great about our country, a hero admired by everyone – had a brother who had been imprisoned for refusing to go to war. It was hard to believe. Two brothers: the hero and the shirker. I was equally disconcerted by the thoughts that started to force their way into my head.*

When a writer uses the phrase 'started to' about a character doing something, the reader would be right to get a little disconcerted too. But what would Boden Black have made of the fact that the later Sir Edmund himself registered as a conscientious objector at the beginning of the war, escaping prison since beekeeping was a 'reserved occupation'? (Rex Hillary spent four years in the detention camp at Strathmore, near Reporoa, one of 800 pacifists imprisoned by the New Zealand government.)

This novel is based on the building of the Empress Hut at 8000 feet on Mount Cook in the early 1950s. When the National Hero himself turns up at the snow hole camp and takes up a hammer to work alongside Boden Black, the latter has 'a sudden bout of nerves, a kind of stage fright, such as I had experienced at school when playing the Porter in *Macbeth*'. If only young Boden Black had learned something from the irreverence of the role. But light-hearted grumbling banter is not the mode of the aptly named Boden Black.

Nor is rocking the boat. At the conclusion of the novel he is suddenly an old man (as indicated by a reference to erectile dysfunction as the novel's only – and rather late – coy hint at any sexual activity) visiting the Mount Cook village where the Empress Hut is apparently now preserved as a historic relic outside the visitor centre. After living uncomfortably with his reputation as a poet having, for much of his later life, rested on a single anthologised poem, Boden Black has accepted a commission for a new poem to be read at the opening of the new museum and visitor centre. He considers, fleetingly, the opportunity to say something about the huge car park now built on very spot that inspired his original famous poem. But, of course, if you've read this far, you know that he'll chicken out – in final words of the novel, 'In the morning I would return and read my poem'. That's the climax of the book and that's as exciting as it gets.

Terry Gifford

My Life, Volume One: To Be Brave
Royal Robbins
Pink Moment Productions, USA, 2009, pp218, $19.95

Royal Robbins is one of climbing's gentlemen. He will be forever associated with trying to set the standards of style in the development of climbing in Yosemite's golden age. At the back of this book Robbins graciously calls for support for 'two non-profit agencies very close to my heart', the Boy Scouts and the Yosemite Fund. But he begins with the story of a committing solo ascent of the west face of the Leaning Tower, partly chosen as a dry place during a period of rain in the Valley, more pointedly chosen as a second ascent statement about its first ascent by Warren Harding in a siege style that included six months with untouched ropes in place between efforts. Robbins admits that he was making 'another move on the Yosemite chessboard' by attempting to 'raise the style ante'. Yet he has the generosity to also admit 'we'd probably be buddies except for this thing about climbing. I don't attack you personally, only the way you do it. For me it's all philosophy. For you it's a big joke, like when you skewer me as a kind of preacher, a "Valley Christian".'

There's a lot going on in this passage. There's no way that Robbins and Harding would have been buddies, but for this climbing thing. Yet Robbins wrote a wonderfully warm obituary for Harding in *High* magazine, despite being 'skewered' by Harding in his time, as he can now boast, admitting that he was a bit of a preacher for style, a keeper of the faith against conquest by bolt and, in practice, an ethical policeman. But it is by no means clear that Robbins won the argument, as it is currently played out around the world's steep faces. Is there such a thing as 'upping the style ante' in a sport where styles have become distinct branches of the activity? Well, just look at the correspondence being played out by Alex Huber and Conrad Anker in the summer 2010 pages of *Alpinist 31* about their 1997 ascent of Latok II. Huber: 'The use of the power drill has nothing to do with an excessive use of bolts.' Anker: 'Power drills encourage a less thoughtful use of bolts.' The defence and regret being engaged here suggest that Robbins' manner of opening his autobiography is not just history, but heritage as continuity – the way past decisions of style define debates about the future. Because what Huber and Anker are arguing about is the future of our rock heritage around the world, just as Robbins' choices of action engaged with Harding's choices for the rock heritage of Yosemite that has been left for us and our children.

It is hard to accept the role of 'Valley Christian' without a certain righteousness, especially if you still believe yourself to have been in the right. So one might have some anxieties about the declaration that these seven volumes will be about conveying 'the message that life is an adventure and that character counts'. To be sure, there are in this first volume regrets as well as defences: the low self-esteem at school, 'young and foolish' dares in early adventures on freight trains, childhood nightmares, the disappearance of two fathers, an attempted robbery. Then his mother allowed him to choose his name – his step-father's with which he had grown up, or his birth name, Royal Shannon Robbins. After joining the Scouts and being introduced to the mountains, the character we know began to form.

The book ends with the final effort on Leaning Tower, when retreat from the overhanging rock is impossible. But the self-reliance that his mother had encouraged is nowhere more needed than *after* topping out, when a swollen Bridalveil Creek has to be crossed: 'I've never seen death so close. After all those wild things on rock – I never thought it would be water.' Perhaps the greatest test of character late in life is the style with which the self-examination of an autobiography is approached. Suffice it to say that I'm very much looking forward to the next volume.

Terry Gifford

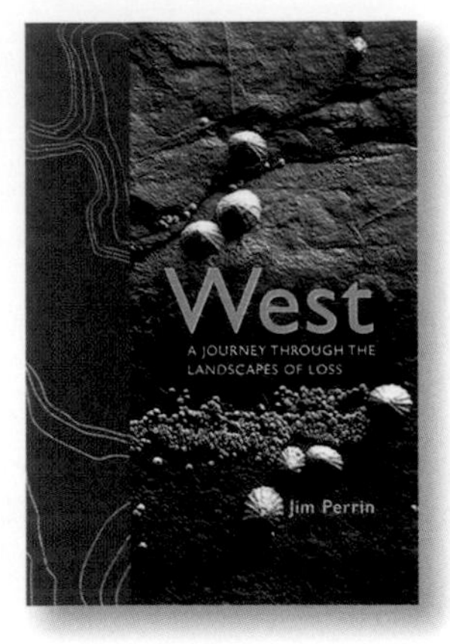

West
Jim Perrin
Atlantic Books, 2010, pp336, £18.99

In *West*, writer and 70s climbing activist Jim Perrin tells of the deaths by suicide of his son William and from breast cancer of his wife Jacquetta, two events that happened within a year of each other.

Jim first meets Jacquetta in the early 70s, at the height of his life as a rock-climber, but loses contact when she, coming to meet him in Wales, sees him on the point of completing a solo ascent of *Cenotaph Corner*. This seems to flip her into a state of shock at the man's lack of responsibility; she drives away and disappears to the other side of the world. Jim is unable to trace her and for 28 years each feels the anguish of lost love – until, at a literary event, they meet again. They 'marry' in a Pagan ceremony on the shore of the Lleyn Peninsula and take up life together in Jim's recently acquired house in Llanrhaeadr, a small and archetypal Welsh village in the Tanat valley between Oswestry and the Berwyns, Jim having decided to leave his haunts around Llanberis for somewhere that has nothing to do with climbing. But within a very short time he sells the house, which he loves, and is once more on the move, this time to a caravan on the other side of the Berwyns, a step that enables him to pay off his new wife's not-inconsiderable debts.

Meanwhile, his son William has been carving out a name for himself as one of Britain's leading 'traditional' rock climbers – that is, an adventure climber very much in Jim's spirit, rather than a sport climber – and is invited on an expedition to the sea cliffs of Cape Farewell in Greenland. On the day of departure Will drives down to Heathrow, drops the rest of the team off at check-in, and then, instead of parking the car, drives back to his house near Llanberis, where he lives in isolation for four days before putting his head in a noose in his bedroom. He is not discovered for several days, by which time the body is already decomposing. A week after Will's funeral Jacquetta, who has never been entirely well, it is assumed because of the gross physical abuse suffered at the hands of a previous lover, is diagnosed with a particularly virulent form of breast cancer. The doctors' initial estimate of a survival time of several years is rapidly reduced to a few months. After her death Jim buys another house in Llanrhaeadr and moves there, but he too becomes increasingly ill. The doctors' prognosis that he also has cancer leaves Jim unconvinced. He thinks the problem psychosomatic, brought on by extreme grief. The memories associated with Llanrhaeadr – perhaps with the whole of North Wales – are too much, and he once again sells up and moves, this time to the Ariège, the eastern end of the Pyrenees, where he writes *West*.

One bows one's head in respect before this harrowing tale. Which is one reason it is a difficult book to review. Another is that over all hangs

Jim's commitment to a highly romantic style, and inseparable from this his insistence on the expression of all feeling and emotion, and all sensuality, however personal. When combined with the subject matter this makes much of *West* fairly extreme, and it will invite in some readers the criticism that the book makes public too much that should have remained in the privacy of Jim's mind. Perhaps the safest that can be said is that if you have read Jim before and admire his writing, you must read this. It is Jim on every page, his testament, his outlook and his mode of expression. Beyond that, so much is a matter of taste. There is, for example, the question of sex. Jim's had a lot of it, and he writes about it explicitly. I have a problem with this similar to that I had with *Cham*, a recent climbing novel. As Victor Saunders pointed out in his review in last year's *AJ*, *Cham* is full of explicit sexual descriptions. Are they necessary? Well, if the purpose is to show what a cold and ultimately unattractive milieu it is that the young protagonists of the novel inhabit, then 'yes'. And I think one can take the same view of Jim's writing when he is describing the wild and liberated climbing scene around Llanberis in the 1970s. The description of his betrayal by an Irish ex-lover immediately after he has lost the two people dearest to him in the world makes one grateful to have missed out on all that. The problem is that he employs the same literary devices when describing his new-found love, and I wish we had been left to use our own imagination over their intimacy. The book could have been – would have been – so much more a work of art. But then, I suppose that just wouldn't be Jim. It would also suppose that the book was written primarily for us, the readership, and it isn't. It is written for Jim himself, as a cathartic act. For me, this is at the heart of the weakness of overly-romantic writing. And it tends to make all such work – as is the case here – too drawn out.

In so many ways Jim is a combination of contradictory outlooks. He is a man of great sensitivity, and quite explicit in his view that this has contributed to his increasingly falling out of love with the climbing scene. He leaves Llanberis for Llanrhaeadr because the former now depresses him, and he feels the need to escape. More and more, climbers have come to seem little more than Ruskin's 'greased pole' merchants, rather unsophisticated people perhaps, who can't see, or experience, beyond the obvious. Part and parcel of this is his growing sympathy and belief in the feminine side of his own character, with all that implies about intuitive feeling as opposed to fact and argument:

> *I love the way that women are, their difference, the subtleties of their approach, the way they move through the world, …I see the men out on the fells, hurrying, hurrying, pressing through, acquisitive, eyes intent on goal and summit and the completion of lists, itineraries, records.*

He is the archetypal rationalist when he takes the view, throughout his suffering, that we just do not know what happens at death, or how consciousness is connected to the physical body, if at all. He is irritated by the Dawkins and Dennets of this world, who he sees as too full of certainty (though he knows their work well; there is no man better read.) He is equally irritated by the certainties of well-meaning New-Age acquaintances who take it upon themselves to tell him what's what and how the world really is. He is surely right when he writes that 'there is nothing more ludicrous than pompous certainty in the face of what cannot be known.' And yet he is full of mysticism and the centrality of feeling – 'the tendency towards magical thinking has long been present in me' – and is more than capable of leaving the facts behind.

Jim is a very bright man, but that doesn't stop him indulging the romantic fantasy of the noble savage, slightly reworded as the spiritual superiority of the past. Possibly it was superior; but to use his own arguments, how can we be so sure? I would be with him on the spiritual superiority of the rural as opposed to the urban life, and perhaps most readers of the *Journal* would; but I'm uneasy about idealising the past. The brutality of the life of the rural poor has generally precluded those finer things of life about which Jim is so passionate, surely. I also find his political views too tribal. And allowing these prejudices to impinge does not improve the quality of his work.

West is infused with Jim's tenacity of spirit, but overall it is, as surely it must be, a sombre read. And it draws on the melancholia that suffuses his take on the world and his tastes in literature in general. Recalling his enthusiasm for 9th century Welsh poetry as a student, he writes:

> *It strikes me as odd that I should have been attracted by such solemnity, such depth of sadness, in the spring years of my life. Though to scan back over the years seems to bring into focus a consistent thread of mourning.*

So it is not surprising that one of the achievements of this book is to convey so effectively an undercurrent of impending disaster. (It made me think of Gavin Maxwell's *Raven Seek Thy Brother*, and the best of the descriptive writing is as good as Maxwell's; perhaps as good as anyone's.) I barely smiled for the first 200 pages, except once, at the wonderful description of seeing off a specimen of the 'countryside police' whilst wild-camping on Harlech beach.

But then we come to the third section of the book, 'Chiaroscuro', and the move to Llanrhaeadr, and I found myself not just smiling but laughing. This is, if you like, the leavening, the relief and innocent joy in the book. And it is wonderfully written – Dylan Thomas all over again. The characters are larger than life, hugely colourful. Jim loves the place, and loves the people, who are of all political persuasions, giving the lie to his too simple analysis of our social ills. The references to sex – plenty of those, of course – are bawdy rather than pornographic. We want it all to last. And of course it cannot.

Jim rather divides opinion in the climbing world. I have always found him the most generous of men. Whether you like his writing must be, ultimately, a question of whether you feel his talents sufficiently outweigh the weaknesses. More than any contemporary writer from our sport, I find he forces me to think and re-evaluate. And for that reason alone I want to read him.

Phil Bartlett

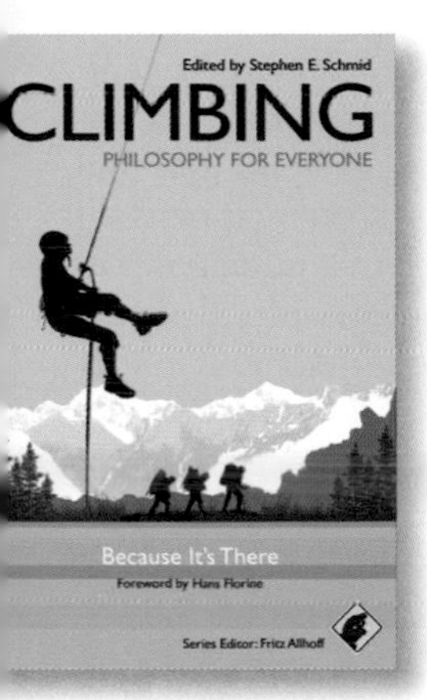

Climbing – Philosophy for Everyone: Because It's There
Edited by Stephen E Schmid
Wiley-Blackwell, 2010, pp242, £11.99

At the 2010 Kathmandu Mountain Film Festival I gave a slide show on the eccentricities of British climbing culture from the perspective of a weekend climber of modest ambitions and even more modest abilities. The audience questions began with one Nepali who said he had three questions: 'Can you smell the difference between rocks? What do you think about falling? What is harder to climb, a rock or a man?' If this had been in the UK I would have suspected the extraction of the Michael. But, whether this man was a Buddhist or not, I took his questions seriously and answered, 'Yes,' 'I try not to', and 'A man'. This book, written by climbers who are also professional philosophers, is an attempt to explore with clarity of thinking questions about climbing, most of them less interesting than those of my Kathmandu questioner.

Familiar questions about ethics, styles, environmentalism, risk and responsibilities tend to come to the familiar variety of conclusions via philosophical routes that you may or may not find interesting. Since most of the contributors are North American, the climbing contexts and examples tend to derive from there and it is mostly European philosophers of previous centuries who are drawn upon for structures of thought and constructions of the issues. It is fun to see some of these essays as in unarticulated dialogue with each other. Joe Fitchen, early partner of Royal Robbins, observes that climbing, in his experience, has not produced 'significantly better people', but a stage for the acting out of already formed personalities. For Paul Charlton, on the other hand, the demands of climbing can 'leave us better equipped to contribute to our societies'. Note that the latter is argument and the former personal observation. Such distinctions are important to philosophers who regularly complain of sloppy and erroneous thinking whilst selecting quite narrow philosophical frames with which to pursue questions of their own precise definition. It turns out from the footnotes that the games philosophers play here render as the single most quoted text *The Games Climbers Play* by Lito Tejada-Flores.

Ben Levey uses Hegel's argument that the slave's restrictions produce more 'self-realization' than in the master to conclude that the trad climbing game demands 'an instinctive questioning and redressing of a deeply held presupposition, as part and parcel of its rules, while the sport climbing game does not'. Nevertheless, a depressing number of other contributors take sport climbing as their model. Debora Halbert argues that climbing is a gift economy in which 'route setters' give their bolted routes to others. Her supreme example is of Rick and Liz Webster's gift to the climbing community of seven miles of crags which they bought in Kentucky's Muir Valley in the late 1990s, building roads and trails so that route setters could bolt the rocks to hell 'while the Websters monitor who can set routes and the procedures for doing so'. Elsewhere Dale Murray asks, 'Is it rational for me to contribute by not climbing?' This is a rather different kind of gift that leaves him free from the gift of those monitoring Websters.

Perhaps the most challenging essay is that in justification of 'hold manufacture', or chipping. William Ramsey makes a cleverly written, clearly argued case that I suspect is more convincing in an American context where 'if you are a serious climber who regularly climbs relatively hard sport routes there is a very good chance that at some point you have done a route with at least a few manufactured holds'. Already guilty? Then manufacture a few more in that forever-I-mean-forever unclimbable blank section, you route setter.

Oh these philosophers! Their internal consistencies can take you to places you never thought you'd be. As one of them says a few pages later, this book is 'an appropriate area for chiselling out some of the common arguments involved in the ethical discussion'. And it's no good squirming in your apparently innocent boots feeling indignant and injured. These philosophers *are* the Moral Mountain Rescue Squad. Take me back to Kathmandu where the answers can be 'Yes,' 'I try not to', 'A man', and the questioner a philosopher from a less 'rational' tradition.

Terry Gifford

In the Footsteps of Mallory and Irvine: The Wildest Dream
Mark Mackenzie
John Murray, 2009, pp 248, £20

So who had the wilder dream: George Mallory in his obsessive bid to be first on the summit of Everest, or Conrad Anker in his search for evidence that Mallory and Irvine had succeeded? Mark Mackenzie's account *In the Footsteps of Mallory and Irvine – The Wildest Dream* is more than the book of Anthony Giffen's drama documentary film, it is a stalwart sifting of the evidence contained in more than 30 books devoted to mountaineering's most famous mystery.

It was Conrad Anker who found Mallory's remains clinging to the flanks of Everest, a discovery that offered no positive answer to the question. But the find was sensational and turned the romantic myth, of two dots high on Everest somehow evaporating into the mist, into an awful reality; Mallory reduced to a cluster of broken bones and tattered cloth, his shoulder smooth as marble in the refrigerating cold.

Mackenzie traces the background to the 1924 expedition leading to the disappearance of the two climbers and Conrad Anker's career in mountaineering, from apprentice to professional climber on the 1999 team hoping to solve the Mallory-Irvine mystery. After the discovery of Mallory's body Anker went on to reach the summit, attempting the famous second step without using the metal ladder put there by the Chinese. The 90ft pitch, which is topped by an overhang, prompts the critical question of whether Mallory, probably the best rock climber of his generation, could have succeeded given the thin air, freezing wind and the clothing and equipment then available. Anker failed when his foot touched the ladder.

Eight years later he was back on Everest with the Altitude Everest Expedition to recreate on film Mallory and Irvine's fateful attempt. With him was Leo Houlding, leading light among today's generation of rock climbers but like Sandy Irvine a relatively inexperienced high altitude mountaineer. Irvine is portrayed as a live wire from the roaring twenties, an all-round athlete, Oxford rowing blue with a liking for theatre, fast cars and women. His affair with the stepmother of a good friend involved making love four times before breakfast. More usefully he proved to be a practical wizard at servicing the oxygen equipment that provided 'English air' to the 1924 mountaineers.

Mackenzie's narrative switches between the 1924 and the 2007 expeditions as Anker and Houlding don period clothing, identical to that worn by Mallory and Irvine, to recreate the climb. They promptly abandoned this nod at authenticity on the North Col when cold, wind and altitude began to bite. Indeed, of the 10 westerners in the film team, five failed to make it on to the mountain and one cameraman developed serious altitude sickness.

When Anker and Houlding reached the second step at 28,000ft the metal ladder that has eased the path of climbers for some 40 years was temporarily removed and Anker, after one spectacular fall, eventually 'pulled himself into the fog created by his own breathing' and he and Houlding plodded to the summit.

Technically the second step would probably have been within Mallory's known capabilities. But the thin air at 28,000ft, deteriorating weather late in the day with the summit still some way ahead and a relatively inexperienced partner, all weighed against success. Mackenzie points out that Mallory's injuries, the lack of frostbite on his fingers and the broken rope suggest he died from a fall lower down the mountain. Conrad Anker was far from convinced that Mallory would have chosen a death-or-glory finale. Although Mallory was obsessed by a desire to reach the summit and knew that subsequent success and status as a great explorer would bring great rewards, claiming the prize meant getting back in one piece.

Ronald Faux

Deep Powder and Steep Rock:
The Life of Mountain Guide Hans Gmoser
Chic Scott
Assiniboine Publishing Limited, 2009, pp384 plus DVD, $50

Writing a biography can be extremely challenging. It contains a kind of duality that can play itself out for better or worse. On the one side, the writer works within the context of the known history, gathering together existing facts and perhaps forming new lines of inquiry that will give the basic shape and structure to the biography. The other side is trickier, for how we write about the past can, and often does, redefine it. The written interpretation of the past therefore becomes the new remembrance, and the new history. The biography writer is therefore both retrospective, and sometimes unknowingly prospective.

The first biography of a recently deceased and esteemed member of a community – in this case the Canadian mountain community – brings its own additional gravity. It is the weight of expectation. Canadian mountain historian Chic Scott moves carefully and purposefully into this terrain with this biography of the guide and heli-ski entrepreneur Hans Gmoser.

When Gmoser died in 2006 at age 73 from injuries sustained in a cycling accident, few could believe it. Gmoser had been such a significant force, played a pivotal role in putting the Canadian Rockies on the world stage, and shaped the lives of numerous guides and clients. His accomplishments would include the adventurous second ascent of the east ridge of Mount Logan in the St Elias Range in the late 1950s and the first ascent of Denali's huge Wickersham Wall in the early 1960s. But it was for his adventures in and around the Canadian Rockies that he became best known. First for the difficult new rock climbs that Gmoser, often in the company of fellow expatriate Austrians, established on the then-virgin walls of Yamnuska. And secondly for his love of skiing – adventures throughout the winter in search of the best snow, often undertaking groundbreaking multi-day ski tours that traversed and connected huge tracts of glaciated terrain.

Gmoser travelled throughout the North American continent, sharing his stories through charming films and speaking engagements. And his invention and development of the sport of heli-skiing, which grew from humble roots into a leading adventure holiday company, was to launch Gmoser into the world of high-pressure business.

Written by Scott at the request of Gmoser's widow, Margaret, *Deep Powder and Steep Rock* makes an admirable job of capturing the chronological essence of Gmoser's life. I use the term chronological with intent because where the book excels is in its comprehensiveness, covering the breadth of Gmoser's life from its austere beginnings in Austria, his move to Canada as a young immigrant, the early, hungry and ambitious years as a climber and skier, to his eventual marriage, family and the growth of his business, Canadian Mountain Holidays.

As evidenced by his other books such as *Pushing the Limits* (a comprehensive history of mountaineering in Canada) and his ski-touring guides, Scott does his research. In writing this book, he was granted full access to Gmoser's personal diaries and letters. One gets the sense, at times, that Scott is treating some of the material with caution – I don't think this coyness was entirely his own, rather it speaks to the circumstances of the book's development and Gmoser's stature as the elder statesman of Canadian mountaineering. That being said, he works effectively with what he has and what is already known. As a result, the best of the book is contained within the first sections. Here are the stories and writing – much of it Gmoser's – that speak to a true love of the mountains and the camaraderie that fuels the spirit. These are the stories of Gmoser's early life as a climber.

There is a marked lack of writing from Gmoser in the later sections of the book. This is when he became busier and, some felt, consumed by business pursuits. When I spoke with Scott about this, he indicated that indeed Gmoser's writing and descriptions of his own experiences had become less frequent. This is a shame, for Gmoser's writing was often simple and beautiful, and along with his films, was an important element of his message about the mountain experience as he saw it. After his landmark first ascent of Yamnuska's *Direttissima*, Gmoser wrote:

> *This mountain to us is not a sports arena. To us it is a symbol of truth and a symbol of life as it should be. This mountain teaches us that we should endure hardships and that we should encounter the difficulties and not drift along the easy way, which always leads down.*

Scott alludes to some of the tensions that existed in the second half of Gmoser's life – the business pressures and the divisiveness that occurred at times when Gmoser was perhaps seen more as an entrepreneur than the young Austrian immigrant who had been so charmed by the mountains. During these times, Gmoser himself seemed more detached and Scott's own writing of that period is more chronological in nature. The DVD of some of Gmoser's own skiing and climbing films from the early days that is included with the book emphasises the joy, adventure and passion of those earlier times.

So in the end, does Scott move into the terrain where a biographer negatively changes our collective memory through stretching of facts? Thankfully not – Scott has captured the history effectively. But nor do we get a full insight into all of Gmoser's character; there is just a start here. This isn't entirely Scott's fault as he was writing this book at the request of Gmoser's widow, something that was no doubt an honour but also came with limitations. Perhaps one day Scott will gather together more of Gmoser's story, and we will get an even deeper understanding of the life of the man who was to change the face of Canadian mountaineering.

Jon Popowich

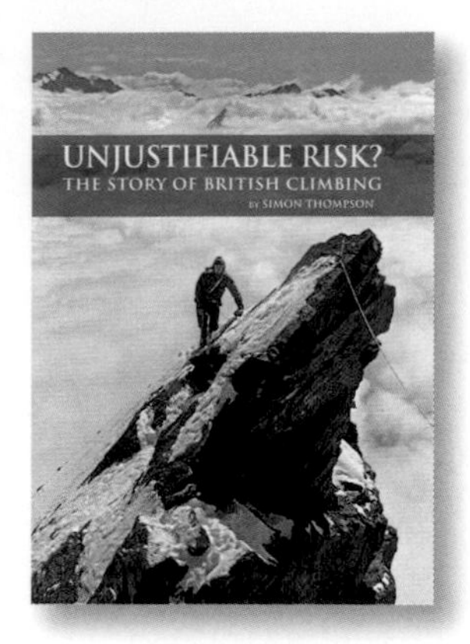

Unjustifiable Risk? The Story of British Climbing
Simon Thompson
Cicerone, 2010, 388pp, £20

This is an ambitious book. Simon Thompson, an Alpine Club member, has aimed to produce a comprehensive history of British climbing, starting with the early British visitors to the Alps in the mid-18th century and ending in the present day: the last new route he records is *Echo Wall* on Ben Nevis, climbed by Dave Macleod in 2008. In the space of 340 pages he thus moves through the entire gamut of British climbing in the British Isles, the Alps and the greater ranges. It is the first such book to be published in at least 50 years. Its closest precedent is R L G Irving's *History of British Mountaineering* (1955). *A Brief History of British Mountaineering* by Colin Wells (2001) is exactly what is says: brief. Wells's *Who's Who in British Mountaineering* (2008) is very readable but is an encyclopaedia of climbers rather than the narrative that Thompson has attempted.

Thompson sets out his stall in his introduction: this book is about the social, cultural and economic conditions that gave rise to the sport in Britain, and the achievements and motives of those who took part. He also boldly takes on the perennial question of why people climb, using as his template the five motives cited by James (Jan) Morris in *Coronation Everest*. Thompson succeeds in some respects and fails in others; he is also often highly contentious, and he set himself some curious limits in the way he conducted his research, with some resultant flaws. The best parts of the book for me are his biographical portraits of a large number of climbers, which are usually entertaining and informative. The index contains hundreds of names, from the Abraham brothers to Geoffrey Winthrop Young, via Bonington, Coolidge, Freshfield, Longstaff, Mallory, Tasker, Whillans, Whymper and many more. It is an impressive distillation of information, much of it taken from obituaries in the *Alpine Journal*.

In between the narrative come historical passages that present Thompson's views of the ideological and sociological roots of climbing. Thompson, in his non-climbing life a successful businessman, is keen to demonstrate the link between social trends and the development of climbing. In Victorian times it was the preserve of the professional and leisured classes, spreading in the 20th century through the classes, thanks to such factors as improved transport, long school holidays, and the dole.

At the same time, Thompson's own biases become clear. He espouses the romantic version of mountaineering, where free spirits pursue their aims devoid of commercial taint. He prefers light, alpine-style ventures to large-scale expeditions. These are reasonable preferences, but his perceptions have led him to devalue some of the most important mountaineering events of his narrative. While he decries the feats of organisation that lay behind the British ascents of the south face of Annapurna in 1970 and the south-west face of Everest in 1975, he does not give sufficient credit to their technical achievement and the extent to which they advanced Himalayan mountaineering to new levels. He also displays a persistent animus towards Chris Bonington in his role as climber-manager which underrates Bonington's record as both climber and expedition leader.

What is strange is how far Thompson has formed these judgments without talking to any of the participants. His approach is that of a historian, using written accounts as his evidence and thus not testing his observations in any conversations with those involved, which seems a wasted opportunity since so many in the latter parts of the book are still alive. All his quotes are recycled from other publications and he fell into the trap of lifting disparaging remarks by Bonington about George Mallory from a book by the jolly thespian (but seemingly less-than-reliable reporter) Brian Blessed, which Bonington now vigorously disputes. Thompson thanks seven people for 'help and advice' in his introduction but the help was mostly practical rather than heeded in shaping his ideas. He is given to making sweeping and often dismissive judgments on topics such as Munro climbers, asserting that most are driven masochists who take part primarily for a sense of achievement and are rarely interested in beauty or adventure. He contends that elite climbers are obsessed and self-absorbed, and that many have unhappy or unfulfilling personal relations.

As author, Thompson is entitled to his judgments. But a problem arises where they are divorced from the known facts. As a Mallory biographer, I was keen to read what Thompson writes about him. For Thompson, Mallory is tarred with the same brush as Bonington, driven by commercial aims. He declares that Mallory thought that his life would be transformed by success on Everest and was prepared to leave behind his wife and children for the chance of fame and glory; and suggests that Mallory chose Irvine for the final summit attempt rather than the more experienced Odell so that he could take most of the glory for himself. There is no evidence for these assertions and Mallory did not voice such thoughts in any of his letters. Mallory's previous attempts to earn a living as a writer and lecturer after the 1922 expedition had ended in failure and he was enjoying his work as an extramural lecturer at Cambridge. Nor was Everest an obsession for him, as Thompson glibly asserts. Mallory had no thought of climbing it until he was invited to join the 1921 expedition. He was less than happy at returning so soon in 1922 and profoundly ambivalent over whether to go in 1924.

I was also interested to see what Thompson made of Dougal Haston. In general, he has Haston right: a dark and driven soul, brooding and flawed. But Thompson writes that during the 37 days that the 1967 British Cerro Torre expedition spent pinned in its base camp by Patagonian storms, 'while the others swore and cursed, Haston simply switched off, displaying no outwards signs of boredom or frustration'. I was in base camp with the expedition and do not recognise this description. I checked the two sources cited by Thompson: Haston's *In High Places* and the biography by Jeff Connor, *The Philosophy of Risk* (2002). Haston writes that base camp was surprisingly peaceful during the storms, and Connor has nothing to contribute. Thompson also writes that Haston 'almost invariably led' the climbing when in fact Haston himself reports that the leading was shared by Boysen, Burke and himself.

These may appear inconsequential details. The problem is that they weaken trust in Thompson's use of evidence to make his judgments, leaving you wondering how much is actually true. The book remains an engaging read, and Thompson's arguments set out points of view that deserve consideration, even if many will disagree with them. It will also be a useful resource and reference work and as such a worthwhile addition to mountaineering bookshelves.

Peter Gillman

Thin Places: A Pilgrimage Home
Ann Armbrecht
Columbia University Press, 2009, pp290, £24 hard cover, £15.50 soft

The 'thin places' of the title are those places where gods have made their mark upon the land, a place to hear the voice of ancestors, or perhaps of the land itself. This is a difficult concept to get over in the English language without coming over as a New Age mystic. Ann Armbrecht succeeds partly because she is an anthropologist with a writer's gift, and partly because, with the Yamphu Rai villagers of Nepal, she shares wholeheartedly in a way of life where thin places exist without need of didactic proof.

If you've hiked up the Arun valley, perhaps en route for Makalu base camp, or higher, you've probably met Yamphu Rai, but you are most unlikely to have gained the insights Armbrecht offers here.

Thin Places was the first book I picked off the stack when lured on to the judging panel for the 2009 Banff Mountain Festival book awards. Nepal and the aid industry are familiar territory and Armbrecht's mix of intimately engaged study and search for connection with people and land looked right up my street, even though it probably raised the eyebrows of her professional colleagues. It's certainly not a work of academic detachment.

I wasn't disappointed – at least for the first two-thirds of the book, and then it started to fall apart, along with the author. For all the personal baggage she eventually unloads on the reader, Armbrecht the anthropologist is a questioning and clear-eyed observer. The Nepal section was genuinely insightful, particularly the portrayal of the hard and often lonely lives of the women in these hill villages; the role of the shamans and their spirit journeying is told in fascinating and affecting detail.

However, the second theme of the book, Armbrecht's personal search (does even she really know for what?) becomes increasingly distant from the first. We're back in the USA now, Armbrecht's marriage is falling apart and the narrative descends into a kind of desperate road trip. 'Home is not a place we ever reach.' It's a pretty bleak conclusion, unless you can shrug it off in Blind Boy Fuller/Robert Crumb style as 'Keep on Truckin'.

For all its faults, I still think *Thin Places* was the most original of the works before the 2009 Banff book jury. It's one of the few entries that I could happily pick up again, though I know that eventually Armbrecht's self-absorption would become too much.

Stephen Goodwin

Murder in the High Himalaya
Jonathan Green
Public Affairs, 2010, pp271, £15.99

Murder in the High Himalaya tells the story of the killing of 17-year-old Kelsang Namtso, a novice nun who was shot dead by Chinese border guards in 2006. There was a lot of publicity surrounding her death, much of it contradictory. This book is an attempt to give a factual account of those events.

For most of the Tibetans who attempt the journey to India, the 'escape' is a pilgrimage to see the Dalai Lama. Many return to Tibet afterwards. In late September 2006 a group attempted to cross the Nangpa La near Cho Oyu. Some made the brutal traverse, others were captured by the PAP, the Chinese border guards, and one, Kelsang, was shot dead. Unusually all this was witnessed by several climbers from the base camp at Cho Oyu.

Green adopts the structure that worked so well in Galen Rowell's *In the Throne Room of the Mountain Gods*, alternating chapters from the westerners' point of view with those from the Tibetans'.

The 'Tibetan' chapters lead up to the escape and give us a swift overview of Tibetan life under the Chinese. By the time we reach the route over the Nangpa La we have become familiar with the main characters. So it is rather moving when, in a passage reminiscent of Younghusband's 1905 military expedition, there is the account of the nuns using pills which had been blessed and pictures of the Dalai Lama to ward off the Chinese bullets. We follow the harrowing tale of the survivors' descent into Nepal and the sickening torture of the captured refugee Jamyang. The errors of topography or orientation slightly impede the flow of the story; Green has the refugees re-crossing the Nangpa La while fleeing, as the captives are dragged off from the climbers' base camp to idling trucks nearby. (In 2006 there was no road closer than several hours' walk from the camp.) These are probably editorial oversights.

In the alternate chapters Green maps the growing paranoia of Luis Benitez, the western guide who sent the story by satellite before he thought through the consequences and how he was going to leave Tibet should the Chinese connect him with the story. This part too is well told, though Green does seem rather down on the commercial operators who exhibit 'the great evil of our age, cynicism... they secretly disdain their Chinese hosts but outwardly act as apologists for them'. (And I thought that it was only journalists who were like that!)

Unfortunately for a supposedly factual account, one detects an underlying Sinophobia paired with a romantic attachment to all things ancient, especially ancient Tibetan. Examples of the former: the new railway to Lhasa is 'a brazen statement of China's will…'; 'The Chinese are fed a steady diet of propaganda'; the Chinese 'appeal to greed over human rights'; their Olympic propaganda recalls that of the Nazis. Meanwhile the Tibetans are imbued with an ancient sagacity: Westerners call it Everest, but the 'Tibetans, without measuring instruments, already knew the peak's dominant status, they simply called it Qomolangma, Goddess Mother of the World'. Yes, that is what you see if you do an undiscerning internet trawl. Actually a little further investigation would have suggested the original meaning of Chomolungma (Green uses the Chinese spelling for this Tibetan word) has been debated for decades if not longer, and may actually be irretrievably lost. My favourite translation is Gary McCue's (*Trekking in Tibet*, 1999) quoting Asian studies scholar Edwin Bernbaum's interesting 'Lady Immovable Good Cow'.

In other passages those historic folks are just better than the modern ones; for example Messner's 'spiritual quest' and Hillary and Tenzing's 'quiet nobility' are contrasted with modern 'rampant egoism'. A little more study might take some of the gloss off his characters. When the Chinese opened up the north side of Cho Oyu in 1987, Green says this led directly to the commercialisation of the peak and violence. The example he gives of this in 1989 concerned two teams that were, a) not commercial expeditions (i.e. those with guides and clients), and b) were operating on the Nepalese side of the hill, not the Tibetan. He seems to have been reading Ed Hillary's intemperate rant about modern commercial trips, and doing so uncritically. According to Green, commercial guiding outfits are known as the 'brotherhood of the rope'... and they watch out for each other in the lawless frontier governed by the almighty dollar. This is news to me, and rather begs the question just how much does Green actually know about the mountains? And in what way does this develop the story of Kelsang?

I think the relevance of these passages to Kelsang is the implied culpability of the Westerners, who are accused of appeasement in the face of the human rights tragedy unfolding in Tibet, of which Kelsang's story is one small but highly visible part. But if we are to trust Green's judgment, we need to believe the accuracy of his reporting. Here I have a problem.

Green likes to attribute to his characters states of mind that cannot be known: she 'was overcome with a greying melancholy... half-formed memories of her family'; ...the water felt silky and comforting in the darkness'. I don't much care for that kind of assumption in a factual account, unless it is a direct quotation. But while not provable, these statements may not be actually untrue. One can even excuse hyperbole on grounds of cultural difference: 'On the high passes... there is no law or morality' and the east face of Everest 'knifed up into the jet stream more defiant and lawless than ever'. Green is fond of his lawlessness.

There are however, several statements that are precisely incorrect. Here is a small selection of the factual errors: Green says that 'the only Westerner to have successfully crossed the Nangpa La is the Swiss photographer Manuel Bauer', in 1995, (The Cho Oyu first ascensionists crossed the pass in 1954); and about Russell Brice's climb of the North East Ridge, he says: 'No one had attempted the route before.' (Oh please DO read some history). 'The Nangpa La is a keyhole pass between two 8000m peaks.' (And some geography too.) 'The crevasses on the Nangpa La are a thousand feet deep.' (And some glaciology while you are at it.)

In the final pages Green at last discloses the aim of his book: after a meeting with the Dalai Lama, he takes the great man's advice to 'simply tell the truth'. Actually I quite like that, unpacking the hidden agenda at the end. It recalls Jim Perrin and his moral coercion trick; telling his readers they have wasted their time reading so far if they disagree with him. I don't disagree with Jonathan Green, it is important to tell the truth, and in parts his book works well. But is it the simple truth?

As with all things Tibetan, telling the truth is anything but simple. There are more than two sides to this story, and everyone seems to have a vested interest, and their own version of the story to propagate. So, perhaps a little inaccuracy here doesn't affect the main line of the story, or, does it? I would like to say this is an important book, it is just that if the fact checking on the easy things is so slack, what about the hard things? Has he made as many mistakes about China and Tibet as he has about mountains? I don't know, because that is not an area I know much about, but I don't trust his accuracy.

Verdict? What should be an important book is marred by sloppy regard for the facts.

Victor Saunders

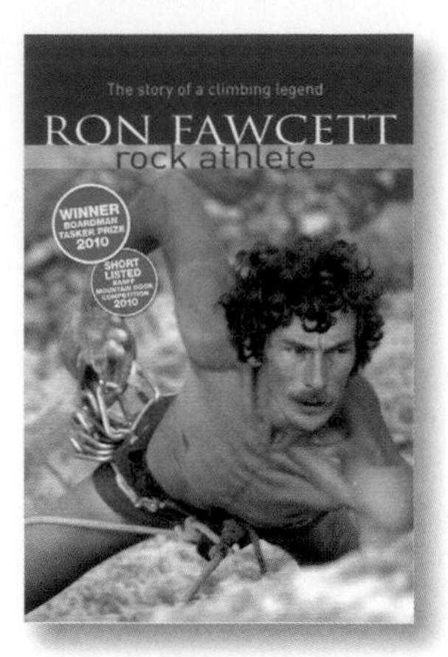

Ron Fawcett: Rock Athlete
Ron Fawcett with Ed Douglas
Vertebrate Publishing, 2010, 240pp, £20

As my old friend and climbing partner Sean Smith puts it, 'I've had two lives. A busy one and a not so busy one.' Back in the days when my own life was not so busy I became a teenage rock climber, obsessed with the sport with an intensity I now find bewildering. So much so, that when it came to make choices about where to go to university, I went to Sheffield. Much of my abundant free time was spent out on the gritstone edges and limestone of the Peak District, with similarly afflicted individuals. It was a different era, with few purpose-built climbing walls, no sports climbing, minimal specialist gear or even clothing. Entry into the sport usually came through some chance meeting with a climber, or on a trip through school or the Scouts. It still felt like a counter-culture activity and you would know by name many of the people on a crag at any given time. All that was set to change.

Arguably, no one individual did more to bring about that change than Ron Fawcett. He was quite simply a climbing phenomenon and for a number of years through the late 70s and early 80s was everywhere, putting up new routes and adorning the pages of the world's climbing media. He even starred in a TV series, entitled, of course, *Rock Athlete*.

Now, many years after his climbing heyday Ron and the journalist Ed Douglas have teamed up to produce a biography detailing his incredible life. From humble beginnings in Embsay, near Skipton, to becoming one of the best rock climbers in the world is quite a journey and Ed has done a great job in capturing Ron's voice. It is a gentle and warm read that comes across like listening to someone reminiscing over a pint in front of a roaring pub fire. Quite rightly, *Rock Athlete* was the winner of the 2010 Boardman Tasker Award for Mountain Literature.

Within a couple of years of starting climbing Ron was putting up difficult new routes and soon began a significant climbing partnership with Pete Livesey. Livesey is widely credited with bringing scientific training techniques to climbing in the UK and was obviously a huge influence on Ron and the way he pursued the sport. His approach is best described as seriously hard graft. While he was obviously very talented, it was his drive, dedication and determination that set him apart. The sheer volume of training and difficult climbing he undertook at his peak is simply staggering.

It was all too much in the end – the obsession ran its course – Ron dropped from the public-eye and for a while became involved in the then rapidly evolving sport of paragliding. Later he became a dad and more recently a veteran fell runner. By the end of the narrative he has come full circle and his love of climbing is rekindled.

It has not all been plain sailing, as you would imagine. Ron was a pivotal figure in enabling athlete-climbers to make a living from the sport, but he made no fortune himself, as rock climbing was then merely on the cusp of becoming the consumer-driven activity it is today. At times money was tight. Nor has Ron been lucky in love, and with two marriages behind him has had his share of heartache. The separation from his second wife – who left him for another woman – resulting in them sharing custody of their children for a time was obviously particularly painful. However, the girls ultimately moved back with Ron full-time and he has been a devoted father to them. Not unexpectedly, a few mates die climbing on the way and others succumb to illness. His own list of falls, fractures and injuries are hardly insignificant either. However, there are few traces of bitterness about any of these misfortunes.

Ultimately, what I took away from this book was something I had already realised when as a shy young man I would say 'hello' at the crag and then watch with a mixture of awe and admiration as Ron did what he does best. Here is a decent, ordinary, down-to-earth man with an extraordinary talent who has led a remarkable life. Thanks to Ron, Ed and the people at Vertebrate for sharing it all with us.

Simon Yates

Thirty Men and a Girl
Elizabeth Parry
*Allegra, 2010, pp423, £18**

Music dominated the life of Elizabeth Parry but mountains and memories of her adventures in the Alps became a lasting backdrop to her life as a singer and opera impresario. *Thirty Men and a Girl* is less radical than the title suggests; the name was chosen to introduce the forces concert party that toured the Middle East during World War II. As the girl in question and soprano soloist with the staff band of the Royal Army Medical Corps, Parry was voted a Forces Sweetheart. After the war she launched and ran the Wigmore Hall Lunch Hour Concerts and had a distinguished career with the English Opera Group formed by Benjamin Britten. She then established her own touring company, the London Opera Players, taking live opera on tour to schools and audiences with more than 3000 performances over half a century.

Her memoirs are detailed, largely drawn from her diaries, and mountains have hardly a mention before page 328 when Parry, then aged 40, developed a passion for climbing them.

Now approaching her nineties she looks back on the time her family spent 21 successive years on holiday in Zermatt, staying at the Monte Rosa Hotel. Mountains were there to admire or to ski down and when friends invited her to climb the rocks of the Riffelhorn she hesitated, claiming she had 'no head for heights'. Parry soon developed one and began studying the sport at a Mountaineering Association evening class in St John's Wood. A rock climbing apprenticeship in the Dolomites with the guide Celso Desgasper, 'heels down, stand well away from the rock', and she graduated to a traverse of the Matterhorn, up the Hörnli and down the Italian ridge. A late starter to the sport, she went through several seasons 'in a sort of climbing frenzy', always modest about her achievements; holding her guide when a hold broke and he plunged into space, a tight rope on the Knubel Crack, robbed by bandits in the Hakkari mountains of south-east Turkey and, as confidence grew, her amazement at including a traverse of the Weisshorn and both the Peuterey and Innominata ridges of Mont Blanc in her list of successes. In 1961, Parry joined the Ladies Alpine Club and is still an AC member.

It has clearly been a rich and fulfilled life but, for the girl with 30 men, there came a poignant wartime truth; the only man she had ever wanted to marry, a soldier in the Parachute Regiment, was killed at Arnhem.

Ronald Faux

* Allegra, Broadmeade Copse, Westwood Lane, Wanborough, Guildford, Surrey, GU3 2JN

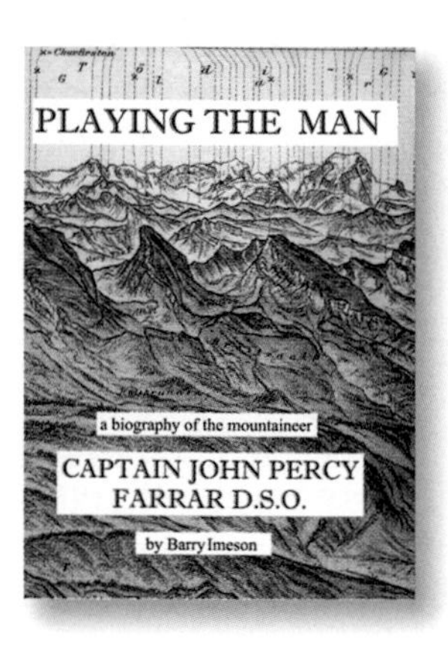

Playing the Man: a biography of the mountaineer Captain John Percy Farrar D.S.O.
Barry Imeson
*Loose Scree, 2010, pp245**

When Percy Farrar died in February 1929, Julius Kugy described him as 'a true servant of the highest mountaineering ideals' while Geoffrey Winthrop Young said Farrar's was probably the strongest single influence modern mountaineering had known, and as editor of the *Alpine Journal* he had 'kept it at a level of literary and scholarly excellence that could challenge comparison with any more celebrated quarterly'.

Young may have been showing some of the fulsome generosity that was a hallmark of the many obituaries Farrar himself wrote for the *AJ*, but even so he cannot have been far off the mark. Farrar was not only one of the leading climbers of his day, with the ascent of more than 170 mountains to his name, but his energy, enthusiasm and cosmopolitan touch were at the service of the Alpine Club for two decades, including as president (1917-19) and joint editor.

If you are only vaguely aware – or worse, totally unaware – of Percy Farrar's contribution to the AC and the mountaineering world, the good captain would not have been surprised at such historical ignorance. In correspondence with one loyal contributor, he noted how 'very few' used the Club's 'superb library' and added: 'You would be astonished to find what a thundering 'mute pack' the bulk of the members are.'

Barry Imeson, who produces the idiosyncratic *Loose Scree* free magazine, has written *Playing the Man* as a modest attempt to restore Farrar to his rightful place in our collective memory. That Imeson felt the need is demonstrated by his decision to self-publish, however his caution in going for an initial print run of only 250 copies suggests he does not feel the 'mute pack' is over eager for a Farrar biography. And that's a pity; it is potentially an interesting story.

Percy Farrar was born in the same year that the AC was founded; made a fortune in South Africa; fought in the Boer War; locked horns with Arthur Hinks of the Royal Geographical Society in planning the 1920s Everest expeditions; handled complicated family affairs and wayward nieces; all the while cramming his seasons in the Alps from 1881 to 1926, including many first or early ascents.

In 1909 Farrar became Assistant Editor to George Yeld and was elevated to Joint Editor in 1919, the pair retiring together in 1926. As T S Blakeney observed in his study of 'The "Alpine Journal" and its Editors', it was an open secret that Farrar was 'the real editor' for much of this time (*AJ*80, p120). Forceful and dogmatic, Farrar could also be wonderfully droll and his sparring, recorded here, with former editor William Coolidge, the 'Sage of Grindelwald', and with Hinks is a delight. While Farrar hoped that Everest could be climbed without bottled oxygen, he rejected Hinks's assertion that oxygen was for 'rotters' and noted that: 'Strictly speaking, I do not think that oxygen is any more of an artificial aid than food.'

Playing the Man is not an easy, flowing read; it's a monograph with lengthy quotes in small type and lots of endnotes. At times, particularly when mired in the politics of South Africa or the affairs of the Farrar family, it can be hard going. But for this reviewer at least the toil was amply repaid by insights into the character and editorial tribulations of an illustrious predecessor. With what fellow feeling I read such ostensibly dry lines as: 'The economics of publishing the Journal continued to concern the Club Committee...'

Stephen Goodwin

* *Playing the Man* is available direct from Barry Imeson at his address in the AC Members' Handbook. There is no charge for the book, but recipients are asked to refund the cost of postage.

The Tiger: A True Story of Vengeance and Survival
John Vaillant
Alfred A Knopf, USA, 2010, pp329, published in the UK by Sceptre, £18.99

John Vaillant's true tale of a man-eating tiger prowling the snow-wrapped forests of Russia's Far East and the men hunting the killer down contains all the elements of a timeless story of man against the wild. From *Beowulf* to *Jaws*, monsters have besieged human towns, and heroes have killed those monsters. In *The Tiger: A True Story of Vengeance and Survival* Vaillant's monster is the Siberian, or Amur, tiger, the largest of all the big cats. In the final years of the exhausted 20th century this animal stalks a post-Soviet landscape whose inhabitants need no introduction to suffering and struggle.

There is no mountaineering in *The Tiger*, but as with his previous book, *The Golden Spruce*, Vaillant inhabits the close-to-the-bone frontier lands that enthral adventure climbers. The connections were acknowledged at the 2010 Banff Mountain Festival where *The Tiger* received a Special Jury Award. John Porter, one of the book judges, described it as 'a book that explores the many levels on which man is losing the natural balance that once existed with human society and the animal kingdom.' As the pages of the *AJ* testify – this volume included – mountaineers know themselves privileged when they come upon the tracks of a snow leopard and are ever hopeful of seeing the beast itself. In the case of Vaillant's big cat, seeing the tracks would be more than enough.

The book tells the story of an animal that appears to be motivated by fury against men. Normally tigers avoid contact with people in Russia: they have learnt that men carry guns. But this creature patiently stalked his victims. By eating his kills, the tiger eradicated their remains. He even demolished several buildings with rabid ferocity. Vaillant's thesis is that the tiger was maddened by persecution. Its corpse, when eventually examined, bore witness in wounds to a lifetime's pain: he 'had been shot with literally dozens of bullets, balls, and birdshot'.

Post-perestroika, the collapse of the area's state-run logging industry led to a steep increase in poaching. A tiger corpse could fetch a high price across the border in China. In the 1990s Inspection Tiger was set up to control the poaching, and it is the unit's senior inspector, Yuri Trush, who is charged with the task of hunting down the rogue man-eating tiger. Trush makes an impressive hero and Vaillant doesn't disguise his admiration for this principled and brave man. He describes Trush in similar terms to the tiger itself: 'Trush's physicality is intense and often barely suppressed... His fists are knuckled mallets, and he can break bricks with them.' Trush takes his team of men and dogs into the mid-winter forest to track the animal on foot. The reader knows a showdown has to be coming and neither the facts of what happened nor Vaillant's narrative disappoint.

By this stage the animal Trush was tracking was wounded, harassed and hungry. It may have been in trouble, but it was still dangerous. Vaillant wants to remind his readers how to feel real fear for an animal in the wilderness. Like so much that was once wild and terrifying, tigers have been tamed in the western imagination. We are most likely to see them caged by zoos or our television screens. Vaillant goes all out in his efforts to make us tremble before this predator: he compares the creature and its body parts to no less than a pit bull, meat hooks, stilettos, an industrial refrigerator, a velociraptor, maces, a boxer, surgical tools, the tail fin of an airplane, a saltwater crocodile and a basketball team. While the reader has to share his 'wonder at our strange fortune to coexist with such a creature', there's a point at which this blazon, unfolding in the space of two pages, ceases to evoke the sublime and instead becomes funny. More effective is the image of tigers hunting along the Russian seashore under cover of fog, swimming into the Bikin River and crawling into fishermen's boats.

Vaillant delivers a heroic conflict, and yet the tiger is not top predator in the Russian forests. Only 450 of these animals remain. Knowing this, we have to ask, between the townspeople and the big cats, who is really under siege? The true success of Vaillant's story lies in its nuance. Trush is a reluctant tiger hunter. He currently works to protect wildlife within a newly created federal park. Though his park is under-funded and surrounded by lawlessness, Trush remains determined: 'Nature has decided there should be a tiger here,' he declares. 'Hope dies last.' For the space of Vaillant's story the tiger is the monster threatening the townspeople's lives. It's a story that makes sense to us on a mythic, visceral level, but reality is darker: not tigers but political upheavals have made life in the Russian wilderness a fight for survival.

Kathleen Palti

Grasping for Heaven: Interviews with North American Mountaineers
Frederic V Hartemann and Robert Hauptman
McFarland, 2010, pp264, US$35

This book is exactly what the subtitle says; the interviewees include Pete Athans, the late Christine Boskoff, Carlos Buhler, the late Charles Houston, Jim Wickwire, Sharon Wood and a dozen more. Interestingly the authors have included three historians, Elizabeth Hawley, Maurice Isserman, and Audrey Salkeld – Audrey being the only real 'foreigner' in the pack, given that Jamling Tenzing Norgay lived for 10 years in New Jersey.

The question-and-answer interviews have been only lightly edited, betraying the interviewee's voice and manner in a way that is often lost in the more interpretative, selective quotes style of most newspaper or magazine interviews and biographies. Climbers who have been interrogated by Hawley in Kathmandu will certainly recognise her sharp tone as she parries Hauptman's occasionally ill-informed questions.

The most interesting interviews were of those climbers I knew least about, such as Christine Boskoff who took over the company Mountain Madness after founder Scott Fischer perished on Everest in 1996. Christine herself was killed in an avalanche in China in 2006 along with Charlie Fowler.

Maybe it's a transatlantic divide, but the downside of this book for me was the ingratiating style of Hauptman's questioning, finding it 'an extremely rewarding privilege to speak with these glorious people'. Steady on, they're only climbers!

That apart, the answers do a good job in fleshing out the lives of 15 significant mountaineers and three 'historians' – though Elizabeth Hawley prefers to be known as a 'chronicler'.

Stephen Goodwin

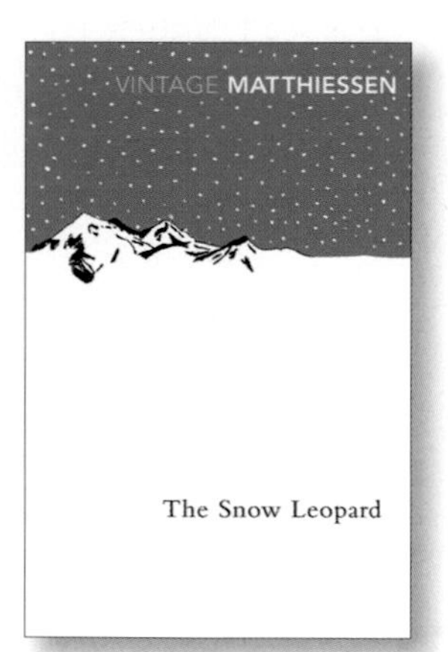

The Snow Leopard
Peter Matthiessen (new introduction by Richard Mabey)
Vintage 2010 (first published in UK by Chatto & Windus 1979) pp328, £8.99

Curiosity drew me to this re-issue of Peter Matthiessen's 1970s' classic. What would Richard Mabey, the UK's pre-eminent 'nature writer' of today make of the work of an American writer in a similar field a generation or more ago? I ended up reading not just Mabey's perceptive new introduction but the whole book once again.

Matthiessen's earnest attempts at self-analysis in the course of his odyssey to the Crystal Mountain in Nepal leave Mabey feeling in need of some spiritual porters. He cannot follow the author through his 'convolutions of Buddhist theory'. And in this Mabey cannot be alone. 'I understand the words, though not always their meaning,' he says.

My guess is that most of the many thousands who have read *The Snow Leopard* – often in the first flush of a love affair with Nepal – treated Matthiessen's deeper philosophical passages as they would, say, the exotic detail of a Mandala or a Persian miniature. Appreciation of the beauty of the whole does not require precise comprehension of each component. Well, that's my excuse.

What carries the book is the sheer luminosity of Matthiessen's description of journeying in the Himalaya. Ten years since I first read it, *The Snow Leopard* still retains a magical, dreamlike quality, punctuated by George Schaller's blunt deflators. (Schaller was the biologist Matthiessen accompanied.) The 'dream' is actually accentuated by the passing of time. Matthiessen's observations of 1973 are no longer the reality of Nepal, at least not in the social sphere. Landscape is relatively constant, though viewed from within greater insulation by today's traveller. And is there about the whole cast of Matthiessen's masterpiece an innocence now lost? Have we, as mountain tourists, destroyed that which we profess to love?

As for the snow leopard, the earthly part of this quest, Matthiessen doesn't get so much as a glimpse of one. 'Have you seen one? No, isn't that wonderful!' he answers his own rhetorical question. The pilgrim has made peace with his demon of desire. As Mabey says: 'Even a materialist can take comfort in this negation of hubris, in its acceptance of the world-as-it-is.'

Thirty-five years ago the snow leopard was an almost mythical beast. Today it is a staple of BBC documentaries and magazine photo spreads (though numbers continue to decline perilously). We think we know this cat. But the magic of the snow leopard, as Matthiessen experienced on the cold hills above Shey Gompa is more elusive than ever. For the last three years I have been pencilled in to the programme of Mountain Kingdoms to lead a trek to Upper Dolpo and Shey Gompa. Long and expensive, the trek has not attracted enough clients to be viable. Not only have I not had a chance to watch for a snow leopard, I haven't even had an opportunity to tread in Peter Matthiessen's footsteps.

'Isn't that wonderful!'

Stephen Goodwin

Climbers' Club Guides to Pembroke
Vol 3 Range East: Stack Rocks to Hollow Caves Bay by Gary Gibson,
Vol 4 Range East: Saddle Head to St Govan's by Gary Gibson, *Climbers' Club, 2011, pp334,342, £20*

Now, I must declare an interest at the outset. I am a member of the Climbers' Club. (I would like to say a long standing member, but smutty *double entendres* aside and given the miracles of modern medicine that would be a far-fetched claim.) In fact I have been recently elevated to vice president (with responsibility for communications). That's one hell of an interest. So, with nepotism oozing from every pore I shall proceed with this 'review' and endeavour not to make it read like promo blurb.

In my defence, I'll claim to have been out of the loop as far as the CC is concerned for some years. Years in which the world of guidebook design

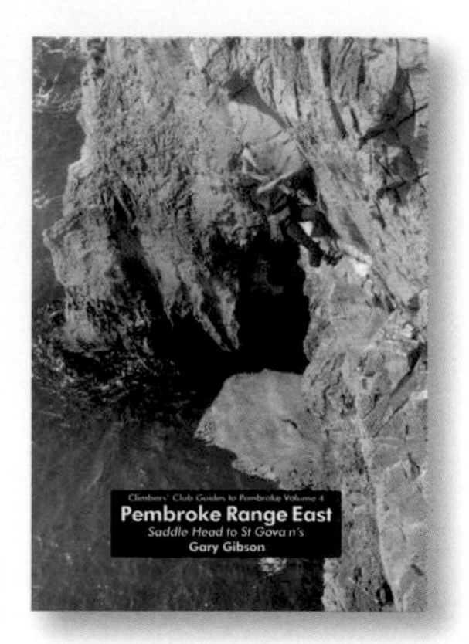

and production has been through a major revolution complete with upheaval, turmoil and casualties and the CC has had its fair share of woes. The catalyst for this cataclysm was the advent of desktop publishing (DTP) which unleashed the power of computing on a printing and design world little changed since the Middle Ages.

At the forefront of this revolution were, of course, the Rockfax team and for years it seemed the rest of the guidebook fraternity either buried their heads in the sand or were playing catch-up. Having said that, perhaps comparing Rockfax to the traditional club guidebook setup was always unfair given the latter's total reliance on large-scale voluntary contributions of time and effort. And as we all know trying to organise climbers is like herding cats.

These days of course, Rockfax is mainstream, almost traditional and it's the conventional guidebooks that are looking radical and nowhere more so than the latest series of guidebooks from the Climbers' Club. Typical of the new-look guides was the magnificent *Lundy* by Paul Harrison in 2008 which helped set the scene for the rest of the series. The latest books, a five-volume definitive guide to the sea cliffs of Pembroke follow suit: superb colour crag shots, detailed maps and inspiring action shots make these 'must-have' guides. Beware when you open them up – it's so easy to lose an hour among the zawns and sun-baked limestone. . . sigh!

If, like me, you're a sucker for climbing history the introduction section is a winner. It's hard to believe that up to 1974 there was only a relative handful of routes on these miles of cliffs. Lakeland heroes Armstrong and Whillance had put up a few gems, Jim Perrin and Colin Mortlock had done a bit and Pat Littlejohn had 'dissed' the place as early as 1970.

This was all to change one Easter weekend in 1980 when the BMC called for an informal meet to Pembroke. Remarkably a whole host of stars turned up as did I – chauffeur and rope-holder to one Steve Bancroft. The group shot on page 32 shows most of the line-up (predictably Pat Littlejohn and Henry Barber were already at the crag) and certainly those young, beaming, slightly hung-over faces would break into ironic laughter if you'd told them that many would go on to become the great and the good of the British climbing establishment! During that long weekend over 150 new climbs were put up, the tide had turned for Pembroke, a handful of routes became thousands.

These latest Pembroke guides showcase the modern trad revolution in British climbing just as the early guides to North Wales and the Lakes proclaimed the talents of Jones, Pigott, Longland, Kirkus, Edwards, Brown and Whillans. The delivery is different of course: the in-your-face colour and youth and flesh of 'now' versus understated good chaps and tweed of 'then'. But no less commitment at the top end, no less risk.

Bernard Newman

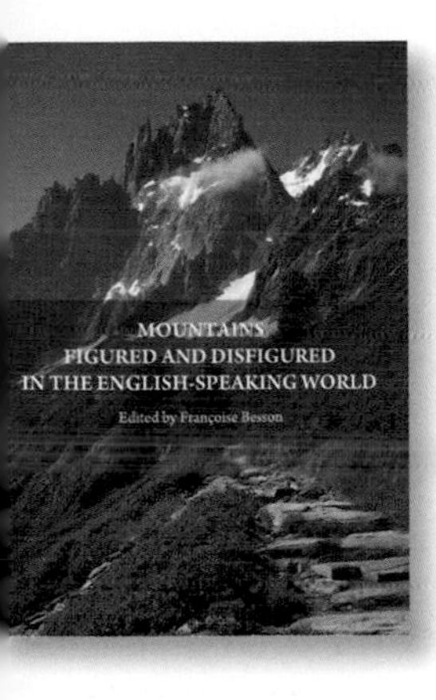

Mountains Figured and Disfigured in the English-speaking World
Edited by Françoise Besson
Cambridge Scholars Publishing, 2010, pp770, £64.99

Victorians in the Mountains: Sinking the Sublime
Ann C Colley
Ashgate, 2010, pp265, £55

Living Waves:
Form & Rhythm in the Art of John Ruskin
An exhibition at Brantwood, Coniston, Aug 2010-January 2011

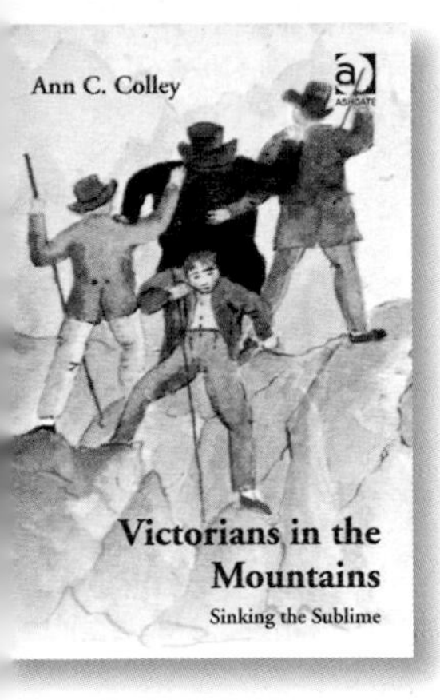

The first two of the titles above are scholarly works; the third is of a modest exhibition at John Ruskin's home in the Lake District, a selection of paintings and drawings celebrating a more impressionistic side to Ruskin the artist than his familiar, precisely observed studies of Venice or Rouen cathedral.

I've grouped the three because Ruskin forms a common link. He could hardly be left out of '*Figured and Disfigured*', a vast work that evokes the representation of mountains in the English-speaking world by poets, painters, philosophers and climbers from the 16th to the 21st centuries. And in *Victorians in the Mountains*, which examines the way the 19th century invasion of tourists and climbers undermined the sense of mountains as sublime landscapes, Ann Colley devotes a lengthy chapter to the influence of climbing on Ruskin's theories of perception.

Ruskin (1819-1900) was an Alpine Club member from 1869 to 1882 when, as his *AJ* obituary put it: 'illness overcame him and shut him off from the outer world' (*vol 20*, p127). Over the years his distaste for AC's 'vanity' and competitive spirit in the mountains softened and he joined after being a guest at a jolly winter dinner in 1868, his qualification being 'Author of the Fourth Volume of *Modern Painters*'. There was certainly no long list of first ascents.

However Colley contends that Ruskin's climbing – 'his physical and kinetic relationship to the mountains over a long period of time' – was essential to his understanding of mountains. She highlights some of his scrambles and glacier excursions around Chamonix and his long day traversing Mont Buet in worsening weather. At 3099m, the Buet was Ruskin's mountaineering high point; his hitherto unpublished account of the 1844 ascent appeared in an article entitled 'Ruskin and the Alps' by A L Mumm in *AJ 32* (328-43). Colley quotes the same diary entry as evidence of Ruskin's immersion in the climb itself, with only a peripheral painterly response. At the summit he found himself in position 'which I did not altogether like – a ledge of snow overhanging a cliff of three thousand feet down'. (Was he standing on a cornice?)

Colley, like Mumm, is trying to make the point that Ruskin was more of an alpinist than we give him credit for. But do they strain too hard? While it is likely Ruskin would have become more of an adventurous pioneer, like his Victorian contemporaries, had he not been held back by over-protective parents, would it really have enhanced his already keen gift for mountain observation? He needed to 'grasp the boulders' in order to study the close detail essential to his way of seeing, but he did not need to set any records to achieve that.

Colley also argues that Ruskin's mountain excursions made him more aware of a weakness in his eyes that caused floaters to interfere with his vision, an imperfection that in a sense gave physical effect to his stated belief that 'nothing is ever seen perfectly, but only by fragments'. This 'vulnerable eye' was paradoxically a privilege for Ruskin for it is an imperfection, says Colley, that 'opens up a space for the imagination and leads one into the spiritual mystery of the landscape'.

The *Living Waves* exhibition at Brantwood demonstrated both the close up intensity of Ruskin's vision and the quality of mystery: a marbled cone shell depicted from above to show its spiral form becomes an abstract suffused with movement, so too does a rendering of snow forms in a pair of mountain studies, probably made in Mornex, Switzerland, in 1862. (Mumm reckoned Ruskin to be first Englishman to draw attention to the beauty of the Alps in winter.)

Living Waves was the subtitle that Ruskin gave to *Deucalion*, his book on geology, and it reflects his conviction that all things are perpetually in motion, with mountains the most dramatic example of that movement. In pencil and watercolour he is able to express this with a fluidity and economy that leave words labouring.

Mountains Figured and Disfigured... is not a book many climbers will be packing to the Himalaya, not unless they can afford an extra porter and expect to spend a month snow-bound. Its 770 pages comprise 56 essays and papers, most of them presented at a conference at the University of Toulouse-Le Mirail and Gavarnie in October 2007. Not surprisingly, French pyreneists have a strong showing among the poets, novelists, academics and mountaineers who have contributed to this multi-faceted work.

Ruskin is the sole subject of an essay by Laurence Roussillion-Constanty, a lecturer in English at Toulouse, who tells us that during the time Ruskin spent in sight of Mont Blanc he did not just look at the mountain. He used his observation of it to build a rigorous appreciation of nature, art and religion, finding inspiration for his philosophy of art and giving it its original shape.

He is also one of three English artists – along with William Gilpin and J M W Turner – deployed by Malcolm Andrews, professor of Victorian and visual studies at the University of Kent, in an essay entitled 'The Emotional Truth of Mountains' – a far higher truth of mental vision beyond the physical facts, as Ruskin contended. Ruskin was championing Turner; for me that 'emotional truth' today is exemplified by the work of Julian Cooper, in paintings of Jannu, the Eiger north face, Kailash and the quarries of Lakeland that go way beyond topography to evoke an interwoven history of man and nature, mystery and, always, movement, those 'living waves' again.

The breadth of *Figured and Disfigured* is too great to be encapsulated here. Some of the essays are in the rarefied realm of the literary theorist, but there is much for anyone interested in literature, art, history or philosophy as inspired or informed by mountains. AC members Robert Macfarlane and Kev Reynolds are among the contributors.

In her introduction, Françoise Besson writes that 'modern man sometimes reads in the mountains' resources, in their mines and parks, a page to be torn off, whereas poets read an alphabet and mountaineers try to meet a dream'. She urges us to listen to the mountains and 'participate no longer in the destruction of wild nature but to be actors in its preservation' – Ruskinian to a fault.

Stephen Goodwin

Presumptuous Pinnacle Ladies:
A selection from the early journals of Britain's first women's rock climbing club
With a history of the Pinnacle Club and notes on the authors by Margaret Clennett
Millrace, 2009, pp176, £13.50

A copy of this book was given to me for Christmas 2009. I already had a full set of the Club's journals, acquired in the early days of my membership during the late 1970s, plus a copy of the Club's history, (*Pinnacle Club: A History of Women Climbing*, Shirley Angell, 1988). Despite having these records of the Club library, I was particularly delighted with my Christmas present. This book is a treasure trove in its own right. It contains around 20 of some of the best pieces of writing from the journals covering the early years of the Pinnacle Club, published in the 1920s and early 1930s.

The Club has been very important to me personally for more than half my life. Until the early 1990s, most of my rock climbing and mountaineering, both in Britain and further afield, was with Club members, who all remain very good friends. It was lovely to re-read the varying pieces after many decades and realise, afresh, that since its foundation, Club members have been doing just what we still do now and recording their experiences for posterity. The invaluable ethos of companionship and shared experiences that comes through in the writing will be familiar to many longstanding members of mountaineering clubs everywhere, not least the Alpine Club.

Each of the articles included in this small and beautifully produced book is highly readable. Some taken from the first journal look back to the years just before the Club was founded and help explain why it was needed by the few enthusiastic women rock climbers of those days. There are articles by the founder, Pat Kelly, and also about her. The pieces range across the British Isles, from the Club's 'home' in Wales, to the Lakes and include some important articles on women's firsts in Scotland. Two stories of the first woman's lead of Crowberry Ridge by *Abraham's Direct Route* and the first traverse of the Cuillin by a party of women are both excellent reads. Another essay discusses and questions the custom for climbers and explorers to claim and record first ascents of various kinds. Some tales in the book are straight narrative and others are in different styles, for example one is like a fairy story and others are satirical pieces, where fun is made of the author herself and other participants in the climbs portrayed. It was also interesting to read the notes on each of the authors, together with the useful concise history of the Club, which sets the overall context very well.

I particularly enjoyed re-reading the description of the 1932 opening of the Emily Kelly Hut in Cwm Dyli under Snowdon, still much loved and cared for by members. Fifty years later, in my first year as Club Secretary, I had great fun coordinating another party to celebrate the half century of our occupation of our Welsh home. All too soon my fellow members will be planning the centenary celebrations for 2021 and I hope they will take on responsibility for producing a second volume of the Club's history, to record activities during the 40 years spanning either side of the turn of the last century.

Meanwhile the Club continues to write and edit a new journal every three years. Perhaps the publishers of this little volume will be producing further editions of the best pieces from the many decades following the extracts in this first book of early tales about the Presumptuous Pinnacle Ladies. There is certainly plenty of material that could be selected from the later journals and re-published for today's readers to enjoy.

Jacqueline Turner

Rising to the Challenge: 100 years of the Ladies Scottish Climbing Club

Helen Steven

Scottish Mountaineering Trust, 2010, pp176, £24

The third of recent SMT history publications, *Rising to the Challenge* is the history of a group of people rather than of a mountain (as seen in the Ben Nevis and Cairngorms books). As with the other national Scottish clubs, the LSCC formed under a boulder, and the intent of long-serving member Helen Steven's book is to bring together the stories that make up the history of the club since its birth in 1908. The compilation of this book

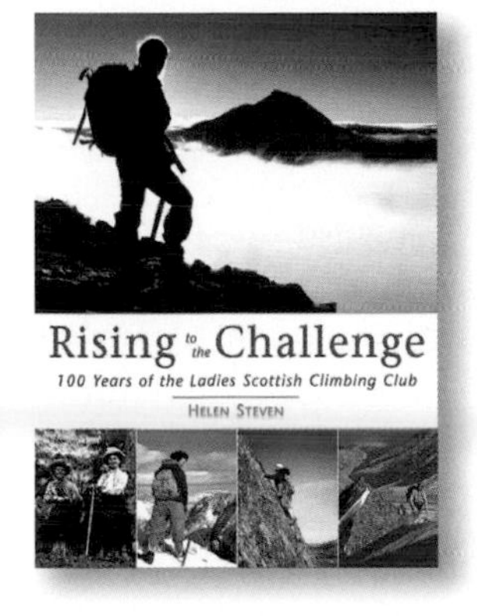

being very much a personal project, she quotes from a variety of sources including newspapers, diary material, journal articles, oral history and her own experience to illustrate the club's first century of activity. The format is similar to that of the other SMT books with copious photos, both historical and contemporary.

Rather than a strict chronology from the club's inception, the chapters of *Rising to the Challenge* are based on activities of the club (walking, skiing, the huts, alpine activity and so on), and within the chapters the anecdotes follow a loose chronology. This structure is both its strength and its weakness: it allows the book to avoid the format of 'this happened, then this happened', but it does not provide a strong narrative linking the within-chapter anecdotes together. The general impression is that the author had a lot of bits and pieces that she thought would be of interest and stitched them in.

Written in the style of an extended journal article and with a small print run, the book has a feel of being written for a specific group rather than a wider audience. The tone of the writing is very much a selected celebration of the club rather than a definitive history, complete with comments intended for insiders to recognise themselves or each other. There is even a recounting of how charades were played out at Hogmanay celebrations. But then there are explanations of mountaineering terms such as 'moving together', which would presumably be unnecessary for members of the mountaineering club.

That doesn't detract from the fact that many strong mountaineers founded and have been members of the LSCC, and fortunately many have left good diaries from which some of the most interesting information has been extracted. An extraordinary number of firsts, including the first all-female expeditions to the Himalaya (1955) and Greenland (1970), and the first female to complete a self-propelled round of the Munros, were accomplished by LSCC members. The current membership, while ageing as much as the other national clubs, is still very active in Scotland, the Alps and Greater Ranges. The book will certainly be a source of inspiration to budding female mountaineers, and of information for researchers looking to add the second X-chromosome to round out their mountaineering histories.

Susan Jensen

Siachen Glacier: The Battle of Roses
Harish Kapadia
Rupa, New Delhi, 2010, pp254, US$25

When thinking back over the history of exploration of the Himalaya, I sometimes imagine a dinner hosted by Harish Kapadia with the spirits of Younghusband, Tom Longstaff, Fanny Bullock Workman and her husband William Hunter, Eric Shipton and Bill Tilman, and a few other select individuals from the Great Game all sat around the table. These guests are among the greatest of the early explorers of the Himalaya and Karakoram. Harish Kapadia, like the famous Belgium detective Hercule Poirot, has called them together to solve a mystery. Like Poirot, Kapadia is rather short, plump and exact, but toughened from years of unexcelled exploration of the region. At this dinner, Kapadia unravels all the mysteries of the 'blanks on the map' that these great explorers had not quite solved. Needless to say, it is a damn jolly evening for like-minded adventurers.

To say that Harish Kapadia is one of the leading authorities on the Indian Himalaya and Karakoram is truly an understatement. For more than three decades through his own books and articles, and as editor of the *Himalayan Journal*, he has provided essential information to anyone hoping to visit the more remote corners of the great ranges in India. For many climbers, the information generates only frustration since so many regions described lie in areas that are restricted or forbidden to foreigners, unless part of a joint expedition with the Indians. His latest book is essential reading for anyone interested in the history of exploration and mountaineering in the Eastern Karakoram of Ladakh, both past and recent, and seeking a fair and comprehensive explanation of the tragic, woeful and costly Siachen War (Siachen means rose in Ladakhi).

There is no aspect of geography, natural history, culture, art, religion, local customs and languages that does not interest Kapadia. However, a new dimension has increased in importance in the past 10 years – conflict and warfare. In November 2000, his son – Lt Nawang Kapadia – was killed in a fire-fight with insurgents in Kashmir. *Siachen Glacier – The Battle of Roses* is dedicated both to his son Narwang and to the soldiers of the Indian Army at Siachen. It is a patriot book, and the arguments set out for the retention of the Siachen with Indian territory are carefully and accurately defended. But for Kapadia, the rights and wrongs are another story, and he is not one to easily allocate blame.

The history of conflict in the region is long and goes back into the times of myth and the great kingdoms of central and southern Asia. Kapadia relates legends from local oral history passed down the Balti inhabitants of invaders from Yarkand. But for many centuries Ladakh was a place for rest and respite for traders before crossing the series of high and dangerous passes linking central Asia to the North, and the rich plains of India to the South. As with many trading centres, tolerance of all religions was a feature of the culture, as it remains today with Hindus, Muslims and Buddhists living together in many areas. But Ladakh is an island in a sea of conflict. To the west is Pakistan Occupied Kashmir (POK), and insurgency in the south and west in the Muslim majority areas of Kashmir is ever likely to flare up. To the north and north-east, there are unresolved border issues with China. Today Ladakh has difficulty concealing its status as a frontier military outpost. There has scarcely been a year over the past six decades when there has been no fighting, hence restricted access to many areas.

> *The Greeks have the perfect word to describe the turmoil in Kashmir, Ladakh and the Siachen – 'oro-politics as Oro means mountains. The armies and the people involved in this are fighting with mountains, about mountains for mountains and in the mountains.*

The 25-year war for the world's longest glacier is rooted in a number of missed opportunities to set boundaries on the true watershed for the Nubra valley. This is the Indian interpretation of an infamous and often repeated phrase that in 1947 set the border from grid point NJ9842 'thence north to the glacier.' At the time of partition in 1946, the geography of the area was still unclear, and no one conceived of a time when it might be fought over. The chance to fix the border at the end of the first Indo-Pak war in 1946-47 and again at the Simla Agreement was missed by Indira Gandhi and Zulfikar Ali Bhutto.

Ironically, climbing and trekking expeditions were the immediate cause for the start of the war in 1985. The ease with which the Siachen could be reached from the Baltoro (compared to the much longer journey from Leh – itself a long journey from central India) meant that climbing expeditions sought permission to go there through Pakistan even after partition. They were actively encouraged by Islamabad to do so and India was slow to protest. Successive expeditions from America, Japan and Austria in the 1970s and early 80s crossed the Bilafond La onto the Siachen, and climbed many of the peaks on both sides of the glacier. The US Defence Mapping agency placed the Siachen with POK in the mid 1970s and thereafter many major atlases accepted 'de facto' that that with so many expeditions travelling into the area through Pakistan, it had become part of Pakistan. Even the air traffic control lines were shown as running from NJ9842 across the Siachen to the East. The point is that this is clearly 'east,' not 'north' as per the agreement in 1947. When Pakistan gave permission to a Japanese Expedition to climb Rimo 1 in 1984, it was 'a peak too far'. It overlooked China and the Karakoram Pass. If this border line was accepted, the road to the Nubra and all of Ladakh was open on two sides.

It is not until late in the book that Kapadia reveals the true theme of the book. It is a subject that has been close to his heart for a number of years, and one that the mountaineering community worldwide would hope to see – the creation of an International Peace Park to encompass all of the Siachen and surrounding area. He is working closely with the Pakistani mountaineering authorities and all of us should join in support. Kapadia summed up the dilemma in his acceptance speech on being awarded the 'Patron's Medal' at the Royal Geographical Society in 2003:

> *We are nations linked by Himalayan geography. Nations, which do not understand and respect geography, are condemned by history. Governments and people of both countries should realise that there is a humanity that binds us together.*

So he concludes with words of hope – almost. When a group of Indian and Pakistani climbers unfurled their flags together on the summit of the Mönch a few years ago, Kapadia comments that one of his companions whispered: 'Raise our Indian flag a little higher.'

John Porter

Challenges for Mountain Regions: Tackling Complexity
Institute of Mountain Research: Man and Environment (ed.)
Böhlau Verlag, Vienna, 2010, pp223, €49

Cruising down sunny Stubaital in a Post bus after a satisfying week's ski touring last spring I was struck by how much this Tyrol valley has changed in the 30 years I've known it. When the kids were small we'd camp beneath old fruit trees on a dairy farm in Neustift; we were there 25 years ago when catastrophic floods forced a night-time evacuation of the site; returning a few years later, the dreamy orchard site had become a swish holiday park with a Billa supermarket on what was once an adjoining meadow; today Stubaital looks like a brash suburb of Innsbruck.

'Tackling Complexity' is the sub-head of this academic book, edited by Axel Borsdorf, Georg Grabherr, Kati Heinrich, Brigitte Scott and Johann Stötter, and the Stubai range exemplifies the tangle of pressures on mountain areas and how we regard and exploit them. At the head of the valley the Stubai glacier is a thriving year-round ski resort (though on the neighbouring Sulztal glacier – separated from the Stubai by the Daunkopf peaks – we'd encountered nobody); both glaciers are retreating and the valley communities have to dam and channel to protect themselves against flash floods and mud slides (old risks perhaps but now seemingly more potent in a warmer climate); then there is all the building in the valley bottom – hotels, holiday homes, commuter homes and all the attendant roads and services. 'Tackling complexity' indeed. On top of all that of course is the effect on the social fabric of Stubaital of so much change and apparent prosperity.

Most mountain inhabitants are not as fortunate as those of the Stubai. Poverty and war is the lot of too many elsewhere – yet more complexity.

Mountains make up a third of the surface area of the world, and while they are home to only a tenth of the world's population they provide more than a third of our resources, from the life-giving rivers that water the plains of India and China, to playgrounds for climbers and skiers. Global warming in the mountains is occurring up to three times faster than elsewhere with all manner of little understood consequences. And since we're too wedded to consumption to make any meaningful attempt at reversing that warming process – even assuming it were possible – we had better get up to speed on understanding change in the mountains, how to adapt to it and mitigate its worst effects.

This is the job of the contributors to *Challenges for Mountain Regions* – their aim being to provide the research data necessary for action to maintain the vital functions of mountains, preserve their rich biodiversity and introduce sustainable economic development to keep communities alive. It is not a book that offers solutions – except in the sense that the search for reliable evidence is an essential precursor to effective action – but a record of the work done by leading research institutes based in Innsbruck. This does, unfortunately, give it a sniff of the self-serving.

Contributors include Harald Pauli, the botantist who took part in the Alpine Club's 'Summits of Learning' conference in 2007, explaining then, as he does here, the work of the Global Observation Research Initiative in Alpine Environments (GLORIA) in tracking the upward migration of plants as the mountains get warmer.

The 'Afterword' goes to Bruno Messerli of the Geographical Institute of the University of Berne. The professor is something of an outsider among the predominately Innsbruck folk, and it is interesting that it is he, who after recounting the decades of effort spent pushing mountains up the international agenda, broaches the dirty business of politics. Preserving the common (i.e. cross-border) goods of the mountains and overcoming common concerns is both a scientific and a political challenge, Messerli points out. 'For us, this means that science will one day be held responsible for both what it did and what it did not do.'

I wouldn't want to misinterpret the professor, who is after all an AC honorary member, but this apparent injunction to his peers to stand up and be counted, put me in mind of the NASA climate scientist James Hansen who giving evidence to the Ratcliffe coal trial in 2010 said he wouldn't want his grandchildren to say to him: 'Pa, you understood what was happening, but you never made it clear.'

Stephen Goodwin

The Cairngorms: 100 Years of Mountaineering
Greg Strange
Scottish Mountaineering Trust, 2010, pp400, £27.50

Ben Nevis: Britain's Highest Mountain
Ken Crocket & Simon Richardson
Scottish Mountaineering Trust, 2009, pp416, £27.50

At first glance these two handsome productions from the Scottish Mountaineering Trust appear to be companion volumes – histories of the two most testing winter climbing grounds in Britain. But although, spine-on, they make a good-looking pair on the bookshelf, in the authors' approaches to their mountainous subjects, the books are of a different flavour.

Ben Nevis was trailed in the last *AJ*. It is the second edition of Ken Crocket's authoritative 1986 history of 'man's interaction with the mountain which is not only the highest in Britain but one of the most ferocious in Europe for weather changes'. For the much revamped 2009 edition, Crocket's research and story-telling is augmented by the expertise of Simon Richardson, author of the 2002 SMC climbing guide to the Ben, *AJ* Area Notes correspondent and insatiable new route activist.

The Cairngorms is an exhaustive – some might say 'exhausting' – history of climbing in the massif, from its beginnings in March 1893 when William Douglas (he of the Douglas Boulder at the foot of Tower Ridge on the Ben) and John Gibson reached the summit plateau of Lochnagar via *Black Spout Left Hand Branch* to the end of January 1993 and second ascents of *Pinnacle Grooves* (VI, 7) and *Winter Face* (VI, 6) on the same mountain. It has the feeling of a monumental labour of love by Greg Strange, also a veteran of SMC climbing guides, and runs to a similar 400-page length as the Ben book. But Strange has not ranged quite so wide.

Crocket begins the Ben book with a chapter on 'early travellers', including John Keates who after his 1818 ascent declared: 'It was not so cold as I expected – yet cold enough for a glass of Whiskey (sic) now and then.' There are sections on the summit Observatory, the SMC hut, whisky distilling, fell running, geology, mapping, natural history and Gaelic place names, though the climbing still dominates. The impression is of a lot more going on in this book; it's concentrated, just as it is on the mountain itself, and more cosmopolitan.

Common to both books is a wonderful range of photos: black and whites of the likes of Tom Patey, Bill Brooker, Jimmy Marshall et al, through to colour of Andy Nisbet, Dave MacLeod, Andy Turner, and so on. Also both make clever use of page margins for portraits, pullout quotes and diverting nuggets such as the progression of ice-axe design to today's acutely bent, leashless tools.

The margins are less busy in *The Cairngorms*. The ice-axes, for example, are one of the bonuses of the Ben book and have no equivalent in the other. Perhaps it is just as well, for a weakness of *The Cairngorms* is that it ends – except for a brief postscript – in 1993. That makes a tidy century for Strange, but it misses almost two decades of development, not merely of tools themselves, but of the evolution of technically extreme climbing so well documented by Richardson in respect of Ben Nevis.

Strange's narrative though has a different appeal, immersing the reader in a world of long walk-ins, bothy weekends and exploration of lonely granite crags. What? 'Long walk-ins… lonely crags? This isn't the Cairngorms scene familiar to most climbers today – the hordes that do the quick trot in to the Northern Corries from the ski resort carpark. No, for Strange the 'Golden Years' were 1950 to 1960, with Malcolm 'Mac' Smith as the central motivator.

Back then, most exploration was still from the Braemar side of the range. However, as Strange explains, in 1960 a new road was built to the foot of Coire Cas. 'At a stroke the Northern Corries of Cairngorm had become the most accessible high mountain terrain in the country.' Although 20 years later Strange would be active in the campaign to halt the spread of ski infrastructure on Cairngorm, at the time the ski road did not rankle that much ' since most skiers… had, by necessity, been hill-walkers and climbers anyway'.

Strange tells the Cairngorms story with great affection; it may not be compartmentalised as in the Ben book, and require a little more reader application, but from the moment you arrive, metaphorically, with Strange at Derry Gates you sense the magic that has drawn him again and again to the deep glens, dark corries and granite cliffs of the 'Gorms.

Stephen Goodwin

Flakes, Jugs & Splitters:
A Rock Climber's Guide to Geology
Sarah Garlick
Falcon Guides, 2009, pp212, US$17.95

'Why does Hueco Tanks have so many huecos?… Why can't you climb at Red Rocks after it rains, even if it's dry?… Why is the Eiger falling down?' Questions, questions… And Sarah Garlick has the answers. *Flakes, Jugs & Splitters* won the 'Mountain Exposition' award at the Banff Mountain Festival in 2009 (the title alone was worth some kind of prize.) As jury member Jon Popowich put it: ' This innovative new book sheds light on the science behind the stone that supports our fingertips.'

Garlick, rock climber and research geologist, has tapped into a new vein here. So far as I know this is the first practical guide devoted to the stuff we climb on. After taking us through plate tectonics and a climbers' guide to geological time (Baffin Island's granite emerged 1,800 million years ago, FitzRoy's pluton a mere 18 million years ago, not so long before first humans at 5 million, and so on) the meat of the book is in Q&A format.

I wish I'd had this book when I visited Utah four years ago. Then I could have looked up: 'Why is Indian Creek so splitter?' The answer is nowhere near as snappy as the question unfortunately, and there is no room for it here. Suffice to say I would have been wiser, though no more able to climb those perfect crack lines.

The downside of the book for most *AJ* readers is that it is primarily focused on rock climbing areas in North America – 114 pages compared to 31 for the rest of the world. The UK gets one paragraph, on the mysteries of gritstone. Garlick expresses the hope that her example will be followed with similar guides for Europe, Asia and South America. It's a nice idea. Rock is our medium yet how much do we really know about it? Can you answer those first three questions even? Me neither. Want to know the answers? Buy the book.

Stephen Goodwin

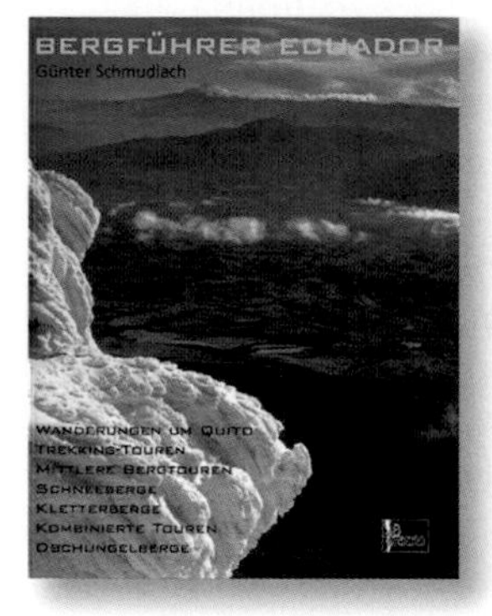

Bergführer Ecuador
Günter Schmudlach
Panico Alpinverlag, 2009, pp328, npq

Edward Whymper, through his famous book *Travels among the Great Andes of the Equator* (1891) lured mountaineers and travellers to fresh territory. Since then the high Andes of Ecuador have been visited by climbers from everywhere. Now, with the latest edition of Günter Schmudlach's *Bergführer*, visitors have one of the most comprehensive guidebooks ever written. The text is complemented by 23 b&w photos and line drawings, 32 sketch maps and 107 colour illustrations.

The Swiss author set himself an ambitious programme for the book: hiking, rock-climbing, trekking, glacier tours, mountain tours and jungle tours. He has methodically covered each of the 80-odd peaks of Ecuador, from peaks of 2900m to 6310m Chimborazo, including history, access, transportation, charts, gear and also a difficulty rating (*schwierigkeit*) attached to each climb or hike. The wealth of text is rounded out by appendices, notes and indexes.

The German text is not difficult to follow. With this third edition, this a guidebook destined to be immensely useful and, one hopes, to command imitation – in English and other languages.

Evelio Echevarría

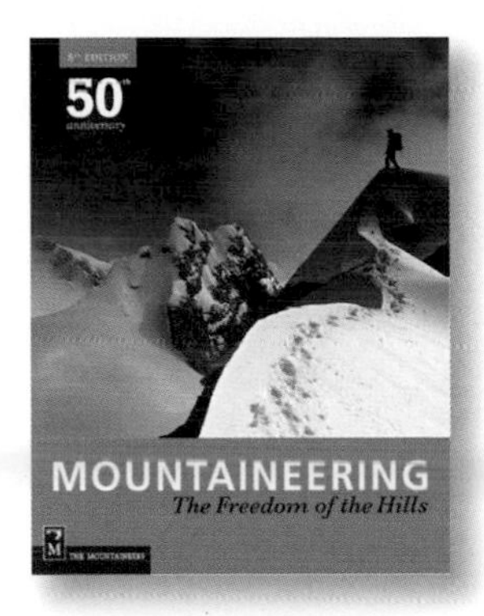

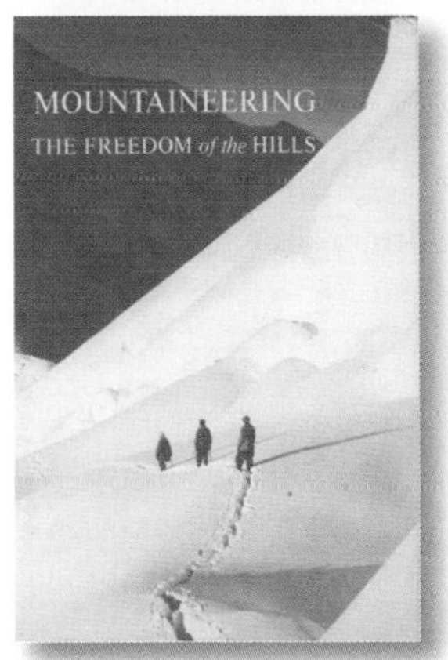

Mountaineering: The Freedom of the Hills, 8th edition
Mountaineers Books, 2010, pp600, US$39.95 hardbound, US$29.95 paperbound

The first time I came across this book, it was the 'Freedom' sub-title that caught my eye in a second-hand store in Carlisle. I was expecting some literary musings on the lines of *Ascent* and was a bit disappointed when it turned out to be the mammoth instructional tome. A wiser man would have acknowledged he had much to learn and not so quickly pushed it back on the shelf.

Ask any North American about *Freedom* and they'll tell you it's their 'bible'. This 8th edition marks 50 years of one the most comprehensive of all mountaineering manuals (1960 first edition cover shown lower left).

It was conceived to meet the needs of climbers in the Pacific North-west who had found the advice of European texts hardly adequate to their wild and complex terrain, where even getting to the mountains required a full set of backcountry skills.

Five years after publication of the first edition of *Freedom*, came its nearest UK equivalent, *Mountaineering: From Hill Walking to Alpine Climbing*, by Alan Blackshaw. For many of us, 'Blackshaw' became *our* 'bible', and anything we've learnt since has been picked up 'on the job' as it were. But *Freedom* has lived on as a general instructional work whereas 'Blackshaw' has been succeeded in the UK by more specific training guides, directed at particularly skills and/or obtaining qualifications.

In the 1960s, when we didn't travel so much, large chunks of *Freedom* would have been irrelevant to most UK climbers; much less so today. It is impossible to summarise this deep well of knowledge, there's everything from how to choose your socks, through the merits of racking gear on harness or bandolier, to snow science. There's a certain American earnestness to the text, particularly in the exhortatory 'Leave No Trace' chapter, but also flashes of droll humour, such as:

> *Good navigators are never truly lost – but, having learnt humility from years of experience, they always carry enough food, clothing, and bivouac gear to get them through a few days of temporary confusion.*

More than 600,000 copies of *Freedom* have been sold since 1960 and it has been translated into 10 different languages. It has always been a collegiate production and this 8th edition is the work of a team of 30 active climbers and 'educators'. I can't help but think part of its continuing success lies in that sub-title – added by Harvey Manning, chief editor of the first two editions. It certainly seems to have been the bait for the free spirits who have endorsed this 8th edition, including Timmy O'Neill, John Harlin III and Will Gadd.

Steve House apparently devoured his parent's 3rd edition not long after he learnt to read. Most important was its promise of freedom, says House: Freedom to explore who I am. Freedom afforded by learned skills to explore any mountain wilderness. Freedom to move, to climb.'

Stephen Goodwin

CD: The Bar Room Mountaineers and other climbing songs from Dennis Gray and friends

When Tom Patey died abseiling from a Sutherland sea stack in 1970, mountaineering lost not only one its leading practitioners but also one of its most inspiring balladeers. I saw him several times at the Rowenlea Hotel in Carrbridge, where landlord Jimmy Ross would lock the doors at closing time and allow the proceedings to continue far into the night. Those occasions usually followed exhilarating days on the hill, the two experiences merging into one glorious composite memory.

Those scintillating evenings are now recalled on a CD produced from a tape of a session at the Clachaig Inn in the late 1960s. The tape belonged to Bill Brooker, Patey's long-standing climbing partner and friend, and was retrieved by Dennis Gray who has produced the CD with recording expert Paul Cherry. It's a priceless recording, Patey accompanying himself on accordion and singing no fewer than nine of his songs. He's at exuberant full pitch, combining brilliantly inventive rhymes with a subversive irreverence and unflinching gallows humour.

Patey is mountaineering's Fool, mocking the luminaries of the climbing world without fear or favour, disarming criticism with the brilliance of his wit, while confronting his audiences with climbing's dark side, its readiness to embrace risk and death. He parodies climbing's representation in the media too – there's a song about Joe Brown, the so-called 'Human Fly'; and since I was the butt of several jokes in Tom's climbing articles, I feel relieved to have been spared mention in his lyrics.

Those who do not escape include friends and climbing partners such as Hamish MacInnes, Ian McNaught-Davis, Peter 'Motley' Crew, and the Alpine Club in its entirety, represented by Patey as irredeemably posh and remote from the demotic strands of mountaineering. Singled out for special mention is Chris Bonington, whose early attempts to earn a living from mountaineering are scrutinised in lyrics too scurrilous to be repeated in a family publication like the *AJ*. (The determined reader can find them in Patey's wonderful anthology, *One Man's Mountains*.) In an aside captured on the CD, a voice sounding remarkably like that of our former president is heard to enquire whether one of the songs is libellous. An unmistakeable Hamish MacInnes reassures him: 'Oh no, that's not libel – it's a good one that.'

The quality of the recording can best be described as mixed, since the original was captured on a cassette recorder against the cacophony of a packed house at the Clachaig. Several of the songs are incomplete and one is marred by a tuneless voice singing along close to the tape recorder. Paul Cherry, who re-mastered the recording at his Cotswold Studio, has nonetheless performed a miracle in retrieving the nine songs from a battered C90 cassette, and the rapture of the evening shines through. Patey's family were consulted throughout and gave their consent; his youngest son Michael wrote expressing his delight at hearing his father's voice again for the first time since 1970.

The magic of the Patey recordings is complemented by other songs on the CD, principally performed by Dennis Gray himself at Paul Cherry's studio. Gray has provenance, as he comes from a musical family and sang at the Rowanlea with Patey on several occasions. He is an aficionado of climbing songs – he gave a knowledgeable presentation at the AC in 2009 – and sings numbers by C Douglas Milner, Showell Styles and John Hirst. He also sings several of his own compositions. In short, it's an irresistible package.

Peter Gillman

The CD is obtainable from Paul Cherry, Delly Breach Farm, Whitings Lane, Hailey, Witney OX29 9XG. Email: riffraff@cherry-consulting.co.uk Phone 01993 868087. Cost £11 to UK addresses.

What Goes Around Comes Around
Paintings by Jim Curran, Alpine Club exhibition, 2009

I was going to call this article 'The Recent Art of Jim Curran' but anyone who knows Jim would leap to my defence as the double entendres came howling their way from Sheffield. Or perhaps they wouldn't, which might be worse. Therefore the title refers not only to the exhibition of Jim Curran's paintings, watercolours and prints exhibited at the Alpine Club in late 2009 but also to the whole subject of Jim's art.

In 1959, at the age of 16, Jim entered Ealing College of Art. How did he get there? That he does not know. Nor, apparently, did his friend and fellow student, Adrian Mallett. They just got there in the autumn of 1959 and it all began. Jim is a bit more forthcoming about how he got to Harrison's Rocks at about the same time. He went by car. The two events may seem remote in the extreme but they are inextricably linked as each has informed the other throughout Jim's long and varied career as a painter, climber, mountaineer, writer and film-maker.

To come back to the exhibition (or should it be around?) the paintings exhibited in the Club's gallery were all created within the preceding two years, so they represent a snap shot of Jim's recent artistic activity, rather than a full retrospective display (which is long overdue). The two main series were Harrison's Rocks on the longest wall of the gallery and the Millstone series, based on a few discarded millstones close to Stanage in the Peak District. In both series stone dominates the canvas. It is deeply, reassuringly stony. It has depth and form, not superficial surface colour on blocks and shapes, and that works. Step back from the stone, and forms hold the viewer's eye. It is the shape of the stones, boulders and crags rather than the landscape they occupy that is striking. I know some works have human figures in them but I cannot recall which ones – they are not of importance, the stones are.

The Millstone series is in some way the most successful because it addresses the tension between the natural and the man made, a tension that exists in our landscape to a greater degree than one might appreciate. I made the trip to see Jim's millstones when I spent a weekend with him in Sheffield in October 2009 and was amused to see, just 10 metres away, two lads happily bouldering on the crag. I don't think for a minute they were aware of the millstones on the ground just a stretch from their packs. But Jim is. Jim the artist that is. He misses nothing and the glorious symmetry of the perfectly circular, heavy stones, that no one man could ever lift, stand both in contrast to and in harmony with the gritty crags out of which they were carved and to which they will in the future return. It is the dialogue between what man makes out of nature and what natures does with man's creation that is the underlying subject matter in this series.

Thousands of hours on the gritstone of Derbyshire and the sandstone of Kent breed a familiarity of routes, shapes, holds but also, to the artist, a pattern of intriguing shapes. Jim does not paint what he sees at a glance, but what he scrutinises, draws, criticises. 'Drawing is the basis for everything I do, even writing,' he says, 'Every few years I draw my surroundings at home as an exercise. It's proof of what a good, long, hard stare can do for you.' Painting is an illusion, like film making on one level, but to be a good illusionist you have to be expert in the art of creating your illusion. To be a good artist, in Jim's mind, you have to be able to create and shape your painting to look like what you want it to look like. He cites Rembrandt and Cezanne as examples: 'close up a Rembrandt hand or a Cezanne rock can be a matter of a series of seemingly random brushstrokes. Stand back and examine the effect on the whole and it is a hand, a rock, a face, a sky.' For Jim, Cezanne was the most inspirational of all the artists he has studied and admired since his first lectures at Ealing, and it is not hard to see why. Cezanne broke away from the Impressionists world of diffused light and colour; he explored form and structure in his paintings. Not in a realistic way but in a way that interpreted the landscape and created an illusion of, for example, the Mont St Victoire, which was a subject that absorbed and

8. Jim Curran's *Millstones at Stanage, 2008* (oil on canvas 30ins by 40ins) at his Alpine Club exhibition in autumn 2009.

obsessed him for 40 years.

Cezanne worked critically, he was never entirely satisfied with what he was creating, and to this extent at least Jim mirrors his artistic hero. He too is seldom satisfied with what he has created and works away at a subject again and again, ever more critical, trying to perfect on canvas an illusion of the sandstone of Harrison's or the gritstone crags of Stanage.

The result in the two series of paintings at the Alpine Club was a visiting and revisiting from different angles, in different lights and from differing perspectives the forms and shapes of the stones. That is the power of these canvases. The intensity and density of the stones. And that is why I didn't like so much the watercolours from Spain, not because they are bad but because they have not been subjected to the same, rigorous, critical, even zealous working that have the stones. I'd even go as far as to say that even the millstones did not get such grinding attention to form during their creation.

Anyone who has not seen Jim Curran's recent work should do so. His art is born out of 50 years' experience of the looking, painting, climbing on stone and staring at it with the equipment he learned at Ealing.

Julie Summers

The Boardman Tasker Prize for Mountain Literature

Space constraints in this two-year volume of the *AJ* prevent us following recent practice and reproducing the speeches of jury chairmen for 2009 or 2010, however most of the books shortlisted have been reviewed in either this volume or 2009. The prize of £3000 commemorates the lives of Peter Boardman and Joe Tasker and is given to the author or co-authors of an original work that has made an outstanding contribution to mountain literature. On 17 May 1982 Boardman and Tasker were last seen on Mount Everest attempting to traverse The Pinnacles on the unclimbed north-east ridge at around 8250m. Their deaths marked the end of a remarkable era in British mountaineering.
The winners, shortlists and judges for 2009 and 2010 were as follows:

2009

Winner: **Beyond the Mountain** by Steve House, *Patagonia Books, USA* (*Vertebrate Publishing in UK*)

Others shortlisted:
Cairngorm John by John Allen, *Sandstone Press*
Hooker & Brown by Jerry Auld, *Brindle & Glass, Canada*
The Longest Climb by Dominic Faulkner, *Virgin Books*
Revelations by Jerry Moffatt, *Vertebrate Publishing*
Deep Powder and Steep Rock by Chic Scott, *Assiniboine Publishing, Canada*

Judges: Phil Bartlett, Kym Martindale and Ian Smith

2010

Winner: **Ron Fawcett: Rock Athlete** by Ron Fawcett with Ed Douglas, *Vertebrate Publishing*

Others shortlisted:
No Way Down by Graham Bowley, *Viking Penguin*
The Hut Builder by Laurence Fearnley, *Penguin Books, New Zealand*
Climbing Philosophy for Everyone by Stephen E Schmid, ed, *Wiley-Blackwell*
Unjustifiable Risk? by Simon Thompson, *Cicerone Press*

Judges: Ian Smith, Kym Martindale and Barry Imeson

In Memoriam

The Alpine Club Obituary	Year of Election (including to ACG)
Chris Astill	1985
Patrick (Paddy) Boulter	1972
Roger Childs	1997
Robert (Bob) Creswell	2007
Robin Day	1968
John Edwards	1982
Nawang Gombu	Hon 1998
Alistair Gordon	1993
Alfred Gregory	1952 (Hon 2004)
Eileen Healey	LAC 1947
Mike Hewson	1994
Frederick Hill	1975
Peter Hodgkiss	1988
John Kempe	1952
Erhard Loretan	Hon 2010
James (Joss) Lynam	1970
John Moss	1972
Margaret Munro	LAC 1956
Mary Noake	LAC 1965
Charles (Hamish) Pelham-Burn	1950
Frederick Robert (Bob) Robinson	1968
Balwant Singh Sandhu	2001
Peter Stone	1970
Pat Vaughan	1954
Chris Walker	2006
Alan Wright	1962

As usual, the Editor will be pleased to receive tributes for any of those not included in the following pages.

Chris Astill. *(Smiler Cuthbertson)*

Chris Astill 1956 - 2009

'Chris Astill was the one on Liathach.'

Avalanches in Scotland on 30 December 2009 claimed the lives of three climbers; the news that Chris was one of them slowly entered my brain, cutting like a chainsaw through my feelings. Since Jimmy Jewel had died so many years ago now, I'd promised myself I would not allow myself ever to get hurt again. Some hope!

Chris and his partner Jo had been in the Highlands, over on his favourite north-west coast, as usual over the Christmas period. He had called me to say 'hello' and to ask where he could get snowshoes. He was obviously aware of the great depth of new snow that had come down and it was still falling. I pointed to Martin Moran for the snowshoe advice and asked Chris and Jo to call in again, like last year, on their way back to Derbyshire.

It wouldn't happen. Nearing the top of a gully on Liathach, the avalanche took him down some considerable way. His pal Oliver climbed down and got to him. Although Chris was talking, things were serious and the helicopter rescue was probably minutes, hours, too late, who knows, as he died later that night in Inverness hospital.

I was, and still am, devastated.

'Eyeeup kid, ow's it goin' youth?' The standard Nottingham welcome was always truly meant with real friendship. Chris was that kind of guy, one of the nicest blokes I've known for nearly 40 years. Intellectually always very smart, a neat and determined man and without question a great all-round climber. To me he had no faults, except maybe even for me, being a touch too keen, ready for any escapade: a Scottish winter adventure, that wet rock climb, our South American odyssey to Aconcagua with my clients, Bill, David and Sandra, an Alpine adventure in Chamonix or even a Himalayan sojourn. He was the true all-rounder; one of my best climbing friends.

I first met him when I was a 19 or 20-year-old. When we were both coming through the ranks, grabbing those elite north faces, I would bump into him everywhere: in the UK, mostly in Llanberis but often in Stoney cafe; in the Alps, on the Bioley, then Snell's Field; and later, Pierre D'Ortaz, legendary campsites used by the best alpinists of the times, as mere breaks between great climbs. Lately he would join fellow AC members and venture up bigger peaks in the Himalaya. (He had joined the club in 1985.)

We soon became good friends. Sadly, as I grew older and slowed down, with my last 14 years being spent up north, and with that golden era of British alpinism long gone, it would be a less regular meeting, with those famous words ringing out across the Llanberis high street, or in Pete's Eats, or as I would unload the sacks at Ynys for the weekend. I was grateful for the climbing clubs we were both in – the AC, Climbers Club and the Fell & Rock. These kept us more in contact over recent years and I hoped would do so for a few more to come.

I was looking forward to some more great times together. Mid December 2009 brought one more such event. I'd intended to fly down to Manchester to avoid the eight-hour drive. Chris assured me he would be waiting at the arrivals for me, and was intent on whisking me to Tideswell and the local pub, to join the boys and of course, Jo, his beautiful lady, would as always be by his side. The plan was thwarted by heavy snow in the Highlands. I tried twice more to fly but on both occasions the runway was out of action. Eventually I had to drive, or I would miss my final CC committee meeting as president. It was dark by the time my sat nav got me to within shouting distance of Chris and Jo's lovely house in their neat little village. Chris stood proudly outside his house, and directed me to a parking spot alongside his brand new garage. He had restricted his free time for quite a while to build it, and a super building it had turned out to be. 'I've only got the loft insulation to put in and that's that,' he announced proudly. So sad to know he wouldn't see the finishing line.

I spent a great weekend with Chris, Jo, and Rachel, one of his two daughters from his first marriage. On the Sunday, Chris and I had a special day together on Kinder Scout. It would be my first visit to this wild place, and not only would we ascend to the bleak plateau, we'd walk through the mire to the Downfall, which I really wanted see, and Chris announced we'd do a rock climb on one of the high crags there. Ok, it would only be a Severe, but in that damp and gloomy atmosphere, you could argue about my keenness. Chris, however, was on fire, and I would not dowse him.

We had a great day, the Downfall was in full flow and I pondered the sight when frozen. Later, on the rock route, I was watching carefully for sandbags. On a convenient ledge I craftily avoided finishing the top pitch with an, 'I'll bring you up. It's not clear where it goes from here?' Chris came up, took the rack and proceeded to show me why I held him in such esteem, as he smoothly climbed the slimy, green groove, which I had been convinced wasn't the normal way forward.

Recently we'd been doing some talking. Our future alpine plans, given some breaks in my annual summer guiding programme, and Chris's ability to break off his 'pole counting' for BT, were for the Frêney, even the Innominata and the Pueterey Integral. How I could put back the clock now. His new day job, recently acquired after a successful and rewarding career in the mining industry, always amused us all, but it secured the finances along with Jo's outdoor centre instructor role, and he was happy strolling along the fells in many different locations in the country, and in all weathers. I'm sure there was much more to it than counting poles, but I never got the chance to find out more. He told me he felt so alive.

Smiler Cuthbertson

Paddy Boulter, Kuala Lumpur, 1993.

Patrick 'Paddy' Boulter 1927 - 2009

Professor 'Paddy' Boulter, who died in November 2009, aged 82, played a key role in establishing the first breast cancer screening centre in Britain. Away from the operating theatre or lecture hall, Paddy was never happier than when he was heading up a hill – be it in Nepal, the Alps or simply Penrith Beacon near his Cumbrian home.

Paddy was born in Annan, Dumfriesshire, in 1927 and always took pride in his Scottish ancestry. The family moved to Wimbledon then back north to Carlisle where Paddy attended Carlisle Grammar School and developed his love of hill-walking and climbing in the Lake District. On one occasion he cajoled friends to cycle from Carlisle to Coniston, where they climbed the 'Old Man', then pedalled home.

After training at Guy's and a spell at the Middlesex, Paddy returned to Guy's as Senior Registrar, before going on to become a consultant surgeon at the Royal Surrey County Hospital, Guildford. It was here, together with a consultant radiologist, that he made his name by developing the use of mammography to detect early cancers; he set up a pioneering unit in Surrey in 1978 with his wife Mary (they had married in 1946) running a team of 100 volunteers who guided people in outlying clinics in the area.

Meanwhile in Edinburgh, Professor Patrick Forrest was working along similar lines. After 10 years their joint study showed that early diagnosis had reduced breast cancer death rates by 25%, an achievement that persuaded the government to adopt such screening nationally.

When Paddy retired from Guildford he and Mary moved back to Cumbria. However Paddy's medical career continued; he became president of the Royal College of Surgeons of Edinburgh from 1991 to 1994 and was made an honorary fellow of the Royal Australian College of Surgeons. He travelled the world lecturing and teaching and was greatly respected by his students, although their enthusiasm dimmed occasionally when they were dragged up mountains in his wake. He never travelled without his boots.

Paddy joined the Association of British Members of the Swiss Alpine Club (ABMSAC) in 1968 and advanced rapidly, becoming a committee member in 1971, vice-president in 1973 and president in 1978. A man of great charm and humour, he was also recognised as a shrewd chairman of meetings and wise counsellor. He became a member of the Alpine Club in 1972.

A past ABMSAC Journal shows that 1971, perhaps a typical year, included two weeks in the Lakes, skiing at Obergurgl, climbing in Chamonix, St Luc and Zermatt, a family holiday in Corsica, and finally an ascent of the Puig de Teix above Valdemosa in Majorca – all this on top of his medical duties. Later he and Mary developed a special affection for Bivio near the Julier Pass in Switzerland. Other shared passions were fly-fishing – their Cumbrian cottage is close by the River Eden – and alpine plants.

Among Paddy's other claims to fame were to have played cricket on the Plain de la Morte, a 22-hour day in Colorado, 200 miles of walking and 56 tops in Galloway and a visit to the Khyber Pass. He climbed with John Hunt in Nepal and he and Mary went ski mountaineering with Harry Archer in the Engadine on many occasions. The meticulousness observed in his medical research was evident also in a record he kept of every hill and mountain climbed from 1961; in 30 years he ascended nearly 4000 named tops.

Paddy is survived by Mary, his two daughters Jenny and Anne, five grandchildren and five great-grandchildren.

Wendell Jones

Roger Childs

Roger Childs 1933 - 2010

Roger Childs, who died in Spain on 8 June 2010 after some years of debilitating illness, was a dynamic man of many parts who combined athleticism with artistic sensibility. Coming relatively late to serious mountaineering, he then embraced it with the same enthusiasm as had characterised his already action-packed life.

Educated at Cranbrook School, Kent, Roger qualified as a chartered accountant and, after gaining his professional experience with an accountancy firm in Rochester, joined UNRWA in Beirut in 1959 when the scars of the 1956 Suez debacle were still manifest. His experiences in this troubled part of the world left him with an abiding interest in Middle Eastern affairs. Apart from skiing at the Cedars of Lebanon, waterskiing in the Mediterranean, and crewing in Beirut Yacht Club races, it was here that he met his wife Belita. They worked together as part of an amalgam of nationalities that comprised UNRWA (UN Relief and Works Agency for Palestine Refugees) and in 1961 were married in Tehran. That same year they moved to Jerusalem where Roger was appointed head of UNRWA operations for Jordan, with particular responsibility for running refugee camps.

After returning to London in 1963, the couple bought an elegant house in Greenwich, and in 1965 Roger joined Rank Xerox where he worked for the next 14 years, at first London based, but with overall responsibility for the firm's Scandinavian operations, and later as second in command of the Paris office. As befitted a proper Englishman, he habitually walked to work through the streets of Paris with a furled umbrella. After Xerox, Roger's independent bent took him into management with several British industrial companies. In 1983 he and his cousin bought MEDC, a tiny electrical design and manufacturing company in Pinxton, Nottinghamshire. This turning point in his career coincided with his first serious essay into ski mountaineering, a High Level Route traverse as a member of a Downhill Only club party. Roger's drive, enthusiasm and management skills were eventually to turn MEDC into a highly successful business venture with an annual turnover of £13m.

For many years, Roger played a pivotal role in the artistic life of Greenwich and Blackheath. He helped revive, and for many years served as Chairman of, the Blackheath Conservatoire which was originally founded to train and encourage young musicians, dancers and artists. He himself had taken up drawing and painting in the 1980s and this remained a solace to the end.

Apart from a life-long love of sailing, especially in the Aegean which he explored with family and friends as part-owner of a 41ft ketch, he was active in many sports including fell running with the annual Trevelyan Hunt in the Lakes, squash, and tennis (with which he persevered even after serious illness). But most particularly, in the years before working in the Middle East, his passion was rugby. He represented his county, Kent, and played regularly for Blackheath, oldest of Rugby Union clubs. In the Club's centenary match against Newport, he scored the winning try.

After his 1983 High Level Route, Roger turned his mind to exploratory ski mountaineering and, in the following year, joined my party with the object of completing a ski traverse of the Cairngorms. Aborted when I dislocated my shoulder, Roger's companionship provided balm when we were holed up for nine hours in the Avon bothy, while David and Anna Williams undertook a hazardous night-time ski to raise a helicopter rescue. Thereafter, Roger became a regular member of the team, completing the three testing final sections of the Pyrenean High Route, the ascent of half a dozen peaks, and a final settling of scores with Aneto and Posets.

We went on to make a skein of Scottish ski ascents together, mixed with the occasional alpine foray, but it was in Spain that Roger's mountaineering penchant found truest expression. One of his many projects had been to rehabilitate Prado Lobero (Wolf Meadow) a wildly beautiful *finca* that he and Belita had bought near Candeleda beneath Spain's Sierra de Gredos. Here, they set about converting derelict farmhouses into dwellings of delight, excavating fresh springs, and transforming unkempt fields into fruitful orchards. Prada Lobero became the launch-pad for many pioneer ski mountaineering expeditions and ascents in Spain's less frequented ranges such as the Gredos, Picos de Europa, Montes Carrionas, and the Cordillera

Cantabrica. Roger's enthusiasm, savoir faire, and his intimate knowledge of the country, its language and people, its paradors and hostels, wines and gastronomy made these unforgettable experiences.

In April 1994 he was a valued member of Derek Fordham's Svalbard expedition which, after long, cold days of pulk slogging, climbed the archipelago's highest peak, Newtontoppen. In 1996, he made a solo ascent of Cotopaxi (5600m), and in 1999 joined a pioneer ski tour to lesser-known parts of Greece including Falakro. We returned the following year to the Pindus and climbed the country's second summit Smolikas (2637m). By now the ill-health that was to blight the last decade of Roger's life had already taken hold, and to have completed that exhausting day in his condition, demanded the exceptional qualities that characterised the man. Fittingly, his last ski mountaineering expedition was to the Lebanon in 2001 but, game to the end, he subsequently attended two ASC meets in Andermatt and Briançon.

Roger became a member of the Alpine Ski Club in 1987, and for several years served as the Eagle Ski Club's honorary treasurer. Already an FRGS, he was elected to the Geographical Club in 1997, and in that same year, with over a dozen unguided ski mountaineering tours, several of them pioneer, and well over 30 ascents to his credit, he was elected an aspirant member of the Alpine Club.

Although Roger's last few years were a struggle against illness, he never lost his zest for living, love of nature, humour, or skills as a raconteur. Ever lovingly supported and sustained throughout those difficult times by his wife Belita, his daughters Sophie, Alexa, Julia and Anya, he confronted every setback with an abiding Christian faith, and with the same courage and determination that had made him such a stalwart mountain *companero*. Roger Childs was a most hospitable, devoted, life-enhancing family man of many gifts. He will be greatly missed by all who shared the numerous fields of activity that he had graced but most of all by his wife, daughters and grandchildren.

John Harding

Robert (Bob) Alexander Creswell 1948 - 2010

The public often assume a head for heights is the first requirement of a mountaineer. But, as Bob Creswell proved, curiosity and enthusiasm will take you a lot further. As a child, his family liked to remind him, he was so frightened of heights that he insisted on being carried down stairs. Yet as an adult, and despite a later than usual start in the hills and a demanding career, he climbed mountains on every continent, often in the company of Jagged Globe guides, who counted him a good friend as well as a capable client.

From early forays in the Welsh and Scottish hills, he went on to explore the Altai in central Asia, climb hills in Antarctica, make an attempt on Denali in Alaska, and have a string of successes in South America, including an ascent of the stunning Alpamayo, the most attractive peak in Peru's Cordillera Blanca. Expeditions to Africa included the *Ice Window* route on Mount Kenya, now a victim of climate change, and to the Atlas and the Rwenzori.

Bob also climbed Carstensz Pyramid, locally known as Puncak Jaua, in the western central highlands of Papua, Aconcagua in Argentina and Elbruz in the Caucasus, all the highest peaks in their respective continents. He thought about completing the list of the seven highest peaks on the seven continents but reached a personal limit attempting Denali. Having sprained his ankle training in Scotland, he wasn't, he explained, enjoying himself, and wouldn't slow down the other expedition members. Being in mountains was about much more than simply reaching a summit. For Bob, it was a glorious chance to fulfil his lifelong passion for learning.

Born in London in February 1948, Bob Creswell grew up in Marlow, Buckinghamshire, and went to school in High Wycombe. He read Chemical Physics at Reading University and graduated with a first in 1970. Bob stayed on to do his PhD under the supervision of Prof Ian Mills, who described him as one of the best research students of his career.

Using microwave spectroscopy to study molecules in the gas phase, Bob then analysed their spectra with quantum mechanics to deduce their structure. His supervisor made two further critical interventions in Bob's life, taking him up Tryfan while they attended a conference at Bangor, an experience that took some time to percolate. The other was an introduction to his secretary Lee, whom Bob married in December 1973.

By then Bob was doing post-doctoral work at Michigan State University, where Lee joined him for a year. Awarded an Alexander von Humboldt fellowship – appropriately enough for someone who later climbed his own share of South American volcanoes – he worked with Prof Gisbert Winnewisser, a dominant figure in spectroscopy and astrophysics, then attached to the Max Planck Institute, based at the Justus Liebig Institute University in Giessen.

From there Bob went to Cambridge, working for Prof Brian Thrush, whose field was the study of the rates of chemical reactions in gases. Lee worked for the head of department in Clinical Biochemistry, where she became friends with Ken Siddle, who shared the young couple's passion for the theatre but also organised laboratory hill-walking trips.

It was on one of these in 1981 that Bob renewed his brief acquaintance with the Welsh hills, climbing Tryfan once more and then moving on to Glyder Fach's Bristly Ridge. Except that in the intervening years his boots had rather decayed and, finding himself with a sole flopping free of its upper, he was forced to descend. From this rather unpromising start, Bob's passion for the mountains blossomed.

Despite changing careers, leaving academia for the Inland Revenue, he became a regular on Siddle's trips, whose personnel numbered anywhere from 10 to 30 souls. They travelled all over the British Isles. A summer camping trip to Torridon revealed an antipathy to camping, which Bob retained, but his stamina for hill walking was prodigious and would think little of driving up on a Friday night to Scotland to pick off a few more Munros. He completed the list at the turn of the millennium. 'They were fantastic times,' Siddle recalled. 'Some of my best days were shared with him.'

In 1990, Ken took a sabbatical, and during his absence Bob decided with a small splinter group to rebel from the programme of damp Scottish hills in favour of a walking tour in the Alps. The experience was electrifying, and Bob found himself in his early forties embarking on a new career as an alpinist. An early attempt on the mighty Finsteraarhorn was curtailed on the advice of his guide, who suggested its more approachable neighbour the Agassizhorn instead. He went back a few years later and finished the job.

Without a network of climbing friends built up through a usual youthful apprenticeship, and rising steadily through the ranks at the Inland Revenue, Bob was understandably short of both time and experienced companions. Nor was he, by his own admission, a natural athlete. But he trained hard for the mountains, running the London marathon in 1997. His relationship with Jagged Globe allowed him to fulfil his growing ambition in the mountains, including his first trip to the Himalaya – Mera Peak in Nepal, with its up-close views of Everest and Lhotse.

His usual gang of friends were roped in, including Ken Siddle. It was typical of Creswell's generous nature that he waited behind the main group on summit day as Siddle caught up, so his friend would have the best chance of reaching the top. 'He said: "Come on, we'll do this together." I wouldn't have got up without him,' Siddle said.

After Mera, Bob embarked on his 15 years of world mountaineering, cramming in an incredible number of adventures. Having transferred to London, but still living in Cambridge, Bob was finally posted to Washington as part of the Anti-Avoidance Group, also becoming a delegate to the Joint International Tax Shelter Information Centre (JITSIC), a co-operation between the tax authorities of the USA, Australia and Canada.

Despite his glittering intellectual credentials, his successful career and passion for the mountains, Bob wore his learning lightly and could seem quietly reserved. He was not the kind to put his head down and push on for the summit: Bob had his camera out, or else was examining flowers or creatures. Constantly learning, he took a pre-degree course in Fine Art, and when climbing in Ecuador didn't miss the chance to visit the Galapagos, knowing intimately the impact the islands had had on Charles Darwin.

In Mongolia, Bonny Masson recalled, Bob was always relaxed and excellent company. 'He obviously enjoyed all aspects of the trip,' she said, recalling jeep rides across the steppes, dairy feasts in herders' homes and throat-singing concerts. With no sherpas to call on, the team had to carry their own loads to high camp. Bob proved himself a strong and competent climber, Masson said, as happy singing Beatles' songs with the kitchen crew as reaching a summit.

Bob could be a perfectionist, without being pedantic, pursuing woodwork to a near-professional standard. He joined an evening woodwork class in Cambridge to have access to tools, working quietly on his own, but impressing his tutor, who persuaded him to sit for a City and Guilds Certificate, earning a distinction. (The same dedication was applied to his deep love for making puddings.) He was also thoughtfully generous. Although a determined atheist, he agreed to be godfather for Ken Siddle's younger son. Knowing the boy's passion for elephants, he made him a jigsaw of one by hand, which remained a treasured toy.

By 2008, Bob had decided that his various passions needed more time than work allowed, so he went part-time as a prelude to retirement. Wanting to get fit for another expedition to South America, he went rock climbing in North Wales with Dave Walsh, who had guided his ascent of Mount Kenya. That evening he experienced inexplicable numbness in his right hand. This was caused by a glioblastoma, an aggressive form of brain cancer. He bore his treatment with great courage and humour, but succumbed to the disease on 21 July.

Ed Douglas

Robin Day OBE 1915 - 2010

Robin Day has been a household name in Britain since the 1950-60s when he had a leading role as a designer in introducing the 'New Look', with its graceful, 'modern' lines to a war-weary Britain; and aimed to bring contemporary design to a mass market at a reasonable price. I first met him, climbing and skiing, in the late 1950s and enjoyed a life-long friendship with him thereafter.

Robin specialised in designing furniture, especially chairs or seating, and produced with the furniture company Hille the first polypropylene stacking chair, reputed to have sold over 60 million world-wide, a brilliant use of the new injection moulding technology which he had mastered. Subsequently he had many significant responsibilities including designing the interior of the Super VC10 aircraft; the seating for the Barbican Concert Hall; and (with his wife Lucienne who was a leading textile designer) as design consultant for the John Lewis Partnership, developing the house-style for some of its department stores and for the Waitrose supermarkets. He and Lucienne were seen as cult figures in typifying the modern style of living at one time, even appearing together in an advert for Smirnoff vodka, as some football star might do nowadays.

In 1959 he was named a Royal Designer for Industry, though he preferred working on design issues to being on committees.

Robin's life as an eminent designer, for which he was awarded an OBE, is recorded in the book *Robin and Lucienne Day, Pioneers of Contemporary Design*, by Lesley Jackson (Mitchell Beazley, 2001).

Robin Day

Robin seems to have developed his interest in the outdoors, the hills and mountains, in his 30s or 40s onwards and joined the AC in 1968, when he was over 50. In addition to climbing and hillwalking in Scotland and elsewhere in Britain, he made a number of trips to the Alps, Greece, Turkey, Africa, Garhwal and Nepal.

From the 1960s onwards he became increasingly interested in ski touring and ski mountaineering, especially long-distance Nordic ski touring. His journeys included Scandinavia End to End, with a series of four linked journeys of about 500 miles each, in the 1970s (*AJ* 83, 90-97, 1978). Robin was not on the original first stage (Banak-Abisko) of this series of journeys in 1973, but made up for it with a journey Sulitjelma-Alta in 1978.

Robin told me a year or two ago that he thought his ski journeys in Scandinavia were some of the most important times of his life. I was interested – even surprised – by this comment at the time, but thinking over it, I can see that long-distance Scandinavian ski touring was something which Robin might find exceptionally fulfilling. This was mainly as a demanding and difficult sport requiring high levels of fitness, stamina and the technical ability to ski easily over varied mountain terrain. But it was also because of his understanding of, and personal commitment to, the Scandinavian way of life and culture, and especially the Norwegian tradition of love of nature. This was linked with a sympathy for the 'small is beautiful' approach, very much on the lines put forward by EF Schumacher in the 1970s.

He was completely at home in any remote Norwegian or Swedish hut; and anywhere in the Scandinavian mountains or huge forests, or on one of the great Norwegian lakes, frozen in winter. He loved the 'simple' but effective approach to making buildings in wood, as the Norwegians had done over the centuries, heated by a wood-stove; and would be delighted to find the occasional old farm-building with its wooden doors and windows as a link with the past. He was in fact very much a Nordic person, not only in appearance, fitness and fleetness of foot, but also deep in his culture, philosophy and approach to life.

An honorary member of the Alpine Ski Club and one-time vice-president, Robin succeeded in remaining very fit into later life and climbed

Mount Kenya (with Rob Collister) at the age of 76. He died in November 2010, less than a year after Lucienne.

Robin is a wonderful example to follow and I feel there is much to learn from what he did, how he did it, and what he stood for.

Alan Blackshaw

Patrick Fagan adds: I first met Robin in Norway in 1972, and shared many ski tours with him over the next 20 years, in the Alps, High Atlas, Jura and Sweden, but most of all in Norway, a country we both loved. (Indeed, with Alan Blackshaw and others, he completed a complete ski traverse of some 3000 km through the length of Norway over four seasons in the mid 1970s). I never climbed with him, but he was sufficiently capable and experienced to climb Mt Kenya (Batian) at the age of 76, at the time at least thought to be the oldest person to achieve this.

Robin was the easiest and most delightful of companions on these ski tours, quietly unassuming and most modest, and always liable to break out in one of his very personal chuckles. He had an enviable ability to connect with people, as I noticed with admiration in a village in the High Atlas when he was able to take photographs of local Muslim women in their homes, a degree of intimacy denied to the rest of us. He was a huge asset, too, when any equipment failed, turning his professional skills and very personal repair kit to the support of those less skilled or prepared for such emergencies.

I had the great privilege of enjoying the company of Robin and his wife, Lucienne, many times at their home in Chelsea, and later in Chichester where they moved some years ago. They rented a cottage near Midhurst for many years from where Robin would invite friends for long walks, another of his pleasures, but one had to be fit and strong to keep up with him.

WG CDR John Richard Wilson Edwards 1933 - 2010

John Edwards was born in Shrewsbury but spent most of his early life in Welshpool. He was a Welshman and a fervent supporter of all things Welsh, in particular Welsh rugby. He took great pride in the fact that he went to Shrewsbury School and at every opportunity would point out to certain friends that Shrewsbury School was older than Repton (Shrewsbury was opened in 1556 and Repton in 1557).

From his earliest days he had a love of the great outdoors and he spent much of the rest of his life in the mountains. At the age of 15 or 16 he and a group of other young men formed the Shrewsbury Rock and Ice Club and climbed in North Wales and the Alps.

He joined the Royal Air Force as a pilot in 1957 but, after earning his 'wings' at flying training school he was not able to continue to advanced flying training. In 1961, whilst he was thinking about the future direction of his career, he was posted to RAF Eastleigh in East Africa. John appre-

John Edwards, and pipe, on the summit of the Ortler – a sponsored climb to raise funds for a church roof. *(Ron Hextall)*

ciated the opportunities presented by this posting where he would have access to the tremendous array of mountains previously visited by his great hero Eric Shipton. Moreover, he would also be in striking range of the many uncharted mountains in the Ruwenzori and the notable peaks in and around Mount Kenya. Whilst he was in East Africa he became a member of the mountain rescue team and in that capacity undertook a number of ascents of Kilimanjaro, both as a member of a rescue party and as a guide for RAF visitors to Eastleigh.

He lost no time before taking advantage of his situation, and together with Harry Archer and others made expeditions into the Ruwenzoris. Some of peaks they climbed in the area were believed to be first ascents. On one particular climb, John recorded finding a very old ice-axe embedded in the snow on the summit ridge of Mount Stanley (5109m). This axe had a note on it dated 1906 and was said to have been left behind by the Duke of Abruzzi.

However, John would say that his major achievement in East Africa was in October 1964 when he and Tommy Thompson made the first ascent of the 1200m sheer east face of Mawenzi – the Eiger of Africa. John described this epic in *AJ 112*, 229-242, 2007. It is believed that that ascent has never been repeated. During the recce in 1963 they found the remains of a DC3 aircraft on a high ledge, complete with dead passengers and crew, that had mysteriously disappeared 20 years earlier. John's photographs of the scene appeared in the national press and he was particularly pleased to receive congratulations from the aircraft tyre manufacturer as the photos showed the tyres still to be in excellent condition even after all those years exposed to the high level elements.

John decided to continue his career in the RAF as a supply officer and subsequently served at RAF Stafford, where he was officer in charge of mountain rescue, RAF Hereford, the Middle East, RAF Old Sarum, MOD London and MOD Harrogate. During this time he set his eyes on the Himalaya and in 1979 went with a small team organised by John Whyte to climb Kwande (6011m) and Mera (6476m). The team received some support from the RGS in return for capturing and returning some leaping spiders, but whilst they were there they took photos of footprints believed to be those of a Yeti, and collected some 'Yeti droppings' for analysis by the sponsors. As far as I can remember, the droppings were identified as being similar to those of apes. Later, in 1983 John returned to the Himalaya with a party that included his son Simon, and together they climbed the unnamed Peak 42.

By now a squadron leader, John lead teams to the Zagros mountains of the then Persia and to the Atlas mountains of Morocco. He was extremely proud to be elected a member of the AC in 1982. After a number of years attending ABMSAC meets as a guest of Harry Archer, with whom he shared many of his previous climbing expeditions in the RAF, he was encouraged to become an honest man and join the ABMSAC. In the years that followed, John was a regular attendee on the annual alpine meets, and became a popular and well-respected member of the club.

He retired from the RAF in 1984 as a wing commander and joined his cousin in a new venture to build and operate nursing homes throughout the UK. The company expanded rapidly, largely due to John's negotiations with health authorities to take care of their elderly patients in new and much better surroundings. John left the company in 1996 and spent more time at his home and with his family in Shrewsbury.

Undeterred by his advancing years, John continued serious climbing in the Alps. He had already climbed all the 4000 metre peaks but had failed, due to bad weather, on two attempts on the north face of the Eiger in the 1960s. This he corrected by completing the ascent with his son Simon as recently as 2008. In 2009, he led a group of students up Mont Blanc and, afterwards, made a successful attempt at the Frêney Pillar, a climb that had previously eluded him.

During these latter years, he gave much of his time to charity work, including a number of lectures on mountaineering to the Women's Institute and other organisations, and worked with the Shropshire Wild Life Trust. One of his major contributions was to his local church, where he was a member of a group attempting to find the money to replace the church roof. As part of that work, John and I made a sponsored climb in the Alps, and carried a small cross, made by his church, to the summit of the Ortler (3905m), placing it by the much larger cross already in-situ. This effort succeeded in raising more than £3500 towards the church roof.

Whilst still in apparent good health, he was planning more ambitious climbs for 2010 but, tragically, he collapsed and died on 19 January due to a pulmonary embolism. John leaves a wife, Enid, whom he married on 3 March 1956, a daughter and two sons, five grandchildren and two great-grandchildren. He will be sadly missed by all who came into contact with him. He loved to talk about mountains and would do so with anyone who showed some interest – providing, of course, that he could smoke his pipe. The world is a poorer place without John Edwards.

Ron Hextall

Nawang Gombu Sherpa 1936 - 2011

Nawang Gombu Sherpa was the youngest member of the successful 1953 Everest expedition. He later reached the summit himself and subsequently became the first person to climb Everest twice. His entrée to the comparatively lucrative world of high-altitude mountaineering was made possible by his uncle, Tenzing Norgay, who reached the summit in 1953 with Edmund Hillary.

Gombu's family came originally from the Karta valley, a few miles to the east of Everest, in Tibet, where his grandfather owned a substantial herd of yaks. In the early thirties the yaks were lost, reducing the family to serfdom. Tenzing's elder sister, Lhamu Kipa, was working as a servant girl in the village of Tsawa when she fell in love with her employer's son, a young monk called Nawang. The couple married and in 1936 Lhamu Kipa gave birth to Nawang Gombu. It may have been the disgrace of a landowner's son marrying a serf which prompted the family to migrate in 1939 across the Nepalese border to Solu Khumbu, the homeland of the Sherpas. However, during the forties they returned to Tibet and enrolled Gombu to study at Rongbuk, the world's highest monastery, at the foot of Everest's north face. Tenzing later recalled meeting the family here in 1947. From the abbot, Trulshik Rinpoche (also a distant relative) young Gombu heard about the English climber George Mallory who had disappeared high on Everest in 1924; he was also told by some of his fellow monks that there was a golden calf on the summit – the only reasonable motivation they could find to explain the Englishmen's incomprehensible attempts to climb the mountain.

Gombu with Ed Hillary at the 1988 Everest reunion, Pen y Gwryd. *(Bernard Newman)*

In the absence of lay schools, Rongbuk gave Gombu an education; but he was a reluctant novitiate who decided that the Buddhist monastic life was not for him. He ran away and recrossed the frontier to Solu Khumbu and it was here, in the market village of Namche Bazaar, in the autumn of 1952, that he again met his uncle, Tenzing Norgay, returning from the second unsuccessful Swiss attempt that year to climb Everest. By now Tenzing's mountaineering experience and international contacts had made him a prestigious figure in the Sherpa community. He had already been asked to act as sirdar for the British attempt on Everest planned for the next spring and he would be deciding who got which jobs. Gombu begged to be included and was promised a place on the team, with the warning that it would be very hard work.

So, at the age of 17, Gombu became the youngest employee of the 1953 British Everest Expedition. Even by Sherpa standards he was short. He was also quite plump. One of the British team members, Wilfrid Noyce, commented that Gombu was the only Sherpa he had ever met who asked a sahib to go more slowly. It should be pointed out that Noyce was phenomenally fit, and that Gombu soon got into his high altitude stride, endearing himself to the team. The leader, John Hunt, noted how 'little Gombu was smiling and cherubic, like an overgrown schoolboy ... always seeking helpful jobs to perform.' And when the big day came to lift 17 loads of food, fuel, tents and oxygen to the South Col for the final summit attempt, Gombu was one of the Sherpas chosen for this vital job.

A few days later his uncle reached the summit with Edmund Hillary, earning international fame not only for himself, but to some extent for his whole Sherpa people, whose traditional trading activities had been curtailed by the recent Chinese invasion of Tibet. For a young Sherpa like Nawang Gombu, who had now proved himself at high altitude, a career in expeditions was a potentially lucrative, if dangerous, alternative to subsistence farming. In 1954 he was one of four Sherpas chosen to accompany Tenzing to Switzerland for alpine training with Arnold Glatthard at Rosenlaui, in the Bernese Oberland. That year he also attempted the world's fifth highest mountain, Makalu, with an American expedition. Then in 1955 he had his first big success, making the first ascent, with an Indian expedition, of Saser Kangri (7518m), in northern Ladakh.

In 1960 he returned to Everest on the first Indian attempt, getting to within 100 tantalising metres of the summit. Then in 1963 Uncle Tenzing wrote to James Ramsay Ullman, the author commissioned to cover the first American Everest expedition, recommending Gombu as sirdar. Gombu got the job and 30 April that year found the five foot tall Sherpa back on the summit ridge, above the South Col, this time sharing a tent with the six foot four American climber Jim Whittaker. The following day, at 1pm, the two men planted the Stars and Stripes on the summit.

Success with the Americans widened Gombu's horizons. He was welcomed with the rest of the team at the White House by President Kennedy and received the Hubbard Medal of the National Geographic Society, to wear alongside his earlier Queen Elizabeth II Coronation Medal. Later, from 1973 to 1993, Jim Whittaker invited Gombu to spend summers working with his guiding company on Mount Rainier, Washington. Meanwhile, back in Asia, he had made his permanent home in Darjeeling and become Director of Field Training at the Himalayan Mountaineering Institute, operating in Sikkim, on the flanks of Kangchenjunga.

In 1964 he reached the summit of Nanda Devi, the highest mountain wholly in India, and holy source of the Ganges. The following year he returned to Everest, with the first Indian expedition to climb the mountain. This time the top camp was placed astonishingly high, just 350m below the summit, enabling Gombu and Capt A S Cheema to reach the top at 9.30 am. Gombu had become the first person ever to climb Everest twice.

His first wife, Dawa Phuti, died in 1957, giving birth to his eldest daughter, Rita. He later married Sita Gombu, with whom he had a son and two daughters; one of them, Yangdu, now runs her own mountain trekking business based in Delhi. Gombu continued to climb well beyond middle age, making his last big expedition, in 1989, to Kangchenjunga. The following year, when I met him for the first time, leading a party of schoolgirls through the foothills of Sikkim, his laughter rang through the rhododendron forest. His sheer good nature and beaming smile endeared him to a wide international circle of friends and he remained particularly close to his American companions. Tom Hornbein, a fellow member of the 1963 Everest Expedition, recalls 'a kind of inner glow: just being in his presence, both in '63 and more recently on a visit to his home in Darjeeling, was a bit like standing by a stove and warming your soul; the heat being emitted was a vitality and joy and unabashed caring and kindness.'

Stephen Venables

Harish Kapadia adds this postscript on Nawang Gombu's cremation at Darjeeling on 28 April 2011:

For three days after his death, Gombu's body was kept in the house and prayers were recited by lamas, according to Sherpa custom. The prayers on the second day were conducted by a large group of Lamas who played drums. Next day morning a group of 21 ladies from Ghoom recited very sonorous and moving prayers. The day of the funeral started early and dignitaries came to pay tributes, beginning with the military establishment at Darjeeling. Wreaths were laid on behalf of many organisations and individuals. The funeral procession started at 1 pm and after a brief circle reached the Himalayan Mountaineering Institute. The body was carried to a specially prepared funeral pyre. The ladies followed it with a slow chant of the Buddhist mantra *om mane padme hum*.

It was a farewell to a great mountaineer, a grand family man and a wonderful soul. Gombu's entire family – his son, daughters and grand children – was present. So too was Col N Kumar, who participated on several major expeditions with Gombu, and many of the two generations of Indian mountaineers who had been taught by Gombu. To me he was always Gombu 'daju' ('brother' as Sherpas call him, also as a mark of respect) and I can recall many happy hours spent together. As the flames leaped skywards and lamas chanted prayers, a heavy downpour blessed Gombu – the heavens were welcoming him.

Alfred Gregory 1913 - 2010

Alfred Gregory, or 'Greg' as he was universally known, died in Emerald, near Melbourne, Australia, on 9 February 2010 just three days before his 96th birthday. As one of the few survivors from the successful 1953 Everest team, of which he was a worthy member, it falls to me to compose this obituary tribute. I am most grateful to Stephen Venables for allowing me to use much of the carefully researched material he incorporated in his excellent obituary published in *The Independent* on 10 February 2010.

I think I first met Greg around a boardroom-size table at the Royal Geographical Society on 17 November 1952 when the newly appointed leader, John Hunt, assembled his UK team members for the first time. He had chosen all of us primarily for our climbing ability and experience as potential summit candidates, but we were also now rather arbitrarily allocated essential subsidiary tasks. Hunt looked around and said, 'Now who knows a bit about photography? Ah – Greg seems to take good pictures.' Greg was already a keen amateur photographer with his own Contax 35mm camera. Promoted suddenly to 'official expedition photographer', he never looked back and it changed his life. In the years that followed, people tended to forget that he had carried a load to Hillary and Tenzing's top camp at 27,900ft (8504m), higher than anyone had camped before, and was remembered instead for capturing some of the 20th century's most evocative images.

Greg occasionally liked to point out the differences between the predominantly upper middle class, public school, milieu of the 1953 team and what he described as his working class background. In fact, his father owned a successful grocery business in Blackpool. Nevertheless, Greg's childhood was quite tough, as his father was killed in the First World War, when Greg was only three, leaving his mother to bring up the children alone whilst struggling to keep the grocery business afloat through the Depression. On leaving Blackpool Grammar School, Greg was apprenticed into the printing trade but he managed, with the help of the new Youth Hostel Association, to escape regularly to the hills, first bicycling, then taking up hill-walking and climbing. By the outbreak of World War Two, when he was 26, he had managed to travel abroad for three alpine seasons.

During the War he served with the Black Watch in North Africa and Italy, recruited as a private and rising to the rank of major. He was delighted to see his war end early with the successful conclusion of the Italian campaign. Free to roam in 1945, he spent a happy summer climbing amongst the deserted summits of the Alps; in 1946, after demobilisation, he set up his own travel business, specialising in guided alpine climbing. He got to know many local alpine guides, including Louis Lachenal, but it was only in 1952 that he was invited by R L G Irving, the Winchester schoolmaster who had introduced George Mallory to mountaineering, to join the Alpine Club. Greg's qualifications included classic routes on more than 30 alpine peaks, mostly climbed guideless and as leader of the party. In those days, there were a

Alf Gregory at work on the 1953 Everest expedition *(George Lowe/Royal Geographical Society)*

few club members who felt perhaps he was 'not the right type' and might use his club membership to further his commercial activities, which he readily refuted. Guide or not, his experience was valued by the establishment and that summer he was asked to join Eric Shipton's expedition to Cho Oyu which was really a training exercise for Everest. The 1951 Everest reconnaissance, initiated by Michael Ward, had confirmed a possible new southern route up from Nepal, but the Swiss meanwhile had smartly booked the mountain for 1952. By way of consolation, the British were given the sixth highest peak, Cho Oyu. They made little impression on this objective, as the only feasible route lay in Chinese-occupied Tibet; instead they enjoyed a feast of exploration, roaming wide over the then untrodden wilds of the Nepalese frontier, crossing passes and climbing numerous smaller peaks. Griffith Pugh, supported by the Medical Research Council, also carried out invaluable physiological research. Fortunately, the Swiss narrowly failed on Everest, despite a second attempt in the autumn, giving the British perhaps the last chance in 1953 to be first up the mountain.

In a surprise decision, the Joint Himalayan Committee of the AC and RGS replaced Eric Shipton as leader with John Hunt who chose a fresh team, but Greg who had performed well was still a natural choice. In his extra role as expedition photographer, he went to see Karl Maydens, one of the leading photojournalists of the day, at *Life* magazine. Maydens gave him another Contax and asked Greg what lenses he would like. 'I said I'd have a 50mm and a 125mm lens. No wideangle! I just didn't appreciate how big these mountains really were. Still, I think I managed okay.' In addition to that modest equipment, he took a medium format Rolleiflex and two lightweight fixed lens Kodak Retina 2 cameras for use above 8000 metres. And that was it. None of these cameras had a built-in exposure meter, so at first all his exposures were calculated with a separate Weston Master meter. However, he quickly learned to judge the dazzling high altitude light and soon found that he could predict exposure perfectly without the meter. He also didn't bother with bracketing – hedging bets with varied exposures – so shot a fraction of the film that would be used on a modern expedition. He later recalled, 'When I photographed Hillary and Tenzing approaching the highest camp, I only took one picture of them. I pointed the camera, clicked and said to myself, "Got that". That was how you did it in those days. I gave myself no second chance, even though Kodachrome had a speed of only 10 ASA.' The rest of us all carried cameras and took many pictures, but Greg ensured that the important shots got taken. As already mentioned, the results of this crash course in professional photography resulted in some outstanding images: goggled Sherpas balancing heavily laden across ladders spanning immense crevasses; baggy-trousered Charterhouse schoolmaster Wilfrid Noyce leading another heavily-laden team up the silent white valley of the Western Cwm; Hillary and Tenzing smiling triumphantly, safely down after their triumphant climb; and, three days earlier, the classic shot of the two men, on their way up, heading for that ledge where they would sleep higher than any man had slept before. Small and wiry, and sporting a purple bobble hat, James Morris, the *Times* correspondent, remembered him 'moving always with a sharp eagerness, always on the move, rather like a Lancashire terrier in the pink of condition'.

On the final leg to that top camp at 27,900ft (8424m), when they came across the depot left by John Hunt and Da Namgyal at 27,350ft (8336m), they had to pick up essential extra items – a Meade tent and a large black oxygen cylinder weighing 20lbs. Hillary took the tent making his load 62lbs; George had over 50lbs. They both looked at Greg. He was small, lean and very fit but had shown little enthusiasm for load-carrying in the past. Now there was no alternative. Hillary handed him the black oxygen bottle. So all of them now had over 50lbs each. With the heavier weight of equipment in 1953, the summit pair could never have established the camp without additional help from Ang Nyima, George Lowe and Alfred Gregory. However, on the day when it really mattered, 28 May 1953, Greg carried his vital load and took his photos. For the only member of the team other than Hunt to have passed his 40th birthday, it was a fine effort.

Everest consolidated Greg's photographic talent: as he put it later, 'I went to Everest an amateur and came back a pro.' Kodak took him on as a freelance lecturer and he packed halls for 20 years. He broadened his photographic horizons, taking on new projects such as photographing, with one of the first Nikon single lens reflex cameras, the life of his old home town, Blackpool – beehive hairdos, Teddy boys and kiss-me-quick hats – before its latter day decline. 'The whole place smelt of sea, chips, beer and candyfloss,' he told an interviewer, 'but there was still the decorum of the old.' His pictures eventually appeared in book form in 1994 as *Alfred Gregory's Blackpool* – a companion volume to *Alfred Gregory's Everest*. The printing was impeccable, the composition classically balanced, and the observation as sharp and kindly as that of any of the great photographic masters. He also consolidated his travel business, now called Alfred Gregory Holidays, leading clients year after year on treks through Nepal and other mountainous areas. He also led two serious mountaineering expeditions. The first, the

199. Perhaps 'Greg's' most iconic photograph: Hillary and Tenzing at 27,300ft on the south-east ridge of Everest on their way to the final camp at 28,000ft. (*Alfred Gregory/ Royal Geographical Society*)

1955 Merseyside Himalayan Expedition, continued where Eric Shipton had left off in 1952, mapping the Rolwaling region to the west of Everest, and climbing a total of 19 summits including Parchamo (6187m), nowadays a popular objective for commercial trekking organisations. The other expedition, in 1958, was an attempt on Distaghil Sar, one of the highest mountains in the Karakoram, which was unsuccessful due to excessive avalanche risk.

Greg never retired. He separated from his first wife, Ninette, a French war widow, in the 1960s. Travel, adventure and photography remained lifelong passions, which he was able to share with his second, Australian wife Suzanne who he insisted was the better photographer. For many years their base was the Derbyshire village of Elton, where guests were always welcomed with an 'Eltonian' – a generously strong gin cocktail of Greg's devising. Then in 1993 they emigrated to Australia to explore a whole new continent, developing a particular passion for the aboriginal rock art of Western Australia. They lived in the small town of Emerald, an hour's drive from Melbourne in the forested Dandenong hills, the haunt of the lyre bird. Whenever my wife and I stayed with our daughter in Melbourne, we made a point of visiting Greg and Sue, enjoying their hospitality and discussing his latest photographic projects. He was dragged reluctantly into the age of the digital image, while insisting on the superiority of film. But it was a losing battle as digital cameras yielded increasingly excellent results. Thousands of his slides were eventually digitised. As he gained recognition in Australia, his pedigree again came to the fore, with exhibitions and the publishing of *Alfred Gregory: Photographs from Everest to Africa* in 2007. He became an Australian citizen in May 2009.

Although Greg never rested on his laurels, and was always seeking new inspiration, he remained proud of the part he played on Everest. He is survived by his wife Suzanne, daughter Yolande, son-in-law John, three grandchildren and four great grand-children.

George Band

Eileen Healey 1920 - 2010

In the late summer of 1959, Eileen Healey trained her husband's new cine camera on two figures setting out for the summit of Cho Oyu, the world's sixth-highest peak. The climbers were the French swimwear designer and accomplished alpinist Claude Kogan and the Belgian star Claudine van der Straten-Ponthoz, members of the first all-female expedition to one of the 8000m giants of the Himalaya.

The footage of dazzling snows and deep blue skies, which lay for years half-forgotten in Healey's attic, captured the two women unwittingly setting out on what proved to be their last climb. An avalanche destroyed their tent at Camp IV, killing them and their Sherpa Ang Norbu. Another Sherpa who attempted to come to their aid was also killed.

It was a bitterly tragic end to an expedition that was very much Kogan's creation. She had almost succeeded in climbing Cho Oyu five years earlier, alongside the Swiss guide Raymond Lambert. Cold conditions and strong winds had driven them back, but Kogan felt they hadn't tried hard enough and was left 'with a boiling, impotent rage'. She wanted to show that far from being weaker in the mountains, women could prove more resilient than men to the trials of high altitude.

To that end, she set about organising not just an all-female expedition but one that was international too. Kogan was invited to lecture to the Alpine Club in London, and Eileen Healey, by then an experienced member of the Ladies Alpine Club, went to hear her speak. Kogan was, she recalled, 'a remarkable person, tiny, attractive, and great fun'.

Healey wasn't a professional filmmaker – she said she only got the job because no-one was more qualified than she was – but a pharmacologist from Kent, who worked as a bacteriologist. She found work at Boots in Nottingham, where she joined the Polaris club, and then moved to Manchester. Born in Brighton, both her parents were keen hill walkers and spent childhood holidays in North Wales and the Lake District. She took up climbing during the Second World War.

Her first alpine season was in 1947. She developed a love for granite climbing and particularly enjoyed hard rock climbs in the Mont Blanc range. She climbed with some of the biggest names from that era, such as Nat Allen and Don Cowan. Healey was a stylish, well-balanced climber whose success was built on skill rather than raw strength. She kept a 13-volume diary of her climbing career, from 1943 onwards, which will become a valuable archive of post-war women's climbing.

Eileen was 38 at the time of the expedition, and had already climbed in the Himalaya, joining a group of women led by Joyce Dunsheath on an exploratory trip to Kulu in India in 1956. They suffered terrible weather but managed to complete a survey of the Bara Shigri glacier. After her companions left for home, Eileen stayed on for another fortnight, making a couple of first ascents, including the first ascent of Cathedral Peak and a new route on the attractive peak of Deo Tibba, a shade over 6000m, with just two Ladakhi porters for company.

Inspired by Kogan's determination, Healey and two other women from the LAC signed up for Cho Oyu: the well-known adventurer Countess Dorothea Gravina and Margaret Darvall, who took on a lot of the pre-expedition organisation. Later recruits included the Swiss climber Loulou Boulaz, famous for her attempt on the Eiger in 1937 and ascent of the Croz, and the two teenage daughters and a niece of Tenzing Norgay. Twelve women embarked for Cho Oyu, with the journalist Stephen Harper from the *Express* following at an appropriate distance.

For Gravina, the expedition was overtly political, to show what women from around the world working as a team could achieve. For Healey, 'climbing was my great hobby'. As she put it herself, 'I didn't care who helped us.' She didn't mind whose rope she tied onto, as long as they were enjoying themselves. In this way she met her husband, Tim, as an experienced expert leading him up a climb in North Wales.

They were married in 1958, and Eileen left for Cho Oyu on the day of their first anniversary. 'She tried to use it as an excuse not to go,' he joked later, but on arriving in the Sherpa village of Namche Bazaar she was enthralled. 'It was beautiful. We were obsessed by mountains so the difficulties didn't put us off.'

Nor did she have any doubts about the wisdom of the enterprise. 'I had every faith in Claude,' she said. It was certainly nothing to do with her gender that caught the expedition leader out, rather her impatience at getting the climb done. Heavy monsoon snow still coated the upper part of the mountain, adding to the avalanche risk.

Base camp was also located at around 5700m, much too high for climbers to recover from the rigours of the mountain. 'It needed to be lower,' Healey reflected. Like Loulou Boulaz, she suffered from the altitude. After the accident, Dorothea Gravina took command, saying she wanted to try for the summit as a 'crowning memorial' for the dead women, but as she admitted herself: 'I was alone.'

In 2003, Healey had an emotional reunion with Tenzing's daughter Pem Pem at the 50th anniversary reunion of surviving Everest members. They had not seen each other since 1959.

A member of the all-female Pinnacle Club as well as the LAC and the Alpine Climbing Group, her adventurous life continued deep into old age, as she followed her passions for climbing and sailing. After living in Uganda for two years, she and Tim brought their family home after Idi Amin came to power, and settled near Chester. Last year, her film work was given the recognition it deserved, presented at the Kendal Mountain Film Festival by the historian and writer Audrey Salkeld. Her husband and her two sons, John and Jamie, survive her.

Ed Douglas

Peter Hodgkiss in the Black Spout of Lochnagar, February 1973, having 'abandoned an intention to climb *Raeburn's Gully* in the face of deep soft snow, high winds, and waves of spindrift'. *(Bob Aitken)*

Peter Hodgkiss 1936 - 2010

Heaven forbid, but if my library of mountain books were to catch fire right now with just a few minutes to rescue treasured volumes, I'd rifle the shelves for those with the image of a Gutenberg-era screw press on the spine – the distinctive logo of The Ernest Press. There would be none of mountaineering's best sellers among them, no *Into Thin Air* or Eiger epics, rather a collection telling climbing's story via *The Ordinary Route*, to employ the title of one of The Ernest Press's real gems.

Of course proprietor Peter Hodgkiss must always have hoped to make money from his titles, and to an extent he did, with a successful run of mountain biking guides providing the company's bread and butter. But look at the chances he took with new authors, even an extraordinary prose-poem imagining the final hours of George Mallory, and it is clear that profit was not his guiding star. Peter was a romantic who published out of a love of mountains and the climbing game, and a belief that if the writing was of quality then that book deserved to be in print. The result was that The Ernest Press enjoyed critical acclaim, its authors picking up a disproportionate number of mountain literature prizes without anyone getting rich.

However Peter's presence in the background of British climbing went way beyond the output of The Ernest Press. Ask about him in the senior clubs – that is the Alpine Club, the Scottish Mountaineering Club, the Climbers' Club, and the Fell & Rock Climbing Club – and many will know the name without knowing precisely what this modest man did. 'I think he helped with the guidebooks,' would be a likely reply.

But to say Peter 'helped' would be to understate his important role as a print broker. For decades he provided the link between club guidebook editors and printing firms; advising editors on what was practical in terms of format, paper quality, reproduction of diagrams and photos and so forth, meanwhile negotiating an acceptable price with printers, usually these days in the Far East.

The happy conjunction of two strands of Peter's life made him ideally suited to this task – a long career in the print business and a passion for climbing. Born in Leeds, Peter Hodgkiss was one of three brothers. The family moved to Nottingham where Peter attended the Becket School in West Bridgford. Hodgkiss senior was a printer and Peter followed his father into the craft, serving a six-year apprenticeship with Thomas Foreman & Son.

Tall and lean, at school he was an enthusiastic rower, West Bridgford being hard by the river Trent. His introduction to climbing came at age 17 when he went on an Outward Bound course in the Lake District. In addition to climbing and strenuous hillwalking, he also became a keen cyclist and in later years Peter and his wife Joy would go on cycling holidays, Scottish islands being a favourite destination. He and Joy Pycock married in 1959. Both came from Catholic families and the romance began at the Church of the Good Shepherd in Woodthorpe. Peter was certainly blessed in the partnership; they had four children, Joy supported Peter when the vicissitudes of the printing trade brought unemployment, her computer expertise was a boon to The Ernest Press, and she endured his frequent absences in the Alps or Highlands.

The couple moved to Glasgow in 1961, Peter working for the Clyde Paper Co and later for other firms. Apart from an unhappy 12 months' exile in Blackburn in the early 1970s, the family have remained on the South Side of the city, first in Netherlee and then in Giffnock.

Prior to the founding of The Ernest Press, Peter's work, or lack of it, followed the fortunes of his troubled industry. But climbing and the hills were a constant. Joining the Glasgow section of the Junior Mountaineering Club of Scotland in the mid 1960s, he found partners for long days on Highland crags, summer or winter. His determination to get out whatever the weather could cause exasperation. If the rock were too wet for climbing he would urge companions over a clutch of Munros. Rain was dismissed as 'just condensation'. He joined the SMC in 1975 and was president of the Glasgow JMCS in 1977.

Peter wasn't interested in pushing the grades or self-advertisement. He rock climbed up to Very Severe and operated on snow and ice at around grade V. A Hodgkiss day on the hills would usually start and end in the dark, plus two or three hours' driving from Glasgow and back. He loved the classic lines. On one long day, recalled by Mike Thornley, they linked the great trad' routes of Ben Nevis – first climbing North-East Buttress, descending Tower Ridge, ascending Observatory Ridge and down Castle Ridge. Any one of those routes would constitute a 'good day on the Ben' let alone all four. 'Actually that day was a bit untypical for Pete,' added Thornley. 'It was a bit showy.'

While Joy was at mass on a Sunday, Peter would be on the hill, excusing himself to the children as an agnostic. So regular was this weekend routine that one daughter told friends that her father didn't go to church 'because he's an agnostic – that means he goes climbing on Sundays'.

In truth, the hills had become akin to a religion to Peter; he loved their remoteness, a place to lose and stretch himself. It's no surprise that while unemployed around 1980 he became actively involved in the successful (so far) campaign to prevent the expansion of the Cairngorm ski area into Lurchers Gully – a wild coire west of the current piste network. In the only book that actually bears his name as author, the SMC's district guide to *The Central Highlands* (1984) Peter bid all those who enjoy a sense of wilderness 'to be both vigilant and active in protection of that value'.

Peter's alpine seasons were also a reflection of this mountain wanderer approach rather than bagger of trophy routes or busy 4000m summits. He shunned the resorts of Chamonix and Zermatt, preferring the relatively quiet side valleys off the Val d'Aosta in north-west Italy. His alpine partner in the 1970s was Ted Maden. They would camp with their families at or near Cogne in the Gran Paradiso national park and take off into the mountains every few days. One notable ascent was the north ridge of La Grivola (3969m). The Italian poet Giosuè Carducci called it *l'ardua Grivola bella* – the arduous beautiful Grivola, which seems to make it a natural Hodgkiss mountain. Later, he had seasons with Richard Gibbens, who had contributed photographs to *The Central Highlands*. Gibbens remember little of technical merit, but long days off the beaten track, Peter 'gliding with absolute poise' on snow and ice, and long conversations about classical music, photography and English grammar. Leafing through Central Highlands as we spoke, Gibbens came across a note from Hodgkiss – handwritten in fountain pen in his fastidious style – thanking Richard 'for good company in the Alps, good conversation when required, peaceful quiet at other times'.

Peter's entry into publishing grew out of his enthusiasm for mountain literature and the discovery at the bottom of a box of books bought at auction of some volumes on Antarctica that he didn't want. He was advised to contact Jack Baines, an antiquarian book dealer in Anglesey. The two met in the back room of Peter's house and sat drinking tea and talking about old classics they would like to see back in print. Each wrote out a cheque for £1000 and The Ernest Press was born. First off the press was a facsimile copy of *Twenty Years on Ben Nevis* by W T Kilgour. It had been out of print for 80 years. Baines, who had also been a mountaineer, died in 1996.

By 2010 The Ernest Press had some 50 books in its catalogue – a good many of them of an esoteric nature that few, if any, other publishers would touch. Top of that list must be Charles Lind's *An Afterclap of Fate: Mallory on Everest*, a haunting prose-poem in the imagined voice of George Mallory. It has not sold 1000 copies but it won the prestigious Boardman Tasker Award for Mountain Literature in 2006. Peter has also championed the novelist Roger Hubank. Climbing novels are a gamble to say the least, but Hubank's *Hazard's Way* won both the BT and the Grand Prize at the Banff Mountain Literature Festival in 2001.

In all, four Ernest Press titles have won the BT and others have been shortlisted. Arguably it should have been five, with Harold Drasdo's *The Ordinary Route* the one overlooked. It was the epitome of an Ernest Press book, well-written, reflective, philosophical in an unflowery way, and set in a landscape comfortable to most climbers. As was noted on the cover: 'even the Ordinary Route is not to be despised.'

I first spoke to Peter Hodgkiss in January 1997 prior to interviewing the critic Janet Adam Smith, literary editor of the *New Statesman* from 1949 to 1960. Peter had enjoyed a long correspondence with Adam Smith and had just republished her engaging *Mountain Holidays* (1946). He warned me to keep my wits about me. Although in her early nineties, this grande dame of the AC had an incisive mind and was a stickler for facts and grammar. And so was Peter, as I was to discover five years later when I was persuaded to become editor of the *Alpine Journal*.

Peter had been elected to the Alpine Club in 1988 and in 1993 the Ernest Press became joint publisher with the club of the *AJ*. He was pleased to have that screw press logo on its spine and gave freely of his time to ensure that the *AJ* looked its best. We spent countless hours on the phone, digressing from production headaches to recent climbs or books old and new. Had I read René Daumal's novel *Mount Analogue*? (A metaphysical adventure.) 'Oh you must.' And two days later it arrived in the post. Sometimes our headaches were novel too. One year the *AJ* was delayed in China after a censorious printer spotted a tiny image of the Dalai Lama within a photograph. It cost us a fortnight but the photo remained unchanged.

Our last meeting was at his Glasgow home six days before he died. Despite the cancer that had racked him for six months, he remained erect and dignified, insisting that we should talk in his office, business as usual rather than retiring to the sitting room. 'Growing old isn't for softies,' he would say when asked how he felt. But Peter Hodgkiss was never a softie and he was concerned to be involved with production of the *Alpine Journal* until his final days.

Stephen Goodwin

John William Rolfe Kempe CVO 1917 - 2010

John Kempe who died on 10 May, aged 92, was born on 29 October 1917 so had outlasted most of his contemporaries. He was elected to the Alpine Club on 8 December 1952, being proposed by Harry Tilley and seconded by A E Gunther. He also became a Life Member of the Himalayan Club in the same year. In the Alps he climbed over three seasons: 1949 in the Dauphine; 1950 in the Silvretta and Dauphine; and 1951 in the Zermatt area. These were mostly guideless climbs in partnership with Gunther. Then in spring 1952, he joined Tilley, David Bryson, a BBC producer, and John Jackson for trekking and climbing in the Garhwal Himalaya which included an attempt on Nilkanta (21,640ft) with bivouacs at 16,000' and 17,000', but they were defeated by heavy snow.

His most notable role in the Himalaya was in setting the scene for the first ascent of Kangchenjunga in 1955, approached from the south-west up the Yalung valley. In April and May 1953 he accompanied Gilmour

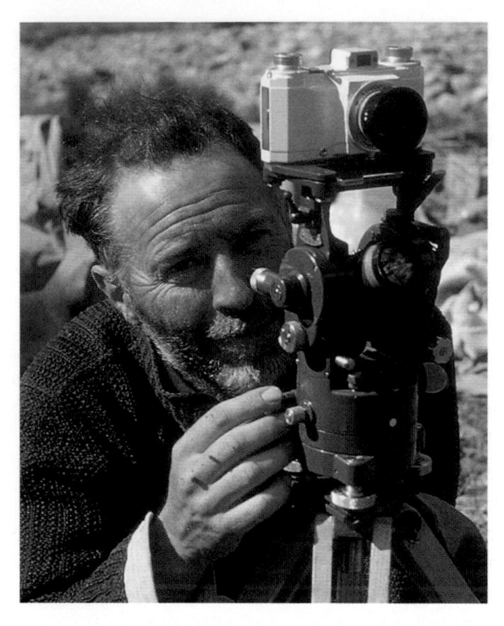

John Kempe photo-theodolite surveying during the British Huagaruncho Expedition, Peru 1956 *(George Band)*

Lewis, attempting Boktoh on the west side of the valley and ascending the northern shoulders of Koktang and north Kabru. Both summits were missed because of misgivings as to the state of the snow on the way down, but from Kabru the south-west face of Kangchenjunga was examined and after reconnoitring the lower defences of the mountain they considered that, in spite of Smythe's opinion to the contrary, a possible route up might be found.

This led to a further reconnaissance of the mountain in April and May 1954 by Kempe, Lewis, Ron Jackson, Jack Tucker, Trevor Braham and Dr Donald Matthews. The expedition had the limited objective of finding a route that would appear to lead to the summit. Three routes were examined: Pache's Grave route, one below the Talung Saddle, and the last by the main ice-face, all with a view to reaching the large ice-shelf which runs across the mountain at about 24,000ft. Kempe's official report of the expedition (*AJ 59*, 428-31, November 1954) together with the photographs and reports of individual members were considered by a sub-committee appointed in April 1954 under the chairmanship of Sir John Hunt. Their recommendation that an expedition to the mountain in 1955 should be sponsored by the Alpine Club was accepted. Charles Evans agreed to lead the expedition with the limited objective of reaching this Great Shelf. (So far no expedition had been above 20,000ft on this face.) At the same time, just in case things proved easier than expected, Evans was planning to take oxygen and sufficient equipment to launch an attack on the summit. This was to be 'a reconnaissance in force'.

The 1954 party climbed a rock buttress on the east side of the Lower Icefall, which became known as Kempe's Buttress, and thought that from there one might climb the remaining 600ft of the Lower Icefall, and continue up the Upper Icefall to the Great Shelf, and thence by way of the snow gangway, reach the west ridge and so to the top. It was a complicated route, and at the time the 1955 team had no great faith in it, for the avalanche dangers, let alone the technical difficulties, might make it totally unsafe or impossible. Kempe's party had considered the top of the Rock Buttress – the highest point they had reached – to be about 21,000ft. But a detailed survey in 1955 by the civil engineer and deputy leader Norman Hardie judged it to be only 19,000ft. This gave another 2,000ft of virgin ground to be covered. But the main achievement was that it got the 1955 expedition launched on the mountain, and it was successfully climbed by two pairs, Joe Brown and myself on 25 May and Norman Hardie and Tony Streather the following day. The ascent was not repeated for 22 years.

John Kempe was born in Nairobi, the son of a Colonial Service officer who sadly died of a fever when John was only four, so his mother took her young son and daughter to live at her family's home in Norfolk. He was educated at Stowe and won an Exhibition to Clare College, Cambridge, where he read Economics and Mathematics. He also joined the University Air Squadron – of the 22 undergraduates who trained with him at Duxford, only two others were to survive the Second World War.

Kempe was about to enter the Indian civil service when war was declared in September 1939, and he volunteered for the RAF. As he was already an experienced pilot, he was kept back from operations in order to train the new intake, so many of whom, to his deep regret, were to die during the Battle of Britain. In December 1940 he therefore asked to move to operations but this was not effected until July 1941, by which time the allies had achieved air supremacy, flying on the front line was a bit safer and he was lucky to survive. He was posted to No 602 Squadron, flying Spitfires, and in May 1942 promoted to squadron leader, and the next year mentioned in dispatches. In June 1944 he was posted to No 125 Squadron, flying Mosquitoes. From a base in North Africa he escorted convoys making for Malta. He commanded Nos 153 and 255 Night Fighter Squadrons, and in 1945 was posted to Algiers as chief test pilot (Middle East). Shortly before being demobilised in 1946 he was again mentioned in dispatches.

After the war Kempe worked briefly at the Board of Trade and in private business, but found himself dissatisfied and restless. Discovering that his former housemaster at Stowe was now teaching at Gordonstoun, he asked whether there was a vacancy for a mathematics teacher. There was, and he got the job. After only three years in Scotland, in 1951 he was appointed the founding principal of the Hyderabad Public School in India with the motto 'Be Vigilant'. He chose the Shaheen (literally 'Royal White Falcon') as the School Emblem, for its sharpness of vision and its innate ability to soar to great heights. He served from September 1952 to August 1954. Among his first acts was to ensure that the dates of the school holidays coincided with the Himalayan climbing season.

In 1956 (by which time he was headmaster of Corby Grammar School, in the Northamptonshire steel town where he remained until 1967) Kempe was the leader of an expedition to the Peruvian Andes which climbed the virgin 18,797ft peak Huagaruncho. Legend had it that the Incas had climbed it previously leaving a cross of gold on the summit, but no such thing was found. Three of the party were from the 1954 Kangchenjunga venture: Kempe, Tucker and Matthews, augmented by Michael Westmacott and John Streetly, the successful summit team, and myself. This was the first time I had really had the opportunity to meet and climb with John and found him a delightful, kindly and modest companion and we became good friends. This was to be his final expedition. He gave up climbing in 1957 after marrying his wife, Barbara Huxtable, the daughter of an Australian doctor who had won an MC and Bar at the Battle of the Somme.

In 1968 Kempe returned to Gordonstoun, but this time as headmaster, a post he held for 10 years. The school was already famous as the alma mater of the Duke of Edinburgh and the Prince of Wales; under Kempe, it also educated Prince Andrew and then Prince Edward, who arrived just before Kempe retired. The school's other claim to fame was its Spartan regime: boys were required to go for a dawn run, whatever the weather, and to take two cold showers a day. But while Kempe retained these traditions, he was also an innovator, in 1972 admitting girls who, within three years, made up nearly a quarter of the pupils. He also introduced individual tutors for sixth form pupils. He himself taught classes in English, logic and philosophy, and would invite groups of pupils to his house for tea, sherry or his own home-brewed beer.

John Kempe was a member of the Mount Everest Foundation Management Committee 1956-62 and chairman of the Round Square International Committee 1979-87 through which young people undertake voluntary work in developing countries. He was also vice-chairman of the European Atlantic Movement committee 1982-92 (and its vice-president thereafter), and a trustee of the University of Cambridge Kurt Hahn Trust 1986-89. In addition to articles in the *Alpine*, *Geographical*, and other journals, he published *A Family History of the Kempes* (1991). He was appointed CVO (Commander of the Royal Victorian Order) in 1980, and is survived by his wife Barbara and their two sons and one daughter.

The last time we met was at his very special 90th birthday celebration at the RAF Club on 27 October 2007. He was by then quite frail but afterwards sent me a photograph of three of us standing together, John, Mike Westmacott and myself, which was a lovely souvenir of the occasion. At the memorial service to celebrate his life, Barbara asked that any donations should go to the Himalayan Trust UK to benefit schools in the very remote valleys below Kangchenjunga. This would have pleased John.

George Band

Robert Lawford 1916 - 2009

With the death of Bob Lawford on 11 October 2009 the Alpine Club has lost one of the most devoted and capable members in its long history.

An engineer by profession, Bob's talents were applied to aircraft production with Handley Page until 1942 when he moved into the oil industry, working for the Anglo-Iranian Oil Company at Abadan. In 1946 Bob joined the Metal Box Company where as a director he played a leading role in that company's affairs while based in Bombay (Mumbai), Madras and Calcutta.

As a young man Bob had acquired the techniques of rock climbing and general mountaineering in the English Lake District which he visited with regular companions on numerous occasions. Like many active enthusiasts of his generation, the Second World War and a heavy workload interrupted the prospect of a natural progression to climbing and exploration in the Alps and greater ranges. However, on his arrival in Calcutta where the Himalayan Club was based at that time, Bob was able to re-establish his links with the climbing scene by making a significant contribution to that club, filling various official posts and being elected as president prior to his return to this country in 1970.

As a former president of the HC, Bob was welcomed at the Alpine Club, to which he had been elected in 1967 and where he soon became equally indispensable. Although any appreciation of Bob's role in the AC, which covered so many aspects of the club's activities over a period of almost forty years, must inevitably be somewhat incomplete and inadequate certain areas of his work call for particular comment.

Bob is perhaps remembered best for his long association with the Alpine Club Library where as honorary librarian for more than 20 years and subsequently as librarian emeritus he dealt quietly and efficiently with all matters in his domain. The library, which had expanded continuously from the early days of the club – a catalogue of books published in 1888 ran to more than 50 pages – and which had been stored for safe-keeping in various locations outside the capital during the war, had become too large to be maintained on a voluntary basis. Understandably in such circumstances, earlier cataloguing systems had not been maintained and by the time of Bob's arrival at the club, in spite of heroic efforts by previous honorary Librarians assisted by a small group of volunteers, several thousand books remained to be sorted, cleaned and reclassified. To this major challenge, including the ongoing need to deal with considerable numbers of journals received from other climbing clubs, and to numerous other problems in the following years, Bob gave countless hours of his time. In addition he took on the daunting task of sorting and cataloguing thousands of photographic prints, negatives and glass lantern slides, when his profound knowledge of the Himalaya enabled him to identify many untitled peaks. Bob also advocated and implemented the sale to members of duplicated books and journals, many of which he himself first repaired or rebound to a professional standard – a scheme which over the years has generated substantial funds for the Library and enabled members to add to their own collections at reasonable cost.

Only brief reference can be made here to further examples of Bob's immense contribution to the Alpine Club over many years. Others have recalled his catalogues of the club's maps and pictures; his card index covering more than 500 Himalayan peaks; his major role during the moves from South Audley Street, first into temporary accommodation and then to the present premises; and his guidance to many members on Himalayan matters.

Bob has been aptly described in the *Alpine Journal* as 'the linchpin of the whole effort'. In recognition of his services to the club he was elected to honorary membership in 1979 and as a further tribute to his work a series of pictures produced by contemporary artistic members and donated to the club to mark its 150th anniversary is now known as 'The Bob Lawford Collection'.

Essentially a practical man of action with an innate love of the mountain world, Bob's work to catalogue and preserve our treasured possessions – work which to a great extent forms the basis of the club's computerised facilities today – is an enduring reminder of his achievements. In offering our condolences to Bob's family the club wishes to express its gratitude for his outstanding contribution over so many years. We were fortunate indeed to have Bob on our side.

Christopher Russell

Michael Baker writes: In the 1970s when I was hon secretary I used to visit the club at lunchtime on most week days in order to attend to correspondence and see to the club's affairs. Almost always there were two people in the South Audley Street premises that we then occupied – Mrs Lewis the formidable, not to say fearsome caretaker, concierge and manager – and Bob Lawford. Mrs Lewis was very sparing with her friendship but in her eyes Bob could do no wrong. This was only partly because of the countless hours he spent in the basement trying to put some order into the club's library, archives and records. There was also about him, as she I think saw very clearly, the deepest sense of loyalty to the club which she appreciated because she shared it.

Bob's involvement with the club at that time was not entirely subterranean, though he rarely contributed to the lively and informed discussion which followed the lectures. To this there was one remarkable exception. In 1974 Dr Terris Moore had come over from the United States to talk on the 1932 expedition to Minya Konka in Eastern Tibet. According to the expedition report (*AJ* 45, 302, 1933) they 'exposed thirty negatives' on the 24,906ft summit in good clear weather. At the end of his lecture Dr Moore showed a panoramic view compiled from some of these negatives and invited the audience to identify any of the numerous peaks it depicted. Given that the area was remote and the ascent had not been repeated this was quite

Bob Lawford in the Lake District c1946. *(Joan Coad-Pryor)*

a challenge. However, a rather tentative voice came from the back of the hall – to this day I believe it to have been Bob: 'I say Terris, I think you have the slide in the wrong way round!' When the necessary adjustment had been made he and a number of other members named almost all of the peaks from one side of the slide to the other.

Robert Pettigrew writes: Bob Lawford merits a special mention in the Himalayan context for creating over many years the unique resource of the Himalayan Index, painstakingly compiled as a card index before the age of computerisation. Bob will forever be remembered as the leading member of a trio of British expatriate mountaineers, the others being Charles Crawford and Bill Risoe, who 'stayed on' in post-partition India in 1947 and who resolved, individually and collectively, to try and ensure the future viability of the Himalayan Club, almost fatally weakened by the inevitable loss of its core executive membership. All successively held office as presidents of the HC.

Bob and Ann Lawford epitomised the perseverance and dedication of those few of the British community who 'stayed on' and by their encouragement and support of young Indian embryonic mountaineers ensured the succession of capable future office holders of the Himalayan Club. A keen rock climber and hill walker in his youth, Bob had no choice but to forgo the call of higher mountaineering and to channel his love of mountaineering into research and administration. His original research of the Himalayan peaks whilst he was in Calcutta, which he recorded on handwritten index cards for each of 500 mountains, was to become the basis for the Alpine Club's Himalayan Index. Of the research he wrote: 'I've been working on a list of all the Himalayan peaks for a chap who is publishing it in book form with photos. What a job! I have recorded about 500 over the years, having checked on over 800 expeditions.'

It was Bob, as honorary secretary of the HC, who invited me to Calcutta to present an illustrated lecture to the club on our first ascent of Kulu Pumori (21,500ft) above the Bara Shigri glacier on the Kulu/Lahul/Spiti watershed of the Great Himalayan Divide in 1964[1]. The young members he has assembled epitomised the fellowship engendered by a love of mountains, where hospitality was of the legendary sort experienced by all the mountaineers who travelled through Calcutta en route to the Himalaya. It was also memorable for a scholarly vote of thanks by Dr K Biswas, then editor of the *Himalayan Journal.* Later Bob, then vice-president in 1966, encouraged my further explorations of Kulu by offering strong support to Jagdish Nanavati and me as we planned and carried through our Indo-British expedition's successful second ascent of Bruce's Solang Weisshorn (19,450ft)[2], since this was his own philosophy translated into practice. Our association resumed on my own repatriation from India when I succeeded Bill Risoe as honorary local secretary of the HC. Bob continued to assist me in that role to the end of his life, a 40-year epilogue to round off a lifetime of service to the greater mountaineering fraternity from Calcutta to London and thence worldwide.

Bob is survived by his wife Ann, his daughters Anna (a member of the HC and AC) and Diana, and three grandchildren.

1 *AJ* 70, 70
2 *AJ* 72, 201

Erhard Loretan 1959 - 2011

When Erhard Loretan and his fellow Swiss climber Jean Troillet reached their advance base camp at 5850m on the Rongbuk glacier late on 30 August 1986 they had set a new standard in extreme alpinism – to the summit of Everest (8850m) and back in less than two days, no sherpas, no rope, no bottled oxygen; for the last 1000m they did not even take a rucksack.

The pair climbed mainly at night, so as not to overheat in their down suits, and rested during the warmth of the day. Meticulous in its planning and beautifully stylish in its execution, their ascent of the mountain's North Face via the Japanese and Hornbein couloirs was described by Voytek Kurtyka as 'night-naked climbing'.

With his ascent of Kangchenjunga (8586m), Nepal, in 1995, Loretan became only the third person to climb all fourteen of the world's 8000-metre peaks, following on from Reinhold Messner and Jerzy Kukuczka. By April 2011, twenty-five climbers had achieved this feat, but few with the verve of Loretan.

Born in Bulle, in the canton of Fribourg, Loretan began climbing at the age of 11 and four years later climbed the east face of the Doldenhorn (3643m) in the Bernese Alps – the same Swiss range where he fell to his death on 28 April – his 52nd birthday – while guiding on the Gross Grünhorn (4043m). He found his true métier as a mountain guide after first working as a cabinet maker, and seemed to derive as much pleasure from sharing trade routes and peaks with clients as he did from expressing his 'fast and light' philosophy in extreme places.

At the time of writing, the precise circumstances of Loretan's accident were unknown. Reportedly, he and a client, a 38-year old Swiss woman resident in Geneva, had left the Finsteraarhorn hut (3048m) at 6am, ascended to a col where they deposited their skis, and had reached about 3800m on the south-west ridge, the Normal Route, when they fell 200m down its north-west face. When rescuers arrived, Loretan was found to be dead; the client was still alive, though with multiple fractures and internal bleeding. She was airlifted to hospital.

The Gross Grünhorn is a fairly standard peak for ski mountaineers in the Bernese Alps; once again it appears that an alpine guide who on his own private account operated at the highest level has died in a manner that on the face of it seems prosaic.

In 1980 Loretan made his first trip to the greater ranges, climbing new routes in the Peruvian Andes, and two years later ticked the first of his 8000ers with an ascent of Nanga Parbat (8126m). The blueprint to his reputation-making Everest climb came in 1985 when he and Triollet made a super-lightweight ascent of Dhaulaghiri (8167m), climbing fast, mainly at night, and carrying no ropes or bivouac gear.

The audacity of the pair's Everest ascent was matched by the literal cheek of their descent – a four-hour sitting glissade of the entire North Face, or to put it in less technical terms, perhaps the longest and highest bum slide in the world. Triollet described it thus: 'It was crazy… we were sitting side by side, looking at each other, laughing, digging our ice-axes into the snow, flying along.' And in their oxygen-starved hallucinations they were accompanied by marching bands.

Reflecting years later, Loretan insisted the feat wasn't incredible at all: 'We just set off and we were fortunate to do it in two days. We were young and in love with climbing. When you're in love, you'll do anything. It wasn't sacrifice, it was normal.'

In 1987 Loretan had his first serious accident in the Alps but returned to climbing with an appetite as voracious as ever: a new route with Kurtyka on the Nameless Tower (6239m), Trango Towers, Pakistan, in 1988; a haul of 13 north faces in the Swiss Alps and an attempt on K2 (8611m) in 1989; then in 1990 came Denali (6194m), Cho Oyu (8201m) by its difficult south-west face in 27 hours, and up and down the south face of Shisha Pangma (8046) in 22 hours – a remarkable year. In 1994, as well as climbing Lhotse (8501m), his penultimate 8000er, he made a fine solo first ascent of Mt Epperly (4508m) in Antarctica's Sentinel Range.

Climbing for Loretan meant fulfilment. 'I have taken the decision to live intensely, flirting with risk,' he said. But his recent years were clouded by tragedy. In 2003 Loretan received a four-month suspended prison sentence after pleading guilty to the negligent manslaughter of his seven-month old son in 2001. Loretan admitted to the police that he had shaken the baby boy 'for a couple of seconds' to stop him crying and that when he put him back to bed the crying stopped. He had later summoned an ambulance. The case led to fresh research showing many parents were unaware that infants, because of weak neck muscles, could die from being shaken for only a few seconds.

Even in his storm years, Loretan did not court publicity – the race for the 8000ers was more a figment of the media than of the climbers, he contended – and after the tragedy he avoided any limelight, focusing on his guiding.

But among mountaineers, Loretan's achievements were never likely to be forgotten and last year he accepted honorary membership of the Alpine Club. He also came to London to take part in 'First on Everest' at the Royal Geographical Society, a charity event organised by Doug Scott. With Everest today more associated with stunts and ego-burnishing, it was a chance to celebrate the boldest and best of climbing on the world's highest peak. Erhard Loretan, unassuming as ever, was back in the fold – albeit all too briefly.

Stephen Goodwin

Joss Lynam

Joss Lynam 1924 - 2011

James Perry O'Flaherty (Joss) Lynam was Ireland's best-known mountaineer. His achievements included many expeditions to the greater ranges and an outstanding voluntary contribution to adventure sports in Ireland. Joss is known to many Irish and international walking enthusiasts for his many hillwalking guidebooks and was the editor of *Irish Mountain Log* (IML) for more than 20 years. He continued as the literary editor of *IML* up to his death.

Laoch ar lár was how the former minister for community, rural and Gaeltacht affairs Éamon Ó Cuív described him, paying tribute to his 'pivotal role' in Comhairle na Tuaithe, the countryside council initiated by the minister to deal with access and development strategies for recreational activity in rural areas. He made an outstanding voluntary contribution to the development of adventure sports in Ireland, and played a key mediating role in disputes over access to the countryside.

Joss was born in London on 29 June 1924, son of Edward Lynam and Martha (nee Perry), both of whom were natives of Galway. Edward was curator of maps at the British Museum, and was author of a number of books about maps and mapmaking. During his childhood the family spent a number of holidays in a cottage at Renvyle, County Galway. It was on one of those trips that he climbed his first mountain – Knocknarea, Co

Sligo – with an aunt. His ashes were scattered there in February 2011.

In 1942, at the age of 18, Joss was sent with the Royal Engineers on military service to India, where he learned to speak Hindi and spent time in the Himalayan foothills north of Delhi. He recalled later that he had a 'quiet' war, being demobbed before Indian partition. However, he lost a close friend who had remained behind and was caught in the ensuing bloodshed.

He subsequently studied engineering at Trinity College Dublin. While a student, he and Bill Perrott founded the Irish Mountaineering Club (1948), initiating an appeal through *The Irish Times* letters page. They were out in Luggala in Wicklow on the day the appeal was published and returned to a sheaf of telephone messages. The first meeting was held in Dublin's Central Hotel and Robert Lloyd Praeger, naturalist and author of *The Way That I Went*, was elected as first president. Joss's aim was to ensure it was mixed sex – at a time when many British and international clubs were male only – and cross-Border.

One of those first IMC members was his future wife, Nora Gorevan, whom he married on his graduation in 1951. Fortunately, Joss's career as a civil engineer brought the couple to work in a number of mountainous regions including Wales, the English Lake District and India. At this stage, he had been to the Alps, and had already undertaken his first international mountaineering expedition – to Kolahoi in Kashmir at the end of the war. He described many years afterwards how much of his technique was self-taught and how he slipped away from base camp with a book to learn how to cut steps on ice. 'How we survived, I don't know... It was the first real mountain that any of us had ever seen.'

He was leader or deputy leader of expeditions to Greenland, the Andes, Kashmir, Tien Shan, Garhwal and Tibet, including the 1987 expedition to Chang-tse (7543m), which was the forerunner to the successful first Irish ascent of Everest in 1993. He was joint leader with Mike Banks of a veteran mountaineering trip to the 6632m-high Jaonli peak in India in 1991 when an earthquake struck less than 15 miles away. His sound mountaineering judgment, knowledge of different ranges, route-finding and navigation ability, perseverance and understanding of the mountain environment all contributed to his considerable leadership skills.

He brought this experience to bear in his role as president of the Union Internationale des Associations d'Alpinisme's expeditions commission in the 1990s, and was instrumental in making the case for greater involvement of the 'host' countries, such as India and Pakistan.

Arguably, one of his finest legacies was the formation with others of a number of organisations supporting adventure sports, including the Federation of Mountaineering Clubs in Ireland, the Association for Adventure Sports, the Irish Orienteers, Bord Oiliúint Sléibhte, Tiglin – the National Outdoor Training Centre in Co Wicklow – and Outdoor Education Ireland.

He was a driving force in developing a national network of waymarked trails, as chair of the National Waymarked Ways Advisory Committee from 1984 to 2007. His vision of a representative body for hillwalking and mountaineering was realised in Mountaineering Ireland, which has grown from very small roots to an organisation of 10,500 members. He also created a 'Celtic fringe' of alliances among Irish and British mountain training organisations in his role as chair of a joint consultative committee.

The early 1980s were a difficult time for him and his family; he was made redundant in 1983, but said afterwards that it was the 'best thing that could have happened', as he undertook consultancy work, lectured and produced a number of walking guides for Gill and Macmillan while also editing Irish Mountain Log, which he had founded in 1979. In 1986, he had a coronary bypass operation, and his son Nicholas died the following year. However, there was some good news also with the arrival of his first grandchild, Christopher.

He served on Cospóir, the national sports council, from 1974 to 1984, and advised on curriculums for outdoor pursuits courses and organisation of outdoor education centres run by Vocational Education committees. Dissatisfied with Ordnance Survey maps of Connacht at the time, he re-surveyed the region's mountains in 1988 and published *Mountains of Connemara* under Robinson's Folding Landscapes imprint. He was also a contributor to *Encyclopaedia Britannica*, and continued his civil engineering work – such as with the Office of Public Works at the Skellig Michael world heritage site off Co Kerry, and on a number of pier and harbour schemes.

His natural style was one of 'benign persuasion', but he could be a tough and determined negotiator when required, though always willing to see the other's perspective. In recognition of his extraordinary voluntary work and achievements, an honorary doctorate from Trinity College Dublin (2001) was conferred on him and he received the Irish Sports Council's inaugural Sport Volunteer of the Year Award (2005).

He celebrated his 80th birthday climbing *Paradise Lost* and abseiling *Winder's Slab* at Dalkey Quarry on his 82nd birthday. Both were to raise money for cancer research, as he had had treatment himself. Joss is survived by his wife Nora, his daughters Ruth and Clodagh, and his three grandchildren.

The editor is grateful to Frank Nugent, Mountaineering Ireland and The Irish Times for their contributions to this obituary.

John Moss 1943 - 2010

Professor Emeritus John Moss took us all by surprise when he contracted cancer in October 2009. After an eight-month battle he died at home in Cape Town on 30 May in the arms of his family.

John's passing created a void that is unlikely to be filled any time soon. He was a rock solid fixture and focal point for visiting climbers to South Africa. His popular *ad hoc* 'slide shows' at home were not to be missed. He delighted us with his deadpan humour in descriptions of his travels, and

John Moss

it was a given, no matter what the travel circumstances, that there would always be a mountain climbed or attempted. These Moss 'soirées' always had an added attraction – you were as likely to meet a Nobel Laureate as a big wall speed merchant from California or a distinguished mountain lecturer from Europe. Charismatic as they come, John had a gift for hosting and entertaining a wide variety of people from academia, mountaineering and sailing (I sailed into his life 22 years ago) all thrown together on the same couch.

British born and educated, with a PhD in inorganic chemistry from Leeds University, he was regular of the British rock-climbing scene in the 60s making many first ascents on Yorkshire limestone, in the Avon Gorge, Cheddar Gorge and in Derbyshire. He was president of the Leeds University Union Climbing Club from 1966 to 1968.

With his PhD in hand, and several summers in the Alps under his belt, John struck out for the Canadian Rockies, finding time to fit in a position as a Postdoctoral Research Fellow at the University of Alberta. Partnered by Brian Greenwood, between 1969 and 1970 the pair made first ascents of Mt. Colin (winter), *Balrog* at Yamnuska, and the north-east face of Mt Babel, which some consider was a decade ahead of its time. Joined by Oliver Woolcock and Chris Jones, he also made the first ascent of the north face of Hungabee in addition to many early ascents of other peaks in the range. In 1971, following in the wake of Chouinard and Tompkins, John and friends drove a wreck from Edmonton to Patagonia and failed on the North Tower of Paine due to bad weather.

With an academic career always on the boil, in 1973 John changed hemispheres and took a position in the chemistry department at Rhodes University, Grahamstown, South Africa, becoming the head of inorganic chemistry from 1977 to 1979. Later in 1979 he 'tied himself in' at the base of Table Mountain in the chemistry department at the University of Cape Town. This suited his mountain passions admirably, allowing him to climb actively for the next three decades at weekends and during school holidays on the warm 'Table Mountain sandstone' that the Western Cape Province is famous for.

In 1995 John was named the Jamison Professor of Inorganic Chemistry at UCT and in 1997 he was made head of the chemistry department. Throughout his academic career he published more than 300 scientific papers and maintained active collaborations with colleagues from Cambridge, the California Institute of Technology, Colorado State University in Fort Collins and Lund University in Sweden. As a visiting research associate with long periods away from base, always joined by his wife Lynn and daughters Tara and Miranda, John was a master of the art of combining the university sabbatical with mountain travel. To wit, you could not imagine him entering into a collaboration with an institution in the flatlands of Midwestern America.

Like many 'university climbers', before a family entered the picture he ranged far and wide during the longer breaks with expeditions to Mt Kenya in the mid '70s, including the north face of Batian, the *Ice Window*, and the fourth ascent (first in a single day) of the north-east pillar of Nelion. In 1976 with Paul Fatti, his partner on many adventures, he climbed a new route on Kilimanjaro's Kersten glacier. Expeditions to Baffin Island, Patagonia and Nepal followed.

A keen offshore sailor, he crewed in many ocean races including the Cape to Uruguay Race in 1982 and the Diaz Race, Lisbon to Cape Town, in 1987. When I sailed in on *Pelagic* in 1988 after my first Antarctic climbing expedition, John found me at the yacht club bar. The next day (with a hangover) we roped up and climbed the airy Africa Crag – the visiting guest's intro to Table Mountain. Thus began two decades of non-academic collaboration between us, climbing far and wide in the Western Cape, and also a memorable junket in 2006 to Namibia to climb Spitzkope. As recently as 2008, with Paul Fatti and other friends, John sailed on *Pelagic Australis* in Tierra del Fuego and attempted and failed on Mt. Frances in the Beagle Channel. Bad weather and possibly age (so the story goes) both played their part.

In 1990, John instigated an ambitious project to sail from South Africa to South Georgia and then to the Antarctic Peninsula to celebrate the centenary of the Mountain Club of South Africa. My team on *Pelagic* was scheduled to meet them on the Peninsula in January 1991 for a united effort on some virgin summits, but as it happened technical problems with their boat *Diel* pushed the schedule back and then an engine failure on the way to South Georgia unfortunately made the Peninsula rendezvous impossible. While on the island, attempts on Mt Paget and Mt Spaaman failed due to the usual ferocious weather, but the team did manage the first ascent of Mt Senderens at the southern end of the island.

During my many sailing visits to Cape Town and since becoming resident in 2002, almost without exception John would be on the phone during the week planning a day out on rock for the next weekend. We were a group of friends straddling the right and wrong side of 60 who were John's followers and we all took it for granted that his unfailing enthusiasm would somehow keep us all fit and moving through the vertical. In scientific jargon he was a constant in a society of variables. No less enigmatic, he was the chemistry professor who struggled with the idea of a cell phone, and we all loved him for it.

Skip Novak

Frederick Robert (Bob) Robinson 1922 - 2010

Bob Robinson

My first meeting with Bob was memorable. Lacking a guidebook and lost on one of the steeper routes in West Virginia, a partner and I debated, over-committed leader calling to distant second, how and where the route might, or might not, progress. Our conversation carried, for detailed instructions emerged from an invisible presence below the tree canopy. The accent was English, the tone gravelly. After our ascent and descent we found Bob and his wife Joan comfortably seated at their camping van. Bob and I started a friendship that lasted until his death on 17 May 2010, but it was at Seneca on that warm summer evening in 1969 that I first experienced Bob and Joan's welcome and natural inclusiveness.

Bob was born on 9 July 1922, the son of an engineer and one of four brothers, all of whom, in varying degrees, shared his zest for outdoor activities. A thoroughly practical and pragmatic man, Bob made consistent contributions to mountaineering and climbing throughout his life where his engineering, inventive, administrative and legal skills could be put to good use. He lived virtually all his life on the Surrey-Hampshire borders, apart from an adventurous four years attached to the British embassy in Washington.

Displaying a natural mechanical aptitude, Bob qualified as a Chartered Engineer at the Royal Aircraft Establishment, Farnborough. His early outdoor experiences were with the Scouts where he was first exposed to camping, mountain walking, caving and canoeing, all of which he continued in later life. His first alpine experience, in 1947, was with the Mountaineering Section of the Camping Club. However it was with AC and Midland Association of Mountaineers members that he completed most of his alpine ascents between 1952 and 1976.

Bob's mountain skills and judgement were exemplary. Rarely flustered, his judgment in extreme situations was impeccable. Many of his climbing companions thank Bob for extricating them from difficult situations. Bob did not climb at the extreme limits but was at his best on mixed ground. Caught in bad weather on the summit plateau following an ascent of Old Brenva with a party that included the AC's Norman Cochran, Bob persuaded his companions that the safest retreat was to reverse their ascent route. He had taken the precaution of recording bearings from the exit couloirs through the séracs. The party was able to retreat, narrowly avoiding a catastrophe when one slipped, pulling four from their steps who were only held by the fifth man. Many years later Bob and I were members of a large club party traversing the Olan when we were caught in a severe electric storm close to the summit. An epic abseil descent in appalling weather followed; Bob in his element, a totally trustworthy and reliable companion.

His alpine routes included many of the classics. Bob's own favourites included the Monte Rosa routes *Topham Arête* and *Cresta Rey*. He knew the ground well and had completed the traverse from Zermatt to Gressoney in a thick cloud, including many of the summits. These were typical of his aspirations towards classic, now perhaps less fashionable, routes with a sense of adventure. Together we climbed the Bumillergrat on the Palu, finally traversing a slushy Palu ridge in the late afternoon sun. This was one of the few occasions when Bob expressed concern at conditions and I was thankful it was him on the other end of the rope. Over a two-week period we climbed many of the classic Bernina routes.

Within the South-east, Bob was a member of an active core of climbers exploring then relatively unknown crags in the Wye Valley. Sadly they failed to retain records of first ascents. He always maintained that many routes attributed to others had first been climbed by his group.

Bob qualified as Chartered Patent Agent and in this capacity he was seconded from the RAE to the Washington embassy between 1967 and 1972. Bob eagerly grasped the opportunity, rapidly establishing contact with the Potomac Appalachian Trail Club Mountaineering Section, of which he subsequently became chair. Over five years, often accompanied by Joan, he undertook regular forays into many of the climbing and wilderness areas in the US with American friends, expatriate British climbers including Roger Wallis of the AC, and visitors from the UK. His own account of the period includes trips and expeditions to the Selkirks, Texas, Bugaboos, Wind Rivers, Wyoming, Yosemite and Mt Rainier as well as the Eastern crags and outcrops. Bob wrote two inspirational articles for the *MAM Journal* describing the North American climbing scene covering not only the climbs and mountains but commenting on the different social and class structure.

He noted that American climbers tended to come from mainly highly educated professional classes. With evident approval, Bob recorded that a climbing newsletter known as *The Eastern Trade* was in circulation. The 'Trade' connotation was a deliberate reference by the editor to Victorian England and the 'lesser business classes'. He thoroughly approved of the emancipation of climbing. While at Washington, Bob wrote the first comprehensive guide to Seneca Rocks and became chair of the climbing group within the local section of the Appalachian Trail Club. Never afraid to voice an opinion, one may imagine his none too gentle cajoling to utilise natural protection rather than the pitons that were spattered liberally across many Eastern US crags in the '60s.

As an engineer and lawyer, Bob made an extended contribution to the BMC, serving on the Equipment sub-committee, South-west committee and the Management committee. Sceptical about unproven theoretical assertions, Bob consistently advocated empirical testing of equipment and techniques. He contributed to the development of glass fibre reinforced wood ice-axes. While significantly improving the strength and despite handling characteristics superior to early metal axes, Stubai turned down the opportunity to manufacture them for the mass market for 'aesthetic reasons'. Bob was a strong advocate of dynamic leader belaying during the late '60s – the practice of allowing controlled slippage of the rope in a leader fall. Arnold Wexler and Bob conducted practice sessions for novices with 'Oscar', an 80-kilo dummy. Bob was elected President of the MAM in 1975, a post he retained for two years.

Naturally inventive, in retirement Bob became an active member of Remap the charity devoted to producing customised technical aids for disabled persons. He took a particular pride in his own designs, all of which involved innovative one-off engineering solutions. When loss of mobility prevented active participation, Bob maintained a strong interest in mountaineering and the exploits of succeeding generations. Bob made his mark in mountaineering. He put back more than he had taken and we are grateful.

Bill Thurston

Balwant Singh Sandhu
1934 - 2010

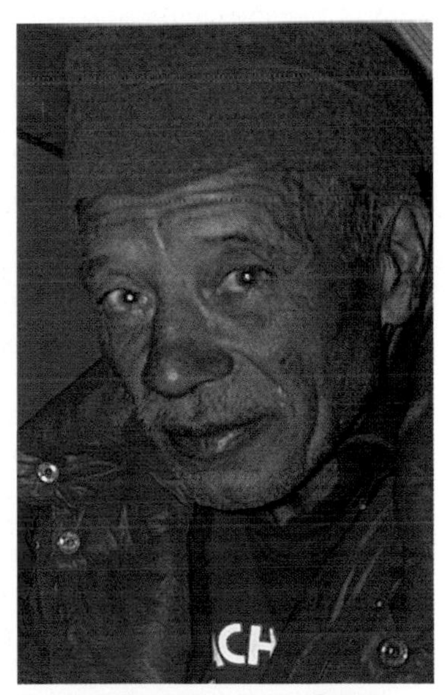

Balwant Sandhu. *(Doug Scott)*

Balwant Sandhu was not as one would imagine a Sikh colonel in the Indian Army to be. On the Indo-British Changabang Expedition of 1974 most of his resting time was spent reading Arthur Miller or chatting away, in his deep baritone voice, interspersed with infectious chuckles of laughter, on every subject under the sun with the odd line or two from Browning or W B Yeats thrown in for good measure.

Balwant was co-leader of the expedition, along with Chris Bonington, although it was Balwant who had overseen its organisation right up to base camp. He had tremendous respect from the Army members of the Indian contingent who helped progress the expedition, as far as the British knew, with very little fuss or bother. Subsequently, Balwant, Chris, Martin Boysen, Dougal Haston, Sherpa Tashi and myself all made the first ascent of Changabang (6864m). We came back with mutual respect for each other enhanced and looked forward to further climbs together, especially with Balwant.

Santokh Singh Sandhu, a Sikh farmer living near Lahore, in what is now Pakistan, had five sons and the eldest was Balwant Singh Sandhu, born 1 October 1934. Since Sikhs are traditionally warriors it was not unusual for at least one member of the family to enter the Army. In 1957 Balwant was commissioned into the Mahar Machine Gun Regiment. Five years later he volunteered for the Parachute Regiment. He later taught at the Army College of Combat for three years and then went on to command the Sixth Parachute Battalion with distinction from 1971 to 1976. In 1980 he became Principal of the Nehru Institute of Mountaineering at Uttarkashi for five years. By this time Balwant had become one of the most experienced Indian mountaineers, a fact recognised by his peers who invited him to become an honorary member of the Alpine Club. He was later elected on to the governing council of the Indian Mountaineering Foundation for six years. He was also an honorary secretary of the Central Himalayan Environment Association, represented India on the UIAA for four years, and was president of the Himalayan Club from 1983-1985.

In 1981 he was given the Arjuna award for excellence in mountaineering in recognition of a lifetime of walking and climbing in remote and little-known regions of the Himalaya. There is only space to mention the highlights of his climbing career, the first being the first ascent of the North Peak of Bancha Dhura solo (c6000m) in 1962. Other first ascents included Shinkun (6065m in Lahaul, 1968), Changabang (6864m, 1974), Phawararang (6349m, 1979), Mamostong Kangri (7516m) in the East Karakoram (1984), Kabru Dome (6600m) via a new route (1985), the difficult west face and west ridge of Kamet (7756m, 1985), Manirang II (6100m) climbed together with his German wife, Helga, whom he had married in 1976 and Chombu East Peak, NE Sikkim (5745m, 1996). In 2001 Rudugaira (5816m) and in 2002 Jogin III (6116m) were climbed during Doon School Expeditions to the Garhwal Himalaya.

This list represents only part of his lifetime love of climbing. He could not, however, as he said, put himself 'through so much torture as to go to Everest' but he did help others to go through organising various training camps for young Indian climbers. He also took part in a variety of expeditions as leader or co-leader with foreign climbers, schools, colleges, the IMF and with his beloved 'Paras'.

In 1973 he led the Indo-British Expedition that put Chris Bonington and Nick Escourt on the summit of Brammah (6416m) in the Kishtwar. In 1975 he was deputy leader of an Indo-French Nanda Devi Traverse expedition. Balwant, with French climbers and also with his great Indian friends Prem Chand and Dorje Lhatoo, climbed Nanda Devi main peak (7816m). The expedition also climbed Nanda Devi East (7434m) but bad weather thwarted achievement of its main objective which was to link the two summits by a high level traverse. Balwant broke a leg, making the descent something of an epic, but then not for the first time. He had injured himself on several occasions previously, from rockfall in 1961 and again in 1964, surviving a 1000m avalanche but breaking a leg. Later on the Indo-New Zealand expedition to Rataban (6166m) he was again injured by rockfall. It seemed there might be some truth in the saying 'old soldiers never die'.

Balwant was physically as well as mentally tough and could move easily and naturally through the mountains, acclimatising well and able to cope with all the usual frustrations without irritation. If ever a man lived his life to the full it was he. Apart from his love of mountaineering and Army life, and the thrill of making over 150 parachute drops, he enjoyed shooting, fishing, horse-riding and riding his Bullet motorbike, usually at considerable speed, not always successfully but he did survive several accidents.

My appreciation of Balwant increased with every meeting – after Changabang, on Shivling (6543m) in 1981 then north-east Sikkim with Suman Dubey and other English and American friends in 1986. None of us on that expedition will ever forget the journey from Delhi on the Raj Dani Express enthralled with Balwant's stories of the partition of India and the more recent history of the Subcontinent. I again joined Balwant on the Raj Dani Express, this time to Guwahati for our attempt to reach Takpasiri on the Indo-Tibetan border with Greg Child and Akhil Sapru in 1999. Balwant had already agreed to and succeeded in reconnoitring the route through the jungles of Arunachal Pradesh the year before. This was a considerable achievement for a 65 year old, alone but for the local Nishi people. Our expedition, after an 18-day 'rumble in the jungle', arrived below our mountain but unable to climb it; only Akhil was fit since I had torn a tendon in my knee, Greg had blood poisoning and Balwant was struck down with malaria. We retreated to recover happily in Balwant's genial company at the Dibrugarh Military Hospital. We never found time to climb together again.

Balwant stayed at my home in 2004 with his wife Helga, where I was able to reciprocate the whole-hearted hospitality laid on four years before at their home in the Shimla Hills of Himachal Pradesh. We made plans to visit Arunachal Pradesh again and also Nepal, but too late.

On 3 December Balwant Sandhu was struck by a speeding car near the Indian Mountaineering Foundation building in New Delhi. He was immediately taken to the Army Research and Referral Hospital in New Delhi where he failed to regain consciousness. On 10 December Balwant passed away leaving Helga and their son Cornelius (Muki) grieving at his bedside and for all of us who knew him everywhere to grieve for a courageous climber and loyal friend.

Doug Scott

David Smith

Francis David Smith 1928 - 2008

David Smith died on 5 April 2008, just over a month after reaching his 80th birthday. He was born in Burnley on St David's Day 1928 and lived all his life in that locality. He attended local schools and completed his education at Burnley College and Accrington College, becoming a chartered engineer, member of the Institution of Production Engineers and of the Institution of Electrical Engineers. He served his engineering apprenticeship with Burco Ltd followed by 43 years with Morley Products Ltd and its various successor firms, in the production of domestic gas and electric appliances, finishing as works manager, with additional roles in graduate and apprentice training in the district.

David's outdoor life started with his family on the local hills, first climbing Pendle at the age of four. He joined Burnley YHA Group in 1944, and the Lancashire Caving & Climbing Club in 1947, the year of his first mountaineering holiday on Skye with Harold Wiseman when he climbed Sgurr Alasdair and the Inaccessible Pinnacle. In 1948 he climbed on Arran and cycled to Cape Wrath, and in 1949 had his first sight of the Alps, cycling from Lyon to Monte Carlo over the Alps and returning via Avignon. In 1952 he climbed almost every weekend in the Lakes with Douglas Spray, and with him completed the Cuillin Main Ridge for the first time, in 10 hours from top to top.

In 1955 David joined the Yorkshire Ramblers' Club, of which he remained an active and devoted member for the rest of his life, with 40 years' continuous membership of the committee in one role or another – the length of his list of offices remains a club record. He gave much time and energy to the two club huts, at Low Hall Garth in Little Langdale and Lowstern, Clapham, where he was renowned for his catering, especially at Christmas meets. He served as president from 1976 to 1978 and was elected an honorary member in 1990.

David climbed in the Alps every year from 1953 to 1966, his first season being at Zermatt when he climbed the Rimpfischhorn, Weisshorn and Dom but was beaten off the Matterhorn by bad weather. From 1955 onwards his alpine climbing was entirely with YRC members, and from 1986 he organised regular alpine meets, attending all from then until 2003, apart from 1997 when he was recovering from a hernia operation. His ascent of the Grépon was amusingly described by the late Roger Allen in *YRC Journal* Vol IX as part of a composite article, 'Shambles in the Alps', the tongue-in-cheek British humour of which was not appreciated by the reviewer in a certain overseas alpine journal who concluded that the YRC were a right 'shower'. In his later years he climbed a number of trekking peaks in Nepal, Bolivia and Peru on YRC expeditions.

David was elected to the Alpine Club in 1961, proposed by Harry Stembridge. Although he was not particularly active with the club as such, he was well known as a YRC representative at club functions. In 1965 he booked to attend the AC Matterhorn Centenary dinner in Zermatt with Roger Allen and others, but their traverse of the Rothorn from Zinal took so long that they only reached Zermatt after the dinner was over.

My own friendship with David began in 1957 at a meet on Hadrian's Wall when we climbed together on High Shield Crag above Crag Lough. From then into the late 1960s we had many times together on the hill and underground, as well as working on the club huts to which he devoted much time and effort. Underground, with his climbing skills, he was always the last in the party to get his feet wet. On the annual YRC Long Walks, I soon found that if I could keep up with him at the outset his steady pace would see me through the walk. Two events in Scotland stand out: the Cuillin Main Ridge in 1961 in mist with him and Roger Allen, David's second traverse, 13hrs 50mins peak to peak, 18hrs 30mins Scavaig to Scavaig, followed two days later by a fine day on the Blaven – Clach Glas traverse, and a rapid descent on Good Friday 1963 from Ben Lui in an avalanche, as a party of six of whom four were actual or prospective members of the AC, memorably described by Louis Baume in *YRCJ* IX. I had just two alpine holidays with David. In 1963 we went with Roger Allen to the Dauphiné. Our first climb was the Aiguille Dibona by the *Boell Route*, where David's insistence that we be prepared for any eventuality resulted in our being so heavily laden that we nearly did have to bivouac, coupled with his mistaking the crux pitch and leading, quite competently I must say, the nearby grade V+ pitch on a much harder route.

After that we had a great trip, traversing the Ecrins by its south face. Difficulty in following the complex route meant that we reached the summit ridge too late to go to the Barre, and satisfied ourselves with the lesser 4000m top Pic Lory, before descending the voie normale to the glacier below the hut, where we tried out our new homemade lightweight bivouac tents rather than face the climb up to the hut. The ensuing glacier tour past the splendid Pelvoux, Coup de Sabre and Pic Sans Nom took us back to the Temple Ecrins hut, where we were greeted by the warden and a reporter from the regional paper, who credited us with the first traverse of the season.

David was a fine writer, with numerous articles in the *YRC Journal*, as well as obituaries in the *AJ*. One useful innovation he made was to invite YRC members to lodge their life stories with him to ease the task of obituary writers for the club journal, and a significant part of this notice comes from his contribution to that file.

In 1966 David married Elspeth, an active member of the Fell & Rock Climbing Club, and throughout their 41 years of marriage they spent many happy days on the hill together and with their two children, while encouraging each other to be active with their respective clubs. He had a strong Catholic faith, which he followed in harmony with Elspeth who is a United Reformed Church lay preacher, and would quietly slip away from a meet on a Sunday morning to attend mass. He actively supported his local church in Nelson which the Catholics and Methodists share, and it was there that his funeral took place, conducted by his Catholic priest with assistance from the Methodist and URC ministers. The church was filled with a congregation of about 250 drawn from family, church, former colleagues and YRC members and their wives, the AC being represented by then president, Paul Braithwaite.

Richard Gowing

Pat Vaughan 1931 - 2009

Pat Vaughan winter climbing on Snowdon. *(Neville Drasdo)*

At Pat's funeral last year, Stephen Andrews, vice-president of the Climbers' Club, recalled that Pat had joined the CC in 1962, but had begun climbing in London with the 'Bar-Room Mountaineers'. Our friendship dates from that earlier era, in the late forties when the Bar Roomers were active at Harrison's Rocks. Apart from the climbing, many of their escapades involved the vehicles used to get to and from the rocks.

I well remember returning from Groombridge one Sunday night, driving up the hill into Sevenoaks on our ex-WD Norton 500 combination, when a retarded ignition caused the exhaust to overheat and become red-hot, with sparks flying and the engine threatening to explode. As I pulled on to the verge, Pat, just behind on his Rudge, had the presence of mind to draw alongside and reach for the petrol tap, below the fuel tank, to switch it off, as we scrambled to abandon ship. Cool, calm, intelligent, and ever ready to meet a challenge, these were the qualities that distinguished him, in life generally and in his climbing.

He was an ideal leader, careful, strong and in control. I remember him on *Great Slab* on Cloggy, leading Jean, to whom he was engaged, and the delicate way he moved across the upper traverse, whilst we contented ourselves with the *voie normale*. Well capable of the sandstone test pieces at Harrison's, Pat, with Dave Thomas and Johnnie Lees, climbed at a notch higher than most of us in North Wales, the Lakes and Scotland. At Tremadog he was involved in the early exploration of the crag, and was responsible for first ascents of *Valerie's Rib*, *Belshazzar* and *Creag Dhu Wall*. He was unfazed by the early Brown routes; Ken Wilson wrote in *The Black Cliff* 'the only repetitions outside the Rock and Ice Group were Pat Vaughan's ascent of *Hangover* in 1952 and Bob Downes of *Octo* in 1955'. In the Lakes in 1951 he got one of the great plums with the ascent of *Fools in Paradise* in Borrowdale.

He had three seasons of guideless climbing in the Alps in 1951/2/3, during the last of which Gwen and I joined up with him in Courmayeur, where he arrived unexpectedly with Geoff Millwood and Dick Tombs from the Bregaglia. We all went up to the Noire hut and encountered Hamish Nicol and Alan Blackshaw. Alan was unwell and decided not to climb, which was fortuitous for us, as it meant that Pat and Hamish could climb together, making three ropes of two. They decided to attempt the south ridge of the Aiguille Noire de Peuterey without a bivouac, which they achieved magnificently, and after a dawn start were back at the hut by 9pm. This was the second British ascent of the route (the first in one day) and marked the apex of Pat's alpine climbing. He was subsequently elected to the ACG and joined the Alpine Club in 1967.

Pat's background had been something of a mystery to us. We knew he was a student, lived alone, and seemed unusually self-sufficient and mature. He rarely mentioned his family, but his daughter has filled in some of the history. He was brought up in London and Sussex by his mother and maternal grandmother, his father having left the family during his infancy. Aged eight he was sent to Kingham Hill as a boarder. He showed an early self-determination by running away twice and pleading to go to day school. He transferred to Steyning Grammar School where he was very happy. Whilst there he set up an enterprise selling eggs and chickens to the villagers. He experimented with crossing the birds to get better layers, showing, at this early stage, both talent as a natural scientist and a good head for business. It was an exciting time for a schoolboy to be living in south-east England. Holidays and weekends were often spent in London where he could see the bomb damage from the Blitz, and he had a grandstand view of the aerial dog fights over the Sussex countryside.

In 1944, when his grandmother died, his mother and stepfamily moved into her cottage, where for a few years they lived a normal family life. In 1948, when Pat finished school, they emigrated to Australia, but he chose to stay in London to study science at university and do his National Service. It was at this stage, after hitchhiking to Skye, that he discovered rockclimbing. He was captivated and it became a lifelong passion, even more consuming than his enthusiasm for motor-sport and driving fast cars.

He was called up in autumn 1953 and began aircrew training at RAF Ternhill as an acting Pilot Officer. Surprisingly, for Pat was exactly the 'right stuff' for a fighter pilot (he even looked like one), he was axed along with 50 percent of the intake, before the end of the course. He transferred to RAF Hendon and was attached to a medical research unit, as assistant to Danny Abse, a consultant radiologist and poet. He developed an interest in ultrasonic physics which led, much later, to a PhD and research into the medical applications of this speciality.

After demob, married to Jean and expecting their first child, Pat began to think seriously about career and family. His first job was as works chemist with a small company in the emerging industry of synthetic polymers. At the same time he became a part-time student of the Plastics Institute to study for their diploma, successfully completing the two-year course in one year to become an Associate.

Their second daughter was born in 1960, and in the same year he went into partnership with an economist colleague. The next 20 years were ones of happy family life and developing the business. Climbing was put on the 'back burner', but he still managed to get away for the odd weekend in Wales with the Drasdo brothers, Eric Herbert and Hugh Banner, maintaining his technical ability in the E1 grades. This busy and productive time ended tragically with Jean's death in 1981, following a long depressive illness.

At this point we began to see more of Pat; our own children were leaving the nest, and like him we had just discovered downhill skiing. For the next decade we worked our way through the major alpine resorts with Pat, enjoying his entertaining and ever good-humoured companionship. Our best week was at Davos in January 1987, when the temperature never rose above zero, the sun shone continuously and we skied till we dropped. During this time Pat sold his business, which had been highly successful and ensured him a comfortable retirement. He bought a converted windmill in Essex, a cottage in Snowdonia and, with a V sign to the RAF, acquired a personal pilot's licence.

Harold Drasdo introduced him to Audrey Jones, who had recently divorced, and the two of them discovered a mutually supportive relationship, marrying in 1989. They retired to a beautiful house on the Menai Straits and spent the summers in Portugal. When Pat became ill with Alzheimer's, Audrey nursed him devotedly, visiting him daily when he entered the nursing home at Menai Bridge for his last two years. It was a very sad time for the family, distressing to see the slow decline of this fine mind and physique. We will remember him as he was: a great character who added a touch of glamour to the climbing scene, a perfect companion, intelligent and sensitive to the needs of others, but with a steely determination within.

Denis Greenald

Neville Drasdo writes: With the demise of Pat Vaughan, climbing has lost one of its most entertaining and charismatic personalities. I climbed with Pat at regular intervals for many years and found it a rewarding experience. A special bonus was the interesting conversations we had on the long drive to Wales, though this was occasionally punctuated by some tense moments due to his preoccupation with the performance of his car. Among my most memorable experiences were several weekends when we climbed Snowdon gullies and ridges on the Saturday in extreme winter conditions – once falling through a cornice above Cwm Glas, and by contrast, spent the following day on the Anglesey sea cliffs in brilliant sunshine.

It never failed to amaze me how Pat, at about fifty years of age, having little or no practice in between our well-spaced visits, could launch himself into the lead on routes such as *Central Park*, *Fifth Avenue* and *Gogarth*, where I often felt we were climbing near to the limit of our performance. But it was the same adventurous spirit and willingness to meet formidable difficulties head-on that pervaded his life from his earliest alpine experiences and allowed him while struggling to establish a successful business in the competitive field of acrylic chemistry, to take a part time PhD in ultrasonic physics and then to work in his spare time in a voluntary capacity on its medical applications. After one of these days on Anglesey I remember vividly, one moment as we sped homewards across the island, accompanied by suitable music, with the whole Snowdon range spread out before us, snow covered and illuminated by the late afternoon sun. I remarked that though life has a limited span we had really had had some fantastic days. Pat agreed contentedly, and that is how I like to remember him.

Chris Walker 1980 - 2010

Chris Walker was born on 16 March 1980 and died on the descent from Buchaille Etive Mor along with his client Robert Pritchard on the 24th February 2010. The accident robbed the mountaineering community and the Alpine Club of a larger than life character, who shared his passion for the mountains easily and willingly with anybody who joined him out on the hill.

I first met Chris whilst he was working on the 'Night Watch' at Glenmore Lodge. We had both topped out of routes on the Mess of Pottage, Coire an 't Sneachda, into a full Cairngorm gale; as I covered my eyes to shield them from the elements Chris looked across and announced 'this is bloody amazing'. The descent into Coire Cas was quickly conducted to the accompaniment of much staggering, struggling against the wind with hoods cinched tightly down – yet the eyes of one member of these parties burned brighter than the rest, despite the wind driven snow. It took a few years to recognise what being in the mountains was about for Chris; yes, it was about climbing, but it was also about sharing an experience with other people, a zest for life and for adventure. It was this humble approach to the mountains that ensured that the last route completed was always the best, regardless of whether it was a small Scottish snow gully or a major Himalayan expedition peak. Of course, being Chris it was always 'the best' followed or proceeded by a string of highly descriptive expletives, which if delivered by anybody else would be most offensive.

A little while later I saw Chris again, this time camped at Les Chosalets campsite in Argentiére. As well as chain-smoking roll-ups and drinking excessive quantities of cheap lager, Chris had also managed to amass a significant collection of mountaineering successes in France and

Chris Walker, Pakistan, 2007
(James Thacker)

Switzerland with Paul Dickson, Neil Pickstock and Neil Johnson. A fraction of these achievements would please any aspiring British alpinist.

Here on Les Chosalets, Chris explained how he had always wanted to be a cowboy. At 16 he had started his adventures by securing some work on a cattle ranch in Wyoming, presumably where he developed his passion for burgers and his loathing of vegetables. He recounted that not long after the ranching he had busked his way around Australia, before returning to work in the UK and making a chance decision to go climbing with his shop manager.

The town of Bury was, in his own words, the scene of perhaps one of Chris's 'greatest achievements' when not only did he witness an armed raid while working at Halfords, but spent the vast majority of the time with a gun held to his head. The ensuing well practised tale took on epic proportions which entertained many folk in warm bars, cold bivouacs, chilly base camps, smoke filled teahouses and finally at a packed funeral in Cumbria, where Chris' favourite line was used again: 'Empty the till or I'll blow your f***ing brains out!!!'

After surviving this episode Chris moved to Llanberis, starting an instructor training scheme based in the mountains of Snowdonia and climbing for himself at every available opportunity. He was taken under the wing of British Mountain Guides Phil and Al George, spending a particularly memorable day at Gogarth where he quietly decided he wanted to become a guide himself. Chris was eternally grateful to the George brothers for taking him climbing on that day, never for a moment considering that they, like many of his climbing partners since, had recognised his zest for life and adventure.

This period in North Wales paved the way for Chris's acceptance onto the Night Watch Scheme at Glenmore Lodge, Chris's strategy at the interviews, to be the last one standing at the bar, seemingly meeting with some success.

Following his time at the Lodge Chris travelled and climbed in many mountain areas including the Himalaya, making many friends who drew him back for numerous visits. Successful trips were made to Aconcagua (6962m), Island Peak (6189m), Lobuche East (6090m), Mera Peak (6476m), Elbrus (5642m) and Baruntse (7220m). One of Chris's proudest moments was summiting Ama Dablam (6856m) in 2005 whilst working for Tim Mosedale. As well as being an accomplished climber, Chris recognised that being abroad for long periods was challenging for family and friends, and it was whilst on Ama Dablam that Chris set to work filming his ascent to show those at home what he had been up to. The resulting DVD not only proved popular with his family but was also used in Sheffield schools as a resource in leisure and tourism classes – Chris's film being a particular hit with teenage girls.

After one such Himalayan trip five years ago Chris, influenced by one of his best friends Ian Boorman, decided to make a new base in Keswick. Within a short space of time he was part of the community, initially working as a freelance instructor for local outdoor centres but soon establishing Chris Walker Mountaineering, rapidly building up an extensive and loyal clientele who provided a basis for his new company Mountain Approach.

While based in the Lakes, Chris also frequently worked in Scotland, living in Fort William over the winter. It was here that he often worked for local mountain guide Alan Kimber, somebody whom he frequently referred to as 'a hero'. Despite having known Alan for only a short while, Chris's superior people skills were evident again as he devoured Sue Kimber's legendary flapjack, did his washing in her machine and linked in to Alan's wi-fi connection, all within a couple of weeks of arriving in Fort William. Of course, this was all well received and Chris became a regular visitor, alongside many guides and instructors, sitting down around the kitchen table to discuss the latest conditions on the hill.

It was this good grounding in the Scottish winter and its sometimes infernal conditions which helped Chris to pass his assessment for the Mountain Instructor Certificate (MIC) with flying colours in the winter of 2009. Shortly afterwards he described how he was feeling relaxed and confident and was looking forward to working in Scotland with all his assessments behind him.

Chris's life ended tragically whilst descending the west spur of Coire na Tulaich when a small section of windslab released, knocking him and Robert Pritchard off their feet. Both were taken down steep ground with tragic results. The last pictures downloaded from Chris's camera were taken that day on *Curved Ridge* and show a friend, climber, instructor and guide climbing the 'latest best route' with the same passion I had witnessed in the Cairngorms years before.

Chris Walker joined the Alpine Club in 2005. He is survived by his parents Gill and Geoff Walker.

James Thacker

Alpine Club Notes

200. John Innerdale, *Rébuffat Route, Aiguille du Midi,* chromacolour, 32 x 45cm, 2008.

PAUL BRAITHWAITE

President's Valedictory Address

Read before the Alpine Club on 4 December 2010

The 2nd June 1953 was my seventh birthday. That morning at the school gates I was surprised to find that everyone was celebrating. Union Jacks were flying from the school tower and at assembly we were told the celebration was, of course, for the coronation of Queen Elizabeth II, together with the announcement that Mount Everest had been climbed by Sherpa Tenzing and Sir Edmund Hillary. From a 7-year-old's perspective all was well with the world; Britain doing what it does best.

I vividly remember gazing at the photos of Tenzing on the summit that were splashed over all the newspapers. They left a lasting impression on me.

Everest had finally been climbed on 29 May, which coincidentally is Doug Scott's birthday. The day of the announcement was 2 June, my birthday. It seems ironic that 22 years later we would both be key players in the second British expedition to succeed on Everest, this time by the south-west face in 1975. Fate – or just plain old coincidence?

I started climbing in 1961 with school friends in the Chew Valley area close to home. The local gritstone outcrops were ideal for beginners but also provided really hard test pieces of the time. These were first climbed in the late 1940s and early '50s by legends Joe Brown and Don Whillans; *Hanging Crack*, *Overhanging Crack*, *The Trident*, *Blue Lights Crack*, etc. The route names alone would send shivers down your spine. Needless to say, we were content with the easier routes at that time. I couldn't imagine how anyone could climb those overhanging horrors and it wasn't until many years later that I managed them (with far better protection than my predecessors). We had our occasional mini-expeditions to the Peak District but our Sundays were mainly spent on local outcrops and moorland scrambles.

One day, friends and I took the train into Manchester to see a lecture by the great French mountaineer Lionel Terry. His presentation was about his successful climbs in Peru and Patagonia. It was truly amazing and completely blew our tiny minds. Vivid memories of the beautiful red granite, sparkling ice and pure white snow – we had never seen anything like it. A complete contrast to our rather drab moorland outcrops.

The following year, at the age of 18, a school friend and I set off in search of that red granite. We hitchhiked from our village of Springhead, near Oldham, complete with moleskin breeches, mountain boots and ice-axes perched on top of rucksacks. On arriving in Grindelwald, we spent some hard-earned cash on a one-day glacier climbing course and a few days later proceeded to follow a guided party up the west ridge of the Eiger. We applied the same

201. Paul (Tut) Braithwaite.

tactic on the Matterhorn's *Hörnli Ridge* a few days later, mindful of keeping a respectable distance from the guide and client in front. We did all this within our two-week annual summer holidays on about £30 each.

This early adventure to the Alps triggered more interest in me for what was happening in top flight climbing and I began to take note of the escapades of leading British mountaineers of the decade – Joe Brown, Don Whillans, Chris Bonington, Tom Patey, Hamish MacInnes, Ian Clough, Les Brown, John Streetly and Robin Smith. I vividly recall the iconic photo of Don high on the Central Pillar of Frêney, wearing a flat cap and plimsolls; reports of Brown and Whillans' route on the west face of the Blatière (outstanding for its time); Chris and team, on Nuptse; and how a few years earlier Joe Brown had led the route to the summit of Kangchenjunga utilising the new technique of hand-jamming. Finally, the climax of that period must be the *Eiger Direct*, first climbed in 1966 by an all-star cast and including a relatively new kid on the block, the young Dougal Haston. The press coverage was truly amazing, showing technical climbing of the very highest standard for the time, which the public could follow closely from the comfort of Kleine Scheidegg. Sadly, the tragic death of John Harlin tainted the success and in many ways marked the end of an era.

I desperately wanted to be involved at a high level, but where to start? In the mid '60s I spent a couple of summer holidays climbing in Chamonix as a complete novice, making all the usual early mistakes. Wrong place, wrong time, too much heavy gear and always being out of sync' with the weather – the characteristics of two-week holiday mountaineering trips! I was always left frustrated and so in 1968 decided to make some fundamental changes to my life. I packed in my job and teamed up with a friend of mine, tough Lancastrian Dave Barton. On his first visit to North Wales in 1967 Dave had made his mark by soloing *Cenotaph Corner* and *Cemetery Gates*. The liaison proved to be the start of a new era in my life and what was to become a lifestyle I could have hardly dreamed of at the time.

That year we acclimatised on the *Hörnli Ridge* and made our second route the *Bonatti Pillar* on the Dru. After a long, night-time slog from Chamonix to the foot of the pillar we realised that Dave had left his share of the climbing equipment, plus our stove and guidebook, at a rest stop on the glacier. Undeterred, off we set with two ropes, 10 karabiners and one set of tape étriers between us. Several pitches up Dave took a long fall and badly injured his hand. For Dave Barton there was no question of retreat. I would have to lead the rest of the route. After a cold, uncomfortable night sitting on a sloping ledge, we set off the following morning with Dave's hand in a poor state. I followed the steep crack lines on the crest of the pillar which lead the way to the summit of the Petit Dru and by late afternoon we arrived on the summit of the Grand Dru; then came the long descent back to Chamonix. It was a baptism by fire for the pair us and my first alpine *grande course.*

Over the following weeks, along with other mates Jack Firth and Pete Hays (the Burnley lads), we did a stack of good quality routes but the time came for them to leave at the end of their summer holiday. I stayed on climbing with different partners, and totted up over 15 big routes in the mountains, eight of which were considered *grandes courses*. The highlight of that year for me was an ascent of the Walker Spur with the American climber John Martz. 'Not bad for a first season,' I was told by Nick Estcourt who in the autumn of 1968 invited me to join the ACG. I could hardly believe it. The importance of the Alpine Climbing Group to young up-and-coming mountaineers of the time was immense. It felt very special to be accepted as a member of this élite group and it certainly put a spring in my stride, giving me just the sort of encouragement I needed. The vision of those founder members of the ACG back in 1952, which allowed the modern 'young guns' of the time to join the Alpine Club, played a huge part in the club's survival and future.

The following year, 1969, I returned to Chamonix with a regular climbing partner of mine – Richard McHardy. We did a range of classic hard rock and mixed routes including the first British ascent of the Croz Spur on the north face of the Grandes Jorasses. Climbing with Richard gave me some of my most memorable days on both British crags and the mountains of the Alps. He was a few years older than me, already established as one of Britain's best climbers, and so I was very much his apprentice in those early days. Both from similar backgrounds, we had to work hard for our free time weekends and trips to the Alps each year. Those halcyon days gave us the very best of times.

Some of the main players I climbed with on the British alpine scene in the late '60s and early '70s were Al and Aid Burgess, Alan Rouse, Rab Carrington, Bill O'Connor, Paul Nunn, Richard McHardy, Pete Minx, Dan Boon, Cliff Phillips and of course Eric Jones and Leo Dickinson, climber and photographer. Also the influence of *Mountain* magazine, at that time edited by Ken Wilson, should not be underestimated as it provided regular and up-to-date articles containing the very latest information from the world's leading mountaineers. Over the next few years, my visits to the Alps were interspersed with a series of small expeditions to the Caucasus, Baffin Island, South America, Peru and the Pamirs.

Late summer of 1974 saw me driving out to the Alps with Chris Bonington and Doug Scott; during that journey, to my surprise (on Doug's recommendation), Chris invited me to join his team for an attempt on Everest's southwest face in the autumn of 1975. Of course I accepted. Before leaving in July 1975 I spent four weeks in the Alps getting into shape mentally and physically, for the big adventure. The rest is history – a life changing experience for me. A big thanks to Chris and Doug for giving me the opportunity to climb on Everest and to Nick for being a solid and dependable partner on our big day climbing the Rock Band.

The following summer, 1976, I joined a road trip to Alaska with the Burgess twins, Paul Moors and Don Whillans. Al, Aid, Paul and I did an alpine-style ascent of the classic Cassin Ridge on Denali over a period of six cold days. On the way down the normal route, we spent some time with two American climbers. One of them commented: 'So you're one of those Everest dudes are you?' Fame at last, I thought. I was somewhat taken aback and asked him which magazines he'd been reading. His reply was: 'None dude, you've got your name and expedition written in felt pen on your overgaiters!' The sort of reality check you need every now and again!

By the mid '70s and early '80s other top British mountaineers had emerged; the next generation if you like. Peter Boardman, Alex McIntyre, Joe Tasker, Dick Renshaw, Roger Baxter-Jones, Nick Colton, Andy Parkin and Mick Fowler, to name a few, were all quick to learn and took their skills and ambitions to the greater ranges, producing a string of impressive climbs, sadly not without heavy casualties.

Future generations of mountaineers can look forward to further advancements in technology with regard to clothing, more instant, accurate weather forecasting and increased understanding of the body's behaviour at altitude, along with activity-specific training and fitness regimes. I believe this will lead to cutting-edge mountaineers, who demonstrate the ever-necessary ability, desire and drive to climb bolder, faster and more efficiently in their constant search for exploration and adventure.

Below, in date order rather than preference, I have listed some routes and expeditions climbed with Alpine Club members.

North face of the Eiger with Pete Holden and Tom Leppart

The start of the 1971 season, a warm-up on the north-east face of Lyskamm then the north face of the Matterhorn. A few days later, a trip to Grindelwald. The weather still good, it was time to step out on the big one – the Eiger, possibly the greatest of all the European north faces and certainly the most formidable. Easy access from high grass pasture to the foot of the face and within an hour or so you're at the Swallow's Nest bivvi site.

From here you have to commit. I couldn't have been with a better team on this memorable climb. After the Eiger, Pete and Tom went on to complete all the six great north faces that year – the first Brits to do so I believe.

East Pillar of Mt Asgard, Baffin Island

1972 and my first trip with Doug Scott. The team included Paul Nunn, Dennis Hennek and I. Just the four of us in total isolation in the desolate Arctic landscape. A long approach walk with light rations and heavy sacks. Beautiful red granite; following crack lines and grooves to an overhanging headwall crack system which Dennis led in fine style. A truly great Arctic classic rock climb and an unforgettable expedition.

Everest south-west face, First Ascent

Everest 1975 – a life changing experience for me. Brilliant organisation by expedition leader Chris Bonington. A big team effort from all involved. The Everest story is well documented in the book and film *Everest the Hard Way*. The *après* Everest experience was an unforgettable few months. Lecture tours, invites to Buckingham Palace and Number 10 Downing Street, lavish awards ceremonies etc.

Mountaineering in Patagonia

My first trip to this region, in 1973, included the first attempt to climb Torre Egger. A tough uncompromising route, Martin Boysen and I were thwarted in the final few hundred feet due to high levels of difficulty and a constant barrage of ice falling from the summit mushrooms. After this disappointment we went on to make the first ascent of the Aig Innominata, a beautiful red granite spire in a wild, grandiose setting. The team included Martin Boysen, Eric Jones, Mick Coffey, Leo Dickinson and the great man himself, Don Whillans. American guest stars Rick Sylvester and Dan Reid were also in attendance.

Grandes Jorasses – Walker Spur (winter)

In February 1982, Roger Baxter-Jones and I did the first British winter ascent of the Walker after three attempts in previous years. The very best days of technical climbing imaginable, in full winter conditions. Those final few pitches to the summit in a heavy snowstorm as darkness approached at the end of day three added to the thrill. A makeshift bivvi on the summit, next morning the long descent to Courmayeur, the traditional hitch-hike through the Mont Blanc tunnel to Chamonix just in time for a late night party with live music in the Bar Nash. Life doesn't get better than this!

The crags of Britain and the mountains of Europe and the rest of the world have played an important part in my life for the past 50 years and I've had the good fortune to meet and climb with some of the most inspiring and extraordinary people imaginable. To Richard McHardy and Doug Scott I owe a great debt, for giving me the inspiration and direction I needed during my formative years. It's been a fascinating journey and the icing on the cake has been my time, over the past three years, as president of the Alpine Club. As my predecessors will know, it's rarely possible to realise all one's good intentions. 'Could haves, should haves' – there will always be those! I now relinquish the role of president to the capable hands of Mick Fowler and wish him well over the next three years.

Finally I would like to thank all the committee members, officers and volunteers of the club for their continued support. Without their loyal dedication and hard work, it's hard to imagine how the Alpine Club could maintain its position as such a highly respected organisation.

It's been a privilege!

STEWART HAWKINS

Pamirs Pilgrimage

This article describes a journey to Central Asia to pay homage to Wilfrid Noyce (1917-62), one of the outstanding mountaineers of his age, a man who inspired in many a love of the mountains and a desire for mountain exploration.

Wilfrid Noyce, after many first ascents in Britain and the Alps in the 1930s and 40s, made a major contribution to the successful 1953 Everest expedition led by John Hunt. He was the one who broke through to the South Col with one Sherpa after several attempts by others, thus preparing the way for the summit assault. In 1962 he accompanied Hunt on the joint British-Soviet expedition to the Pamirs; there, while descending Pik Garmo (6601m), Wilfrid and the young Scot Robin Smith fell to their deaths. As it was too dangerous to bring the bodies down they were buried in a crevasse on the mountain. By the time the British group returned to base the Russians had already built a memorial cairn to Wilfrid and Robin overlooking the Garmo glacier, not far from their first base camp.

Wilfrid Noyce taught me French at school and introduced me to the mountains. He was also my senior scoutmaster. Having travelled in Central Asia I had the desire to visit the Garmo memorial partly as an adventure but also to express my debt to Wilfrid. After discussions with Graeme Nicol and Ian McNaught-Davis, members of the 1962 expedition, I established where the memorial was. The Garmo valley is one of the more remote and inaccessible of the western Pamirs and several miles from the nearest road or habitation. I discussed the idea with Rosemary Ballard, Wilfrid's widow, and with Jeremy, their younger son, who agreed to go with me.

Through the website **Pamirs.org** I made contact with various people who had worked and trekked in Tajikistan, but there was only one Tajik organisation responded to my emails requesting assistance. This was Pamir Adventure, run by Surat Toimastov, a biologist by training and an expert photographer. He knew the area and had tried several times to get into the Garmo valley.

I had planned to go in June 2008 but detailed research indicated the Kyrgyz Ob river, which flows across the entrance to the Garmo valley, might be impassable at this time as the glacier melt would be rising. The memorial is some 12-13 miles up the valley from the Kyrgyz Ob. Jeremy and I decided to delay the trip until the glacier melt would be at its lowest and before the snows arrived. The window was the last two weeks in September and first week in October. We decided to go in 2009.

However, I felt that a reconnaissance might be useful and continued

202. At the memorial to Wilfrid Noyce and Robin Smith, Garmo Valley, Pamirs, 27 September 2009. Left to right: Barry Cooper, Peter Norton, Jeremy Noyce, Stewart Hawkins. *(Hawkins Coll.)*

with the original idea: in June 2008, with Surat, his son and a local guide, I went over the route as far as the Kyrgyz Ob. Surat has a number of local contacts and our requirements for horses and assistance for 2009 were discussed with the Tajik farmers.

In 2009 the party was completed with another pupil of Wilfrid, Peter Norton, and a friend of Jeremy, Barry Cooper. Wilfrid, with Peter and me, had founded the Mallory Group, for mountain and outdoor activities, at Charterhouse.

We arrived in Dushanbe, the capital of Tajikistan, on 21 September and the following day left with Surat and Zaffar, an ex-wrestler, the cook/chauffeur, in a big Mitsubishi 4x4, travelling the main road which leads via Gharm and Jirgatal through Kyrgyzstan to Kashgar in Xinjiang, western China. The vehicle bowled along for first 60 miles or so through Kafarnihan to Abigarm on good tarmac; thereafter the main road was spasmodically tarred until Darband. Shortly afterwards we turned off on to the Pamir Highway, a grand term for a mountain track, albeit marked in red on the maps. There was a terrific storm and after half-an-hour on the Highway – about 20 miles – we were diverted into a ravine. The bridge over the river had been washed away and two torrents had cut the road as well. Tortuous, steep, muddy bends led us to the bottom of the ravine and across the river and up in similar manner on the other side. The latter was complicated by a Chinese 18-wheeler that was stuck and even with chains could not make more than a slither to give just enough room to pass. We spent the night a little further along at a farm at Khur. The Tajik farmers are very hospitable and provide simple accommodation.

The second morning was still wet. Shortly after Tavildara, 112 miles from Dushanbe, we turned off the Pamir Highway, continuing up the Khingow valley. Coaxing the car over a ford that we had to reconstruct, we travelled on broad cultivated terraces above the river. Beyond the terraces the mountains rose to 4000m and higher. We ourselves were already at nearly 2000m. However we had not expected the mudslide that formed a 2m-high barrier across the road. On one side was the mountain and on the other was a steep drop to the river – no way round. Fortunately some other travellers were behind us and we set to with stones and bare hands to make the lump safe to drive over with caution. We spent that night in Russian ex-army caravans at an abandoned mining camp at Sangvor. This was now used as a rest-camp looked after by the village headman, Hairat-ullah, a friend of Surat's whom I had met last year. He accompanied us for the rest of the trip. It had taken two days to do what we had done in one the previous year.

Day three was more agreeable, although the road deteriorated. The scenery was impressive: at the top of the valley, where we could see into the Garmo valley, we could see fleetingly Pik Ismail Somoni (formerly Pik Kommunizma 7495m), and Pik Garmo. Shortly after midday we arrived at Arzing the highest habitation in the Khingow valley at 2500m, some 180 miles from Dushanbe. Two stallions and another horseman and a guide were provided and the four of us, Jeremy, Peter, Barry and I set off to walk to the deserted village of Pashimghar, five miles further on, where we camped with a splendid view into the Garmo valley. In 2008 I had seen bears just above the village.

Although there were just four of us, we now had, in addition to the two Tajiks who had come with us from Dushanbe, two local guides, their sons as horsemen, four horses, one filly who followed her mother all the way, and three dogs. It was quite a caravan. We crossed the fast-flowing Kyrgyz Ob on horseback behind the horsemen and then we walked. There were no paths as only the occasional hunter ventured there. The primary forest was impenetrable. At one stage it took two hours to cover 1.75km. There was a little open parkland but we made best progress in the wide riverbed. We saw plenty of wildlife, including a bear, a golden eagle, a snake, ibex, hare and many traces of wild boar.

After two days we reached the lower base camp of the 1962 expedition. Our Tajik friends recognised the camp from the pictures in *Red Peak*, Malcolm Slesser's account of the expedition. There we spent two nights: on the first we had another terrific storm and wondered how long we would have to wait before the weather allowed us to complete our pilgrimage.

However the morning of Sunday 27 September dawned fair, and after breakfast our guide from Arzing, Abdul Sha'id, who had been up there once hunting, led us some 200m above the camp to the five memorials to

203. The memorial to Wilfrid Noyce and Robin Smith with the new commemorative plaque, Garmo valley, Pamirs, 27 September 2009. *(Stewart Hawkins)*

Russian climbers who had died in the 1970s, and then some 600m further to the Noyce-Smith cairn at 2976m. It was in the same good state as in the 1962 photographs. Jeremy arrived first and spent a little while on his own in front of the memorial – a final closure with a father who had died when he was eight years old. It was a moving moment.

Jeremy and his mother had arranged for a commemorative plaque to be made and we affixed this to the stone on which the two names had been engraved in 1962. Jeremy said a few words and Peter gave a short eulogy. Abdul Sha'id knelt and recited verses from the Qu'ran. Having taken all the necessary photographs we returned to the camp. The glacier that the memorial had overlooked 47 years ago has receded some two to three miles and all that remains are the slagheaps of the moraine – 'the foulest ground imaginable', according to Slesser.

On our return, understanding the country a bit better, we stayed as much as possible in the Garmo riverbed, leaping the small streams and using a horse to cross the main torrent when necessary. The weather was exceptionally kind to us and we had the towering mass of Pik Garmo as our backdrop all the way to the Kyrgyz Ob. We reached Arzing in two days, having walked more than 40 miles in the five days in trackless country. We returned to Dushanbe with very similar experiences as on the way out, but the weather was better!

MICHEL BATAILLON AND ANDRÉ MOULIN

An Alpine Trophy – The Legendary Grépon Ice-axe

Historical Background

(by Michel Bataillon – translated and edited by Jerry Lovatt)

Until a few months ago, I only really associated the name Mummery with a crack on the Grépon and that of Burgener with the slabs of the Grand Dru. Then, at the end of the summer 2010, these names became forever tied to a venerable ice-axe, more than 100 years old. I saw it for the first time on 12 July 2010 in a mountain chalet in the village of Les Étages, a short distance down the valley from La Bérarde in the Oisans, where I had been taken by my friend and neighbour, André Moulin, a major collector of alpine literature and prints and member of the Alpine Club.

Albert Frederick Mummery was born in 1855 and started climbing in the Alps at the age of 16. However, it was in 1879 that his alpine career took a decisive turn when the Valaisan guide Alexander Burgener led him up a new route on the Matterhorn, the Zmutt Ridge. Ten years older than Mummery, Burgener was already famous: he had been Clinton Dent's guide on the Zinal Rothorn in 1873 and then made the first ascent of the Grand Dru, also with Dent, in 1878. He was well known for his physical strength and fortitude and for his understanding of alpine topography. In Chamonix they were at the same time envious and even a little fearful of him.

From then on, Mummery climbed with Burgener in the Valais, notably on the Furggen Ridge of the Matterhorn, and in the Chamonix Aiguilles. When they reached the summit of the Grands Charmoz on 15 July 1880, they were accompanied by Benedikt Venetz, a man who had been a worker on the Burgener farm in the Saas valley. Venetz, known as 'The Indian', was by all accounts an outstanding rock-climber.

One year later, on 30 July 1881, Mummery and Burgener made the first ascent of the Charpoua Face of the Aiguille Verte. Hard on the heels of this, with Venetz who had by then joined them, they made an attack on the Grépon, first of all by the Mer de Glace face and later by the Nantillons face, which led to the North summit, on which they placed an ice-axe. On 5 August 1881, their third attempt was successful: after returning to the North summit, they reached the highest point, the South summit (3482m) via the Vire à Bicyclette.

Reading Mummery in *My climbs in the Alps and Caucasus*, it is clear that each played his part. After having attempted in vain to throw a rope, they decided to act according to 'the fair methods of honourable war'. It seemed to make sense that Venetz should be charged with the delicate final pitch. Standing first on Burgener's shoulders and then on an ice-axe wedged in the crack, he made a famous lead to the top of the Grépon. Mummery made an attempt to climb the last pitch unaided but had to be pulled up the last part by the other two. On the summit, three rock seats awaited them – there, champagne and the planting of the ice-axe.

Mummery entrusted Burgener with the task of fixing in place the ice-axe that would become the object of a challenge met by the Frenchman, Henri Dunod, four years later. Mummery wrote:

The summit is of palatial dimensions and is provided with three stone chairs. The loftiest of these was at once appropriated by Burgener for the ice-axe, and the inferior members of the party were bidden to bring stones to build it securely in position. This solemn rite being duly performed, we stretched ourselves at full length and mocked M. Couttet's popgun at Chamonix with a pop of far more exhilarating sort.

On returning to Chamonix, Mummery described the rock difficulties that they had faced and overcome. He confirmed that the ice-axe would have plenty of time to get rusty before it received another visit to the South summit and that he was ready to offer the sum of 100 francs to the person who brought it back: 100 gold francs of the Third Republic of Jules Grévy. To provide a point of reference, one knows that in 1885, for the sum of 200 francs, the guide François Simond and three other Chamonix men led Henri Brulle to the summit of the Dru.

François-Henri Dunod was born in 1865 and was thus 16 years old when the Mummery, Burgener, Venetz team made the first ascent of the Grépon. Four years later in 1885, after a swift initiation on the Dent du Géant, the Matterhorn and the Dru, he teamed up with the Chamoniards, the brothers François and Gaspard Simond and Auguste Tairraz to attack the Grépon. Between 6 August and 2 September, they make six attempts. To replace the ice-axe of the Mummery team, they carried up successively a two metre long pine tree, then a French flag which, for want of a better place they had left on the Grands Charmoz, then a beam three metres long which they left up there with a view to a fourth try. On the sixth attempt, on 2 September 1885, they carried up three metal ladders with a total length of 11 metres, even at that insufficient for Auguste Tairraz. François Simond, however, employed the technique of throwing a weighted rope and gained the summit.

The Yearbook of the French Alpine Club for 1885 records:

Henri Dunod gives an interesting account of the month he spent besieging the Aiguille des Charmoz (which he names incorrectly the Aiguille du Grépon) having continuous sight of the ice-axe of Mr Mummery, until the final attempt of 2 September 1885.

In 1892 and 1893, Mummery repeated his ascent of the Charmoz and of the Grépon, this time guideless, but accompanied by a photographer with a camera having 13x18 plates, which was used to photograph him at work in the crack that bears his name, a celebrated shot that has been endlessly reproduced. On the South summit, he discovered that the axe which had been well anchored by Burgener was there no longer. Henri Dunod had taken it down to Chamonix.

Next, the guide François Simond sought to exchange the ice-axe for the reward promised in 1881. Mummery refused. For what reason? According to some, because he felt that too much time had passed; according to others, because Dunod and his team, the brothers Simond and Auguste Tairraz, had not truly followed the route of the first ascent and above all had used metal ladders – means 'unfair'.

Fifty years later, that is to say in the 1940s, François Dunod, the son of François-Henri the alpiniste – he had died in 1946 – replied to a messenger from the Alpine Club, who wanted to exhibit the Grépon ice-axe in London: *'Too late, Mummery did not meet his commitments – the ice-axe will stay in France.'*

Olivier Dunod, a man of about 50 years of age and a frequent visitor to the Oisans, both on foot and on ski, had always seen the ice-axe in the house of his great-grandfather in Les Étages, until the moment when his father, by this time more than 80 years old, had lent it to the museum in Saint-Christophe-en-Oisans. Later, realising that this small local museum, packed with alpine history, was going to change its management and thus perhaps its point of view, Dunod had judged it wise to end the loan and had recently requested the return of the ice-axe. He now wished to dispose of the axe, not by means of a donation, but to cede it to the Alpine Club for an amount at least equal to the value of the gold francs of the original Grépon challenge. A 'compensation', he tells us, finally to fulfil the promise made all those years ago by Mummery.

The Axe *(Michel Bataillon, translated and edited by Jerry Lovatt)*

Although ice-axes of the period were notable for their size, this one is a giant among giants. Of total length 112 cm, it weighs no less than 1.45 kilos. Under the pick are engraved the initials 'BV' followed by a small cross. Although it is possible that they could stand for Burgener Venetz, it seems unlikely that they would have represented both their names on the same axe. Ice-axes normally belong to one person, not two, and it is therefore almost certainly the case that they are the initials of Benedikt Venetz. Under the adze there is an italic 'M' and although tempting to associate this with Mummery, it is perhaps more likely to be the mark of the maker.

However, Ruedi Bhend, whose company has supplied some of the greatest names in mountaineering history and who ranks as one of the leading authorities on early ice-axes, has failed to identify this mark. Likewise, Konstanz Willisch, who has been responsible for the restoration of numerous historic ice-axes, was unable to associate the mark with any known early maker in the German speaking part of Switzerland. Added to the fact that the Chamoniards were some years ahead of the Swiss in ice-axe manufacture, this leads to the hypothesis that the Mummery team was supplied locally

204. Paul Braithwaite, the then AC President, with Mummery's ice-axe and its generous donor, André Moulin, at the Alpine Club Library, 9 November 2010. (*Tadeusz Hudowski*)

in the Chamonix area. Jackie Masino, who has worked all his life in the Charlet factory, indicates that the founder Josef Charlet forged his first axe in 1880. Having said that, when shown photos of the axe, Masino concluded that it was most likely the product of an artisanale forge which had used the mark they normally applied to agricultural tools.

Investigations at the Heimat Museum in Grindelwald and at the Musée Alpin in Chamonix have also failed to reveal any other axe with the italic M mark. Research continues, but it seems likely that this axe originally belonged to Benedikt Venetz and was made by an artisan toolmaker in the Valais.

The Acquisition *(André Moulin)*

I first heard of this in a call from Jerry Lovatt, Keeper of the Artefacts at the AC. Following a communication to the Alpine Club from Olivier Dunod, concerning the ice-axe, Jerry asked me if I would be able to contact M Dunod to establish exactly what he had in mind, as this was not entirely clear. In the event, I decided to visit him at his house in La Bérarde. It seemed a good idea to take someone with me, not least to act as a witness to the proceedings. To fulfil this role, I chose my friend and neighbour, Michel Bataillon, a mountaineer with a major interest in the history of the sport.

On arrival, we checked the axe, which proved to be very large and heavy, with the letters 'B V' under the pick, as mentioned above by Michel. It appeared to us most likely to be the axe left by Mummery.

Olivier Dunod explained that the axe had been kept in the Dunod family and had been handed down from father to son. Following its retrieval from the museum in Saint Christophe, he had no particular reason to part with the axe, unless he was made 'an interesting proposal'. He was thus waiting to hear what we had to say.

In response, I made him a dual proposal. First, he would be appointed a life member of the Alpine Club, without any subscription fee, and that the transfer of the axe would be covered in articles with photos in the next *Alpine Journal*. Second, we would pay him the discounted present value of the money his ancestor did not receive and round it up. He immediately turned down the first proposal, as of no interest to him. After a look at official statistics of conversions of francs in euros that I had brought with me, even rounded up, he rejected the second proposal. Dunod said that his bottom price was 10,000 euros. I advised him that this was way beyond what we could envisage and that I would revert to the Alpine Club.

Michel and I agreed that the price was very high: 10,000 euros is a large amount of money, from any point of view. I tried to contact Jerry on the phone to ask him the sort of money the Club could afford to pay but I failed to get hold of him. My friend, who had observed the conversation between Dunod and me, told me that Dunod was only interested in money, that the negotiation was closed in advance and that Dunod would not lower his price. I regarded this axe as an extremely rare relic of the great period of British Alpinism and that it had to be at the Alpine Club. This opportunity to acquire it being the first in 125 years, I felt that I should not miss it for a matter of money. It also occurred to me that the Alpine Club was probably short of cash and that I should provide the necessary financial assistance, bear the cost of the axe and donate it to the club.

The same afternoon, we went back to Dunod, worrying that he might change his mind. I gave him a 10,000 euros cheque from one of my personal accounts. He delivered me a receipt 'du cheque de 10,000 euros en paiment du piolet de Mummery'. However, he said he was not prepared to hand over the axe to me until his bank account had been credited. I thus requested he hand it over personally to me in Serre Chevalier.

On each of the following mornings, I had a look at my bank account on my computer. When my account was debited, I phoned Dunod. He answered he was not available for the next few days. I did not care for that very much, so we went immediately to La Bérarde and I took possession of the axe.

Not long after, on 9 November, I visited the Alpine Club and had the pleasure of presenting the axe to the president, the keeper of the artefacts and the committee. After its four years on the summit of the Grépon, and 125 years in a chalet in the Oisans, this important artefact has now finally found its true home in the clubhouse of the AC in London.

ALPINE CLUB LIBRARY ANNUAL REPORT 2009 – 2010

Hywel Lloyd, chairman of the Council of Trustees of the Alpine Club Library writes: One of the key achievements has been the improved library operation which all visitors compliment. The organisation and work by Jerry Lovatt, our hon librarian, and our new librarian, Tadeusz Hudowski, exudes capability and shine; gone are some of the old dreary approaches. New computing equipment has appeared in the library reading area to give better, digital access to several collections (and this access will continue to increase in scope); special thanks are due to John Town for this installation.

Finances have been difficult but we believe we are through the worst due to careful money management. Thus our hon treasurer, Richard Coatsworth, has been able to decide to retire, after 10 years in post. Special thanks to Richard for such splendid work. So we are seeking a new treasurer – is there a volunteer out there? John Mellor has looked after our investments and the change to new fund managers; John has also now decided to retire. So, thanks to John for many years service, and a welcome to Kimball Morrison in this role.

On a sadder note, I record that Mike Hewson died after a short but sharp fight against cancer in the summer of 2010. Many readers will know Mike because he ran the operation to sell books that had been donated to the library but which were triplicates or quadruplicates of books already held; this service helps members find the book they want and gains a steady and important income for the library. Mike was also the company secretary of the Library Charity and looked after the essential paperwork. He is very much missed by us all. Barbara Grigor-Taylor and Jerry have taken over the task of cataloguing books for sale, taking orders and posting out books sold.

The work of the hon archivist, Glyn Hughes, continues unabated and we have received several important donations of diaries and papers. The Himalayan Index also gains entries through the careful compilations by Sally Russell.

The photo library is still the Herculean task facing us. Anna Lawford's work has piloted a comprehensive cataloguing system. A book is easier to catalogue because it has a title and, usually, an author. A photograph might be by an unknown photographer and of persons unknown; although we can probably recognise any mountain. So, cataloguing is taking a tremendous amount of time. However, with trained volunteers from NADFAS (National Association of Decorative and Fine Art Societies), previously Philip Pepper and now Harry Melville, Anna has supervised a large amount of conservation work on the historic glass slides and albums of prints in the photo collections. Anna will be retiring from the keeper of the photographs role in March 2011; meanwhile, Sue Hare continues to run the operation of sales of photo reproductions; another steady and important income for the library.

Peter Berg, previously our hon archivist, has written and published a book about Whymper's Lantern Slide Show of around 140 years ago. Peter Mallalieu has published a second, enlarged edition of *The Artists of the Alpine Club*. These, and several other publications due out soon, contain many photographs from the collections of the Alpine Club.

As I write this in spring 2011 we are welcoming Roland Jackson as the new library hon secretary and Peter Roland to the task of being curator for the photographs. They will have plenty to do because nothing stands still in the library work.

I conclude by quoting Mike Westmacott, a previous chairman of the library, who wrote in 1989: 'We have the duty ... of keeping faith with the many people who have generously contributed to the library, making it the important collection we have today.' Since then, many new donations of collections, money and time have made his words even more true. We can be proud that the library team of splendid volunteers are doing this.

PRESIDENTIAL ELECTION

Mick Fowler was elected President of the Alpine Club on 4 December 2010 following what is thought to be the first contested election to the prestigious post in the Club's 153-year history. Mick pledged to devote his three years as president to attracting more active alpinists into the AC.

Though AC rules provide for ballots to office holders, traditionally that of president has been passed on by invitation rather than contested election. During 2010 the Club committee discussed potential candidates and unanimously concluded that Mick be asked to stand as successor to Paul Braithwaite.

When a challenger emerged in the form of Henry Day, the committee and wider membership was faced with something of a dilemma. Mick exemplifies the style of exploratory mountaineering championed by the AC, and it was thought that having as its public face a climber still pushing the boat out on big mountain routes could only be of benefit to the club's image. However Henry, climbing leader of the Army Mountaineering Association team that made the second ascent of Annapurna (8091m) in 1970, is also a popular figure in the AC, having served the club in several roles, including vice-president (1986-87).

Under the club's antiquated rules (now changed) only members who actually attended the AGM would be able to vote in the Fowler-Day contest. But annual meetings are often thinly attended and the AC membership is scattered worldwide. The committee therefore decided to conduct a consultative poll among the club's 1200 members. It was to be non-binding but would clearly be difficult to ignore.

Come the day, members filled the AC's clubroom in Shoreditch for a hustings session with the two candidates followed by a secret ballot. Despite much prior uncertainty, in the end the result was clear-cut – Fowler 59 votes, Day 21 votes. The poll was even more emphatic – Fowler 241, Day 60. If the turnout does not look too impressive, bear in mind two things – nobody loves AGMs, and it was a weekend when winter climbing conditions in the UK have seldom been better. From now on, the AGM decided, postal and proxy votes will be provided for in club elections. ***SG***

NEW HONORARY MEMBERS

Since publication of the 2009 *Alpine Journal*, the following have been appointed:

Peter Habeler, Austrian guide, best known for his partnership with Reinhold Messner on fast climbs of the Eiger and Matterhorn north faces, an alpine-style ascent of Gasherbrum I (8086m) and their groundbreaking ascent of Everest in 1978 without the aid of bottled oxygen.

Tom Hornbein, American doctor who in 1963, with Willi Unsoeld, made the first ascent of Everest's west ridge and then descended by the south ridge, thus completing the first traverse of the mountain.

Silvo Karo, Slovenian alpinist and filmmaker, best known for his first ascents of the south face of Cerro Torre in 1987 and the west face of Bhagirathi III in 1990 – both routes with the late Janez Jeglic. Karo's 16mm film of the Cerro Torre climb won first prize at the Trento Mountain Film Festival.

Erhard Loretan – deceased. See his obituary, page 436.

Jeff Lowe, American alpinist with more than a 1000 first ascents to his name. Best known for introducing modern European ice climbing to the USA, for his attempt on the north ridge of Latok I with Jim Donini, Michael Kennedy and George Lowe in 1978, and for the first ascent of the north face of Kwangde Ri, Nepal, with David Breashears in 1982.

OFFICERS AND COMMITTEE FOR 2010/2011

Note: This list covers two years. Where an officer or committee member served for only one of those years, that year is given in brackets.

PRESIDENT .... Paul Braithwaite (2010), Mick Fowler (2011)
VICE PRESIDENTS . Derek Buckle (2010), Simon Yates, Jim Milledge (2011)
HONORARY SECRETARY .... Françoise Call (2010)
John Town (2011)
HONORARY TREASURER .... Rupert Baron
HONORARY LIBRARIAN .... Jerry Lovatt
HONORARY EDITOR OF THE *Alpine Journal* .... Stephen Goodwin
COMMITTEE .... Anna Lawford, Mike Mortimer
John Porter, Tracey Quine, Stuart Worsfold, Dave Wynne-Jones
Stephen Hunt (2010), Martin Scott (2010), Bill Thurston (2010)
Duncan Tunstall (2010), Derek Buckle (2011), Jamie Goodhart (2011)
Peter Holden (2011), Roger James (2011), Mike Pinney (2011)
ADMINISTRATOR .... Iwonna Hudowska
LIBRARIAN .... Tadeusz Hudowski

OFFICE BEARERS

BMC LIAISON .... Alison Stockwell
LONDON LECTURES .... Derek Buckle
MEETS .... Dave Wynne-Jones
MEMBERSHIP .... Stuart Worsfold
WINTER DINNER .... William Newsom
HONORARY ARCHIVIST .... Glyn Hughes
HONORARY KEEPER OF THE CLUB'S PICTURES .... Peter Mallalieu
HONORARY KEEPER OF THE CLUB'S PHOTOGRAPHS ... Anna Lawford (2010)
Peter Rowland (2011)
HONORARY KEEPER OF THE CLUB'S ARTEFACTS .... Jerry Lovatt
HONORARY KEEPER OF THE CLUB'S MONUMENTS .... William Newsom
CHAIRMAN OF THE FINANCE COMMITTEE .... Richard Morgan
CHAIRMAN OF THE HOUSE COMMITTEE .... Françoise Call (2010)
Roger James (2011)
CHAIRMAN OF THE ALPINE CLUB LIBRARY COUNCIL .... Hywel Lloyd
CHAIRMAN OF THE MEMBERSHIP COMMITTEE .... Stuart Worsfold
CHAIRMAN OF THE COMPUTER WORKING GROUP .... David Baldock
ASSISTANT EDITOR OF THE *Alpine Journal* .... Paul Knott
PRODUCTION EDITOR OF THE *Alpine Journal* .... Bernard Newman
NEWSLETTER EDITOR .... Dick Turnbull
WEBSITE EDITORS .... David Baldock, Robin Quine
TRUSTEES .... Michael Baker, John Harding (2010), Stuart Beare
CLIMBING FUND .... Derek Buckle, Toto Gronlund,
Paul Knott, Martin Scott, Chris Watts

Contributors

SANDY ALLAN is a freelance British Mountain Guide favoured with a worldwide list of ascents, climbs and travels. Based from Newtonmore, Scotland, Sandy is a passionate mountaineer and Scottish winter climbing activist who feels it is imperative to maintain our natural wilderness areas in pristine condition and pass on to all, the unique sense of freedom, kinship and responsibility we experience in wide open spaces.

MALCOLM BASS lives with his partner Donna James on the edge of the North York Moors. Between expeditions he enjoys bouldering, sport and trad climbing, and driving up and down to Scotland in the dark. He works as a clinical psychologist in the NHS. He has climbed new alpine routes in Alaska, India and China, but is currently in the grip of an unhealthy obsession with Kilnsey.

MICHEL BATAILLON was artistic adviser of the Théâtre National Populaire from 1972 to 2004 and a translator of contemporary German playwrights. He now divides his time between the theatre, libraries and archives and his mountain home in the Oisans. His interest in mountain history led to his involvement in the retrieval and research into the celebrated Grépon ice-axe.

ANTONIO GÓMEZ BOHÓRQUEZ lives in Murcia, Spain. A librarian and documentalist (information scientist), he specialises in ascents in the north Peruvian ranges. He has written two books: *La Cordillera Blanca de los Andes, selección de ascensiones, excursiones y escaladas* and *Cordillera Blanca, Escaladas, Parte Norte*. He has climbed since 1967, with first ascents including *Spanish Direct* on the north face of Cima Grande di Lavaredo, Italy (1977), *Direct* on La Visera (1981) and *Pilar del Cantábrico* on Naranjo de Bulnes, Spain (1981), *Canal Central* on the south-west face of Alpamayo (1983), east face of Cerro Parón (La Esfinge, 5325m), Peru (1985) and the south-east face (1988).

PAUL BRAITHWAITE was AC president 2008-2010 and is the managing director of specialist contracting company Vertical Access Ltd. He started climbing in 1961 at the age of 14 with school friends on local Pennine outcrops. For more than 35 years he climbed extensively at a high standard in the UK, the Alps and greater ranges (winter/summer) and became one of Britain's leading mountaineers of his generation. He was a member of many climbing expeditions to remote regions including Arctic Canada, Alaska, South America, Russia, Nepal and Tibet and has taken part in many first ascents including the south-west face of Everest in 1975.

KESTER BROWN is the managing editor/designer of publications for the New Zealand Alpine Club. He produces the club's quarterly magazine *The Climber* and the annual *NZ Alpine Journal*. He is a rock climber and mountaineer of many years' standing and lives at Taylors Mistake beach, NZ.

DEREK BUCKLE is a retired medicinal chemist now acting part-time as a consultant to the pharmaceutical industry. With plenty of free time, he spends much of this rock climbing, ski touring and mountaineering in various parts of the world. Despite climbing, his greatest challenges are finding time to accompany his wife on more traditional holidays and the filling of his passport with exotic and expensive visas.

ROB COLLISTER lives in North Wales and earns his living as a mountain guide. He continues to derive enormous pleasure as well as profit from all aspects of mountains and mountaineering.

HENRY DAY considers his real legacy to climbing to be the expeditions to the Himalaya he helped organise that gave many climbing friends great introductions to high mountains, such as on Shisha Pangma. Summiting Annapurna I (2nd ascent), Tirich Mir (4th), Trisul II and Indrasan were personal bonuses. Helping to carry the top camp on Everest (3rd British) was just as important.

PAT DEAVOLL has been a rock, ice and mountain climber for 35 years. These days she specialises in mountaineering in the greater ranges and has taken part in 10 expeditions to Asia in the past 10 years. In 2011 she will travel to Afghanistan to attempt the first ascent of the NW ridge of Koh-e-Baba-Tangi (6516m) in the Wakhan Corridor and is getting ridiculously excited about this. She (only just) manages to fund her expeditions by working for the New Zealand Alpine Club as events and activities co-ordinator... and scrounging grants.

DEREK FORDHAM, when not dreaming of the Arctic, practises as an architect and runs an Arctic photographic library. He is secretary of the Arctic Club and has led 21 expeditions to the Canadian Arctic, Greenland and Svalbard to ski, climb or share the life of the Inuit.

MICK FOWLER works for Her Majesty's Revenue and Customs and, by way of contrast, likes to inject as much memorable adventure and excitement into his climbing ventures. He has climbed extensively in the UK and has regularly led expeditions to the greater ranges for more than 25 years. He has written two books, *Vertical Pleasure* (1995) and *On Thin Ice* (2005). In December 2010 he was elected president of the Alpine Club.

TERRY GIFFORD was director of the annual International Festival of Mountaineering Literature for 21 years. Former chair of the Mountain

Heritage Trust, he is the author of *The Joy of Climbing* (Whittles, 2004) and *Al Otro Lado del Aguilar* (Oversteps Books, 2011). Visiting professor at Bath Spa University's Centre for Writing and Environment and *profesor honorario* at the University of Alicante, Spain, he acted as *burro* for the making of Gill Round's walking guide, *Costa Blanca* (Rother 2007).

MARTIN GILLIE enjoys classic routes whilst 4000m peak bagging, and also exploring out-of-fashion corners of the Alps. Having to work as a university lecturer in Edinburgh to fund his addiction means that there is never sufficient time to do either to the extent he would like. He compensates by spending too much money on climbing guides, old and new.

PETER GILLMAN has been writing about mountaineering for 45 years. His biography of George Mallory, *The Wildest Dream*, co-authored with his wife Leni, won the Boardman Tasker prize in 2000. Other titles include *Eiger Direct* (written with Dougal Haston) and two editions of an Everest anthology. A devoted hill-walker, he completed the Munros in 1997.

STEPHEN GOODWIN renounced daily newspaper journalism on *The Independent* for a freelance existence in Cumbria, mixing writing and climbing. A precarious balance was maintained until 2003 when he was persuaded to take on the editorship of the *Alpine Journal* and 'getting out' became elusive again.

LINDSAY GRIFFIN lives in North Wales, from where he continues to report on the developments in world mountaineering. An enthusiastic mind still tries to coax a less than enthusiastic body up pleasant bits of rock and ice, both at home and abroad.

DAVID HAMILTON has been leading climbing, skiing and trekking trips in the greater ranges for 25 years. He has made multiple ascents of each of the '7 summits'. He has worked for seven seasons in Antarctica, leading climbers on Mt Vinson and skiers to the South Pole. In his spare time he enjoys small-scale travels in quieter mountain ranges closer to home.

STEWART HAWKINS was introduced to the mountains by Wilfrid Noyce when at school and has been a member of the Climbers' Club for more than 50 years. He has climbed in Wales, Scotland, the Alps, Arabia and the Tien Shan and has explored other ranges in Asia and Africa. He lives in the southern French Alps where he is writing a biography of Noyce.

ANDY HOUSEMAN is from North Yorkshire but lives in Chamonix, France, where he is training to become a UIAGM guide. In spring 2011 he resumed his partnership with Nick Bullock for an attempt on the south pillar of Kyshar (6769m) in Nepal.

JOHN INNERDALE is an architect, landscape painter and beekeeper based in the Lake District. A lifetime of walking and climbing in the UK, Alps, Norway, Pyrenees, Himalaya and Patagonia has helped him understand and interpret mountain architecture. He is a trustee of the Mountain Heritage Trust.

DICK ISHERWOOD has been a member of the Alpine Club since 1970. His climbing record includes various buildings in Cambridge, lots of old-fashioned routes on Cloggy, a number of obscure Himalayan peaks, and a new route on the Piz Badile (in 1968). He now follows Tilman's dictum about old men on high mountains and limits his efforts to summits just a little under 20,000 feet.

HARISH KAPADIA has climbed in the Himalaya since 1960, with ascents up to 6800m. He recently retired as honorary editor of both the *Himalayan Journal*. In 1993 he was awarded the IMF's Gold Medal and in 1996 he was made an honorary member of the Alpine Club. He has written several books including *High Himalaya Unknown Valleys*, *Spiti: Adventures in the Trans-Himalaya* and, most recently, *Siachen Glacier: The Battle of Roses* . In 2003 he was awarded the Patron's Gold Medal by the Royal Geographical Society.

PAUL KNOTT is a lecturer in business strategy at the University of Canterbury, New Zealand. He previously lived in the UK. He enjoys exploratory climbing in remote mountains, and since 1990 has undertaken 14 expeditions to Russia, Central Asia, Alaska and the Yukon. He has also climbed new routes in the Southern Alps and on desert rock in Oman and Morocco.

PAT LITTLEJOHN is known for a 'clean climbing' ethic and adherence to the lightweight, alpine-style approach. His worldwide portfolio of first ascents includes the NE Pillar of Taweche (Nepal), Raven's Pyramid (Karakoram), Poi N Face (Kenya) and Kjerag N Buttress (Norway). He succeeded Peter Boardman as director of the International School of Mountaineering in 1983. Pat enjoys passing on the skills acquired over four decades of alpine climbing and is keen to ensure that climbing's unique 'spirit of adventure' is kept alive, both on the rock and in the mountains.

JERRY LOVATT is the Alpine Club's honorary librarian, a former AC vice-president and a book collector with a particular interest in early Alpine history. His mountaineering activities continue, albeit at a rather more sedate pace than his book collecting, this year taking him with other AC members to a largely untouched range in north-west China.

ANDRÉ MOULIN is a French entrepreneur, former Lloyd's member – and member of the AC since 1988. A major collector of mountaineering books and Mont Blanc prints, he enjoys hiking in the Alps and spending time in a former military lookout post isolated on a mountain top in the southern Alps that he has turned in a private hut.

BERNARD NEWMAN started climbing the day England won the World Cup, so you'd think he'd be better at it by now. He joined the Leeds University Union Climbing Club in 1968 when Mike Mortimer was president and was closely associated with that exceptional group of rock climbers and super-alpinists which included Syrett, MacIntyre, Baxter-Jones, Porter and Hall, without any of their talent rubbing off. One-time geologist, editor of *Mountain* and *Climber*, Bernard is now a 'freelance' writer, editor and photographer.

BRUCE NORMAND is from Scotland but lives in China, where he works as professor of physics at Renmin University (People's University) in Beijing. Author of more than 20 first ascents and new routes on 6000m peaks in the Trans-Himalaya, he has also climbed K2.

SIMON RICHARDSON is a petroleum engineer based in Aberdeen. Experience gained in the Alps, Andes, Patagonia, Canada, the Himalaya, Alaska and the Yukon is put to good use most winter weekends whilst exploring and climbing in the Scottish Highlands.

GEORGE RODWAY is a physiologist, mountaineer and an expert on mountain medicine. An assistant professor at the University of Utah, he has written extensively on the history of high-altitude physiology and is the editor of George Ingle Finch's *The Struggle for Everest* (2008).

C A RUSSELL, who formerly worked with a City bank, devotes much of his time to mountaineering and related activities. He has climbed in many regions of the Alps, in the Pyrenees, East Africa, North America and the Himalaya.

BILL RUTHVEN is an honorary member of the Alpine Club. Before being confined to a wheelchair he had built up more than half a century of mountaineering experience, which is invaluable to him in his work as hon secretary of the Mount Everest Foundation. He is always happy to talk to and advise individuals planning an expedition.

MARCELO SCANU is an Argentine climber, born in 1970, who lives in Buenos Aires. He specialises in ascending virgin mountains and volcanoes in the Central Andes. His articles and photographs about alpinism, trekking, and mountain history, archaeology and ecology appear in prominent magazines in Europe and America. When not climbing, he works for a workers' union.

DOUG SCOTT has made almost 40 expeditions to the high mountains of Asia. He has reached the summit of 30 peaks, of which half have been first ascents, and all were climbed by new routes or for the first time in lightweight style. Apart from his climb up the SW face of Everest with Dougal Haston in 1975, he has made all his climbs in alpine style without the use of supplementary oxygen. He is a former president of the Alpine Club.

BOB SHEPTON was fortunate enough to find the cliffs of Lulworth and Portland unclimbed in the 1960s and 70s and set about steadily developing them. In latter years he has led Tilman-type expeditions to the west coast of Greenland and Arctic Canada, sailing and climbing new routes from his boat, culminating in the 'Big Walls' expedition that was awarded a *Piolet d'Or* in 2011.

JOHN TOWN is a retired university administrator. He has climbed in the Alps, Caucasus, Altai, Andes, Turkey and Kamchatka, and explored little-known mountain areas of Mongolia, Yunnan and Tibet. He is old enough to remember the days without satellite photos and GPS.

PHIL WICKENS studied biology at Imperial College in London. After completing his PhD in plant pathology he worked for two winters and three summers as a field guide for the British Antarctic Survey, and currently works as a freelance guide, lecturer and photographer in the polar regions. He has led numerous climbing and skiing expeditions to remote areas, including the Alpine Club's expeditions to the Pamirs and Antarctica.

JEREMY WINDSOR is an anaesthetist and researcher at the Institute of Human Health and Performance, based at University College London. Despite limited ability, he has climbed widely throughout the UK and the greater ranges. As an expedition doctor he has undertaken trips to East Africa, South America, Greenland and the Himalaya.

DAVE WYNNE-JONES used to teach before he learnt his lesson. He has spent over 30 years exploring the hills and crags of Britain and climbed all the Alpine 4000m peaks. By the 1990s annual alpine seasons had given way to explorative climbing further afield, including Jordan, Morocco, Russia and Ecuador, though ski mountaineering took him back to the Alps in winter. Expedition destinations have included Pakistan, Peru, Alaska, the Yukon, Kyrgyzstan, Nepal, India and China with a respectable tally of first ascents.

Index 2010-2011

C

D

N

O

P

X

Y

Z

www.berghaus.com
berghaus Lead. Don't follow.

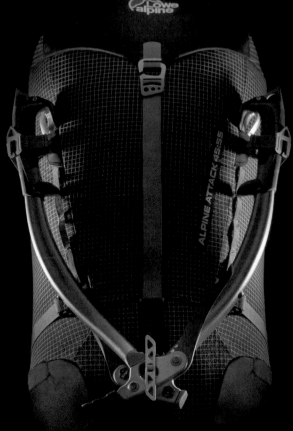

Rope tests.
Somewhere between heaven and earth. Safe hold and support whenever you need it. 30 international climbing athletes put the high performance of the Mammut technical climbing brand to the test on the Klausen Pass. With impressive results: optimally equipped with the very best technical hardware and climbing harnesses from Mammut, you can climb any route with passion.
SWISS TECHNOLOGY
Absolute alpine.

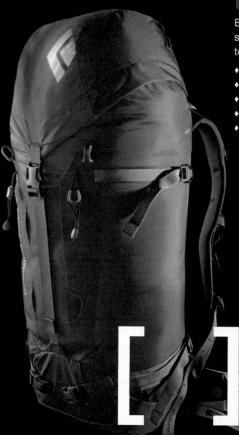

MOUNTAIN
EQUIPMENT